God is Beautiful

God is Beautiful

The Aesthetic Experience of the Quran

Navid Kermani

Translated by
Tony Crawford

polity

The translation of this work was funded by Geisteswissenschaften International – Translation Funding for Humanities and Social Sciences from Germany, a joint initiative of the Fritz Thyssen Foundation, the German Federal Foreign Office, the collecting society VG WORT and the Börsenverein des Deutschen Buchhandels (German Publishers & Booksellers Association).

Polity Press
65 Bridge Street
Cambridge CB2 1UR, UK

Polity Press
101 Station Landing
Suite 300
Medford, MA 02155, USA

ISBN-13: 978-0-7456-5167-5
ISBN-13: 978-0-7456-5168-2 (pb)

A catalogue record for this book is available from the British Library.

Library of Congress Cataloging-in-Publication Data

Kermani, Navid, 1967–
[Gott ist schön. English]
God is beautiful : the aesthetic experience of the Quran / Navid Kermani.
pages cm.
Includes bibliographical references.
Translated from German.
ISBN 978-0-7456-5167-5 (hardback)
1. Aesthetics in the Qur'an. 2. Aesthetics–Religious aspects–Islam. 3. Qur'an as literature. I. Title.
BP134.A38K4713 2014
297.1′2232–dc23

2014021613

Typeset in 10 on 11 pt Times NR MT
by Toppan Best-set Premedia Limited
Printed and bound in United Kingdom by Clays Ltd, Elcograf S.p.A

For further information on Polity, visit our website: politybooks.com

Contents

Preface

Religions have their aesthetics. Religions are not collections of logically reasoned norms, values, principles and doctrines. They speak in myths, in images, rarely in abstract terms. They bind their followers not so much by the logic of their arguments as by the aura of their proponents, the poetry of their texts, the appeal of their sounds, forms, rituals, even their interiors, colours and odours. The insights they strive for are brought about more through sensory experience than through mental reflection; they are aesthetic rather than discursive in nature. The operations that make up their practice are not didactic lessons but rather occurrences that move the faithful physically as much as mentally. This is true of all religions, and it is nothing new.

Turning to Islam, however, we encounter an odd paradox: Islam's aesthetic dimension is of central importance to the Muslim self-image, if only because the Muslim Prophet's greatest – and, according to many theologians, his only – confirmatory miracle is the beauty and perfection of the Quranic language; yet, at the same time, the aesthetic dimension has hardly figured at all in the Western view of Islam, art historians' research aside. Hardly any academic writer would deny that Muslims experience the Quran aesthetically – as a poetically structured text and as a musical recitation – and that the reception of the scripture as an aesthetic phenomenon is one of the essential components of Islamic religious practice, at least in the Arabic-speaking world. Nonetheless, although the aesthetic reception of the Quran is so important and obvious, it has never been proportionately reflected in Oriental studies: researchers noticed it early on and occasionally stated it, but are only gradually and sporadically beginning to address it. The limited resonance of such efforts is evident not least in the fact that general descriptions of Islam as a rule still completely ignore the importance of aesthetic considerations within the Muslim religious world. The formal properties of the Quran, for example, which are of capital importance for Muslims' faith, have only recently interested at most the philologists among Orientalists – and most of those who passed judgement on the Quran's form condemned it. That the Quran could excite aesthetic pleasure, 'that it could even be simply the best book in regard to language, rhetoric and literature and, beyond that, literally unsurpassable for all individuals and peoples, and that this supremacy is evidence – the strongest evidence – of the authenticity of the revelation' – as Angelika Neuwirth precisely stated the import of the doctrine of *iʿjāz*, the miraculous nature of the Muslim revelation[1] – that doctrine was long seen by Western readers as absurd, explicable if at all by religious fanaticism. The catalogue of offences compiled in 1910 by Theodor Nöldeke, to date probably the most important scholar in German Oriental studies, under the harmless-sounding title *Zur Sprache des Koran* [On the language of the Quran], remained the paradigm for Western assessments at large until the 1970s (recall, for example, Wansbrough's harsh words in his *Quranic Studies*, the most-discussed work on modern Quran research). Consequently, Western scholars of Islam have never been able to take the *iʿjāz* of the Quran quite seriously, even though it is a foundation of Islamic faith and, strictly speaking, the only miracle in Islam. Instead, they have treated it 'as a theologoumenon of particular exotic charm, a model of dogmatic partiality, not to say an aberration of an entire culture – at best, as a vagary of exaggerated Arabic cultural pride', as Neuwirth critically notes,[2] and this foundation of faith has remained beyond the scope of the general Western awareness of Islam. When the Western layman wants to know why people believe in the Quran, he takes up a translation and studies its content. The interjections of Muslims, in particular those of Arab origins, that the substance of their revelation cannot be grasped by means of a translation, are acknowledged marginally at best. Often the insistence that the Quran is untranslatable is interpreted as evidence of the closed-mindedness or even fundamentalism of Muslims, as when discussion turns to Turkish children in Germany who learn the Quran by heart in the original Arabic without understanding a word. And yet the objection – common even among enlightened Muslims – to reading (much less reciting) the Quran in a language other than Arabic involves axioms of the world of Islamic faith.

The purpose of the present book is not to refute the value judgements of the early and middle periods of Oriental studies and to follow the Muslim theoreticians of *iʿjāz* in drawing on literary scholarship to affirm the beauty of the Quran. Rather, this book describes Muslims' relation to the Quran and the meaning of the aesthetic dimension for that relation. Its focus is not on the work but on its reception by an audience. The Quran itself is examined only to the extent necessary to discern whether it presupposes or at least suggests a specific aesthetic mode of reception. In Western Quran studies, an approach has long [been predominant] that either centres on the presumed author Muhammad's intentions, influences and motives or else analyses what the Quran *is* – that is, what its words *really mean* (when no longer 'burdened'[3] by theological exegesis, winnowed from the 'chaff of often errant scholasticism', which may sometimes contain 'an occasional grain'),[4] what genre it belongs to, whether it is complete, authentic, flawed, ethically acceptable, or well written. This book, on the other hand, aims to explore what the Quran is *for* Muslims, and hence sees it as a structure – not as a concrete object but as a system of relations. The relations discussed in this book are those between the text and its recipients. No text exists – let me assert at the outset – except in such relations. When we consider those relations, however, the diverse and often fabulous forms of testimony, argument and interpretation of an aesthetic reception of the Quran step forth out of the exotic or not rationally understandable sphere, and it becomes easier to see why Muhammad's relation to the poets is particularly delicate or how a theology could arrive at the wondrous dogma of the Quran as a literary miracle.

The entire history of Muslim and primarily Arabic literature and theology up to the present is permeated with testimony of aesthetic appreciation, accounts of individual situations in which recitations of the Quran provoke ecstatic reactions, and acclaim for certain reciters. They appear in all genres, in all kinds of contexts and eras, and every scholar of Islam must inevitably encounter them regularly. A history of the Quran's reception that places all of these testimonies in order and includes all the relevant considerations would be too ambitious a goal at present. As a beginning, we can do no more than collect evidence from individual segments of this history, discuss them, and let them speak for themselves. Since I cannot exhaustively treat the subject in general, especially in view of the number of blank spots in the scholarship to date – still too great – I would like to look at six points in depth to discover the general in the particular.

Numerous issues are touched on only briefly or not at all in this book. All those effects, for example, that are not linguistic in the narrow sense, such as the influence of the Quran on the fine arts, are not discussed, in spite of their aesthetic relevance. Likewise the reception of the Quran in non-Arabic-language communities is mentioned only in passing, since it is too different from that in the Arabic-speaking countries to be incorporated in the scope of the book's argument. The Persian authors cited treat the Quran as an Arabic text and discuss its reception by an Arabic-speaking audience. If individual occurrences, accounts or views of earlier Muslim authors are often set in relation to interpretations of modern philosophy, aesthetics or literary scholarship, this is not done with the intention of showing that knowledge was already present in Islam that occurred only later to Europeans. People have always reflected on the reception of texts, images and sounds that they find beautiful or moving. It goes without saying that they have sometimes come to similar conclusions. Although most of the sources with which I am concerned are quite old, they often speak – in their different terminology – of experiences and impressions which are not foreign to us, and which may emerge more clearly in their singularity, and also in their familiarity, when contrasted with experiences and impressions from other contexts.

In closing, a word about the word 'aesthetics': in the pages that follow, it is not used to indicate some doctrine of the beautiful rooted in the

Quran. Rather, the 'aesthetic' should be taken, in reference to the word's etymology (*aisthesis*), to mean that which is perceptible with the eyes and ears, hence that aspect of an object or an occurrence which can be experienced artistically and gives pleasure – in contrast to its discursive content, consisting of abstract concepts. An 'aesthetic reception' is a reception that is oriented primarily towards the sensory appearance of an object – that is, its visual, auditory, tactile, olfactory and gustatory properties – or towards its expressive qualities. An 'aesthetic' idea is thus an idea conceived through the senses, not – to use Baumgarten's and Wolff's terminology – a distinct rational idea. Furthermore, the aesthetic dimension encompasses those aspects of the Quran and its reception that can be discussed with reference to criteria that are also applied to works of art. In this sense, every book, and especially every revealed scripture, has an *aesthetic* dimension, the Bible no less than the Quran. The meaning accorded to this dimension is different in each culture, however. Islam is, as far as the aesthetic reception of its sacred text is concerned, not an exception. On the contrary, as I hope to show, it is a striking example of the close correlation, grounded in a common origin, between art and religion, revelation and poetry, religious and aesthetic experience.

I submitted the present work in 1997 as a dissertation in Islamic studies at the University of Bonn. That which is good in it is also the work of my wife, Katajun Amirpur, my teacher, Professor Stefan Wild (Bonn), and Professors Monika Gronke (Cologne), Hartmut Bobzin (Erlangen) and Angelika Neuwirth (Beirut and Berlin). The support they all gave me exceeded all ordinary bounds, and I thank them for making this book possible.

I am also grateful for valuable information to Professor Naṣr Ḥāmid Abū Zaid (Leiden), Professor Annemarie Schimmel (Bonn), Andreas Jacobs (Cologne), Friederike Pannewick (Berlin), Dr Manutschehr Amirpur (Winterscheid) and Dr Khalil Kermani (Siegen). I would like to thank Wolfgang and Mahrokh Beck and Dr Maria Stukenberg for welcoming me so cordially into the family of their publishing house. I thank the German National Academic Foundation for its generous financial support of my research. Finally, I thank my parents, Dr Djavad Kermani and Sakineh Schafjzadeh-Kermani: without their love and trust, everything would have been meaningless.

Navid Kermani
Cologne, February 1999

1

The First Listeners

Beauty saves the world.

Dostoevsky, *The Idiot*

The greatest of Arabia's poets was Labīd ibn Rabīʿa.[1] His poems hung on the doors of the Kaaba as a sign of his triumph. None of his fellow poets dared to challenge him by hanging their verses beside Labīd's. But, one day, some followers of Muhammad approached. Muhammad was decried by the heathen Arabs of that time as an obscure magician and a deranged poet. His followers hung an excerpt from the second surah of the Quran on the door and challenged Labīd to read it aloud. The king of the poets laughed at their presumption. Out of idleness, or perhaps in mockery, he condescended to recite the verses. Overwhelmed by their beauty, he professed Islam on the spot.[2]

Countless stories like this one are recorded in Islamic literature: stories that tell of the overwhelming effect of Quran recitation on Muhammad's contemporaries, of people who converted on hearing a verse of the Quran, or who wept, cried out, were enraptured or fainted. If those stories are true, the Quran enchanted, delighted, unsettled or shocked its adherents and its opponents – at any rate, it inspired them, often hypnotized them, moved them to ecstasy, and in extreme cases killed them. The Prophet's follower Zurāra al-Ḥarashī, for example, is said to have let out a cry and then fallen over dead as he recited from the Quran during public prayer.[3] A similar fate befell other believers of his day and later times, including one of the best known *tābiʿūn* (successors of the Prophet's companions), Abū Juhayr aḍ-Ḍarīr, who lived in the eighth century. When the famous Quran reciter Ṣāliḥ al-Murrī (d. 792 or 793) recited a verse to him, he 'uttered a loud groan and departed this world', as one account that is often cited by mystics put it.[4]

The Shafi'i theologian Abū Isḥāq Muhammad ath-Thaʿlabī (d. 1035) wrote an entire book[5] about the *qatlā l-Qurʾān*, those 'slain by the Quran'. At least as prominent as those cases in the history of the Quran's reception, however, are the conversions. 'He who has heard cannot do otherwise than to submit perforce to the Quran': thus the Egyptian Muṣṭafā

Ṣādiq ar-Rāfiʿī (d. 1937) explained this phenomenon, so frequently discussed by Muslim scholars. He analysed it as follows:

> Every part of his spirit was touched by the pure, musical sound of the language, and section by section, tone by tone, he absorbed its harmony, the perfection of its order, its consummate form. It was not as if something was recited to him, but rather as if something had been burned into him.[6]

The Muslim and especially the folk traditions concerning the life of Muhammad tell of a number of people who, on hearing the word of God, spontaneously began to revere the Prophet, or at least were so deeply moved that they abandoned their hostile intentions. Of course, the authenticity of such conversion stories is dubious, if not altogether impossible, as in the case of the episode about the poet Labīd that opens this chapter.[7] Many of these stories have a distinctly apologist character. In this respect the Muslim missionary accounts, miracle stories and prophetic traditions differ from those of other religions only in degree, if at all.[8] Nonetheless, those texts have value for researchers. They most certainly have implications for the role played by the Quran in the consciousness of the Muslim community and for that community's view of the revelation and of their own salvation history. The kinds of miracles that are told give an inkling of the horizons of the faithful. And the greatest miracle of Islam, later declared a dogma, is the beauty of the revealed text.

Where Western treatises on the history of Islam tend to offer ideological, political, psychological, social or military reasons for the success of Muhammad's prophetic mission, Muslim authors of all ages have identified the literary quality of the Quran as a critical factor in the spread of Islam among the Arabs of the seventh century. Accounts of the rapture, amazement and ecstasy that Muhammad's recitations are supposed to have provoked in his first listeners continue to embellish every good orthodox treatise on the Quran and are advanced by Muslim authors as the most convincing evidence of its divine origin.[9] Through the biographies and works of hadith, the Quran commentaries and the treatises on *nubūwa*, Muhammad's prophecy, and through modern writings, whether oriented towards edification or academic study, on Muhammad and his life – all of which are permeated with examples of the overwhelming effects of Quran recitation – a past takes shape in which the Quran's linguistic form is a fundamental element of the salvation history, and its metaphysical quality appears as a historic fact. 'God, the Sublime, assisted Muhammad with something with which he had never assisted any other mortal, and He distinguished him with special qualities that are above and beyond the measure of the miracles that are attributed to the prophets and the degrees that are proper to the saints', writes Abū Nuʿaym al-Iṣfahānī (d. 1038) in his *Dalāʾil an-nubūwa* [The proofs of prophethood], in a chapter that he tellingly titled 'How the Quran and the sight of the Prophet captured hearts, so that many of the wise converted to Islam on their first encounter'. Abū Nuʿaym writes further: 'There is no sign and no token that could be more wonderful (*abdaʿ*) and more magnificent (*arwaʿ*) than the sign (*āyāt*) of Muhammad, the clear Quran, the wise exhortation, the precious book.'[10]

To question the authenticity of reports on the reception of the Quran in early Islamic times, to doubt Muslims' claims of the factuality of the Quran's effect, is legitimate, but trivial. If one wished to understand Judaism, it would not suffice to expose the Jews' departure from Jerusalem as historically false; the topography of the Christian salvation history is no less meaningful for being fictional. Those who see only a rigid dichotomy of fiction and reality fail to recognize the significance of even the most subjective and improbable testimonies of faith – and hence of the accounts of the reception of the Quran – for cultural history and the phenomenology of religion. From such a point of view, the stories of the Quran's listeners must continue to appear as pretty but uninformative fairy tales with the transparently pious purpose of outfitting Islam with a miracle of its own. Such observers continue to overlook the fact that they offer an approach to the specific way in which revelation, faith and salvation history appear to Muslims.

Consequently, the accounts collected in these chapters about the reactions of Muhammad's contemporaries to the recitation of the Quran are not intended as a critical historical approach to 'what really happened'. They draw a picture that follows from the *Muslim* sources. With reference to the time of Islam's origins, this means we are dealing with a phenomenon that the Egyptologist Jan Assmann called 'cultural memory'. Let me begin by quoting his own explanation of the concept:

> Cultural memory refers to one of the exterior dimensions of the human memory, which initially we tend to think of as purely internal – located within the brain of the individual, and a subject of encephalology, neurology, and psychology but not of historical cultural studies.... However, the contents of this memory, the ways in which they are organized, and the length of time they last are for the most part not a matter of internal storage or control but of the external conditions imposed by society and cultural contexts.[11]

Assmann's theoretical reflections on culture can make an important contribution to a more precise view of the formation of Islamic identity. There is no space here for a detailed translation of his explanatory models to the culture of Islam, but I will briefly present at least a few of his insights before returning to the early Islamic accounts of individual actualizations of the Quran. Assmann's reflections may provide a matrix against which these accounts appear, not simply as fictions with little significance for historic reality but as an integral, indispensable part of a cultural memory in which history is always a construct and never a given quantity.

Remembered History

'Societies conceive images of themselves, and they maintain their identity through the generations by fashioning a culture out of memory', Assmann writes.[12] He emphasizes that the collective 'memory of a shared past'[13] is essential for a community's identity. Along with their 'adherence to the same laws and values', collective memory is what enables individuals to feel they belong to a community and to say 'we'. This identity, or, as Assmann also calls it, 'the connective structure of common knowledge and characteristics',[14] is formed of those two elements, memory and adherence. The first is expressed in the form of stories, the second in the form of behavioural norms.

> Just as an individual forms a personal identity through memory, maintaining this despite the passage of time, so a group identity is also dependent on the reproduction of shared memories. The difference is that the group memory's basis is not neurological, but cultural: a complex of identity-shaping aspects of knowledge is objectified in the symbolic forms of myth, song, dance, sayings, laws, sacred texts, pictures, ornaments, paintings, processional routes or – as in the case of the Australians – even whole landscapes.[15]

Myth illuminates the present by reference to its origins: it is 'the past condensed into foundational narrative'.[16] Through the remembrance of this past, through the representation of its foundational figures of memory, a community reassures itself of its identity.[17] From this point of view, the origins of Islam also belong to a mythical time. As historic facts, Muhammad's life and his prophetic acts are the object of historical research. In addition, however, they have become the foundational narrative of the Muslim community – hence myth. That says nothing about whether the traditions of the Prophet are historically true or false; it only describes their function and importance for the cultural memory of the Muslim community: 'Myth is a story one tells in order to give direction to oneself and the world – a reality of a higher order, which not only rings true but also sets normative standards and possesses a formative power.'[18]

No part of the past is remembered for its own sake: remembrance must fulfil certain functions. Hence the past is always a social construction, one shaped by the particular need for meaning and the frame of reference of a given present.[19] For this reason Assmann called memory an 'internalized past'. Memory does not distinguish between the past as fiction (myth) and the past as reality (history), and indeed Assmann finds the distinction obsolete in any terms: the remembered past 'is myth, regardless of whether it is fact or fiction'.[20] No memory is untouched by reconstructive imagination and value-directed interest. In the cultural memory, the factual is transposed into remembered narrative, and thus into myth. 'This does not make it unreal', Assmann stresses; 'on the contrary, this is what makes it real, in the sense that it becomes a lasting, normative, and formative power.'[21]

The belief in the literary art of the Arabs and the stylistic supremacy of the Quran, the claim that no one among the poetically gifted Arabs was able to meet the Quran with anything better, more beautiful, more enchanting, has been an identity-forming element of the Muslim community since the tenth century at least. The inimitability of the quranic language is taken as a clear proof that what connects the individual members of this community, and what separates them from other communities – that is, their religious faith – is objectively true and eternally valid. Myth and history go together, each depending on and determining the other: the belief in the scriptural miracle as the consequence of a certain reception history and the reception history in which the miracle is seen to be confirmed. Just as it would be absurd to claim that a doctrine such as that of *iʿjāz* could be a synthetic product of scholarly study, removed from reality, created in a vacuum with no real experience of beauty on the part of the faithful and no memory of the experience of past generations, and yet be universally accepted within just a few decades, it is likewise all too natural that, as an established dogma, the poetic miracle has influenced the community's cultural memory, and that those events in the community's history that indicate the authenticity of the miracle become objects of attention, emphasis and imagination. 'Only an important past is remembered, and only a remembered past can become important', Assmann writes, and he adds, 'Remembering has always been an act of semioticizing.'[22]

The fact that cultural memory most strongly preserves those events that stabilize the community's identity, ornaments them with new details or even constructs them outright does not detract from their significance in the slightest. To understand a culture, even narratives that are clearly contradicted by history must be considered as 'the past' if they are so held in the consciousness of the community. In this view, their significance is defined less by historic fact than by the function of the narrative in the cultural memory. This point is especially noteworthy in regard to *iʿjāz*, the miraculous nature of the Quran, since Islamic studies have long challenged the idea that the dogma has its roots in the Quran itself. The passages that are most often cited in support of *iʿjāz*, called the *taḥaddī* verses, in which God 'challenges' the unbelievers to produce a surah equal to those of the Quran,[23] apparently did not originally refer to the stylistic perfection of the quranic language. Nöldeke's finding to this effect[24] has been confirmed several times over in recent years. In spite of this conclusion, which is inescapable upon a close reading of the passages concerned, the fact that later Muslims understood these verses as referring to an aesthetic challenge is a remarkable phenomenon in religious and cultural history. And the various traditions that speak of Arab poets striving in vain to create a work the equal of the Quran are just as significant as reflections on the cultural memory of the Muslim community – and hence on its identity – as if they were indisputable historic fact. 'One must simply bear in mind', Assmann states, 'that memory has nothing to do with the study of history.'[25]

The old Muslim scholarship sometimes expresses the amazing insight that factual history is not identical with the image of that history that we form and project in the present. The authenticity of the *sīra* or biography of the Prophet by Ibn Hishām (d. 833), which some treat today as a collection of undoubted historic facts, was for a long time the subject of a controversy which did not substantially reduce the text's normative function.[26] In dealing with traditions of the Prophet (except those that were relevant for making laws), some theologians favoured a certain amount of acknowledged indulgence (*musāmaḥa*), especially towards pious stories, edifying sayings and ethical sermons that were compatible with traditional notions and values: 'It may be a weak ḥadīth but one feels content with it', the legal scholar an-Nawawī (d. 1277) was wont to say.[27] In some circles, inventing false traditions was even encouraged if they served pious purposes. Storytellers, called '*quṣṣāṣ*', entertained audiences in public squares by recounting largely fictitious stories and proverbs from the life of the Prophet, much to the displeasure of serious theologians.[28]

There is no contradiction between this seemingly almost permissive way of treating history and the fact that the remembered past as a whole generally has an aura of immutability, inviolability, because of its constitutive function for the collective identity. Indulgence was shown only to those traditions that were compatible with and complementary to the collective memory. The Prophet himself is said to have declared that any statement attributed to him that is consistent with the Quran actually originates with him, 'whether I have in fact said it myself or not'.[29] Thus we can consciously disregard the criterion of authenticity if – and only if – there is a consistency with the accepted canon. Conversely, doubt as to the credibility of the overall picture, indications that things couldn't have happened the way we always imagined them after all, and the production of undeniable facts, realizations and experiences that disprove the version inscribed in cultural memory have drastic consequences for the community's self-image and necessarily meet with determined resistance. This is true even when the historicist criticism does not cast doubt on the actual principles of faith, as in the case of Ṭāhā Ḥusayn's (d. 1973) book about the poetry of the Dschahiliyya. Ḥusayn doubted neither the divine revelation of the Quran nor the works of the Prophet. By denying the authenticity of pre-Islamic poetry as it has been handed down, he merely shook 'the opinion which arose, and which the ancients were convinced of, and which many more recent authors are no less convinced of, namely, that the Arab nation in its entirety is a nation of poets and every Arab is by nature and inclination a poet.'[30] But because this notion, like the Arabic Abraham myth also contested by Ṭāhā Ḥusayn, is part of the collective self-image, and because it is also closely intertwined with and serves as a historic foundation of the dogma of *iʿjāz*, criticism of it is felt to be sacrilege: after all, God specifically gave the Arabs a degree of verbal skill 'such as no other people had been given', as Qāḍī ʿIyāḍ (d. 1149) puts it:

> God had implanted this special potential and ability in the nature and essence of the Arabs so that they were able to improvise the most wonderful speeches and find the right words for every occasion. At every conceivable opportunity they spoke in verse, spontaneously and without stopping to think, to taunt, berate, praise or scold others. In this way they tried – and succeeded – in raising a person up, or reducing him to nothing: such art can justly be called permissible magic.[31]

The consensus questioned by Ṭāhā Ḥusayn is expressed by Muḥammad Abū Zahra, professor of Islamic law at Cairo University, who says that historians of every age agree 'that the Arabs had outstanding works of literature and possessed a fine taste for language that allowed them to distinguish estimable from poor oratory and a beautiful speech from a base one.'[32] Ṣādiq ar-Rāfiʿī goes so far as to say:

> In the time of the Quran, the Arabs had achieved a degree of eloquence that they had never known in their prior history. In every previous era, the language had developed continuously, undergoing improvement and refinement, and had begun to shape the social customs.... The kingdom of language (*dawlat al-kalām*) had become established among them, but it had had no king until the Quran came to them.[33]

Another aspect of the Islamic community's historical self-image is the notion that the high poetic level the Arabs had attained at the time Muhammad won them over by the eloquence of his proclamation has never been surpassed since. 'If we know that the people of that time were unable to produce anything equivalent', as al-Bāqillānī (d. 1013), for example, puts it: 'At best, those who came later have approached or equalled the ancients. But surpassed or exceeded them? No, that never happened.'[34]

The fact that Islam's proof of faith is a poetic one is thus closely linked to the paramount importance attached to the poetically exalted language, used primarily in recitation, of early Arabic culture. The logic of the miraculous proof involves not only the Arabs' recognition of the Quran as a divine work by its stylistic perfection but also the fact that the Arabs, the nation of poets par excellence, were the ones who were obliged to admit the poetic miracle: a people who appreciated the art of oratory above everything else, and who could only be persuaded by a miracle of words. The connection between the Arabs' mastery of language and the doctrine of *iʿjāz* is expressed in cultural history by the explanatory model which al-Jāḥiẓ (d. 869) was probably one of the first to propose, and which appears again and again when Muslim scholars address the foundation of that dogma: God granted to each prophet, the Muʿtazili al-Jāḥiẓ wrote, the gift that his people would value most highly. In Egypt, where magic was highly regarded, Moses outmatched the arts of Pharaoh's sorcerers by turning his staff into a snake, and was thus confirmed as a prophet. In a time when the healing arts were particularly valued, Jesus' raising the dead was the miracle that authenticated him. Muhammad is the prophet of a nation that prided itself on poets above all else, therefore his sign had to be a miracle of words;[35] in the words of Muḥammad Abū Zahra, it had to 'fit' them: 'If the miracle of the Islamic prophet lay in his celestial language that surpassed human ability, that naturally accords with those people who initially received it, without controverting its eternal validity.'[36]

If we accept the traditional image of the pre-Islamic Arabs as a people of poets and admirers of eloquence, 'a people that breathes poetry', as Nizār Qabbānī puts it,[37] the Muslim scholars' ethnopsychological theory takes on a surprising plausibility, and even some Orientalists are susceptible to it. Philip K. Hitti, for example, seems to adopt it when he writes:

> By virtue of its peculiar structure Arabic lent itself admirably to a terse, trenchant, epigrammatic manner of speech. Islam made full use of this feature of the language and of this psychological peculiarity of its people. Hence the 'miraculous character' (*iʿjāz*) of the style and composition of the Quran, adduced by Moslems as the strongest argument in favour of the genuineness of their faith. The triumph of Islam was to a certain extent the triumph of a language, more particularly, of a book.[38]

It is revealing that Islamic studies, while ignoring the Muslims' aesthetic appreciation of the Quran and rejecting the 'myth' of its stylistic supremacy as nothing less than absurd and ridiculous, at the same time rarely questioned the historic substratum of *iʿjāz* – apparently because, at first glance, it had nothing to do with the theological miracle itself. What Wilhelm Ahlwardt identified in the mid-nineteenth century as characteristic of 'the Arabs' has hardly ever been doubted:

> But what they took the greatest pride in and valued more highly than all gifts and all possessions, apart from their religion, was their language, the works of their literature. For if ever a whole people cherished the works of its language with general interest, even with sacred adoration, and rejoiced in them with admiration and wonder as in the song and the sound of speech, and so delved into the wonderful working and forming of the word, into the inconceivable diversity of forms and into the secret of meanings, it is the Arabs, from the earliest times through the entire course of their history.[39]

While that part of the remembered past that directly concerned the credibility of the quranic proof was subjected to rigorous historical criticism, Orientalism took the myth of the Arabs as a nation of poets almost at face value. The scepticism of the historian, one is inclined to conclude, is less pronounced where it is not fed by religiously motivated doubts.

The Quran and the Traditions

The realization that remembered history is always a construct does not necessarily imply that it is completely random and composed of arbitrary inventions. Naturally there must be something on which the 'myth' is founded, although that foundation will often have been different in fact than it appears in cultural memory. By any stretch of the imagination, the entire reception history of the revealed scripture could no more have been made up out of thin air than the remembered context of the revelation itself.

At least the statements that Muhammad addressed his compatriots with recitations that he represented as divine inspiration, and that his recitations had an effect of some kind, can be considered as being founded on an 'established' historic reality, provided one attributes to the Quran a minimum of authenticity as a historic document.[40] Even such a strictly factually oriented Quran scholar as Tilman Nagel states that Muhammad's reading cast 'as it were a spell on many Meccans'.[41] And Jacques Berque states,

> And it would be preposterous to deny that this text, which came down over twenty years in periodically interrupted and unordered fragments, and was collected twenty years later, could [not] have gained the acceptance it has if it did not possess its, let us say, truly unique qualities.[42]

The Quran itself documents its own reception history and testifies to its aesthetic appeal – for example, in verse 39:23:

> God has sent down the most beautiful of all teachings (*aḥsana l-ḥadīth*): a Scripture that is consistent and draws comparisons; that causes the skins of those in awe of their Lord to shiver. Then their skins and their hearts soften at the mention of God.[43]

It is worthwhile to examine the wording more closely: *taqshaʿirru minhū julūdu l-laḏīna yakhshawna rabbahum thumma talīnu julūduhum wa-qulūbuhum ilā ḏikri llāhi* – literally, something like '. . . at which the skin of those who fear their Lord will become rough, but then their skins and their hearts will soften in remembrance of God.' The passage precisely defines the postulated effect of a quranic recitation: it first causes gooseflesh (this is exactly the process indicated by the verb *taqsha'irru*),[44] then soothes the hearer in body and soul, making him ready to celebrate God. The passage clearly says that religious insight is communicated aesthetically by the hearing of a speech that is called beautiful and makes the listener shiver, gives him gooseflesh: it is communicated by *aḥsanu l-ḥadīth*, 'the most beautiful speech', an experience of beauty. Yet the ultimate purpose of the act of communication as formulated by the speaker is not mere pleasure or Kant's 'disinterested satisfaction', but a cathartic process that fosters the readiness to celebrate God (*ilā ḏikri llāhi*). In Schiller's words,

> Only through beauty's morning gate
> Didst thou the land of knowledge find.[45]

In praising the speech as 'beautiful' (*ḥasan*), the speaker in the Quran verse posits a formal excellence. At the beginning of the twelfth surah we are told, 'We will relate to thee / the fairest of stories (*aḥsana l-qaṣaṣ*)',[46] and another passage refers to the Quran as the 'most beautiful explanation' (*aḥsanu t-tafsīr*).[47] Rudi Paret is, as far as I can see, the only German translator to read *ḥasan* and the superlative *aḥsan* almost always as 'good' and 'better'. However, the quality attributed to the Quran in these verses is not general in nature but refers specifically to formal properties.[48] The root *ḥ-s-n* in Arabic (including quranic Arabic) has the semantic field 'good, excellent, beautiful, comely': it encompasses both moral and aesthetic senses, expressing a philosophy that is not foreign to the Classical mind. Plotinus' sentence that the good and the beautiful, goodness and beauty, are identical[49] corresponds exactly to the semantic reality of the Quran. While Arabic terms with this root always carry both connotations, translators must choose one meaning or the other, depending on the context, and thus restrict the meaning of the expression. For example, people tend to translate *wa-ḥasuna ūlā'ika rafīqan*[50] in the sense of 'what good companions they are', because, in modern usage, companions called 'beautiful' would suggest outwardly attractive people. In the Arabic, however, 'beautiful' can just as well be understood in the sense of 'morally good', and vice versa. Even in passages in which *ḥasan* or *aḥsan* occurs in connection with *'amal* (work) or *ya'malūna* (the corresponding verb), the word can only be translated as 'good', since it denotes a moral category.[51] In other contexts, Paret's translation of *ḥasan* as 'good' is an unnecessary generalization – that is, when the term evidently denotes an aesthetic category, as in verse 95:4: *laqad khalaqnā l-insāna fī aḥsani taqwīmin*, 'We indeed created Man in the fairest stature'.[52] Here *aḥsan* means neither morally 'good' nor an unspecified superlative quality ('best'), but 'well-formed', hence beautiful, fair.[53] This sense is evident even to Paret in verse 55:70, in which the women of paradise are called *khayrātun ḥisānun*: here the quality of goodness (of character) is distinguished from the quality of beauty, and the root *ḥ-s-n* clearly stands for an aesthetic quality.

Leaving aside the question whether the quranic speaker is right to call his recitation *aḥsan*, the occurrence of the assertion itself is remarkable in a revealed scripture. From the point of view of reception aesthetics, it assumes a certain prior resonance on the part of the listeners. A speaker would not emphasize, with no further explanation, that he is narrating 'the most beautiful of stories' if such a claim could be expected to be met with surprise and bewilderment as being diametrically opposed to the audience's expectations. That the Quran presents the realization of a metaphysical truth as a sensual experience is also implied by the continuation of verse 39:23, which refers to the trembling that seizes the Quran's listeners, and by verse 5:83, which says that 'thou seest their eyes overflow with tears because of the truth they recognize'.[54]

The statement that something happens to the listeners when the Quran is recited may have been met with protest, and the claim of having caused such a reaction is not necessarily congruent with the reality of the time. Subjectively, however, from the speaker's point of view, such a reaction must have occurred in order for him to refer to it. And, even if one doesn't share the Muslim view that the narrator is God and hence omniscient, one must nonetheless conclude from the account of an aesthetic effect of the recitation that such an effect in fact occurred, although it may not have been as universal or as overpowering as the speaker claims. Gustav Richter is one of the few Western Quran scholars to perceive that 'we comprehend the force of the experience under which the faithful stood at the proclamation, since the Prophet describes it to us himself.'[55]

Ultimately, a word like 'beautiful' is of course only an empty shell, expressing little more than that something is formally or sensually attractive, or that one likes it, or that it feels pleasant or has a positive value. The Quran is found to be 'beautiful', but the texts do not say what the quranic speaker sees as its specific quality, or how the 'creators' of a traditional biography of the Prophet – an author such as Ibn Isḥāq (died c. 767) and an editor such as Ibn Hishām, say – imagine the fascination it evokes. What beauty is, which qualities were associated with the term *ḥasan* in seventh- and eighth-century Arabia, and what constituted a beautiful text for Muhammad's contemporaries cannot be determined on the basis of such remarks, and the question can't really be resolved anyway. There is no doubt that the concept is something fundamentally different from what a person of the twenty-first century imagines. It is remarkable, however, that the quranic speaker seems to use *mutashābih* in verse 39:23 and the passage *aḥsana taqwīm* in verse 95:4 to denote beauty as a kind of formal harmony or proportion: this is reminiscent of the definition of beauty in the aesthetics of Classical European art as a harmony between the parts of a whole. It is perhaps a universal aspect of the experience of beauty, and in any case one found in classical antiquity, that the ordered form of aesthetic objects – their measure, proportion – is what distinguishes them from the ugly, formless and chaotic and makes them appear to the recipients as pleasant, soothing or generally 'impressive'. Whether we call such a category 'beautiful' is not critically important:

> How all that is brought in and transformed and put before you, how one theme is led up to and another left behind, taken apart; yet in the process something new is getting ready, so that there is no empty or feeble passage; how flexibly the rhythm changes, a climax approaches, takes in tributaries from all sides, swells like a rising torrent, bursts out in roaring triumph, triumph itself, triumph 'in and for itself' – I do not like to call it beautiful, the word 'beauty' has always been half offensive to me, it has such a silly face, and people feel wanton and corrupt when they say it. But it is good, good in the extreme, it could not be better, perhaps it ought not to be better...[56]

No, this is not a comment on the Quran, although in the course of this study we shall encounter a number of such commentaries that express similar sentiments, in similar diction. This quotation is from Thomas Mann's *Doctor Faustus*, and what the speaker is referring to here is a musical composition.

We can infer from the Quran that the Prophet regularly visited the Kaaba in the early years of his vocation to recite the revealed verses.[57] The first few believers, who threw themselves on the ground or wept during his recitation, gathered around him,[58] along with increasing numbers of curious listeners. Muhammad's opponents were often present as well. At first they treated the new prophet with scorn and demonstrative contempt; their reaction to Muhammad's growing audience was apparently marked by increasing unease and hostility. They could not accept his claim to speak with divine authority and sought to dismiss him as an ordinary poet, soothsayer, sorcerer or fanatic.[59] Up to this point, the account of Muhammad's preaching given by the later tradition matches the recitation scenario that we can infer from the Quran itself, which has some actual historical value.[60]

Yet it is more instructive, and in a certain regard much more exciting, or at least more colourful, to see how the quranic scenario is illustrated in the collective memory, and how the quranic narrative of reception, which is only hinted at in the text, appears as the narrative of a miraculous aesthetic effect. The attraction exerted by the Quran, to which some allusions in the text itself attest, is interpreted poetically in the cultural memory and described from many points of view and in great detail. The extra-quranic documents too attest, much more strongly than the scripture itself, that the revelation was not only persuasive in content but also to a great extent aesthetically experienced. Thus the later Muslim exegetes considered it obvious that *ḥasan* or *aḥsan* in the Quran's self-referential remarks referred more to its linguistic form than to its salvific message. The passage cited above, for example, *naḥnu naquṣṣu ʿalayka aḥsana l-qaṣaṣi bi-mā awḥaynā ilayka hāḏā l-qur'āna*, was always understood by Muslim commentators as meaning, in the words of az-Zamakhsharī (d. 1144), that God 'recounts the story in the most beautiful way'.[61] In the verse 'God has revealed the most beautiful message', they likewise read the postpositive attribute *mutashābih* ('resembling one another') as referring to the style or the verbal composition (*naẓm*) of the Quran, and hence saw a praise of its linguistic form as implied in *aḥsanu l-ḥadīth*.[62] For the exegetes – who did not encounter the text immediately but rather perceived it in the context of their expectations, which were shaped by collective memory – there could be no doubt that the beauty of the message was poetic in nature, because to them the aesthetic impact of the recitation on Muhammad's contemporaries, which is only alluded to in the Quran, was a historic fact documented by numerous reports.

Two premises are fundamental for the early history of the Quran's reception as it is preserved in the cultural memory of the Muslim community: first, the notion that the pre-Islamic Arabs were a cultural community substantially characterized and identified by their language and poetry, and, second, the tremendous and inescapable fascination that the recitation of the Quran is supposed to have exerted. These two premises underlie all of the accounts of individual situations of reception, within which certain patterns or memory figures can in turn be perceived. These figures include the spontaneous converts as well as the opponents who publicly rail against the Prophet while secretly consumed with longing to hear the Quran. We also encounter the villains, who know no other way to defend against the power that the Quran exerts than to attack anyone who recites it, and the poets, who are unable to match the Quran with a work of equal poetic perfection. We meet the Prophet's followers who vie with one another in their love for Quran recitation; we hear anecdotes about the art of individual reciters; and naturally there is the Prophet himself, to whom the most beautiful voice is attributed. A key element of the early reception history is also the irritation caused by the language of the Quran, because it does not belong to any of the known genres of verse and yet has a great but inexplicable attraction. A related phenomenon is the curiosity that brought people from the entire Arabian peninsula, and even from other countries, to Mecca or Medina to hear the Quran for themselves, and the ensuing frantic efforts of the Quraysh to deter everyone in the country and abroad from that intention.

In order to familiarize ourselves with the remembered history in its present-day form, the following presentation is not limited to a strictly circumscribed corpus of source texts from the hadith and the biography of the Prophet.[63] I will also draw on a complementary selection of later presentations of early Islamic history as explicitly Muslim readings of the original Muslim sources. Some of these are theological writings from the ninth to thirteenth centuries in which accounts of the founding period are no longer merely recounted, but much more clearly arranged and embedded in a religious world view;[64] others are modern books about the Quran and early Islamic history, widely accepted in theological and traditionally religious circles, that evaluate and sometimes selectively elaborate, psychologically or exhortatively, on the original sources – that is, the early hadith collections and the *sīra* works – or use them to support a particular interpretation.[65] To be exact, we can distinguish three layers of memory. To avoid confusion and repetition, however, I will not separate them at the outset, although I will, when occasion arises, point out differences in the presentation of remembered history in the different discourses. Towards the end of this chapter I will include some remarks on how the history of Quran reception allows us to observe the transformation of certain facts in cultural memory. It goes without saying that the following exposition is selective and merely highlights individual themes of the reception history, namely those that are aesthetically relevant. This is not meant to suggest that Muhammad's listeners, in the cultural memory of Muslims, perceived the Quran exclusively as 'beautiful', or that the success of his prophetic mission is attributed to poetic excellence alone. On the contrary, a number of very important conversions are recorded – including the first, that of Khadīja – with no indication of an aesthetic reception of the Quran. Nowhere does the Muslim literature overlook other factors, such as the Prophet's charisma[66] or the justice of quranic doctrine,[67] but they are not the topic of this chapter. Without denying the importance of other well-known facets, this chapter is devoted exclusively to an aspect of the Quran's reception history that is largely neglected in Western research. Let me emphasize once more that none of the traditions presented in the following is considered historically true, although for the sake of readability I relate them here without quotation marks. Nor are they considered as 'falsifications', however. Whether they are factual or not does not need to be resolved, since this investigation is not concerned with reconstructing the 'true' historic events. What interests us here is rather the construction of a memory as an element of identity formation. The present investigation assumes that truth and falsehood are not the only categories that are of interest to cultural studies.

Conversions

In many Muslims' view of their own history, the conversions of the early Islamic period were not due simply to the Prophet's arguments, his preaching, his presence or his charisma. Where the conversion stories mention the immediate cause at all, Arabs most often converted upon hearing the Quran, whether as a recitation or as part of ritual prayer or *ṣalāt*.[68] However, I must hasten to add, the accounts do not often relate the immediate cause. Although the biographies of the Prophet record the exact names of hundreds of converts, in most cases they merely note who embraced Islam when, or succinctly report, 'The Messenger of God offered him Islam, and he converted to Islam (*fa-ʿaraḍa ʿalayhi l-islāma fa-aslama*).[69] The assertion that the poet Bujayr ibn Zuhayr, the subject of a report by Ibn Kathīr (d. 1372), was counted among the more dangerous opponents of the Prophet and, as the context implies, had no intention of converting when he met Muhammad raises the question how to explain such a radical and sudden change of heart and how we should picture the encounter between the two men: what were the words, gestures or actions in which the Prophet expounded Islam? That Muhammad recited from the Quran, and that the quranic recitation was the principal medium of his prophetic mission, is supported by those accounts that enlarge but little on the act of conversion. 'The Messenger of God spoke, and he recited the Quran (*talā l-qur'āna*) and summoned [the listeners] to God and commended Islam': Ibn Isḥāq usually describes Muhammad's exhortation in these and similar words.[70] Ibn Sa'd (d. 845) is no different, recounting Muhammad's encounter with the representatives of the Khazraj at the first covenant of 'Aqaba in the tersest possible words: 'He sat down with them, summoned them to God, and recited the Quran to them, whereupon they followed him.'[71] Another variation on the pattern of early Islamic conversion is the case in which a heathen hears or recites the Quran by chance and then converts. 'Ali ibn Abī Ṭālib, for example, one of the very first converts, met the Prophet at *ṣalāt* and then converted to Islam.[72] The report says nothing about what impression the recited text made on young 'Ali, or what about it moved him to convert. Likewise, 'Uthmān ibn Maẓ'ūn, who heard the Prophet recite verse 16:90 ('God commands justice...'), is quoted as saying, 'Then faith was fixed in my heart and I began to love Muhammad.'[73] Other converts are quoted as uttering general exclamations of pleasure. An example is the Bedouin who heard a Muslim recite the Quran and then exclaimed, 'I declare that nothing in Creation is able to produce such oratory.'[74] We may also consider the anecdote about the young Jew Īyās ibn Mu'āḏ, whose tribe, the 'Abdulashhal, had come from Yathrib to Mecca to persuade the Quraysh to ally with them against the Khazraj. When Muhammad visited them and recited to them from the Quran, Īyās exclaimed, 'O my people! By God, this is better than that (*khayrun mimmā*) for which you came', and he converted to Islam.[75]

The judgement of the healer Ḍimād is similarly imprecise. After Muhammad recited the profession of faith to him three times, Ḍimād gave up his attempt to cure Muhammad of the obsession that his countrymen thought afflicted him. Ḍimād exclaimed, 'I have heard many words from the sorcerers, the soothsayers and the poets, but never anything like this', and he embraced Islam.[76] This account gives us to understand that Ḍimād finds Muhammad's oratory better than the verses of other inspired speakers, but what makes it superior is unspecified. In another version, Ḍimād at least mentions 'beauty', although without indicating what kind of beauty he means: 'Never have I heard a speech more beautiful (*aḥsan*) than that', he exclaims, and asks Muhammad to recite it again, whereupon he converts.[77]

The conversion accounts presented thus far, couched in general terms, rather hint than make plain that the Quran was received as an aesthetic phenomenon. The aesthetic aspect emerges more clearly, however, when these accounts are placed in the context of those that do relate the listener's specific impressions. Several other stories describe the recitation of the Quran as *ḥasan* or *aḥsan*, such as the story of the poet Suwayd ibn aṣ-Ṣāmit, an official of the city of Yathrib, who was called 'the Consummate' because of his strength, his eloquence, his dignity and his lineage. Some months before the Hijra, Suwayd had come on the heathen pilgrimage to Mecca, where the Prophet visited him personally to invite him to embrace Islam. The account of this meeting is the same in Ibn Hishām's and Ibn Kathīr's biographies of the Prophet:

> [Suwayd] said, 'Perhaps you've got something like that which I have.' 'And what is that?' asked the apostle. 'The roll of Luqmān', meaning the wisdom of Luqmān, he answered. 'Hand it to me', said the apostle, and he handed it over, and he said, 'Truly, this discourse is fine [*ḥasan*]. But that which I have is better still [*afḍal*]: a Quran which God has revealed to me which is a guidance and a light.' And the apostle recited the Quran to him [*talā 'alayhi l-qur'āna*] and invited him to Islam; he did not withdraw from it but said, 'This is a fine saying.' Then he went off and rejoined his people in Medina and almost at once the Khazraj killed him. Some of his family used to say, 'In our opinion he was a Muslim when he was killed'; he was (in fact) killed before the Battle of Bu'ath.[78]

The recitation of the Quran is sometimes also described as *jamīl* or *ajmal*,[79] which can only be understood as praise of its poetic form. While the root *ḥ-s-n* covers a semantic field from (morally) good to (outwardly) beautiful, *jamīl* is more clearly an aesthetic category that almost always refers to the sensory impression of a phenomenon. The following episode perhaps expresses most succinctly that the Quran listeners were reacting to an aesthetic experience:

> Abū 'Ubayd mentions that a Bedouin listened to a man reciting *fā-ṣda' bi-mā tu'mar* ('So proclaim openly what you have been commanded').[80] He prostrated himself in worship and said, 'I have thrown myself down before the eloquence of this oration (*sajadtu li-fashāḥatihī*).'[81]

The best-known of all conversions in Islamic history is also among those that imply an aesthetic experience: that of 'Umar ibn al-Khaṭṭāb, who later became caliph. Originally one of the most dangerous opponents of the young Muslim congregation, 'Umar was a man of thirty or thirty-five who was endowed with enormous muscular strength and energy, loved gambling, wine and poetry, and was considered both sentimental and short-tempered.[82] 'We could not pray in the Kaaba before 'Umar had converted to Islam, and when he converted he fought the Quraysh until he was allowed to pray there himself, and we prayed with him.'[83] This statement by 'Abdullāh ibn Mas'ūd, a companion of the Prophet, indicates the importance of the conversion for the cause of Islam.[84] On the day of the events recounted, 'Umar had originally intended to kill the Prophet, but, just when he wanted to go to him, he learned that his sister Fāṭima and her husband Sa'īd ibn Zayd had embraced Islam. Enraged, he ran to their house. From the street in front of their door, he heard someone reciting the Quran to them. 'Umar stormed into the room. The reciter hid as quickly as he could, while Fāṭima took the pages of the Quran and hid them under her legs.

'What was that murmuring I heard?' 'Umar shouted at her.

'You didn't hear anything', said Fāṭima and her husband, trying to calm him.

'Umar shouted, 'Yes, I did, by God, and I know you are following Muhammad in his religion!'

He wanted to attack his brother-in-law, but Fāṭima threw herself between them so that 'Umar unintentionally struck her a violent blow.

'Yes, we have converted to Islam, and we believe in God and His Messenger – so do what you want', Fāṭima and Sa'īd cried.

'Umar already regretted his behaviour; the blood on his sister's face moved his heart. In a gentle voice, he asked her for the scripture. After Fāṭima had made him promise to return the manuscript undamaged and had also persuaded him to perform an ablution, since an unclean person must not touch the Quran, she handed it to him. 'Umar began to recite the surah *Ṭa Hā* (no. 20). After just a few verses he stopped, and exclaimed,

'How magnificent, how beautiful these words are (*mā aḥsana hāḏa l-kalāma wa-akrama*)!'

Once he had read to the end, he immediately went to Muhammad to profess Islam before him. 'The Messenger of God was so vociferous in his thanks to God that the whole house heard of 'Umar's conversion', the story goes. This is a slightly abridged form of the version given by Ibn Hishām and Ibn Kathīr.[85]

According to another version that both biographers also present, after 'Umar had looked in vain for his drinking comrades, and for the wine merchant, he came by the Kaaba, where Muhammad was at *ṣalāt*. Curious, 'Umar slipped behind the black stone of the Kaaba without the Prophet noticing. 'Umar is then quoted as saying, 'When I heard the Quran, my heart softened, and I wept, and I was penetrated by Islam.' After Muhammad had finished his prayer he started home, and 'Umar followed him to profess his conversion to Islam before him.[86]

Although the plots are quite different, the two versions have some essential elements in common. In both of them, the recitation of the Quran causes the sudden and unexpected conversion of one of Muhammad's most formidable opponents, and in both versions 'Umar's own comments indicate a subjective experience of an aesthetic nature. ʿUmar does not say he has now seen the truth, or that the message has convinced him, or that he has finally understood after long deliberation or through a sudden insight, or anything of that sort. Instead, he tells of 'beauty' and that his heart was 'softened', that he wept on hearing the Quran and that something 'penetrated' him. Taken all together, these descriptions can only refer to a sensual event, not to a rational decision or some kind of crucial moral-ethical experience.

In this and other episodes, who recites the revealed text seems not to be essential. The traditions include spontaneous conversions to Islam as well as outbursts of joy and delight by Quran listeners even without Muhammad's presence. The difference between Muhammad's own language – the language he uses when calling people to Islam – and that of the Quran is conspicuous even in the early sources. And it is only to the language of the Quran that an aesthetic quality is explicitly attributed. Muhammad's missionary sermons, on the other hand, seem, by his own account, to evoke rejection from most listeners.[87]

Very often the conversion accounts are about poets, or at least include – as in ʿUmar's case – the remark that the person concerned is renowned for his rhetorical gift. The literature has a penchant for affirmations of the superiority and uniqueness of the quranic language by such 'experts' as al-Walīd, aṭ-Ṭufayl, Ḥassān, Labīd, Kaʿb and Suwayd.[88] This can also be observed in the account of aṭ-Ṭufayl ibn ʿAmr ad-Dawsī's conversion.

Aṭ-Ṭufayl was a wealthy poet and a nobleman of the Banu Daws. Ibn Isḥāq reports that several of the Quraysh visited him on his arrival in Mecca. They warned him against Muhammad's rhetorical sorcery, which was sowing nothing but discord among the people. If aṭ-Ṭufayl were to approach the Prophet and listen to his oration, he and his people would become embroiled in dissension and conflict (by the powerful effects of Muhammad's preaching, adds Maḥmūd Rāmiyār, who retells this episode from the *sīra*). The Quraysh urgently advised aṭ-Ṭufayl to exchange no words with the Messenger of God, and above all not to listen to his recitations. 'They were so insistent that I decided not to listen to a word or to speak to him', Ibn Isḥāq quotes aṭ-Ṭufayl as saying. He even plugged his ears with cotton, 'fearing that I might overhear a word or two against my will'.[89] In the Kaaba, aṭ-Ṭufayl finally encountered the Prophet, who was at prayer. Unintentionally, he overheard some of the recitation. While Ibn Isḥāq at this point merely notes that aṭ-Ṭufayl heard a beautiful oration, the impression of that speech on the listener is described by the present-day author Rāmiyār in these terms:

> It was a sweet and inspired recitation. It beguiled the heart and caressed the mind. So great was the attraction of that recitation that no man of poetry and rhetoric could escape it. A wave of gentleness flowed towards him in what he heard; it contained a wealth of spiritual meanings such as he had never encountered in any human oratory.[90]

In any case, what he heard was so attractive that aṭ-Ṭufayl abandoned his resolution and decided to listen more closely. 'I am a prudent man and poet; I can distinguish what is beautiful from what is vile!' he said to himself. 'What is there to keep me from listening to what this man is saying? If what he propounds is beautiful, I will accept it; if it is vile, I will leave it.'[91] He followed Muhammad home and asked him to recite something to him. Ibn Hishām quotes his judgement: 'By God I never heard anything finer or anything more just. So I became a Muslim and bore true witness.' Aṭ-Ṭufayl returned to his people and won most of his comrades over to Islam.[92]

Besides poets, another group of people who were particularly receptive to the beauty of the Quran, if we believe the traditions, were Muhammad's particularly aggressive enemies: Meccans such as Unays and ʿUmar ibn al-Khaṭṭāb, who at first fiercely opposed the Prophet but then spontaneously joined him when they heard his recitation. 'Let us just consider the effect that hearing the verses had on the opponents', Maḥmūd Rāmiyār comments. 'In this regard alone, we know the names and full biographies of dozens of people who went to the Messenger of God to dispute with him, disagree with him and protest against him, and they no sooner sat down with him, heard his preaching and God's verses, than they became Muslims.'[93] A well-known example is that of Muṭʿim ibn ʿAdī, who, after his closest relatives had fallen in the Battle of Badr, went to the Prophet to ransom his cousin and two of his comrades. The Prophet was at prayer and was reciting the surah *Ṭūr* (no. 52), which warns of the Day of Judgement and proclaims the bliss of Paradise. When he reached the last verse, Muṭʿim converted to Islam.[94] 'It was as if my heart had split open!' Abū Nuʿaym quotes him as saying.[95] In al-Wāqidī's (d. 822) version, Muṭʿim falls asleep in the mosque in Medina and is awakened by the Prophet's recitation. 'It was on that day that Islam first penetrated my heart', he says in this account.[96]

ʿUthmān ibn Maẓʿūn's conversion takes place in a similar way: filled with wrath, he sought out the Prophet, who invited him to sit down. The ensuing conversation was suddenly interrupted when Muhammad received a revelation. When he came to his senses, ʿUtmān asked him, 'What was said to you?' The Prophet recited verse 16:90 ('God commands justice...'). 'Then faith was established in my heart, and I loved Muhammad', ʿUtmān said according to the tradition.[97]

Still more spectacular are the conversions of the Medinans Saʿd ibn Muʿād and Usayd ibn al-Ḥuḍayr, the leaders of the Banū ʿAbdilashhal, immediately before the Prophet took up residence in the city. When they heard of the arrival of two of Muhammad's followers, one of whom was Saʿd's cousin, Saʿd asked his comrade Usayd to go to them and drive them out of the neighbourhood. To prevent them from tempting the weaker members of the tribe, he wanted Usayd to ban them from setting foot in the territory of the ʿAbdulashhal ever again. Full of wrath, Usayd took his lance and went to the two strangers. How dare they lead his comrades astray, he cried, and threatened to kill them.

'Won't you first sit down and hear us?' Muṣʿab ibn ʿUmayr, one of the two Muslims, asked him. 'If you like what you hear, you can accept it, and if it displeases you, you can stop.'

Usayd agreed, planted his lance in the ground, and sat down. Muṣʿab spoke to him of Islam and recited from the Quran. Even before Usayd spoke, the tension in his features was released, so that the two Muslims saw 'Islam in his radiant, transfigured face'.

'How magnificent, how wonderfully beautiful these words are (*mā aḥsana hāḏā l-kalāma wa-ajmalahū*)!' Usayd cried. 'What must one do to join this religion?'

Shortly thereafter, Usayd returned to his brother and assured him that he had found nothing wrong with the two strangers. He also mentioned that the Banū Ḥāritha had set out to kill Saʿd's cousin Asʿad to expose the head of the tribe and to punish him for having given protection to the two Muslims. Enraged, Saʿd jumped up, anxious about the Banū Ḥāritha's intentions. 'By God, I see you have failed', he said, and hurried to the two Muslims. But Muṣʿab was able to persuade him, with the same words as before, to sit down and hear the recitation for himself. When he recited to him from the Quran, Saʿd too joined the new religion on the spot. With an exalted expression on his face, the head of the tribe returned to his people, who all converted to Islam immediately.[98] 'Those who showed the most obstinacy and hostility embraced the faith fastest when the Quran was recited to them', Muḥammad Abū Zahra comments.[99] Naturally the Quran's conquest of its bitterest opponents, or of the poets for that matter, from one second to the next is hardly surpassable as a confirmation of its supernatural force.

Conversions caused by the sound of the Quran are also presented as collective acts by larger groups,[100] even including members of other scriptural religions. Twenty Abyssinian Christians who had gone to Mecca to obtain news of the new Prophet converted on their first meeting with him. 'When they heard the Quran their eyes flowed with tears, and they accepted God's call, believed in Him, and confessed His truth', the tradition tells. 'God, what a wretched band you are!' the Quraysh railed indignantly. 'Your people at home sent you to bring them information about the fellow, and as soon as you sat with him you renounced your religion and believed what he said. We don't know a more asinine band than you.'[101]

The Negus of Abyssinia is also said to have wept, together with all his bishops, 'until his beard was wet and . . . until their scrolls were wet',[102] when the Muslim emigrants recited part of the surah *Maria* to him. Abū Nuʿaym presents both that version and another of the same event. The other version recounts:

> When he heard it, the negus knew that it was the truth, and he said, 'Recite to us more of this good oration!'
> Then they recited another surah, and when he heard it he knew the truth, and he said, 'I believe you, and I believe your Prophet.'[103]

The episode demonstrates the importance attributed to the mere sound of the Quran, for we cannot assume that the negus spoke Arabic, nor is there any suggestion that the Muslims recited a translation. The problem of comprehension is not mentioned in the traditions. A later scholar, Qāḍī ʿIyāḍ, infers from that fact that it was not only Arabic-speaking listeners who were enchanted by Quran recitations. In support of his conclusion he presents one anecdote about a Christian who 'neither understood the meaning of the Quran nor knew the explanations of it', but nonetheless wept on hearing the Quran. Asked why he was weeping, he answered, 'because it is moving (*li-sh-shajā*) and because of the poetic composition (*naẓm*).'[104] In another case, ʿIyāḍ tells of a Byzantine general who heard a Muslim prisoner recite a verse of the Quran, and thereupon travelled to Mecca expressly to profess Islam before ʿUmar.[105] Reports of this kind are what Muḥammad Abū Zahra has in mind when he says,

> The Quran was of such musical (*mūsīqā*) and poetic quality that it made any listener shiver, even if they understood no Arabic at all. For the words, with their intonations, nasalizations, rhymes, verses and pauses were arranged in such a way that they exerted an attraction on non-Arabs as well, even though they did not understand the meaning of the words. It was the melody (*naġam*) that produced a wondrous image in them.[106]

Other Muslim authors of the twentieth century too, such as Ṣādiq ar-Rāfiʿī,[107] Labīb as-Saʿīd,[108] Moḥammad Taqī Sharīʿaṭī-Mazīnānī,[109] Maḥmūd Bustānī[110] and the poet Adonis (Adūnīs),[111] emphasize the acoustic dimension of the quranic miracle, an aspect that is completely absent from the earliest traditions and appears only marginally in the classical *iʿjāz* tracts. However, Maḥmūd Rāmiyār writes,

> Quran recitation, with that beautiful sound that is proper to it, with the attraction and charm inherent in its rhymes, with the low and high tones of its words and the density of its melody, produces in the listener a condition of tenderness and evokes a movement in his soul that occurs with no other speech and no other song. Its wonderful attraction affects even those who do not understand Arabic and do not know Islam; even they are shaken.[112]

Even the jinn converted when they heard the Prophet reciting the ritual prayer at night in the desert between Ṭā'if and Mecca.[113] According to the Quran, they said, 'We heard a wonderful recitation that led to righteousness, and therefore we believed in it.'[114] The Prophet is said to have known that they flocked around him when he recited the revelation. One time, to give his companions the opportunity to see the jinn, he led them outside the gates of Mecca at night. There he moved a short way away from the group and recited from the Quran. ʿAbdullāh ibn Masʿūd reports what happened:

> Great black creatures surrounded him so that they blocked our sight and I could no longer hear the Prophet's voice. After a while they dissolved, like a cloud, but among them a group remained. As the day dawned, the Prophet ended the recitation and departed. He came to me and asked me where the group that had remained was.
> 'There they are', I said.
> The Prophet took a bone and some camel dung and gave them to them as provisions for their journey, and said that those things were unclean for humans.[115]

The last example I would like to offer of a sudden conversion caused by Quran recitation is one I have found in no biography of the Prophet in this form but which I heard told years ago in Iran and have heard many times since.[116] I present it not only because it has made a particular impression upon me, but also because it indicates that by no means all the stories about the life of the Prophet have found their way into the canon of biographies and traditions. The story tells of a scout from Yathrib who went to Mecca to investigate the mysterious reports of the appearance of a new prophet. People had warned him beforehand against the prophet's magic tricks, and urged him to plug his ears before he encountered people reciting from the revelation. As the man walked through the streets, he met a group of the faithful listening to a Quran reading. He thought to himself, I am a man of reason and experience. Why am I making a fool of myself by plugging my ears just because someone is reciting a text? He removed his ear plugs, heard the sound of the Quran, and professed Islam on the spot. The sirens in the twelfth book of Homer's *Odyssey* cannot have been more alluring.

The peculiarity of such conversion accounts, which always have the same structure – one or more protagonists who are hostile to the Prophet or know nothing about him hear a few verses of the Quran and convert to Islam on the spot – becomes especially conspicuous when we search for something analogous in other religions. The phenomenon of a conversion caused by an aesthetic experience in the narrow sense, as is proclaimed to have occurred in Islam even in later centuries,[117] is hardly found in Christianity, for example. Neither in the Gospels nor in other sources can such accounts be found, much less with any comparable frequency. The great conversions and initiations of the Christian narrative – Paul,[118] Augustine,[119] Pascal[120] and Luther[121] are perhaps the first names that come to mind in this connection – are caused by experiences which, although they may be just as remarkable to the outsider, are, according to the autobiographical testimony, not primarily aesthetic in nature. It is not the beauty of the divine revelation that stands out in the protagonist's perception, but its moral, ethical meaning for the individual. This is not to say that the development and practice of Christianity or of any other religion could be imaginable without the aesthetic fascination of certain places, texts, songs, images, smells, acts, gestures or vestments,[122] or that Protestantism, for example, could have spread so rapidly in the German-speaking countries without the poetic force of the Luther Bible. But however important it may be in the practice of the faith, the aesthetic moment plays a subordinate role in the image that the Christian – or, more specifically, the Protestant – congregation forms of its own past. Few Christians if any would claim that Jesus drew flocks of disciples because they perceived a formal perfection in his oratory, and no Christian religious instruction teaches that the triumph of Christianity has its cause in the poetic beauty of the Gospels. Even Johann Georg Hamann, who has emphasized the aesthetic character of revealed scripture in his writings as no other Christian thinker has done, does not interpret his own spiritual experience of 31 March 1758, which followed immediately from reading scripture – namely the fifth chapter of Deuteronomy – as an experience of beauty. In his notes about that spring day in London, Hamann says that he came to have a concrete, personal experience of the idea of salvation and felt himself, after years of confusion and depression, amid conditions 'too abominable to tell', as Wilhelm Dilthey hints in his biographical essay,[123] to be liberated from Egypt's bondage. According to Hamann himself, he fell 'into deep contemplation' while reading, thought of Abel, and identified himself with Cain:

> I felt my heart thump, I heard a voice sigh in its depths and wail like the voice of blood, like the voice of a slain brother who wanted to avenge his blood if I did not hear it betimes and went on stopping my ears to it saying that it was just this which made Cain a wanderer and a fugitive. All at once I felt my heart swell, and pour out in tears, and I could no longer conceal from my God that I was the fratricide, the murderer of His only begotten son. The Spirit of God went on, in spite of my great weakness, and the long resistance I had made against His witness and His stirring of me, to reveal to me more and more the mystery of the divine love and the benefit of faith in our gracious and only Saviour.[124]

The passage bears witness to an extraordinary, undeniably poetic attraction of the biblical text, without which Hamann's experience and hence his repentance would be inexplicable. However, he himself emphasizes the sudden comprehension of his own depravity and the redeeming, beatifying message: he does not mention its rhetorical splendour, nor does he compare the Bible with works of poetry to proclaim its supremacy or stylistic uniqueness.[125] Although Hamann's experience comes closest to those of the Quran listeners presented in this chapter, this distinguishes it from them: they explicitly mention the poetic form of the Quran as the force that causes their conversion. Not even among the many examples that

William James has presented and analysed in what is probably the most prominent collection of Christian conversion accounts is there a conversion story comparable with that of Labīd or ʿUmar.[126] The spontaneous professions of faith that James cites are 'all with a sense of astonished happiness, and of being wrought on by a higher control',[127] a description that could probably be applied equally to ʿUmar's subjective state, but the critical event in James's narratives is usually of moral or emotional importance: a person is in a state of existential despair or psychological distress when an event or a feeling makes them aware of the vanity of their lives to date, and from one second to the next they begin a new life. The alcoholic abandons his addiction; the miserable man becomes blessed; the rich man becomes a philanthropist; the doubter finds peace; the vicious man is purified. They follow the pattern of Augustine's conversion, his renunciation of the sensual pleasures that 'tugged at my fleshly garments', and his turn towards the 'chaste dignity of continence... cheerful but not wanton, modestly alluring me to come and doubt nothing':

> Thus I was sick and tormented, reproaching myself more bitterly than ever, rolling and writhing in my chain till it should be utterly broken. By now I was held but slightly, but still was held. And thou, O Lord, didst press upon me in my inmost heart with a severe mercy, redoubling the lashes of fear and shame.[128]

James cites no conversion that has its immediate cause in the aesthetic experience of revealed scripture. Where a scripture reading leads to a conversion, the cause is the 'impressions of the meaning of suddenly presented scripture texts'[129] – that is, passages whose meaning one suddenly comprehends, not verses that are so pleasing to hear that one cannot help feeling they are divine. Doubtless there are conversions to Christianity that are caused by the beauty of scripture, but accounts of such cases play, as far as I can tell, no significant part in the overall corpus of Christians' testimony on the spread of their religion. They are not a topos of the literature on the salvation history, not a figure of the collective memory. In the Muslim self-concept, however, the aesthetic fascination that the Quran exerts is a constitutive influence in the Muslim tradition of faith. It is this act of collective identification and interpretation, not the experience of beauty that occurs during the reception of sacred texts, that is specific to the religious world of Islam.

The Community of Quran Listeners

If even the jinn were unable to resist the Quran, if even the devils (*shayāṭīn*) were converted by the 'miraculous recitation',[130] it is no wonder that human beings too, once they had heard it and converted to Islam, could not get enough of it. A prototypical example is ʿAbbād ibn Bishr, who read the sixteenth surah with such passion that he did not stop even when an enemy shot arrows at him, eventually hitting him.[131] Some accounts suggest that the Muslims under the four 'rightly guided caliphs' (*al-khulafā' ar-rāshidūn*) had a Quran reciter with them at every battle to gladden the warriors' hearts, starting with the Battle of Badr at the latest.[132] 'Abdullah ibn 'Amr could not stop reciting the Quran after his conversion: not a day went by without his reciting the entire scripture at least once. He pursued his passion to such excess that in the end his wife had no other recourse but to speak to Muhammad, complaining that her husband had turned his back on the world, had declared eating and sleeping sinful. The Prophet told 'Abdullah to exercise moderation.[133] According to some sources, it was this event that moved him to issue the well-known command to allow at least three days for a complete reading of the Quran.[134]

Again and again we see that the ardour with which the Muslims listened to the Quran is attributed, among other causes, to the delight afforded by the euphony of the quranic language. The Prophet's prohibition against reciting even a short surah, such as no. 112, in a single breath is explained by a Shiite commentator with the observation that only an unhurried recitation 'preserves the beauty of the Quran'.[135] The Iranian scholar Mohammad Taqī Sharī'aṭī-Mazīnānī is overflowing in his description of the first listeners' delight:

> The Arab, already besotted with the beauty of language, suddenly heard an oration like none he had ever heard before. Everything about it was pleasure to him: its alluring melodies, its exquisite expressions, its harmonious structure, its novel style, and its argument too. His thoughts were opened, his intellect was stimulated, his heart illuminated; his soul became as light as a feather; his feelings and inclinations were moved and caressed; he thrilled to this oratory and was enraptured, he was amazed and astonished; it transformed, changed and delighted him.... What can I say, what words can describe the Quran, can explain its power? Once more, I must fall back on the Quran itself: its words have fallen like rays of light on the eloquent Arabs, so that the listener found himself immersed in light; it enveloped his whole being and every particle of his existence, illuminating his heart and mind. The Quran was a light that shone into the soul through the aperture of the ear; it transformed the soul and, as a result, the world.[136]

The manifestations of pleasure and fascination attributed to Muhammad's comrades are numerous. When the Prophet dictated the 23rd surah to the scribe 'Abdullāh ibn Abī Sarḥ, for example, 'Abdullāh was so enraptured at the description of the act of creation in the twelfth verse ('And we made Man from a lump of clay') that he cried out, 'Praise be to God, the most excellent Creator!' According to the Muslim interpretation, his words unintentionally anticipated the subsequent verse of the Quran.[137]

Al-Ġazālī (d. 1111) mentions that Khālid ibn ʿUqba once went to the Prophet and heard him recite part of the sixteenth surah:

> 'Recite it again', Khālid requested, and the Messenger of God recited it again. Khālid cried, 'By God, there is a sweetness (*ḥalāwa*) and a grace (*ṭalāwa*) in it; its floor is covered with leaves and its branches bear plentiful fruit: this is not the word of a human being.'[138]

Another companion of the Prophet, the future caliph Abū Bakr, is said to have been too moved by reciting the Quran, and a too 'gentle person' (*rajul raqīq*), to lead *ṣalāt* at common prayers.[139] Once, when the Prophet was sick and wanted to ask him to lead the prayers, ʿĀ'isha intervened, saying, 'If Abū Bakr takes your place, the people won't understand a word (of the Quran) because he'll be weeping so loudly. Send ʿUmar to recite the *ṣalāt* to the people.'[140] When the Quran was recited to him, however, Abū Bakr was as still as a piece of wood,[141] like Ibn Masʿūd, who looked like a 'garment thrown down'.[142] Ibn Masʿūd is reported to have said about the Quran, 'Its sweetness is never-ending, and its spring never runs dry',[143] and, on another occasion, 'When I contemplate the *ḥā'-mīm* surahs,[144] it is as if I had entered ever-green gardens with soft and lovely meadows. I am always searching for them.'[145]

Among those who indulged in blissful listening to the Quran were the angels. Usayd ibn al-Ḥuḍayr was reading the Quran one night when his horse began to jump about nervously. Usayd was worried that his little son, who lay next to him, might get trampled, and so he stopped. But every time he resumed his reading the horse began to jump again. Above its head Usayd saw something like a shadow with many lights in it rising up into the air out of sight. The next day, Usayd went to the Prophet and asked him about the vision. 'Those were the angels, listening to you. If you had continued, the people would have been able to see them in the morning, for they would not have concealed themselves.'[146] This narrative corresponds to a hadith cited by al-Ġazālī in his theological and aesthetic praise of the Quran (*faḍīlat al-Qur'ān*):

> A thousand years before the creation of the world, God the Exalted recited the surahs *Ṭāhā* and *Yāsīn*. When the angels heard them, they said, 'How happy are they to whom this will be revealed! How happy are the hearts that will carry this in them! How happy are the tongues that will pronounce it!'[147]

Of course the Prophet himself is said to have had a particularly beautiful voice. 'God listens to no one as attentively as a prophet reading the Quran with a beautiful voice', he says himself,[148] and the first Umayyad caliph, Muʿāwiya (d. 680), later told his comrades: 'If I weren't afraid of attracting a crowd, I would imitate for you how the Prophet recited.'[149] About Muhammad's rendition of the 95th surah, Al-Barā' ibn ʿĀzib said he had 'never experienced anything more beautiful than his recitation'.[150] In the Shiite literature, the imams are also said to have had extraordinary voices, which is not surprising, since the Shiite salvation history includes the lives and deaths of the imams who succeeded the Prophet. In the *Kāfī fī 'ilm ad-dīn*, for example, one of the four canonical hadith collections of the Shia, we read that the fourth imam, Zayn al-'Ābidīn (d. 712), had the best voice of his day. When he recited the Quran, the water bearers stopped in front of his door.[151] When he recited outdoors, 'it happened that passers-by swooned because of the beauty of his voice. Truly, when the imam let his voice sound, no one could withstand its beauty.'[152]

In spite of the popularity of his recitation, the Prophet preferred to hear others recite the Quran than to recite it himself.[153] He often told his companions, 'There is no end to its wonders and, no matter how often it is recited, it will not grow dull.'[154] To his followers, he cried, 'Embellish the Quran with your voices, for a beautiful voice increases the beauty of the Quran!'[155] and 'Learn this Quran! When you recite it, you will be rewarded with ten merits (*maḥāsin*) for every word.'[156] If he heard a voice reciting the Quran as he passed by a strange house at night, he knew who lived in the house.[157]

According to the traditions, the Prophet never missed a chance to hear a good Quran recitation. The Prophet's wife 'Ā'isha once came home very late at night, when Muhammad had been waiting up for her.

'What kept you?' asked the Prophet.

'I heard the recitation of a man whose voice was more beautiful than anything I have ever heard', his wife replied.

Muhammad hurried to the mosque, where he listened to the recitation for a long time. Then he returned home and said, 'It is Sālim Mawlā Abī Ḥaḏīfa. Praise be to God who made such a man among my people.'[158]

The Prophet's favourite reciter was Abū Mūsā l-Ash'arī. After hearing his recitation for the first time, the Prophet said, 'This man has been given one of David's flutes.' When Abū Mūsā heard that, he said, 'Messenger of God, if I had known you were listening, I would have recited more beautifully.'[159]

Numerous anecdotes present the second caliph, 'Umar, as a particularly enthusiastic Quran listener.[160] When he recited the surah of Joseph at public morning prayers, 'the tears flowed down on his scapula*'.[161] Many Sufi treatises report that 'Umar 'sometimes nearly choked on his tears when he came to a Quran verse in his daily prayers, and he collapsed and could not leave the house for a day or two, and received sickbed visitors.'[162] When 'Umar was angry, one had only to read him a few verses of the Quran to soothe and cheer him.[163] Even as caliph, he was wont to stroll across the marketplace of Medina reciting the Quran, pacifying other people's disputes in this way.[164] His favourites among his companions were those who had mastered the Quran, or large parts of

* Apparently the Arabs at that time wrote on the scapulae of animals – Trans.

it, by heart.[165] It was ʿUmar too who is said to have created the office of the Quran reciters, who were responsible for recitation during *ṣalāt*, one for the male and one for the female congregation.[166] The biography of ʿUmar, a great lover and connoisseur of poetry and an influential enemy of Islam until his conversion, is paradigmatic of the power both of the Quran, which came to occupy the traditional place of poetry, and of the radical transformation of ideological, ethical and aesthetic norms in Arab society.

From the beginning, Quran recitations, whether in the form of ritualized *ṣalāt* or actual recitation, were the distinguishing outward feature of the young congregation, displacing poetry.[167] Quran recitation was the credential of belief and disbelief,[168] the identifying badge in battle, at once a standard and a fanfare.[169] It is no coincidence that those inhabitants of Yathrib who had heard the Quran and converted to Islam before the Hijra, unlike the first Muslims of the tribes of ʿAdal and al-Qāra,[170] were not so eager to ask Muhammad to send them a reciter.[171] Reciting from the Quran was so common in the houses of the early Muslims that a sound 'like the buzzing of a swarm of bees' filled the streets far into the night, Rashīd Riḍā (d. 1935) wrote.[172] 'He who has not sung the Quran is not one of us', the Prophet himself said,[173] and some of his statements can be read as claiming a monopoly on aesthetic experience for the Quran, as for example when he declares, 'God has permitted the beauty of the voice for nothing else than for the Quran.'[174] What is hinted at here – that the Quran usurped the place traditionally held by song and poetry in old Arabian society – is expressed unambiguously by the philologist Ibn al-Aʿrābī (d. 845): 'The Arabs delighted in practically all forms of singing (*ġināʾ*) and songs (*nashīd*). When the Quran was revealed, they loved to make it the object of their customs in the place of singing.'[175]

In the customary Muslim view of the life of the Prophet, the Quran challenged the status of poetry in the society not only by its ideological orientation but also with regard to questions of stylistic quality. The Meccans initially situated the revelation in the context of poetic works, as the Quran itself repeatedly attests.[176] In several conversion narratives, too, the protagonists compare the Quran with the works of the poets, then acclaim the uniqueness of the quranic language. According to Muḥammad Abū Zahra's interpretation, which is in keeping with theological tradition, most poets would have recognized the impossibility of challenging God in a battle of poets, setting their own verses against the Quran, or at least would have quickly retreated from such an undertaking, as did the twelve poets who had gone to Mecca with their hero Unays expressly to put the Prophet in his literary place.[177] Anyone who was foolish enough to try it 'was humiliated, reaped only scorn and derision, while the Quran only gained further renown.'[178] Naḍr ibn al-Ḥārith likewise failed to convince Muhammad's listeners that the Quran's literary merit was only average when he stood up during a recitation and cried,

> 'By God, I am a better storyteller than he! Come to me, for I will tell you a better story than he!' Then he told them of the kings of Persia, of Rustam and Isfandiyār, and asked them, 'In what respect is Muhammad a better storyteller than I?'[179]

In another context, Naḍr is quoted as saying, 'By God, Muhammad is no better storyteller than I, and his speech consists only of the ancestral fables (*asāṭī r al-awwalīn*), which he has learned from others just as I have mine.'[180] Sayyid Quṭb, who later became the mentor of modern Islamism, represented the scene in his book *Artistic Imagery in the Quran* as a competition for the audience's attention. While Muhammad recited the Quran in the mosque, Naḍr in another corner of the mosque told the people the story of Rustam and Isfandiyār 'so that they would turn away from Muhammad and the Quran, but no one turned away.'[181] According to the account in the *sīra*, Naḍr's vain rivalry left its echo in the Quran, for example in the passage: 'And when Our signs were being recited to them, they said, "We have already heard – if we wished, we could say the like of this – this is naught but the fairy-tales of the ancients."'[182]

The degree to which the Quran appears as a literary quantity in the Muslim discourse about the founding period, and not just as a religious message, is revealed in an unpretentious way by an anecdote recounted by Qāḍī ʿĪyāḍ in the context of stories about the first Quran listeners: The grammarian Abū Saʿīd ʿAbdul-malik al-Aṣmaʿī (d. c. 828) reproached a singer in his employ (*jāriya*), 'May God kill you for your enchanting oratory!'

'How can my speech be considered eloquent in comparison to God's?' she replied, and recited verse 28:7 as an example of true mastery in the use of language.[183]

In the Muslims' understanding of their own history, anecdotes such as this that attest to the mystique of quranic language must not be read as suggesting that the propagation of the Quran succeeded because of its literary qualities alone, that the Meccans were only attracted and persuaded by its beautiful words. The descriptions of the Quran as a fascinating break with the traditional norms of structured text refer both to its form *and* to its theme, which departed from the existing literary and social tradition. The revelation was felt to be not only beautiful but also true: it also moved people by the religious, social, ethical, moral or other aspects of its 'content'. However, none of this detracts from the impression that the Quran was perceived and appreciated aesthetically, inasmuch as practically all works of literature are appreciated by the receiving community using a complex system of norms of various kinds, including norms that refer to the argumentative, ideological aspects of the works. In some cases, the appreciation of a work's argument and ideology can push the perception of its formal elements into the background without making it cease to be an *aesthetic* object or casting doubt on its artistic character. 'In the perception of a given work of art with thematic elements, the relation between the life reality and its values, on the one hand, and the reality mediated by artistic means, on the other, always prevails, so that an appreciation is always the result of a complex process that is conditioned by the whole contemporary structure of life and its values',[184] writes the Czech literary scholar Felix V. Vodička, one of the founders of Prague structuralism. He continues:

> Any work that becomes the object of an appreciation runs up against the habits and conventional notions of the perceiving collective in these respects as well, so that those habits and notions form the background against which a contemporary concretization of the work takes place, whether the appreciation is positive or negative. A work with an unusual theme which is not supported by the literary and social tradition and a work with a new artistic treatment of a non-conforming theme are equally perceived as a violation of norms.[185]

Thematic and formal aspects are thus intertwined in the perception and appreciation of a work; the aesthetic and the extra-aesthetic areas, as Vodička's colleague Jan Mukařovský calls them, 'are in a constant, mutual contact which can be described as a dialectical antinomy.'[186] Nonetheless, there are significant differences between an aesthetic reception that also encompasses the thematic or ideological motifs of the work and a purely thematic or ideological appreciation. Such an appreciation occurs, according to Vodička, 'the moment the appreciation of a work considers only the reality about which the work says something and ceases to be interested in the work itself and its structure; the moment the work is judged only with regard to the truthfulness of its statement and not with regard to the quality of the poetic expression in the given text.'[187] Research in cultural history or religious studies may bring to bear such an exclusive interest in the message, but would then no longer be concerned with an aesthetic reception in the strict sense of the term. Aesthetic reception entails the notion that the complex of signs perceived has more functions than the mere communication of a message. The accounts mentioned clearly bear witness that, even if what moved Muhammad's audience was not only the language which they perceived as beautiful, it cannot have been just the content either. The cause of the audience's interest is presented as the intertwining of a specific message, which many found scandalous and others liberating, with an unusual linguistic form, which the majority of the audience found appealing. In this regard, however, the force of the Quran is qualitatively similar to that of many other literary works, exceeding them at most quantitatively. Neither in Aeschylus nor in Lessing nor in Brecht can aesthetic reception be surgically separated from the reception of argument or ideology, and the immanent poetic form of their works is by no means intended to permit such a separation.

As the vitalist philosopher Jean-Marie Guyau (d. 1888) concisely states, quoted by Mukařovský in his discussion of the intertwining of aesthetic and extra-aesthetic functions in art:

> The keenest aesthetic emotion, the one least mingled with sadness, is met with in those cases where it converts itself immediately into action, and in this way it satisfies itself. The Spartans felt more intimately all the beautiful verses of Tyrtaeus... when these verses led them in combat. The volunteers of the Revolution were never so moved by the 'Marseillaise' as the day when it inspired them with its song on the hills of Jemappes. So, two lovers bending over some love poems like the heroes of Dante and living that which they read will experience deeper enjoyment, even from the aesthetic point of view.[188]

Only since the advent of the modern period has it been possible to conceive of art as restricted to purely aesthetic or simply entertaining functions. There is nothing in the literary practices of earlier eras that corresponds to light fiction or the opposite phenomenon of *l'art pour l'art*.[189] This said, the fact that the Quran induced states that were anything but epicurean, and was hardly listened to out of mere hedonism, does not imply that it was not received aesthetically. The tradition leaves no doubt that the recitation touched the audience deeply. The Prophet himself often wept when he heard the Quran[190] and made sounds as if his insides were a 'boiling kettle' (*mirjal*);[191] at times he fainted,[192] and he said of the surah *Hūd* (no. 11) and its sisters[193] that they made his hair turn white.[194] Once when he read surah 37, *aṣ-Ṣaffāt*, to a delegation from Hadhramaut who had come to Mecca to find out about him, he was unable to get past the fifth line. 'Then God's Messenger was silent, and his soul was still, nothing in it moved; only the tears flowed over his beard.'[195] The Prophet's contemporaries reacted no less impetuously, as even the Quran indicates, prostrating themselves in tears or in worship on hearing the revelation.[196] To some Yemenites who had come to Abu Bakr after Muhammad's death, and who wept when they heard the Quran, the first caliph said, 'It had the same effect on us.'[197] ʿIkrima, the son of Abū Jahl, every time he took the *muṣḥaf*, the written Quran, is said to have cried out, 'This is the word of my lord! This is the word of my lord!' and then fainted.[198]

ʿUmar is said to have cried out on hearing verse 52:7 ('Your Lord's punishment is coming') and then fallen unconscious. Friends carried him home, where he lay sick for a month out of fear of God's punishment.[199] According to the tradition, Salmān al-Fārsī shouted and put his hands on his head when he was present at the revelation of verse 15:43 ('Hell is the promised place for all these'), whereupon he ran away and could not be found for three days.[200]

For all the beauty attributed to the Quran, accounts such as these strike a note of awe and horror, alarm and grief: the divine revelation evokes not only fascination but also fear. But not fear alone: we must suppose that the fright and tears are accompanied by pleasure as elements of a cathartic experience, and that the Quran is perceived as beautiful, exerts an almost irresistible aesthetic attraction, not in spite of, but because of the existential experiences that it induces. For precisely those who, like ʿUmar, Abū Bakr or Muhammad, weep, collapse, cry out in fear, or faint on hearing it are presented as the greatest lovers of Quran recitation.[201] In the cultural memory of the Muslim community, their desire to hear the Quran occurs as an aesthetic desire; it is taken for granted that the poetic form of the text was, if not the sole cause, an essential part of its effect on Muhammad's contemporaries. We must not imagine their delight as purely musical enjoyment, however: rather as a sensually perceived, non-discursively occurring, in every respect unsettling process of realization, as the Quran itself describes it in verse 39:23.[202] The ambivalence of the experience of beauty that is apparent in this Quran verse and in the traditions – the *promesse du bonheur* and at the same time the shock and even terror that it can produce – is universal, and is felt in encounters with great works and described in aesthetic theory even today. No matter how often art has been yoked to purposes of mere entertainment in the age of the *feuilleton*, since the rise of popular literature and the triumph of the culture industry, the cathartic element of the Quran's reception that is alluded to in many testimonies is an unchanging part of the history of aesthetic experiences. And this catharsis too, just like the Aristotelian concept, could be described as the effect of elements of '*Entsetzen*' [horror] and '*gewaltige Rührung*' [powerful emotion], to use the Classical philologist Wolfgang Schadewaldt's translation of Aristotle's terms *phobos* and *eleos*, fear and pity.[203] Although it has nothing in common with mere enjoyment, however, such a catharsis is inconceivable without a feeling of pleasure. In his discussion of tragedy, Aristotle calls this the 'proper pleasure' (*oikeia hedone*).[204] 'I love to hear it [the Quran] from someone else', the Prophet says to Ibn Masʿūd, and breaks out in tears on hearing him recite the surah 'The Women' (no. 4).[205] What else could this mean but that he loves to hear what makes him weep or, on other occasions, makes him shudder or swoon, or turns his hair white. Hans Robert Jauss quite correctly defines catharsis as 'the *enjoyment* of affects as stirred by speech or poetry which can bring about both a change in belief and the liberation of his mind in the listener or spectator'.[206] The sirens' song in the *Odyssey*, for Jauss, is not only the epitome of aesthetic pleasure but 'also promises a knowledge which is the prerogative of the gods and therefore fatal to man.'[207]

> For beauty is nothing
> but the beginning of terror, which we still are just able to endure,
> and we are so awed because it serenely disdains
> to annihilate us,

as Rilke put it.[208] And the Quran, in a verse that has occasioned many exegeses on the enormous force it exerted on Muhammad's contemporaries, says, 'If We had sent this Qur'an down to a mountain, you would have seen it humbled and split apart in its awe of God.'[209]

In the collective memory of the Islamic mystics, the moments of wailing and fear, the emotion, and likewise the euphoric ecstasy that the Quran is supposed to have evoked in Muhammad's contemporaries are particularly emphasized, and their tracts show a penchant for those anecdotes – often not found in the *sīra* or in the canon of hadith – that recount such moments. In the last chapter of the present work, when we try to characterize the experience of the Quran listeners as recorded in Sufi texts, we will need to clarify how the reception of the Quran varies between *tremendum* and *fascinans*, and the extent to which such an experience can be understood as aesthetic when it has little to do with art and the enjoyment of art.

The Adversaries' Impotence

Not all of those who heard the Quran converted to Islam on the spot, as Qāḍī ʿIyāḍ explicitly states.[210] Even Muhammad's fiercest antagonists were moved by the power of his recitation, however. Rashīd Riḍā makes a distinction between the effect of the Quran on unbelievers and its effect on the faithful:

> The effect on the first [listeners] was one of being overpowered (*rawʿa*) by its poetic art and amazed (*dahsha*) at its composition, which enticed them to hear the Quran's invitation and to believe in it. Thus its beauty was not hidden from any of them, even if there were great differences in their appreciation of it, depending on their degree of rhetorical mastery and their intellectual understanding.[211]

A frequently cited example of the helplessness of Muhammad's fiercest opponents is al-Walīd ibn al-Muġīra, a Quraysh nobleman who was widely famed for his eloquence and rhetoric. Ibn Kathīr relates, with a reference to Ibn ʿAbbās, the following story from the early days of Muhammad's mission:

> When al-Walīd ibn al-Muġīra came before him, the Messenger of God recited the Quran to him, so that al-Walīd's heart was softened (*raqqa lahū*). When Abū Jahl heard this, he went to al-Walīd and said, 'O Uncle, the people have decided to take up a collection for you.'
>
> 'Why?' asked al-Walīd.
>
> 'They want to give you money to go to Muhammad and oppose him face to face.'
>
> 'But the Quraysh know that I myself am the richest among them', replied al-Walīd.
>
> 'Then say something, anything, about Muhammad, so that your people know you reject him.'

> 'What shall I say? There is no one among you who knows more about poetry than I. I know all kinds of qasidas and the *rajaz*, and I am familiar even with the poems of the jinn. But, by God, his recitation is like none of them. By God, there is a sweetness and a grace in it; its branches are heavy with fruit, and much water springs from its ground. It surpasses everything, and nothing surpasses it; it crushes what is beneath it.'
>
> 'Your people will not be content if you say nothing about him', Abū Jahl insisted.
>
> 'Leave me alone so that I can think about it', said al-Walīd. After he had thought, he said, 'It is nothing but sorcery handed down from earlier times; he copied it from someone else.'[212]

Al-Bayhaqī (d. 1066) recounts another version of the story of al-Walīd. In his account, when the Prophet had recited verse 16:90 ('God commands justice…'), al-Walīd asked him to repeat the passage. After Muhammad had read the verse again, al-Walīd cried, 'By God, there is a sweetness and a grace in it; its branches are heavy with fruit, and much water springs from its ground. This is not the word of a human being.'[213] In Abū Nuʿaym, we read:

> 'I have heard poetry, in the metre of *rajaz*, of *qarīḍ*, and of *mukhammas*. But never have I heard a speech like this' – by which he meant the Quran; 'this is no poetry. It has a sweetness and a grace, it has light and many shadings, it surpasses everything and nothing surpasses it.'[214]

The episode reads slightly differently in Maḥmūd Rāmiyār's *History of the Quran*. According to Rāmiyār, the Quraysh instigated a public meeting between al-Walīd and the Prophet, in the hope that al-Walīd would prevail. The Prophet was able to win the debate by reciting the beginning of surah 41:

> At first al-Walīd was haughty and arrogant as he listened to the verses. The longer the Prophet's warm voice carried on, however, the more meek and subdued al-Walīd became. This went on until the Prophet came to verse 13: 'If they turn away, say: "I have warned you about a blast like the one which struck ʿĀd and Thamūd."' At that point, a change came over al-Walīd. A trembling seized him, and he was beside himself. The session was adjourned and the audience went away. After this event, several people went to al-Walīd to complain that they had not expected him to conduct himself in such a way, and that they had been humiliated and dishonoured because of him. Al-Walīd thought a while, and then said,
>
> 'No, you know that I fear no one and cannot be bribed. You know that I am a good judge of eloquence. But the oratory that I heard from Muhammad cannot be compared with any other speech. It is both captivating and

deeply moving. It cannot be called poetry, nor prose. It is deep and full of substance.'[215]

On that or another occasion, al-Walīd also called Muhammad's recitation 'sweet and magical' and prophesied that it would prevail against all other oratory.[216] In any case, after his lost 'duel', the Quraysh pressed him to say something against Muhammad's recitations that they could use as propaganda. Al-Walīd asked for three days to prepare his answer. When the Quraysh came to him after that delay, he said, 'Muhammad's speech is witchcraft and sorcery, and beguiles the people.' Since that incident, and on al-Walīd's advice, the unbelievers are said to have called the Quran *siḥr* (witchcraft) and threatened the Meccans to prevent them from listening to the recitation.[217]

According to the Muslim commentators and the chroniclers of the *asbāb an-nuzūl* ('occasions of revelation'), this episode is reflected in the Quran.[218] They see God's words in the following verses as referring to al-Walīd:

Leave Me with him whom I created alone,
and appointed for him ample wealth,
and sons standing before him,
and made all things smooth for him;
then he is eager that I should do more.
Nay! He is forward unto Our signs;
and I shall constrain him to a hard ascent.
Lo! He reflected, and determined –
death seize him, how he determined!
Again, death seize him, how he determined! –
Then he beheld,
then he frowned, and scowled,
then he retreated, and waxed proud.
He said, 'This is naught but a trumped-up sorcery;
this is nothing but mortal speech.'
I shall surely roast him in Sakar;
and what will teach thee what is Sakar?[219]

Ibn Hishām offers yet another version of the meeting between al-Walīd and the baffled Quraysh. It was shortly before the time of heathen tribes' annual pilgrimage to Mecca, and the Quraysh were afraid that Muhammad with his recitation would bind all the pilgrims under his spell, as he had enchanted so many Meccans.

'Let us call him a soothsayer', one suggested, but al-Walīd objected that the soothsayers' mumbling and rhymed prose was something quite different.

'A madman', another suggested, but al-Walīd rejected this too as inapt – likewise the proposal to call Muhammad a poet. One said he should be called a sorcerer, and again al-Walīd commented that the characteristics of the sorcerers, such as ritual spitting or tying knots, hardly applied to Muhammad.[220]

'But what shall we say then, O Abū 'Abd Shams?' the Quraysh asked.

'By God, his word has a sweetness, its root is that of a palm tree whose branches are full of fruit', said al-Walīd, and added that anything they said about Muhammad's oratory would be false. In the end, however, he recommended calling Muhammad a sorcerer after all, because that would offer the best hope of discrediting the self-styled prophet's outrageous recitation and making it explicable as the ordinary work of a mortal man.[221]

It is expressed again and again in the Muslim traditions that the Quran caused great confusion among the Arabs because it did not resemble any of the familiar forms of structured discourse – neither poetry (*shi'r*) nor rhymed prose (*saj'*) – yet nonetheless had an overwhelming attraction. As a last example we may mention the poet Unays, from the tribe of the Ġifār. He reported to his brother Abū Ḏarr al-Ġifārī about a man he had met in Mecca, who claimed that God had sent him.

'What do the people say about him?' Abū Ḏarr asked.

'They say he is a poet, a soothsayer or a sorcerer', Unays answered, and went on to explain, 'I have often heard the words of the soothsayers, but his is not like theirs. I have compared it with all kinds of poetry and found that it cannot be called poetry. Indeed, he speaks the truth; the people lie.'[222] Abū Ḏarr then travelled to Mecca, listened to the Quran, and converted on the spot to Islam,[223] as did his brother and their mother a short time later.[224]

The Arabs' inability to classify the Quran among the known classes of structured oratory is often mentioned by twentieth-century Muslim authors too, such as Ṣādiq ar-Rāfi'ī:

> The Arabic rhetoricians saw that it [the Quran] belonged to a class (*jins*) of oration that was different from theirs; that its composition incorporated the spirit of the language, and they had no alternative but to keep it away from the soul of each individual Arab, or to prevent it from entering into that soul. For it was the face of linguistic perfection which their souls recognized and which revealed itself to their hearts.[225]

The text of the Quran is at the centre of the conflict between the Quraysh and Muhammad as it appears in Muslim sources. In order to put him in his place, the Prophet's opponents were obliged not so much to vilify him personally as to defame the form and content of his recitations, to cast doubt upon them and make them dismissible as witchcraft or poetry. This was their only hope to undermine his mission: his credibility would stand or fall with the Quran. They needed to expose the text as an ordinary, mortal work. The Quran itself seems to record the heat of this debate in some of its Meccan verses:

The Messenger says, 'O my Lord, behold, my people have taken this Qur'an as a thing to be shunned.'
Even so We have appointed to every prophet an enemy among the sinners, but thy Lord suffices as a guide and as a helper.
The unbelievers say, 'Why has the Qur'an not been sent down upon him all at once?' Even so, that We may strengthen thy heart thereby, and We have chanted it very distinctly.
They bring not to thee any similitude but that We bring thee the truth, and better in exposition.[226]

Some voices mocking the Quran are also recorded, although evidently none of them was of lasting influence – at least according to the sources other than the Quran. The triumph of Islam, which is held to be primarily the triumph of a text – Muhammad is supposed to have inveighed against the unbelievers with the Quran and nothing else, says verse 25:52 suggestively – is proof, according to Muslim historians, that the objections to the rhetorical quality of the Quran found little acceptance among the Meccans. If expressions of disapproval had been widespread, the argument goes, the unbelievers would certainly have used them as an argument against Muhammad and refuted his claim to prophecy with the same argument that they had advanced against the pseudo-prophets Musaylima and Sajāḥ: the Meccans had rejected their prophecies ostensibly because of their coarse and crude rhetoric. 'This speech is not that of a divinity', Abū Bakr perceived at once when a man asked him about Musaylima's verses. Al-Bāqillānī cites this response in connection with the Quran's stylistic superiority.[227] Muḥammad Abū Zahra's commentary on the failure of the prophets competing with Muhammad sums up the traditional Muslim view:

> But their oration had so little substance, and their reason was so base, that the Quraysh orators would not recite their words, because they had heard the divine word and knew its worth. The Quraysh orators might deny the truth, acquiesce in the depravity of their convictions, flout religion and declare the divine message a lie, but they would not sacrifice their eloquence and their taste for beautiful language in their struggle against the Quran.[228]

In this connection, Muslim authors refer again and again to the Quran's 'challenge' (*taḥaddī*) to the unbelievers: in several verses in the Quran, God invites the unbelievers to produce something to rival it. In verses 52:33–4 for example, we read:

> If they say, 'He has made it up himself' – they certainly do not believe – let them produce one like it, if what they say is true.

Even if humans joined forces with the jinn, they could not produce such a text:

> Say: 'If men and jinn banded together to produce the like of this Koran, they would never produce its like, not though they backed one another.[229]

In the surah *Hūd*, the challenge is phrased more precisely:

> Or do they say, 'He has forged it'? Say: 'Then bring you ten suras the like of it, and call upon whom you are able, apart from God, if you speak truly![230]

And in the surah 'Jonas', God makes the unbelievers' task still 'easier' – to mock them, according to the traditional interpretation. Here just a single surah that rivals those of the Quran would be enough to claim victory over Muhammad.

> Or do they say, 'Why, he has forged it'? Say: 'Then produce a sura like it, and call on whom you can, apart from God, if you speak truly.[231]

In verse 2:23, the invitation is repeated, but this is followed by a warning that the opponents will not be able to present a surah of similar quality: 'And if you do not – and you will not – fear the Fire, whose fuel is men and stones, prepared for unbelievers.'[232]

Whatever the original sense of this challenge may have been in Muhammad's day, later Muslims saw it in the context of the customary battles among poets and interpreted it as proof of the historic supremacy of the Quran, of its quality as a literary miracle. 'The Messenger of God challenged them with the Quran; he allowed them to hear something that seemed to be not of their world, such was its eloquence, style, rhetorical mastery, and elegant expression', writes Abū Nuʿaym.[233] In the Jahiliyyah as it is represented in the customary view, which Orientalism has largely adopted, public duels between poets were a part of social life. Over and above their artistic or literary attraction, such events often had great political importance, since they could definitively decide conflicts between factions and tribes. It is unlikely, al-Jāḥiẓ declares in his now classic argumentation, that the Prophet's opponents would have agreed not to use the kind of oratory they mastered as no other people, which was their pride; not to use it while they gave their lives and property and left their homes to destroy his cause and its consequences. It is more likely that they would have said – if not all in unison, then at least one alone among them:

> 'Why do you sacrifice your lives, waste your wealth and leave your homes, when the means to combat him is simple and the most obvious course of action against him is this: let one of your poets and your orators compose a speech in the style of his, as long as the shortest surah which he has said you

> cannot imitate, and like the smallest verse which he has challenged you to imitate.'[234]

It is inconceivable, the author of the best-known *iʿjāz* compendium, al-Bāqillānī, agrees, that the Arabs would not have thought of silencing the troublesome agitator by rebutting him. Yet they did not make the attempt. If they had, the result would have been handed down, as the poetry of the Jahiliyyah and the oratory of the early Arabic speakers were handed down.[235] Only later poets, such as Ibn al-Muqaffaʿ (d. 756), Ibn al-Rāwandī (d. mid to late tenth century), al-Mutanabbī (d. c. 965) and Abū l-ʿAlāʾ al-Maʿarrī (d. 1058), are said to have tried – and failed, of course – to rise above the Quran stylistically.

The Quran recitations increasingly caused shock, dismay and, finally, panic among the Quraysh. By defeating and humiliating them on their own ground, in the field of their greatest mastery, the arena of poets, the Prophet had robbed them of their sharpest weapon, their superior use of language. In the face of the power and sweetness of the divine word, even the greatest verbal artists among the Arabs (*bulaġāʾ al-ʿarab*) admitted they were powerless and, in the words of Rāfiʿī,

> abandoned all hope of being able to exercise their vested right [of rebutting their rival's speech]. They found in the Quran that which exceeds all forces and transforms the inner being and stuns the wits as after a collision, and that which makes vain all efforts to prevail by cunning or deceit.[236]

Unable to fight the Quran with its own weapon – that is, language – the Quraysh were forced to resort to other means of putting an end to the menace. ʿUtba ibn Rabīʿa attempted to persuade the Prophet, by warm words and tempting promises, to leave off his recitations, but he too failed. ʿUtba was not only an elder of the Quraysh but was also famous for his eloquence and wit.[237] He said to the troubled leaders of the Quraysh, shortly after Ḥamza had converted to Islam, 'Why don't I go to Muhammad, talk to him, and make him some proposals. Maybe he'll accept some of them: we'll give him whatever he wants, and he'll leave us alone.' The Quraysh took hope, because they were confident in his persuasiveness. ʿUtba went to Muhammad and offered him wealth, honour, power and even, if the demon did not release him, therapy – if he would only stop bewitching the people and vilifying their old gods with the Quran. Muhammad patiently heard ʿUtba out.

'Have you finished?' he asked him.

'Yes.'

'Then listen to me carefully', Muhammad entreated his opponent, and recited the beginning of surah 41. Deviating only in elegant stylistic details from Ibn Hishām's original account, Maḥmūd Rāmiyār tells what happened then:

> ʿUtba fell silent. As if bewitched, he clapped his hands in the air and shook his head. He listened to the Quran verses. When Muhammad came to verse 37, he bowed and then asked, 'Abū Walīd, have you heard what you needed to hear? That is you, and those are the signs.'[238]

ʿUtba stood up and went away. When he returned to his companions, they saw he was changed. They asked him what had happened.

'I heard a word such as I have never heard before. By God, that is not poetry, not sorcery, and not soothsaying. O ye Quraysh! Take my advice: do as I do and leave him in peace, for, by God, the word that I heard will spread like fire.' And ʿUtba endeavoured by many arguments to persuade his companions that it was more prudent not to pursue Muhammad any longer.

But they said, 'By God, his tongue has bewitched you too, O Abū Walīd!'[239] The Quraysh felt that it was the inexplicable attraction of the new oratory that was pulling the rug out from under them and threatening the old power structure. Finally, right after the Hijra, even their wives assembled at night before the cell of Khubayb ibn ʿAdī, who recited the Quran until dawn, and they 'wept, and it touched their hearts'.[240] When their leaders assembled to take counsel for their next steps against Muhammad, they heard some of their number ask, 'Do you not see the beauty of his oratory, and how he captures men's hearts?'[241] Worried not least about the effect of the Quran on the women and children,[242] and baffled to find themselves speechless and even their poets powerless, and their very resolve endangered by the aesthetic power of the Quran, the Quraysh tried to put pressure on Muhammad and his followers with verbal and physical attacks. But the Prophet only defended himself against their violence with the Quran, continuing his recitation unperturbed. Al-Jāḥiẓ writes:

> God sent Muhammad at a time when the Arabs were greater poets and orators, their language more established, and their power of resistance in this field stronger than at any other time in their history. With a clear proof Muhammad invited the great and the small among them to believe in God, and to acknowledge his prophecy. Because his opponents had no other recourse, and the doubts that had arisen with Muhammad's appearance could not be allayed, and only their stubbornness and ire kept them from accepting his message; in ignorance and confusion they took up swords; they declared war on him, killed his most respected followers and his uncles and cousins, and in all this time he defended himself against them only with the Quran, entreating them day and night to produce something like it to prove him a liar, even just one surah or a few verses. The more often he challenged them with the Quran, the more apparent it became that they were unable, and their impotence became obvious.[243]

Especially the sight of the Prophet praying, and hence reciting from the Quran, enraged his opponents.[244] Once ʿUqba ibn Abī Muʿayt crept up behind him and dumped the entrails of a camel on Muhammad's back.[245] Another time, he went to strangle the Prophet from behind as he was at prayer, but Abū Bakr was able to stop him just in time.[246] It was Abū Bakr too who intervened when a whole troop of the Quraysh seized the Prophet by the collar to kill him. When he recited to them, sobbing yet with a loud voice, from the surah 'The Forgiver' ('How can you kill a man just for saying, "My Lord is God..." '),[247] the attackers suddenly let Muhammad go.[248] Attempted murder, and in general the greatest hostility, is also attributed to Abū Jahl, the most powerful and most brutal of the Quraysh princes. It is only thanks to the archangel Gabriel, the tradition holds, that the Prophet was not harmed when this arch villain of early Islamic history tried to kill him with a big stone while he was praying: just as Abū Jahl was about to throw the stone, he suddenly turned around, his face pale with fright, and ran back to his companions, whom he had told in bold words of his intentions. A bull camel had blocked his path, he stammered, its head, shoulders and teeth more frightening than anything he had ever seen, 'and he made as though he would eat me.' But the Prophet knew it was Gabriel who had routed his enemy.[249]

There was nothing the Quraysh could do. To prevent the spread of Islam, they resorted to prohibiting public recitations in their own and the neighbouring tribes. In Ibn Hishām's biography of the Prophet we read the following account from the time when the dominance of the Quraysh was still relatively secure. Abū Bakr had taken refuge from their persecution with Ibn ad-Duġunna:

> Beside his house, which was situated in the Banū Jumaḥ quarter, Abū Bakr had a mosque in which he performed *ṣalāt*. A soft-hearted man, he was moved to tears every time he recited the Quran. The young men, slaves and women would stand around him and wonder at his behaviour.
>
> Some men of Quraysh went to Ibn al-Dughunna saying, 'Have you given this fellow protection so that he can injure us? Lo, he prays and reads what Muhammad has produced and his heart becomes soft and he weeps. And he has a striking appearance so that we fear he may seduce our youths and women and weak ones.'[250]

Although in this instance they were successful, since Ibn ad-Duġunna revoked his protection and Abū Bakr was forced to go back to Mecca, the Quraysh soon saw more and more of their people turn their backs on the heathen poets to attend the recitations of Muhammad and his companions. Even many of the poets themselves followed the Prophet and placed themselves at the service of his mission. In order not to succumb to the attraction of the Quran, the Quraysh fled or closed their ears the moment they heard the sound of it. The Quran itself points out that the unbelievers tried to withstand the recitations by turning away or feigning deafness. The Muslim exegetes at least take the following verses quite literally:[251]

> A revelation from the Lord of Mercy, the Giver of Mercy, a Scripture whose verses are made clear as a Quran in Arabic for people who understand, giving good news and warning. Yet most of them turn away and so do not hear. They say, 'Our hearts are encased against what you call us to; our ears are heavy; there is a barrier between us and you. So you do whatever you want, and so shall we.'[252]

But the unbelievers were not always content to turn away when the Quran was recited. They sometimes clapped their hands as if to drive out an enchantment, or they began to sing or to call out, as verse 11:5 suggests.[253] They forbade their own people to listen to the Quran,[254] and they reviled or threw rubbish at people who prayed or recited.[255] When Muhammad's companion ʿAbdullāh ibn Masʿūd dared to defy them by reciting the 55th surah, they were so angry that they fell on him and beat him. 'God's enemies were never easier for me to bear than at that moment', he assured his companions afterwards. 'If you want, I'll go back and recite to them again tomorrow.'[256]

Wherever the Muslims went, they brought the words of the Quran, and increasingly 'the Quraysh were in panic lest for God's sake anyone should listen to the Prophet speak and Islam should spread', as Maḥmūd Rāmiyār puts it.[257] The Quraysh were so afraid of the Quran's power that, at the time of the pilgrimage, when many visitors were expected in Mecca, al-Walīd ibn al-Muġīra posted sixteen of his followers on the roads leading into town and ordered them to make the pilgrims afraid of Muhammad's proclamations. But the pilgrims heard the Quran nonetheless, and praised the Prophet.[258]

The pure terror that increasingly took hold of the Quraysh is perhaps most clearly illustrated by the following episode in the commentaries on verse 36:9, which al-Bayhaqī included in his *Signs of Prophethood.* Some of the Banū Makhzūm, among them Abū Jahl and al-Walīd ibn al-Muġīra, planned an assassination:

> When the Messenger of God performed *ṣalāt* and they heard the sound of his recitation, they sent al-Walīd to kill him. Al-Walīd set out and came to where the Messenger of God was still at prayer, but he could not see him, although could hear him. Al-Walīd went back and reported to his companions what had happened. Then Abū Jahl and some others went with al-Walīd. They came to the place where Muhammad was praying. They heard his voice, but when they approached it, they suddenly heard it from behind them. They turned around and followed the sound, but, whichever way they went, they suddenly heard the voice at their backs. They went back without having been

able to find the Prophet. This is the explanation of the verse cited: 'And We have put before them a barrier and behind them a barrier; and We have covered them, so they do not see.'[259]

Not all of the opponents reacted with such confusion. Although the Quran mentions the power of its recitation, it admits, remarkably, that not all listeners are susceptible to it. The reason, according to the traditional interpretation, is not that the Quran was rhetorically imperfect, but that God purposely closed the listeners' ears to the peculiarity of the recitation, so that they heard nothing unusual in it: 'And among them are some who [appear to] listen to you, but we have placed covers over their hearts – so they do not understand the Qur'an – and deafness in their ears.'[260] Thus some of the Meccans simply shrugged their shoulders at the Quran recitations, while others were all the more consumed with a forbidden yearning. 'Although they were heathens, and inwardly resisted admitting its magnificence, they felt attracted to it and wanted to hear it', Muhammad Abū Zahra explains. He adds:

The melody of the words and their attraction, the sublime expressiveness and the whole unique arrangement, more beautiful than a string of pearls, was a source of pleasure to them. But because they knew of their desire to hear the Quran, and knew the effect it would have on their souls, they forbade one another to listen to it, and commanded noisemaking whenever it was heard. And still, no matter how often they forbade it one another, every one of them listened to the Quran on his own. When they met one another, this secret was revealed, and they discovered that none of them had kept their agreement.[261]

We mentioned above that Mecca's poets skulked around the Kaaba when Muhammad recited the Quran there. Even ʿUqba ibn Abū Muʿayṭ, one of the leaders of the Quraysh, had to be confronted by his closest friend Ubayy ibn Khalaf to stop secretly attending Muhammad's recitations. 'Do I hear that you have sat with Muhammad and listened to him?' his friend admonishes him. 'I swear I will never see you or speak to you again (and he swore a great oath) if you do the same again, or if you do not go and spit in his face!'[262]

This conflict of emotions is most evident in the story of Abū Sufyān, Abū Jahl and al-Akhnas ibn Sharīq, who were three of the most important persons among the Quraysh, and who most vociferously railed against Muhammad and insulted his listeners.

The Messenger of God was in the habit of holding evening prayers at his house. One night, Abū Jahl, Abū Sufyān and al-Akhnas ibn Sharīq went, unknown to each other, to the Messenger of God's house and hid there to listen to the Quran recitation. All three of them stayed hidden behind the wall all night long. As dawn broke and they left their hiding places to go

> home, they ran into each other in the street. Each of them rebuked the others. 'Don't come back here again', they said to each other. 'If one of the fools saw you, it would only aggravate their curiosity.' Then they went their separate ways.
>
> But the next evening, all three men returned to their hiding places, unseen by each other, and listened to the recitation until dawn. When they set out to go home, they met again, and they rebuked one other again as they had the night before. The third night too, they hid and listened to the Quran until dawn and ran into each other afterwards. Finally they said, 'There is nothing else for it but to swear an oath that we will never do that again.' And they swore an oath and made a pact. Then they went their separate ways.[263]

After that, Abū Jahl, Abū Sufyān and Akhnas ibn Sharīq's behaviour towards Muhammad's followers was even more hostile and aggressive. They and their liegemen spared no effort to keep the Meccans away from the Quran recitations. Muhammad's followers were met with curses, threats and bitter mockery and sometimes pelted with dung. The Prophet himself fared no better, suffering the most offensive insults. Abū Jahl in particular was unbridled in his belligerence: he beat Muhammad and pulled his beard. When Muhammad knelt in the Kaaba during *ṣalāt*, Abū Jahl crept up behind him and threw the placenta of a sheep at his head. Rāmiyār attributes Abū Jahl's wrath to his unsatisfied desire, resisted but unvanquished, to hear Muhammad's preaching. Interpreting the three secret Quran admirers' state of mind after they had made their pact, he writes, 'A guilty conscience sometimes torments a person. In their hearts they asked themselves what kind of oratory it was, so unlike the speech of other people, made of different stuff, put together differently.'[264] Az-Zarkashī (d. 1392) offers a similar interpretation: the fascinating thrill (*raw'a*) that the Quran produced in the hearts and ears of its listeners, whether believers or deniers, was incomparable.

> If the listener is a believer, the blissful thrill and the sublime feeling seize him straight away, and his heart feels an unceasing attraction to and love for the Quran. And if the listener is a denier, he still feels this thrill in his heart, but it is mixed with something distressing and admonishing that makes his agitation gain the upper hand over the beauty of what he is hearing.[265]

Qāḍī 'Iyāḍ sees the fascination and the agitation as greater when the listener is an unbeliever, 'so that their hearts find listening troublesome and their resistance grows'.[266] According to al-Bayhaqī's account, the three Quraysh leaders stayed away from Muhammad's house after the third night, but they were unsettled, and wanted to know each other's opinions about what they had heard. 'Naturally, they were quite apprehensive that, being leaders of their people, their inner disturbance would someday be discovered by their followers and sap the morale of the whole community', explains Muḥammad Ḥusayn Haykal (d. 1956), the author of what has probably been the most popular biography of the Prophet in the past century.[267] Only Abū Jahl's resolve prevented the other two from converting to Islam, according to the *sīra*. The Muslim tradition interprets the following verses as God's revealed words about the three men:

> We know best the way they listen, when they listen to you and when they confer in secret, and when these wrongdoers say, 'You are only following a man who is bewitched.'[268]

The Power of the Word

A fundamental premise of Muslim historiography, and *a fortiori* of modern Muslim Quran scholarship – a premise which Islamic studies have almost completely ignored – holds that hardly anyone was able to resist Quran recitation, and that neither the Prophet's opponents nor his followers could attribute his success to his charisma or his message alone; all of them are supposed to have seen the unexpected attraction of Muhammad's oratory as a direct explanation.[269] Sādiq ar-Rāfiʿī, for example, writes:

> The Arabs could resist no longer, since the Quran had paralysed them in their very eloquence (*faṣāḥa*), which was their most important and greatest art, and in oration, which they placed above all other activities. They retreated before it, although they were a strong, fearless people of warriors and raiders, as numerous as the pebbles on the ground, and Muhammad had no one but himself and a few companions who only revered him and committed themselves to his victory after they had heard and got to know the Quran, which enchanted them and multiplied their strength and made them greater than themselves.[270]

Muslim authors regularly explain that Muhammad overcame his enemies' physical violence primarily through the verbal force of his oratory. 'Muhammad is he whose tongue God has made into a sword, and that sword is plain Arabic', says ʿAli ibn Rabbān aṭ-Ṭabarī (d. approx. 857).[271] Some felt that only very great men, such as Khadīja and Salmān al-Fārsi, converted to Islam without being influenced by the stylistic quality of the Quran, while lesser men needed this miracle to persuade them.[272] Rāmiyār comments, 'It is certainly uncontested that the fame and predominance that Islam attained were nothing other than a consequence of its nature as a verbal miracle (*iʿjāz*), and only the splendour and magnificence of the Quran are to thank for everything that happened.'[273] Similarly, Sayyid Quṭb points to the Quran – and he means the effect of

Quran recitation – as 'the decisive factor, or at least as one of the decisive factors, that persuaded those who joined the faith in the early days of Muhammad's mission, in the time before he had weight or force, before Islam had either power or strength,'[274] And Muḥammad Abū Zahra writes:

> The Quran drew the Arabs towards faith by its terrible splendour (*raw'a*) and the force of its rhetoric (*bayān*), by its astounding succinctness and because it contains abiding words, long and short stories, and many small and great admonitions, because its long expressions delight and its short sentences omit nothing in their clear wording and plain instructions. In fact, their faith originated not in a desire for upheaval nor in their weakness – weak though they may have been. If their faith was strong, it was because of the Quran: it was the Quran that had driven them to believe because of its rhetoric, which plainly surpassed human ability.[275]

Rashīd Riḍā draws the scope of the Quran's verbal power still wider: it 'changed the Arabs' souls, and the Arabs in turn changed the other nations', he writes, and so comes to the conclusion that the frequent recitation of the Quran brought about 'the most tremendous intellectual and social revolution in history'.[276] Among contemporary authors, this interpretation of early Islamic history is not limited to the devout, traditionally oriented circle of scholars who are primarily cited in this chapter. A secular intellectual such as Adonis essentially follows this interpretation too when he states:

> But the initial amazement that the Quran produced among the Arabs was of a verbal nature. They were beguiled by its language, by its linguistic beauty and art. That language was the key that opened the door through which they could enter the world of the Quran and accept Islam as a religion. Hence it is impossible to draw a dividing line at any level between Islam and language. One may even say that the early Muslims who formed the first hard core of the Islamic mission believed in the Quran primarily as a text whose linguistic expression had taken possession of them: they believed in it not because it revealed to them the secrets of being or of human existence, or brought a new order to their lives, but because they saw in it a scripture that was like nothing they had known before. Through language their nature was changed from within, and it was language that changed their lives.[277]

In the view of the authors cited, the literary superiority of the text is at least as important for the triumph of Islam as Muhammad's words and deeds. This interpretation is all the more remarkable because it is not supported by the Quran, or even by the early traditions. Instead, a gradual change in perspective has taken place over the course of Muslim history: certain details have been accentuated in the cultural memory in a very particular way. While the *sīra* also mentions the attraction that Quran recitation exercised, the subtext at least of the accounts from the Meccan period is that the Prophet met primarily with rejection; the Hijra is of course a consequence of that rejection. Apart from a very few from the lower classes (*qalīlan mina l-mustaḍa'fīn*), the Meccans gave Muhammad's oratory no acknowledgement at all.[278] The tribes outside Mecca likewise all rejected him at first.[279] In this phase, the effects of the Quran as described above are the exception, not the rule. In the hindsight of later times, the perception changed, and the irresistibility of Quran recitation shifted to the foreground. This shift is of course most visible in a comparison of texts from different contexts, such as the Quran and the exegesis, that refer to the same events. Certain verses that, taken alone, at first seem unspecific are transformed in the Quran commentaries or the *asbāb-an-nuzūl* works into references to the aesthetic effect of the Quran. Such an interpretation of these verses is not necessarily wrong, but it cannot be strictly inferred from the Quran alone. This transformation is characteristic of the interpretation of the original recitation situation in the collective memory. Verse 41:26, for example, reads: 'The unbelievers say, "Do not give ear to this Koran; and talk idly about it; haply you will overcome."'[280] The verse appears at first to relate the unbelievers' instigation not to heed the Quran – that is, not to follow its commandments, to reject its message. On closer inspection, the verse is seen to refer to a specific situation: it relates the Meccans' injunction not to listen to a certain recitation (*lā tasma'ū li-hāḏā l-qur'āni*) but instead to disrupt it with noise and loud talking (*wa-lġū fīhi*).[281] According to the Muslim commentators, the Quran alludes here to the fact that the Meccans, after a number of conversions prompted by the sound of the Quran, had tried at least to diminish the effects of Muhammad's recitations in the Kaaba by clapping, singing and loud talking (*laġw*);[282] ar-Rāzī (d. 1210) adds the loud reciting of poems and fairy tales.[283] Thus the commentators explain the Quran's repeated admonitions to Muslims to pay no attention to the unbelievers' *laġw*.[284] Muḥammad Abū Zahra's commentary on the verse summarizes the traditional Muslim reading:

> The greatest of Muhammad's opponents feared that the Quran would affect them strongly, since they preferred disbelief to faith and aberration to guidance. So they agreed not to listen to this Quran. They knew that everyone who heard it was moved by its sublime expressiveness, which was above human power. They saw that the people – even the great personalities, the dignitaries and the powerful – believed in it one after another, that Islam was growing stronger, the faithful more numerous, polytheism weaker, and its adherents fewer.[285]

The following verse is likewise understood by Muslim commentators as a reference to the uncontrollable urge of even Muhammad's enemies to listen to the Quran:

Behold, they fold their breasts, to hide them from Him;
behold, when they wrap themselves in their garments He knows what they secrete and what they publish;
surely He knows all the thoughts within the breasts.[286]

The verse does not seem at first glance to be about Quran recitation. It apparently refers, without naming it explicitly, to a certain event among Muhammad's opponents. We have little chance of understanding the passage without adducing a commentary. It is interesting to see how Muslim scholars explained it. Maḥmūd Rāmiyār writes in his *History of the Quran* that the Meccan poets went to great lengths to avoid being seen and recognized when they listened in secret to Muhammad's recitations in the Kaaba, and he sees this as one of many indications of 'the force and power of the divine message'.[287]

Many Quran verses, like the one above, appear in the light of Muslim exegesis as evidence of the Quran's spellbinding aesthetic power. The scholars are eager to supplement the often unspecific allusions to events in Muhammad's surroundings with stories about the reactions of individual Meccans to his recitation. No matter how those reactions looked 'in reality', only the tradition – and hence, one might say, the *remembered* history – records how strongly the language of the Quran enthralled its first listeners. And of course the later commentaries on such Quran passages, and on their alignment with the Prophet's biography, are not the only instance in which the later congregation interprets its own sources as evidence of an aesthetic power of the Quran and accords that power an increasing importance for early Muslim history. The accounts in the extraquranic traditions of specific recitation scenes demonstrating the Quran's irresistibility likewise undergo continuing embellishment over time. If we may consider the works of *sīra* and hadith as a first layer of memory, the image of the Quran's miraculous aesthetic power that continues to prevail today was formed only in the second layer. The reference to the Quran's linguistic perfection and the claim that no one among the eloquent Arabs was able to meet the Prophet's challenge and produce something better, more beautiful, more captivating than the Quran did not become defining figures of memory for the identity of the Muslim community until the formation of the *iʿjāz* doctrine in the ninth and tenth centuries. The linguistic perfection and historic supremacy of the Quran, although certainly conceived and expressed as a subjective impression in the preceding centuries, was now taken as clear evidence that what the individuals in that community share, and what distinguishes them from individuals in other communities, is objectively true and valid for all time.

In contemporary treatises that deal with the effect of the Quran, we can see the lasting presence of the principal figures of memory and the knowledge stored in the cultural memory, but we also see how each successive present has related to these fixed points in the past – in Jan Assmann's words, how it has set itself 'in an assimilating, exploring, preserving and altering relation'[288] to them. The traditions on specific recitation situations that demonstrate the irresistibility of the Quran are not invented afresh, but they are interpreted again and again; or conversion stories from the *sīra* that originally contained no indication of a crucial aesthetic experience, such as that of the Christian ʿAddās,[289] come to be presented, as in Rāmiyār's *History of the Quran*, as evidence of 'that forceful and profound effect'.[290] The latter example is telling, as the author is an extremely conscientious scholar who uses only sources that are credible – from a Muslim point of view – and carefully documented. Thus, while his work is largely free of the ornamentation and certain glorifications that popular piety applies to episodes from the life of the Prophet, he cannot entirely avoid the effusive style of his chapter on the 'Effect of the Quran' (*ta'thīr-e Qor'ān*).[291]

To judge from the accounts of the Meccans' reactions to Muhammad's recitations as presented in this chapter, the Quran's aesthetic effect on its first audience (and the succeeding generations) was like that of no other literary text in the world. And even if we deny their authenticity completely, and read them merely as the invention of a later era, as an apologetic construct, it is still extraordinary in cultural history that the aesthetic reception of the revealed scripture takes on such outstanding importance even in the image that the later Muslims formed of the origins of their religion. No other text has given rise to so many extreme attestations of such an intense reception. Those who believed in its message found the sound of the Quran nothing short of divine, we are told, while its opponents took it 'merely' as spellbinding magic. Even the latter classification, intended as moderate, indicates a powerful experience. Furthermore, the Quran is said to have had such effects regardless of the listener's ideological orientation, social position or personal intention. That is, the accounts of the listeners' reactions assume a uniform aesthetic sensitivity, a condition that generally accompanies the reception of literary works in a given era. Regardless of the questions of the Quran's divine origin, the truth or falsehood of *iʿjāz* or the literary quality of the revealed scripture – none of which is the subject of the present study – the uniformity of the audience's aesthetic sensitivity emerges not so much from the literary structure of the work as 'from certain common properties of context, as on the whole the study of context most easily facilitates our separation of subjective elements from characteristics of the period', to quote Felix V. Vodička.[292] He and the other structuralists of the Prague circle, the precursors of reception aesthetics as it was later conceived in Germany, studied the concretization of aesthetic objects – that is, the reproduction of such objects in the consciousness of the community of recipients in a specific context. Vodička defines a context as 'the set of circumstances making it possible to perceive and evaluate a work esthetically':[293]

> Only by being read is a work aesthetically realized; only reading makes it an aesthetic object in the reader's consciousness. Aesthetic perception is closely

linked to *appreciation*, however. Evaluation presupposes criteria, but standards of value are not stable, so that the value of a work, from the perspective of historic sources, is not a fixed, immutable quantity.[294]

Recipients within the same context can come to quite different results in appreciating an aesthetic object, yet the context largely determines the nature of the appreciation and the aspect of aesthetic experience on which it is based. Accordingly, the same work in a new context may be perceived in a completely new dimension of meaning and, again, variously interpreted and appreciated in that context. Over the course of its reception history, there have been profound changes in audiences' perception of Homer's *Iliad*, for example. And the twentieth century made Chopin's originally aristocratic music into a mass-market item that issues from telephones, airline headphones, restaurant loudspeakers, and the like.[295] The Quran too has been received very differently in the religious discourse of present-day Egypt, for example, compared with its reception in the founding period of Islam. Certain properties of the work come to the fore while others recede into the background; previously unmentioned aspects of the work begin to be perceived while others are neglected and become insignificant. The Quran's linguistic form – a critical aspect of the work in remembered history, and one which agitated the spirits of opponents and adherents in the extreme during its earliest reception – has shifted away from the centre of contemporary reception (as has the quranic eschatology), while the moral and ethical parts of the discourse and those that pertain to legislation and social norms have come to dominate what some decry as an excessively narrow perception.[296] With a change of context, not only can different aspects of a work become dominant in its reception, but 'precisely those properties of the work can be perceived as aesthetically effective that were not felt to be so before, so that a positive appreciation is based on entirely opposite reasons', Vodička explains.[297] Inevitably, different aspects of a work evoke aesthetic effects in audiences in non-Arabic-speaking countries than in Arab audiences. But even when we compare the reception of the Quran during the Prophet's lifetime with its reception by an Arab or Saudi Arabian audience of today, we cannot assume that the criteria for a positive appreciation of the work remain identical. The supraindividual aesthetic consciousness of the Muslims has changed too drastically in the intervening period, even in remote areas, if only through the influence of foreign civilizations with their technical innovations (consider, for example, the technical ability to record and reproduce a recitation, or the introduction of microphones and loudspeakers) and their aesthetic norms. Even, or perhaps especially, the mainstream aesthetics of today's culture industry, from Sky Television to easy-listening music, inevitably influence the aesthetic consciousness of the receiving community, if only by provoking a backlash, a turn towards what the community conceives as aesthetically traditional. Yet a context-dependent change in the supraindividual aesthetic consciousness occurred even during the Prophet's lifetime, as even a superficial comparison of the appeal structures of early Meccan and Medinan surahs reveals. Whereas the early Meccan revelation, with its vociferous threats and promises, its forcefully worded reflections on the incomprehension of the unbelievers and the obviousness of God's signs, appeals to an audience which for the most part has yet to be persuaded, the later surahs are addressed to an already Islamic *umma* which needs less persuasion than admonition and instruction. Thus the fact that the recipients' context underwent a critical change in just a few years is manifest even in the text itself. The Quran is no more a constant than a work of art is. As an aesthetic object it changes with each shift in its social, religious and artistic environment, because with each such shift it is perceived through a different prism.[298]

To identify the different concretizations of an aesthetic object, we must examine each one in its given context with its referential system of expectations. Only by elucidating the cultural context of the revelation and the polarity of the text and its addressees can we understand the incredible-sounding stories about the effects of Quran recitation on the Meccan audience and that audience's reactions within their specific linguistic, mythological and sociocultural environment. Only in this way can we go beyond the categories of 'faith' or 'disbelief' and historic 'truth' or 'falsehood' in our discussion of such stories and see that Muhammad's contemporaries' reactions to the mere recitation of a text as described in the traditions are, in the context of their time, unusually intense but *qualitatively* perfectly consistent with that society's horizon of expectations, to the extent that we can reconstruct it – again, from Muslim sources. Naturally the reconstruction of the context is or could be the same kind of projection as our image of the reception itself, and we must bear this in mind. What we are examining is still remembered history. In any case, there is no doubt that the inhabitants of the Arabian peninsula in the early seventh century had a completely different kind of relation to language and poetry than that to which we are accustomed in the present day. I am not talking – at least not primarily – about the Arabs' love of poetry that has been so romanticized by later authors. There is every reason to assume that 'poetry', *ash-shi'r*, had an extremely important, even an existential function in early Arabic society, but it was not primarily a medium of artistic expression as we understand it today, and the *shā'ir* was not an author of literary works of art. Ignaz Goldziher pointed out the magical or mantic function of ancient Arabic poetry in *Abhandlungen zur arabischen Philologie* [Discourses on Arabic philology], his unsurpassed presentation of inspiration and poetry in ancient Arabic culture: 'The word brings with it a sense of the magical.'[299] The wealth of examples in Goldziher's work indicates that language to the Arabs of the Jahiliyyah was not primarily a vehicle for information. It must have seemed to them more like a powerful organism with a life of its own, a creature from another world, but one with a literally monstrous influence on this world. As in other ancient cultures, language was not a mere tool, but a subject which could be mastered only by a chosen few, something objectively real that interacted with people as a magical entity. The power of the Quran can be called *magical*: this assessment by the first recipients is still tenable today if we add that, for Muhammad's contemporaries, structured speech in itself possessed a magic, of which only vestiges remain in the modern world. The section that follows develops this concept to a certain extent.

In saying that language possesses, for lack of a better word, a certain 'magic', we are not talking about hocus-pocus but referring to those speech acts by which beings, whether people, spirits or gods, attempt to exercise power over the natural course of events; by which they influence other beings, whether animals, plants or gods – whether by revelations, incantations, invocations, verses, curses or blessings. In this sense, verbal magic is a universal phenomenon. The occult term 'verbal magic' or 'language magic' is the 'viceroy and discoverer of an altogether usual "side of language", but one which is rarely known as such in spite of its familiarity', writes Winfried Menninghaus in his study of Walter Benjamin's theory of language.[300] Verbal magic in this sense is a universal phenomenon. It is a necessarily vague expression of a certain experience of language which is difficult to define but which, whether or not we are aware of it, is still present, and, in premodern societies such as that of pre-Islamic Arabia, omnipresent.

About Verbal Magic

In the German-speaking countries alone, the magic of language has interested such diverse twentieth-century authors as Gershom Scholem,[301] Ernst Cassirer,[302] Walter Benjamin,[303] Karl Kraus[304] and Ludwig Wittgenstein.[305] As disparate as they are ideologically, they share the awareness that the authority of sacred texts is rooted in the 'magical' power of ordinary language, whether they see it, with Scholem, as a positive principle of language-based theological mysticism or, with Wittgenstein, as the negative starting point of a critical analysis aimed at demystifying language. The authors named are also united in distinguishing between a modern, 'instrumentalist' concept of language, in which words are more or less arbitrary symbols for things, and an earlier concept, still immanent in certain speech acts (especially in poetry, which posits an inherently necessary relation between a name and a thing), in which the essence of things is expressed *in* words (not *by means of* words) – that is, a concept of language in which substance is compounded with its designation. Those who make this distinction are the heirs of the Romantic philosophy of language, which developed out of reflections on language's origin.[306] Another notion conserved from the Romantic period is that, while poetry is the epitome of verbal magic, that magic is not limited to poetry, and, as August Wilhelm Schlegel emphasized in his Berlin lectures on language, 'because poetry is originally native to language, language can never be so thoroughly depoeticized that a number of poetic elements will not be found scattered everywhere in it.'[307] The Romantic language philosophers' view that poetry is the true, natural language of human beings[308] was formulated in Arabic by the Syrian poet Nizār Qabbānī. 'Man is the animal that composes poetry' is the beginning of an essay[309] in which Qabbānī reflects on the language of the revealed scriptures and the universality of verse:

> Ever since this inhabited star first rotated on its axis, there has been poetry; ever since the first man's hand reached for the first wildflower to take it to the woman waiting for him in his shelter, with the words, 'I bring nothing for us to eat today. Instead I have brought you this beautiful creature, which I found hidden in a rocky crevice. It is like the opening of your mouth, my love.' That was the first time in the history of gifts that beauty was given; it was an opening line in the book of the science of the beautiful, a first letter in the first collection of poetry.[310]

Its lyrical style notwithstanding, Nizār Qabbānī's statement is not entirely unrealistic. Poetry is a basic form of human speech that exists in all known cultures and is far older than literary prose. Yet Qabbānī's insight is not as new as he suspects.[311] It was expressed by the eighteenth-century Christian philosopher Johann Georg Hamann in words whose influence extended far into the Romantic period and to the modern philosophy of language:

> Poetry is the mother-tongue of the human race, as the garden is older than the ploughed field; painting, than writing; song, than declamation; parables, than logical deduction; barter, than commerce. A deeper sleep was the repose of our most distant ancestors, and their movement was a frenzied dance. Seven days they would sit in the silence of thought or wonder; and would open their mouths – to winged sentences.[312]

Speech, composed in a formula, styled in rhyme and rhythm, transformed into songs, poems, hymns or myths, is an anthropological constant which, unlike prose, is found in all known peoples at every stage of human history. The Italian philosopher Giovanni Battista Vico (d. 1744) tried to conceptualize this phenomenon in a cyclical view of history divided into three epochs – the mythic age or age of the gods, the age of heroes, and the age of men – after which a new mythic age begins the next cycle. Each of these ages produces its own language: the first is the hieroglyphic ('a sacred and secret language'); the second, a symbolic language ('using resemblances'); and the third, the epistolary ('or vernacular language, which was used for the common business of everyday life').[313] Vico adds, however, that in reality each form of language never exists alone but can be at most only a dominant form among several: 'The gods, heroes and men all originated at the same time, for it was after all men who imagined the gods and who believed that their own heroes were a mixture of divine and human natures. And their three languages also originated at the same time.'[314] Vico's intention is not to reconstruct a historic sequence but to present a model for the constantly recurring conditions for the origin and development of language.[315] His theories of human language development may lead us to a more precise definition of the power that words had in the oases of the Arabian peninsula, the power that Goldziher vaguely describes as 'magic'.

Vico assumes that language, in an original time that he conceives as an ideal, was metaphorically connected to man's experience of nature and only later came to be organized in relatively arbitrary systems determined by convention. The Canadian literary scholar Northrop Frye took up Vico's theory and identified an inexact distinction between subject and object as characteristic of the first age:

> In this period there is relatively little emphasis on a clear separation of subject and object: the emphasis falls rather on the feeling that subject and object are linked by a common power or energy. Many 'primitive' societies have words expressing this common energy of human personality and natural environment, which are untranslatable into our normal categories of thought but are very pervasive in theirs: the best known is the Melanesian word *mana*. The articulating of words may bring this common power into being; hence a magic develops in which verbal elements, 'spell' and 'charm', and the like, play a central role. A corollary of this principle is that there may be a potential magic in any use of words. Words in such a context are words of power or dynamic forces.[316]

In the mystic age described by Vico, there can have been no linguistic abstraction, no 'empty words'; there would have been no 'just talking', no colloquial language of the kind Karl Kraus derided: 'Vernacular results when people have their way with language, finding their way around it, as if it were the law; sneaking their way past it, as if it were the enemy; when they speak straight away, without waiting to be spoken to.'[317] What one said or left unsaid was never irrelevant or inconsequential and was always specific. There was no need to follow words with deeds, as the saying goes. In this sense, Goethe's Faust was wrong to posit the deed as primordial in translating the biblical verse 'In the beginning was the Word'. In old cultures, the word *is* an act – as in the ancient Greek, where *logos* stands for both word and deed, like *dabār* in Hebrew, and is also comparable with the Arabic word *qāla* ('to say'), which originally encompassed all kinds of acts.[318] Faust merely chose a different translation of the Greek word – but in doing so, as the visionary Goethe grasps, he also takes the real separation of word and deed, which could be called the starting point of modern civilization, to its logical conclusion.

If we bear in mind that Vico's three linguistic ages are intended as a model, and that in reality all three exist simultaneously, with differing degrees of dominance, then his theory of language development can accommodate later observations as well. Cultural historians, anthropologists and ethnologists offer a wealth of examples of the imagined unity of word and deed, or even of word and thing, in ancient cultures. A woman among the Germanic tribes who was accused of witchcraft or fornication would be punished accordingly unless another person was willing to take 'revenge' (*uphaevelse* – literally, 'setting up again') for the accusation. Whether or not she was 'guilty' was not the issue. A word made her guilty, and only another word could rehabilitate her.[319] In a world so conceived, there can be no love without a declaration of love,[320] and an oath sworn has the power to make something true or untrue. We must bear this in mind when we study the much discussed oaths in the Quran, which some have dismissed as abstruse and purely ornamental affirmations or as conventional introductory forms. In the language of the Quran, they are without a doubt primarily shrewdly used literary devices for emphatic effect, but the form in which they appear, like the oaths in the Bible, reflects[321] the still older function of oaths as producing magical influence or legal obligation.[322] Even in more advanced Islamic times, the instinctive belief in the power of mere words endures, if we take seriously an anecdote related by Ibn ʿArabī (d. 1240) at any rate. The legal scholar Mālik ibn Anas (d. 796) was asked whether it was permissible for the faithful to eat the meat of 'water swine' (*khinzīr al-māʾ*, a term for cetaceans in general and dolphins in particular). Pronouncing a legal opinion, he said (*aftā*), 'It is forbidden.'

The person who had consulted him then objected, 'But don't they belong to the family of aquatic beasts?'

'They do, but you called them swine.'[323]

Words have become, but were not always, labels, a kind of wrapper around things or acts. The function of words as merely conventional symbols, and the concept that the relation between an object and a word that symbolizes it is extrinsic and arbitrary, is not 'natural' but the mark of a rationally oriented, 'modern' mind, the characteristic of an epistolary language, as Vico called it. The beginning of metaphysics as a philosophical discipline in the place of – or at least side by side with – religion can be thought of as the moment when the identity of word and object became a problem, and the question arose, in Adorno's words, 'whether concepts are mere signs and abbreviations, or whether they are autonomous, having an essential, substantial being in themselves.'[324] On the other hand, to the immediate or hieroglyphic linguistic mind, which we find in ancient or so-called primitive peoples (and in children) and which is implied by many creation myths, the objectness of words is taken for granted: words exist independently of people and are not the organon a person uses to structure reality.[325] A word is one with, and even calls into being, the object or the act that it names. Things do not exist first to be named afterwards: on the contrary, naming gives them existence. This is probably reflected in one way or another in all religions: when God taught Adam the names of things, that was an act of creation.[326] Accordingly, many myths describe the time before the Creation as a state in which heaven and earth are still unnamed, and the names of all things were unknown.[327] In the beginning was the Word.

The power of the word can be felt in the creation myths of many cultures, as in the Bible, and it is almost always allied with the supreme god of creation, as the tool with which he or she brings forth the world, or as his or her very being.[328] The Sumerians held that everything that exists was created by the word of the god Enki. Like the Egyptian god Ptah, who creates humanity by the word, the religious traditions of perhaps all peoples, from the mythology of the South American Witoto tribe and the African Dogon tribe[329] to the Quran, attest that God creates by His word: there is no more trenchant expression of such a creation than *yaqūlu kun fa-yakūnu*, 'He said, "Be," and it is.' The imperative 'be' here in verse 40:68 is at once both word and act, so that we might go so far as to conclude, with Adonis, that all of Creation is 'nothing but words of God'.[330] In many religious traditions it is the word itself that creates: the word is object, as concrete as any natural object. In India, *vāc*, 'speech', is a primordial being or a creating divinity in its own right. The power of words is so great that gods are named after them: *Brahman*, the Vedic god, denotes the One who is filled with the power of the sacred Word, a magical incantation. In such conceptions, the sacred Word is a living entity, often conceived as a supernatural person.[331] This is the notion expressed in the following words of Yahweh:

> For as the rain cometh down, and the snow from heaven, and returneth not thither, but watereth the earth, and maketh it bring forth and bud, that it may give seed to the sower, and bread to the eater: So shall my word be that goeth forth out of my mouth: it shall not return unto me void, but it shall accomplish that which I please, and it shall prosper in the thing whereto I sent it.[332]

Words condensed into rhythmic formulas or verse, like incantations, are not only as real as objects or acts: they are also just as powerful in their effects. To pronounce them is, in the words of van der Leeuw, 'like firing a loaded pistol'.[333] A blessing is an effective power for good, comparable to a self-fulfilling prophecy; a curse is not an unfriendly remark but a real threat; it is a weapon, a living substance that bores into the soul to do harm. In the Quran, the fear of the effect of a curse is reflected in the fact that the strongest form of affirmation of a statement is a willingness to curse oneself if it is not true.[334] In highly developed cultures too, including the Hellenic, the ancient Persian and the Far Eastern civilizations, practically nothing was as widespread as the belief in the magical power of structured or formulaic speech, of blessings, oaths, declarations of love, and the like. The hereditary curse in a Greek tragedy was conceived as something personal, like a demon living in the family's house and inexorably working its evil. People and their actions are nothing more than its tools.[335] Although today we understand such conceptions only as metaphors, originally they must have been quite concrete.[336] In ancient Japanese culture, it was considered appropriate not to speak sad news so that the words could not cause any harm.[337] Other peoples avoid speaking words and syllables that sound like the name of a dead person.[338] It is no wonder, then, that in many ancient literatures words are metaphorically called 'arrows' or 'lances'. In the Psalms, tongues are a 'sharp sword'.[339] Cultural historians and anthropologists affirm, and even a scholar of the Quran and of poetics such as ʿAbdulqāhir al-Jurjānī (d. 1078) thought it possible, that a well-wrought invective verse can devastate an enemy, while a rhymed declaration of love can engender love in the heart of the addressee. Al-Jurjānī called poetry a 'kind of magic (*ḍarb min as-siḥr*)',[340] and wrote:

> From matter of value, it creates new things of wonder that are precious and of great value; it transforms the substances and changes the physical qualities so that alchemy seems to become true and the existence of an elixir obvious, except that this alchemy is purely mental in nature and has to do with conceptions and thoughts, not with lifeless matter and objects.[341]

Traces of verbal magic can be found today primarily on religious occasions: in church rituals, weddings or funerals; even here, however, words are progressively losing their magical-spiritual association, in the same way as they have lost it already in formulaic greetings, oaths and curses. In poetry, on the other hand, it is still invoked today. Octavio Paz explains:

> Poetry is metamorphosis, change, an alchemical operation, and therefore it borders on magic, religion, and other attempts to transform man and make of 'this one' and 'that one', that 'other one' who is he himself.'[342]

In this century, a number of European and Latin American poets, as well as Arabic and Persian writers, have been conscious that poetry is the epitome of verbal magic.[343] In addition to Octavio Paz, quoted above, we may cite here Adonis, Nizār Qabbānī, Sohrāb Sepehrī, Borges, Valéry, Hugo, Celan, Georgia and, of course, Rilke:

> That it shall bind the divine,
> The word soars to the conjuring.[344]

Words in a poetic text are not mere representatives of the object they designate, indifferent references to reality: in their specific composition, they exercise an effect that cannot be explained merely by their declarative content.[345] It is precisely in this effect that the connection between poetry and verbal magic as we have defined it here has its roots. Rilke and many other poets have appealed to this magical function of language which transcends the immediate sense in part because they felt the magnitude of what had been lost with the change to a one-dimensional linguistic consciousness. The present age may be anything but untouched by 'verbal magic', but it suffers more than any other, as the Japanese cultural historian and scholar of Islam Izutsu remarks, from the 'ravages' of that magic:

> Why? Because the verbal magic has, so to speak, gone underground; it has altered its ways, has disguised itself, and has assumed more insidious forms than before. It has to a great extent been neutralized and enervated, but by suffering this loss it has succeeded in becoming the warp and woof of all our thinking without our being in the least conscious of the fact. And herein lies a great danger.[346]

Horkheimer and Adorno make similar observations in the *Dialectic of Enlightenment*:

> For the more completely language coincides with communication, the more words change from substantial carriers of meaning to signs devoid of qualities; the more purely and transparently they communicate what they designate, the more impenetrable they become. The demythologizing of language, as an element of the total process of enlightenment, reverts to magic.[347]

Numerous writers and thinkers of the twentieth century have responded to the depletion of language in the modern world and given tangible expression to the arbitrariness and meaninglessness of words, culminating in the shredded speech of Lucky's monologue in *Waiting for Godot*, in which the words are – how shall I describe it? – violated or vomited. The only further escalation possible is a demonstrative silence, an *Act without Words*, as two of Beckett's later plays were titled[348] – or the talk-show discourse of our mediatized reality. In this way all speech returns to its origin, to non-speaking; all the acts of naming since God taught Adam the names come to a close – only the end is not the fulfilled stillness of mystical enlightenment or the silence of those who, like Hölderlin or Rimbaud, have transcended the entire sphere of the utterable. What befalls us is rather a regression to the condition of aphasia, as Beckett sketches it, or the babbling non-communication of the information society that encloses the subject; what the subject experiences is not the fulfilled universality that stands at the end of the mythic-religious cycle, where it comes face to face, in the end as it was in the beginning, with the nameless

Divine[349] – everything is one – but only the great Indeterminate: since everything has been named, there is 'information' about everything – everything is the same. This is the context in which we can understand that a poet such as Octavio Paz concentrates his mission in the sentence: 'Against silence and noise I invent the word.'[350]

Of those who have repeatedly addressed the writer's struggle to find words that have not been completely depleted and petrified to cliché by mass use, Kafka is probably the most prophetic.[351] He had a distinct sense that the functionalization of language into mere signs threatened to backfire in violence and regression when demagogues infused it with new meaning, filled it with new magic, their magic. George Steiner explains this in the following words:

> From the literal nightmare of *The Metamorphosis* came the knowledge that *Ungeziefer* ('vermin') was to be the designation of millions of men. The bureaucratic parlance of *The Trial* and *The Castle* has become commonplace in our herded lives. The instrument of torture in *The Penal Colony* is also a printing press. In short, Kafka heard the name Buchenwald in the word birchwood. He understood, as if the bush had burnt for him again, that a great inhumanity was lying in wait for European man, and that parts of language would serve it and be made base in the process…[352]

What does all this have to do with the Quran? A great deal: the awareness of our own, historically very specific linguistic world, and the elucidation of the relics it contains of an earlier, 'mythic' way of dealing with language, demonstrates how very different the function and power of language must have been for Muhammad's contemporaries. The effects of Quran recitation on seventh-century Arabs cannot be explained without bearing in mind the magical function of structured or formulaic speech, which may seem strange to us at first, and with it the cultural and linguistic context of the revelation or, in Jauss's terms, the 'transsubjective horizon of understanding'.[353] An awareness of the magic that can be inherent in language helps us to understand why the linguistic structure of the Quran was *necessarily* so critically important at that time and reveals that such reactions as weeping, wailing, fainting, rapture and spontaneous conversions, in relation to the first listeners' horizon of expectations, are extraordinary but not unrealistic.

Language and Poetry in Ancient Arabic Society

Through the lens of the semantic theory that Leo Weisgerber called linguistic ideology (*sprachliche Weltanschauungslehre*), which builds on Humboldt's concept of a language-specific world view or *Weltansicht* and draws on postulates that are ultimately traceable to Leibniz, the ponderous importance of language in the collective consciousness of the Arabs of Muhammad's time is visible not least in the language itself.[354] An illustrative example is the term *aʿjamī*. The Arabs of the Jahiliyyah divided what they knew of the human race into two categories: Arabs (*al-ʿarab*) and non-Arabs (*al-ʿajam*). The distinction was based on race, blood, customs, and the like, yet the most important criterion to determine which of the two groups a person belonged to was a linguistic one: the Arabic language. From this fact we can see, among other things, that the fundamental meaning of the root *ʿ-j-m* is probably an 'extreme unintelligibility of speech'. People who were of pure Arab ancestry, but could not speak Arabic correctly, were called *aʿjamī*;[355] animals too were *aʿjam*. That is, the term referred to all living things that were unable to articulate in Arabic in accordance with the norms, and it was decidedly pejorative: it implied a contemptuous attitude on the part of the Arabs against anyone who did not master their language. Even today, *aʿjam* means both 'non-Arab' and 'barbarian' (the latter word is of course analogous, being derived from a Greek term for those who did not master the Greek language). To Muhammad's contemporaries, being unable to express oneself in the Arabic language was almost the same as being mute.[356]

In view of the political situation and the tribal structure of their society at that time, the fact that the Arabs considered themselves a unit, to be contrasted with non-Arabs, was not something inevitable. Just as they classified the world by a linguistic criterion, their community too was engendered by the language. The Arabs of the Jahiliyyah were not confederated, nor did they share a common political platform. On the contrary, clans raided one another, and blood feuds tore across the country. The most important organizational form by far was the tribe: it dominated the individual's world view and personal alliances. Nonetheless, the countless clans constantly warring with one another considered themselves a single, uniform people – and the language on the Arabian peninsula in the early seventh century was considered the element that united all factions in spite of their conflicts. Every tribe had its own dialect, which was difficult for other tribes to understand, but the formal language of poetry, *ʿarabīya*, reigned over all dialects.[357] Poetry, in accordance with Vico's conception, produced a common identity; it was the foundation of the uniform memory that spanned all the divisions. We may compare this situation with that of Germany at the end of the eighteenth century, when literature was what fostered a common, specifically 'German', self-image among the small and tiny states. Shelomo D. Goitein writes:

> This phenomenon of pre-Islamic poetry was a miracle in more than one respect. First, we see primitive people, camel breeding bedouins, developing an accomplished and refined means of expression, and, secondly, and even more astonishing, one and the same literary language, with small negligible dialectical differences, was used by mostly illiterate persons scattered over an

area as large as one third of Europe. From Yemen in the south to Syria in the north, from the fringes of Iraq to the borders of Egypt, pre-Islamic poetry used one and the same idiom and the same literary techniques. How this was achieved we do not know and most probably shall never learn.[358]

According to the traditional notion, *'arabīya*, long since relieved of everyday use, was passed down from generation to generation. Children received strict and careful initiation into its refinements; adults listened reverently to the recitations of their poets. Naturally a person who spoke Arabic particularly well acquired a special dignity, a distinct power within the tribal community. Eloquence (*faṣāḥa*), in the pre-Islamic world view, was one of the three chief abilities of the 'perfect man' (*al-insān al-kāmil*), alongside the arts of hunting and riding.[359] The poets occupied the highest rank within a community. They were poet princes in the true sense of the word: leaders of their tribe, heroes in battle, lords of oratory. Their commands were to be obeyed unconditionally.[360]

The plenary power of the poet did not stem primarily from his ability to bring forth pleasing things; it was founded rather in his performance as an oracle of secret knowledge and in the magical powers that were attributed to his oratory. The belief in his inspiration referred to the insights that the poet received from higher powers and divulged in poetic language.[361] An old Arabic saying, 'There is more to the poem', alludes to the poet's store of arcane knowledge.[362] As we know, prophecy and poetry in Arabic culture, as in most cultures, have been related since the earliest times. Just as the Prophet's revelation is poetic, the poetry of the Jahiliyyah is prophetic.[363] In the beginning, poets and soothsayers were no doubt practically indistinguishable. Like a kind of shaman, the poet (*shā'ir* – literally, 'one who knows') imparted supernatural, mantic knowledge[364] that lent him importance and prestige within his tribe, such as poets and seers also enjoy in other cultures.[365] The *shā'ir* had little in common with our idea of a poet, and the first duty of a study aimed at the relationship between divination and poetry, as Nora Kershaw Chadwick emphasizes in a comparative investigation of primitive forms of divination, is to put aside our modern concepts of poetry.[366] For people of the ancient world, and for the remaining primitive peoples of our time, poetry is not simply an artistic genre, much less a pleasant pastime. It is a source of supernatural knowledge and an instrument of real power. In such contexts, repetition, parallelism, refrain and alliteration are not merely 'artistic devices' but magical-religious means of exercising power. Because spiritual knowledge has been communicated in poetic language all over the world, the history of human thought, as Chadwick underscores, has over long periods been a history of human poetry.[367]

From a present-day perspective, and with a certain chutzpah, the pre-Islamic poet could be described as a hybrid between head of state, priest, pop star, general, demagogue, artist, international player and press secretary. Among his most important duties were deciding on tactical procedures in military campaigns, consulting oracles to determine the destination and the time of departure for migrations in the desert, and acting as an arbiter in conflicts. Depending on the occasion, his poems could be news broadcasts, call signs, pastimes, defence and spiritual edification.[368] In spite of its limited thematic repertoire, the poetry of the Jahiliyyah is *the* means of intertribal communication: to quote a proverb attributed to Ibn ʿAbbās, it is 'the Arabs' archives (*dīwān*)'.[369] Even today, almost all of what we know about ancient Arab society is drawn from its poetry.[370]

When Muhammad began his preaching, Arab civilization was no longer in a purely mythic epoch in Vico's terms. The original unity of seer (*kāhin*) and poet had given way to quite distinct profiles. While the seer was still primarily responsible for communicating transcendental knowledge, the poet had the particular function of representing the group externally. In the reception of his texts, 'artistic' elements increasingly came to the fore; his presentation was evaluated more and more by aesthetic criteria on the basis of literary norms. The poet no longer bore much resemblance to a shaman.[371] In addition to supernatural inspiration, he had to have skill in his craft; he had to master the poetic language, which was different from the tribal dialects, know the genealogy and history of the tribes, and be familiar with the themes and stylistic techniques of poetry. To acquire this knowledge, he was usually first apprenticed to another poet as a rhapsode (*rāwī*).[372] But, although the poetry of the Arabian peninsula in the early seventh century increasingly resembled an art form, language had not completely lost its magical connotations. A great deal of evidence attests to the formidable power of certain phrases, which moved the rhetorician Ibn Rashīq (d. 1063) to devote a chapter to 'those whom poetry elevates and those whom it brings low'.[373] Like the Indians, the Greeks and the Romans – consider the prehistory of the Latin *carmen* – Muhammad's contemporaries continued to attribute poetic inspiration to supernatural, personified powers: to a jinn (*jinn*, *jinna*, more rarely *jānn*) or a demon (*shayṭān* or *ṭābīʿ*) who possessed the poet and spoke through him.[374] To what degree the invocation of the jinn was still felt to be a real operation during Muhammad's lifetime is a subject of debate.[375] But the vehement repulsion of any suspicion that Muhammad was *majnūn*, 'possessed by jinn', which occurs at several places in the Quran,[376] the frequency and intensity with which the Quran addresses the phenomenon of demonic possession, indicates that such attribution had not entirely decayed into a mere verbal convention. As Goldziher states, 'some significant vestiges' of the old notions would 'still have been present in the minds of the poets and their audiences'.[377]

The Quran itself attests to the magical power of language. A good word (*kalima ṭayyiba*) 'is as a good tree – its roots are firm, and its branches are in heaven; it gives its produce every season, by the leave of its Lord', while 'the likeness of a corrupt word (*mathalu kalimatin khabīthatin*) is as a corrupt tree – uprooted from the earth, having no stablishment.'[378] The

Quran's warning in surah 113 against the 'women who blow on knots' indicates the presence of mythic thinking in Vico's sense of the term, for all verbal magic begins, in the beliefs of many peoples, including the Arabs, in breath, the locus of the soul and the origin of all speech.[379] Another such indication is the custom of taking off a sandal before uttering a curse.[380] Like similar customs in many ancient cultures, it was a means of heightening the power of the curse,[381] and it was widespread among Muhammad's contemporaries before it was proscribed in Islam. Islamic culture adopted the heathen notion of the power of a curse, but with a particular transformation. The Prophet is said to have warned, 'Beware the curse of him whom you have wronged, for it is carried on the clouds', and that the curse rises into the sky 'as if it were a fountain of fire'.[382] One of the worst sins, he said, was to cause one's parents to be cursed by provoking others to the point that they pronounce a malediction.[383] And he describes the curses of an innocent person, even an unbeliever, as arrows and missiles that cannot fail to strike the evildoer.[384] A legend from a later time recounts that an Abbasid ruler who planned to terrorize the population of Baghdad scornfully asked his potential victims what means they had of preventing his scheme. 'We will fight you with the arrows of the night', they cried. The ruler immediately gave up his plan, because such curses were considered especially dangerous: they were arrows 'straightened by lips that murmur prayers, by eyelashes that sprinkle tears'.[385]

We may at this point mention another characteristic of the first of Vico's three ages: namely, taboos against speaking certain words. The power of language in the mythic age prohibits mentioning dangerous objects or persons by name. In some cultures, even the word 'no' is taboo. In many such contexts, lying becomes an art, and poetry originates in the impossibility of calling things by their names.[386] The taboo against pronouncing certain words is due to the vocative power that names originally had. 'My father and my mother told me my name, and it has remained concealed in my body since my birth, so that no sorcerer may have power of sorcery against me', says the Egyptian sun god Ra.[387] In the Jahiliyyah, as in many other cultures of the ancient world, it was apparently not customary in an encounter, even one of an intimate nature, to ask a person's name – at least not right away. Ordinarily, people took pains to conceal their names. In important negotiations, the parties entered into a special agreement by mutually undertaking to disclose their names. The reason for keeping one's name secret, Goldziher suspects, probably lay in the practical danger of 'exposing oneself to blood vengeance due to a blood guilt, which one hoped to avoid by concealing one's identity.'[388] The custom must also be considered in relation to the magical meaning of names in societies that did not distinguish clearly between objects and their names, however: on giving their names, people in such societies must fear risking part of their souls, since the self is inseparably entwined with one's name. For similar reasons, slaves in Roman law had no right to a name, and a person who lost the status of a subject of law had their name annulled.[389] In the early seventh century, the conception of names illustrated in these examples was more than vestigially present not only in Arabia but also in Japan during the Manyo era, where a woman's name was known only to her parents and her husband.[390] From ancient Egypt comes the tradition, like the custom of devout Muslims on mentioning the Prophet, that royal names were regularly pronounced in conjunction with the formula 'life, salvation, health'. Simply speaking the king's name would have exposed him to danger, but the salvific formula was supposed to work as a counter-charm.[391] In the Bible, such notions are reflected in Yahweh's injunction against swearing falsely by His name or profaning it.[392] But the words of Jesus are still more telling: 'For where two or three are gathered together in my name, there am I in the midst of them.'[393] The early Christians, for whom calling a name meant calling a thing or person into existence, must have understood this as invoking Christ's real presence.[394] As late as Shakespeare's time, and outside religious contexts, we find names attributed their original meaning: in *Julius Caesar*, the mob lynch Cinna the poet simply because he shares the name of another Cinna: 'I am not Cinna the conspirator!' cries the unfortunate victim. 'It is no matter', a citizen replies, 'his name's Cinna; pluck but his name out of his heart, and turn him going!'[395]

The Prophet's clear admonition not to conceal one's name suggests that the tendency to do so still existed in his time.[396] In the light of these considerations, the implications of Muhammad's claim – like that of the Hebrew prophets before him – to speak 'in God's name' are all the more striking. It was more than merely claiming to act and speak in accordance with God's will. It meant that God's spirit was at work in him, spoke out of his mouth, and gave his words their power.[397] The same principle is conserved today in the Muslim concept of the ninety-nine most beautiful names of God.[398] Especially in the mystical ritual of *ḏikr* (and also, with reservations, in day-to-day religious practice), speaking the names is in principle nothing short of conjuring God's presence. By concentrating on a specific name and pronouncing it again and again, the mystic feels increasingly filled with the divine presence, until ultimately – in the ideal case – he feels one with God.

Another phenomenon whose existence harks back to a mythic age of language development, and which was evidently of great importance for the sociocultural context of Muhammad's revelation, is the public poets' contest, a custom that is known to have existed in many variations – including competitions between seers or shamans – in many cultures: among the early Greeks, the Tatars, the Anglo-Saxons, the Celts and the Norsemen. The criterion for success in such contests is not so much the quantity of the poet's knowledge as the rhetorical skill and the literary style of the recitation.[399] Even today, poets' duels take place in the Arab world as cultural and social events.[400] In the Prophet's time, they determined the hierarchy within the tribe. They were also a form of intertribal political contest, a kind of vicarious conflict between poets as champions of their respective tribes. The market (*sūq*) at ʿUkaz, which Philip K. Hitti has called 'a kind of *Académie française* of Arabia', was particularly important in this respect:[401] there the greatest orators met and competed each year during the three sacred months, when the code of honour prohibited armed conflict.

The role of the poet as a spokesman and leader of his tribe was most important in connection with *hijāʾ*, the highly developed genre of flyting or poetic taunts. Even in the late Jahiliyyah, *hijāʾ* had clear ties to the mantic origins of poetry. This was the genre in which the functions and powers of poets and soothsayers most obviously overlapped. For Muhammad's contemporaries, *hijāʾ* was not a mere form of entertainment, an amusing recitation of mocking verses, as it was in later centuries. Originally, *hijāʾ* was a curse and a charm used as a weapon: it was used at the beginning and during the course of a battle, and was 'just as important as, perhaps even more important than, the battle itself', as Goldziher emphasizes.[402] A ceremoniously declaimed, well-phrased insult could devastate its target and make a whole army run away ashamed and demoralized. For its victims, it was a lasting stigma. In the words of a taunting poem by D̲ū r-Rumma (d. 735 or 736), their biting pain never ends, and their shame 'is forever renewed and increased with time'. Once unleashed, 'what is in circulation everywhere cannot be guided back again.'[403] These expressions echo the mythic concepts of words as living beings presented in the preceding section. In such an environment, a formula or a verse hurled at the unbelievers could have a far greater effect than the Prophet's coaxing – not primarily because of the content of the text but because of its overall verbal structure – that is, most of all because of its word order, its rhythm, its intonation, the brilliance of its rhymes, and the like. Even during Muhammad's lifetime, poets are said to have brought about their tribes' victory over its enemies by invocations and curses, and in many cases the poet is presented as the leader of his tribe. Hawd̲a ibn ʿAlī sends the Prophet the message *anā shāʿiru qawmī wa-khaṭībuhum*, by which he expresses his lordship over the tribes of central Arabia: 'I am the poet of my people and their spokesman, and the Arabs revere my position.'[404] Expressions such as this, in a context in which verbal magic as described above was considered real, allow us to understand why the Prophet is considered to have won his victory on the field of poetry and why specific recitations are said to have routed whole armies.[405] Certain sayings of the Prophet suggest that it was not only the Quran that had effects that seem unbelievable from a present-day perspective: rather, it seems that structured oratory in general was very powerful. Muhammad prompted his personal poet Ḥassān ibn Thābit to taunt his adversaries with verse, saying: 'Your mockery plagues them more than a volley of arrows at dawn.'[406] Ibn Hishām's biography mentions the Prophet's advice that a man being cursed should 'throw himself to the ground sideways so that it misses him'.[407]

Muhammad's contemporaries must have found the artistic appreciation of poetry inseparable from its magical function.[408] 'Eloquence has an enchantment', they are supposed to have said.[409] Conversely, the soothsayers' oracular rhymed prose (*saj'*) was considered a form of poetic expression that had an aesthetic appeal.[410] It is only natural that an engagingly phrased pronouncement was more effective than a lukewarm one, and it must have been part of universal human experience that words that sound banal or ordinary in day-to-day use take on an unexpected richness and force when they are recited in metrical or rhythmic form. The Quran was revealed in a cultural milieu in which language in general and poetry in particular had an outstanding importance, one in which poetically structured oratory was associated with supernatural origins and was considered indispensable for asserting and maintaining a claim to leadership. The revelation incorporates the facts of the times. This is not a new idea even to Muslims: after all, the Quran teaches that God addresses all nations in the language and the form that they understand. In view of its first audience's expectations, it would be absurd for a teaching that claims to be divinely inspired, and which demands that people submit to a new authority, to be propounded in prosaic speech. In other words, the language of the Quran is necessarily poetic. To paraphrase Nietzsche's sentence that he would only believe in a God who could dance, we might say of Muhammad's contemporaries that they could only believe in a God who could make poetry.

2

The Text

God is not ashamed to strike a similitude
Even of a gnat, or aught above it.

Quran 2:26 (trans. Arberry)

Is the Quran poetry? From the point of view of Muslim theology, the answer is a definite negative. By the criteria of classical Arabic literary theory, the Quran contains poetic elements (and must therefore be susceptible of *tafsīr adabī*, or 'literary exegesis', according to Amīn al-Khūlī [d. 1967]),[1] yet its style and subject matter are not those of the genre called *shiʿr:* it neither conforms to the metrical scheme of ancient Arabic poetry nor deals with the customary themes.[2] To a modern literary scholar, the answer would not be as clear-cut. Just because the Quran does not conform to the literary norms of Arabic poetry, Roman Jakobson, for example, would not place it outside the 'line of demarcation between poetry and nonpoetry'.[3] As Jakobson has shown, poetic means and motifs are innumerable, and the establishment of a few conventional ones, which vary with time and place, is never more than temporary. Such conventions appear from an outsider's point of view almost arbitrary, and the history of literature documents the changes they constantly undergo. In the German Neoclassical or Romantic period, for example, it would have been unthinkable to consider a text about rubbish or soft-boiled eggs as poetry, since rubbish and soft-boiled eggs were not on the 'list' of poetic themes and motifs of that time. Customary set pieces included the moon, the sea, the nightingale, the cliffs, the castle, and other things of that sort. Today, however, the subject matter of a poem is irrelevant to the question whether or not a text is poetic. A twentieth-century poet such as Pablo Neruda is free to proclaim:

> This is the poetry we search for, worn with the work of hands, corroded as if by acids, steeped in sweat and smoke, reeking of urine and smelling of lilies soiled by the diverse trades we live by both inside the law and beyond it.

> A poetry impure as the clothing we wear on our bodies, a poetry stained with soup and shame, a poetry full of wrinkles, dreams, observations, prophesies, declarations of love and hate, idylls and beasts, manifestos, doubts, denials, affirmations and taxes.[4]

No one today would hesitate to call Neruda's texts poetry. Yet if Neruda had lived a hundred years earlier, nineteenth-century readers would not have considered the same verses poetic. Conversely, a work that is perceived by its first audience as poetry may be read in later eras primarily as a historic document or, like the Song of Songs, as a religious text.[5] And, finally, it is also possible for many readers to extol a personal document of an informational nature such as Kafka's *Letter to His Father* as a poetic work of genius, or for a modern recipient such as the Syrian poet Nizār Qabbānī to call a religious text such as the Quran, which explicitly and repeatedly proclaims its dissimilarity to poetry, a 'divine qasida'. Qabbānī writes, in his essay quoted in chapter 1,

> When God wanted to speak to man, He chose poetry (*ash-shiʿr*), euphonious song, the fair word, the graceful verse. In His omnipotence He could have commanded man: 'Believe in Me', and man would have believed. But He did not. God chose the more beautiful way, the more noble means. He chose poetry.[6]

Of course Qabbānī knows that the Quran is not a poem by the standards of ancient Arabic poetry. But he is also aware that a generic term such as 'poetry' does not represent an entity, something fixed for all time. What poetry is at a given time or in a given culture may be important to philologists, anthropologists or religious scholars but, since the broad acceptance of structuralist literary theory, it is no longer a standard by which to determine the poetic character of a text. To answer the question whether the Quran is poetry from a present-day perspective, it is not enough to point out that it does not belong to the genre *shiʿr* in an ancient Arabic context. That fact implies at most that the Quran does not consist of poems in the sharply defined sense of the Arabic literary tradition. But something that is not *shiʿr* can still be poetry. The Arabs classed pre-Islamic Persian poems in the prose genre (*nathr*) because their metre was not familiar.[7] This indicates that the Arabic notion of literary genre is itself relative. All the stylistic criteria that a reader with common sense generally musters in deciding whether a text is poetry or prose – metre, rhyme, line and stanza structure, rhythm, etc. – are only valid within a given culture. Furthermore, as the German language makes somewhat finer distinctions than most others in this point, '*Prosa*' (prose) is a complementary category, not to '*Poesie*' (poetry), but to '*Gedicht*' (poem): '*Prosa*' can be '*Poesie*' – prose can be poetic – yet *nathr* cannot be *shiʿr*. The fictional nature of a text, another criterion that the unreflecting mind applies on this question, has little to do with its poetic or literary character.[8] Heinrich

Heine's *Travel Pictures* or Dostoevsky's *House of the Dead*, for example, do not fit into the dichotomy of historic reality versus literary fiction. Yet, in spite of their documentary pretensions, both of these books are without a doubt poetic. In any case, even for 'true' literature, the author's intention in creating any work of art should not be taken as absolute. After all, in the creative process it is 'only one element in the artist's relation to the art-work and hardly the definitive one', as Adorno pointed out in rebuttal to psychoanalytical interpreters of art.[9] Moreover, some Muslim philosophers, such as Avicenna (Ibn Sīnā, d. 1037) and Averroes (Ibn Rushd, d. 1198), explicitly exclude fictionality as an identifying characteristic of the poetic.[10] And it is by no means taken for granted that the Quran is a non-fictional text through and through. Muḥammad Aḥmad Khalafallāh, a devout Egyptian scholar, sustained the thesis – opposed by equally devout scholars – that the quranic narrative is fictional and only metaphorically true.[11] So is the Quran poetry after all?

This is not the place for a definitive answer to this question. The introductory discussion above is intended primarily to question the all too often foregone conclusion that Muhammad's prophecy cannot be poetry because it is not *shi'r* as defined by classical Arabic literary theory. Before we could decide whether the Quran is poetry, we would have to define that genre – and that is a problem. Every culture, every period and every poetics has produced its own definition, and today the 'borderline dividing what is a work of poetry from what is not is less stable than the frontiers of the Chinese empire's territories', as Jakobson puts it.[12] It might be possible to pick a given definition and then apply it to a discussion of the 'poetry of the Quran', but it would also be quite arbitrary – as indeed such discussions of the Bible seem to be.[13] In any case, that is not the purpose of the present work. As announced in the explanatory introduction, this is not a study of the 'artistic nature' of the Quran. It is not an analysis of the Quran's language, style or rhetorical devices as they are objectively present in the text. It is irrelevant to the present study whether the Quran, as Muslims say, is of divine beauty, or whether Muhammad, as Nöldeke and his colleagues instruct them, was an 'average stylist'.[14] Hence I make no attempt to determine what literary genre the Quran should be assigned to. The present work is concerned – and its recourse to the methods and approaches of structuralism and reception aesthetics follows from this focus – with how the Quran is aesthetically received. Strictly speaking, this book is not even about the Quran and what it may or may not be, 'objectively'. In the ternary relationship between the sender (God/Muhammad), the message (the Quran) and the receiver (the Meccans/the Muslims), we are interested in the receiver, and specifically in the extent to which the Quran is actualized as an *aesthetic object* in the receiver's mind.

Such a study cannot be based exclusively on documents about individual actualizations, however. The reception of a text is not completely arbitrary, nor is it dependent only on who the recipient is and in what context the reception occurs; the sender and the message are not completely negligible. 'The psychic process in the reception of a text', writes Hans Robert Jauss, 'is in the primary horizon of aesthetic experience, by no means only an arbitrary sequence of merely subjective impressions, but rather the carrying out of specific instructions in a process of directed perception.' Like other texts, the Quran 'predisposes its audience to a very specific kind of reception by announcements, overt and covert signals, familiar characteristics, or implicit allusions.'[15] We don't need to conduct an audience survey to know that a poem by Friedrich Hölderlin is read differently than the Cologne telephone directory: the texts themselves tell us that. In addition, the Quran in particular is a highly self-referential text, a text that, more than any other scripture in the history of world religions, reflects, comments on, and discusses its own linguistic form in numerous passages.[16] Even if our intention is to examine only the reception of the Quran, we must at least touch upon the extent to which the Quran itself guides the process of reception into certain channels and on the specific effects of such a predisposition in the history of the Quran's reception among Muslims, including the perceptions of the revelation to which the dialectic process between work and audience has led. In this second chapter, I would like to examine these issues at the textual level, before turning to acoustic features in chapter 3. I must emphasize that the structural elements of the quranic language to which I refer in these two chapters as causes of an aesthetic reception (such as its openness or some of its phonetic figures) are only examples that may serve to illustrate how the text guides or at least elicits certain perceptions and other phenomena in its reception history.

The Poeticity of the Quran

Reception, the perception and assimilation of a message, is an essential part of an act of communication between a sender and a receiver. The Quran, like any other linguistic or non-linguistic message in such a communication, is a system of symbols with various functions. For this structuralist view, the genre to which the text assigns itself and the terms that its receiving community may apply to it, or explicitly refuse to apply to it, are secondary considerations. While the genre 'poetry' is conditional upon the given context, and hence temporally contingent and ultimately hypothetical, we can discern certain attributes of an aesthetic message whose existence does not depend on whether or not the participants in the act of communication identify them as aesthetic elements. A poem by Bertolt Brecht, the Book of Job and a speech by Martin Luther King can all be experienced as poetic texts. All three can also be considered as historic documents, ideological manifestos, testimonies of a certain experience of the world, or normative appeals, depending on the recipient's situation, inclination, personality and environment. What all three texts have in common, in spite of the very different genres to which they are commonly understood to belong today – what they all bring with them to make their aesthetic reception *possible* – is the *poetic function* of their linguistic symbols, or their *poeticity*, as Jakobson termed it, following the Russian formalists. Accordingly, the first question to ask with regard to the Quran is not what genre it belongs to, but whether it shows poeticity – that is, the property of a text that makes an aesthetic reception possible (aesthetic in the sense that its signs are perceived in their sensory appearance) and, when this property is sufficiently developed, usually evokes such a reception.

The Prague structuralist Jan Mukařovský published various treatises in the years following 1936 in which, building on the organon model presented by Karl Bühler in his *Theory of Language*, he identified four basic functions of human speech. The representational, the expressive and the appellative function dominate in purely informative utterances, while the fourth function, the *poetic*, takes on greater importance in poetic speech.[17] In this model, the first three functions refer to entities and goals outside language: representation refers to reality, expression refers to the sender, and appeal refers to the receiver. These functions thus have practical informative value or practical effects. In all of them, the entire purpose of the linguistic symbol is its extralinguistic reference. The sender is interested not in the message itself, only in its meaning. The ideal of such a referential language is to make it as easy as possible to understand the content – that is, to communicate an idea.[18] The poetic function, on the other hand, tends to separate the speech act from its practical purpose of communicating non-linguistic information. A poetically structured text is not only 'meaning' (whether discursive, mystical, practical, emotional or any other kind) that is 'clothed' in a certain form; its linguistic symbols are not only used to indicate an extralinguistic referent. They are not mere representatives of a designated object, arbitrary pointers to reality. Rather, they refer, in their specific composition, to themselves; they make the symbol visible as a symbol or, as others have termed it, an icon.[19] Very generally speaking, this takes place by means of a conscious deformation of the referential language, such as parallelism, all kinds of rhyme and assonance, word repetition, epanalepsis, anaphora, epiphora, and the like, as well as metaphor, parable, clausulae, tropes, unexpected inversions, acoustic effects by means of puns and rhythm, semantic incongruities, surprising collocations, suspenseful plot devices, etc. All of these create an aesthetic stimulation in the recipient's mind that draws his or her attention to the linguistic signs themselves, or, more precisely, to the composition, the 'style', as it is commonly called, or, in the corresponding and more precise term of classical Arabic literary studies, *naẓm*, the 'order'. To a certain degree, which varies with the degree to which the poetic function dominates in a given text, the linguistic sign becomes autonomous, freed from the task of transporting a contextual message, and approaches music or at least the musical principle.[20] The poet Hermann Hesse expressed this idea without the structuralist vocabulary: 'Only pure poetry is capable of such perfection; only it attains the ideal form, completely saturated with life and feeling, that is otherwise music's secret alone.'[21] Likewise: 'A poem is not just content: the more it transforms its content, following the alchemy of art, into form, line, melody, the more poetic it is.'[22] As the philosopher Schopenhauer discerned, musicality is the epitome of poetry, or of the aesthetic function, as we should say in this instance, because music is not 'the copy, the repetition, of any Idea of the inner nature of the world', but in itself 'immediate...objectification'[23] of the will. The medium is the message, we might say in more concise and more contemporary terms: the text is its own content; it is the information it contains.[24]

None of the four functions of language[25] ever appears in isolation from the others. Even in everyday speech or, more generally, in day-to-day interpersonal relations, the aesthetic function permeates every activity and often contributes substantially to furthering a person's material interests (in education, in crafts, in industrial production or in advertising),[26] and conversely even the most poetic expression transports some information of practical relevance about the speaker, the recipient or the surrounding reality. Even a Dadaist poem is not only self-referential. According to Jakobson, poetry is any text in which 'poeticity, a poetic function of determinative significance',[27] predominates. In practice, however, the 'practical' functions are predominant in many texts that are called poetry by the receiving community but serve primarily non-artistic purposes,[28] such as social criticism, panegyrics or didactic verse, or much ancient Arabic poetry.[29]

All four functions of language are clearly discernible in the Quran. The lawgiving parts of the Quran, for example, are primarily appellative, but so is a prayer such as the *Fātiḥa* (no. 1), since it is, at least on the superficial textual level, a human speaker's appeal to God. This is not changed by the fact that, in the Muslim understanding, the text is on a second level not that of a human speaker but a speech prescribed for humans by God – that is, as everywhere in the Quran, the actual speaker is God.[30] The constant shifting between speakers on various levels, from the divine Authority to the Prophet to the various classes of people who are quoted, makes it particularly difficult to isolate the functions immediately intended in each passage, and is one of the causes of the structural complexity of the quranic language. The authoritative speaker of the Quran is of course not the person Muhammad but is 'situated on a much higher level, in contrast to the ancient poets, which lends a peculiar and absolutely unprecedented suspense to the diction overall', as Gustav Richter wrote; yet, at the same time, by no means all of the text is formulated in the royal 'we': the Prophet also speaks in God's name about God 'anaphorically, as if in contraposition to Himself'.[31] The change of speaker often occurs without warning, sometimes within a verse or even within a sentence, and does not necessarily coincide with a change of themes or of the rhetorical and stylistic elements used. To add to the confusion, the first-person singular does not always indicate the human speaker but sometimes expresses God's self-revelation.

Nonetheless, we can still discern different functions as dominant in different passages. Most verses of the Quran have a more appellative or representational function, such as the threats, promises and exhortations, for example, and the narrative, descriptive or contemplative parts. Passages with a predominantly expressive function are rare, and most of them are verses in which the immediate speaker is not God but the Prophet or the people. God seldom talks about himself in the Quran, and on the whole we may consider the Quran, following Naṣr Ḥamid Abū Zayd, as a text whose linguistic organization is oriented wholly towards the addressee.[32] In addition to representation, appeal and expression, the poetic function occurs in the Quran with varying intensity in the individual verses and surahs. In the instructions on inheritance and family law, weaning children and fasting – although Muslims would hardly doubt the linguistic perfection of these verses – the poetic function recedes into the background, and the dominant character of the text is informative.[33] Accordingly, the Muslim literature contains little on aesthetic effects of such passages. On the contrary, even the rather conservative theologian al-Ġazālī states unequivocally that such verses are little suited to *samā'*, the mystics' ritualized 'listening', and hardly elicit the desired state of ecstasy.[34] Nonetheless, the poetic function is eminent even in the most prosaic parts of the Quran, if only because the language in those passages too stands out from colloquial speech and features many rhetorical elements, such as rhyme, which is sustained even in the laws, marking the speech units. This does not mean the poetic function is dominant in such passages, of course. In many other excerpts, such as the sequences of oaths and the eschatological prophecies, in the surahs *al-Fātiḥa* and *al-Ikhlāṣ* (no. 112), and also in a dramatic narrative such as the surah of Joseph (no. 12), we may ask whether the totality of the words, their effect as an overall composition, dominates in the text over their 'practical' or informative function. That would be an indication of poeticity in a text: all the lexical signs are interrelated; none of them can be reduced to its denotatum in isolation from the others. The recipient's attention is drawn to *how* the information is communicated: the message becomes self-reflexive and produces, in a very broad sense, pleasure. This is easy to demonstrate in the Quran.

The phrase *mā anzalnā 'alayka l-qur'āna li-tashqā / illā tad̲kiratan li-man yakhshā* at the beginning of the surah *Ṭāhā* (no. 20) is the passage that causes 'Umar in the famous conversion story to leave off his violence, to turn pale and then to cry out, 'How beautiful, how sublime is this oratory!'[35] Every sign in this passage can be clearly seen to be related to the others, and to develop its full character only in interaction with them. These verses – which we may translate literally as 'Not to distress you did We send down the Quran to you / but as a reminder to him who fears' – contain the essence of the revelation in a nutshell: an admonition that God has charged the Prophet to transmit to the people. No element of it can be isolated from the others: without the preparatory *mā anzalnā ʿalayka l-qurʾāna li-tashqā*, the *illā taḏkiratan li-man yakhshā* would lose its effect, since it is the affirmative resolution of the negation in the first line, which is at the same time an admission of the distress that God has laid on the Prophet. The second line provides the justification of *tashqā*, which in return gives the word *yakhshā* its comforting character and its sonorous force. In order to receive the message, the listener must perceive the interrelations of the signs. If we remove the signs from their relational system, by examining the individual parts of the verse separately or by studying a paraphrase of the content, the message changes; its information content (in the semiotic sense) is reduced; it loses the fullness that results from its complex linguistic structure.[36] For ʿUmar at the time of his conversion, the relational system of the signs in the first two lines of the surah is not the complete composition. In Ibn Hishām's version, after the first two verses have filled ʿUmar with such a surprising degree of amazement and rapture, he recites the rest of the surah in great agitation before running to the Prophet to announce his entry into the Muslim congregation – into the community of Quran listeners, one is tempted to say.

The present book does not answer the question whether the poetic function predominates in the surah in question, so that it would have to be called poetry in the Jakobsonian sense of the term, as Michael Sells claims for several passages of the Quran.[37] In any case, an answer based on a consideration of the text alone, as Jakobson proposes, and not the history of its reception, would be insufficient. With good reason Umberto Eco doubts whether it is possible to analyse and describe a poetic text 'like a crystal', as a pure, meaningful structure, without regard to the history of its interpretations: 'When Lévi-Strauss and Jakobson analyse Baudelaire's *Les Chats*, are they bringing to light a structure that *precedes* all possible interpretations, or are they not rather offering a new performance of it, one that is only possible today, building on the cultural heritage of our century?'[38] Unlike the Prague structuralists Mukařovský and Vodička, Jakobson does not see clearly enough that the dominance of the poetic function cannot really be determined objectively; it is not inscribed in the text for all time but dependent on the reception, on each successive actualization of the text. Ultimately, the conclusion that the poetic function predominates in a text would be nothing but the result of a specific actualization of that text. Accordingly, Mukařovský points out that a preponderance of some extra-aesthetic function is a frequent occurrence in the field of art. Only when the object is perceived as a work of art does 'the definitive synthesis of its functions take on an aesthetic hue in such a degree that even a dominant extra-aesthetic function appears as an aesthetic fact, as a factor contributing to artistic value.'[39]

Let me stress once again that all four of the basic functions of language described by Mukařovský, building on Bühler's work, are present in every text. In the Quran – as in literary works, and also in other revealed scriptures – the fourth function, the poetic, is of special importance: we can at least state that it is a poetically structured text. In other words, it possesses the *potential* for aesthetic reception. What function predominates in the text, whether the informative or the poetic, depends ultimately on its actualization, since the interplay of the linguistic functions is only synthesized in the recipient's mind.[40] Both the poeticity of the text and the corresponding sensitivity on the part of the listener are necessary in order for it to be received as an aesthetic object. *How* the text is received is the result of the dialectical interplay between the recipient's individuality, the paths of reception inscribed in the text, and the context of the specific, unique actualization. In short, the Quran, like any other text, *is* nothing: it can only be something *to* someone. Depending on how it is read or heard, the Quran can be a poetic text. We can thus identify the Quran as potentially poetic: thanks to the highly developed poetic function of its language, it offers the potential for actualization as a poetic text in the mind of a recipient. This is why Nizār Qabbānī can call the Quran poetry in spite of his awareness that it is not poetry in the sense of the classical Arabic genre. When he reads it as poetry, the text is a qasida – not ontologically, but in its manifestation in the moment of communication between some sender and the receiver Nizār Qabbānī.

Creating Horizons and Altering Horizons

If the poetic function in the text is a precondition of and the impetus that stimulates an aesthetic reception, then we can now examine that function more closely with regard to the Quran, indicating some examples of features that cause or call forth an aesthetic reception. A predisposition to aesthetic reception on the part of the listener begins at an elementary level – that is, with the revelation's code. The language of the Quran is not ordinary language, nor was it so to Muhammad's contemporaries.[41] Its preachings are in the language of the ancient Arab poets, *ʿarabīya*, a standard dialect used exclusively for literary and ceremonial purposes.[42] Texts in *ʿarabīya* are conspicuously distinct from everyday language by their inflectional suffixes and by unusual syntactical patterns. This outward property of the quranic language, as banal as it is to say so, is enough, even on a recitation of the first verse, to draw the listener's attention to the signifier, the vehicle of meaning, regardless of the signified, the meaning or meanings it carries. The sender's choice of this specific code for communication automatically places the text in a generic group: that of *ashʿār*, the works of the ancient Arab poets.

Because the English-speaking world has no specific *poets' language* analogous to *ʿarabīya*, there is no communicative situation in English that corresponds to that of the Quran. But we can imagine, to continue with banal observations, what normally happens if the inhabitant of a remote village in a sparsely populated region informs his neighbours that the bus to Richmond leaves at 11:34 a.m. by the new timetable, or if a customer in a department store asks for an *eau de cologne*: nothing special. The referential linguistic function of such messages directs the listener's entire attention to an external object – in Umberto Eco's words, to 'the contextual meaning of the words, and from there to the referent. We are now outside the universe of signs; the sign has been used up; what remains is a series of behavioral sequences that constitute the response to the sign.'[43]

But if the villager were to address his neighbours unexpectedly in the Queen's English, or the department store customer were to ask for a product singing in a tenor voice, although the message remains the same, the receiver's attention would be on the sign itself: its form, and hence its poeticity, would be the centre of interest. Up to this point, the communication has nothing to do with art or poetry. The example shows only how a sender, merely by using a different code from the everyday one, can guide the reception of the message from the informative function to a different linguistic function – to the poetic function of the lexical signs, so to speak, which is potentially present even in sentences such as 'The bus to Richmond now leaves at 11:34 on weekdays' or 'I'd like to buy this *eau de cologne* please.' In the case of the Quran, its linguistic code is not just different from the everyday code but also associated in the receiving community's mind with poetry. The listener therefore immediately situates the text in the complex of previously existing literary works and norms, instinctively subjecting it to an aesthetic appreciation,[44] as soon as he or she hears the words *iqra' bi-smi rabbika llaḏī khalaq / khalaqa l-insāna min ʿalaq*, ostensibly the first revelation.[45] This is the beginning of the continuous process of creating and altering expectation horizons.

Of course, the language of the revelation is distinct from everyday language not only in the use of the *ʿarabīya* but also in its structural complexity – that is, in its persistent use of stanzas[46] and formulaic structures, refrains, rhyme, line structure,[47] acoustic stresses, rhythm,[48] and regularly interspersed clausulae that transcend the given narrative theme;[49] many kinds of parentheses in the flow of discourse; shifts in the narrative level and dramatic changes of speaker;[50] repetition,[51] diction, tropes, metaphor[52] and many other devices. In Muslim Quran studies, these poetic structures in the Quran are fully recognized and investigated in such works as the *Badīʿ al-Qur'ān* of Ibn Abī l-Iṣbaʿ al-Miṣrī (d. 1356), which is devoted entirely to the analysis of the text's stylistic features. Nowhere in the Muslim discourse do the commentators minimize the difference between the Quran and poetry. However, they see that difference not in the simplicity of the quranic language but in its perfect fulfilment of all rhetorical norms and ideals. To put this appreciation concisely: the Quran is not poetry, because it is more, and more exquisite, than poetry. The notion of *more* also implies a common ground, however, since a thing that exceeds another cannot be completely different in kind from what it exceeds. In spite of all its differences from the genre *shiʿr*, the Quran undeniably has a number of features in common with that genre above and beyond the shared 'code', the *'arabīya*: its use of rhyme, for example, which in many cases conforms to the rules of poetry; or the structure of certain units of oratory, which have evoked distant comparisons with the structure of the classical qasida or, in the case of surah 111, the invective *hijā'*.[53] Other stylistic elements known from the established genres of structured discourse, *kahāna* and *shi'r*, include oaths,[54] puns,[55] parallelism,[56] the frequent use of dual forms,[57] onomatopoeia, word accents and rhythmic homogeneity.[58] Moreover, the Quran was recited publicly in a melodious voice, like the works of the poets,[59] and, to the young Islamic congregation, its *place in life* was comparable in several respects with that of qasida recitation in the pre-Islamic society.[60] Taken all together, these considerations leave little doubt that Muhammad's preaching had a poetic aura. His opponents' claim that the Quran was *shi'r* cannot have been purely polemical: it must have reflected the actual perception of many people – not because the Quran was identical with poetry in the minds of the receiving community, but because poetry and the other genres of inspired oratory were the only things they could relate it to; they were the 'least different'. The Muslim tradition documents this in its repeated reports that the Meccans consulted poets and other masters of the literary language to ask them what Muhammad's recitations should be called. And, by the consistent answer of the 'experts' that the Quran is neither *shi'r* nor *kahāna*, the tradition indicates that less sophisticated people had a hard time drawing such clear distinctions. A poet among the Prophet's followers, 'Abdallāh ibn Rawāḥa, is said to have been surprised and confronted by his wife as he was leaving the chamber of a concubine. His wife had suspected for some time that he was unfaithful to her. Because she knew 'Abdallāh had once sworn never to recite the Quran without being ritually clean (which he would not be if he had lain with the concubine), she challenged him to recite from the Quran. 'Abdallāh immediately recited three lines of a poem that sounded so much like the Quran that his wife was convinced of his innocence. She 'thought it was a Qur'ān' (*ḥasibat hāḏā qur'ānan*).[61]

Although they demonstrate very early usage in the use of *qur'ān* as a common noun, not a proper name, this anecdote and others like it are of course not historically documented. As a part of the remembered past, however, and considering the linguistic character of the revelation as it happens to exist, such anecdotes permit inferences as to how the Quran appeared to its first recipients in regard to the relation between the structure of the work and the ambient structure of norms. 'The Quran should not be underestimated as a document of the reception of ancient Arabic poetry, among other things', Angelika Neuwirth notes. 'The Prophet's listeners had long been sensitized to poetic forms, and the Quran was able to take advantage of their stylistic expectations.'[62] According to Neuwirth's Egyptian colleague Abū Zayd, who like her has a literary orientation, the Quran 'assimilated the pre-Islamic texts', just as 'all later texts assimilated it'.[63] The first Muslims were aware 'that the text is not isolated from reality', so that it must be understood 'in the light of other texts, especially poetic ones'.[64] Such a comparative understanding was necessary precisely where the Quran differed from those other texts and had to be understood as something new, something that went beyond their linguistic habits, as the familiar saying of the Prophet's grand-nephew Ibn ʿAbbās indicates: 'When something about the Quran is unclear to us, we follow the ancient Arabic poets.'[65] Certainly this statement refers primarily to semantic problems in the Quran that can be solved by reference to the works of the poets. But, at the same time, it underscores the notion that the language of God is none other than the language the Arabs knew as poetic, and hence they must see the Quran within the horizon of the older texts, applying the same mechanisms to decrypt it that they would use to interpret metaphor and other rhetorical topoi in the profane poetic language, as demonstrated by many quotations that as-Suyūṭī (d. 1505) presents in this context.[66] The Prophet himself is said to have recited a poem when he was asked for something from the Quran.[67] Abū Zayd writes:

> And so poetry was transformed into a reference system for explaining the Quran. That does not mean that the Quran's relation to poetry must be seen as identity, but as a relation between texts within one culture. That the ancients understood the text in the light of other, earlier texts indicates that they had an awareness of the 'correspondence' as well as the 'difference' in the relation between the texts.[68]

In the traditions and the Quran verses mentioned in the previous chapter, we saw that even those listeners who found in the Quran something different from poets' verses still compared it with them – to conclude that it is not poetry. But the basis for comparison, the norm against which the Quran was measured (in later times too, by the way, as for example in the *iʿjāz* literature, and commonly in Arabic literary criticism[69] and in the discussions on correct Quran recitations),[70] the horizon of expectations in which it appeared, were the same as those that applied to the known forms of structured oratory, *shiʿr* and *kahāna*. That the Meccans positioned the Quran, or at least parts of it, in the context of poetry, and Muhammad's opponents accordingly sought to fight it with poetic means, is also evident in the behaviour of Umm Jamīl, to cite a somewhat different kind of example from the tradition. The Prophet had circulated surah 111, which is in the style of *hijā'*, the ancient Arabic invective poem, about her and her husband Abū Lahab. Umm Jamīl stormed into the mosque, shouting that she would 'smash his mouth with this stone; by God, I am a poet!' But the poetic insults that she then unleashed against Muhammad missed their mark, because God hid him from her sight.[71] Although this episode says nothing about the stylistic quality of the Quran, it is conspicuous that the natural answer to Muhammad's oratory, in Umm Jamīl's mind, is poetry, *hijā'*.

By its linguistic code first of all, and still more by its linguistic form, the Quran evoked the horizon of expectations, linguistic mechanisms and norms that was familiar from other, poetic texts. It awakened the audience's memories of things they had heard before, put them in a certain emotional mood and made them instinctively anticipate how the text must continue, in accordance with the rules of the genre or type of text. Ideally, however, the text does not continue as anticipated, because surprise, as we know at least since Aristotle's analysis of tragedy, is the driving element in generating attention and aesthetic experience. However, the horizon of expectations in which a work such as the Quran arises is determined by more factors than just other, earlier works. It comprises the aesthetic conventions, postulates and experiences of the Meccan audience, as well as their way of thinking and the reality of their lives and beliefs. In structuralist terms, all of these elements can be considered as norms by which the work is appraised. These norms are applied in the work itself too, sometimes positively, sometimes negatively. Usually, literary tastes lag behind actual literary development – that is, the norm evolves only with repeatedly occurring violations – although the opposite case can occur as well: critics can voice demands, advocating a development of the literary norm, which authors carry out only later. And a work that conforms to the norm is not necessarily evaluated positively, since aesthetic expectations can also be directed towards something new and different, although overall the history of art can be seen as a history of rebellion against the prevailing norms.

There is a complex, dynamic interdependency between the development of the norm and the development of literary reality. Indeed, as Vodička emphasizes, 'the whole living diversity of literary works arises precisely from the dynamic tension between work and norm.'[72] This tension is the outstanding element in the early history of the Quran's reception. Although Muhammad's prophecy arises in a clearly circumscribed horizon of expectations and rules because of the linguistic properties mentioned above, it does not conform at all harmoniously to that horizon. It varies and corrects the norms, and even flagrantly violates them, far more than it complies with them: 'The custom of those who went before is past (*maḍat sunnatu l-awwalīn*)', as the Quran says;[73] a new linguistic era has dawned. The words of the phenomenologist of religion Friedrich Heiler are superbly applicable to Muhammad's revelation: 'All the major periods in the history of religion are linguistically creative and have a tendency to revolutionize the fixed linguistic forms by the charismatic word.'[74] Just as the Quran presents Arabic culture with a new source of inspiration, *al-lāh*, the one God, it also introduces new themes, motifs and ideological attitudes, as well as a new form of poetically structured language. The text's deviations from familiar patterns and from the aesthetic norm are more significant than its conforming features in determining the first audience's reaction and appreciation of it. From the standpoint of literary history, this is the normal case. What is unusual about a work, what deviates from the norm, naturally receives greater attention than the features it has in common with other works. The Meccans must have perceived the Quran primarily as a break with literary tradition, almost as a negation of poetry, especially since the Quran itself emphasizes that break as its agenda. Stylistically, several of the early surahs might have passed as *saj'*, inasmuch as their rhyme, the series of oaths, and the initial encryption and subsequent explication of the message resembled the oratory of the soothsayers. Yet the essential feature of divinatory rhymed prose, the actual soothsaying, was lacking. The Quran had still less in common with the familiar styles of poetry, especially since its subject matter was of a completely different kind. The themes and motifs of Muhammad's recitations aside, their overall character stood in contradiction to the ancient Arabic poetry, which was conservative and aristocratic by nature, affirming the existing value system and the legal norms of tribal aristocracy.[75] The whole appellative structure of the Quran, on the other hand, especially the older surahs, is oriented towards change. Where the Quran used topoi that were known from *shi'r* or *kahāna*, it modified them, sometimes beyond recognition. For example, the jinn appeared with a completely new character,[76] and the oath, a standard element of *kāhin* texts, was purposely de-mythologized.[77] In the traditions of the life of the Prophet, we also see that Muhammad explicitly rejected certain outward characteristics and rituals of poetic oratory and replaced others with new symbols. That certainly helped to distinguish the Quran from the familiar genres, unmistakably proclaiming its deviation from traditional norms. Muhammad's curiously emphatic admonition to wear sandals on both feet or on neither foot, for example, is obscure at first, but is evidently connected with the ancient Arabs' custom of taking off one shoe to pronounce a *hijā'*.[78] As for the language of the Quran, it was *'arabīya*, yet neither the Quran's extremely irregular – should we say ingeniously free? – metre nor the structure of its surahs conformed to the known patterns of poetry. Even the use of rhyme, which by and large adheres to the norm of *shi'r*, must have sounded strange to the early listeners, if only because the interruption of the flow of speech by an *iskān*, which occurs consistently in the Quran, must often have produced a different sound from the familiar poetic recitation with long-drawn-out final vowels that carry over to the next line.[79]

Although Muhammad's recitation was not like any kind of oratory known at the time, it is supposed, according to the testimony presented in chapter 1, to have had an incomparably powerful aesthetic attraction, producing a delightful and at the same time disconcerting effect. The polarity between the Quran as a work and the Meccans as an audience is fuelled by the dialectical relation between the expectations created in the audience by certain signals (such as the use of *'arabīya*, rhyme or the style of recitation) and the work's contravention of norms (such as its violation of the familiar stylistic rules of poetry or its almost diametrically opposed ideological alignment). This makes the Quran one of those works in the history of literature that, in Jauss's words, 'evoke the reader's horizon of expectations, formed by a convention of genre, style, or form, only in order to destroy it step by step – which by no means serves a critical purpose only, but can itself once again produce poetic effects.'[80] Jauss sees the relation between the audience's expectations and its reaction to a work as 'a criterion for the determination of its aesthetic value'.[81] The distance between the given horizon of expectations and the new work, between the previous aesthetic experiences and the alteration of that horizon implicitly demanded by the negation of familiar experiences or the new awareness of experiences vocalized for the first time,

> determines the artistic character of a literary work, according to an aesthetics of reception; to the degree that this distance decreases, and no turn toward the horizon of yet unknown experience is demanded of the receiving consciousness, the closer the work comes to the sphere of 'culinary' or entertainment art [*Unterhaltungskunst*]. This latter work can be characterized by an aesthetics of reception as not demanding any horizonal change, but rather as precisely fulfilling the expectations prescribed by a ruling standard of taste, in that it satisfies the desire for the reproduction of the familiarly beautiful; confirms familiar sentiments; sanctions wishful notions; makes unusual experiences enjoyable as 'sensations'; or even raises moral problems, but only to 'solve' them in an edifying manner as predecided questions.[82]

Whether or not one adopts Jauss's criterion, and consequently attributes a particularly high aesthetic quality to the Quran, it is remarkable that the criterion provided by reception aesthetics for determining the aesthetic value of a literary work – the way the work, 'at the historical moment of its appearance, satisfies, surpasses, disappoints, or refutes the expectations of its first audience'[83] – has often been articulated, and has influenced the evaluation of the text, in the course of the Quran's reception history. The almost stereotypical appreciation of a Muslim scholar is that of Sharīʿaṭī-Mazīnānī: 'Neither was it poetry, nor was it prose, but it had the merits of both without the detriments.'[84] 'It is prose, but not like prose; it is poetry, but not like poetry', writes Adonis too.[85] Centuries earlier, as-Suyūṭī wrote, 'It unites the beauties of all styles, without conforming to any of them',[86] and ar-Rummānī (d. 994) saw the break with the familiar styles (*naqḍ al-ʿāda*) as an indication of the Quran's miraculous nature:

> The 'break with the familiar' is grounded in the fact that the known forms of oratory up to then were *shiʿr*, *sajʿ*, *khaṭab*, *rasāʾil* and spoken prose, and the Quran came with a unique idiom that was different from everything familiar and at the same time attained a degree of beauty with which it exceeded all other forms, and even the art of verse, which is the most beautiful speech of all.[87]

The Quran itself takes great pains to emphasize that it is different from all known genres, and the tradition contains, as we saw in the first chapter, a multitude of accounts of the first listeners' confusion, amazement, and inability to classify Muhammad's oratory. 'I know all kinds of qasida and the *rajaz*; I am familiar even with the poems of the jinn. But, by God, his recitation is like none of them', murmurs al-Walīd ibn al-Muġīra in fascination.[88] 'Utba meanwhile heard a 'speech – by God, I never heard such a one before; it is not poetry, not divination, not spellcasting.'[89] Similar statements by many of their contemporaries have been handed down. Muhammad's critics, on the other hand, criticize precisely what is new about the quranic style, calling it poetry, divination, magic or fables such as the ancestors told. Indeed, the multitude of labels they use is the clearest illustration of their perplexity in the face of the new text. Some authorities went so far as to say the Quran owed its uniqueness to its *ġarāba*, its 'strangeness' or 'peculiarity', and praised that as its actual literary quality.[90] The innovative character of the language, as it is conceived in reception aesthetics, perceptibly becomes an aesthetic category, underscoring Adorno's conjecture: 'Probably no important artwork ever corresponded completely to its genre.'[91] In this view, what is really remarkable and admirable about the quranic style is precisely the break with aesthetic norms – a break which is apparently unmotivated by events in the history of literature, and for which even Western scholarship has no explanation, in spite of its efforts to discover all of Muhammad's possible (and impossible) influences. If one believes in Muhammad as a prophet, it is not far-fetched to point to the originality of his language as evidence of his divine mission. If one sees him as an artist, one is at least tempted to infer from the unprecedented character of his work that he was a genius. In Western Quran studies, however, the dominant tendency for a long time was to see the text's stylistic peculiarities and deviations from the ancient Arabic norm simply as errors that were due to Muhammad's clumsiness and insufficient mastery of *'arabīya*.[92] An unbiased analysis – this would seem to be established today – would find that the peculiarities of the quranic language are too pervasive to be explained by incompetence or by the Prophet's 'settling for easy answers', as Nöldeke puts it.[93]

But the vitality of a work does not require simply that it is new, deviates from the norm and at the same time moves and captivates the audience. If that were the case, the work's aesthetic power would be exhausted with the passing of an ephemeral norm. The essential thing, according to Vodička, is 'what properties it potentially contains in regard to the development of the literary norm'.[94] In the history of literature, the only literary provocations that have made a lasting mark are those that contributed to a change in the norm: those that did not simply place themselves outside the existing horizon of expectations, but engendered a new horizon. By that standard, the Quran can be considered to surpass all the literary works of Arabic culture. Although most Western researchers have been hesitant to appraise the linguistic qualities of the Quran, hardly any of them have denied this. 'There is no event in the history of the Arabic language that influenced its development more permanently than the rise of Islam', Johann Fück writes in the opening of his book on *'arabīya*.[95] The comprehensive shift in norms that the Quran caused throughout an enormous geographical territory, encompassing in particular the use of language and the aesthetic norms, is incomparable. As Bernard Lewis once remarked, that norm shift is actually the wondrous thing about the Arab expansion.[96]

With the progressive change in norms caused by the Quran, naturally the reason for the Quran's power also changed: it no longer owed its effect, as Angelika Neuwirth states, 'to the force of the unfamiliar, but to the grandeur of the undoubted focus of the new culture taking shape'.[97] Building on the Quran's status as the word of God, and therefore stylistically unique and unsurpassable, the Arabic language had a model whose validity was unbroken from then on, a model after which all other texts had to be patterned if they were to be considered serious literature. In this logic, the respect that a text elicits is connected with how closely it approximates the style of the Quran. Down to the present day, the status of *'arabīya*, the Arabic of the Quran, as the language of classical literature has been unchallenged. Not until the twentieth century did reformers dare to question its monopoly, although without complete success, as Shouby notes in an essay on the influence of the Arabic language on the psychology of the Arabs:

> In spite of the numerous cries for reform in both the language and the style of Arabic literature, it is still impossible for any Arab to write with no consideration for such grammatical, idiomatic, or stylistic requirements as are exemplified in the Qur'an without running the risk of being denounced as an ignorant or a stupid person, if not as an impudent abuser of the integrity of Arabic as well as of the sacredness of the revealed word of God.[98]

What other book of world literature can be said to be considered by its admirers, centuries after its 'publication', not only as beautiful and linguistically perfect but as exemplary and worthy of emulation in their own stylistics? One may think what one likes about those admirers, one may shake one's head, cite them ironically or dismiss them as motivated by religious conceit – but one cannot deny that they exist and have specific, unmistakable effects on people's history, culture and day-to-day lives in a large geographic area. To my knowledge, Arabic is the only language, with the exception of Sanskrit, whose rules of grammar were historically fixed – in principle and to a high degree in practice as well – not by the reality of usage but on the basis of a single book. The actual grammar of that text, which was the same as that of pre-Islamic poetry, was raised to the status of a norm, without regard for day-to-day communication, and made absolute, in the truest sense of the word. Johann Fück points out the peculiarity of Arabic that stems from the normative power of the quranic language: 'The dogma of classical *ʿarabīya*, which is binding on every Arabic writer, makes it extraordinarily difficult even today to gain insight into the evolution that Arabic, like every living language, has undergone in a period of more than 1300 years.' On the other hand,

> the rules, compiled with untiring industry and admirable dedication by the Arabian national grammarians, describe the classical language in all its aspects, phonetics, morphology, syntax and lexicon so thoroughly that the state of perfection which their normative grammar has reached permits no further development at all.[99]

Roman Jakobson once asked, 'How would the norms of the Russian literary language ever have been relaxed had it not been for the Ukrainian Gogol' and his imperfect Russian?'[100] There could have been a Gogol in the Arab world too but, faced with the existence of a divine paradigm, it would have been harder for him to instigate a shift in the norms. In contrast to other cultures, the grammar rules and the aesthetic norm do not adapt to the inevitable changes of the times. Instead, a historic manifestation of the language remains the fixed ideal over centuries, considered unattainable yet prescribed as the model which every writer and orator must approximate, while grammarians only study and describe it in ever increasing depth and detail.[101] Arabic is thus an extreme example of the way sacred languages are intentionally kept static and, although they do not completely stop the natural evolution of language, can slow it considerably. Yet, at the same time, the colloquial language continues to change like that of any other people, because outside influences penetrate it, for example, and because otherwise the capacities for living perception and representation in a changing world would soon be exhausted. This paradoxical development led to what the anthropologist Clifford Geertz called the 'famous linguistic schizophrenia of Arabic-speaking people':[102] the existence and continuing validity of the 'classical' (*muḍarī*) or 'pure' (*faṣīḥ*) Arabic, on the one hand, and the continuous evolution and diversification of the unwritten dialects, called 'vulgar' (*ʿāmmīya*) or 'common' (*dārija*), on the other. The classical language is hardly used outside of public, literary and religious life, while the dialects are seen as suitable only for day-to-day communication.[103] None of the dialects has been able to develop into a formally autonomous language, as Italian did. Because of the Quran, Sādiq ar-Rāfiʿī writes, classical Arabic remained a living language, unlike other languages of antiquity such as Latin, and the Arabs today, although they are as fragmented as they ever were, with more political and social divisions than common traits, still consider themselves a unit.[104] That is why ar-Rāfiʿī's countryman the literary scholar Amīn al-Khūlī considers the Quran

> the greatest book and the most powerful literary work in the Arabic language, for it has made that language immortal and preserved its essence,

> and the Quran has become immortal with it; the Quran is the pride of the Arabic language and the jewel of its tradition, and the Arabs know this quality of the Quran, though they may differ in their faith or in their inclinations – they feel that it is the essence of what distinguishes Arabic (*'arabīyatuhū*).[105]

In such an appreciation of the text by the receiving community, it is striking, although not unusual in literary history, that the violation of norms with which the Quran confronted its immediate addressees – both aesthetic and ideological norms – diminishes with the lengthening perspective of hindsight. Just as the theologians considered that Islam reinstated the original religion of Abraham, the Arabophile intelligentsia from the Abbasid period on, if not before, saw it not as a negation, but as the definitive formulation of the values, world views and aesthetic norms that were supposed to have existed in a glorified pre-Islamic past. Similarly, the literary critics of that era, and of the centuries that followed, placed the Quran in the literary tradition of the Jahiliyyah, celebrating it as the culmination of that tradition.[106] The focus of perception was no longer the break with earlier traditions that had been critical for Muhammad's contemporaries, but the continuity of earlier traditions and their attainment of perfection.

In the Muslim conception, by addressing people in wonderful Arabic language, by selecting Arabic from among all languages, God accorded it a rank that many Arabic speakers even today feel as an obligation, an elevation, and sometimes a burden. Anyone who has experienced a well-formulated, stirringly delivered public speech in an Arab country has observed the powerful, 'magical' effect that the language has on the audience. This became particularly clear to me in Cairo in 1991, when I attended a meeting of a political party in opposition to the government. The meeting was at first quite peaceful. Taking advantage of a brief pause between two speakers, a man in the audience suddenly stood up and declaimed political slogans in spontaneously improvised verse for at least half an hour, while the rest of the audience in the small hall, stuffy and overfilled with several hundred guests, responded with a refrain. The way in which, by the power of structured oratory alone, the mood of the meeting was raised to the boiling point and a shared feeling, a mixture of self-assurance, fighting spirit, solidarity and a bit of enjoyment, was created among those present, was impressed on my memory as a crucial cultural experience – one that is hard to imagine occurring in a Western European context.[107]

The impression that the choice of words, their intonation and the melody and rhythm in Arabic oratory are at least as important as the content in persuading the listeners (not only in impressing or pleasing them) is confirmed by many Arabs, both in conversation and in books. Shouby, for example, writes, 'Arabic literature and language seem to overemphasize the significance of words as such, paying less regard to their meaning than is usually the case in Western literature and language.'[108] It is significant that one of the points of contention in the heated debate about the Egyptian literary and Quran scholar Naṣr Ḥāmid Abū Zayd, who was forcibly divorced from his wife because of accusations of apostasy, was his controversial skill in speech and writing. Abū Zayd's eloquence was mentioned again and again in articles in his favour, while his critics said his Arabic was disgraceful and marred by loan words and neologisms. To us, a scholar's mode of verbal expression would be a negligible criterion in a discussion about his professional and religious views – but in an Arabic context it is considered quite pertinent. In centuries past, clumsy language was one of the first reproaches typically made against theological opponents, and especially so-called heretics.[109]

Education in the mother tongue – perfect mastery of its morphology and syntax and familiarity with its finest lexical and prosodic nuances – is an essential part of the formation of a Muslim scholar or man of letters even today, and a central focus of theological training in particular. No branch of learning is cultivated to such a degree as linguistic scholarship in its various disciplines, although, as Goldziher jibes, it cannot be denied 'that this *enfant chéri* of the Arabic academic world was not completely at home with some of those who called themselves "scholars"'.[110] Down to our own time, the position claimed for classical Arabic as the language to be used in poetry and public oratory has remained unchallenged. In the course of the Arab awakening movements, it even gained an explicit political relevance and was at the centre of national consciousness.[111] Rashīd Riḍā, for example, saw the crisis of Muslim societies as a crisis of language:

> The Muslims have lost His [God's] guidance only because they no longer know the secrets of His language, and therefore their atheist and colonialist enemies attack them by way of His language. The Muslims know that, and they strive to preserve their religion by preserving their language and keeping alive its conventions and the secrets of applying its rules.[112]

To realize what that means, perhaps we must imagine what such a thing would sound like in English – the constant presence of a 1400-year-old form of expression in the society, in its religion, its literature, its politics.[113] In an Arabic context, the apparently 'mythic' power of the language is visible. A politician, a preacher, a poet who raises his voice in classical Arabic uses an instrument that is sufficient in itself, depending on his mastery of it, to fascinate his listeners. His language works as a kind of time machine, transporting the audience back to a mythical past – in Assmann's sense of the term, as described in chapter 1. Even a televised excerpt of a speech by, say, Arafat, Qaddafi or Saddam Hussein conveys an impression of that power; recordings of the great speeches of Nasser still more – many Egyptians say his rise to power would have been unthinkable without his magnificent rhetorical talent.[114] A film titled

Nasser 57, which was shown throughout the Arabic world some time ago, permits an observation of how perfectly Nasser (or the actor Aḥmad Zakī) was able to play on the different levels of Arabic, switching between popular and standard registers, achieving persuasiveness and attention simply by his linguistic demeanour. In retrospect, one can hardly remember what he said, but how he said it is unforgettable. The film illustrates how, by ostentatiously pronouncing standard Arabic sentences at the right moment, even by throwing a simple 'antiquated' formula such as *yā ayyuhā l-ikhwa* (O ye brothers!) at the audience, the speaker can electrify the masses and claim a 1400-year lineage. The packed Beirut cinema where I saw the film was filled with that incomparable suspense, and in the final scene, every time Nasser addressed his audience with the classical vocative particle, pressing it out of a face hardened to a mask by the tension, you could feel the audience holding their breath. And at the end of that speech, when the socialist Nasser from a lectern at Al-Azhar University cries *Allāhu akbar* four times with brief, significant pauses, he closes the circle, returning to where his own history began: he becomes a prophet.

Modern Arab leaders, such as the Mubaraks, the Assads, and the young monarchs, do not possess Nasser's rhetorical skill, which accounts for their lack of effect. Rival leaders are driven all the more to resort to the *ʿarabīya*, the ancient language of the poets, the language of the Quran, which is both a treasure and a weapon. The fascination of fundamentalism is also bound up with language. The fundamentalist leaders try to speak pure Arabic, untainted by dialects or foreign words. Except superficially, this generally has little to do with the Quran or its dynamics, since the Quran vibrates with energy and a richness of sound, and its fascination lies in its breach of norms. The Arabic spoken by modern fundamentalists is often appallingly trite, puritanical, conformist and, in fact, artificial. Yet it is perceived as pure and religious, mythical and, in a dull, banal sense, sublime. The mere code of the language becomes a tool used to legitimate their claim to the status of a sacred authority.

On the first day of the American air offensive on Afghanistan, Osama bin Laden made his first video broadcast. What amazed me was that Osama bin Laden spoke exquisite Arabic. Not once did he slip into dialect, as usually happens with the modern generation of Arab leaders, nor did he confuse the complicated inflectional endings, as even intellectuals sometimes do. He chose antiquated vocabulary, familiar to educated Arabs from religious literature and classical poetry, and avoided neologisms. It was, in a way, the stiff, puritanical, conformist, even artificial Arabic already mentioned, with one significant difference. For the first time, I witnessed a person use the puritanical form so naturally that even I fell under its spell.

The crucial rhetorical point of the speech was not its beauty in itself: Osama bin Laden evoked the unadulterated purity of the language. It sounded like a traditional speech. In reality, though, his rhetoric represents a complete break with tradition. The real heirs of this tradition, the Arab theologians of today, speak very differently – if they are rhetorically well educated – with their exquisitely varying enunciation of high Arabic consonants, precise modulation and length of vowels, the result of many years of learning Quran recitation and elocution. Osama bin Laden lacked this training and, although he spoke antiquated Arabic, it sounded simple, clear and modest. In fact, his rhetoric worked precisely because of the lack of rhetorical ornament and the conscious modesty of expression. This linguistic asceticism marks a rejection of the burden of tradition, a return to pure roots – also symbolized by his attire and setting, namely the cave – all the props needed to create a prophetic aura. Even the lack of accentuation in his rhetoric echoed the puritanical Wahhabi spirit, which is allegedly identical with the divine spirit of the Prophet. This break with prevailing tradition was most obvious when Osama bin Laden cited phrases from the Quran: while other speakers grotesquely raise and lower their voices when they recite the revelation, Osama bin Laden proceeded in the same solicitous tone, as if his own words were on the same level as the Quran.

Osama bin Laden rejected the factual history of Islam in order to return to an alleged primordial origin, but he also turned his back on the predominant rhetorical tradition. He rejected ornamentation of any kind, rhetorical devices – in fact, the entire history of interpretation of the Quran – to return to the unadulterated, original wording, the pure, naked scripture. It is no coincidence that, in Christianity, this explicit restraint from aesthetic splendour is found in Protestantism, particularly Pietism. The rejection by the new Muslim puritans of excessively musical Quran recitations, especially in Saudi Arabia, is an essential one. A fundamentalist reading of a source text could be defined in literary terms as the assertion of a single, eternally valid, literal interpretation. A fundamentalist exegesis negates the diversity of the possible interpretations which, in the theologicial tradition of Islam, as in that of Judaism, was always seen as praiseworthy. Classical Muslim interpreters agreed that no verse of the Quran could be reduced to one single, absolute meaning. Today virtually all secular readings by modern Muslim scholars subscribe to this fundamental principle of Muslim exegesis: they insist upon the heterogeneous meaning of the text, including – implicity or explicitly – the poetry of the Quran, its poetically structured language, since any poetic text can be read and interpreted from many perspectives without affecting its irreproducible singularity. The very heterogeneity of meaning defines the text as poetic; indeed, it stops being poetic once it is unambiguous. It is then reduced to a mere treatise, an ideological manifesto or – in the case of the revelation – a mere book of laws. For scholars such as the Egyptians Amīn al-Khouli, Muḥammad Aḥmad Khalafallāh and Naṣr Ḥāmid Abū Zayd or the Iranians ʿAbdolkarīm Sorūsh and Moḥammad Mojtahed Shabestarī, this insistence on the heterogeneous meanings of the text and the innovative, variable act of interpretation is related to an emphasis on its aesthetic features.[115] They know that, if the Quran is accepted as a revelation and as a literary monument and body of sound, this will open up a whole cosmos of signs, meanings and interpretations and allow it to be read in a multitude of different ways. This attitude towards the revelation is diametrically opposed to the claim to a monopoly of interpretation as advocated in varying degrees by Islamist movements, who warn against arbitrariness, stressing the clarity of the divine word and neglecting its beauty. The intellectual and often physical conflict surrounding the Quran that is being played out today in the Islamic world is also a conflict about its aesthetic dimension, which some feel is in danger of being lost.

The conviction that the Quran is a perfect, eternally valid model of linguistic practice – that is, the confidence that God has provided a divine corrective for human language – is further reinforced by the habits, rituals and typical epochs of a Muslim lifetime, and, conversely, those rituals are at the same time an expression of that conviction.[116] Practically every traditionally raised Muslim has attended a Quran school, for example, where he or she memorized the Quran or parts of it and, most importantly, practised reciting it correctly. Educated people were and to some degree still are assumed to know the Quran, so that allusions and quotations are possible anywhere at any time.[117] The strong presence of the Quran in the day-to-day life of Islamic and especially Arab societies is striking and goes beyond the religious sphere. Anyone who has learned Arabic knows that even simple conversations are impossible without quranic expressions.[118] Elaborating on his own experiences and studies in Morocco, Clifford Geertz writes:

> Aside from the specifically religious contexts...ordinary conversation is laced with Quranic formulae to the point where even the most mundane subjects seem set in a sacred frame. The most important public speeches – those from the throne, for example – are cast in an Arabic so classicized that most who hear them but vaguely understand them. Arabic newspapers, magazines, and books are written in a similar manner with the result that the number of people who can read them is small. The cry of Arabization – the popular demand, swept forward by religious passions, for conducting education in classical Arabic and using it in government and administration – is a potent ideological force, leading to a great deal of linguistic hypocrisy on the part of the political elite and to a certain amount of public disturbance when the hypocrisy grows too apparent. It is [in] this sort of world, one in which language is as much symbol as medium, verbal style is a moral matter, and the experience of God's eloquence wars with the need to communicate, that the oral poet exists, and whose feeling for chants and formulas he exploits as Piero exploited Italy's for sacks and barrels. 'I memorized the Qur'an', one such poet said, trying hard to explain his art. 'Then I forgot the verses and remembered the words.'

> He forgot the verses during a three-day meditation at the tomb of a saint renowned for inspiring poets, but he remembers the words in the context of performance. Poetry here is not first composed and then recited; it is composed in the recitation, put together in the act of singing it in a public place.[119]

Although the complex relations between the Quran and poetry that arise from their competing aspirations will be discussed in more detail in chapter 5, I should at least mention at this point, where we are concerned with the normative ramifications of the Quran, that it had a strong influence on Arabic literature as a literary monument very early on, soon after its revelation.[120] That influence continues to a certain extent today; its modern forms include intentionally flouting the paradigm of quranic language. The Quran liberated Arabic poetry from the narrow limits of known genres and opened up new ways of treating language, metaphor and motifs. Written standards and the theoretical study of language and literature arose from Quran hermeneutics, and, even after Arabic literary scholarship had developed into an independent, secular discipline, it never completely abandoned its orientation towards the Quran as a linguistic model.[121] It is significant in this connection that rhetoric was still called the 'science of *iʿjāz*' after it had left its theological origins far behind it. A later author, Ḍiyā'uddīn Luṭfullah (d. 1625), wrote a whole book on *'iʿjāz* in the science of *iʿjāz'*, which was not about the Quran and addressed the relation between expression (*bayān*) and meaning (*maʿnā*) only in general terms.[122] The movement of the 'Moderns' (*muḥdathūn*) in Arabic poetry, beginning in the eighth century, drew motivation and legitimacy from the Quran's imagery and stylistic departures from the strict formal rules of poetry to weave a succession of new rhetorical figures into poetry, modernizing the received norms.[123] A work of literary scholarship such as the highly influential 'book of rhetorical figures' by Ibn al-Muʿtazz (d. 908) bases its method in large part on the Quran, which provides the author with examples of all the stylistic innovations he proposes. This book deals with the revelation exclusively in its quality as a literary monument and a stimulus for what at that time was an avant-garde poetry.[124] The innovative power of the aesthetic 'provocation' that the Quran caused in the history of Arabic literature is still effective today, and it moved the Syrian-Lebanese poet Adonis – who is not exactly the most pious of Muslims – to note that what is modern in Arabic poetry has its roots in the Quran.[125] While this proposition, which refers specifically to the stylistic possibilities of the poetic language, is somewhat surprising, the uniqueness of the Quran's influence in literary history, viewed broadly, with consideration of the intertextuality of Quran and poetry or the broadened spectrum of themes, metaphors and poetic ideas, is unquestioned. And it is by no means limited to Arab culture. A work in Persian, Rūmī's thirteenth-century *Mathnawī*, is in a way just as much a poetic dialogue with the Quran as Ibn ʿArabī's divan or certain poems by Adonis himself.

More could be said about other linguistic and artistic aspects of the horizon shift that the Quran caused, such as the integration of its compositional structures in music or in the fine arts and calligraphy.[126] I should at least mention in passing what is probably the Quran's most momentous deviation from the literary tradition of the Jahiliyyah: the importance that Islam attaches to the text's written form. The North Arabians had developed a true script only shortly before Muhammad's time, and it was by no means generally established.[127] Poetry was transmitted only orally and conserved in memory, and this was the responsibility of a specific profession, the rhapsodes (*ruwāt*). The transition from an oral to a written culture marks the beginning of the entire Arab-Islamic civilization, which Naṣr Ḥāmid Abū Zayd correctly calls *the* culture of the Book.[128] Without this transition, the subsequent spectacular development of the sciences and arts would be unthinkable.[129] The event in European history that is most comparable with the changes in the Arab world that were triggered by the written Quran is the invention of printing. Paradoxically, however, the oral form of the Quran, the theological necessity of reciting it and transmitting it orally, which persisted in spite of the transition to a written culture, has at the same time ensured that the spoken word and the oral communication of information have continued to play a fundamental role in the society even after the Gutenberg revolution, especially in education and the academic world.[130]

The normative power of the Quran is by no means limited to the religious or even the social sphere. A history of its aesthetic influence would to a large extent entail a cultural history of the Islamic or at least the Arab world. For the purposes of the present study, I would like to let the foregoing remarks suffice and return to the Quran itself. To identify the specific nature of the communication that takes place between it and its recipients, let us examine, as a representative example of its other properties, one that is perhaps the most salient characteristic of its poeticity.

The Quran as an Open Text

If the ideal quality of an informative language is the greatest possible clarity and articulation, then the openness of the message, its ambiguity, is an essential part of all aesthetic communication, 'an intrinsic, inalienable character of any self-focused message, briefly, a corollary feature of poetry', as Jakobson writes;[131] in Roland Barthes's words, openness is 'the very being of literature, carried to its paroxysm'.[132] Or, as al-Jurjānī said about metaphorical language in general:

> One of its main advantages is that it lets this poetic expression of ideas appear in ever new forms that lend it higher rank and nobility, adding further excellence to that which it has; and that one and the same word gains several expressive values, so that, repeated in different places, it has a different value

and an individual rank in each of them, captivating and graciously beguiling the eye each time anew.[133]

In the Quran, which al-Jurjānī has in mind as much as poetry in these remarks, we can clearly observe how the text, because its word signs cannot be reduced to a unique denotation, elicits an aesthetic reception on the part of its recipients. The most famous of its ambiguous verses, 24:35, may serve as an illustration.

allāhu nūru s-samawāti wa-l-arḍi
God is the light of heaven and earth.
mathalu nūrihī ka-mishkātin
The image of His light is that of a niche
fīhā miṣbāḥun
in which a lamp is burning,
wa-l-miṣbāḥu fī zujājatin
a lamp in a glass.
wa-z-zujājatu ka-annahā kawkabun durrīyun
And the glass sparkles like a star
yūqadu min shajaratin mubābarakatin
ignited by a blessed tree.
zaytūnatin lā sharqīyatin wa-lā ġarbīyatin
An olive tree, neither eastern nor western,
yakādu zaytuhā yuḍī'u
whose oil almost glows
wa-law lam tamsashū nārun
although no fire touches it –
nūrun ʿalā nūrin
Light over light!
yahdī llālhu li-nūrihī man yashā'u
God leads to His light whom He wants.
wa-yaḍribu llāhu l-amthāla li-n-nāsi
And God makes parables for people.
wa-llāhu bi-kulli shay'in ʿalīm
And God knows of all things.

Those who compare the translation with the original will find the original linguistically more elegant. But it is not clearer or easier to understand. The translation cannot really conserve the openness of the Arabic text; it is obliged at various points to choose between possible interpretations. The mysterious quality of the original results first of all from its condensed word formations, such as *mathalu nūrihī ka-mishkātin fīhā miṣbāḥ*. It is further obscured by the difficulty of determining the subject of each individual clause. It takes a good deal of thinking, for example, to understand what a blessed tree ignites (see the sixth line): the star, the glass or the lamp. Some of the images are not immediately understandable, which is slightly disturbing. One could easily imagine the sun or a star as a metaphor for God's light, or even a lamp – something bright in any case. But the comparison with a niche (and not with the light that is in that niche) is unexpected; it raises questions. It is equally unusual and unnaturalistic for a lamp – if that is what is meant – to be lit by a tree, by an olive tree no less, and one whose oil almost glows. Since when do trees light lamps, and what does the *almost glowing* oil of the olive tree mean? In a modern poem, these images would be read as a bold, almost absurdist surrealism, or at least as needing some interpretation. But the mysterious and suspenseful aura arises not only from the meanings of the words. Almost more important is the sequence of nouns that creates a slow but steadily beating rhythm. These are accompanied by appositions that at first do not quite seem to fit, or to explain anything, like the olive tree, which is *lā sharqīya wa-lā ġarbīya*, which may refer to the cardinal directions but could also indicate that the glowing that has no rising and no setting – in any case, 'neither eastern nor western' is not the expression that we as recipients expect in a statement about an olive tree. By breaking through the probabilistic order of the language, the text increases the number of possible meanings. This cause and effect are familiar from other literary texts, and form one of the factors that make up the uniqueness of poetic communication. With an extremely sparing application of rhetorical ornamentation, the niche, the lamp, the glass and the olive tree without place or direction, whose oil almost glows without being ignited, form an image of the divine light that practically demands a proliferation of explanations because its allusions conceal more than they reveal. It is no coincidence that 'Light over light!' has become the torch primarily of mystical exegetes, who have put forward ever more fantastical interpretations of the celestial illumination. 'No other passage of the Koran is surrounded with so much mystery', Goldziher notes disapprovingly in regard to the interpretative history of the Light verse, in which 'one allegory could be heaped on another'.[134]

Perhaps the first listeners had an immediate understanding of the comparison developed here; perhaps they were familiar with the olive tree and knew what the Quran was alluding to in calling it *lā sharqīya wa-lā ġarbīya*. Or perhaps they were just as confused, unsure or inspired to form their own interpretations as the recipient of today is on hearing or reading this verse for the first time. The openness, the ambiguity of the short sentences and the cryptic images, is responsible for the poeticity of this verse. For, as Eco writes, 'a message that holds me in the balance between information and redundancy, that forces me to ask what it is supposed to mean, while through the clouds of ambiguity I glimpse something that guides my basic decoding – such a message is one that I begin to study *to see how it is made*.'[135] Az-Zamakhsharī's answer to the question why all verses of the Quran are not unambiguously explainable betrays a closely related view. If the Quran were so easy to understand, the theologian says, 'people would have simply followed the easily comprehensible, superficial sense and turned away from that for which one must search and meditate, which requires deeper observation and intellectual reflection.'[136] Al-Jurjānī too writes:

> If you are offered an idea in the form of a comparison, it usually becomes clear to your mind only after it has forced you to search for it by thinking, to meditate on it and apply your will to it. The finer and the more subtle the idea is, the more it will resist you, the more clearly it will refuse you, the more severely it will close itself to you.
>
> But it is in human nature that, when a person acquires a thing only after searching or feeling desire for it, and has withstood longing for it, the possession of it once achieved seems sweeter and more splendid; that the soul prizes it and values it more highly and loves it more jealously and ardently.[137]

Both of these theologians have a clear view of the idea that a message, precisely by resisting immediate comprehension and not permitting spontaneous referral to a denotatum that exhausts its potential meaning, directs the recipient's attention to its specific composition of lexical signs. In structuralist terms, the lexical sign in such a message is self-referential, and hence its function is poetic. In more ordinary words, such a message can be compared to a stone that one turns back to look at after one has stumbled over it. Only as a result of such a process, directed by the text, does the recipient discover the multitude of possible meanings which, as Eco writes, 'expand at every new look, to the point that they seem to offer me a concentrated image of the entire universe.'[138] Otherwise, az-Zamakhsharī warns, 'the sole path by which one can attain knowledge of God and His unity is laid waste.'[139] Of course, the Italian semiotician and the Persian Quran commentator in these quotations are not talking about the same thing: one means works of poetry; the other, a revelation. But their analyses of the process of reception are unmistakably related. This kinship would not be possible if the kind of reception they are discussing were not likewise related. What az-Zamakhsharī describes is none other than the essentially aesthetic reception – or, to phrase it more cautiously, a reception that takes place through aesthetic processes – of a religious message.

John Wansbrough has called the language of the Quran a 'torso',[140] which suggests incompleteness, a fragmentary transmission. More illuminating and fitting is Norman Calder's comparison of the quranic style with a Chinese painting:

> When, in such a painting, a high pagoda or a mountain top emerges into the sky, the observer is compelled to fill the adjacent absences with rural valleys or firm foundations. Nor in this exercise is the imagination free: the heights

> of a pagoda do not rest on a set of Corinthian pillars, and the lower slopes of a Chinese hill are resistant to details derived from a landscape by Constable. The independent structures of Chinese poetry inform us that bamboo, lotus and cherry blossom, and a lonely scholar dreaming of his distant home, are precisely what lies in the emptiness of a Chinese landscape. Likewise when quranic narrative offers its usual provision of incomplete detail, the imagination has never been simply free to fill the gaps; the filling has to be measured against independent structures.[141]

It is obvious as soon as one sits down to peruse the Quran that it is not easy reading, that it sometimes places great demands on the recipient and can hardly be read *and understood* over longer passages (although it may be enjoyable in a purely musical way) without constant reflection, association and interpretation. Jacques Berque aptly notes that the language of the Quran creates 'the impression of a rather paradoxical contrast between a kind of unembellished wording, in spite of the depth and complexity of meaning, combined with a great economy of means'.[142] The economy of the narrative is particularly striking in the stories of the prophets. Whatever the speaker does not consider essential is at most touched on, and what is unnecessary is systematically omitted, to direct the audience's attention to motifs that are central to the intended message. Other manifestations of this narrative pattern include the extremely sparing use of adjectives, the fact that individual characters in the stories, such as Jacob and Sulayha in the surah of Joseph, remain anonymous throughout or over long passages, and that times and places are rarely mentioned, and then vaguely, usually with a simple *iḏ* ('then') or *lammā* ('when').[143] The corresponding stylistic techniques, and in particular the ellipse so highly praised by masters of Arabic rhetoric (*iʿjāz*), are found in the Quran outside the stories of the prophets as well. They do not make the text more easily accessible to unprepared recipients who do not share the knowledge of the immediate addressees. Confused by unfinished sentences, anacolutha and frequent changes of grammatical person, confronted with enigmatic metaphors and ambiguous allusions, surprised by the unusual treatment of motifs that at first seem familiar, fatigued by tautologies, repetitions and passages that are mysterious and sometimes even completely inexplicable at a first literal reading, and thrown off balance by unannounced changes of subject, interruptions of the flow of discourse, unexpected jumps between levels of narrative, and a sometimes apparently arbitrary compilation of the individual discursive units and their still more incomprehensible arrangement, the recipient often has trouble following the text, keeping sight of the theme, and making sense of all its contents as they occur. The Orientalists complained at length about such difficulties and saw themselves confirmed by prominent lay readers of the translated text. A typical opinion is that of the Scottish essayist Thomas Carlyle (d. 1881), who found only a 'wearisome confused jumble' in the Quran and felt repelled by endless repetitions, long-windedness and perpetual chaos:

'I must say, it is as toilsome reading as I ever undertook.... Nothing but a sense of duty could carry any European through the Koran.'[144] It would be unjust to ascribe such harsh judgements only to ill will or to pure ignorance. After all, Arabic authors still quote Carlyle favourably for his positive portrait of Muhammad.[145] And even the devout Muslim scholar Seyyed Hossein Nasr finds that 'it is as if human language were scattered into a thousand fragments like a wave scattered into drops against the rock at sea.'[146] The judgement of the British archaeologist Stanley Lane-Poole is similar: 'The sentences are short and full of half-restrained energy, yet with a musical cadence. The thought is only half-expressed; one feels the speaker has essayed a thing beyond words, and has suddenly discovered the impotence of language and broken off with the sentence unfinished.'[147] Frithjof Schuon, a convert to Islam, also confesses that the Quran, from an outsider's view, appears as 'a collection of sayings and stories that is more or less incoherent and sometimes incomprehensible at first approach', in which the reader 'runs up against obscurities, repetitions, tautologies'.[148] Feelings such as these – which can also assail readers of the Old Testament, according to Martin Luther[149] – may creep up not only on the readers of translations but also to a certain degree on Arabic audiences as well, and were in fact mentioned as early as the ninth century by a Christian Arab critic of the Quran, ʿAbdulmasīḥ ibn Isḥāq al-Kindī.[150] Of course, recipients who listen to the Quran in Arabic do not experience many of the difficulties in comprehension, since they hear the text as it is structured and interpreted by the reciter. Recitation is discussed in detail in chapter 3. Muhammad's contemporaries, furthermore, were also familiar with the Quran's language and its world of ideas, and the sender based his message on knowledge he shared with this particular set of recipients. We can thus identify the addressee of the quranic stories as an audience who already know at least the rough outlines of the plot. Nonetheless, even Muhammad's audience must sometimes have found it difficult spontaneously to decrypt the many allusions to earlier texts, to make meaningful connections between parts of a surah that are sometimes hard to relate to one another, to interpret the metaphors and to follow the Quran's unusual language as it breaks through the restrictions of the existing literary conventions and sets its own norms. Furthermore, the terminology of the revelation, which takes some getting used to, and its numerous allusions, sentence fragments and references to things past require so much historic, political and linguistic knowledge on the part of the recipient that it is hard to imagine that the Meccans would have understood every detail with crystal clarity. The Muslim tradition of *ġarīb* seems more plausible: these are the 'peculiar words' in the Quran that needed to be explained to Muhammad's contemporaries and whose interpretation was not always certain even to an authority such as Ibn ʿAbbās.[151] As-Suyūṭī quotes a devout Muslim: 'What heaven shall shelter me and what earth shall receive me if I say what I do not know about the Quran?'[152] 'I say nothing at all about the Quran', the legal scholar Saʿīd ibn al-Musayyib (d. 712) is said to have cried as a result of his amazement (*dahash*).[153] And al-Gunayd (d. 910) is filled with respect when, on being asked why he does not lapse into rapture and movement on hearing the Quran as other mystics do, he says, 'The Quran is the word of God, and it is hard to understand.'[154]

Although these statements are by later recipients, there is no doubt that a number of key words in the Quran, such as *amr*, *qadr*, *hudā*, *waḥy*, *albāb* and *ṣamad*, as well as many inconspicuous expressions, not only have challenged the later exegetes and translators, evoking a variety of interpretations by their polysemy, their capacity for multiple meanings,[155] but also must have appeared cryptic or ambiguous in some passages to the original, immediate addressees. One of the accusations of Muhammad's opponents was that his revelation was obscure: it was nothing but 'muddled dreams' (*aḍġāthu aḥlām*),[156] they said. The Quran itself frequently mentions the need for interpretation of the eschatological passages in particular – where the text quotes the Meccans' questions about earlier revelations, for instance.[157] Michael Sells has convincingly demonstrated, taking two shorter surahs as examples, that the text intentionally leaves certain terms ambiguous, and guides that ambiguity by subtle signs that evoke far-reaching associations in the listener, yet without really explaining the word in question.[158] This process is an artful use of the text's openness as a poetic technique that creates an arc of suspense spanning groups of verses and sections. The enigmatic lexical character of certain terms is only one of several factors that make the text open. More important are the deviations from the syntax and grammar of the familiar, expected style, which we touched on in our discussion of the 'Light' verse and which Sells's meticulous analysis exposes more clearly. For a brief example, consider the beginning of surah 101:

1 *al-qāriʿa*
The pounding.
2 *mā l-qāriʿa*
What is the pounding?
3 *wa-mā adrāka mā l-qāriʿa*
What makes you know what the pounding is?

The word *qāriʿa* in the first verse is extremely difficult to define lexically. For one thing, its root, *q-r-ʿ*, covers a broad semantic field from 'beat' to 'shock' to 'break'; for another, the participial form used here is hardly known.[159] Both lexically and syntactically undetermined, *al-qāriʿa* simply stands there at first, with no function or relation in the sentence. As in other surahs, the Quran confirms the lexical indeterminacy in the second verse by posing the question *mā l-qāriʿa*.[160] The surah then draws out the suspense that begins with the ambiguity and the exclamatory character of the first verse by delaying the answer while at the same time feeding the expectation of it. The expression *mā adrāka mā* in the third verse appears in the Quran whenever a word or phrase is introduced that is assumed to be puzzling to the listener. In this case, it not only confirms the admitted lexical indeterminacy of the opening word but also creates a new syntactical mystery: the answer that follows can now refer both to the first question relationship (What is the *qāriʿa*?) and to that which provides the answer to it (What makes you know what the *qāriʿa* is?). In the surah, the answer takes the following form:

4 *yawma yakūnu n-nāsu ka-l-farāshi l-mabthūth*
A day when people are like scattered moths,
5 *wa-takūnu l-jibālu ka-l-ʿihni l-manfūsh*
And the mountains are like carded wool.

Instead of resolving the semantic and lexical ambiguity as expected, this syntactically and grammatically indefinite construction heightens it, as if the passage were intended as an anticipatory confirmation of what Roland Barthes would one day write: 'To write is to jeopardize the meaning of the world, to put an *indirect* question that the writer, by an ultimate abstention, refrains from answering.'[161] Even the first word, *yawma*, as simple as its lexical meaning seems to be, is grammatically ambiguous: the exegetes interpret it both as the direct object of an implicit verb ('Think of a day...') and as a temporal accusative ('On a day when...'). In the first case, the sentence would refer to the question 'What is the *qāriʿa*?' In the second, it would answer the second question, 'What makes you know what the *qāriʿa* is?' What place we assign to the metaphors that follow, which seem mysterious enough in themselves and indeed are intended to be mysterious, hinges on the word *yawma*. The confusion has a threatening feeling, and arises not from the lexical or syntactical obscurity of the terms (the words themselves are familiar, taken from day-to-day life) but from their unusual arrangement, from the oracular uncertainty of the image: we know what *farāsh mabthūth* and *ʿihn manfūsh* mean, but we can hardly imagine a day on which the people are like scattered moths and the mountains like carded wool.

As Michael Sells has shown, the feeling that something momentous but not quite definable is going to happen, or is about to befall the addressee, permeates the entire surah and is heightened by the sonorous quality of the spoken words. The openness is thus not accidental, nor is it the result of inexact sentence constructions. On the contrary: it is calculated, and it is the primary factor responsible for the surah's suggestive effect on the listener. The 'transmission of information' takes place not only, indeed only to a very limited extent, on a discursive level. It involves other levels of communication as well: the auditory, the emotional, the poetic – in the broadest terms, the sensual or aesthetic level. That also means that there is no simple way to distil a 'practical', unambiguous message from the surah. The complexity of the statement, the fact that it is communicated sensually, by sounds, moods, rhythms and images, and cannot be reduced to a clear concept, is part of the message. The complexity cannot be unravelled without changing the message, without losing the richness of its 'information' (in the semiotic sense). Beckett's statement that he would have had no reason to write his novels if he had been able to express their subject matter in philosophical terms[162] indicates an essential characteristic of poetic communication. The semantic reference of large parts of the Quran, as of any other poetically structured text, goes far beyond the immediate meaning of its linguistic signs and cannot be identified unambiguously. That does not mean the Quran has to be 'accessible with difficulty, almost closed', as Tilman Nagel finds it.[163] What Nagel calls *closed* can also be understood as *openness*. 'All artworks – and art altogether – are enigmas; since antiquity this has been an irritation to the theory of art', writes Adorno, and his words are no less applicable to revelations. 'That artworks say something and in the same breath conceal it expresses this enigmaticalness from the perspective of language.'[164] The enigmatic quality itself is the source of an aesthetic stimulation: if the essence of the aesthetic phenomenon were directly definable, the recipient's interest would quickly fade. Every poet knows, and many have said in one way or another: when art is understood, when its linguistic or dramaturgical texture is exposed, when its content has been decoded once and for all, it is finished. As-Sakkakī (d. 1229) describes the ungraspable nature of the aesthetic phenomenon: 'The Quran's *iʿjāz* can be discerned but not described, just as we can discern but not describe its regularity of metre or its grace (*malāḥa*), or hear the euphony that this voice produces but not know how to capture it.'[165] In his analysis of aesthetic experience, Rüdiger Bubner says,

> No name goes to the heart of it. It appears again and again, showing new facets, eliciting further interpretation. The fact that the actual structure never comes to the surface and exposes itself to our understanding is responsible for the ostensible meaningfulness of artworks, for the untiring search for their content, the successions of interpretations they elicit.[166]

The Muslim concept of the revelation recognizes and emphasizes the Quran's ambiguity. No person, not even the Prophet himself, can presume to understand every verse perfectly. Because Muhammad is not considered the author, but a medium and at the same time the first recipient of the message sent by God, it is logical that he could not always immediately comprehend the rich meanings of the verses. His own words, carefully separated from those revealed to him, are not the commentary of the 'author' but a first interpretation of the text, and, in spite of all the authority Muhammad may have as the Prophet, a fallible one.[167] Hence the open nature of the revelation, its enigmatic quality, is not a theological dilemma but a necessary consequence of a message whose sender is God. 'If a person were given a thousand insights for every letter in the Quran, he would still not reach the end of the ideas that God has put in one verse of His book', said the mystic Sahl at-Tustarī (d. 896). 'For it is the word of God. But His word is proper to Him.' And as-Sarrāj (d. 988), who quotes at-Tustarī's statement, adds, 'As God is without end, likewise the understanding of His book has no end.'[168] The idea that revelation is necessarily open has been similarly expressed in modern Christian theology (if we may read 'concealment', *Verborgenheit*, in the following quotation from Paul Tillich's inaugural lecture at Leipzig as a manifestation of the Incommensurable, as openness certainly is):

> Only what is essentially hidden, what is not accessible by any path of knowledge, is communicated by revelation. By being revealed, it does not cease to be concealed, for its concealment is part of its being; and if it is revealed, then the fact that it is concealed is also revealed.[169]

Orientalists, on the other hand, because they assumed Muhammad was the inspired but ultimately autonomous author, had difficulty with the Quran's ambiguity. For what defies unambiguous definition also defies explanation: it is not so easy to point to Muhammad's influences and his conscious or unconscious cues, which Orientalists searched for so long and so industriously.[170] Because it could not consider him as the mouthpiece of a third party, namely God, the discourse of Oriental studies intuitively assumed – although we might not jump to the same conclusion today – Muhammad as the author was completely conscious of what he was preaching to his countrymen. This was not only a negation of his claim to be the prophet of a message that was not his own, it also accorded him a lower status than that of a poet in the European tradition: poetic genius, in an age-old tradition, is seen precisely as obedience to an unconscious impulse. The investigative zeal to make everything explainable, to detect all Muhammad's motives and influences, to expose every stylistic peculiarity, betrays an ignorance of the nature of poetic language which becomes obvious if we imagine Hölderlin, Nietzsche or Kafka (or the poetic passages of the Old Testament) as the suspect in question. What does it explain if one declares that, in the *nūr* verse quoted above, the lamp in the niche (or in the window, since *mishkāt* can mean either one) is an allusion to altars set with lamps in churches and abbeys, as D. B. Macdonald and Frantz Buhl surmise?[171] Even if this conjecture is true, it only supplies the context from which the components of the image were taken – but what the image means, what depths of spiritual experience nourished it and to what perceptions, associations, ideas, attitudes or acts it can drive its listener, remains as enigmatic as ever. After all, it is not enough simply to interpret Goethe's '*Über allen Gipfeln ist Ruh*' as alluding to the peak called Gickelhahn that Goethe had climbed near Eisenach, or to interpret Brecht's 'Changing the Wheel' simply by naming the places and political systems to which the poet referred in the lines 'I do not like the place I have come from / I do not like the place I am going to', or to find out what country road Brecht had experienced a breakdown on.[172] The poeticity of a text is evident precisely in the fact that its meaning goes beyond the author's intentions and associations, that it outlasts the author and continues to produce meaning, to evoke associations, in new contexts that he or she could not have anticipated (although in the Muslim assumption, of course, the Quran is special in that its Author is omniscient, and hence did know in advance all the future resonances that His words would have). The Quran's poeticity consists primarily in the fact, not that it is composed in rhyme, but that a single signifier contains a multitude of signifieds, that its potential is not exhausted in a single interpretation, or even in a finite number of interpretations. It always elicits new experiences, depending on the listener's receptivity and creativity, and different aspects of the transmitted message come to the fore in each such experience. Whereas a traffic sign can be understood only in one sense, and ceases to be *this* traffic sign with its particular meaning if we fancifully reinterpret it, a poetic text can be seen and understood from many perspectives without losing its irreproducible uniqueness.[173] From the point of view of modern art theory, the text's variability and lacunae – that is, exactly those properties of the Quran that have often been considered defects by Western Quran studies – suddenly become the criterion of its quality. This is why Norman Brown, for example, who evidently knows the Quran only in translation and has an altogether un-Orientalist approach to it, since he is interested in it as a literary monument, can declare Muhammad's preaching to be the original model of a literary avant-garde, considering it more avant-garde than Joyce (who had a similar inkling himself):

> [W]e are the first generation in the West able to read the Koran, if we are able to read *Finnegans Wake*. In fact Carlyle's reaction to the Koran – 'a wearisome confused jumble, crude, incondite; endless iterations, long-windedness, entanglement' – is exactly our first reaction to *Finnegans Wake*. The affinity between this most recalcitrant of sacred texts and this most avant-garde of literary experiments is a sign of our times.... In both the Koran and *Finnegans Wake* this effect of simultaneous totality involves systematic violation of the classic rules of unity, propriety and harmony; bewildering changes of subject; abrupt juxtaposition of incongruities.[174]

Only the fundamental ambiguity of the artistic message creates the necessary condition for its perception as poetic. This implies that any aesthetically organized form (not just poems, and not just works of art) is open in Eco's sense of the term. The Quran is such a form, and, as every scholar of religion knows, so are all other sacred scriptures.[175] But, while every poetically structured text in every era must have a minimum of openness, not every poetics is self-aware. And this is true of poetics in either sense: poetics understood as the study of the poet's art and a system of obligatory rules, and poetics as the formal and structural plan which the artist explicitly or implicitly proposes and which underlies his or her work.[176]

Openness as a conscious goal of the process of artistic production is a modern phenomenon in the West. Although earlier theoreticians did note the subjective component of the reception of a work of art, reflections such as Plato's on perspective led in precisely the opposite direction: like other ancient philosophers, Plato felt the artist must minimize the viewer's subjective contribution by technical devices to ensure that the viewer sees the work in the only correct way.[177] Another example of intentional closedness of the work is the medieval theory of allegory, which developed out of biblical exegesis but was subsequently applied to poetry and the visual arts. In this theory, a text contains three other potential levels of meaning in addition to its literal meaning: the allegorical, the moral and the anagogical. Obviously, the openness of this poetics is strictly limited to exactly four equally important possible interpretations.[178] The dominant tendency in the history of Christian exegesis, at least in the view of the Bible scholar Stephen A. Geller, has generally been to curtail the richness in meanings that texts potentially have when read as poetry. 'Competing interpretations of a passage are often subjected to a ruthless process of amputation until only the "fittest" survives as bearer of the sole true meaning. Ambiguities are only problems to be eliminated, not opportunities for exegetical enrichment.'[179] A conscious poetics of the 'open work of art' began to form in Europe only during the course of the Enlightenment, and became explicit in the symbolism of Verlaine and Mallarmé in the second half of the nineteenth century. By an attitude of suggestion and an intentionally created atmosphere of indeterminacy, these authors wanted to open their works to permit as free a response as possible on the part of the reader. Then, in the twentieth century, the programmatical rejection of a specific prescribed meaning – as in the plays of Beckett and Heiner Müller or the new music of Stockhausen and Pierre Boulez – became a characteristic of all kinds of works and art forms. Umberto Eco points to Kafka's novels and stories as exemplary of the intentionally open art work:

> Trial, castle, waiting, passing sentence, sickness, metamorphosis, and torture – none of these narrative situations is to be understood in the immediate literal sense. But unlike the constructions of medieval allegory, where the superimposed layers of meaning are rigidly prescribed, in Kafka there is no confirmation in an encyclopaedia, no matching paradigm in the cosmos, to provide a key to the symbolism. The various existentialist, theological, clinical, and psychoanalytic interpretations of Kafka's symbols cannot exhaust all the possibilities of his works. The work remains inexhaustible insofar as it is 'open', because in it an ordered world based on universally acknowledged laws is being replaced by a world based on ambiguity, both in the negative sense that directional centres are missing and in a positive sense, because values and dogma are constantly being placed in question.[180]

To return to the Quran, the seventh verse of the third surah says:

> It is He who sent down upon thee the Book, wherein are verses clear (*muḥkamāt*) that are the Essence of the Book, and others ambiguous (*mutashābihāt*). As for those in whose heart is swerving, they follow the ambiguous part (*mā tashābaha*), desiring dissension, and desiring its interpretation; and none knows its interpretation (*ta'wīlahū*), save only God. And those firmly rooted in knowledge say, 'We believe in it; all is from our Lord'; yet none remembers, but men possessed of minds.[181]

Muslim theologians have speculated abundantly from the earliest times on the division of the verses by interpretability undertaken here, as well as on the two key terms *muḥkamāt* and *mutashābihāt*.[182] Some have also taken this verse as an opportunity to present their hermeneutic methods.[183] The interpretation of this passage is one of the longest in Aṭ-Ṭabarī's (d. 923) Quran commentary, which is not exactly condensed to begin with. Aṭ-Ṭabarī alone lists five different readings that were discussed in his day. In his own interpretation, the distinction of *muḥkamāt* and *mutashābihāt* is not between unambiguous verses and those that require interpretation, but between those that are susceptible of interpretation by scholars and those that no one but God can comprehend. Az-Zamakhsharī, on the other hand, reads *muḥkamāt* as those verses that admit of no other interpretation than the simple literal sense, while the *mutashābihāt* are ambiguous and can be variously interpreted. Both of these exegetes say that the *mutashābihāt* cannot be understood unambiguously. This is attested to in the verse by the word *ta'wīl*, which is used in the Quran in the sense of 'explication' or 'interpretation' (of dreams, for example).[184] There is controversy, however, as to whether the *mutashābihāt* are interpretable at all – that is, whether only the *definitive* interpretation is reserved to God, while mortals can and should strive to interpret them to the extent of their ability. As for the *muḥkamāt*, scholars differ as to whether they require interpretation or are so plain in their meaning that no exegesis is necessary. No matter which of the two readings one is inclined to follow, it is clear that the Quran shows a distinct awareness of the ambiguity of at least some of its verses. From the point of view of literary history, that fact is remarkable. It makes Muhammad's revelation an early example of a text that not only implicitly builds on a poetics of openness but also discusses that openness explicitly.

Yet that is only one side of the coin. The Quran declares and discusses its openness, but it does not make a manifesto of it. As a religious teaching, the Quran is designed to communicate a message that is comprehensible to human recipients. It is 'an illuminating Qur'an (*qur'ānun mubīn*)'[185] that Muhammad recites 'in a clear Arabic tongue (*bi-lisānin 'arabīyin mubīn*)',[186] and anyone who is not blind and deaf can understand the verses

(*ʿaqala*).[187] One of the reasons for this strange-sounding insistence on the clarity of the revelation (expressed in other verses by other words derived from the root *b-y-n*), which seems almost perfunctory and which has hardly been discussed in Islamic studies to date as far as I can see, probably lies in the notions that were associated in pre-Islamic times with the genre called *waḥy*.[188] With the word *waḥy*, the Quran classified itself as a type of text that was relatively well defined in the Jahiliyyah. *Waḥy* stood for a communication that was mysterious and obscure to the outsider, that had something diffuse or cryptic about it, 'a teaching in concealment' (*iʿlām fī l-khafāʾ*), as it is defined in the *Lisān*.[189] Thus the inspiration of a poet or soothsayer by a jinn was called *waḥy*, but so was the birds' twittering to one another, which is unintelligible to humans. In calling God's communication with the Prophet *waḥy*, while at the same time emphasizing the clarity of the message (which makes it different from the obscure verses of the soothsayers), the Quran adopts a pre-Islamic concept and develops it further in a dialectical process. The term *waḥy* is given a new usage, no longer associated with the mysterious and arcane or with the esoteric, often incomprehensible speaking in tongues of the pre-Islamic inspired texts. The Quran made the word serviceable as a technical term for revelation. The 'clarity' of the recitation does not refer to an unambiguously decodable meaning, just as *ʿaqala* does not mean a complete, rational understanding of the verses. Otherwise the Quran would not designate some of them as *mutashābih* and would be quite different in its linguistic structure. Nevertheless, the repeated emphasis on clarity gives it a weight in the quranic 'poetics' that pushes the concept of openness into the background, although without directly contradicting it. ʿAbdulqāhir al-Jurjānī, whose sensitivity to the specifics of poetic – including quranic – oratory has remained unsurpassed, and who knows that ambiguity is an essential part of the trope, clearly states that God 'would certainly not have given His book the character of a miracle by making it unclear and enigmatic'.[190] The Quran's self-concept is evidently opposed to 'evoking acts of conscious freedom' on the part of the interpreter, in Eco's words; to an understanding of the work as work independent of its creator, as philosophical hermeneutics proposes; to the intentional inclusion of lacunae for a creative reader to fill, as discussed in reception aesthetics.[191] The text itself leaves no doubt that it is concerned with the communication of a certain contextual message, not with an author's poetic expression, which might be interpreted independently of his or her intentions. The Quran is therefore not a suitable model for an intentionally open, *avowedly* ambiguous text.

Nonetheless, it is precisely on this point that we can observe a new and surprising shift in emphasis when we move our perspective from the sender's to the receiver's end. While the sender (whether God or Muhammad) emphasizes the clarity of the message and only once very hesitantly addresses its ambiguity, stating it as a fact rather than a policy, a majority of the receivers have identified and emphasized the openness and unfathomability of the Quran as a characteristic of the divine. In the mystical exegesis in particular, the Quran is assumed to offer a limitless degree of interpretability. Every verse of the Quran admits 60,000 explanations, said one late mystic; the Quran contains 277,000 sciences, says another; and ash-Shaʿrānī (d. 973), the famous disciple of ʿAlī al-Khawwāṣ (d. after 941), said his teacher had discerned no fewer than 240,999 sciences (*ʿulūm*) in the *Fātiḥa* alone.[192] The *saykh al-akbar* ('Great Master') of mystical Quran exegesis, and probably the most fascinating hermeneuticist that the Islamic world has produced, the Andalusian Ibn ʿArabī, taught in his *Meccan Revelations* that everyone finds what he or she endeavours to find in the Quran. To Ibn ʿArabī, the openness of the Quran – the fact that it can be perceived and experienced from many points of view and endlessly reveals new facets and responses in the interaction between the listener and the text, without ever ceasing to be itself, the divine Word – is the mark of its celestial nature. He quotes Sheikh Abū Madyan (d. 1126) as saying, 'A recitation that does not contain this richness is not really Quran.'[193] To Ibn ʿArabī, whose own work is one great commentary on the Quran, and who claimed that everything he ever wrote, or said in Sufi conclaves, was drawn from the treasure of the Quran,[194] the accessibility of the meanings that appear through subjective experience is an essential property of the text – not because the meaning is arbitrary but, on the contrary, because in the Quran, and through the Quran, God speaks to Man, and every person is different: 'God knows all these meanings, and there is none that is not the expression of what He wanted to say to the given person.'[195] The radical theoretical underpinnings that Ibn ʿArabī offers for the openness of the Quran are not representative of Islamic scholarship. Sunni circles in particular still seek today to exclude him, sometimes even by parliamentary action.[196] But even the orthodox exegetes have always underscored the plurality of possible interpretations, at least until a few centuries ago. 'Every verse can be understood in 6,000 ways, and what then still remains to be understood is more still', writes az-Zarkashī, quoting unnamed authorities,[197] and Qāḍī ʿIyāḍ says that one of the Quran's miraculous qualities (*wujūh iʿjāzihī*) is that 'under every expression' there are 'many and varied chapters'.[198] Ignaz Goldziher comments:

> Precisely the spectrum of possible interpretations in this *fecunditas sensus* is for Muslim theologians indicative of the superiority of the Holy Book, evidence of its inherent riches, its inner variety. The Koran is *dhū wujūh*, i.e. ambiguous, literally, having several facets, i.e. possible interpretations. These correspond precisely to the manifold *pāmīm* (faces) which Jewish scribes find in the Torah. The admittance of different traditional interpretations was recognized as a laudable prerogative of theologians to find a variety of explanations (*wujūh*) for one and the same phrase. 'You have not reached the grade of perfect knowledge until you discover the diversity of versions in the Koran.' The attitude is a graphic description to be found in any

> comprehensive work on Koranic exegesis. From one verse to another you find behind the most appropriate explanation always a number of alternatives, introducd by *wa-qīla*, 'and it is said.' These are the *wujūh*, legitimized as a tribute to the multitude of ideas of the Holy Book.[199]

Surprisingly, this notion of the 'faces of the Quran', which is so important to Muslim exegesis, has no basis in the Quran itself. The term *wujūh* does occur, but never in the sense of an ambiguity of the scripture. The concept of an inexhaustibility intentionally created by God developed in the course of the Quran's reception history, sometime between Muhammad's first revelation and the writing of the oldest extant commentaries. It is obvious that the concept has grown out of the experience of reception: that people who encountered the Quran had the feeling their interpretations did not exhaust its wealth of meaning, like the exegete who, Ṣādiq ar-Rāfiʿī recounts, spent thirty-six years interpreting the second surah 'and died without having finished it'.[200]

A word such as 'unfathomable' or 'inexhaustible' in this connection refers not only to an openness of the text's meaning. The *wujūh* that are felt to be infinite also include explanations of its linguistic structure.[201] The 'formal' elements are just as unfathomable as the 'content' in the sense that the recipient faced with an unusual sequence of lexical signs that he or she finds both stimulating and irritating instinctively tries to fathom what Paul Valéry called '*l'action qui fait*':[202] after all, the mystery of its production is an essential quality of the sirens' song. This impulse is clearly visible in the efforts of the Arab rhetoricians and grammarians to explain the linguistic mechanisms of the Quran. 'What is this grandiose uniqueness, this exquisite splendour and the astounding art of presentation that first appeared with the Quran, so that it has made all creatures incapable of reacting, and even exceeded the powers and abilities of the speakers (*bulaġā'*) and masters of beautiful oratory (*fuṣaḥā'*)?', asks al-Jurjānī in the introduction to his *Arguments of the Miraculous Inimitability of the Quran*:

> What is it, that it captivated all minds and all thoughts so completely that all idle talk ceased and all speakers fell silent, to the point that no tongue moved, not another word was spoken, no one could act, no stone gave off a spark, no sword cut, and the Quran flooded the valley of language with impotence (*ʿajz*) and blocked the paths of speech?[203]

It would be nonsensical to see al-Jurjānī's obsessively meticulous works as mere theological apologies – it would have been a strange fanaticism indeed that could make a literary genius like him rise to such exalted efforts out of piety alone. For several hundred pages he examines nothing else but the nature of poetic language, whether from the Quran or from poetry. For him as for many other Muslim linguists, as we shall see in more detail in chapter 4, the proof of faith is rather the external inducement to study the language of a text that has visibly affected them aesthetically, a language that, in Berque's words, they unstintingly admire without being able to fathom 'the reasons for their admiration'.[204] Near the end of his book on *iʿjāz*, al-Bāqillānī illustrated the inadequacy of human categories in the face of divine beauty in the following anecdote:

> A Bedouin travelling by night lost his way. The moon rose and showed him the path. 'What shall I say to you?' the Bedouin asked the moon. 'Shall I say, "May God raise you up"? But He has already raised you up. Or shall I say, "May God enlighten you"? But He has already enlightened you. Or shall I say, "May God grant you beauty"? But He has already granted you beauty.'[205]

In the Muslim biographies of the Prophet, the listeners' emotions on being confronted with a text of unfathomable depth are recorded or, more precisely, traced and projected on the past as a source of identification. Not only do we frequently read about believers who meditate for nights on end over a single surah or a single verse,[206] but the accounts emphasize that the ambiguity of the message does not impair the aesthetic experience: on the contrary, it seems to be directly proportional to aesthetic pleasure.

'Did you like it?' the worried Quraysh asked their leader ʿUtba ibn Rabīʿa when he returned from hearing the Prophet recite the beginning of Surah 41.

'Yes!' said ʿUtba, and added, 'I understood nothing of what he said, except that he warned of a thunderbolt like that of the ʿĀd and the Thamūd.'

'Woe!' cried the Quraysh. 'The man spoke to you in Arabic, and you don't know what he said?'

'No, by God, I understood nothing of what he said, except that he mentioned a thunderbolt.'[207]

When Muhammad's opponent al-Walīd compares the Quran to a tree whose branches are heavy with fruit and to the ground bubbling with water; when the biography recounts how ʿUtba, dumbstruck, clapped his hands together and shook his head; when one report follows another of Meccans paralysed, falling down as if struck by lightning, or moved to tears, confessing themselves amazed and fascinated, never having heard such a recitation before – the listeners in these accounts do not completely 'understand' the text; on the contrary, what they hear is more than they can understand or explain. Everyone who has ever been entranced by a book, a poem, a picture, a composition or a stage performance knows this experience. The works of art that we can immediately 'grasp' are not the ones that captivate us; the ones that compel us to read, listen and watch again and again are the obscure, the open, the formally surprising, the unsettling and the amazing. The *sīra* describes the same thing in the story of the three Quraysh, Abū Jahl, Abū Sufyān and al-Akhnas, who hide outside Muhammad's house night after night to listen in secret to his recitation.[208] Of course, we must view the legend not as a historic reality but as remembered history. It tells how the community of the Muslim faithful imagines the reception of the Quran in Muhammad's day. But, because that community distinctly imagines that reception as being aesthetic or based on aesthetic processes, we may suppose that their own relation to the Quran is similarly aesthetic. Although the attraction that the Quran had for the three Meccans is not seen as real from a historian's point of view, the experience that this narrative projects on the initial phase of Islam is very real and observable today in large parts of the Arab world. Such an attraction is familiar to every art lover – except that the legend has inflated its power to infinite proportions, to a divine scale. The experience recounted is comparable with the experience of works of art – not in the sender's intention, the message or the conclusion that the receiver draws from it, but in the *structure* of the act of reception. And this process, miraculous only in its intensity, not in its essence, is not shrouded in religious mystery; it is describable. We can trace what happens when we perceive a text as unfathomable and it holds us spellbound so that we want to receive it again and again. We can reconstruct the act of communication that takes place as a structural model, just as we can estimate the extent to which a text predisposes its audience for an aesthetic experience. An aesthetic stimulus can only appear ambiguous, 'siren-like' and unfathomable even after repeated reception if the receiver cannot isolate each individual signifier and relate it unambiguously to its denotative signified; if the receiver is obliged to grasp the denotatum of the entire expression, because, in al-Jurjānī's words, 'the meaning of the whole is a single meaning, and the verse from beginning to end is a single word.'[209] In a message with a purely referential purpose, the receiver separates the components of a sentence to determine the meaning of each one. A message with a predominant poetic function is not susceptible to this operation. To quote al-Jurjānī once more, it is 'like an iron chain that cannot be broken'.[210] The signified appears polymorphous and indefinite, and the first phase of the process of understanding is satisfying by its very complexity; at the same time it elicits a desire to look again more closely, to receive the text again. On a subsequent contact with the message, the receiver encounters a pattern of complex signifieds that inevitably evoke memories of earlier experiences. The sequence of associated memories enters into an interaction with the signifieds that are realized on the second contact, which are different from those of the first contact because the second reception takes place from a different perspective, with a new hierarchy of stimuli. The recipient's attention is now drawn to stimuli that were perceived only incidentally. Umberto Eco writes:

> This transaction between the memory of previous experiences, the system of meanings that has surfaced during the first contact (and will again reappear as a 'harmonic background' in the second approach) and the new system of meanings that is emerging out of a second contact automatically enriches the meaning of the original message – which, far from being exhausted by this process, appears all the more fertile (in its own material constitution) and open to new readings as our understanding of it gets more and more complex.[211]

Drawing on the quranic metaphor of the lamp, Ibn ʿArabī says something not so very different:

> The servant whose inner eye (*al-baṣīra*) is illuminated – who 'walks in light from his Lord'[212] – gains with each recitation a new understanding of that verse different from the one he attained during the previous recitations, and different from the one he will attain in the recitations that will follow. It is the one that God answers to his prayer, which was addressed to Him with the words, 'Lord, increase my knowledge!'[213] But he whose understanding is the same in two successive recitations is betrayed (*maġbūn*). He whose understanding in each recitation is new, he has gained by God's grace (*rābiḥ marḥūm*). But he who recites with no understanding at all is lost (*maḥrūm*).[214]

It is impossible to look at a picture the same way twice, or to hear in a song exactly what one has heard before; we can never read the same book twice: at each new observation, the free flow of reflection focuses on different details, newly discovered aspects of the artistic message, integrating them anew or better in the contemplated whole, and in this way the supposed unity of perception is transformed each time.[215] As the contemporary Moroccan scholar ʿAzīz Lahbābī puts it: 'The revelation is not the text itself, but the new discovery that the believer makes each time he reads it.'[216] The sensory experience initiates a reflection that is theoretically endless, and in practice ceases only when our attention weakens and the sign is no longer aesthetically stimulating because we have become accustomed to it; it is 'unable to entice either our imagination or our intelligence into new perceptual adventures', as Eco writes.[217] In the hadith we find the insight that even the word of God can produce a kind of saturation, and the recipient should take a break from it to renew his or her sensitivity: 'Recite the Quran until it is worn out, and if it does not wear out, you are not reciting it.'[218] 'Recite from the Quran what caresses your hearts and stop when it divides you.'[219] Al-Ġazālī phrases this idea clearly and sees no fundamental difference between the Quran and poetry in regard to the possibility of a habituation that is detrimental to experience.[220] The mystic Hojwīrī (d. c. 1071), on the other hand, says one of the miracles of the Quran, and a contrast to human texts, is that the spirit 'never tires of hearing and reciting the Quran, so powerful is the emotion'.[221] Az-Zarkashī too counts among the miraculous qualities of the Quran the fact that it 'is always fresh and flourishing in the ears of the listener and on the tongue of the reciter'.[222] This may be an echo of the following sentences by Qāḍī ʿIyāḍ:

> One of them [the miraculous properties of the Quran] is that the reciter never tires of it and the listener cannot forbear it, and, on the contrary, the delight of the recitation only increases the longer one devotes oneself to it and repeats the words, so that one cannot but love it. Its bloom and its freshness never cease. Other recitations, even if they equal the Quran in beauty and eloquence, finish by producing weariness if constantly repeated. But our book fills one, as often as one returns to it in seclusion, with enjoyment, and the recitation of it brings happiness even in adversity. This is not found in other writings, so that their admirers (*aṣḥābuhā*) have composed melodies for them and devised external means of enlivening their recitation. That is why the Messenger of God described the Quran with the words that it does not grow stale no matter how often one recites it, and that its teachings never run dry and its wonders have no end.[223]

We must realize that this testimony to a miracle is perfectly aligned with Umberto Eco's description of the reception of works of art: according to Eco – and no one would contradict him – we cannot imagine that an aesthetic form would not be 'exhausted' if we receive it too often in too short a time, and it 'is beautiful to us only because we have long considered it such; and the enjoyment we now draw out of it is merely the memory of the pleasure we once felt while listening to it.'[224] When that happens it is necessary to put the work of art away for a while in order to be affected by its suggestions anew. Eco would deny that any text could be immune to this process of habituation: it would contradict all empirical findings and could only be called a miracle. Qāḍī ʿIyāḍ would agree, with one exception: to him, the Quran is exactly that miracle.

Perhaps it would help us understand what made Abū Jahl, Abū Sufyān and al-Akhnas hide outside Muhammad's hut night after night if we examine what goes on when a person finds a text fascinating and attractive. And if we disregard for a moment the absolute inexhaustibility that Qāḍī ʿIyāḍ and others claim for the Quran's reception experience, it is really not so strange for a text to seem renewed rather than worn out on repeated reading. When al-Ġazālī tells of Quran readers who recite the surah *Hūd* for six months without breaking free of its fascination, or who, like Abū Sulaymān ad-Dārānī, repeat one verse for four or five nights in a row and get past it only by refusing to meditate on it any longer;[225] when, alluding to a hadith of the Prophet, he says that the miraculous (*ʿajā'ibuhū*) and astounding (*ġarā'ibuhū*) qualities of the Quran never end, and no oft-repeated reading could make it seem old and worn out,[226] he is indicating the same thing that Eco describes from the semiotician's point of view. Of course, the theologian al-Ġazālī is talking about a different text, one conceived as divine, but the reaction provoked in the recipient is structurally the same feeling of inexhaustibility, of semiotic richness, of seemingly endless configurations of meaning in all its varieties, semantic and aesthetic, religious and musical. At times al-Ġazālī's quranic hermeneutics shows a quite modern understanding of the essence of poetic expression, of the diversity and the ultimately infinite number of potential layers of meaning, and of the subjective component of the act of understanding. He recounts that the Prophet recited the Basmala twenty times and realized new meanings at each repetition.[227] The semantic reference of the signs, we might say in contemporary terms, was not limited to a single signified, but was enriched on each successive reception by the altered referential situation of the recipient. 'For those who have understanding', al-Ġazālī writes in the eighth book of *Iḥyā'*, there is 'a great deal of space in the meanings of the Quran'.[228] Al-Ġazālī approvingly cites the statements of older authorities that every Quran verse has sixty different meanings, and no one should call himself a *faqīh*, a legal scholar, who reduces a verse to one meaning.[229] 'If I wished', al-Ġazālī quotes Imam ʿAlī as saying, 'I could load seventy camels with interpretations of the *Fātiḥa* alone.'[230] He cites the Prophet as saying 'that the Quran has an outside and an inside, a limit (*ḥadd*) and a point of ascension (*maṭlaʿ*)', and that the faithful should recite the Quran and explore its peculiarities.[231] However, al-Ġazālī rejects the idea that an interpreter can attain an absolute understanding: every interpretation can be only an approximation. The Quran listener is like an animal, he says, to whom a human speaks with sounds and gestures: he may perceive a good deal, and perhaps understand the elementary message, but he can never comprehend the whole 'beauty, elegance and uniqueness of its composition (*badīʿ naẓmihī*)'. When al-Ġazālī calls the word a 'key to the precious treasure-chambers' and a 'veiled king whose countenance is hidden, but whose command penetrates outwards, like the stinging sun, whose hidden material takes on visible form, and like the shining stars that give guidance even to those who do not know their course',[232] he recalls Goethe's subtle words in the *Divan* about understanding poetic expression:

Correct are those I've chided, too:
A word can't bring all things to view –
That would defy poetic odds.
The word's a fan! Between the rods –
A glancing pair of comely eyes:
With fans, a gauze we will devise,
That even if it shade her face
The maiden-beauty we may trace.
Her eye! – that is the loveliest:
It lightnings into mine! I'm blest.[233]

The poet's word does not have a simple value; it is ambiguous, complex; it is like a fan that conceals what I am looking at but, in so doing, attracts my attention to the essence, to the eye looking at *me* – which also means that it looks at each person differently; every observer sees himself or herself reflected in it. What Goethe says about poetry is related to al-Ġazālī's statement about the Quran quoted above. This association is not meant to imply that the theologian considers the revelation to be poetry. But it does indicate that his approach to the Quran is intrinsically poetic, not content with its external sense, but conceiving the lexical signs as doors behind which an immense wealth of meanings awaits. The temptation to explore them is hard to resist:[234] there are 'in the Quran courtyards and gardens and palaces and brides and brocades and meadows and inns' in which the reciter can stray, yielding to their allure.[235]

Al-Ġazālī is not alone in his aesthetic approach to the Quran. The mystics and poets especially have been aware of the Quran's openness and the different pleasure that it offers each recipient.[236] Rūmī (d. 1273), for example, composed the following comparison for understanding the Quran:

> The Quran is a double-sided brocade. Some enjoy one side, and some the other. Both are true, inasmuch as God most High desires that both peoples should derive benefit from it. In the same way a woman has a husband and a suckling child; each enjoys her in a different way. The child's pleasure is in her breast and her milk; the husband's pleasure is in intercourse with her. Some men are infants of the Way; they take pleasure in the literal meaning of the Koran, and drink that milk. But those who have reached years of full discretion have another enjoyment and a different understanding of the inner meanings of the Koran.[237]

It may be a bit bold, but at the same time it is not entirely absurd to see, in such statements about the different kinds of enjoyments that the reception of the Quran offers each different recipient, a kinship with or a presage of the 'typology of the pleasure of reading' that Roland Barthes devised in regard to poetic texts:

> The fetishist would be matched with the divided-up text, the singling out of quotations, formulae, turns of phrase, with the pleasure of the word. The obsessive would experience the voluptuous release of the letter, of secondary, disconnected languages, of metalanguages (this class would include all logophiles, linguists, semioticians, philologists: all of those for whom language *returns*). A paranoiac would consume or produce complicated texts, stories developed like arguments, constructions posited like games, like secret constraints. As for the hysteric (so contrary to the obsessive), he would be the one who takes the text *for ready money*, who joins in the bottomless, truthless

> comedy of language, who is no longer the subject of any critical scrutiny and *throws himself* across the text (which is quite different from projecting himself into it).[238]

If we can imagine applying Barthes's typography to one type or another of the Quran's readers of today, including Western readers, it is no coincidence. The text's highly developed poeticity inevitably makes the field of possible approaches as broad as the quotation suggests. That the correct way of reading the Quran can be a controversial and politically sensitive question is evident in the case of Naṣr Abū Zayd, whom we have quoted frequently in this chapter. Reviled as a heretic in his native Egypt and forcibly divorced from his wife after a sensational trial, Abū Zayd lived the last fifteen years of his life in exile in the Netherlands. Like his intellectual predecessors Amīn al-Khūlī, Bint ash-Shāṭi' and Muḥammad Aḥmad Khalafallāh, Abū Zayd advocated reading the Quran not just as a collection of laws but also as an aesthetically enjoyable, poetically structured and hence open text. 'How much remains concealed by the limitation to commandments and prohibitions!' said Abū Zayd. 'In reality, no one enjoys the Quran. We read the Quran and are afraid, or dream of Paradise. We transform the Quran into a text that motivates or intimidates. Into a carrot and a stick.'[239]

Abū Zayd was aware that the restriction of the Quran to its lawgiving function was a curtailment of its variability, its 'multitude of meanings and hints'.[240] As early as the 1940s, the Egyptian literary scholar Amīn al-Khūlī had emphasized in his methodological exposition on Quran interpretation that the interpreter of a literary text – and he treated the Quran as belonging to that category – influences it by his subjective understanding. 'It is he who determines the intellectual horizon and lays the meaning and the intention on the expression', al-Khūlī wrote. 'One cannot understand a text without laying one's ideas and one's intellect on the text.'[241] As al-Khūlī's successor, Abū Zayd emphasizes the importance of the interpretative act in understanding a text: he sees interpretation as 'the other side of the text'.[242] Abū Zayd was influenced by Gadamer's philosophical hermeneutics, like the Iranian theologian Moḥammad Mojtahed Shabestarī,[243] and seems to be representative of a broader intellectual current in the Islamic world. The importance attributed to hermeneutics for the exegesis of religious scriptures is connected with the fact that hermeneutics, unlike linguistic analysis and positivistic methods, conceives of understanding primarily as a function of subjectivity. Following the idealist principle that the subject participates in constructing the world, the hermeneutic concept, unlike pure language-analytical approaches, sees the understanding subject as reflecting its own conditions: hence knowledge can never reflect a reality that is independent of the subject. Applied to the Quran, this would imply that the text contains no 'objective' meaning accessible to humans (including theologians), and that we cannot make a clean, 'scientific' distinction, as logical empiricism does, between subject (the interpreter) and object (the text), but that instead every interpretation is the product and reflects the particularity of a specific relation between the text and the interpreter, and hence can never be identical with an interpretation that belongs to a different time – that is, a different historic and sociocultural context.

To Abū Zayd, the Quran is a literary text as far as its linguistic structure is concerned, and as such it is unchanging only in its wording. In contact with the human mind, 'it loses the property of immutability, it changes, and its meanings become manifold.'[244] Islamists, legalists and righteous quibblers of every stripe and of all religions contest precisely this openness, however. They are united in appealing to a 'true' meaning of their scripture, one that is fixed and independent of the subject, and they are united in their insistence that it is unambiguous. The subject can analyse and explain that meaning but must not interpret it (this is an altogether positivistic point of view). Like Barthes's hysterical reader, they take the text at face value, rejecting any other, less obvious meaning, dimension or relevance of its message. We might summarize their exegetic principle by saying that they negate the poetic function of the linguistic signs.

The literary scholar and his Islamist opponents are well aware that, if the Quran is received as a literary monument and an acoustic work – and there is a long tradition of such a reception in Islamic history – then a whole cosmos of signs, meanings and interpretations opens up, just as Homer, Shakespeare, Baudelaire and the Old Testament are open to many different ways of reading. This kind of relation to the revealed scripture is diametrically opposed to the monopoly on interpretation that the Islamist currents practically claim by definition. So they warn against arbitrariness, emphasize the clarity of the divine words, and neglect their beauty. This is apparent in their rejection of excessively musical Quran recitations. The intellectual and often physical struggle that is going on in the Islamic world today is not least a struggle for the aesthetic dimension of the Quran that some feel is in danger of being lost.[245] If so, it would be a grievous loss: 'Now the sirens have a still more terrible weapon than their song, namely their silence.'[246]

Idea and Structure

Throughout the entire history of the Quran's reception, ever since Muhammad's promulgation, Muslims have constantly said it could never really be translated or conveyed in different, simpler language, such as prose. Moḥammad Taqī Sharīʿaṭī-Mazīnānī expresses a consensus that has dominated Muslim Quran scholarship nearly always and everywhere: 'It is because of the choice of beautiful words that not a single word of the Quran can be replaced with a synonym or an analogy without diminishing the beauty of its diction or the specific nature of its meaning.'

Sharīʿaṭī-Mazīnānī also mentions 'the constellation of the words, the construction of sentences, the unique expressions and finally the style and the language', which are impossible to change, and attest to the divinity of the Quran.[247] No matter how great we assume the apologetic content of such an assertion to be, it is still motivated by the particular character of the quranic idiom and bears witness to a fundamental understanding of poetic language. 'The writer's thought is realized in a particular artistic structure', the Russian semiotician Yuri M. Lotman wrote.[248] The 'method of considering the "idea-content" and the "artistic features" separately, a method so firmly established in our schools', is due to a misconception of literature 'as a lengthy and ornate method of expounding thoughts which could be expressed simply and briefly.'[249] It would be tempting to confront some scholars of Islam who speak of the Quran as a 'quarry' or a 'reference work' with Lotman's words:

> The literary scholar who hopes to comprehend an idea independent of the author's system for modelling the universe, independent of the structure of a work of art, resembles an idealist scholar who tries to separate life from that concrete biological structure whose very function is life. An idea is not contained in any quotation, even one felicitously chosen, but is expressed in the whole artistic structure. The scholar who does not understand this and who searches for an idea in isolated quotations is rather like the man who, having discovered that a house has a plan, begins to break down the walls in search of the place where the plan has been immured. The plan is not bricked up in a wall, but realized in the proportions of the building.... The dualism of form and content must be replaced by the concept of 'idea' as something realized in a corresponding structure and non-existent outside that structure.
>
> An altered structure will convey a different idea to the spectator or reader. It follows that poems do not have 'formal elements' in the usual sense of the word. The artistic text is an intricately constructed thought. All its elements are meaningful elements.[250]

We can demonstrate the truth of Lotman's thesis by comparing two translations of an arbitrary surah. For the present discussion, a very brief example may suffice. In surah 112, *al-Ikhlāṣ*, the confession of the unity of God is condensed into a linguistically very elegant formula.

qul huwa llāhu aḥad
Sprich: Gott ist Einer,
allāhu ṣ-ṣamad
Ein ewig reiner,
lam yalid wa-lam yūlad
Hat nicht gezeugt und ihn gezeugt hat keiner
wa-lam yakun lahū kufuwan aḥad
Und nicht ihm gleich ist einer.

[In Arberry's English translation: 'Say: "He is God, One, / God, the Everlasting Refuge, / who has not begotten, and has not been begotten, / and equal to Him is not any one."']

Rückert's German translation quoted here strives to conserve the poeticity of the text. In translating the word *ṣamad*,[251] which is difficult to define, it is willing to deviate from the literal sense in order not to lose the literary character of the original. Although we may disapprove of that choice from a theological or scientific perspective, Rückert is clearly the only German Quran translator who has managed to outfit the linguistic signs of the German with a similar kind of poetic function. In doing so he allows his reader to have at least a similar reception experience to that of an Arabic listener. Both recipients are moved by the aesthetic stimulus of the structured language and the composition of words not simply to determine a signified for each signifier, but also to pay attention to the whole composition of signifiers (that is, at the most elementary level, to perceive them as pleasant, to enjoy their sound). The lexical sign is not just a reference to a denotatum but is also partly self-reflexive; it also refers to itself: its function is poetic.[252] Paret's translation, on the other hand, reveals what happens when the surah is reduced to its contextual message:

Sag: Er ist Gott, ein Einziger, Gott, durch und durch (er selbst) (?) (w. der Kompakte) (oder: der Nothelfer (?), w. der, an den man sich (mit seinen Nöten und Sorgen) wendet, genauer: den man angeht?). Er hat weder gezeugt, noch ist er gezeugt worden. Und keiner ist ihm ebenbürtig.

[An English translation of Paret's German version might be as follows: 'Say: He is God, a single one, God, through and through (Himself) (?) (lit. the compact one) (or: the helper in need (?), lit. the one to whom one turns (with one's needs and cares), more precisely: to whom one goes?). He has neither begotten nor has he been begotten. And no one is his equal.']

What Jakobson stated about poetry is also true of the Quran: it is 'untranslatable'; the most that can be done with it is 'creative transposition'.[253] A surah such as *al-Ikhlāṣ* cannot be conveyed in ordinary language without destroying its structure. But in doing so we not only destroy, admittedly, the elegance of the verses, their aesthetic attraction, we also change the message or, in Lotman's terms, the 'idea'. It is a mistake to think, as Paret does, that a translator can intentionally disregard the form to render the meaning faithfully.[254] By its very studied precision, his translation is not just bad; it is false: it conveys a false idea of the Quran. Paret's translation does not convey to the reader anything like the same information contained in the original verses. The notion that information is transported only by the content of the message, while the poetic form is merely the outer hull – the form is the glass, the content the wine – is based on a misunderstanding of the nature of poetic language. If it were so, Lotman writes, poetic language would lose its *raison d'être*: 'But it is not so: the complex artistic structure created using the material of natural language makes it possible to convey a volume of information that would be impossible to communicate using an ordinary, elementary linguistic structure.'[255]

As early as the tenth century, the philologist Ibn Fāris (d. 1005) recognized that the volume of information contained in a poetically structured message such as the Quran could never be conveyed in ordinary speech, that the information in it is condensed in a way, and that translation appears (at least at first glance) impossible.

> Do you not see that, if you wanted to translate His words *wa-immā takhāfanna min qawmin khiyānatan fa-nbiḏ ilayhim 'alā sawā'*[256] into another language, you would not find any expression that yields the meaning contained in it exactly enough, and you would be forced to dissolve what is compounded, combine what is separate, and expose what is concealed, so that you would say: 'If between you and another people a truce is in force and a peace treaty has been concluded, but you fear betrayal and a breach of the pact, then make it known that you will not keep your obligations towards them, and declare war on them so that both sides will be equally aware of the breach of peace.' It is the same way with His words *fa-ḍarabnā 'alā āḏānihim fī l-kahf.*[257] Is there anything like it in the Arabs' known styles? The word of God, it is said, is so majestic and excellent that no other speech can match, equal or compare with it – and how could it be otherwise? It is the word of the Almighty and Supreme, the Creator of all languages and tongues. But even in the poets we find passages that can hardly be translated except by resorting to discursive circumlocutions and wordiness.[258]

Like the philologist Ibn Fāris, the Quran commentator ar-Rāzī understands that a text such as the Quran does not consist only of contextual information. It is true, he writes in his extended reflection on the translatability of the Quran,[259] that there is much in the Torah and the Bible, for example, that coincides in content with the Quran, such as the praises of God and the pronouncements on the next life, but nonetheless one must not recite the substantially equivalent passages from the other revealed scriptures in prayer. The surplus meaning that ar-Rāzī sees in the Quran is situated not on the level of information, since on that level the statements in the Quran, the Bible and the Torah mean the same thing in many instances. Rather, to translate his statement into contemporary terms, he sees the surplus in the additional aesthetic information – aesthetic in the sense that it cannot be expressed in discursive form. Accordingly, ar-Rāzī rejects the argument of those who would allow non-Arabs to read the prayer in Persian in order to understand its meanings. To know and recite in prayer only the content of the Quran is not at all the same thing as to use its form of expression.[260]

Ar-Rāzī is right. Where the Quran in verse 7:44 has the denizens of heaven crying *qad wajadnā mā wa'adanā rabbunā ḥaqqā* ('We have found true what our Lord promised us'), he communicates in a grammatically and syntactically correct way something which his listeners have already heard and which the faithful have already accepted as valid: namely, that God's promise will be fulfilled. The communication takes place using precisely chosen words that are arranged in an unexpected, unusual way and coordinated with one another. The resulting fusion of the semantic content with the acoustic material, the rhythm and the speech melody of the sentence, makes it new, forceful and especially memorable. The volume of information conveyed is greater than that of a less concise phrasing of the same content would be: the surplus, however, is not a semantic knowledge about the external referent (God's promise) but additional aesthetic information. It affords the listener a sensual and emotional experience of the message being communicated, which means it expands the levels of communication and hence the message itself. Communication in a purely informative sentence, on the other hand, is restricted mainly to the discursive, practical level. 'Things can be said in verse for which there are no means of expression in non-verse', Lotman explains. 'The simple repetition of a word makes the word unequal to itself.'[261] While the abstract of an article in an academic journal can be translated – that is, the information can be transferred from one physical medium to another without significantly altering its content – a poetic text is tied to the signifiers involved and depends on their meaningful composition.

The difficulties in translating a poetic text into another language lie not only on the lexical and syntactical levels – or, in more general terms, on the semantic level. In many cases, the acoustic problem is more serious. The more a text depends for its vividness on the acoustic figures of its letters, on rhythm and on speech melody, and the more it approaches musicality, the more hopeless the attempt to translate it must seem. With the Quran, translation is futile to a degree rarely seen in the poetry of Occidental languages, because its recitative character is not only emphasized by the text itself but is also obvious from the first verse on, so that it does not properly exist as a text when read silently. Similarly untranslatable is perhaps Goethe's '*Über allen Gipfeln ist Ruh*', in which the artistic message is conveyed far more by the melody of the verse, the triple cadence from high to low vowels, than by the semantic meaning of the words.[262] How strongly the Quran, at least in its sonorous shorter surahs, produces meanings and emotions by acoustic means, by rhythmic sequences and by the assonance, consonance, euphony, paronomasia, alliteration, onomatopoeia and phonetic parallelism of its acoustic figures, will be discussed in more detail in chapter 3 in connection with its recitative character. For now, it is important to note that the Quran's message is not conveyed by its content alone, to which the so-called formal aspects would be a pretty ornamentation, but is realized in its specific linguistic or artistic structure, and does not exist independently of that structure.

Paret's efforts to abstain from all form and distil the putative meaning out of the Quran betray a fundamental misunderstanding that afflicts his Orientalist discipline, Quran studies: the idea that a poetically structured text can exist outside its specific form. In rebuttal we may refer to what Rilke once said: every word of a poetic text is semantically unique; it has its own world of contexts and its own tonality.[263] Not every translator can realise what Goethe demands of him in his *Notes and Essays* or Benjamin in his essay on 'The Task of the Translator' – that is, go towards the work linguistically and open himself to it, 'identify with the original', as Goethe said,[264] or 'lovingly and in detail incorporate the original's mode of signification', as Benjamin glosses Goethe's sentence.[265] But when Paret's version, which is not only the most widespread, but considered by Islam scholars 'the standard German translation',[266] says that on Judgement Day '*die Sache brenzlig wird*' ('the matter will be risky'; 68:42), or that a miracle of creation is '*reine Milch, ein süffiges Getränk*' ('pure milk, a pleasant drink'; 16:66), or that God '*sich kein Kind zugelegt hat*' ('has not got himself a child'; 25:2), or asks the Prophet in regard to Creation, '*Kannst du (irgend) einen Defekt feststellen?*' ('Can you detect (any) a defect?' 67:3),[267] that is nothing less than a *taḥrīf*, a distortion, of the Quran.

Another example of the shortcomings of the Orientalist strategy of understanding by reducing the verses to their bare informational content can be seen in Paret's treatment of the words *fu'ād* and *qalb*, two of the Quran's several expressions for the heart. Verse 46:26, for example, says, 'We had granted them such power as We had not granted you, giving them ears, eyes, and hearts; but neither their ears, eyes nor hearts availed them in any way, for they blasphemed against God's signs.'[268] Here and in countless other verses, the heart is mentioned in the same breath with ears and the eyes: in the Quran, these are the organs with which humans perceive the signs of God.[269] *Fu'ād* and *qalb* are thus presented as organs of perception; they are not understood as the seat of emotions, unlike the heart in its customary usage in Western symbolism. Nonetheless, they cannot be simply equated with 'reason' ['*Verstand*'], as Paret proposes in his translation.[270] There are other expressions in Arabic for 'reason' or '*Verstand*', but they are intentionally avoided in these verses. While Paret's translation of verse 46:26 implies that all of ʿÂd's and his men's thinking was of no avail, the Arabic text is explicitly and not arbitrarily concerned with sensory perception and the corresponding organs (one of which is the heart, according to the Quran), not with reason and understanding. The same can be said of verse 16:78: 'It is God Who brought you forth from the bellies of your mothers, knowing nothing. And it is He Who created your hearing, your sight and your hearts (*af'ida*). Perhaps you will render thanks.' In the context of the other verses that mention the heart, it is clear that it is not separate here from the ears and eyes but, like them, one of the organs of perception that make it possible for people to perceive God's grace and to be grateful for it.

Of course, it is natural to interpret the heart's perception, like vision or hearing, as a metaphor for understanding in the intellectual sense, as is vaguely implied in words such as see, hear, insight and grasp. But that is a metaphor. The words are neither synonymous nor interchangeable. The trope is not used simply as ornamentation that can or must be ignored by a person who wants to understand the content; it is not an outer wrapping that the interpreter must painstakingly remove. It makes the verse the vehicle of additional information, containing an ambiguity that cannot be produced in any other way. And there is no reason to pare down its abundance of meaning. Al-Jurjānī recognized as early as the eleventh century: 'This kind of error is like a cankerous disease that has to be eliminated with the hot iron and with treatment, for there are no words to say what it has already done to the most beautiful poetic thoughts.' The deplorable custom of treating poems or Quran verses as mere informative manifestos, collections of theses, admonitions and declarations and disregarding the particularities of poetic language cannot be more clearly denounced than he has done in his *Mysteries of Eloquence*:

> This error is the source of those twisted, absurd interpretations and abominable assertions that many an interpreter expounds. Anyone who hesitates to admit that these nouns look back to their first meanings, and imagines that they have been so cut off from them that any connection between those first meanings and the figurative meanings into which they have developed is dissolved, is like someone who, on examining the Quran verse *Inna fī ḏālika la-ḏikrā li-man kāna lahū qalbun* ('There is truly a reminder in this for whoever has a heart'),[271] realizes that the meaning amounts to 'insight' and 'understanding', but then takes the word bare and by itself and says 'Heart' is here in the sense of 'understanding', instead of approaching the expression from the right side and penetrating the meaning as that of a metaphor, saying, He who does not use his heart and has no insight, although the heart is the organ of insight, is held up here as one who has no heart at all, whose heart has been removed from his breast, just as one might hold up a person who cannot receive wisdom and does not think about what his eye perceives and his ear hears as someone who has no hearing and no sight, who is blind and deaf. Such an interpreter misses the idea that, when a person says *Qad ġāba 'annī qalbī* ('My heart was absent from me'), or *Laysa yaḥḍurunī qalbī* ('My heart is not with me'), he wants to evoke the fantasy in the listener that he has lost his heart, and does not simply mean to say 'My knowledge is absent' or 'My understanding is far away', even if the sense on a closer examination can be traced to these ideas.[272]

Perhaps the minimum of poetic sensitivity that the Persian theologian demands is too much to ask of Quran studies – whether Muslim or

Western. Is it inappropriate to expect the reverence that Goethe, Benjamin and Rilke show a poetic text, the awareness of the difficulty of translating it into another language that Octavio Paz expressed in his warning to translators: 'It is impossible to wound one word without wounding the whole poem; impossible to change a comma without upsetting the whole edifice'[273] – is it presumptuous to expect such scruples and such respect from Quran interpreters and translators too? 'My purpose in this discussion', al-Jurjānī adds to his digression on the quranic heart, 'is to show you that a deviation from the path to something hidden leads to a failure to recognize what lies open; that a little error brings a big one after it, and a small deviation results in losing the way completely.'[274]

The fact that Muslim recipients, knowing nothing of Lotman or Adorno, have always considered the so-called formal elements as meaningful, and not as mere ornament, is evidence of an aesthetic approach to the Quran, as we shall see more clearly from studies of the theoreticians of *iʿjāz* in chapter 4 and the mystics in chapter 6 of the present work. Modern authors too regularly affirm the unity of form and content. Ṣādiq ar-Rāfiʿī, for example, explains:

> One of the most astounding things that we can see about the miraculous nature of the Quran and the perfection of its style is that we think its forms of expression (*alfāẓ*) fit its contents (*maʿānī*). Then we study it more closely and delve into it, and in the end we think its contents fit its forms of expression. Then we think it is the other way around again. We study it further and with the greatest care, and in the end we are always led to the opposite opinion, and we are torn back and forth in the conflict between these two opinions until we finally refer back to God, who created the Arabs with a linguistic talent, only to produce something out of this language that surpasses that talent.[275]

Kristina Nelson, who attended numerous readings in Cairo and spoke with many reciters, scholars and listeners in the course of her research for her book *The Art of Reciting the Qur'an*, observes:

> Ultimately, scholars and listeners recognize that the ideal beauty and inimitability of the Qur'an lie not in the content and order of the message, on the one hand, and in the elegance of the language, on the other, but in the use of the very sound of the language to convey specific meaning. This amounts to an almost onomatopoeic use of language, so that not only the image of the metaphor but also the sound of the words which express that image are perceived to converge with the meaning.[276]

In the light of statements such as these, the belief in the untranslatability of the Quran appears no longer as an arbitrary dogma but as the expression of a reception experience comparable to the feeling on reading a poem

– expressed in Western literature at least since Diderot – that says: this is such an imitable expression; there is no way to translate this. (For Muslim Arabs, of course, the sentiment is further reinforced by the fact that the aesthetic experience is supported by a tenet of faith and confirmed by the collective judgement of the congregation.) This is why Muslim translators of the Quran generally avoid declaring their work as translation. Instead they use titles such as 'the approximate meaning' of the Quran (Rassoul) or *The Message of the Qur'ān* (Asad). The British translator Muhammad Marmaduke Pickthall, the first Muslim to translate the Quran into a European language, makes a somewhat paradoxical assertion right at the beginning of his introduction to that work: 'The Koran cannot be translated. This is the belief of old-fashioned Sheykhs and the view of the present writer.'[277] Likewise, Muhammad Asad makes

> no claim to have 'translated' the Quran in the sense in which Plato and Shakespeare can be translated, for, unlike any other book, the sense of the Quran is inseparably tied to its linguistic presentation. The position of the individual words within a sentence, the rhythm and sound of its phrases and their syntactic structure, the way in which a metaphor almost imperceptibly changes into a pragmatic statement, the use of acoustic intonations not only as rhetorical devices but often as a means of allusion to unspoken but clearly associated ideas – all that makes the Quran unique and ultimately untranslatable.[278]

The Quran itself points to the essential importance of its own linguistic form for the transmission of its message. 'We have never sent a messenger who did not use his own people's language to make things clear for them', says verse 14:4. The concept of a revelation whose content is substantially uniform and whose form is adaptable, which is given to each people in their particular language, is all the more remarkable since it conflicts with the historic situation at the time of Muhammad's revelation. Christianity at least was a religious community and not a linguistic or national unit. Muhammad would have known that the Byzantines spoke a different language than the Christians in Abyssinia. 'The historical situation, of which he must have been aware, was also at variance with his theological formula, that each people had received its revelation in its own proper language', Andrae notes, and sees this theological idea as so remarkable 'that one can hardly believe that Muhammad, whose strength certainly did not lie in the realm of theoretical speculation, could have evolved it himself.'[279] Although Andrae's own explanation – that this conception of revelation is due to a Manichaean influence – is entirely within the current of traditional Oriental studies and can hardly be called anything more than speculative, the fact remains that revelation and language are closely connected in the quranic view of the world. The language of a book is like that of an 'artistic text' in Lotman's analysis: 'by virtue of its entire structure, it is a part of "content" and carries information.'[280] There is probably hardly any text in the world that refers so emphatically to the obvious fact that it is written in *a specific* language. In the conceptual world of the Quran, a non-Arabic Quran is a self-contradiction.

> These are the verses of the Scripture that makes things clear – We have sent it down as an Arabic Qur'an, so that you may understand it.[281]

The Quran leaves no doubt that its specific linguistic structure is what makes it possible for the Arabs to comprehend it as a divine message.

> If We had made it a foreign Qur'an (*qur'ānan aʿjamīyan*), they would have said, 'If only its verses were made clear! What? Foreign speech to an Arab?'[282]

Every people must receive revelation in their own language if they are to understand the message. The idea that one might translate a book, change its linguistic structure, is foreign to the Quran. Muhammad has been sent as an Arab prophet to preach the message to his people in Arabic:

> If We had sent it down to a foreign speaker (*ʿalā baʿḍi l-aʿjamīna*) and he had recited it to them, They still would not have believed in it.[283]

In Muhammad's defence against the accusation that another person, a 'foreigner', had instructed him, the Quran submits that that person spoke a foreign language (and apparently Muhammad's acting as translator was out of the question):

> We know very well that they say, 'It is a man who teaches him', but the language of the person they maliciously allude to is foreign, while this revelation is in clear Arabic.[284]

To be understood, a revelation must be formulated in the language of the people to whom God speaks. The Quran's insistence that it is an Arabic book – 'in a clear, Arabic tongue'[285] – and its statement that God sent each people a Prophet speaking their own language, contrasts with its claim to universality – to Muhammad's designation in the Quran as 'the seal of the prophets' (*khātam an-nabīyīn*),[286] to the Paraclete predicted in the Gospel of John,[287] and to Muhammad's proclamation, 'People, I am the Messenger of God to you all.'[288] The Quran is the book that God sent down to the Arabs, and Muhammad is the Arabs' prophet. But at the same time it is the last and eternally definitive revealed scripture, 'a message for all people'.[289] For Muslims, there is no question that the quranic message is directed to all people, including non-Arabs. A number of Orientalists, on the other hand, including Grimme,[290] Snouck Hurgronje[291] and, most of all, Frants Buhl,[292] were convinced that Muhammad aimed his preaching only at his country and his compatriots. Others, among them Goldziher[293] and Nöldeke,[294] thought that the Prophet had become conscious of the universality of his mission during the period of the revelation, if not before. Regardless of which answer one favours, Islam's connection to the Arabic language cannot be seriously challenged. It is distinctly rooted in the Quran, and is confirmed by Islamic history to date: there is no Muslim education in which prayer is not taught in Arabic, no conversion without the pronunciation of the *shahāda*. Where translations are not prohibited, they are at least problematic. The knowledge of Arabic is considered 'a part of one's religion',[295] and the grammarian Ibn al-Farrā' (d. 822) of Kufa ascribed greater religious value to the study of Arabic grammar than to the study of religious law (*fiqh*).[296] ʿUmar ibn Hubayra tried to enhance the attractiveness of studying Arabic by promising religious benefits: of two who are equal in faith, that one will be preferred in Paradise who speaks more correct Arabic.[297] The admonition of the legal scholar ash-Shāfiʿī (d. 820) sounds more serious:

> Every Muslim must strive to learn as much Arabic as he can, so that he is at least able to attest that there is no God but God and Muhammad is his servant and messenger, and to recite God's book and pronounce the *takbīr*, *tasbīḥ*, *tashahhud*, and the like, according to the duty that has been laid upon him.[298]

Although there were some early on who sought to relativize the duty to learn Arabic, the elegant solution set down in the following hadith has not prevailed: 'The non-Arab among my people (*ar-rajul al-aʿjamī*) recites the Quran in a different language from Arabic, and the angels elevate it into Arabic.'[299] Wherever the Muslims went, they brought the language of the Quran with them, and Arabic's status as the sacred and liturgical language of Islam, like that of Hebrew in modern Judaism or the Hindus' Sanskrit, has rarely been seriously challenged to date. The language of Jesus has a different status in Christianity: little is known about it, and until the modern era it hardly drew the exegetes' attention. (Other languages have nonetheless taken on the character of sacred languages in Christianity: Old Church Slavonic in the Russian Orthodox liturgy; Latin in the Roman Catholic Church; Luther's German in Protestant worship.) The New Testament was written in what is known as Koiné Greek, which was not the native language of its authors, and the Hebrew text of the Old Testament was not consulted by broader circles of theologians before the Renaissance. The '*translatio*' of Christ's and the apostles' message into the vulgar languages was a central concern of the pious and the learned, beginning with the miracle of Pentecost, when 'cloven tongues like as of fire' appeared to the apostles and they 'began to speak with other tongues',[300] through the Church Fathers, St Jerome and Luther, down to the missionary societies of the nineteenth century, which set themselves the long-range goal of translating the Bible into every existing language. To date, this endeavour has led to Bible editions in more than two thousand languages and dialects.[301] George Steiner does not hesitate to say that the theory and practice of translation in the Occident developed out of the need to introduce foreign peoples to the Gospel, and that every reformative impulse from inside the Church brought with it a call for more understandable versions of God's Word: 'There is a very real sense in which reformation can be defined as a summons to a fuller, more concrete translation of Christ's teachings both into daily speech and daily life.'[302] The urgent necessity of preaching the Gospel has even led at times to the invention of written languages where there were none before, with alphabets created expressly for them. In our time, and where the literary ambitions of the addressees have been estimated as particularly low, that concern has also found expression in 'youth Bibles', colloquial versions of the holy scripture that have been purged of all the beauties and stumbling blocks of the Luther Bible or the King James version.

In Islam we see almost a mirror image of this picture. Transposing the Quran into modern Arabic, to say nothing of dialect, would be a sacrilege, and the idea of translating the Quran for the purposes of proselytism in non-Arab countries has occurred to Muslims only in the past few decades. The tradition has been that the missionaries taught their beneficiaries Arabic. Muslim translations of the Quran in any case remained rare into the twentieth century, and those that were written were not widely distributed; they were often published in Europe and only in the form of an interlinear gloss.[303] Moreover, their legitimacy was always contested.[304] And, although early on translations were not categorically rejected in the dominant view, they were not recognized in the same way that some Jewish scholars accepted the targumim but were always considered a more or less provisional expedient, suitable for 'household use' at best, for educational purposes, permissible in exegesis or as quotations accompanied by the Arabic text, and by no means appropriate in liturgy or for memorization (*ḥifẓ*), not even for the purpose of spreading Islam.[305] Some staunch Christians saw the untranslatability of the Quran as the critical 'handicap' of Islam. Samuel M. Zwemer, for example, wrote, 'From the missionary standpoint we have nothing to fear from modern translations.'[306] The specific quality of the Bible was precisely that it could be translated into every language without losing its beauty and spiritual force. Rückert expressed this insight nicely:

> The Christian books possess a great advantage
> which those of Islam, humbled, cannot boast:
> the fact that they are easily translated
> into every tongue spoken around the world.
> Where the Quran's ornamental language is lost,
> the simplicity of the Bible is reborn.
> Hence this gives its blessings more than that,
> like a seed that flourishes in every soil.[307]

As far as we know, the first complete Persian translation to appear in its entirety dates from the eighteenth century, and it was published far from the centres of orthodoxy: in New Delhi, by Shāh Walīyollāh (d. 1762).[308] Even into the twentieth century, scholars in Cairo expressed their opposition to Turkish or English Quran translations. One of them was the reformer Muḥammad ʿAbduh (d. 1905), who thought that such translations would only play into the hands of the Christian missionaries: 'Knowledge of Arabic is one of the obligations of the Islamic religion. Our vocation to the Quran is a vocation to the Arabic language.'[309] In Turkey, Mustafa Kemal Atatürk's project of 'Turkicizing' Islam (part of which had muezzins calling to prayer in Turkish only, for a time) met with considerable resistance. When he asked the poet Mehmet Akif (d. 1936), lyricist of the Turkish national anthem, to produce an official Turkish version of the Quran, Akif is said to have gone into exile in Egypt instead.[310] Around the same time, Zwemer reports from Lahore that a respected lawyer reaped criticism for the following proposal:

> 'The reason why Christians succeed is because wherever they go they have the Bible and say their prayers in their mother-tongue; whereas we have wrapped up our religion in an Arabic dress. We should give the people the Koran and let them say their prayers in their own language.' The only answer he received was, 'Thou art thyself an unbeliever to say such things.'[311]

Much has changed in recent decades, and the number of Quran translations in the languages of Muslim countries is considerable.[312] Even in European languages there are now a growing number of versions by Muslim translators. Whether one welcomes this development or deplores it as the abandonment of an essential principle of Islam, one would have to be blind not to see that a modern, 'protestant' concept of the scripture, like so many other protestant notions, is spreading in Muslim countries. One thing, however, has not been changed by Muslim translation efforts: the Quran has a different role in Arab countries than in other parts of the Islamic world. Its importance in Arab culture goes far beyond the religious sphere and, as Abū Zayd puts it, has 'a dimension and a presence in all areas',[313] but such an absolute statement cannot be made in regard to Iran at least, in spite of the large number of translations now available. Of course there are Quran recitations in Iran, and of course no devout Iranian Muslim would dispute the divine beauty of the Quran's language, but the importance of the Quran as an enjoyable text for recitation is secondary in Iranian society. People turn to the Quran for consolation, legal guidance and admonition; people recite it to come closer to God and pronounce it in prayer. But when people want to recite a poetically beautiful text, to take pleasure in the sound of the language or indulge in mystical religious feelings, they tend to turn to the works of the Persian poets, such as Hafis (Ḥāfeẓ, d. 1389), Saadi (Saʿdī, d. 1292) or Rūmī. Perhaps it is no coincidence that, of the founders of the four schools of Islamic jurisprudence, the one theologian who at first considered it permissible to conduct ritual prayer in another language besides Arabic was of Iranian origin, Abū Ḥanīfa (d. 767),[314] or that it was the Iranian Kharijites who did not consider it obligatory to pronounce the confession of faith in Arabic.[315] And, in modern times, it is likewise a non-Arab, the Iranian reformist philosopher ʿAbdolkarīm Sorūsh, who has put forth the thesis that the Arabic language is an accidental property of the Quran, not an essential one.[316] When Sorūsh expressed this idea at a conference in the autumn of 1995 at the Haus der Kulturen der Welt in Berlin, it provoked a shaking of heads and muted jeering from the Arab members of the discussion panel. The panel included such diverse thinkers as Mohammed Arkoun, Naṣr Ḥāmid Abū Zayd and ʿAbdulwahhāb al-Masīrī, the first two of whom at least are not considered blind followers of dogma. The objections, some of them derisive, from the Arab participants in the discussion and Sorūsh's surprise and incomprehension at their reaction are indications of their differing perceptions of the Quran. For Muslims of other backgrounds who are less sensitive to the aesthetic power of the quranic language than Arab listeners, the linguistic *form* (and hence recitation) is apparently of lesser importance, and the emphasis in a non-Arab yet Muslim context is rather on the discursive content of the revelation. Hence the fact that the Quran was revealed in clear Arabic language, frequently emphasized in the text itself, is to some degree negligible where it remains abstract – that is, where it cannot be felt as an essential quality for lack of language skills.

Incidentally, comparable discussions took place in early Islamic times too. While the Arabs and many Arabic-speaking Persians insisted on the Arabic nature of Islam and inferred from it a superiority of Arabic over all other languages (and of the Arabs over other peoples), the followers of the '*shuʿūbīya*' movement and other Iranophiles sought to demonstrate that Arabic had not been honoured by God before all other languages, and that the non-Arabs, particularly the Greeks and Persians, had a richer language and more beautiful poetry than the Arabs. This dispute continued over several centuries, often with political and social implications, and has left an extensive literature.[317] The pro-Arabic faction took full advantage of the circumstance that God had spoken to mankind in the Arabic language. The opponents did not deny that premise but rejected the inference that Arabophiles such as Ibn Fāris drew from it: that God had chosen the Arabic language because it was the most beautiful sounding, the richest and the most excellent, the mother of all languages, which God had taught Adam; the language of Paradise, the only one with no imperfection; the language that offers the clearest and most beautiful expression of every thought. In this theory of the origin of language, which was widespread among Muslim scholars and remained a subject of reflection long after the *shuʿūbīya* controversy had died down, Adam was obliged to speak Syrian after the Fall. After the Flood, Ishmael and his descendants were permitted to speak Arabic because God had accepted Abraham's repentance.[318] But only a prophet could truly master Arabic; no ordinary person would be able to use all the nuances of expression and grammar, to know all five hundred names of the lion, each with its particular meaning, or to distinguish the more than four hundred different terms for 'misfortune', two hundred words for 'beard', seventy names for a stone.[319] 'The language of the Arabs', says ash-Shāfiʿī, 'is the one which is stylistically the most completely ordered and offers the most extensive vocabulary, and no one except a prophet can ever comprehend the whole science of it.'[320] According to this argument, the miraculous nature of the Quran consists in the perfect use of the Arabic language (which is why proponents of this theory deny the existence of loan words in the Quran).[321] Furthermore, this revealed Arabic is thought to be different from the Arabic that was spoken in the Prophet's lifetime. As-Suyūṭī quotes a tradition in this connection in which ʿUmar, later the second caliph, asks the Prophet, 'How is it that you are the most eloquent among us, even though you have never left us?' The Prophet answered, 'The language of Ishmael had disappeared, but the angel Gabriel brought it back and taught me it, and I have retained it.'[322] In this tradition, the language of the Quran is identical with that of the angels and of Paradise, while all other revelations – and herein lies their inadequacy – were translated by the given prophets from that original Arabic language.[323]

The theory of the origin of language that we have touched on here is a fascinating chapter in the history of ideas. Scholars such as Ibn Fāris, ash-Shāfiʿī and as-Suyūṭī have implicitly based their answers to the famous question of the perfect language on it. And even if we leave aside this special model of historical linguistics, which is not always free of nationalistic vanity (the protagonists of a certain Persian cultural pride, for example, refused to admit that people had spoken Arabic before the Tower of Babel),[324] and focus on Arab-Islamic culture as a whole, that culture, and in particular the doctrine of the Qur'an's *iʿjāz*, has made a contribution all its own to this fundamental field of human inquiry. Regardless of the objections, qualifications and psychological explanations that may occur to outside observers, the aesthetic proof of the truth of a religion, a community's claim to hear God speaking, in miraculous human language no less, is a fascinating phenomenon. Since the Babylonian catastrophe, mankind has wondered about the original single and perfect language that was lost and dreamt of regaining it. In the cultures of the Jewish Bible, the search for the original language has captivated thinkers in every century since Christ and given rise to innumerable theories, visions, linguistic philosophies and practical projects. Some variant of that dream is found in nearly every civilization.[325] Only the Arabs – that is, the Muslims among them – did not join the search. Apparently the idea of exploring the possibilities of a perfect language, or of creating one, never became a topic of scientific, philosophical or alchemical research in Arabic-Islamic intellectual history. The Arabs no longer dreamt of finding that language: they had found it. Mankind's utopian dream of the perfect language, most of them believed and still believe today, is realized in the Quran. It is a linguistic heaven on earth.

Is the Quran Poetry?

In the light of the preceding discussion, we can return to our initial question and finally offer an answer. Is the Quran poetry? To most of its recipients, it is not. The reason lies in the text itself. Although the Quran is aesthetically received by its addressees, the sender's intention as manifested in the text is unambiguously and exclusively that of a real message referring to something outside the text itself. This fact, at the level of the message and its sender, makes it fundamentally different from poetic texts. The Quran refuses the autonomy of a work of art (and even the most politically 'engaged' poetry must retain a scrap of that autonomy if it is to be understood as poetic in the sense we have defined above, and not merely to have an ideological appeal);[326] it is teleological, in the purest sense of the word. When the Quran emphasizes that it is not poetry, it advances precisely its teleology as a distinguishing characteristic:

> We did not teach him poetry,
> Nor does this befit him.
> It is nothing but a Remembrance,
> and a Manifest Qur'an,
> *Therewith* to warn him who is living
> And *to fulfil* the Word against the unbelievers.[327]

As conceived by its sender, the Quran is the opposite of *l'art pour l'art*: it is purely a means of transporting God's promise and warning, so that people return to the *ṣirāṭu l-mustaqīm*, the straight path. The Prophet is responsible only for the *balāġ mubīn*, or 'clear communication'.[328] As poetic as the form of that communication may appear in places, the Quran is primarily and essentially concerned with communicating a non-aesthetic message so that it is accepted, not as beautiful, but as true. *That* makes the Quran a religious text. Its purpose is outside itself: it is not the listeners' aesthetic experience but their ethical and religious conversion and guidance. The revolution it intends is not artistic but ideological, religious and social.

At this point one might object that the receiver does not necessarily have to respect the sender's declaration that the message is directed at a non-linguistic entity: the receiver may ignore the message's insistence on its informative character and practical relevance. There are many cases in literary history in which the author's intentions are at variance with the audience's perception. It sometimes happens that an author publicly protests against the aesthetic perception of his or her works, because he or she is concerned with their political or social effect, for example.[329] A person's protestations that he or she is not a poet often cannot obscure the poetry of his or her works. The observation that Muhammad declared he was not a poet, or even an author in the conventional sense, but only the bearer of a divine message answers the question of the Quran's genre only in a theological sense, not in a literary sense. If we were to accept that observation as a literary argument, we would also have to call all of Tolstoy's later works unpoetic, since he had publicly renounced poetry, rather than as examples of new, fresh literary forms. The Quran claims not to be a work of poetry and points to the fictional nature of poetry as a distinguishing criterion,[330] but, as Jakobson writes, one does 'not believe a poet who, in the name of truth, the real world, or anything else, renounces his past in poetry or art.'[331] The artist is playing games when he announces that he is concerned this time not with *poetry* but with the naked *truth*. When the actor on stage takes off his mask, what we see is his make-up. When he claims to be showing bare reality, he has to work hard to make his audience believe it. And, even if they do believe it, they can still receive his performance as an artistic event, and the real or simulated authenticity may in fact heighten the experience.

For a poetic communication that is not bound to a single moment, it generally becomes less important as time goes by what effect the sender (the author) originally intended by the message (the literary work). Only literary scholars, dramaturges and English teachers need to know what Shakespeare intended with his plays: a contemporary theatre audience can receive them as an artistic event (rather than a museum exhibit) because they have become detached from the author and taken on a life of their own. For the Quran this is true only in a very limited sense. The self-definition in the text has a stronger influence on its reception than would be possible in the case of an artistic work. For those receivers who consider God the author, the continual reference to the sender's original intentions has a fundamental religious meaning. Whereas a theatre critic such as Jan Kott can naturally treat a Shakespeare tragedy as an autonomous work, and evokes no objections when he sets it in relation to the reality of life today without regard for what the author had in mind when he wrote the play,[332] a theological Quran exegete, on the other hand, and indeed any believing receiver, must inevitably and continually refer back to the sender's originally intended message. 'He who interprets the Quran for his own convenience shall take his place in hellfire',[333] says a hadith, indicating that the Quran is not autonomous, not detached from its sender. As a revelation, it cannot be – not to the faithful. Accordingly, the independence of a work of art from its creator, propounded by Heidegger and Gadamer, is the only central point that the Muslim author Abū Zayd rejects in his discussion of European hermeneutics and the applicability of its principles to Quran interpretation. For a believer in the usual sense of the term, such autonomy in the case of this text would exceed the limits of possibility.[334] Even Ibn ʿArabī, whose theory of interpretation may be the most rigorous in the history of Muslim thought, seems to suggest the necessity of referring back to the sender, and to do so in his own argumentation when he posits a distinction between 'understanding the speech and understanding the speaker' to justify looking past the text's literal meaning:[335] the mystic approaches the intention of the speaker precisely by transcending the ordinary understanding of the text.

Because the sender himself has so strongly called attention to the informative function of the Quran, and because that sender is considered to be God, an exclusively aesthetic reception of the Quran is out of the question. Within the Muslim *conception* of the quranic text, its beauty and the aesthetic pleasure that it elicits can be neither ends in themselves nor the message itself. They are only the natural expression of its truth, and hence evidence of its divine origin. Although its Arab listeners perceive the Quran as aesthetically powerful and formally perfect, and although an outsider may admire the art that communicates its ideological appeal not only on the level of discursive content but also by the structure of the text, that content is a solid barrier against a purely aesthetic reception. It is not like Brecht's plays, for example, which are also intended as an ideological appeal but are often perceived 'only' as poetic: Muslims – generally – make a strict distinction between the Quran and the artistic sphere. The authors of the *iʿjāz* summaries have no greater concern than to respect the boundary between the Quran and poetry. Where the distinction begins to blur, the preservers of the Word are quick to protest. We see this in the mystics' *samāʿ* debate on the correct way of listening to the Quran and in the books still written today about reservations against recitations that are too musical.[336] In the countries of the Arab world, a number of state agencies, educational institutions and the media are responsible for educating reciters and listeners to preserve the religious character of Quran recitations and ensure that the audience's attitude is pious and God-fearing (and not merely one of enjoyment, as at a concert). In this way they maintain the distinction from musical entertainment. Of course, the insistence on the referential character of the Quran in the *ādāb at-tilāwa*, the detailed 'etiquette' outlined by theologians for correct behaviour during a Quran recitation, arouses a suspicion that, in the momentary communication between the reciter and the listener, the poetic function of the recited text can become dominant after all, or that 'the emotion and the sanctification and the delight and the joy that one thinks come from the Quran' are actually due to the beautiful voice of the reciter, as as-Sarrāj conjectured.[337] The distinction between referential and poetic function involves how the text is used more than its structure, and we could name a number of referential sentences that, when communicated to a certain person under specific circumstances, would take on an emotional value (and vice versa).[338] In the popular Quran recitations in Cairo or elsewhere in the Arab world, the boundaries between Quran and music, between religious and aesthetic experience, are more flexible than in theory. Reciters not only take almost every liberty of artistic, creative interpretation, depending on their individual temperament, but, what is more, they improvise in accordance with the rules of music. Of course, no reciter would improvise on the literal text of the Quran. But what else could one call it when the singer begins a verse, breaks off, begins again, then jumps backwards again in the text, and finally recites the whole passage with all the verve that he has built up? What should we call it when the reciter, egged on by the cries of the audience – *Allāh yiftaḥ ʿaleek*, 'May God shed his blessing on you'; *yā bulbul en-nīl*, 'O nightingale of the Nile'; *khudnā maʿāk*, 'Take us with you' – rises to ever greater acoustic heights, or when he even repeats a verse because the audience requests it again in spontaneous exclamations of joy? And is it not music when a singer sings and the audience answers '*Allāh*' in chorus, so that everyone present is filled with something like rhythm?

No, most theologians would say, and they would insist that it cannot be, because it must not be. The concept of an ideal recitation situation that has been developed by the discipline of *ādāb tilāwat al-Qurʾān* does not provide for a predominantly aesthetic reception of the Quran. If such a reception is often apparent in the practice of recitation, that is another story. In the next chapter, we will examine the extent to which the tension between religious message and musical performance that we have touched on here, which results in an extremely rich subjective experience, is ultimately caused by the Quran itself. To be precise, since this tension occurs in all religions, and leads to conflicts in all religions between apologists and critics of an aesthetic communication of the revelation, we will investigate the extent to which the specifically Islamic version of this tension[339] is inherent in the linguistic structure of the Quran. We will be concerned with the fact that the Quran is primarily an oral text and with the implications of its oral nature for the aesthetic experience of its recipients.

3

The Sound

Overwhelm me, Music, with your rhythmic raging!

Rilke[1]

On March 23, 1959, in the assembly hall of the 'General Society for the Conservation of the Noble Quran' in the 'Ābidīn district of Cairo, representatives of the Egyptian Ministry of Culture, the Egyptian broadcasting company and Azhar University met to discuss a national project that had been proposed by the society's president, Professor Labīb as-Sa'īd of 'Ayn Shams University: to record and distribute an official recitation of the Quran. The recording was to include all seven reliable readings (*mutawātir*) and the three recognized variant readings (*mashhūr*), each in its eight different subordinate traditions (*ṭuruq*), but not the four non-canonical (*shādd*) readings. The official recording would thus consist of eighty complete recitations of the Quran. The Egyptian reciters were to be selected by a committee formed expressly for the purpose and recorded under the supervision of the greatest Quran scholars using state-of-the-art sound engineering. The result would be published as an audio companion to the official Cairo print edition of the Quran.

After the proposal was generally approved in that meeting, Lābīb as-Sa'īd presented it to the public in a press conference the next day and invited all interested parties to express their opinions, help with preparations, and submit suggestions. The reactions were animated and quite controversial, but after many debates, some of them public, the proponents prevailed, and the production work, which was to take several years, began. The director of Azhar University, Sheikh Muḥammad Shaltūt, expressed his approval in a declaration that was printed in all the major newspapers on 3 and 5 April 1959.[2] The minister of religious endowments (*wazīr al-awqāf*) promised organizational and financial support, and the minister of finance allocated currency for the purchase of technical equipment. The title agreed on for the finished recording was *Al-Muṣḥaf al-murattal*, which can probably best be translated as 'The recited edition [of the Quran]'. In May 1960, the first part of the recording began: the recitation after the reading of Ḥafṣ 'an 'Āṣim, which would be spoken by the master reciter (*shaykh al-maqārī'*) of Egypt, Maḥmūd Khalīl al-Ḥuṣarī. It was published on 23 July 1961, the ninth anniversary of the Egyptian Revolution, and distributed to the broadcasting agencies of the Arab world. The organizational committee, in cooperation with the Ministry of the Economy and the prominent record company ash-Sharq, also released the recording for sale on the open market in large quantities at a low price. The following year, the reading of Dūrī ʿan Abī ʿAmr, which is customary mainly in Sudan and Central Africa, was produced, followed by other *mutawātir* and *mashhur* readings. By 1967, forty-four recordings had been released and distributed internationally. They were said to be no less authoritative than the printed text. Labīb as-Saʿīd wrote a book describing the various phases of the project in detail and discussing possible continuations of it. His book *Al-Jamʿ aṣ-ṣawtī al-awwal li-l-Qur'ān aw al-muṣḥaf al-murattal* includes an elaborate rationale, and was published in an American edition in 1974 as *The Recited Koran*. The central idea of as-Saʿīd's book is the essentially oral nature of the Quran. The author sets forth that the Quran was revealed as a text to be recited orally and has been treated as a text for recitation throughout Muslim history. For Muslims, recitation and oral tradition had always taken precedence over the written text, although in the present day they were in danger of neglect. It was therefore necessary to accompany the official edition of the Quran, which is the model for all print editions, with an equally exact recording of its recitation, so that it might serve as a corrective for all time.[3]

The Quran leaves no doubt that Muhammad was not given a written text, as a common error has it, but received his revelation orally and later recited it to his contemporaries in the same way – in short, that hearing is the presumed mode of reception. *Iqra'* was the first word that God addressed to Muhammad through the angel Gabriel, according to the prevailing Muslim tradition: 'Recite!'[4] The Quran is neither a sermon about God, nor spiritual poetry, nor prophecy in the sense of the ancient Hebrew genre. Its composition is not that of a book that one ordinarily reads and studies alone, in silence. Rather, the Quran presents itself as a liturgical recitation of direct speech by God.[5] It is a text for oral delivery. The written page is secondary; it is in principle nothing more than a reminder.

God speaks when the Quran is recited. Strictly speaking, we cannot read His word; we can only hear it. The Quran describes what is still the most common form of its delivery and reception – oral recitation and listening, not reading – in these terms: *Waiḏā quri'a l-qur'ānu fa-stamiʿū lahū wa-anṣitū*: 'And when the Quran is recited, listen and be still.'[6] The Quran draws a sharp terminological distinction between the recitation of the verses and their reception. The delivery is called *talā*, *rattala* and, most of all, *qara'a*, all terms that denote an oration or recitation, not silent reading. The reception of the recited verses by the faithful is consistently called *samiʿa* or *istamaʿa* – that is, 'hearing' or 'listening'. Only *samiʿa*, not simply *qara'a*, leads to the act of understanding (*ʿaqala*).[7] The difference between the reciter's *qara'a* and the congregation's *sami'a* can get lost in English if we translate the words as 'read' and 'hear', since we associate both reading and hearing primarily with the receiver of a message, not the sender. Reading is an act of reception, not of performance. But the Quran makes a distinction between the reader's and the listener's functions. The organ that receives the verses is the ear. Where the Quran refers to its own reception – and Muhammad himself is considered its first recipient – it mentions hearing – not seeing, not reading, not studying.

> If any one of the idolaters should seek your protection, grant it to him so that he may hear the word of God (*ḥattā yasma'a kalāma llāhi*).[8]

> The disbelievers say, 'Do not listen to this Qur'an; drown it in frivolous talk' (*lā tasma'ū li-hāḏā l-qur'āni wa-lġū fīhi*).[9]

After the verb *qara'a*, 'declaim, recite', the revelation itself is called *al-Qur'ān*, a gerund of the quite common *maṣdar* form, which appears about seventy times in the Quran. *Al-Qur'ān* can be literally translated as 'that which is to be recited' or 'the reciting'. In most instances, especially in the early passages, *qur'ān* simply means 'reading aloud' or 'recitation'.[10] Only in later centuries and especially in the modern period have Muslims and scholars internalized the term *al-Qur'ān* as a proper noun for the revelations as recorded in writing and collected in a book, to the point that its original meaning as a term for the act of recitation has been more or less forgotten.

The Quran has existed as a book in the proper sense of the term – that is, as a uniform written or printed document of a certain size, held together in some way – only since the codification of the scattered manuscripts under 'Uthmān, which Gregor Schoeler is to a certain extent justified in calling a 'publication',[11] and which was by no means uncontroversial at the time. Zayd ibn Thābit, for example, objected, on hearing of 'Umar's proposal to compile the scattered manuscripts, 'How can we do something that the Messenger of God himself never did?'[12] Before the compilation around the year 642, there was no complete corpus of the collected revelations in writing that *al-Qur'ān* could have referred to. While the Quran contains a number of verses in which the word is used as a proper noun for the revelations promulgated by Muhammad, it never refers to a written, finished codex.[13] According to the predominant Muslim understanding, Muhammad intended to collect the recorded texts but did not finish before his death.[14] Labīb as-Sa'īd explains the phenomenon as follows: 'Because the Quran in its essence was the orally transmitted word of God, to be heard and repeated and preserved in the heart, there was no need for an authoritative written text as long as the Muslims could be sure [because the Prophet was among them] that their Quran recitation was correct.'[15]

The concept of *kitāb*, which is also grounded in the Quran itself (and with which Islam refers to the earlier scriptural religions, heralding the beginning of textual coherence), is not identical with the present-day notion of a book. The *kitāb* of the Quran escapes the dichotomy of the oral or written nature of the revealed word, since the revelation is a scripture that must be recited.[16] That is, although the transition from ritual to textual coherence so accurately described by Assmann[17] is initiated by Muhammad himself, and must be assumed to have taken place before the production at least of the long surahs in their present form, the recited word nonetheless remains dominant in the performative sphere, both in the liturgical context[18] and in the dissemination of the text. According to the Muslim tradition, the text continued to be spread during Muhammad's lifetime mainly through the system of oral transmission by Quran reciters (*qurrā'*). When Muhammad wanted to spread his message beyond Mecca and Medina to neighbouring regions, he sent Quran reciters, not written texts.[19] Even the Arabic term for a person who has learnt the Quran by heart – *ḥāfiẓ*, literally, 'preserver, guardian' – suggests that memorization is seen as the primary and surest method of transmission. In the Muslim literature, the generally recognized principle of oral conservation and transmission is called *tawātur*, which could be translated as 'continuous succession'. The concept holds that a great number of Quran readers who know the text by heart, spread over a large geographical area, offer the best protection against corruption and distortion of the revealed text.[20]

Oral Scripture

The oral nature of the Quran cannot be explained simply by stating that writing was not usual in late seventh-century Arabia. Not only are there a number of inscriptions that are significantly older than the Quran as evidence that writing was widespread in pre-Islamic Arabia, but the Quran itself also contains clear references to writing paraphernalia, such as the oath 'by the pen' at the beginning of surah 68, which must have been known at that time.[21] Furthermore, it is by no means settled that Muhammad could not read and write, as the predominant Muslim tradition maintains, and, even if we did assume that, it would still be conceivable that he might *first* have dictated the revelation to the scribes and only then circulated it. Theoretically, the revelation could have been presented from the very beginning as a primarily written text, even as a book, like the scriptures of the Jews and Christians among the Arabs – but it was not.[22] Unlike the prophets of the Old Testament, Muhammad did not receive from his Lord the commandment, 'Take a large tablet, and write on it in easily readable letters.'[23] The Quran explicitly denies any written revelation like the Ten Commandments received by Moses:

> Had We sent down on thee a Book on parchment (*kitāban fī qirṭāsin*) and so they touched it with their hands, yet
> the unbelievers would have said, 'This is naught but manifest sorcery (*siḥrun mubīn*)'.[24]

The Quran itself describes the revelation as the oral transmission of an oral text:

> We will make you recite,
> and you will forget nothing,
> except by God's will!
> Truly, he knows what is spoken
> and what is concealed.
> And We will make it easy,
> so that it will be easy for you.[25]

The concept of revelation that is touched on here has been expressed in more concrete terms in the traditions, which tell that the archangel Gabriel visited the Prophet – every night during Ramadan – and instructed him in the recitation (*kāna yudārisuhū l-qur'ān*).[26] In the words of the contemporary Egyptian scholar Ḥusayn Muḥammad Makhlūf, the Prophet 'listened strictly and with extreme concentration, until Gabriel had finished the message of his Lord, then he recited what had been revealed to him of the Quran, in the words and the manner of oration in which he had heard it. Then he delivered it to all mankind as he had received it.'[27] Because receiving the revelation was assumed to be an auditory process, Muslim theologians later simply called it *sam'*, 'hearing'.[28] According to a conception that has its roots in the Quran, the original text of the revelation is contained in the celestial *umm al-kitāb* (the 'mother of scripture') or the *lawḥ maḥfūẓ* (the 'preserved tablet');[29] Muhammad was inspired with or taught excerpts of that text bit by bit and passed them on to his fellows in the same form.

> We have sent thee not, except
> good tidings to bear, and warning;
> and a Koran We have divided,
> for thee to recite it to mankind
> at intervals, and We have sent it down successively.[30]
> The disbelievers also say,
> 'Why was the Qur'an not sent down to him
> all at once?'
> We sent it in this way
> to strengthen your heart;
> We gave it to you in gradual revelation.[31]

The surah *al-Wāqi'a* explicitly describes the relation between the earthly recitation and the celestial scripture:

> This is truly a noble recitation (*qur'ān karīm*)
> in a protected Record (*kitāb māknūn*),
> that only the purified can touch,
> sent down from the Lord of all being.[32]

The *kitāb* is accessible to humans only in the form of revealed recitation. The material scripture, the letters on paper, are only a *muṣḥaf*, a human, fallible transcript of the divine recitations from the celestial book, and must not be confused with the celestial *kitāb* or with the recited revelation, the *Qur'ān*. Why did the early Muslims 'hesitate to call the written compilation of the recitations "Quran" or "written Quran"?' Labīb as-Sa'īd asks.

> Why did they insist on using the word *al-muṣḥaf*? The reason is evidently that the word Quran in the Muslim vocabulary does not refer to the written word, nor even to the word heard from human lips or stored in human memory. It refers only to the eternal oration of God, which is part of God's being and above all earthly phenomena, including the written text.[33]

The written page has always been subordinate to and dependent on the recitation and memorization of the *ḥuffāẓ*. Since even the official written scripture was not considered infallible, 'Uthmān had a Quran reader accompany every copy.[34] The tradition recounts that, on finding incorrect expressions in some of the finished copies, he said, 'Do not change them, for the Arabs will correct them with their tongues.'[35] The caliph tolerated obvious errors in the manuscripts only because he could rely on recitation to correct them. Even the scholars who met in Cairo in the early twentieth century to agree on an official version of the text relied less on the existing written editions than on the knowledge of the most reliable readings (*qirā'āt*) that has been preserved in memory and transmitted orally over hundreds of years. In the early 1930s, Gotthelf Bergsträsser wrote about this 'Cairene Quran' which is now the model for nearly all printed editions:

> It projects an ancient Islamic scholarship with vitality and power into our days; it is evidence of the surprisingly high state of development of present-day Egyptian scholarship on Quran recitation. One is tempted to say even that *only* the spirit of *'ilm al-qirā'āt* could have performed such a task: the most meticulous, careful collation of European philology would hardly have attained the almost absolute correctness that the Egyptian Quran scholars have achieved by mnemonic mastery of *every* detail and religious devotion to minutiae.[36]

The Islamic concept of a scripture that requires oral recitation leads William A. Graham to a fundamental observation:

> If the Muslim treatment of the Qur'ān – that clearest, even purest and most radical instance of 'book religion' – presents us with a scripture that is oral as well as written, then certainly orality can characterise 'scriptural' as well as 'prescriptural' or 'nonliterate' forms of religious life.[37]

That the Quran must be recited aloud is not only a theological requirement that follows from the Islamic concept of revelation. The recitative character of the Quran is also manifest in its linguistic structure: in the sound figures of numerous surahs, for example, and in the juxtaposition of more or less autonomous parts and episodes, a typical technique in oral texts. The structure makes it possible to begin and end a recitation with any sentence, as is actually done in practice, and to interrupt it and start in again at another place in the text without distorting the overall composition.[38] Other characteristics of an oral text include the frequent shifts between narrative levels – only the speaker's intonation allows the recipient to follow them – and elements such as repetition, refrain (most prominently in surah 55) and the rhyming cadences at the ends of long verses, which are pointless, and even irritating, when pronounced in a normal speech rhythm but contribute substantially to the euphony of a cantilena-style recitation.[39] Stefan Wild cites the Quran's recitative character as one of the primary reasons for the striking differences between Muslim and Western scholars' assessments of the quranic style. Down to the present day, Orientalists have applied their familiar scriptural concept to the Quran, arguing as if it were intended as a collection of sermons or an edifying book suitable for sequential, silent reading by solitary lamplight. They generally neglected its oratorical nature, if they were aware of it at all. Wild writes:

> Parallelismus membrorum, clausula verses with various functions, and scattered meditative passages may appear superfluous, boring, or naive to the Western reader's eye.... To the ear of the listener prostrate on the floor in worship, they give liturgical structure to a continuous text, providing pauses, marking transitions and lending a meditative tone to the mood of the recitation. The recitative form brings with it frequent changes of grammatical person, unfinished sentences, anacolutha, the whole breadth of living speech. In the often dramatic dialogue, the changes of speaker and the beginnings and ends of direct speech are sometimes unmarked. The reciter can mark them with little effort, and the listener can understand them with less still. But the reader-only of today loses the thread and complains of a lack of logic and a 'pleasing form'.[40]

The necessity of recitation is inherent, and a certain musicality of delivery is an obvious component, in the Quran's 'poetics' – that is, in the work's implicitly and explicitly expressed plan for itself. Friedrich Rückert is therefore not wrong to translate the phrase *rattili l-Qur'āna tartīlan* in verse 73:4 as 'sing den Koran ab sangweise' ['chant the Quran songwise']. Certainly *tartīl* in context is not to be understood as a loud trilling away to a melody composed for the text, but neither does it mean the 'regular arranging' that a number of European translators, including Bell and Paret, have suggested. We should probably imagine it as something like a cantilena-style chant.[41] However, the text itself has hardly anything to say about the style of delivery beyond the unspecific instruction *tartīl*. The Quran is practically silent about *how*, while leaving no doubt *that* it is to be recited. Nor has the tradition too much to add on this topic. Although the importance of a beautiful and melodic recitation is more strongly emphasized in the works of hadith than in the Quran,[42] the quotations only hint at how Muhammad's recitation may have sounded. He sang (*taġannā bi*) the Quran,[43] and he recited it with a mellow, quavering voice (*qirā'a layyina wa-huwa yurajja'*),[44] drawing out the long vowels (*madd*),[45] 'not halting and not hurrying, but pronouncing each letter in turn'.[46] The Prophet instructs the faithful to recite the Quran 'with the Arabs' melodies (*alḥān/luḥūn*) and voices (*aṣwāt*)',[47] more fluidly than prose, but more slowly than works of poetry.[48] The reciter should also fear God.[49] Quran recitation makes sense only if the reciter's devoutness is not feigned:

> A believer who recites the Quran is like an orange: its aroma is good and so is its taste. A believer who does not recite the Quran is like a dried date: it has no aroma, but its taste is sweet. A hypocrite who recites the Quran is like basil: it smells good, but tastes bitter. And a hypocrite who does not recite the Quran is like a colocynth: it has no aroma, and its taste is bitter.[50]

Even putting aside the question of the authenticity of such stories, they give only a sketchy impression of the initial form of Quran recitation. The idea that the early Muslims sang the Quran to simple melodies, as Talbi claims,[51] is nothing more than a plausible surmise. What is beyond a doubt is that, whatever it may have sounded like, some form of melodic recitation that has generally been accepted by the scholars, and probably originated with the Prophet himself, was established early on. This can be inferred primarily from the protests against deviant modes of recitation that have been handed down from relatively early times. At the court of Damascus in the late seventh century, ʿAbdullāh ibn Abī Bakr, for example, is said to have introduced a *new* style of recitation, called *qirā'a bi-l-alḥān*, 'recitation with melodies', that was not far removed from ordinary singing. The numerous traditions in which conservative scholars argue against this innovation (*bidʿa*) document the existence of a highly stylized form of Quran recitation, patterned after the Arabo-Persian art song, in the centuries that followed.[52] As this development was taking place, professional singers also added the Quran to their repertoires, sometimes treating it, if we may believe the opposing polemics, as a normal lyric to be sung to whatever popular melodies would suit,[53] and occasionally even sung as a dance tune.[54] We may judge how popular this kind of melodic Quran performance was by the vehement protests of theologians such as Ibn al-Jawzī (d. 1200)[55] and aṭ-Ṭurṭūshī (d. 1126–31).[56] Occasionally the *muḥtasib*, the defender of public order, was called upon to intervene against such sacrilegious entertainment,[57] and one al-Ḥārith al-Miskīn, supreme qadi in Egypt, beat those who sang the Quran to secular melodies with his own hands.[58] Conversely, the fact that music lovers used it as an argument for the legitimacy of music is a further indication of the spread of *qirā'a bi-l-alḥān*. The Andalusian literary scholar Ibn ʿAbd Rabbih (d. 940), for example, rebutted the puritanical proponents of a general ban on music with the words, 'If melodies ought to be prohibited, then you should start by keeping them out of the recitation and the call to prayer.'[59]

Concurrently with this development – and certainly influenced by it – an extensive set of rules began to develop beginning in the ninth century, if not before, called *tajwīd* (literally, 'to make good or beautiful'). These rules specified the phonetics of the correct recitation in a degree of detail that outsiders may find inexplicable. As far as can be discerned from written documents, the principal doctrines of *ʿilm at-tajwīd*, and of the closely related *ʿilm al-qirā'āt*, the science of interpretations, had taken shape by the tenth century.[60] Thereafter they were continually refined and, ultimately, laid down systematically in the works of such scholars as Muḥammad Makkī Naṣr (d. 1045),[61] Abū Zakarīyā n-Nawawī (d. 1233)[62] and Ibn al-Jazarī (d. 1429).[63] The *tajwīd* codex still applied today includes precise instructions on places of articulation, the pronunciation of specific sounds and sound combinations, and prosody. For example, it contains rules for lengthening (*madd*) and shortening (*qaṣr*) vowels, nunation (*tanwīn*) and contextual pronunciation of the letters *nūn* and *mīm* (*aḥkām an-nūn wa-l-mīm*), stopping and starting (*al-waqf wa-l-ibtidā'*), complete and incomplete assimilation (*idġām kāmil* and *idġām nāqiṣ*), and the doubling (*tashdīd*), reduction (*ikhfā'*) and nasalization (*ġunna*) of consonants. It specifies the shading of vowels, indicates peculiarities of the pronunciation of pronouns, suffixes and final *yā'*, and many more fine details, such as when to apply a vibration (*qalqala*) at the place of articulation, and in which combinations certain sounds should be pharyngealized (*tafkhīm*). The *ʿilm at-tajwīd* also defines the 'etiquette' of recitation (*ādāb at-tilāwa*), including when, where and for which occasions the Quran should be recited and how the listeners must behave.

As extravagant as the recitation rules may seem to a Western observer, especially in the precision of their phonetic nuances, their importance for Muslim religious doctrine and practice can hardly be overestimated, as Kristina Nelson correctly states:

> *tajwīd* preserves the nature of a revelation whose meaning is expressed as much by its sound as by its content and expression, and guards it from distortion by a comprehensive set of regulations which govern many of the parameters of the sound production, such as duration of syllable, vocal timbre, and pronunciation. Furthermore, *tajwīd* links these parameters to the meaning and expression, and indicates the appropriate attitude to the Qur'anic recitation as a whole.

> *Tajwīd* is believed to be the codification of the sound of the revelation as it was revealed to the Prophet Muhammad, and as he subsequently rehearsed it with the Angel Gabriel. Thus the sound itself has a divine source and significance, and, according to Muslim tradition, is significant to the meaning.[64]

Although the *ʿilm at-tajwīd* brings the influence of high theological authority to bear in the extensive and still steadily growing literature, it has been only personally transmissible, since the nuances of the phonetic rules cannot be represented in writing. The *tajwīd* works are conceived as teaching aids and must be studied under a teacher who can demonstrate practically the theoretical postulates as the repository of an ancient, mainly oral tradition[65] (although today CDs and DVDs are marketed for use in independent study). This is one reason why the *ʿilm at-tajwīd* has hardly attracted the attention that Western Quran studies has devoted to the primarily written branches of Quran studies such as *tafsīr* (exegesis), *luġa* (philology), *rasm* (orthography), *balāġa* (rhetoric) and *naḥw* (grammar). (Another reason is of course the fact that distance alone prevented Western Quran scholars, especially in the early period of their discipline, from swapping a desk at home for the living Quran teaching of a *muqriʾ*.) Frederik M. Denny emphasizes another aspect of the Western perspective: 'Western scholarship, engaged in by people of Christian or Jewish background mostly, has to some extent imposed its own view of scripture on its approach to the Qur'an by emphasising exegetical, historical and philological concerns.'[66] A scholarship that is not based on the Occidental concept of writing but refers only to the oral and ritual character of its holy 'scripture', and depends moreover on the oral transmission of its findings, must almost inevitably be neglected or even dismissed as irrelevant by Western research.

The *tajwīd* codex, which is theoretically valid and in practice largely observed throughout the Islamic world, includes no rules on the melodic styling of the recitation. Yet, even in the absence of written specifications, certain characteristics of melodic lines have developed, across all regional variations, that are not found in any other kind of singing. This is primarily because the *tajwīd* codex, which is strictly observed wherever possible, necessitates certain melodic figures and caesurae and a rhythmic and temporal organization that do not exist in art songs. The interplay between the articulation, cultivated to a degree found nowhere else, and the rhythm that results from the *tajwīd* rules makes Quran recitation so stylized in contrast to other forms of spoken expression that it immediately elicits a certain receptive attitude in the listener.[67] These acoustic dimensions are an unavoidable part of the code of communication between the reciter and the listener, no less than *ʿarabīya* on the linguistic level. The recipient is predisposed to an aesthetic (or partially aesthetic) reception by the sound alone. It puts him in a state of particular attentiveness and expectation that permits the sensory perception and meditative reflection of even the finest nuances of the recitation. The listeners' attention is directed to the message itself; the aesthetic function of the linguistic signs comes to the foreground.

Yet the relevance of the sensory and primarily auditive perception is not originally the consequence of melodic recitation according to the rules of *tajwīd*. Rather, the art of Quran recitation is the consequence of an acoustic level of communication that is built into the text. The Quran guides its listeners' reception of both by its linguistic properties in the strict sense (which we discussed in chapter 2) and by its purely acoustic qualities, as we will show in this chapter. In many works of ancient Middle Eastern poetry, and in the fine classifications of the *tajwīd* scholars, every sound of the speaking voice is associated with a specific emotional effect; a soft *zād* has a different use than the rough *khā'*, the emphatic consonants produce a different atmosphere than the close vowels and the bilabial *bā'* elicits different moods than the uvular *ġayn*.[68] To those who know how to compose poetically, language is 'not a function or means of expression but a sacred substance, as tones are to a musician', Hermann Hesse wrote.[69] The Quran illustrates how poetry is the transition from language to music, and how a text develops its aura only when it is spoken aloud. The eschatological sections of the Quran, for example, which are often praised for their rich imagery, owe their oppressive atmosphere at least as much, or rather still more, to their rhythmic homogeneity, the unifying assonance of *saj'*, and the rhetorical questions frequently used as a melodic interval. Rückert's German translation makes it possible to a certain extent to appreciate these peculiarities of the quranic language:[70]

1 *wa-l-'ādiyāti ḍabḥā*	Bei den schnaubend Jagenden,	By the snorting chargers,
2 *fa-l-mūriyāti qadḥā*	Mit Hufschlag Funken Schlagenden,	by the strikers of fire,
3 *fa-l-muġīrāti ṣubḥā*	Den Morgenangriff Wagenden,	by the dawn-raiders,
4 *fa-atharna bihī naq'ā*	Die Staub aufwühlen mit dem Tritte	blazing a trail of dust,
5 *fa-wasaṭna bihī jam'ā*	Und dringen in des Heeres Mitte!	cleaving there with a host!
6 *inna l-insāna li-rabbihī la-kanūd*	Ja, der Mensch ist gegen Gott voll Trutz,	Surely Man is ungrateful to his Lord,
7 *wa-innahū 'alā ḏālika la-shahīd*	Was er sich bezeugen muß,	and surely he is a witness against that!
8 *wa-innahū li-ḥubbi l-khayri la-shadīd*	Und liebet heftig seinen Nutz.	Surely he is passionate in his love for good things.

9 *a-fa-lā ya'lamu iḏā bu'thira mā fī l-qubūr*	O weiß er nicht, wann das im Grab wird aufgeweckt,	Knows he not that when that which is in the tombs is overthrown,
10 *wa-ḥuṣṣila mā fī ṣ-ṣudūr*	Und das im Busen aufgedeckt,	and that which is in the breasts is brought out –
11 *inna rabbahum bihim yawma'iḏin la-khabīr*	Daß nichts vor ihrem Herrn dann bleibt versteckt?	surely on that day their Lord shall be aware of them!

Angelika Neuwirth has provided an impressive analysis of this surah's fascinating imagery.[71] What I am interested in here is its acoustic composition. The surah is composed of three parts plus an envoi, and each part has not only its own rhyme but also its own unique phonetic palette. The sequential oath (verses 1–5) is distinguished first of all by the initial syllable *fa-* from the second verse on, which sets the rhythm and signals the beginning of each recitative unit. It also contrasts with the emphatic phonemes in the rhyming words (*ḍabhā*, *qadḥā*, *ṣubḥā*, *naq'ā*, *jam'ā*): the velarization of these words centralizes the final */ā/* (that is, it shifts the place of articulation towards the centre), which makes the intonation fall as low as possible at the end of the unit. The interplay between the high initial and low final syllables creates a dramatic tension. This acoustic cadence is reinforced by the progressive shifting of the place of articulation of the last syllable towards the soft palate, from */b/* in the first to */'/* in the fourth and fifth verses. The */ḥ/* and */'/* in the final syllables of the first to fifth verses are the two pharyngeal sounds among the gutturals in the alphabet (*ḥurūf ḥalqīya*). The result is that the sequential oath sounds heavy, dark, threatening, as if something is about to happen or someone is standing at the door and knocking with a blunt object. The passage gets its characteristic beating rhythm from the short, choppy phrases, which consist of a series of nouns and adjectives, always repeating the same guttural, dark rhyme. The overall effect is breathless, heavy, like a heart beating too fast, or like the approaching gallop of the horses that 'strike sparks with their hooves'.

The core of the surah, verses 6 to 8, contains the statement that is sworn by the introductory oath and emphasized by the envoi. Close vowels dominate this part. The resolution at the end of each verse is accentuated by the emphatic particle *la-*, whose vowel sound is repeated in the first syllable of the rhyming word (*ka-nūd*, *sha-hīd*, *sha-dīd*) and by the vowels */ū/* and */ī/* in the final syllables. The clarity of the sound complements the argument: a reproof issued unambiguously, its urgency reinforced by the contrast to the threatening mood of the introduction. A musical causality results: the deep threatening mood of the first part is resolved by the higher voice of the admonisher in the second part; the admonishing voice in turn clearly states the reason for the danger described in the beginning: man is ungrateful to his Lord.

The questions in verses 9 and 10 vary the melodic line of the three preceding verses, yet the /q/ and /ʿ/ and the emphatic consonants recall the sound of the introductory oath – as if to recall the threatening mood of the beginning to underscore the central admonition. Verse 11, however, which begins with the Arabic emphatic particle *inna*, not a conditional clause, sounds like a final chord that continues the warning, and the rhyme (*la-khabīr*), of the central section.

No matter what we call it – poetry, rhymed prose, song or musical composition – it is unmistakable that the Quran does not simply state its message, which could be summarized in one sentence: Man consciously rebels against his Lord, even though he should know that he will be called to account on Judgement Day. Rather, the Quran's composition creates an aesthetic experience of the message by purposely evoking the poeticity of its lexical signs. And inevitably that puts it close to poetry, and hence close to music. 'The interpenetration of poetry and music is so close that their origin is indivisible and usually rooted in a common myth', George Steiner writes. 'Still today the vocabulary of prosody and poetic form, of linguistic tonality and cadence, overlaps deliberately with that of music. From Arion and Orpheus to Ezra Pound and John Berryman, the poet is maker of songs and singer of words.'[72] It is no different in Arabic. The ancient Arab imagination sees the jinn as both the initiators of poetry and the inventors of musical instruments,[73] and, in works of *samāʿ*, a beautiful voice is almost a synonym for a pleasing melody (*laḥn ṭayyib*, *naġama ṭayyiba*). *Sawṭ* not only means 'linguistic sound', 'voice', or 'tone' but can also mean 'song', 'melody' or 'verses set to music'.[74] Similarly, the word *taġannā*, lexically related to *ġināʾ*, 'song', denotes both singing a song and reciting a poem or the Quran. From ad-Dārimī (d. 869)[75] to Ibn Qayyim al-Jawzīya (d. 1350)[76] to Labīb as-Saʿīd, numerous authors have titled their studies on Quran recitation *At-Taġannī bi-l-Qurʾān*, and as-Saʿīd begins his with a treatise on the great importance in Arab society, not of the spoken word but of music and song, setting them in relation to the power of the Quran.[77] That is nothing extraordinary: Ibn Khaldūn (d. 1406) too, in his *Muqaddima*, discussed Quran recitation in the chapter on 'The Art of Song'. He criticized the fact that many reciters 'recite the Quran and ornament it with the melody of their voices as if they were playing the flute, and they delight in the beauty of what they are doing and in the harmony of their melodies.'[78]

Poetry recitations in the Jahiliyyah, we are told, were often musical events, and the poet was at the same time a singer and a musician.[79] In such traditions, it is difficult to keep poetry and music or recitation and singing apart. In the religious literature of Islam we often encounter texts in which the Quran and music are mentioned in the same context: from Muhammad's canonical saying that 'God listens more attentively to a man reciting the Quran in a beautiful voice than the master listens to the song of his slave girl (*qaina*)'[80] to the words of the modern Iranian Quran scholar Moḥammad Taqī Sharīʿatī-Mazīnānī:

> If all the masters and scholars of music came together and tried to compose a melody from the 28 Arabic letters, even without forming words, they would not be able to compose so many different, varied and harmonious melodies with the richness of meaning that the Quran achieves by forming and connecting words. With this salient quality of the Quran in mind, the Prophet and his glorious people gave definite and repeated instructions to recite the Quran with the melodies of the Arabs.[81]

Gustav Richter, in his analysis of the quranic style, finds many passages in which the acoustic element is not just a side effect of the quranic discourse but becomes the actual vehicle of the message itself, and often dominates both the semantic content and the imagery.[82] Such passages are not found in all surahs; they are more rare in the Medinan than in the Meccan surahs, but they are by no means limited to the eschatological sections. The power of the sounds is particularly evident in the polemics against the Meccans, with their menacing exclamations of woe and their incantatory questions, where the word 'aspires to the condition of music', to use George Steiner's phrase.[83] It aspires all the more keenly the more brilliant the recitation is, since the sonorous component of the Quran unfolds its full power only when the reciter applies the subtleties of articulation in accordance with the rules of *tajwīd*. The 'keyboard' of the quranic instrument includes not only the Arabic language's twenty-eight consonants, six vowels and two diphthongs. A trained reciter must also know about twenty-six *tajwīd* symbols that scholars have defined over the course of time: circles, small rectangles, various letters, lines, and the like, indicate the correct pronunciation of consonants, their possible assimilation with an adjacent sound, places where caesuras are possible or prohibited, and similar instructions. In contemporary editions of the Quran these symbols are printed, sometimes in colour, below, above or beside the letters or in the middle of the text. In transcription they are generally omitted, and a translation offers no hint of them. As a very limited example, the frequently occurring expression *innā anzalnā* ('truly, We have sent down') may serve to convey a certain impression of the degree to which the sound of the recited text is altered and refined simply by the observation of *tajwīd*.[84] The phrase is characterized by a number of different *a* and *n* sounds: *in/nā/'an/zal/nā*. In accordance with the *tajwīd* rule of *ġunna*, the double *nūn* in the untranslatable emphatic particle *innā* is lengthened and nasalized. It is followed by a long */ā/*, which is drawn out further following the *tajwīd* rule of *madd*. *Madd* applies when */ā/* is followed by the glottal stop *hamza* ('). The closed, nasalized *nn* creates a rhythmic suspense and a feeling of restrained energy, which is released in a moment of semantic-auditory eruption in the long */ā/*. In the next syllable, the auditory effect that arises from *ġunna* and the *a* vowel occurs again in a new formation: *an/zal/nā*. Due to the *tajwīd* rule of *ikhfā'* (lowering and nasalization of the voice on the combination of */n/* and */z/*), the sound sequence */anz/* is vocally emphasized. The */an/* of the first syllable is symmetrically echoed by the final syllable /*nā*/. Sells describes the effect produced by this subtle combination of *n* and *a* sounds:

> The result is an intricately intertwined series of echoes, partial echoes, inverse echoes, tensions and releases, constructed of *a* and *n*-sounds and hinging on the liquid. These effects are amplified by the anti-metrical and lapidary rhythm of the five consecutive long syllables – the continued sequence of long syllables forcing the reciter and hearer to dwell upon the aural aspect of the sound-unit.[85]

In two detailed articles, Sells has shown how such sound figures, which can be perfectly heard only when the reciter observes the *tajwīd* markings, occur in many variations within a single surah and are repeated in ever-changing arrangements, so that they can form an important channel in the communication between text and listener. An acoustic analysis of a longer Quran excerpt, including the pronunciation codex, would take us too far from our present theme and require a study of its own. However, even a brief glimpse of a few surahs will allow us to see how the text's sound figures produce semantic, emotive and acoustic interrelations, transporting information. As in the discussion of surah 100 above, let us use an example for which we have a translation that carries over the phonetic composition into German – surah 111, *al-Lahab*.

1 *tabbat yadā Abī Lahabin wa-tabb*
2 *mā aġnā ʿanhū māluhū wa-mā kasab*
3 *sa-yaṣlā nāran ḏāta lahab*
4 *wa-mraʾatuhū ḥammālatal-ḥaṭab*
5 *fī jīdihā ḥablun min masad*

One does not have to be a native speaker of Arabic to realize that these verses must be spoken aloud. And it takes little knowledge of Arabic to hear – if the recitation is good – that they express a curse of hellish proportions, and to sense that the very first verse is already an apodictic judgement, one that brooks no contradiction or appeasement. It is a reckoning, the speaker is burning a bridge, speaking his final word about this Abū Lahab, alias ʿAbdulʿuzzā, the Prophet's half-brother.[86] The 'music' of this surah tells us as much, and we begin to believe those reciters who claim they can convey the meaning of the Quran to a non-Arab simply through the sound of their recitation.[87] Rückert translated the almost onomatopoeic composition into German:

1 Ab sind die Händ' Abulahab's, und er ist ab;
2 Es half ihm nicht sein Gut und Hab.
3 Heizen wird er des Feuers Brast,
4 Zuträgt sein Weib des Holzes Last,
5 Um ihren Hals ein Strick von Bast.

Perish the hands of Abu Lahab, and perish he!
His wealth avails him not, neither what he has earned;
he shall roast at a flaming fire
and his wife, the carrier of the firewood,
upon her neck a rope of palm-fibre.*

Various Orientalists have given ample attention to interpreting the surah[88] and have found different significations for certain words, such as *wa-tabb* at the end of the first verse. However, they have ignored the acoustic component that results from the triad of *tabbat/Lahab/wa-tabb*, composed of the short front vowel /a/ and the labial and palatal consonants. They were not interested in the fact that the final *wa-tabb* not only has a referential meaning but, as a repetition, also functions as an important element in the acoustic composition and the rhythm of the verse, and as such points to itself and to the surrounding lexical signs. Indeed this may be its primary purpose. The message is conveyed not only by the lexical meaning of the words but even more strongly by the auditive thrust which results from the acoustic repetitions, but which is only realized when the text is recited. Likewise, in the second verse, the initial negation *mā* is doubly accentuated by the homophonous relative pronoun and by the first syllable in *māluhū*, so that it begins to speak for itself, like a tone that is repeated several times in a piece of music. The word *lahab* at the end of the third verse, an untranslatable pun on the name of Abū Lahab introduced in the first verse, is a poetic surprise, sprung right in the middle of the surah. The word is thematically, formally and acoustically the central word of the surah, but only the recitation brings out its bitter double meaning. The words, syllables and sounds in this surah are exemplary of the poetic use of words and of an acoustic structure that gives a sensory presence to the theme, a menacing curse. As clearly as Abū Lahab's doom is pronounced in the first verse, we seem to hear the axe fall in *ḏāta lahab*. Such a text cannot simply be read off in an ordinary speaking tone without doing violence to it. It urges even a mere 'reader's' voice to rise and fall, to set accents, pause, pay attention to phrasing, and so fall into a melody – if only a very simple one – something that does not occur in everyday speech. Labīb as-Saʿīd writes:

> The Quran itself attests that it cannot be recited in a normal voice. Among the great multitude of rhetorical figures (*badā'iʿ*) that it contains are some that can be considered essentially musical, not in the sense that they represent musical forms introduced into the Quran, but in the sense that they generate musical vibrations which are inherent in the quranic language and can be heard when it is sung appropriately.[89]

* Arberry's English translation is given here for the sense – Trans.

The recipient's instinctive tendency towards a 'singing' recitation is emphasized in numerous personal testimonials. It is impossible, Lamyā' al-Fārūqī quotes an Azhar graduate as saying, simply to read the Quran. The correct pronunciation of the words and phrases makes a musical arrangement unavoidable.[90] The art of Quran recitation, even in the merely chant-like *murattal* or *tartīl* style, which is usually preferred for edifying or didactic purposes, requires musical talent and at least basic knowledge of classical Arabian music, its *maqāmāt* (modes) and *naġamāt* (melodies).[91] The recitations in the famous *mujawwad* style of Cairo (or *qirā'a bi-l-alḥān*, as it was called until a few decades ago, although it is different from the medieval mode of recitation designated by the same term), which are practically organized as recitals, would by Western standards be called music or singing rather than recitation. The American researcher A. H. Johns calls it 'a great art form, one of the greatest achievements of the human voice',[92] and Gotthelf Bergsträsser observed in the late 1920s:

> Where the Quran is recited without a didactic purpose, the listeners' edification is generally accompanied by artistic enjoyment: the text is recited in the fully musical form, *bi-l-alḥān*. That is the usual form of Quran recitations as practised in the nights of Ramadan and at all kinds of public and family religious feasts.... In this connection we are no longer dealing with recitation in the strict sense but with vocal music: a full singing voice in a high tenor range; rich melodic motion with many embellishments. Minor differences in this mode of recitation are the fact that verses or verse fragments are often repeated (when no correction is called for), that pauses are greatly extended, and that linguistic quantities are shifted more for the sake of musical effect. The listeners too respond differently to such a recitation: even in al-Azhar, such a recitation immediately evoked the rapturous moaning, the *allāhallāhallāh* of admiration, and so on, which would be inadmissible in response to a purely didactic-edifying recitation.[93]

The fine chromatic distinctions in singing – typical of quarter-tone music – are those of the various modes of classical Oriental music, which are freely chosen by reciters. Some modes, such as *bayātī*, are particularly popular. Yet the Quran reciter usually strives for a significantly wider range of melodic motion than is typically found in secular *maqām* melodies, spanning up to two octaves from the initial tone. In its use of the scale, cadenzas, many kinds of modulation, and register shifts, and in regard to melody, rhythm and tonality in general, *mujawwad* recitation approaches classical art music but never merges with it.[94] The differences from secular singing are due to the special religious veneration of the Quran. Veneration calls for the emphatic, distinct pronunciation of every single syllable and the observance of all the Quran-specific pronunciation rules, such as the possible assimilation of consonants with adjacent sounds.

In art music, on the other hand, the singer is free to deform sounds in the text for the sake of a desired melodic line, so that the text may become unintelligible. The *tajwīd* codex ensures that the *sacred* text is not 'drowned out' by *human* music. At the same time it also necessitates a basic rhythm maintained without regard to melodic considerations, which does not exist in vocal music. Additional characteristics that are specific to Quran recitation include the absence of instrumental accompaniment and the total dominance of vocal improvisation in originating the melody: while the melody adheres to the chosen tonal mode, it is determined by the rhythm of the language, not the other way round.[95] The differences from all other known forms of Arabic vocal music are unmistakable, so that the strict separation of the Quran from music is not simply dogmatic. Significantly, however, secular singers appreciate Quran recitation highly for precisely these particularities, whose causes are originally theological. The great reciters are considered experts and exemplars of classical art music primarily for their skill at complex *maqām* improvisation. Many singers feel that studying *tajwīd* is an indispensable prerequisite for singing secular art music because it trains the singer's voice, improvisation skills and sense of rhythm, as well as pronunciation and correct inflection (*iʿrāb*).[96] This explains why the Quran has been used since the Middle Ages in training secular singers[97] and why many performers of classical Arab music in the twentieth century, including Sheikh Sayyid Darwīsh (d. 1923), Sheikh ʿAlī Maḥmūd (d. 1946), the legendary Umm Kulthūm (d. 1975) and the Christian singer Fayrūz learned *tajwīd* and began their careers as Quran reciters or made their mark in both disciplines.[98]

Although Muslims are usually careful not to refer to Quran recitation as music (*ġīnā'* or *mūsīqā*), or to the reciter (*muqri', qāri'* or *tālī*) as a singer (*muġannī*), in order to avoid implying any equivalence between the holy scripture and songs created by humans, theologians nonetheless call for a strong melodic component in recitation, not merely for populist reasons, as Islam scholars and Muslims in general often assume, but for the sake of the ideal recitation as it is conceived in the countless treatises on *tajwīd* and *ādāb at-tilāwa*. Consequently, musical quality is one of the evaluation criteria of the various institutions concerned with training, examining and honouring reciters.[99] Reciters and their listeners also use terminology that is largely congruent with that of music.[100] An anecdote that Ibn ʿAbd Rabbih recounts from the early years of Islam may illustrate how ambivalent the relation between Quran recitation and music has always been. A man is arrested for having allegedly sung loudly in a mosque, an offence against public morals. Fortunately, a Quraysh gentleman who had been praying in the mosque hurries to the police and testifies that the accused did nothing but recite the Quran. The misunderstanding is cleared up and the prisoner released. Outside on the street, the gentleman says to the offender, 'If you hadn't sung so well, I wouldn't have defended you.'[101]

The ambivalence also affects the reception of Quran recitation. In many cases, the recipient's outward behaviour is the same as that of the audience at a musical performance, even if that runs counter to the theological requirements for the practice of recitation. Kristina Nelson writes:

> The dichotomy of the perception of Qur'anic recitation as a unique art and response to it as music could perhaps be more easily explained if the two operated in mutually exclusive arenas. For example, it would be clear enough if we could identify those who respond to Qur'anic recitation as music as those who are unaware of the nature of the text or those unequivocably seeking only aesthetic stimulation. But even Muslims who insist that Qur'anic recitation is not music and who participate in recitation with correct appreciation and sincere intent are also able to regard it as the highest example of vocal improvisation in the Arabic music tradition and may often find themselves responding to it as they would to music.[102]

In a country such as Egypt, a Quran recitation by a well-known singer is not just a religious event. It is one of the major artistic events of traditional Arab societies and is attended by Christians and Muslims, aesthetes and devotees. The best singers appear in international competitions that are broadcast live and are honoured throughout the country, as the following press release from the 1930s about the famous Quran singer Sheikh Muḥammad Rifʿat illustrates:

> No sooner has the clock reached nine in the evening on any Friday or Tuesday than the mosques are packed full of visitors, and people at home or in the streets gather around the wireless. Everyone pricks up their ears in humble anticipation to hear the recitation of the noble Quran by the ingenious reciter Muḥammad ar-Rifʿat.[103]

Labīb as-Saʿīd, who quotes this account in his book *Singing the Quran*, also mentions an occurrence from the 1960s which seems revealing and at the same time disconcerting: four people were killed and dozens injured in a fight in Cairo's al-Maḏbaḥ district after the supporters of a certain Quran reciter made disparaging comments about the quality of another reciter. Of course, the author notes, that is not appropriate behaviour for the audience of a Quran recitation,[104] but it indicates how popular such events still are in modern times. In a Western context we would find nothing comparable in churches or in traditional concert halls. The passion of pop fans might reach similar levels. The answers of Egyptian cab drivers never failed to amaze me when I asked them why, when caught in a traffic jam in scorching heat, they put on a cassette of Quran recitations. The reasons they give are not the uplifting words or the depth of their meaning, or even the listener's devotion. Rather, the answer I heard again and again was, 'It's so beautiful (*gamīl giddan*)!'

We could offer numerous examples illustrating how Quran recitations are received in a way that is situated outside the predominantly religious sphere, and would have to be called artistic in many respects, from the listeners' reactions – including shouts, hand-clapping and sighs of delight – which are sometimes indistinguishable from those of a concert audience, to the star cult that fan communities, tabloids and music periodicals produce around certain reciters, the fuss made about spectacular appearances and important new publications, to the numerous regularly held *nadwa*s, at which the adherents of this art meet in private to listen jointly to new and old recordings of Quran recitations and discuss their musical aspects. It is apparent from certain traditions, and especially from the polemics against the *qirā'a bi-l-alḥān*, that this tendency was already rife in the early history of Islam. Sālim al-Bayḏaq, a contemporary of the Prophet who had come to Medina to pray, had only two words to say about a reciter who had been highly recommended to him: 'Singing, singing (*ġinā', ġinā'*)!' Ibn al-Jawzī (d. 1200) expressed a prototypical indignation about those who 'recite the Quran with melodies (*alḥān*), overstepping the bounds of custom, for they have made song (*ġinā'*) out of it'.[105] The conservative Hanbali legal scholar from Baghdad quotes his predecessor, Ibn ʿAqīl (d. 1119):

> Know: to leave the state of sobriety and enter the state of sensual rapture (*ṭarab*) and intoxication is a temptation for those whose natural urges have gained the upper hand over their power of reasoning. Reality can only be apprehended through the intellect and in a state of sobriety not impaired by ecstasy.[106]

To Ibn al-Jawzī, a permissible reception of the Quran is no longer possible when the sensory or emotional – in a general sense one might say aesthetic – functions of the transmitted signs impair the receiver's intellectual understanding of the message. The term *ṭarab* denotes the aesthetic enjoyment that the perception of sensual phenomena produces, in particular hearing sounds, music, or the recitation of poetry or the Quran. The theologian rejects this enjoyment if it causes other functions of the linguistic signs besides the informative function to be dominant. Where the limit lies – What aesthetic forms are permissible? When does the recitation become a primarily artistic event? – is at the centre of most discussions about the legitimacy of musical Quran recitation. This question is addressed in one way or another in all textbooks on the proper comportment of the reciter and his listeners. Such texts emphasize constantly that understanding and reflecting (*tadabbur*) on the content, and conducting oneself in keeping with the Quran, take priority over the recitation and the pleasure that it may offer.[107] That means the boundary between 'right' and 'wrong' reception is drawn exactly where the aesthetic function of the recited text, its poeticity, begins to dominate – that is, exactly where Jakobson marks the beginning of the sphere of poetry or art in general.[108] The complaint of Muḥammad ʿAbduh (d. 1905) makes plain that this boundary is often overstepped in the modern era as well: 'What kind of behaviour (*adab*) is that which most people display?' the Egyptian reformer asks, and goes on to disparage the fact that the listeners at Quran recitations could not properly listen for all their noise and cries.

> And those who do listen carefully delight in the voice and take pleasure in the melodies of the reciter. When the listeners praise and commend the recitation, they say the same things they say about a singing performance (*majlis al-ġinā'*); the recitation stimulates them in the same way and elicits the same sounds from them as they make when listening to singing, and of the meanings of the Quran they perceive only what they deem suitable as a pretext for their enjoyment, as in the story of Joseph, peace be with him, and they do not heed the admonition and inspiration to noble aims, especially to decency and faith.[109]

Labīb as-Sa'īd describes the issue in more neutral terms: 'Among the unmistakable facts, which we will here neither approve nor critically discuss but only record, is the fact that the people are more strongly moved by the melody than by the meanings of the Quran.'[110] The discussion that still goes on today about the admissibility of *mujawwad* recitation, the melodic singing of the Quran, likewise hinges on the different importance attached to the aesthetic function of the linguistic signs. According to Andreas Kellermann, who wrote a musicological dissertation on Quran recitation:

> The more the reader exceeds the at least relatively redundant use of melody as an 'embellishment' (*tazyīn*) in his *maqām* improvisation, the greater the internal aesthetic tension in the melodic development, and the more the recited text, as an aesthetically defined unit of different dimensions of complexity, threatens to lose its balance in favour of this dimension.[111]

In such discussions, it is practically never disputed that the Quran can and should be recited melodically and in a beautiful voice. The scholars' criterion for the admissibility of a singing recitation has always been the observance of the *tajwīd* rules, which ensure that the text is intelligibly and distinctly articulated, and not the excessive musicality of the reading. The criticism that has been and continues to be directed at certain forms of Quran recitation concerns mainly faults in articulation, which impair the communication of the message. Such faults include the incorrect application of the rules governing the partial or total assimilation of nasals with consonants that follow them, the particular *tarqīq* and *tafkhīm* pronunciations of the letter *rā'* (a rolled, pharyngeal /r/) and, perennially, the excessive lengthening of the long vowels where it is not called for.[112] When such deficiencies are so great that 'the meanings become unintelligible, then the recitation is prohibited by unanimous doctrine', says the Maliki exegete

Abū ʿAbdillāh Muḥammad al-Qurṭubī (d. 1272).[113] Scholars have seldom rejected the melodic presentation of the text, even in the polemics against the medieval *qirāʾa bi-l-alḥān*. As-Saʿīd sums up these rare cases as follows: 'The majority of those who have disapproved of Quran singing or declared it forbidden did not deny nor contest the obvious fact that the Muslims have always considered singing the Quran and delighting in it acceptable, and that they are by nature disposed to respond to it.'[114] The Muslims, or at least most of those who attend Quran recitals in the *mujawwad* style, are generally well aware of the necessary and desirable musicality of recitation and see it as grounded in the Quran itself. Ṣādiq ar-Rāfiʿī finds the text 'almost pure music, in the order and the interaction of the letter tones and the harmony between the character of the meaning and the character of the sound'.[115] Abū Zahra cites the sonorous properties of the Quran as an explanation of its effect on non-Arabs,[116] Adonis calls the Quran a 'melody whose harmonies are not limited by any particular arrangement or fixed metrical system',[117] and as-Saʿīd includes its musicality in the evidence of its miraculous nature,[118] saying anyone who recites it knows it is musical.[119] Egyptian reciters have confirmed this attitude in interviews with Kristina Nelson: Sheikh Hāshim Hayba, for example, says, 'Recitation is a matter of melodies and their ordering'; Sheikh ash-Shaʿshāʿī maintains that 'music is necessary, as long as *tajwīd* is the basis'; and Sheikh Muṣṭafa Ismāʿīl, who died in 1978, said quite distinctly that 'the art of recitation is *mūsīqā*, and the better one can use the *maqāmāt*, the more effective the recitation.'[120] Nelson also quotes an article on musical Quran recitation from an Egyptian music periodical:

> How many eyes have filled with tears and how many hearts with awe and apprehension when the Qur'an flowed over these hearts...from whence does the Qur'an derive this magic which dazzles the mind and shakes the heart? From its phrases? its meanings? from both?...the nerve which touches it all...is the apparent and hidden music in the verses of the Qur'an.[121]

In such remarks, and of course in the recitations themselves, the musical component is accorded greater importance for the realization of the text than is usually observed in the regard to works of classical Arabic poetry: these are also recited, but not with anything like the same rhythmic and harmonic complexity. When they are performed as song lyrics, they are presented not solo but with instrumental accompaniment; when they are improvised, they are still sung to previously composed music. Labīb as-Saʿīd justifies his rejection of instrumentation and composition for Quran recitation by citing the supernatural musicality of the sacred text: unlike human poetry and the scriptures of other religions, it makes musical art superfluous.[122] The Quran reciter Sheikh Ruzayqī argues similarly, rejecting recitation to composed tunes 'because the Qur'an has its own mūsīqā, and you cannot clothe the Qur'an in any other mūsīqā.'[123] Those modern poets who, like Yeats and Hesse, have sworn by the musicality of poetry have invoked the same logic in defending their reservations against setting poetry to music. A poem that needs a tune to be effective is not worth much, Hesse says: 'the more individual and nuanced a poem is, the more it resists the composer.'[124]

The Text as a Musical Score

A text which exists primarily for recitation, which is so obviously composed to be recited and can only be actualized in keeping with its own poetics when it is recited or, in more general terms, performed – such a text can better be compared with a musical score, as Paul Valéry once proposed for poetry, than with a work of literature.[125] A musical score can also be read alone at home, silently or humming quietly. But listening in a concert hall is the form of reception for which it was made. The Quran is similar. A believer does not always have the opportunity to listen to the Quran recited publicly by a trained reciter, and even in Muhammad's day people surely read it or recited it without intonation in private, in nocturnal worship services among close relatives, as related in the tradition of ʿUmar's conversion, or in ritual prayer, *ṣalāt*. But even individual reading, at least in a traditional Arabic context, is coloured by the believer's memory of prior experiences of listening to recitations at school, in the mosque or at religious celebrations, just as an opera lover cannot pick up the score of Pamina's G-minor aria from *The Magic Flute* without recalling the music, and possibly its interpretation by a certain singer (the quranic word for a recollection of that kind is *ḏikr*), without hearing in his or her mind the diminished seventh chord of 'Fühlst du nicht der Liebe Sehnen' ('If you do not feel the longing of love') that, desperate and exhausted, is resolved in the four-bar orchestral coda – 'so wird Ruh' im Tode sein' ('I will find peace in death').[126] And just as the aria was created for the concert hall, the Quran, other possible forms of reception notwithstanding, was created primarily as a liturgical discourse for an audience that initially was not limited to the faithful, with one person reciting and others listening. One might almost think Valéry had the Quran in mind when he said,

> To speak of a poem in itself, judge a poem in itself, has no real and precise meaning. It is to speak of a potentiality. The poem is an abstraction, a piece of writing that stands waiting, a law that lives only in some human mouth, and that mouth is simply a mouth.[127]

'...cette bouche est ce qu'elle est', said Valéry. The inevitable consequence of the Quran's recitative character is that we can never receive the text in itself, but only a person's musical *and* thematic interpretation – the two are inseparable – even if the reciter and the listener are the same person.

This aesthetic implication is accompanied by a theological one which was controversial when the revelation began but has been progressively defused by later generations of scholars: the Quran has its existence not in the state of written or printed words but only in recitation – and thus only in the present moment. 'The Quran is a recorded scripture between the covers of a book; it does not speak', Imam ʿAlī is supposed to have said. 'It is the people who speak through it.'[128] The statement can be applied to the *tafsīr*, the exegesis of the Quran, as well as to *qirāʾa*, its recitation. Only the recipient as interpreter and reciter (and the first such person was Muhammad himself at the moment of revelation) brings the Quran to its present existence and 'frees the text from the material of the words', to use an expression by Hans Robert Jauss.[129] The operation Jauss mentions may refer generally to any perception of a poetic or religious text. Yet, in the case of the Quran, the nature of reception as an occurrence in the present moment is more than just an inevitability: by defining the mode of its reception as listening to recitation, the text itself suggests and emphasizes the nature of its actualization as an event. The text *is* when it is recited – and that means it is when *a person* recites it. Every reading is a unique event, developing through improvisation, nourished by interaction with the listeners; it is not repeatable nor does it aspire to repeat the details of a prior reading. The reciter is free to use stylistic devices including melodic lines, establishing and in certain situations shifting between rhythmic patterns, repeating specific text passages, and even choosing among different traditional wordings.[130] The reciter is thus accorded a significant role in the actualization of the text – a role that is greater the farther back we go in Islamic history. The first manuscripts, written under the Prophet's personal supervision, were hardly more than a 'graphic outline', without vowel signs and without the consonant pointing considered indispensable today. In that form, most letter sequences were capable of multiple readings, so that only interpretation and oral tradition made the text understandable.[131] Muhammad himself is said to have read the same verses differently on different occasions.[132] A Muslim scholar would not go so far as to regard the Quran, in Angelika Neuwirth's words, as the '"overheard" discourse of Muhammad speaking to his listeners, reacting to those listeners and ritually communicating together with those listeners'.[133] But some currents of Muslim theology certainly have recognized that the Quran owes its form to a dialogue situation, with listeners reacting to the recitation and evoking reactions in turn on the part of the reciter.[134] The inevitable emergence of numerous variant texts cannot be explained, as Nöldeke and his colleagues suggest, simply as the result of the Prophet's poor memory;[135] they are not 'corruptions' of an initially unambiguous original. They are the results of a history of reception in which the Quran has been perceived primarily as an oral text, and the *qāriʾ*, like the *rāwī* of ancient Arabic poetry before him or the rhapsode and the troubadour in other societies, is not the mere 'reader' of a work whose every detail was fixed in writing, but the virtuoso interpreter of an orally created, orally transmitted and orally performed text. A hadith alludes to this situation as follows: 'The Quran is something singular, sent down by Someone singular, but the variation (*ikhtilāf*) is due to the transmitter (*ruwāt*).'[136] In such a context, the demand for a definitive text version, something taken for granted in today's world of high print runs and general availability of written media, is inconceivable in an essentially orally oriented culture.[137] In an oral culture, the recitation's nature as a momentary event and the reciter's ability to improvise on the verses, which are preserved primarily in memory, are as self-evident as our ability in our culture to push the same DVD or the same CD into the recorder or player several times. The codification of the scattered Quran manuscripts under ʿUthmān did not serve to determine the unique, unequivocal wording of the revelation but only established – for admittedly pragmatic reasons, in view of an increasing number of different, significantly diverging manuscripts and versions – the written text for practical use, the *muṣḥaf*. The purpose of the Uthmanic recension is quite clearly exposed in a parable cited by Ibn Qayyim al-Jawzīya:

> It was as if the inhabitants of a house had been faced with different paths to get to the house, and there was dissension and confusion among them about which path to take, which was to the advantage of their enemy. In this situation, their leader decided to permit only one path and abandon the others. He did not abolish the other paths: they still led to the house. He only forbade their use in the interest of the community.[138]

The Uthmanic codex (*rasm*) is not a definitive, much less a divinely authorized version of the text: the editors who produced it, unlike the Greek translators of the original biblical text, for example, are not considered to have been divinely inspired. The Muslim tradition contains multiple reports of the Muslims' debates over the correct wording of specific passages during the compilation of the written codex, arising from differences of opinion or from divergent transcriptions. Each such dispute was decided in favour of the oral tradition that was deemed most reliable,[139] yet those decisions were not clothed in any doctrine of infallibility, neither at the time nor since. And what the recension yielded was a framework rather than the content of a recitation: it did not obviate the need for the orally transmitted knowledge of a *qāri'*. Because it was produced before the development of Arabic orthography, it contained no vocalization or consonant pointing, so that even the authoritative codex, once it existed, was not sufficient to know how to read the text.[140] As a result, different readings continued to exist concurrently. Furthermore, the codification did not lead to a uniform Quran text. Other recensions – primarily that of Ibn Masʿūd – were still in circulation, and individual readers were self-assured enough to deviate intentionally even from the Uthmanic codex where they felt it appropriate to do so.[141] Goldziher goes so far as to conclude that the sacred text was established 'in an atmosphere that spanned from liberalism to individualism'.[142] The 'tendency to dogmatic uniformity' was foreign to the early Muslims; only later did a 'strictly defined dogmatics and the appearance of some kind of regular pattern' come to the fore.[143] The Orientalist betrays amazement as he notes the persistence of other variant texts alongside the *textus receptus*, which was itself ambiguous and read in various ways:

> The presumed original text which – more so than the divine scriptures of other religions – purports to represent literally in each and every word – and even in every letter – the *kalām Allāh*, the Word of God, the real text of which has been recorded for time immemorial on the *law mahfūz*, the Well-guarded Table, whence it was orally revealed to the chosen prophet by the angel Gabriel. From the earliest time of Islam, this text displays a large number of *variae lectiones* of sound tradition which cannot always be dismissed as being negligible.[144]

In a culture of orally recited texts and in a society in which the spoken word, in spite of the progressive spread of writing, was still the chief mode of transmission, because of the prevailing infrastructure if for no other reason, the existence of variant readings is not surprising. What should be surprising to our more philologically oriented present-day understanding of the text is the fact that the de facto textual plurality was subsequently sanctioned by theology as a grace. As Goldziher states: 'Contrary to what might be expected in the case of a divine text which can claim divine authenticity only in one form – uniform and generally accepted – such variant readings are not eliminated to favour the one and only divinely decreed version. In such a case, the authenticity and the divine origin of the variants are admitted side by side.'[145] Although from the late eighth century on, if not earlier, the variant readings were addressed as a problem again and again, and became the subject of a whole branch of quranic research called *qirā'āt*,[146] Ibn Mujāhid (d. 936) and his successors still saw it as their responsibility, not to arrive at a uniform text, but to prevent excessively eccentric readings: to separate the wheat from the chaff and choose those readings that approximated the presumed original, the celestial recitation, as closely as humanly possible. The seven, or by other accounts eight, ten or fourteen, readings established by the scholars of *'ilm al-qirā'āt* are not, as they might appear in retrospect, a *textus receptus* and its variant readings but equally valid *variae lectiones*: if any of them is considered a *textus receptus*, then they all must be. At least in the formative period of Islam, educated Muslims who were called upon to choose (*ikhtiyār*) among the traditional textual variants of a given Quran passage, or even, like aṭ-Ṭabarī (d. 923) as late as the tenth century, to arrive at a single text, were 'brought up to a surprisingly productive freedom in dealing with his holy scripture', as Angelika Neuwirth remarks.[147] The attitude of tolerance to variations is supported by hadith such as the following:

'Umar ibn al-Khaṭṭāb said, 'I heard Hishām ibn Ḥakim ibn Ḥizām recite the surah *al-Furqān* [no. 25] differently than the Messenger of God taught me it. I wanted to scold him, but I waited until he had recited it to the end. Then I caught him by the throat and took him to the Messenger of God, and said, "O Messenger of God, I heard this man recite the Surah *al-Furqān* differently than you taught me it."

'The Messenger of God told me to let go of him, and asked him to recite. So he recited the Quran, just as I had heard him do. The Messenger of God said, "That is how it was sent down." Then he told me to recite, and I recited it. He said, "That is how it was sent down. The Quran was sent down in seven readings (*aḥruf*). So recite it as it is easiest for you." '[148]

Ubayy ibn Kaʿb is said to have had a similar experience when he met two Muslims in the mosque who recited the Quran differently from each other, and differently than he was accustomed to do. He led both of them to the Prophet, who listened to them recite and then approved both of their recitations, although they were different from each other and although they deviated from the reading of the famous Quran reciter Ubayy. Ubayy was unsettled, possibly fearing damage to his reputation, but Muhammad allayed his fears by telling him how the seven *aḥruf* were sent down. Afterwards, the angel Gabriel had given him God's commandment to recite the Quran only in one way (*ʿalā ḥarfin*). Apologizing, Muhammad is said to have explained to Gabriel that his people were unable to recite the Quran in only one way, and asked him whether he could ask God to ease the restriction. The next time Gabriel appeared to the Prophet, he brought him God's commandment to recite the Quran in two ways. Again Muhammad apologized, said it would by difficult for the people to obey, and asked Gabriel to petition God for an easier commandment. This process was repeated as Gabriel appeared to the Prophet a third and a fourth time, but Muhammad thought limiting the people to three or four ways of recitation was expecting too much. Finally Gabriel returned and said, 'God has commanded you to recite the Quran in seven ways. Whichever way they read it is correct.'[149] The number seven is of course not meant literally – that is, as yet another limitation on the number of readings – but in its sense as a symbol for infinity, as Ibn al-Jazarī, Abū Bakr ibn al-ʿArabī (d. about 1151), as-Suyūṭī and other Quran scholars have emphasized.[150]

The hadith appears to contradict the whole concept of an authoritative revealed scripture. It almost reminds us of modern compositions by Stockhausen or Boulez that leave it up to the interpreter not only to follow the composer's instructions more or less strictly, as in traditional music, but also to choose between various ways of structuring the piece. The analogy is flawed, of course. Whereas the openness of the artistic message and the performance character of the concert are explicit objectives of the New Music creators, they are only implicit in the hadiths and in the concept of text that they express. Nonetheless, the hadiths manifest a fundamentally aesthetic approach to the revealed text – not because they conceive the Quran as a work of art or praise its beauty, but because they recognize that the communication between God and Man that occurs in the recitation has the essential nature of an event.

Unlike a textbook, an ideological manifesto or a law, the Quran does not exist in a definite form independently of the people who read it. Like a musical composition or a poem, it must be recited (even if silently, as in *ḏikr* or *ṣalāt*), it must transpire, in order to exist for its recipient. And no two actualizations can be the same, because each one is evoked only by the interpretative act of a reciter and transpires only in the mind of the recipient. Such a concept of text is of course irritating to the adherents of literal faith and of orthodoxy – any orthodoxy: which of the possible 'letters' should they cling to?

The numerous scholars who have fervently tried to defuse the hadiths with harmless interpretations have involuntarily underscored the fact that the ideas in them are theologically hard to swallow. Their chief strategy has been to trace all readings back to the Prophet, thus eliminating human production. Muḥammad ibn Aḥmad ibn Ḥibbān al-Bustī (d. 965) alone was able to list some forty different attempts to explain the seven *aḥruf*. A popular solution was to interpret the seven *aḥruf* as referring to the various Arabic dialects in which the Quran was supposedly revealed; however, ʿAbdulḥaqq ibn ʿAṭīya (d. 1151) and as-Suyūṭī rejected this interpretation, pointing out that ʿUmar and Hishām were both Quraysh – that is, they spoke the same dialect – so that the interpretation was hardly applicable to the hadith cited. Other scholars explained that the seven *aḥruf* referred to the seven languages from which words occur in the Quran, or to its seven senses (one outer and six inner senses), or to the seven objects in the Quran (namely narrative, commandment, prohibition, etc.), or the readings of the seven later readers, and so on.[151] None of these attempts to reduce the hadiths to banalities is any more satisfying than the Orientalists' response of shrugging their shoulders. The authors of the *History of the Qur'ān*, the most important Western book on the readings to date, had no difficulty listing reasons why the different text variants existed – 'All such variations, which we can easily explain, caused great troubles for Muslims'[152] – but they had nothing to say on the question why they were tolerated, which is the more important one for the history of ideas. The hadiths of the seven *aḥruf* contain a more fundamental and profound statement than their minimizing interpreters pretend, even if the doctrine's meaning exceeds the intentions of its anonymous 'author', or of Muhammad himself if it originated with him: such traditions must be understood as the expression, not the cause, of the conception of the text that they illustrate. Muhammad's preaching was documented in the original, and the differences between the individual versions were not so momentous (to Sunnis) that they would have made subsequent agreement on a uniform *textus receptus* impossible. But no such consensus was reached. Even if one were to go so far as to claim that practical considerations were the reason why no single reading prevailed – there was no way to enforce compliance – the fact remains that no proposal was ever made to agree on a uniform, definitive version of the text's wording. The theologians' reticence to restrict Muslims' freedom to choose a textual reading of the Quran is a phenomenon that Goldziher calls 'a puzzling perplexity'.[153] The conception of a text with parallel, equally valid wordings is rooted in the text itself. As a transcription of the poetically structured, orally revealed word of God, the Quran had the inherent potential for the formation, over the course of its reception history, of a *modus procedendi* in regard to the canonical wording of the text that Angelika Neuwirth describes as follows:

> Ultimately we must understand that Islam, in its classical period, found a wise and elegant solution to the problem of the textual uniformity of a holy scripture which confronts all scriptural religions – a solution that combines tolerance towards the elusiveness of an absolutely unified text with the legitimate need for unity of the cult, and that at an admirably high level of linguistic culture.[154]

Seen in the light of the quranic concept of revelation, which in an elementary sense is a communication between God as the sender and humanity as recipients, with Gabriel and Muhammad as mediators, the notion of the seven *aḥruf* seems to attest to a fundamental knowledge that the divine Word in human hands is necessarily relative. From the moment God had Gabriel recite the revelation to the Prophet, each successive actualization of the Quran is produced by humans; yet this is seen not as a shortcoming but as the revelation's essence as a 'sending down', as an event which joins the divine with the human. In every recitation, the divinity of the sender is joined anew with the humanity of the recipient. Because people are different, so are the recitations, the 'Qurans' – to use a plural that of course must not exist in Arabic; let us say, the *qirā'āt* are different. In this conception, the perfect recitation is reserved to God, and only it, the unattainable celestial recitation, is ultimately authoritative. Because a human reading cannot claim general validity, it is theologically imperative to accept different readings (and, in the melodic dimension, different recitative styles) as equally valid. This view resolves the paradox and allows us to understand that, precisely because the presumed original text is held to be the Word of God in the strictest sense, no human being can claim to place a definitive restriction on the de facto openness of the memorized and transcribed version.

In view of the foregoing, the history of the Quran's reception can also be seen as a history of its restriction and reification, a normal process in religious history and psychology: people need something they can hold on to, both in the material and in the figurative sense. It becomes apparent that the Quran, as important as the aesthetic function is in its reception, is perceived not as a work of art but as the definitive and normative Word of God; and, hence, that the propensity to determine the indeterminate, so as to possess something fixed and clearly outlined as an orientation in ritual, faith and life, manifests itself in a way that occurs only in relation to texts that are conceived as sacred. What distinguishes a religious message from an artistic one is not so much its form, and not necessarily the intention, but the degree of normativity and sanctity that the sender (or promulgator) or the receiver attaches to it.

Restriction and Reification

The Uthmanic *rasm* was a restriction that was seen in its day as necessary in view of a proliferating pluralism of recitations. 'The Quran was many books (*kutub*); you have forsaken them all except one', ʿUthmān's critics complained.[155] The tradition says in his defence, 'If ʿUthmān had not had the Quran written down, we would have found the people reciting poetry [when in reality they were reciting the Quran]'[156] – that is, the people would have improvised on the Quran with the same freedom that the poets and rhapsodes exercised in regard to poetry. Before the publication of the *rasm*, there were a number of Quran readers who felt it was permissible and appropriate to treat the text quite liberally in public recitation, as readers of poetry did, remaining faithful only to its argument (*riwāya bi-l-maʿnā*). 'What was not only tolerated, but normal and to a certain extent even welcome in ancient Arabic poetry, the diverse, variable nature of the text of a poem', Gregor Schoeler explains, 'had to be scandalous sooner or later in regard to the revealed Word of God. The disputes that then erupted over the correct text of the holy scripture threatened the very unity of Islam.'[157] In view of such concerns, the attempts to attach harmless explanations to the traditions of the seven *aḥruf* appear understandable and the establishment of the written text inevitable. While the *rasm* requires interpretation by Quran readers, it is at the same time a first check on their oral traditions. This was the beginning of the end of the 'very great freedom',[158] as Edmund Beck called it, that the Quran reciter of pre-Uthmanic times enjoyed – like that of the rhapsode reciting a poem.

In the centuries that followed, unification proceeded on three levels.[159] The first objective was to eliminate other textual variants and impose the Uthmanic codex everywhere as an authoritative basis for recitation. This alone took until the eighth century, and it was not until the ninth century that the legal scholars reached agreement on the ritual unsuitability of the non-Uthmanic text variants. At the same time, however, the techniques of script were refined so that, by the tenth century, a text could be transcribed unambiguously. And the restrictions on the Quran reader's and teacher's interpretative freedom continued to increase. Where the codex had allowed him to determine the values of ambiguous consonants (*ikhtiyār bi-l-ḥurūf*) and the vocalization (*ikhtiyār bi-l-qirāʾa*), which were not originally fixed in Arabic script, several firm criteria soon evolved (most importantly, the criterion of grammatical accuracy and the principles of majority and tradition) which led to Ibn Mujāhid's establishment in the tenth century of seven equally valid versions of the text. This restriction made it inadmissible to combine parts of different readings, so that the reader could no longer arrive at an individual reading while observing the criteria. Ibn al-Jazarī expanded this system to ten *qirā'āt*. For each of the ten text versions, there are two *riwāyāt* (transmissions) and numerous sub-transmissions (*ṭuruq*, literally, 'ways') that fix details of prosody and phonetics. Thus there are 126 transmissions of the reading of Dūrī ʿan Abī ʿAmr alone and eighty-three of Qālūn ʿan Nāfiʿ's reading. In addition to the ten canonical readings, four more which do not conform to the criteria were established but excluded from the practice of Quran reading. They are used only in the Muslim secondary literature. The seven or ten *qirā'āt*, on the other hand, are mastered by professional readers even today, and sometimes used in recitation. On occasion they are even combined, in a technique called *jamʿ*.[160] Day-to-day practice almost always uses only one version, however – most often that of Ḥafṣ ʿan ʿÂṣim; in some regions, especially in the West, that of Warsh ʿan Nāfiʿ. It also happens that less knowledgeable listeners, when exposed to recitation of a different reading than the one with which they are familiar, mistake it for a faulty recitation.[161] Moreover, variations and mistakes due to typographical and transmission errors that were still in circulation up to the beginning of the twentieth century have since been eradicated by the 'official Quran' published in Cairo – a meticulously edited authoritative version which nearly all later printed editions have followed. Because its reading markings follow the Hafṣ ʿan ʿÂṣim recension, which was dominant in Egypt, this has become a de facto *primus inter pares*, and, although the recognized readings are still equally valid in theory, many Muslims today consider the Cairene edition the definitive text of the Quran.

Concurrently with this process of unification and restriction of the textual variants and readings, we can also observe an increase in the importance of the *muṣḥaf*, the written Quran, during the Quran's reception history.[162] Very early on, the written text acquired a status that is not supported by quranic statements: this is manifested in the events in the year 657 at the Battle of Ṣiffīn, where the militarily outmatched Muʿāwiya stuck leaves with passages of the Quran written on them on their spearheads to deter the caliph ʿAlī ibn Abī Ṭālib from attacking. The ploy was successful, with far-reaching consequences for the further history of Islam.[163] In the aesthetic sphere, the turn towards the written text was also manifested in the rise of calligraphy and the fine arts that developed from it. In popular devotion, the veneration of a *muṣḥaf* often takes on a fetishistic character, and *baraka*, magical forces, are attributed to it.[164] The statement in the Quran that only the pure were permitted to touch it,[165] which in the text clearly refers to the celestial original, was soon adapted to the material copy, which the devout touch only when in the state of ritual purity.[166] In consequence, some tried to prevent non-believers from touching the Quran and admonished travellers and soldiers not to take it along to foreign countries.[167] Even today, it is seen in devout circles as a sacrilege to give 'copies of the Qur'aan to *kuffaar* who are perpetually in the state of *hadth* and *janaabat* [minor and major impurity]'.[168] In general practice, a copy of the Quran must be carefully wrapped, kissed before and after each reading, and stored higher than all other books. Especially devout Muslims show further signs of respect. Ibn Fūrak (d. 1015) is said never to have slept in a house where there was a copy of the Quran.[169] Such veneration has been and continues to be criticized from various quarters, however. In modern Egypt, both Labīb as-Sa'īd and Naṣr Ḥāmid Abū Zayd, one a representative of orthodoxy and the other a reformist thinker condemned as a heretic, have been prominent exponents of the oral nature of the Quran. As-Sa'īd bemoans the decline of the art of Quran reading, the neglect of the variant readings and the decline in the numbers of people who know the whole Quran by heart, which leads to an endangerment of the *tawātur*, the system of oral transmission of the Quran, and to a dependency on the material, written text.[170] Abū Zayd denounces the iconic status given to the *muṣḥaf*[171] and the reification of the Quran (*tashyī'uhū*) as an 'ornament to women and a magical object to children'.[172] Criticism of this sort almost seems to confirm Plato's warning against the dangers of writing – that it weakens memory and, in contrast to spoken language, communicates only the illusion of knowledge; that it does not engender new insight, but only recalls what a person already knows and has already experienced.[173]

One manifestation of the contemporary tendency to project the existence of a book onto the early period of Islam is the tendency in modern biographies and – as I personally experienced – in popular Quran lessons to represent the Prophet's famous first experience of revelation as the reading of a written page or tablet, even though the Muslim sources (such as Ibn Hishām, Ibn Kathīr, al-Bukhārī [d. 870], aṭ-Ṭabarī, and also az-Zarkashī and as-Suyūṭī) unanimously mention a simple repetition of a text spoken by an angel.[174] The earliest versions do not mention anything like a written text;[175] in others, Gabriel carries a silk cloth with something written on it but does not read it: he recites something that the Prophet retains in his heart as a revelation.[176] Muhammad's cry to the angel in this second version, *mā aqra'*, which could mean either 'What shall I recite?' or 'I do not recite', is reinterpreted in many later accounts as the statement 'I cannot read'.[177] In this interpretation, the miraculous part of the story is that the illiterate Muhammad under divine influence was suddenly able to read. The sources say no such thing.

All of these indications of a 'scripturalization' of Islam[178] must not obscure the fact that the Quran in an Arabic context is still conceived as a primarily oral text, and the necessity of reciting it is, at least theoretically, undisputed. In the communication between the reciter and the listener, the recitative character of the Quran is much more important than the textual variability (which has great symbolic importance but few consequences in practice) because it implies a freedom of artistic style for the reciter. The reciter's freedom is in fact a requirement, since there are no specifications in regard to the scope of a recitation, phrasing or melodic lines. The recitative character of the text is responsible more than anything else for the reception of the Quran as a unique event. *Taqlīd*, the imitation of another person's or of one's own previous recitation, is explicitly rejected.[179] When the celebrated Egyptian singer ʿAbdulwahhāb, who also attained fame as a Quran reciter, announced his intention to transcribe the melody of a recitation, the reaction was so vehement that he was forced to apologize. The thrust of the criticism was that no man might fix in writing what God has left undetermined.[180] The principle of melodic variability has brought about the development of regional recitation styles, corresponding to the regionally varying tonal systems and musical traditions. Outside the sphere of influence of Arab-Persian art music, in Senegal and southern Morocco, for example, forms of melodic recitation have arisen that are tonally patterned after the regional musical cultures;[181] Henry George Farmer once wrote, without exaggerating too much, that one could hear the Quran recited, from the coast of Morocco to the borders of Turkistan, in as many different ways as there are mosques.[182] And the musicologist Andreas Kellermann, who stresses the *performance* character of Quran reading events, writes about the absence of melodic rules:

> Especially in this regard, every act of recitation is dependent on the given context, occasion and moment, on the reader (his background, training and abilities) and his listeners. As a result, Quran recitation has a very great degree of individual and regional variability on this level in particular, which fulfils an important function if we regard the acoustic result, from the point of view of information theory, as an 'artistic text'. Leaving aside the possibility of reproducing a given reading identically by means of recording media, the quasi-mandatory freedom or 'openness' of the melodic rendition guarantees a comparison of necessarily variant realizations of an invariant text defined by the written codex and by the rules of pronunciation and rhythm determined by *tajwīd* and *uṣūl*.[183]

Kellermann also rightly refers in this connection to Lotman's concept of an 'aesthetics of identity'.[184] What Lotman calls the 'freedom of improvisation' and the fetters of the strictly observed *tajwīd* codex are mutually dependent. If there were only inflexible rules, then every new realization would be a copy of the preceding one and would lose its informational value, which lies precisely in what is new and specific to that realization compared with others, however minimal that may seem. Redundancy would take the place of the discovery of ever new layers of the recited message, which is already familiar from previous reception experiences. Only improvisation creates the entropy that is indispensable for aesthetic communication. Nor is it necessary to compare readings of one and the same passage by different reciters to see the importance of improvisation for the 'performance' of the Quran – that is, the importance of the human contribution. Even one and the same interpreter never reads a text the same way twice; and in any case the reciter generally does not aspire to copy an earlier recitation, since that would violate the imperative of improvisation. Improvisation is grounded in the dynamic relationship between reciter and listener, even more directly than in customary concerts of European music, even jazz. The numerous repetitions of text passages, for example, in ever new melodic variations, presenting the same text from different perspectives and making it different from itself, which in turn increases its information content, are directly influenced by the audience's exclamations and cheers. According to Sheikh Rifʿat, even the tonal mode is chosen in relation to the audience. He feels that each listener has a *maqām* to which he or she is particularly responsive, and he therefore varies the *maqāmāt* to touch as many people as possible with the recitation.[185] Not only is the interaction between the reciter and his audience one of the most imposing elements of a successful Quran recitation – and one that has been extolled by all Western observers – it is also inherent in *mujawwad* or *bi-l-alḥān* recitation, which are only permitted in front of an audience and must not be done in private, even for the purpose of practising. For this reason Bergsträsser called them the concert form of Quran recitation.[186] The term is fitting: when a Quran reader wants to practise melodic recitation, he must use a different text than the Quran.[187]

Today, however, a levelling trend is unmistakable in tonal geography, although it is not as extreme as the restriction of textual variability. As a consequence of the age of technical reproduction, certain forms of Quran recitation are listened to and have become popular throughout the Islamic world. Inevitably, the historically evolved diversity of Quran singing has suffered from this development. In addition to the customary media such as audio recordings and public radio, the ascendancy of the Egyptian and to a lesser degree the Saudi recitation styles is secured through international broadcasting networks, satellite dishes, DVDs and the opportunities presented by modern means of communication and transport.[188] Every year at Ramadan, Egyptian Quran reciters are sent in ever greater numbers to more and more countries to give the major recitations. Conversely, there are more and more opportunities for international students to learn the Egyptian or Saudi recitation styles in the respective country. At the same time, the supervision of recitation and the enforcement of the recitation codex have made such advances that there is no comparison with the situation several decades ago, before telephones, automobiles and television, when the observation of the rules was relatively lax outside the direct sphere of influence of the major centres of Islamic scholarship. This development too has had a levelling effect, which is not necessarily to be welcomed from a theological point of view. Certain contrary trends can be observed as well, however. The rise of the Egyptian style encouraged by authorities and the media in various regions has also stimulated an awareness of the local recitation traditions and raised people's consciousness of their religious, cultural and aesthetic value.[189] In such cases, technology can also support pluralism in recitation precisely by making it possible to document the different traditions and so help to conserve and cultivate them and make them better known.

God Speaks

A quite different effect of technical progress on Quran recitation must also be mentioned: the recordings of well-known reciters such as ʿAbdulbāsiṭ ʿAbduṣṣamad, Maḥmūd Khalīl al-Ḥusarī and Muḥammad Rifʿat, which are sold worldwide today by Arabian, Japanese and European distributors on CD, have not only brought about a unification of aesthetic norms but also – leaving aside live recordings – represent completely new conditions of performance and reception, which were broadly criticized at first. As many scholars asked at the turn of the twentieth century, when the phonograph was introduced: Can the Quran be recited by means of a machine?[190] In the atmosphere of the recording studio, there are no dynamics of recitation, reception and response, which unavoidably leads to a reduction in the improvisational component, as a comparison of Sheikh ʿAbdulbāsiṭ's older live cassettes with his newer studio CDs makes plain.[191] Nonetheless, there is no need to fear that the 'canned' Quran recitations will supplant the concert form. The latter is favoured both by religious authorities and by popular taste. Attendance of a public recitation in a mosque remains the usual mode of Quran reception and is still conceived as the norm. The mass media and recordings tend to increase rather than decrease the popularity of such events. In such a performance context, the principle of melodic variability and the imperative necessity of improvisation are durable guarantees that every Quran recitation must be a new, irreproducible event. The convergence of recitation styles may restrict the freedom of melodic variation, but it does not inhibit the *performance* character, the ambience and reciprocity, of the recitation. Quran recitation thus retains its status as the locus of living communication of the revealed words because it makes possible what no technical apparatus can: to share in an occurrence, to participate in producing it, to celebrate it, to accept the unpredictable conjunction of text, singer and audience, to perceive the slightest nuances in the acoustic message, to surrender oneself to the audible text and follow it in all its subtlest movements, to open oneself to it, respond to it, to hear the echo of one's own reaction to it – in a word: to experience it.

The sacred scriptures of all religions are originally texts for recitation or singing; they were originally heard and not read. This is true of the Torah and the Bible, of the Avesta no less than the books of Mani, and of the Vedas, which for a long time it was sacrilege to write down, still more than of the Quran. William A. Graham, who has written a number of works about the oral character of revealed texts, says, 'It is *written word that is spoken*, because it is (ontologically as well as chronologically) spoken word before it is written.'[192] The modern approach to the Bible, for example, primarily reading it – that is, perceiving it through the eyes and hence the mind – became feasible with the printing revolution, if only because there were not enough copies of the Bible or other texts before that. Even long after Gutenberg, reading usually meant reading *aloud*, in European Christianity as elsewhere. Not until the modern period has the divine word been perceived as printed matter between two book covers, available to anyone at any time for silent reading – and this aspect of religion become a private matter.

Although all holy scriptures are thus primarily texts for recitation, they differ in their recitative character. Revelation – that is, God's revelation of Himself to the world – is an act of communication; in Islam, however, it is a direct linguistic communication. God did not send down a book or inspire people to preach the divine message: He spoke, in clearly understandable human language.[193] In the Muslim concept of revelation, the Quran is the direct speech of God, and the *muṣḥaf* is its transcription. Because the Word as revealed to and promulgated by Muhammad is a recitation, not a book, the oral character of the Quran is fundamental to Islam and prevails in spite of the invention of book printing and CD-ROM publishing.[194]

It has often been remarked in the phenomenology of religion that there is a correspondence, not between Jesus and Muhammad, but between Jesus and the Quran.[195] They are the theological centre of their respective religions because one is the Word of God become flesh, and the other is the Word of God become speech. Christ is the accessible, earthly manifestation of God and humanity's link to Him; no man cometh unto the Father but by Him. In Islam, the scripture has that mediating role, not the Prophet. Muhammad himself said, 'Nothing can bring the servant as near to God as that which comes from Him',[196] and the Muslims understood that he was referring to the Quran.[197] 'Recite the Quran!' says another hadith, 'for on Judgement Day it will be an intercessor (*shafīʿ*) for its people',[198] and no intercessor has 'a higher rank with God than the Quran: no prophet, no angel, no one.'[199] Some went so far as to imagine the Quran as a human being with a heart and a tongue, pleading for the righteous at Judgement Day.[200] The Quran was at the service of the great even in this world: Ibn ʿArabī testifies that the surah *Yāsīn* stood at his sickbed and brought about his cure. And the surah *Fātiḥa* fulfilled every wish of his spiritual mistress in Seville, Fāṭima bint al-Muthannā (d. thirteenth century).[201] The Quran is the 'beloved etiquette (*adab*) of God',[202] 'God's strong rope, His radiant light, the most reliable support (*al-ʿurwa al-wuthqā*) and the perfect sanctuary'.[203] The Quran's precedence 'before all other speech is the precedence of God before His creatures'.[204] Abū Ṭālib al-Makkī (d. 996) explains the statement by the Prophet's contemporary Ibn Masʿūd that those who love the Quran love God, and those who do not love it do not love Him, by saying that, 'if you love one who speaks, you love his word; and, if you hate him, you hate what he says.'[205] Every verse of the Quran, said another companion of the Prophet, ʿAmr ibn al-ʿĀṣ, 'is a step towards Paradise and a light in your houses',[206] and Sahl at-Tustarī (d. 896) teaches, 'Love for God is shown in love for the Quran.'[207] Whereas in Christianity Jesus is worshipped as divine, the Islamic prophet is merely a mouthpiece, the medium through which God speaks to humanity. 'Each letter of the Quran is better than Muhammad and his house', says a hadith (albeit a 'weak' one).[208] It is important for dogma to declare Muhammad incapable of reading and writing in order to exclude the possibility of his corrupting God's word, just as Mary must be 'immaculate' in Christianity in order to give birth to the Son of God.[209] The hadiths rather than the Quran itself should be seen as the Islamic texts that correspond to the Gospels: they are inspired words about God, not by God. In many respects, Muhammad is more comparable with St Paul than with Jesus. If being a Christian means, in a fundamental sense, first and foremost accepting Jesus Christ and imitating him by acts, then Islam means accepting and 'imitating' the Quran (the term used by Muslim scholars, *hikāya*, which I will discuss in a moment, means exactly that).

The phenomenological differences between the two religions are similarly connected with the fact that Christianity's holy night, Christmas, is the celebration of Jesus' birth, while *laylat al-qadr* in Islam is the night in which Muhammad received the first revelation.[210] The evangelist John says of Jesus' *acts*, 'if they should be written every one, I suppose that even the world itself could not contain the books that should be written';[211] and a similar comparison in the Quran says of God's *words*:

> Say: 'If the sea were ink
> for the Words of my Lord,
> the sea would be spent before the Words of my Lord are spent,
> though We brought replenishment the like of it.[212]

The last words of the founder: 'I have left you something that, if you hold it firmly, will never let you err', said the Islamic prophet in the farewell address of his last pilgrimage. 'Clear instruction, God's book and the example (*sunna*) of His prophet.'[213] The example of the Prophet, the sunnah, is a prophetic commentary on the Quran. The Quran is everything – all that matters is the faithful literal reading of the original Quran, the celestial scripture – everything else is exegesis. Jesus' last words, on the other hand, underscore the Passion as the completion of God's work, whether in Matthew's and Mark's version, 'My God, my God, why hast thou forsaken me?',[214] in that of Luke, 'Father, into thy hands I commend my spirit',[215] or in John's concise formula, 'It is finished',[216] which says essentially the same thing as the other Gospels: that the revelation of God is fulfilled with the death of Jesus. The consolation that the disciples offer after the death of the founder is likewise different in the two religions. The

Gospels close with accounts of the Resurrection: when Jesus has risen through the power of God, Matthew transmits the comforting sentence, 'I am with you always, even unto the end of the world.'[217] The first caliph, Abū Bakr, on the other hand, said, 'O ye people, he who has worshipped Muhammad, let him know: Muhammad is dead. But he who worships God, truly he lives and shall not die.' Then he recited verse 3:138 ('Muhammad is naught but a Messenger…').[218] And when the Prophet's companions meet to settle his succession, 'Umar assures them: 'God leaves you His book with which He guided His messenger, and, if you follow it, God will guide you as He did him.'[219] The consolation is the sacred text and the knowledge that the deceased has completed his task. The congregation have what they need: the Quran. 'The Prophet has left nothing but what is between the covers of the book', said his companions and successors.[220] Al-Ġazālī illustrates this idea with the following anecdote about the Prophet's contemporary Abū Hurayra:

> Abū Hurayra went to the market one day and said to the people there, 'I see you are all here, but the Messenger of God's inheritance is being distributed in the mosque.'
>
> So the people left the market and hurried to the mosque, but there they found no inheritance being distributed. When they came back to where Abū Hurayra was, they said, 'O Abū Hurayra, we saw no inheritance being distributed.'
>
> 'What did you see?' Abū Hurayra asked.
>
> 'We found a group of people paying reverence (*ḏikr*) to God and reciting the Quran.'
>
> 'That is the Prophet's inheritance.'[221]

While in Christianity two or three are gathered in His name and He is there among them, in Islam people recite the Quran, so that the *sakīna*, the divine Presence, descends and angels join the company.[222]

The parallelism continues in numerous areas, such as salvation history: whereas the prototypical conversion in early Islam is caused by hearing the Quran, the Gospels describe the overpowering aura of the Messiah: it is His person that fascinates people. Accordingly, the message of salvation is spread after Christ's ascension by His disciples' testimony of Him and His acts – the Gospel, the testimony of His life – while the chief means of Muslim proselytizing after Muhammad's death is reciting the Quran. In its inner structure, its addressee and its telos, the Quran is something completely different from the Gospel. Its content is not Muhammad's biography but the direct speech of God entrusted to the Prophet, and it is thematically highly heterogeneous, by no means a continuous narrative like the Gospels.

In the one case, revelation means God's incarnation in a man; in the other, His 'inverbation' in the spoken word. Inevitably, this has radical consequences for the reception of the revelation by the faithful and for the status of the scripture in the given religion. Theological discussion in Christianity, for example, has focused on the question of Jesus' human-divine nature, while Islamic scholars have devoted themselves with similar ardour to the question of the 'creation of the Quran' (*khalq al-Qur'ān*) – that is, whether the Quran is part of God's eternal Being, or whether God created it at a point in time. In both religions, differences in theological positions – however minimal they appeared to outsiders – were so serious that the adversaries often resorted to suppression, inquisition and mutual excommunication. Endeavours in the aesthetic sphere have been analogous to those in theology: a theological aesthetics such as that which was proposed for Christianity by Hans Urs von Balthasar, and present in a rudimentary form in medieval scholasticism, centres not on the beauty of the holy scripture, and the historical interpretation of its poetic form, but on the figure of Jesus Christ, in Whom humanity 'has been shown the glory of God'.[223] Where Muslim scholars have theorized on aesthetically relevant issues, however, these have been related primarily to the Quran, the study and theological appraisal of God's pronouncement with regard to its linguistic perfection and fascination.[224]

Still more striking is the correspondence in the rites by which the presence of God is sensually experienced in the two religions. The church congregation has a specifically religious-sensual experience of the person of Jesus Christ. The central ritual of Christianity is not, or at least not primarily, the reading of scripture: it is consummated in the sacraments, culminating in the Eucharist, the ritual assimilation of the body of Jesus Christ. It is not a mere representation, but a 're-presentation' in a literal sense: a renewal in the present of the sacrifice of the cross. By performing the prescribed acts and speaking the authentic words, the priest invokes Christ's presence.[225] In Islam, which contains nothing called sacrament or communion, the central ritual is listening to or reciting the divine oration, *ṣalāt*, the ritual prayer performed three to five times daily, in which short surahs or excerpts of surahs are recited at the beginning of the first and second *rak'a*, representing a form of ritualized scriptural reading. There is a different word for the soul's dialogue with God, for invoking and supplicating Him for comfort and aid – that is, for prayer in the strict sense: *du'ā*. It is only secondary, however, in comparison with the ritual importance of *ṣalāt* and of Quran recitation in general. The Prophet is supposed to have said, 'The best worship service of my congregation is the recitation of the Quran',[226] and 'Nothing will bring you back to God better than that which has its origins in Him, that is, the Quran.'[227] The following extraquranic word of God (*ḥadīth qudṣī*) is likewise significant: 'He who has been so busy reciting the Quran that he forgets to pray to me (*du'ā'ī*) and to call upon me, to him I grant the most excellent reward of gratitude.'[228] *Ṣalāt*, not silent prayer or *khuṭba*, the sermon, is also the central ritual act in the Friday worship service. The Quran itself does not mention a *khuṭba* to be held on Fridays.[229] Longer excerpts of the Quran are generally recited as well. The Quran is also recited at ceremonies of passage, such as circumcisions, weddings and funerals. The actual liturgical place where the longer surahs of the Quran can be identified as a whole is rather in the context of private devotion: in the numerous Quran circles, many of which meet regularly, or in the thirty nights of Ramadan, over the course of which the full text is recited.[230] Here, in the encounter with His word, is where humans experience God's presence; where the human being is infused with God, addressed by God. Those who devote themselves to the Quran (*ahl al-Qur'ān*) are, as a hadith has it, 'God's family and His intimates'.[231] Some theologians, inferring a pseudo-etymology from a chance assonance, have stated that prayer is called *ṣalāt* because it is a link (*ṣila*) between Man and God.[232] 'When I want to talk with God', one believer said, 'I read the Quran, and I speak to Him endlessly in private, and He to me.'[233] Pronouncing the Word of God with one's own mouth, receiving it in one's ears, holding it in one's heart, is essentially a sacramental act, even if Islam does not use that concept. The faithful do not simply recall the Divinity: like Christians taking communion, they absorb it physically (which is why the believer must carefully rinse his mouth and clean his teeth before beginning the recitation and, in an especially strict view, should avoid pungent or strong-smelling vegetables such as garlic, onions and leeks);[234] the Divinity appears or, more precisely, sounds at the moment mortals speak His words: 'Your mouths are paths of God.'[235] For that reason, quotations from the Quran were sometimes prefaced originally with the present-tense form *yaqūlu* ('God says') instead of the perfect *qāla llāhu* ('God said . . .') that is common today. The objection was raised against the present tense, however, that it does not convey the supertemporal nature of God's word.[236] Theologians were and still are unanimous, however, that it is God Himself Who speaks when the Quran is recited, and that the original situation of communication between Gabriel and Muhammad can be experienced anew in every recitation. Az-Zarkashī, for example, mentions as one of the miraculous characteristics of the Quran that the reciter 'experiences a renewed revelation from God to him in the form of an oration that is God's speech to His messenger'.[237] The mystic Muslim ibn Maymūn al-Khawwāṣ also felt himself directly addressed by God in the recitation:

> I recited the Quran, but found no sweetness in it. So I said to myself: Recite as if I were hearing it from the Messenger of God himself. Then the sweetness came. Then I wanted more of it, and I said to myself: Recite as if I were hearing it from Gabriel, when he revealed it to the Prophet. Then its sweetness increased. Then I said to myself: Recite it as if I were hearing it from God Himself. Then I savoured its whole sweetness.[238]

The more prosaic Muḥammad ʿAbduh describes a similar experience: 'When I hear or recite the Quran, I feel I am in the moment of the revelation, and the Messenger is pronouncing what was sent down to him – that is, what Gabriel brought down to him.'[239] The sacramental character of Quran recitation explains why some early Arabic grammarians are said to have refused to teach Arabic to Jewish and Christian Arabs because the grammatical rules had to be illustrated with examples from the Quran.[240] This is an extreme example, but it expresses at bottom the same instinctive unease that devout Christians may have when an unbeliever attends Holy Mass. In Catholic canon law, *communicatio in sacris* is expressly forbidden, and even today more than a few would doubtless take offence at the participation of non-Catholics in the sacrament.

Because in the recitation of the Quran and in *ṣalāt* the situation of revelation is realized anew, Muslims may well conceive it as an experience of concrete remembrance of the initial event of their salvation history,[241] as Jews and Christians conceive other, different experiences in their respective rites. Of course, the aspect of remembrance is more evident and probably more conscious in the rites of those two older religions. The destiny of Israel, marked by covenant, exodus, exile and the hope of the Messiah, is commemorated by scriptural recitation and the accompanying prayers and hymns; the Exodus as the founding myth of Israel is celebrated in the Pesach festival. In Christianity, the commemoration of the Passion of Christ, the sacrifice of God become man, and hence the commemoration of the world's atonement, culminates in Holy Communion. Although Islam, even in its initial phase, had a relatively clearly circumscribed corpus of text that was considered revealed, it is noteworthy that the reading is not a commemoration of the founding events. Unlike the stories and accounts in the Old and the New Testament, the Quran recounts only partially the founding myths of the community of its listeners. The speaker assumes that his audience knows those narratives, and so does not recount them but rather comments and reflects on them, often in allusions, sentence fragments, references and admonitions. The historic reason is that – unlike the holy scriptures of the Jews and Christians – the Quran's origins and the major milestones in its canonical formation are situated in the time of the salvation history itself. The only necessary reference to earlier time is to the monotheistic pre-Islamic past, and this is provided in the form of relatively clearly circumscribed narratives of the prophets. The most popular example of these narratives is the surah of Joseph (no. 12). The new community forms its identity by attributing to itself a certain past, a 'new' past so to speak, by reference to an Abrahamic genealogy. But *this* pre-Islamic past is not the one that is at the centre of Islamic culture. The remembrance of it takes place within the text and is only a secondary meaning of the cult. The initiating event of the Muslim congregation is rather the text itself. The history of the Muslim community and its inclusion in the salvation history of the other scriptural religions begins at the moment when God speaks to Muhammad's people in their language, as he has addressed other peoples before. And this is the event that is re-enacted in Quran recitation and *ṣalāt*. Although, for the person reciting or praying, the primary function of the text is not the narration of the salvation history, the Muslim cult is nevertheless an act of remembrance in which a past historic event – the revelation (*tanzīl*) of the divine discourse – is not 'commemorated' but re-enacted; not narrated but experienced anew. That is why it doesn't really matter which or how long an excerpt of the Quran is recited: the important thing is that the Word of God is spoken. And that is why, when the Quran is read regularly over a long period in the context of ritual acts, passages are not chosen by thematic or narrative criteria: the text is simply read sequentially from beginning to end. What is important is the completeness of the recitation, not a dramaturgical function – the ritual act of reciting and listening, not receiving, repeating and understanding a coherent, edifying, didactic or suspenseful narrative. A saying of the legal scholar Aḥmad ibn Ḥanbal (d. 855) exemplifies this attitude:

> I saw the Almighty in a dream, and I asked him,
> 'O Lord, what is the best way to come closer to You?'
> He answered, 'Through My word, O Aḥmad.'
> 'With understanding, or without understanding (*bi-fahmin aw-bi-ġayri fahmin*)?'
> 'No matter whether you understand it or not.'[242]

Listening to the Quran has an intrinsic value; intellectual understanding of its content is not necessary, or at least is not essential to the value of the act. The first thing that is necessary is sensory – meaning primarily auditory – perception. Unlike the rather artistic performances of the renowned Quran singers, which are attended by Christian as well as Muslim Arabs, such a religious reading does not permit any emphasizing, selecting or repeating of individual excerpts as particular favourites or as important for the congregation. Its goal is *khatma*, 'completion'. That is, the individual or the group recites the complete text within a predetermined time. The text is divided for this purpose into thirty fixed sections (*ajzā'*), corresponding to the days of Ramadan, the month of the revelation. The sections are determined by mathematically equal length, without regard for the beginnings and ends of the surahs. On reaching the end, the reciter immediately returns to the beginning and recites the *Fātiḥa* and the first five verses of the second surah.[243] This practice does justice to the Quran's nature as an eternal and perfect text whose authority (*ḥujja*), in az-Zarkashī's words, 'endures in all ages and all time, for it is the Word of the Lord of the inhabitants of the worlds.'[244] The duration of a *khatma* is also derived from the story of the Prophet: the practice of reciting the Quran each night in Ramadan is explained by the belief that Gabriel visited Muhammad in that month – called 'the Spring of the Quran'[245] – each year to study the revelation (*yudārisuhū l-qur'āna*) with him.[246] Because Muhammad is said to have recited the entire Quran to the archangel Gabriel twice in the year of his death – after reciting it only once each year up to then – it is considered desirable to read at least two *khatmas* per year.[247] Divine grace (*raḥma*) is believed to descend on the participants at the end of each *khatma*.[248] A scene with Muhammad and the archangel is also presented as an explanation of ritual: 'The Messenger of God said, "Gabriel came down and led me in *ṣalāt*. Then I prayed with him again and again and again..." – and he counted five prayers on his fingers.'[249] The recitation of the Quran joins the human with the divine; it lifts man out of his earthly world; it makes God's voice present in the earthly world. To the mystics in particular, Quran recitations really do have the character of a revelation, inasmuch as they renew God's 'self-unveiling', as Abū Ḥafs ʿUmar as-Suhrawardī (d. 1234) calls it, and create 'mirrors' that reflect His majesty, both for the reciter and for the listener.[250] An angel kisses the reciter's forehead, the famous ascetic Sufyān ath-Thawrī (d. 778) proclaimed, and the reciter 'is raised to prophethood from both sides, without receiving a revelation', said ʿAmr ibn al-ʿĀṣ.[251] The following non-canonical hadith tends in the same direction: 'He who recites a third of the Quran receives a third of prophethood, and he who recites half of the Quran receives half of prophethood, and he who recites the whole Quran shall be given the whole prophethood, without receiving a revelation.'[252]

Another of the Prophet's sayings practically commands an association with the Last Supper: 'The Quran is the feast (*ma'duba*) of God: he who takes part (*dakhala fīhi* – literally, enters into it) is safe.'[253] He who recites the Quran – whether Gabriel, Muhammad, a trained reciter or an ordinary Muslim thirteen centuries later in the chain of speech acts – pronounces not words about God but the Word of God. To quote Muḥammad ibn Kaʿb ibn Sulaym al-Quraẓī (d. 736), it is 'as if God spoke with him',[254] or, in the words of al-Muḥāsibī, 'as if one heard it from Him'.[255] Ibn al-Farrā' (d. 1066), a Hanbali author, goes further still: 'God himself recites through the tongue of every person who recites the Quran. When one listens to a reciter's Quran recitation, one hears it from God.'[256]

Not all theologians went so far as to say, with Ibn al-Farrā' or the Sālimīya, the school founded by Sahl at-Tustarī, that God himself speaks through the tongue of every person who recites the Quran, and those who listen to the recitation hear Him in person and in the present. But even a Muʿtazili such as Abū ʿAlī al-Jubbā'ī (d. 915) cannot help declaring that the participants in a Quran recitation hear God just as Moses did on Mount Sinai.[257] The medieval Christian discussion of the implications of the ritual of communion was surprisingly analogous: conservative theologians repeatedly invoked the real presence of Christ in the Eucharist – something that went without saying to the early Christian community – 'which holds that bread and wine after consecration are not only sacred symbols but the true body and the true blood of Christ, and are handled by the priest and bitten by the teeth of the faithful – not only in a sacramental sense but in sensually experienced reality and truth.'[258] And just as the musical varieties of Quran recitation appeared, as we have seen, too *stimulating* to some 'puritanical' scholars of Islam, who demanded a largely unornamented recitation and reflection on the meaning of the text, likewise the Catholic rite, which must have been in the Middle Ages much more than today a multimedia drama that embraced the believer's senses of sight, hearing, smell, touch and taste – that is, 'all his capacities of sensory perception', as Horst Wenzel demonstrates, was in its splendour and sensual richness the object of persistent criticism that was not so different from the polemics of an Ibn al-Jawzī, for example.[259]

The quasi-sacramental character of Quran recitation is also connected with the tremendous value placed on memorizing the Quran in traditional Muslim societies. For centuries, all school education in the Islamic world invariably began with learning Quran verses by heart.[260] To an even greater degree than merely listening to the recitation, the meditative repetition (*ḏikr*) of the revealed verses, and ideally their complete memorization (*ḥifẓ*), represents the absorption of God's word and hence, to draw a parallel to the sacrament, the assimilation of God. If lessons in Quran schools (*katātīb*) from Kuala Lumpur to Duisburg consist primarily of memorizing the Quran, this is not a manifestation of obsolete teaching methods but the logical consequence of the Muslim concept of revelation. Just as baptism is a step on the path of Christian life, and religious instruction is centred on preparation for the sacraments of communion and confirmation, true Muslim education necessarily involves learning a number of surahs by heart. As a rule, every student knows at least the *juzʾ ʿamma*, the last thirtieth of the Quran, which starts with the word *ʿamma*, 'about what', at the beginning of surah 78.[261] The obligation of *ṣalāt* alone has the effect that every half-way devout Muslim knows at least parts of the Quran. The reputation of being a *ḥāfiẓ* – that is, one who preserves the whole Quran in his memory – brings prestige and reverence to the believer and his family, since such a person carries God's word (and is therefore called a *ḥāmil* or 'bearer') and so upholds the 'banner of Islam', as Fuḍayl ibn ʿIyāḍ (d. 803) said.[262] If a child recites the Quran daily and so becomes a *ḥāfiẓ* (which usually occurs around the age of ten, but often earlier), the grateful family celebrate with a feast that is no less lavish than the initiation celebrations of other religions. Complete memorization of the Quran was and in some places still is expected of respectable religious scholars as a matter of course. For students of theology at Azhar University, for example, it was until recently strictly obligatory, and the great scholars of Islamic history, such as ash-Shāfiʿī and as-Suyūṭī, are known to have acquired the title of *ḥāfiẓ* at the age of just seven or eight years.[263] Many of the religious scholars of today, and even reformist thinkers of a more secular orientation, learned the complete text by heart in childhood. The masters of Quran recitation, moreover, know all the canonical readings of the text.[264]

In Christianity, too, the holy scripture was and is still recited – but it is rarely learned by heart, at least not in its entirety. That is due not only to the fact that the Bible is less suitable for memorization than the Quran but primarily to the different function and importance of the scripture in the worlds of the two faiths. Whereas in a consciously Christian environment the person of Jesus Christ is omnipresent, most visibly through the cross, which artists carve, paint and mould and which is displayed on walls, steeples, tombstones, doorways, mountain peaks and necklaces, in a Muslim context it is the words of the Quran that the faithful keep in their hearts, and whose blessings were such, in the words of the Prophet's companion Abū Hurayra, that 'the house in which the Quran is recited brings its occupants happiness and prosperity; it is populated by angels and avoided by devils.'[265] Or, as the Prophet himself is quoted, 'The house in which a Muslim is reciting the Quran shines to the inhabitants of Heaven as the sparkling star in Heaven shines to the people on Earth.'[266]

As a book, talisman, calligraphy, recitation or quotation, the revelation becomes in a traditional Muslim's day-to-day life what Kenneth Cragg calls 'a sort of accompaniment to life, in the musical sense of the word – the theme by which the believer is articulate, like the singer in the song'.[267] It is the Quran that impresses itself on the senses of hearing and sight, that people carry with them, that as a whole is appreciated, praised, admired, defended, vaunted, revered and, most of all, memorized. 'My congregation was given no fewer than three things', says a hadith concisely, 'beauty (*al-jamāl*), the beautiful voice, and memory.'[268] Cragg, who devoted one of the best chapters in his rich books on the Quran to memorization, writes:

> The sequences of the Qur'ān are apprehended as the setting that runs parallel to daily life. They are a sort of 'key' in which the emotions and aspirations find a vicarious context in the patriarchs or in the Prophet, in the events and phrases of the Quranic scene. The humane situation is 'set to words' – to *these* words, which warn, or chasten, or exhort, or encourage it, in a sort of engagement of these with those, of now with then, in the fabric of the text. *Ḥifẓ* means its prompt availability for guidance or for the imagination, not as something to be tediously recalled out of near oblivion, but as a familiar framework of imagery and theme.[269]

Besides traditional schooling and the obligation of *ṣalāt*, which require rote memorization, one driving force of what Paul Nwyia has called the 'Koranization of the memory'[270] is Quran recitation. Still more prominent, however, is the presence of Quran recitation in day-to-day life.[271] In many regions, loudspeakers outside mosques, television, radio and cassette and CD players produce a tapestry of sound that accompanies the lives of the faithful with the voice of God. Especially in cities such as Cairo and Damascus, late afternoon strollers are as if clothed in the verses of the Quran. William A. Graham sums up his recollection of the first Ramadan he spent in Cairo, which sparked his academic interest in the recitative character of the Quran, in these memorable words:

> It was there, walking the streets of the old city amidst the animated bustle of the nocturnal crowds of men, women, and children, that I first heard at length the compelling chanting of the professional Qur'ān reciters. It seemed that wherever I wandered in the old city, from Bāb Zuwayla to Bāb al-Futūḥ, the drawn-out, nuanced cadences of the sacred recitations gave the festive nights a magical air as the reciters' penetrating voices sounded over radios in small, open shops, or wafted into the street from the doorways of mosques and from under the canvas marquees set up specially for this month of months in the Muslim calendar. If it was only an introduction to the living tradition of Qur'ān recitation, it was also an unforgettable one.[272]

The rites of the Christian and Muslim religions, Holy Mass and listening to, speaking and memorizing the Quran, do not simply commemorate the initial event of the given salvation history: rather, they are mimetic acts in which the believer re-creates the situation of the revelation. The rules for the behaviour of readers and listeners at a Quran recitation, as set down in the pertinent chapters of as-Suyūṭī, al-Makkī or the best-known authority, al-Ġazālī, are aimed at making the recitation a close symbolic approximation of the original act, the revelation, just as the phonetic code of *tajwīd* is aimed at producing its authentic sound, which Gabriel taught the Prophet and he transmitted to his companions.[273] The participants are expected to project themselves emotionally into the situation of the revelation and to be conscious of their own position in the chain of recitation acts that descends from God's speech to Gabriel.[274] Before beginning the reading, the reciter is expected, al-Ġazālī writes, to 'bring to mind the majesty of the Speaker and to realize that what he is reciting is not the word of a human being'.[275] Ibn ʿArabī goes still further, saying that every Quran recitation is a 'renewal of the revelation (*mujaddidu l-inzāl*) on the heart of him who recites it. Whenever it is recited, the revelation (*tanazzul*) from God, the Wise and Revered, is renewed. The hearts of the reciters are the throne on which He sits when He comes down in this way.'[276] He who recites the Quran should be aware, Ibn ʿArabī stipulates, that the Quran 'is new each time it is recited',[277] and that in the moment of the recitation God is in the reciter's heart, so that he receives a revelation:

> But not every reciter is conscious of His descent (*nuzūl*), because his mind is busy with his natural condition. In this case the Quran comes down to him obscured by the curtain of his personality and affords no pleasure (*iltiḏāḏ*). That is what is meant when the Prophet says that there will be some among those who come after in whose throats the Quran will stick fast when they recite it.[278] Such a Quran descends upon the tongues, but not on the hearts. But God says of those who feel His descent: 'With it (viz. the Quran) the true Spirit descended upon your heart.'[279] Such a reciter is he who finds in His descent upon him an immeasurable bliss exceeding all pleasures. When he

experiences this, he is one who has received the new and inexhaustible Quran.[280]

The idea of re-enactment is the basis for the weeping (*bukā'*), sorrow (*ḥuzn*), anguish (*shajā*), humility (*khushū'*) and ritual purity (*ṭahāra*) which all the scholars of *ādāb at-tilāwa* demand of those who attend a reading: these reflect the inner and outer state that corresponds to the act of revelation. Statements to this effect are attributed to the Prophet himself: 'The Quran is sent down with sorrow. When you recite it, recite it with sorrow',[281] or, as another tradition has it, 'put yourselves in a state of sorrow (*taḥāzanū*)'.[282] Such traditions convey a clear awareness that the state of sorrow is part of the ritual – like a physical posture or a certain gesture – and does not necessarily have to 'arise' within the listener.

'He who weeps when I recite a surah to you, Paradise shall be his', said the Messenger of God. And he recited a surah, but no one wept. Then he recited a second, and a third (but no one wept). Then he said, 'Weep, and if you do not weep, then act as if you wept (*tabākaw*).'[283]

The term *ḥuzn*, as it is used in writing on Quran recitation, contains more than a translation such as 'sorrow' could express. It denotes the state of mind of the creature vis-à-vis his Creator: humility, awe, the awareness of one's mortality and insignificance in the face of His infinite splendour and magnificence.[284]

The stipulation of an emotional attitude goes hand in hand with the requirement of mental reflection on the recited verses and their origin.[285] 'Do not scatter it as one scatters dates; do not rush, as one rushes through the recitation of a poem; but stop by its wonders, let your heart be set in motion by them, and beware of merely wanting to reach the end of the surah', Ibn Mas'ūd warns.[286] Pure enjoyment is considered possible, but generally inappropriate. As-Sarrāj (d. 998), for example, characterizes the motives of those listeners who prefer qasidas to the Quran as follows:

He who prefers listening to qasidas to listening to the Quran does so because he considers the Quran holy and sees it as something very serious. For it is something divine (*ḥaqq*). But the souls draw back before its holiness, and their excitements die and their desires and pleasures cease when the lights of the divine reality (*ḥuqūq*) shine on them with their brilliant radiance and reveal to them their wisdom. These people say: As long as human nature persists and we have our attributes and our attributes of desire (*ḥuẓūẓ*) about us, and our spirits delight in stirring melodies and sweet voices, it is more right, in view of the existence of these attributes of desire, if we devote ourselves to the enjoyment of the qasidas than if we were to devote ourselves with them to the word of God, which is God's attribute and His word, which appeared from Him and returns to Him.[287]

This attitude is not typical of Muslim, much less Sufi, discourse on Quran recitation: the stronger delight that the Quran's reception engenders is typically one of the reasons why the recitation of the Quran is preferred to poetry, and why the listeners' sensations of pleasure and enjoyment are considered normal and legitimate. Some Sufis even go so far as to claim the Quran is the only legitimate source of aesthetic recreation;[288] they can point to a hadith that says God permitted the beautiful voices (the expression is understood as a synonym for musical euphony) only for the recitation of the Quran.[289] But the Sufis whom as-Sarrāj presents give reasons for their attitude that are by no means foreign to the *ādāb tilāwat al-Qur'ān*: there is consensus among scholars that, because the Quran comes from God, it demands a different receptive attitude than a poem and must not be enjoyed *only* aesthetically.

Just as Christian theologians have always sought to understand what it means to celebrate Holy Communion, their Muslim colleagues have sought a theological definition of the act of recitation. While it is not false that, as the anthropologist Clifford Geertz puts it, a person who sings the verses of the Quran 'chants not words about God, but of Him, and indeed, as those words are His essence, chants God Himself',[290] how are we to understand this 'God speaks'? Is it really He Who speaks every time the Quran is heard from a human mouth, as Sālimīya claimed? When a mystic such as Ibn ʿArabī, referring to his spiritual experience, emphatically affirmed it, and when a man of practical devotion such as Ibn Ḥanbal refused to reflect on such fine points,[291] the Muslim scholastics were obliged to deny it: they found it inadmissible by the same natural logic by which we would deny that it is Hölderlin himself who speaks when someone recites his poems. The scholastics considered presumptuous the idea that God was the active speaker in the recitation and felt that it negated the essence of the religious practice as a symbolic act. On closer examination, the overly literal understanding of the Quran as the word of God raised at least two problems. First, Ibn Kullāb (d. c. 855) and, later, the Ash'arites considered it an unacceptable anthropomorphism to attribute an audible voice and human language to God. They thought God had given the Prophet the discourse as an *ilhām*, a kind of intuition. Where the divine sense was transformed into human speech – whether at the level of God, the angel Gabriel or the Prophet – remained subject to debate. Yet it was obvious that God does not speak in human language, and ultimately even Moses was addressed by God only in a figurative sense. Only the Hanbali took these passages quite literally. They insisted that the divine discourse consists of sounds like human speech, and in the Quran itself even the vocalization marks of all the recognized readings are divine and eternal.[292]

The second difficulty that results from the view of the spoken Quran as the word of God concerns the act of recitation and is more relevant to our present context. When the Quran is recited, a human being undeniably plays a part in the linguistic expression, in the pronunciation of the words (*alfāẓ*). Regardless of the exact nature of the divine discourse, the Mu'tazili and Ash'ari theologians agreed that it cannot be reproduced by mortals: a recitation can only be an approximation of what was once spoken, a *muḥākāt* or *ḥikāya*, an 'imitation' of the divine oratory.[293] Such subtleties were hardly reflected in public opinion: people were and still are content in the knowledge, or the experienced belief, that God spoke to Muhammad in human language, and they hear God when the Quran is recited without worrying about *how*.[294] Nonetheless, the solution that the scholastics found for the intellectual problem they faced, the theory of 'imitation', is remarkable because it is based on an eminently aesthetic understanding of the process of recitation. It is no coincidence that *ḥikāya* is the term that Arab translators use to render the Greek *mimesis*, the key concept of Aristotelian aesthetics.[295] In Classical art theory, mimesis denotes the artist's creative activity as the imitative representation of an independently, previously existing reality (in contrast to the idealistic concept of the artistic act as an autonomous act of creation – for example, a reincarnation of beauty out of the artist's mind). In contrast to the identity principle and the categorial approach of conceptual knowledge, the Muslim concept of *ḥikāya* instinctively perceives the act of recitation as a mimetic behaviour which seeks to preserve the text in its essence as something indeterminate and singular, transcending the meaning of all individual moments and eluding human conception. We may clarify the aesthetic view that underlies *ḥikāya* by drawing on Adorno's aesthetic theory, in which 'similarity' is a fundamental principle. Adorno writes:

> The Aristotelian dictum that only like can know like, which progressive rationality has reduced to a marginal value, divides the knowledge that is art from conceptual knowledge: What is essentially mimetic awaits mimetic comportment. If artworks do not make themselves like something else but only like themselves, then only those who imitate them understand them. Dramatic or musical texts should be regarded exclusively in this fashion and not as the quintessence of instructions for the performers: They are the congealed imitation of works, virtually of themselves, and to this extent constitutive although always permeated with significative elements. Whether or not they are performed is for them a matter of indifference; what is not, however, a matter of indifference is that their experience – which in terms of its ideal is inward and mute – imitates them. Such imitation reads the nexus of their meaning out of the *signa* of the artworks and follows this nexus just as imitation follows the curves in which the artwork appears. As laws of their imitation the divergent media find their unity, that of art. If in Kant discursive knowledge is to renounce the interior of things, then artworks are objects whose truth cannot be thought except as that of their interior. Imitation is the path that leads to this interior.[296]

The recitation of the Quran (and listening to it) is understood in Islamic theology and in the works on *ādāb ḥamalat al-Qur'ān* as a re-enactment of the initial situation of speech between Gabriel and Muhammad. Just as Muhammad transmitted the lexical content and the manner of recitation (*adā'*) of the orally revealed text as he had received it, others are expected to conserve and be guided by Gabriel's recitation as he presented it. A hadith affirms this duty of mimetic behaviour: 'God wants the Quran to be recited as it was sent down.'[297] It is also expressed in the Quran itself, where God admonishes the Prophet to recite the revelation exactly as it is recited to him, not to rush, but first to listen and then to repeat it:

Move not thy tongue with it to hasten it;
Ours it is to gather it, and to recite it.
So, when We recite it, follow thou its recitation.[298]

For the reciter, this theological view of the original situation implies that he or she must produce the text in its own objective constitution; theoretically, the reciter's rendering (beyond the choice of a reading) does not follow his or her own topical predilections or aesthetic interpretations but the text's implicit formal laws alone. The common definition of the word *tajwīd* indicates this attitude: *i'ṭā' kulli ḥarfin ḥaqqahū*, doing justice to each letter. This is why a modern Egyptian scholar said that recitation is following, not inventing (*at-tilāwatu ttibā'u lā btidā'*).[299] This is not to deny the interpreter's creative power or contribution to the success of a Quran recitation, but to circumscribe the area in which that creativity operates. The ideal recitation is aimed at realizing what is immanent in the text; it does not use the text as material for the reciter's artistic self-realization or for a subjective interpretation (as, for example, an actor, finding something of himself in Hamlet, might explore himself through that role, turning his interior outward, or as pianists today often – and often with great success – act as composers, treating an existing piece merely as raw material). Lamyā' al-Farūqi records her observations on reciters' attitudes:

> Durational features of *tartīl* are no less demonstrative of its abstract, non-programmatic nature. Regardless of word content expressed, this improvised musical expression of Islamic culture retains a continuity which cannot be dissected into sections of greater or lesser activity, of greater or lesser frivolity, of greater or lesser grief. No rhythmic aspect of any portion of *qirā'a* by any reader seems to express a mood or to depict an emotion or state which is different from any other portion by that same reader. No durational relation to programme could be discovered in the readings; neither did any informant feel that such a relation was proper in *qirā'a*.[300]

It is doubtful whether the melodic line has no relation at all to the content of the text, as al-Fārūqī suggests. The frequently used term *taṣwīr al-ma'nā* ('illustration of the meaning') seems to denote such a relation, and various

Muslim scholars emphasize that the recitation must correspond with the *maʿānī*, the meanings,[301] or that the music must be 'descriptive' (*mūsīqā waṣfīya*).[302] That would indicate that the musical design is not completely unconnected to the content of the recited text. At the same time, however, we must note that *maʿnā* is not necessarily synonymous with the meaning or content of a verse. When, for example, a reciter says, 'a verse with one meaning [*maʿnā*] got a particular melody, and one with glad tidings got another',[303] he is referring to the basic mood or the emotional function of a passage rather than to the sense to be illustrated. Obviously, the *mujawwad* reading at least must change with the character of the recited verses; the story of a prophet is read differently than a sequence of oaths. The variation, however, is not simply due to the varying content to which the reading must conform. Rather, it is due to the passages' completely different artistic structure (in Lotman's sense of the term), which calls for a different melodic and vocal composition. In the theory of recitation, this textual structure that determines the form of the recitation is referred to by the term *tawāzun*; this denotes the relation between melodic line and argument which results from the poetic treatment, and which the reciter must observe. In this sense, Labīb as-Saʿīd says the recitation must be 'expressive' (*qirā'a muʿabbira*).[304] The reciter must not 'interpret' the text beyond the requirements of *tawāzun*, by taking an emotional attitude in quotations within the Quran, for example, or by acting the text, no matter how well the stories of the prophets, dramatically structured and narrated as dialogue, may lend themselves to dramatization.[305] The reciter's interpretation is a musical, mimetic, at most a representational one in the sense of non-European traditions of theatre; it is not aimed at a psychological identification of the actor with the text in the way that European illusionistic theatre or the aesthetics of film and television is. The reciter's relation to the text can be symbolized by a hand that gently traces the contours of an object:[306] clinging to it as a separate thing without holding it fast; letting its forms emerge rather than moulding it. Just as a musician follows the sheet music, the reciter follows the minimal impulses of the text and in a certain sense doesn't know, as Adorno said, what he or she is singing.[307] On another level, however, the same is true of the ideal listener as described primarily in Sufi treatises. The audience do not interpret the recited text, do not confront it with their thoughts, emotions, wishes, but empty themselves and surrender themselves to it altogether. Al-Ġazālī characterizes the ideal attitude as 'presence of the heart and cessation of the soul's own train of thought';[308] Abū Naṣr as-Sarrāj writes in the Sufi work *Kitāb al-lumaʿ* that the ideal listeners 'offer no resistance and do not oppose God in regard to the movement and the stillness that come over their hearts in the moment of listening'.[309] To Ibn ʿArabī, it is God himself who calls on the listener 'not to dwell on his own meanings', because in that case he would

> forsake Me in his thinking and reflecting. He needs only to incline fully to Me, open his ear only for My word, so that I am present in his recitation.

> And as it is I Who recite to him and make him hear, it is also I Who explain to him My word and translate its meaning. This is My nightly conversation with him. He takes knowledge from Me, but not by means of his reason and deliberation. He does not give another thought to Paradise or hellfire, to the reckoning of his deeds and the Day of Judgement, to this world or the next, because he no longer judges with his intellect or seeks to understand the verses with his reason, but only opens his ear for what I say to him. In such a moment he is a witness to My presence, and I Myself instruct him.[310]

The Islamic mystics devoted more attention than others to the receptive end of Quran recitation – that is, to the act of listening. Although they do not use the term *ḥikāya*, they conceive listening too as a mimesis that defies conceptual identification, as the theologians conceive recitation. Adorno calls this the immanent experience of the work that occurs in contemplation of it without grasping it discursively, which is 'necessarily immanent and transparent right into its most sublime nuance'.[311] In the practice of artistic experience, the mimetic capacity manifests itself 'as the imitation of the dynamic curves of what is performed; it is the quintessence of understanding this side of the enigma.'[312] To arrive at a conceptual understanding, such an experience is dependent on exegesis; the *qirā'a* needs the *tafsīr*, the other major area of Muslim Quran reception, just as Adorno said art needs philosophy, 'which interprets it in order to say what it is unable to say, whereas art is only able to say it by not saying it.'[313] Only a person's experience of the work, whether as a reciter or as a listener, can momentarily resolve this convolution; only the experience conveys the self-evidence of an understanding – shocking, gratifying, but never expressible in words – which can only be called gnostic, an understanding that can never be attained by intellectual reflection. We will attempt an explanation of this experiential understanding towards the end of this book when we discuss Sufis who listen to the Quran.

4

The Miracle

But the infinite finitely displayed is beauty.

Schelling[1]

In his essay 'Of the Difference Between a Genius and an Apostle', published in 1847, Søren Kierkegaard describes the fundamental incomparability of sacred and profane inspiration. To discuss aesthetic aspects of an apostle's preaching would be sacrilegious: 'you must not presumptuously set about criticising the form.'[2] What is essential for the quality of the preaching is not the statement itself, 'but the fact that it was Christ who said it'.[3] While the genius's work can be discussed with reference to formal and thematic criteria, the word of the apostle, because of his divine authority, is purely apodictic; it is 'not to be understood or fathomed, but simply believed'.[4] Only ignorant clerics, guided by the notion that, 'as long as one says something good about St. Paul all is well',[5] could make the mistake of praising the apostle's message in aesthetic terms for, if 'St. Paul is to be regarded as a genius, then things look black for him':[6] he 'cannot be compared either with Plato or Shakespeare, as a coiner of beautiful similes he comes pretty low down in the scale; as a stylist his name is quite obscure; and as an upholsterer: well, I frankly admit I have no idea how to place him.'[7] The question whether the revelation is excellent and profound is an attempt to judge and evaluate God's apostle as if he were sitting an examination.[8] '[O]ne not infrequently hears priests, bona fide, in all learned simplicity, prostituting Christianity. They talk in exalted terms of St. Paul's brilliance and profundity, of his beautiful similes and so on – that is mere aestheticism.'[9] Kierkegaard accuses the theologians of his day of having erred – led astray by research – in softening the paradox of Jesus Christ's existence by pointing to the stylistic and thematic excellence of the Gospels. 'To believe, in the eminent sense, corresponds quite rightly to the marvelous, the absurd, the improbable, that which is foolishness to the understanding',[10] Kierkegaard wrote about the same time in *The Book on Adler*, finding that orthodox apologetic efforts were intended 'to make *Christianity probable*'.[11]

Kierkegaard is neither a typical nor an institutionally authorized thinker on Christianity. He was a dissenter; his voice was one of protest against his church's willingness to adapt to the demands of his time. He had no desire to play along, as Theodor W. Adorno writes:

> He did not want to make the truth alluring in ways like playing jazz at worship services so that young people would not be bored. The 'short worship service', a popular term today, would have been Kierkegaard's nightmare. In his idiosyncratic examination of the church, he was perhaps the first to discover the phenomenon of neutralization: spirituality, now assimilated or, as the enthusiasts say, integrated – that is, separated from the potential for its own realization – has degenerated into culture, and ultimately to a commodity, devoid of any commitment.[12]

We must not be misled by the fact that he was a loner, largely isolated as a Christian author in his era in his country, or that the official representatives of his church often attacked him, sometimes rudely:[13] Kierkegaard's protest against the aestheticization of religion in the liberal theology of the nineteenth century, dominated by Schleiermacher and Herder, places him in a long-standing tradition in church history. Like the later philosopher Maurice Blondel (d. 1949) in France and the earlier Hamann in Germany, Kierkegaard opposed what he saw as the nefarious influence of an aestheticizing Enlightenment rationalism in the religious sphere and demanded a return to a pure faith that neither questioned nor rationalized the revealed truth. With his categories of inwardness, or religious subjectivity, the Dane took a stand against the objectivism of Hegel.[14] In this respect he is the successor to Pietism, which from its inception had been opposed to gushing talk of the beauty of scripture.[15] The well-known hymn author and preacher of penitence Johann Caspar Schade (d. 1698) found that God had 'accommodated Man's weak and foolish mind and had presented clear and understandable topics, parables and concepts and circumstances which are not unusual in common speech, yet in which the most profound wisdom is concealed'. The search for stylistic subtleties is a sign of human foolishness; one would do better to wonder at and delight in the 'exuberant wisdom of God, Who was able to present high things to all people with simplicity and clarity incomprehensible to reason, and to conceal such spiritual power in the simple words'.[16] Nikolaus Ludwig von Zinzendorf (d. 1760), another proponent of Lutheran Pietism, declared the aesthetic principle per se to be human and therefore absent from holy scripture: 'If something divine is to be in a song, what is humanly beautiful must go out.'[17] The truths of the Bible

> are true to us, they are so *à la lettre*; it is no longer flowery speech, no longer figurative or hyperbolic expression, but the simple, innocent, dry truth that brings its own attraction with it. Spiritual poetry loses all its embellishment, all its beauty, which it has from Nature; for [in beautiful poetry] a little bit of truth must be added or subtracted, even though so much may be possible,

> probable, that exceeds the *ordinaire*; but when everything we have is true, it all becomes peasants' language, and the *idiom* which was previously called *sublime*, and which was a scholarly language, can now be recited by a child six years old, because it is so; it is no longer *tropus* or figure, but his nature; it is a proper everyday thing; it is the *simplicity* of the first beginners; it is part of our learning to spell and to speak, of the first formulation of our thoughts.[18]

The attitude conveyed in these quotations is directly descended from Luther. Yet it was his translation of the Bible that had an aesthetic attraction that is perhaps unique in the history of German literature, and it was in the developing Protestantism that the aesthetic dimension of the recited scripture (as Luther often emphasized) took on not merely great, but foundational importance: 'When I am without the Word, when I do not think of it or occupy myself with it, then no Christ is at home, nor even air or spirit', said Luther in one of his weekly sermons. 'But as soon as I take up a psalm or a proverb from scripture, it shines and burns so in my heart that I take new courage and purpose.'[19] One could hardly be more firmly convinced than Luther of the central importance of the scripture for faith, yet at the same time his placing the biblical word at the centre of religious life makes the difference from the world of Islamic faith all the more obvious. For Luther, the unambiguous clarity of every passage is critical, without regard for any ideal language. Hence there is no question of an aesthetic appreciation of the Bible that might reinforce the truth of his convictions.[20] He is concerned rather with combating the 'whore Reason', who will resort even to aesthetic arguments to confuse God and man: 'If rhyme is required, we will retain not a single article of the faith.'[21] Much as Luther cherished and praised the linguistic form of the Bible,[22] it was secondary: the content was what mattered.[23] Similarly, Calvin wrote:

> Our hearts are still more firmly assured when we reflect that our admiration is elicited more by the dignity of the matter than by the graces of style. For it was not without an admirable arrangement of providence that the sublime mysteries of the kingdom of heaven have for the greater part been delivered with a contemptible meanness of words. Had they been adorned with a more splendid eloquence, the wicked might have cavilled, and alleged that this constituted all their force. But now, when an unpolished simplicity, almost bordering on rudeness, makes a deeper impression than the loftiest flights of oratory, what does it indicate if not that the holy Scriptures are too mighty in the power of truth to need the rhetorician's art?[24]

With their emphatic focus on the Bible's content, their emphasis on the 'dignity of the matter' to the point of ignoring the subtleties of the language, or discounting them as ornament, Calvin and Luther are members of a tradition that reaches from St Luke to St Augustine, and further to the Reformation, Pietism and Kierkegaard, and to the twentieth century: to the imageless and shapeless interiority of Bultmann, and to the so-called Christian fundamentalists. Augustine (d. 430) lent an expression to this view of the Bible that has been influential down to the present:

> Those clear truths it contains it speaks without subterfuge, like an old friend, to the hearts of learned and unlearned alike. But even the truths which it hides in mysteries are not couched in such lofty style that a slow, uncultivated mind would not dare to approach them, as a poor man does not dare to approach a rich one.[25]

This idea has made its most distinct appearance in the concept of *sermo humilis*, the low or humble manner of speech, whose basic principles are found as early as Origen's (d. 254) reference to 1 Corinthians,[26] and which has been kept alive throughout the Middle Ages into the modern period: just as Jesus Christ humbled himself in becoming human, the language of the Bible is likewise intentionally without splendour in order not to distract attention from its content. The philologist and literary historian Erich Auerbach describes the idea of *sermo humilis* as follows:

> The lowly, or humble, style is the only medium in which sublime mysteries can be brought within the reach of men. It constitutes a parallel to the Incarnation, which was also a *humilitas* in the same sense, for men could not have endured the splendour of Christ's divinity. But the Incarnation, as it actually happened on earth, could only be narrated in a lowly and humble style.[27]

Kierkegaard's opposition to all aesthetic appreciation and praise of the holy scripture thus touches on an axiom of Christian faith. Of course the Bible contains excellent poetic passages; it contains the Psalms, the Song of Songs and Genesis; there is pleasure to be found in the language of Isaiah; the Gospels too can be experienced as beautiful. But their rhetorical splendour, while it may be analysed, admired and aesthetically received, is not seen in any Christian doctrine I have found as evidence of the truth of the message. In Christian dogma, the reason for believing cannot be the aesthetic quality of the scripture but only the acts and the nature of the person to Whom it bears witness: Jesus Christ. Well into the modern period, the language in which He preached attracted scant interest among the exegetes. Because even early Christian scholars knew that the books of the Bible had been edited by various authors, many of whom had access only to inspired translations of the originals, it was unlikely from the outset that a conception of their style as miraculous could become dogma. Where the doctrine of verbal inspiration – that is, the notion that the Holy Spirit inspired the authors of the Bible with the words to write – has been advanced in Christianity, it has referred to the accuracy and correctness of the content, not to the individual style or linguistic superiority of the scripture. The poetry of the Bible, the scripture as a verbal work in a special, immutable form and language, has never been a substantial element of Christian teaching, nor has any edition of the Bible been accorded a sacred status comparable to that of the Quran.[28]

The Bible was discovered – or, to do justice to Jewish and early Christian scholarship,[29] rediscovered – as a literary monument by a wide audience only in the eighteenth and nineteenth centuries. The evaluation of religious teaching by poetic criteria, using the methods of literary scholarship to expose its exemplary linguistic character and supposing a relation between religious and artistic inspiration, was a relatively new phenomenon for Christianity in Kierkegaard's lifetime. In classical Islamic scholarship, on the other hand, it was taken for granted. The aesthetic argument – which in biblical apologetics was at best controversial, never dominant, much less a condition of faith – is essential in Muslim theology. Especially in the beginnings of Islamic history, the works of *sīra* and hadith, the Quran commentaries and the treatises on *nubūwa* or prophethood are rich in new examples of the overwhelming power of Quran recitation. Although Kierkegaard insists that 'God cannot help men by providing them with physical certainty that an Apostle is an Apostle',[30] it was this *tangible* certainty, their aesthetic experience, that moved many of Muhammad's contemporaries to recognize his prophethood when they first heard a Quran recitation. And while the Danish Christian considers it a mockery of God to accept His words 'because they are clever or profound or wonderfully beautiful',[31] exactly that was reason enough for the well-known Baghdad physician ʿAlī ibn Sahl Rabbān aṭ-Ṭabarī to convert to Islam. In his *Kitāb ad-dīn wa-d-dawla fī ithbāt nubūwat an-nabīy Muḥammad*, an apology of Islam written in 855 on a commission by the caliph al-Mutawakkil (d. 861), aṭ-Ṭabarī writes:

> When I was a Christian, I did not cease to say in accordance with an uncle of mine who was one of the learned and eloquent men among Christians, that rhetoric [*balāġāt*] was not a sign of prophetic office [that is, a confirmatory miracle] on account of its being common to all nations. But when I waived tradition and customs, and broke with the promptings of habit and education, and examined the meanings of the Ḳur'ān, then I found that the question was as its holders believed it to be. I have never met with a book written by an Arab, or a Persian, or an Indian, or a Greek, which contained, like the Ḳur'ān, unity, praise, and glorification of the Most High God; belief in His Apostles and Prophets; incitement to good and permanent works; injunction for good things, and prohibition of evil things; exhortation to heaven and restraining from hell. Who has ever written, since the creation of the world, a book with such prerogatives and qualities, with such influence, sweetness and charm upon the heart, and with such attraction, felicity, and success, while its producer, the man to whom it was revealed, was unlettered

> [*ummī*], not even knowing how to write, and having no eloquence whatever? This is without doubt and hesitation a mark of prophetic office.[32]

To show that such a book could not possibly have been produced by a human author, Muslim scholars from the early ninth century on went to great lengths to demonstrate its thematic profundity and its formal perfection. They developed literary theories and poetic standards and compared their holy book again and again with the works of the poets, and continue to do so in our time. In other words, they did in principle exactly what Kierkegaard later accused the theologians of his day of doing with their literary apologies of the Christian scriptures: infected with doubt, they placed God 'on the same level as genius, poets and the thinkers, whose sayings are judged from a purely aesthetic or philosophic point of view; and then, if the thing is well said, the man is a genius – and if it is unusually well said, then God said it!'[33] Centuries of Muslim theologians must have thought differently: is not the vast majority of the literature on *iʿjāz*, the miraculous nature of the Quran, an attempt to demonstrate the Quran's rhetorical superiority compared with the works of the poets – 'mere aestheticism'?[34] What Kierkegaard rejects is even today one of the most important lines of argumentation of Muslim apologists: 'by evaluating the content of the doctrine aesthetically or philosophically... I will or can arrive at the conclusion: *ergo* the one who has delivered this doctrine is called by a revelation, *ergo* he is an apostle.'[35] And while to Kierkegaard an apostle does not 'recommend himself and his doctrine with the help of beautiful similes', but must '*prevent* any aesthetic impertinence and any direct philosophic approach to the form and content of the doctrine',[36] the Muslim tradition, on the other hand, presents Muhammad as a prophet who intentionally challenges the unbelievers to appreciate his doctrine aesthetically and to compare it stylistically with other texts, advancing the poetic perfection of his message as the strongest evidence of its divine origin – in Qāḍī 'Iyāḍ's words, as a 'most illuminating sign and most compelling indication'.[37] We know that Muhammad did not heal the sick or walk on water. His only confirmatory miracle was the Quran itself. A frequently quoted hadith says, 'There is no prophet who is not given signs so that people believe in him. What I have been given is nothing but the words that God revealed to me, and I hope that I will have the greatest following on the day of resurrection.'[38]

Al-Bāqillānī, author of the classical foundation of *iʿjāz*, writes that every prophet is outfitted with an individual miracle as his specific sign,

> for the mission of a prophet is not authentic unless he provides an indication and identifies himself by a sign. He is not distinguishable from a liar by his appearance or by what he himself says, or by anything else, but only by the evidence (*burhān*) that has appeared for him, so that by it he can prove his veracity.[39]

People can see that the prophet is sent by God, al-Bāqillānī maintains, only because they are incapable of imitating his sign. In the context of this general prophetology, Muhammad's authenticating miracle, conceived in the same sense as those of the Old Testament prophets, is seen in the fact that his opponents were unable to produce a recitation of the same linguistic quality as his.

> When the members of his language community saw that none of them was capable of challenging the Quran, of finding fault with it and producing something to match it, they were in the same situation as those who saw Moses' white hand or the transformation of his staff into a snake, the miracles that made their lies obvious.[40]

If they had been able to meet the challenges documented in the Quran, al-Bāqillānī argues, it would have been easy for Muhammad's opponents to refute him. They would have been spared the disputes and wars, the emigration and captivity, the loss of all their power, their prestige and their wealth, for, if they really had stylistically outdone the Quran, Muhammad's pretensions would have collapsed. But in spite of all their efforts, and even though they had the time and the ambition and were masters of eloquence, they have remained mute until today.[41] And the silence of the opponents down to the present day (the efforts by Musaylima and others,[42] al-Bāqillānī finds, are too clumsy to be taken seriously) proves that the linguistic composition of the Quran is a miracle that exceeds human ability and defeats every attempt to revolt against it or unseat it. In Tor Andrae's definition, the word *iʿjāz* denotes this 'quality of the Quran by virtue of which it makes people incapable, *aʿjaza*, of producing anything equal'.[43] Andrae has accurately identified the active element that resonates in the word. Strictly speaking, *iʿjāz* means not 'inimitability', as it is commonly translated, but an 'incapacitation', an 'undoing' of any attempt to match it.[44] A person who hears the Quran, al-Bāqillānī wrote, knows that it is God's own speech: the same certainty arises in him that came over Moses when he heard the voice behind the thorn bush.[45] And only the Quran has this quality; the miracles of the Torah and the Gospels lie only in secondary properties, such as their 'messages about the unseen' (*akhbār ʿan al-ġayb*), not in the linguistic composition itself. As-Suyūṭī later added that Muhammad's miracle was greater and more permanent than those of his prophetic predecessors, such as the camel that was given to Ṣāliḥ according to verse 7:73, or the staff that Moses transformed into a snake. Those signs were merely outward, and visible only to the eyes; but Muhammad's proof, because it is experienced inwardly and 'seen by the heart',[46] is verifiable at all times, he wrote. Perhaps it is no coincidence that there was among the early Orientalists a Christian theologian (and bishop), Tor Andrae, who was one of the very few, alongside the poet Friedrich Rückert, who had a feeling for this particularity of Islam:

> In spite of all we know of Muhammad's independence from his models, we must admit that the way in which he inwardly assimilated and refined the foreign words and ideas, the personal pathos with which he was able to claim all this as his own, is the true miracle of his prophethood. We understand it differently, but in a sense we must agree with Qāḍi Abū Bakr that the doctrine of *iʿjāz* of the Quran is based in reality.[47]

We know today, and I have pointed out in chapter 1, that the principal Quran passages that have been cited in defence of the dogma of *iʿjāz* – the *taḥaddī* verses, in which God 'challenges' the unbelievers to produce a surah to equal those of the Quran – could hardly have been originally intended as indications of the miraculous nature of the text's linguistic quality. That the later Muslims understood them in this sense, however, is more remarkable in the phenomenology of religion, more astonishing, than if the doctrine had been clearly formulated in the Quran and the origin of the dogma of the stylistic miracle were explainable as the consummation of a quranic instruction. Within just a few decades between the ninth and tenth centuries, a theological argument became established throughout the Islamic world that could hardly be more peculiar: I believe in the Quran because its language is too perfect to have been composed by a human being. Or, as ar-Rummānī (d. 996) taught, 'The Quran had a unique style that was different from everything known and held a rank in beauty (*ḥusn*) that exceeded all other forms of oratory, and even verse, which is the best form of discourse.'[48] We can understand this only as a kind of aesthetic proof of the existence of God. Nothing comparable can be found in the religious sphere in a Western culture. At best, one might think of the subjective impression of certain musical or linguistic compositions that move some listeners spontaneously to call them 'divine', 'inimitable' or 'immensely beautiful'. It is the poet's task, Valéry explained,

> to make one think of [inspiration], believe in it, to make sure that one attributes only to the gods a work that is too perfect or too moving to be the product of a man's uncertain hands. The very object of an art, the principle of its artifice, is precisely to impart the impression of an ideal state in which the man who reaches it will be capable of spontaneously producing, with no effort or hesitation, a magnificent and wonderfully ordered expression of his nature and our destinies.[49]

We find the same idea, or only a higher degree of the same experience known to everyone who is sensitive to art – the assertion of poetic perfection that Valéry posits only as hypothetical – in Ṣādiq ar-Rāfiʿī's commentary on a phrase in verse 28:38 (*qāla firʿawnu yā ayyuhā l-mala'u mā ʿalimtu lakum min ilāhin ġayrī fa-awqid lī yā Hāmānu ʿalā ṭ-ṭīni fa-jʿal lī ṣarḥan*):[50]

Look carefully: can you find anything more excellent and artful in the mystery of its eloquence and in its awe-inspiring miraculous splendour than this? What eloquent Arab ever heard such oratory and expression (*tarkīb*) who was not overwhelmed by his emotions, did not taste the truth about himself, did not fall into delirium and rapture and did not say, 'I believe it; God is the Lord, Muhammad the Prophet, the Quran the miracle.' Contemplate how it says of the fired brick, *fa-awqid lī yā Hāmānu ʿalā ṭ-ṭīn*, and note the position of the acoustic agitation (*qalqala*) that lies in the letter *dāl* of one word, *awqid* – 'burn'[51] – and how it is resolved in the recitation in the softness of the letter *lām*. Truly, during the recitation something occurs whose beauty cannot be expressed in words; it is as though one's soul were wrenched from one.[52]

When the scholars of *iʿjāz* insist that Muhammad was no 'mere' poet – that the Quran is not 'merely' poetry – their statements imply that he was that and more. For they were well aware that he was a poet: Al-Jāḥiẓ, for example, says that God sent 'Muhammad as the Arabs' greatest poet and orator';[53] al-Jurjānī calls him 'the most eloquent of the Arabs', who 'surpasses the poets in the beauty of his expression and the nobility of his diction';[54] and ar-Rāfiʿī sees the 'incapacitating' power of the Quran as a superlative of the effect of great works of art:

This is the way that we know from the works of inspired geniuses, each of whom is unique in his area of art. But the miracle (*muʿjiz*) of their works, if we may so call it, their inimitability (*iʿjāz*), lies only in the degree to which they contain perfection of an artistic nature. From the effect of such a work of art, imagine what would be an absolute feeling in your soul, a pure longing. Imagine someone took up this work who wanted to imitate and surpass it (*miʿāraḍa*). He sees comparisons and images in the work, so that he does not doubt his ability to surpass it, even to bend it to his will. He turns to it to surpass it, but no sooner does he turn towards it than a feeling and a longing arise in his soul that are beyond all artistic ability.[55]

Some Orientalists would say that is, if not mere sanctimony, then at least a highly subjective, personal sentiment brought about by religious convictions, and hence not noteworthy. But what else is an aesthetic experience if not an absolute dominance of the subjective? What ignorance in regard to all artistic phenomena is inherent in what Stefan Wild criticized as the 'spiteful attitude: "The Muslims may believe the Quran is beautiful, but we say, 'It is by no means beautiful; from a scientific viewpoint it is boring' "'[56] – an attitude that accords no objective value to the reception experience described so often in the Muslim literature? Although the question goes beyond the theme of the present study, it is worth asking: Does not subjective experience, if it is the collective experience of a community of listeners, constitute an objectivity that is more verifiable, more 'scientifically' convincing than the judgements of taste delivered under the desk lamps of European philologists? Or, as Rückert said,

> Wol eine Zauberkraft muß seyn in dem, woran
> Bezaubert eine Welt so hängt wie am Koran.
>
> A magic power must there be in that whereon
> a world hangs as spellbound as on the Quran.[57]

Of course the aesthetic experience and the positive appraisal of it are reinforced by the knowledge that what one is hearing is the Quran, and hence the direct speech of God – but that does not diminish its subjective reality or the objective reality of its multiplicity and intensity. 'The aesthetic judgement on the Quran as a work of art cannot be separated from the reverence it enjoys in a certain cultural milieu', Wild rightly remarks.[58] In other words – those of the translator Ibn al-Muqaffaʿ (d. 756) – because the Quran was declared the norm, it now appears, after a process of habituation, to be one.[59] The later poet Abū l-ʿAlāʾ al-Maʿarrī (d. 1058) thought along the same lines. A legend, probably fictional, tells how, after he had allegedly recited his imitation of the Quran, a listener objected,

> 'This text is excellent, but it does not have the brilliance of the Quran.' Al-Maʿarrī answered: 'Just wait until the tongues in the prayer niches have polished it for four hundred years, then see what it will have become!'[60]

Besides habituation and convention, other extra-textual factors in the Quran's aesthetic appreciation can also be named. Just as art has always been consumed and appreciated for non-artistic reasons, such as prestige, fashion or the appreciation of experts, the Quran too is felt to be beautiful in many ways because the environment dictates, suggests and reinforces that judgement – that is, because its reception takes place in a context in which the Quran is most highly appreciated, aesthetically as well as otherwise. That may be reason to regard the general public's judgement as sceptically as that of Ibn al-Muqaffaʿand al-Maʿarrī, but such scepticism would be equally appropriate in regard to every great and famous work of literature. Ludwig Wittgenstein once wrote, 'When I hear the expressions of admiration of Shakespeare by the important men of several centuries, I cannot help feeling a certain suspicion that it is a convention to praise him, even though I must say to myself that it is not so.'[61] It is impossible to separate the personal and the social influences in the subjective judgement, for listening to the Quran is, like the experience of any artistic text, 'a product of social cooperation and an expression of intellectual community', as the art sociologist Arnold Hauser writes, 'a result of authoritarian achievement and subordinating adaptation'.[62] The Requiem in D minor is considered masterful and evokes a gratifying shiver because, among other reasons, the listener knows it is by Mozart and was composed just before his death. A text by Heine, spoken on stage in a solemn mood by a sonorous voice with judicious articulation, accompanied by reverent sighs from the highly cultivated audience, can be expected to evoke stronger emotions than the same poem encountered in a banal context without knowledge of its authorship. On the reception of works of art, Hauser writes,

> We usually have no idea how extensive and widespread, intricate and tortuous this way is, and how clumsily, helplessly, and confusedly we would face even the most important and appealing artistic creations without being prepared for what to expect from them and how to adapt to them in order to make sense of their symbolic language, which is often a sort of secret language.[63]

From a certain point in Islamic history on, probably in the late eighth or early ninth century, Muslim scholars began to understand the listeners' reactions to the sound of the Quran, attested to in the Quran itself, in the traditions and most of all in the biography of the Prophet as miraculous signs. The doctrine would not have been thinkable without the two hundred years of the Quran's reception history that preceded it. Angelika Neuwirth is the only one of the Western *iʿjāz* researchers to have clearly mentioned this connection between reception and doctrine, although without going into detail:

> What ultimately led in the ninth century to the formulation of the dogma of the inimitability and uniqueness of the Quran is a central experience of inner life and inner radiance, a very real experience of metaphysical beauty of the revealed scripture – not mere theological speculation or scholarly sophistry. The doctrine was the rationalization of a fundamental experience of the whole religious community – even if this experience was limited in its horizon and its rationalization did not take sufficient notice, or sufficiently serious notice, of the experience of other groups.[64]

Of course a reception history, no matter what form it may take for the community of faith, does not automatically lead to a doctrine like that of *iʿjāz*. But it forms the soil in which such a doctrine can develop. Other impulses are necessary for that to happen. In explaining the reasons for the origin of the *iʿjāz* doctrine, Angelika Neuwirth names six other factors but prefaces them with the remark that none of them could have had such a strong influence if it had not been for the prior reception experience.[65] In a nutshell, these additional factors were:

1 The Quran exegesis required an explanation of the *taḥaddī* verses.
2 Muhammad had to be accommodated in the theory of confirmatory miracles which followed from the quranic prophetology.[66]
3 The scholastic dispute over the eternal nature of the Quran – that is, whether it is created or uncreated. (At first it was mainly the Mu'tazili who tried to prove the incomparability of the Quran, while those who, like the Hanbali, considered it uncreated had nothing to prove: its incomparability followed from its uncreated nature. To scholars of later centuries, these questions overlapped, and the question of *iʿjāz* was separated from the dogmatic debate over the nature of the Quran.)[67]
4 The polemic against the other scriptural religions: there was a need to demonstrate that Muhammad is a worthy culmination of the history of the prophets.
5 Arab national pride and the conflict with the Persian *shuʿūbīya* movement: a linguistic confirmatory miracle also seemed to be evidence of the intellectual and linguistic superiority of the Arab people.
6 Interest in literary history in conjunction with the rise of 'modern' poetry in the early Abbasid period.

As an additional motivation of the theoreticians of *iʿjāz*, Heinz Grotzfeld mentions the figurative character and the resulting greater interpretability of a language recognized as poetic:

> The fact that a passage could be interpreted as *ījāz* – that is, as an example of concision – meant that it could be glossed and expanded almost limitlessly. Metaphor solved all the difficulties that the theologians (except the most orthodox) encountered in the Quran's anthropomorphic representation of God and the afterlife.[68]

I have found no other reasons given for the emergence of the *iʿjāz* doctrine in the Western literature. In Muslim scholarship, there have understandably been few efforts to show historic and extra-textual reasons for its specific argumentation: to date, *iʿjāz* has been seen mainly as originating in the *taḥaddī* verses alone and explained by the Quran and its reception history.[69] Only in recent years has the doctrine's development been embedded in the context of the history of theology in general.[70]

The word *iʿjāz* was established in the late ninth century as a term of art for the miraculous nature of the Quran, but was used as early as the beginning of the century, usually in the sense of a stylistic inimitability as it was conceived by the Mu'tazili literary scholar al-Jāḥiẓ.[71] Very early in the *iʿjāz* discussion, another theory was also put forward, the *ṣarfa* doctrine. Another Mu'tazili theologian, an-Naẓẓām (d. c. 840), was probably the first to advance it. This theory holds that the Quran is by no means stylistically unique, but that God prevented (*ṣarafa*) the unbelievers from producing a text to rival it, although they otherwise would have been able to do so. In this view the miracle is rooted not in the Quran itself but in the fact that no one was able to meet the challenge formulated in the Quran. Most of the theologians who followed an-Naẓẓām were Mu'tazili, such as Hishām al-Fuwāṭī (d. 833) and Abū Muslim al-Iṣfahānī (d. 934), but his theory was also accepted by the Shiites as-Sayyid ash-Sharīf al-Murtaḍā (d. 1044) and Sheikh Mufīd (d. 1032), the Zahiri Ibn Ḥazm (d. 1064) and the Ash'arite Abū Isḥāq al-Isfarā'īnī (d. 1027),[72] and ostensibly with slight modifications by more prominent scholars such as al-Ash'arī himself (d. 935) and al-Juwaynī (d. 1085).[73] It is not true that, as an oversimplification one sometimes hears has it, the *ṣarfa* doctrine is the Mu'tazili teaching while the miraculous nature of the Quranic style is part of Sunni orthodoxy. In fact, both propositions have been advanced in both camps, and several of the most important theoreticians of linguistic inimitability, such as 'Abduljabbār (d. 1025),[74] have been Mu'tazili. Some theologians have also seen the miracle both in the text and outside it, both in the excellence of the Quran and in the divine 'prevention' of the opponents: this position is hinted at in al-Jāḥiẓ's writings,[75] documented with reference to ar-Rummānī, the author of one of the oldest extant treatises on *i'jāz*,[76] and the exegete Abū Muslim al-Iṣfahānī.[77] Finally, even an-Naẓẓām, who has been labelled a 'satan among scholastics' (*shayṭān al-mutakallimīn*) for his authorship of the *ṣarfa* doctrine,[78] did not deny the linguistic beauty of the Quran: he too called it *i'jāz*, and indeed most of his successors accepted the thesis of inimitability in principle and only maintained that it was not the actual confirmatory miracle.[79] It is also important to remember that the proponents of *ṣarfa*, who were clearly in the minority, grew fewer with time and dwindled away completely in the twelfth century. Later authors who survey the various conceptions of *i'jāz*, such as as-Suyūṭī and az-Zarkashī, devote only a few lines to *ṣarfa*.[80]

Consistently, the principal argument of those who see the miracle of Islam in the Quran itself is the book's linguistic excellence.[81] Other aspects (or, as the Arabic books call them, other 'faces', *wujūh*) of the Quran's miraculous nature are sometimes mentioned in addition, such as the knowledge of the past and future that it contains; the statements about God, the world of spirits, the universe or, more generally, the 'hidden'; the wisdom about human beings and society that Muhammad could not possibly have produced himself; the absence of any model for the Quran and hence its transcendence of all experience (*kharq al-'āda*); and the analogy with the miracles of earlier prophets.[82] In many cases, the miraculous nature of the Quran's content is explicitly contested on the grounds that it is not different from that of the older revealed scriptures, and what distinguishes the Quran from them is its linguistic form.[83] Qāḍī 'Iyāḍ notes that the *wujūh al-i'jāz* that the scholars mention are too numerous for him to list them all and, besides, most of them concern the art of rhetoric rather than the Quran. One should not call every linguistic peculiarity of the Quran an aspect (*wajh*) of its miraculous nature, he writes.[84] Ibn as-Surāqa, on the other hand, says, 'The scholars differ on the miraculous qualities of the Quran, and they have named many different ones, all of which are correct and wise'[85] – an attitude that some have found all too conciliatory, and that later prompted Ṣādiq ar-Rāfiʿī to remark that Ibn as-Surāqa had achieved the mathematical maximum, 'but if his book had benefited people, it would have been preserved... and God knows better.'[86] In the twentieth century, several more aspects, some of which may seem laughable, were added to the catalogue of quranic miracles. Several authors have claimed to find scientific or medical insights and theories in the Quran that were centuries ahead of the time of the revelation;[87] others have become Cabbalists, detecting a mathematical regularity in its linguistic structure and its composition that can only be explained by divine providence;[88] and Muḥammad Abū Zahra saw God's work in the principles of Sharia formulated in the Quran.[89] But, in general, in the modern period as well as earlier, *iʿjāz* is understood as referring to stylistic inimitability. This is still the most important and, to many scholars, including the Mu'tazili ʿAbduljabbār (d. 1025) as well as the Shafi'i muhaddith and poet al-Haṭṭābī (d. 998) and the Ash'arite ʿAbdulqāhir al-Jurjānī, the only substantial and verifiable miracle. Even those of the great *iʿjāz* theoreticians who saw the content of the Quran as miraculous, such as al-Bāqillānī and ar-Rummānī, concentrated on the linguistic argument. This emphasis is evident, for example, in ar-Rummānī's *Remarks on the Miraculous Inimitability of the Quran*: it lists seven *wujūh* in all, but the discussion of the quranic rhetoric takes up nearly nine-tenths of the volume. A similar weighting can be observed in the works of Qāḍī ʿIyāḍ and as-Suyūṭī. The two best-known contributions to *iʿjāz* in modern times, ar-Rāfiʿī's *The Miraculous Inimitability of the Quran and the Prophetic Rhetoric* of 1922 and *The Quran's Nature as a Linguistic Miracle* (1971) by ʿĀ'isha ʿAbdurrahmān, alias Bint ash-Shāṭi, likewise concentrate on the aspect of literary superiority.

While such a remarkable consensus regarding the nature of the miracle is observable among Muslim scholars across the centuries, the debate on what constitutes the Quran's stylistic unsurpassability has been all the livelier. Is it the individual words, or is it their composition? Is it the selection and sound of the letters, or is it the rhetorical figures and imagery? Is it the recitative qualities, the *ḥusn an-naġam*, the beauty of its inner melody? Or is the miracle to be explained, as al-Khaṭṭābī suggests, by the incomparable emotional effect that its sound provokes in the hearts and souls of the listeners (*ṣanīʿuhū fī l-qulūb wa-ta'thīruhū fī n-nufūs*), against which there is no defence whether or not one believes in the Quran?

> You hear no other oratory, in verse or prose, that fills the heart with pleasure (*laḏḏa*) and delight (*ḥalāwa*), and at the same time with trembling (*rawʿa*) and awe (*mahāba*), as the Quran does the moment it strikes the ear.[90]

Or is it as as-Sakkākī (d. 1228), one of the greatest rhetoricians of his time, proclaimed in his *Key to the Sciences* (*Miftāḥ al-ʿulūm*):

> Know that the *iʿjāz* of the Quran can be grasped, but not described, just as one can grasp but not describe its correct metre or its elegance (*malāḥa*), or as one hears the melody that the voice produces, but no one but the naturally gifted know how it produces it.[91]

But most of the *iʿjāz* scholars are not content with this widely held opinion. It is not enough, al-Khaṭṭābī for example admonishes, to acknowledge the claim of *iʿjāz* yet be unable to explain the grounds for it; it is too vague merely to claim that a kind of indefinable, yet undeniable certainty arises when one listens to the Quran. Feelings on the listener's part such as sweetness, serenity of the soul, beauty and awe must have specific, comprehensible causes, and it is an essential responsibility of the Quran scholar to identify them.[92] And, in the endeavours to find these causes, theology is transformed into literary scholarship, for, as al-Bāqillānī says, only he who

> achieves the highest degree of knowledge of the Arabic language and masters all its capabilities and forms of expression knows the degree of eloquence (*faṣāḥa*) that the ability of an orator can attain and realizes what exceeds that ability and all bounds of skill, and the *iʿjāz* of the Quran is not concealed from him; its difference from all other oratory is as clear as the differences between the various genres of discourse, between sermons, tracts and poetry, or between a good and a bad poem.[93]

In order to understand the Quran and to figure out what makes it unique among all other texts, Muslim scholars began in the ninth century to collect ideal examples of Arabic poetry to compare them with the Quran. The primary goal was to develop a poetics, to define criteria that could be used to identify a verse as excellent, exemplary, effective and beautiful. The extremely broad and ramified research activity that developed in the centuries that followed prompted Max T. Grünert to remark, 'Give credit where credit is due: the Arabs have done for their language what no other people on earth can claim.'[94]

For Arabic literary scholarship, the Quran is more than just a central text: the discipline owes its very existence in large part to efforts to analyse, and not merely describe, the experience of the Quran's beauty and poignancy on the basis of understandable, empirical evidence.[95] There were certainly other factors that also favoured the progress of literary scholarship, such as the rise of a novel poetry in the early Abbasid period, which was called 'modern' (*muḥdath*) at the time, and the resulting exploration of its unusual rhetorical devices and figures of speech (*badāʾiʿ*). But this literary–aesthetic discussion too concerned the Quran from the outset, for the 'modern' poets justified their violation of the rules that had been recognized up to then by pointing out that the Quran itself contained such *badāʾiʿ*. Conversely, chapters about the linguistic and stylistic properties of the Quran were a standard component of legal scholars' works (*uṣūl al-fiqh*). In short, the prevailing atmosphere in the cultural centres of the Islamic world in the ninth to eleventh centuries was one in which all aspects of language and the verbal arts were discussed spiritedly, numerous lasting works of literary theory appeared, and the same scholars who appraised the new poetry tried to describe the stylistic properties of the Quran in greater detail. The need for objective criteria of literary criticism arose not only from the study of the Quran but from the reception of poetically structured texts in general, of which, it was understood, the Quran was one.[96] 'The science of poetic expression and rhetoric (*'ilm al-badī' wa-l-bayān*)', az-Zarkashī wrote, 'is the most magnificent pillar of the Quran commentator.'[97] The best example of the justice of this statement is 'Abdulqāhir al-Jurjānī. A recognized Ash'arite – that is, solidly orthodox – theologian, he is also probably the most important scholar of Arabic poetics to date: the first to bring together the ideas, concepts and insights that were current in his time to form a coherent literary theory. He wrote a celebrated book on the *Mysteries of Eloquence* (*Asrār al-balāġa*), an equally weighty work on the *Arguments of the Miraculous Inimitability of the Quran* (*Dalā'il al-i'jāz fīl-Qur'ān*), numerous books of poetry, major works of grammar (including the thirty-volume *Muġnī*)[98] and numerous theological and legal treatises. The breadth of his subject matter was not viewed as extraordinary. There is no lack of references to poetry in his works on the Quran, or of examples from the Quran in his studies of rhetoric and grammar. To al-Jurjānī, the Quran and poetry were situated in the same sphere: he was interested in both; they were parts of *one* discussion. The unhestitatingly aesthetic view of the Quran that is apparent even in his bibliography becomes more distinct upon a closer look at his book on *i'jāz*. While the title might suggest a theological treatise on doctrines of faith and accounts of miracles, the book itself deals with such apparently secular and poetic matters as *faṣāha* (eloquence), *balāġa* (verbal art), *tamthīl* (comparison), *naẓm* (linguistic composition), *isti'āra* (metaphor), *lafẓ* (expression), *kināya* (metonymy), *majāz* (trope), *ḥaḏf* (ellipsis), *ījāz* (concision), *ta'rīḍ* (allusion, irony), *iḥsās* (sentiment), *ḏawq* (taste, experience), *qaṣr* (abbreviation) and *ikhtiṣāṣ* (development of particularities). His view is so exclusively linguistic that Max Weisweiler was prompted to suppose that the Quran was merely a pretext for al-Jurjānī's 'actual, inner purpose', namely 'to show what is relevant in evaluating all oratory'.[99] If that were true, then we should be able to answer the simple question why al-Jurjānī wrote that book with that title and that content and opened it with a detailed introduction in which he names his theological motivation quite precisely: namely, to solidify the proof of Islamic faith. What reason is there to assume that al-Jurjānī, a man famous for his piety, who did not interrupt his ritual prayer even when a thief robbed him in front of his own eyes,[100] would practically deceive his readers by pretending his motives are different from what they are? And for that reason go to all the effort of writing several hundred pages about *i'jāz*, in which he not only quoted dozens of Quran verses but also discussed and analysed them stylistically, in unsurpassable detail and with admirable precision? In al-Jurjānī's day, the study of rhetoric no longer needed to be justified by religious motives (if it ever had), and al-Jurjānī himself also wrote another work in which he discussed general criteria of eloquence and poetic expression without special regard to the Quran. But this book, as its title announces and as the author emphasizes in the introduction, is about the Quran, exploring its 'sublime uniqueness and brilliant excellence and marvellous art of presentation'.[101]

What is characteristic about Weisweiler's comment is that, while the Orientalist can explain the dominance of poetics in a book about the Quran only by interpreting the author's religious interest as an alibi for his aesthetic interest, the author himself sees the two fields as one and the same: to him the Quran is a revealed text to be experienced aesthetically and described using the insights and concepts of poetry. If Weisweiler's suspicions were well founded, then we should expect al-Jurjānī's reception to have been limited essentially to literary circles; he would not have interested theologians. But the opposite is true: no other work on *iʿjāz* enjoys such undivided esteem among Muslim scholars of all stripes and of all periods. Al-Bāqillānī's pietistic work may be widespread and often cited in the Islamic world – it has become almost the canonical work on *iʿjāz* – but it is al-Jurjānī's *Arguments* that has been praised in the twentieth century by such diverse readers as Muḥammad ʿAbduh,[102] Rashīd Riḍā,[103] Muḥammad Abū Zahra,[104] Sayyid Quṭb,[105] Muḥammad Khalafallāh[106] and Naṣr Ḥāmid Abū Zayd[107] as the pinnacle both of Muslim *iʿjāz* literature and of Arabic literary scholarship.

Al-Jurjānī is certainly the most poetically sensitive of the major *iʿjāz* theoreticians in Islamic history, and the first to have examined all aspects of poetic discourse in such detail and to have arrived at a fundamental theory of poetics. Those who came after him, such as Fakhruddīn ar-Rāzī, Ḥāzim al-Qartajannī (d. 1285), Ibn al-Athīr (d. 1239) and as-Sakkākī, contributed new material and attained some new insights but showed nothing like the same originality and consistency. In the linguistic analysis of his Quran commentary, Az-Zamakhsharī displays a similar sensitivity and sheds light on numerous rhetorical elements, but he does not develop a systematic approach. The later authors, such as az-Zarkashī, Ibn Khaldūn and as-Suyūṭī, saw it as their task to provide an overview of past findings rather than to present new theological or poetological approaches of their own, and, as for the modern period, a comparison of recent achievements with al-Jurjānī is almost disenchanting.[108] In Sayyid Quṭb's literary-aesthetic analysis of the Quran, for example, or the widely praised *iʿjāz* book by Ṣādiq ar-Rāfiʿī, which the Christian intellectual Yaʿqūb Ṣarrūf (d. 1927) ennobled with his statement that every Muslim must possess it alongside the Quran,[109] the shortcomings are unmistakable. Ar-Rāfiʿī is not at a loss for eloquent words to express his enthusiasm for the beauty of the Quran, but he rarely feels the need to provide textual examples of what constitutes the poetic quality he praises.[110] Quṭb is in this regard more conscientious, but his declared attempt to surpass al-Jurjānī and early Arabic rhetoric through his analysis of the Quran's imagery[111] is hardly abreast of contemporary methods (although visibly influenced by Western literature and its aesthetic norms) and is rather naive in its treatment of the text compared with al-Jurjānī. Neither ar-Rāfiʿī nor Quṭb works as closely with the exact wording, or supports his theses with so many examples analysed in such detail and with discussions of all sorts of objections, even the most absurd, as al-Jurjānī does. But, most importantly, no one goes beyond the Quran as resolutely as he does to arrive at general standards of linguistic perfection. The criteria he developed were truly groundbreaking in his time, and many of them are not obsolete even today. Among the twentieth-century authors of whom I am aware, only Bint ash-Shāṭi', the grande dame of Egyptian Quran studies, who has since drifted into the orthodox camp, penetrates to the core of the quranic language. Yet even her work shows but modest progress, if any, in comparison with authors such as al-Jurjānī or az-Zamakhsharī, considering the nearly one thousand years that have passed.

In the section that follows, I would like to present al-Jurjānī's interpretation of the quranic miracle, not simply by reporting the content of his book[112] or presenting his literary theory as a whole,[113] but primarily by investigating what he sees as the particular quality of the Quran in comparison with other texts and what the book reveals about his and his milieu's attitudes towards the revelation. Then, to bring to light what is specific to al-Jurjānī's work, I will contrast it with Bāqillānī's *The Miraculous Inimitability of the Quran* (*Iʿjāz al-Qur'ān*). As an approach to the doctrine of *iʿjāz*, it seems to me more suitable to examine an individual author than to present a survey of all the major writings on the subject in the form of brief summaries, as is customarily done in the Western literature on *iʿjāz*. And, for a study devoted to the aesthetic reception of the Quran, there is no more suitable representative of the *iʿjāz* literature than the man from northeastern Iran.

Al-Jurjānī's 'Science of Composition'

There is no way to prove Helmut Ritter's surmise[114] that the originality of Majduddīn Abū Bakr ʿAbdulqāhir ibn ʿAbdirraḥmān al-Jurjānī was due in part to the fact that he never left his native Jurjān and, unlike many of his learned colleagues, showed no ambitions to collect as much knowledge from as many sheikhs as possible. That he was a creative and a groundbreaking author through and through is impressively demonstrated, however, by his book on the 'arguments of the miraculous inimitability of the Quran', even more so than by his book on the 'mysteries of eloquence', which is better known in the West and has been translated into German by Hellmut Ritter. Al-Jurjānī excels not only in the striking precision and the obsessive detail of his analyses of specific figures of speech, but he is also the first to have devised a poetics that is as comprehensive as it is systematic, based on the concept of *naẓm* and derived from several fundamental insights of textual linguistics. Depending on the context, I would translate *naẓm* – literally, 'order' – as 'construction' or 'composition', and sometimes as 'structure' or 'artistic structure', because, as we shall see, it corresponds in many contexts to what Lotman, for example, means by that term in modern literary theory. If we remember that the Latin word *textus* is derived from the verb *texere* and means 'fabric', we might even render *naẓm* as 'text'. *Naẓm* is not just 'style' in general, as Weisweiler thinks (al-Jurjānī uses the term *uslūb* for that). Nor can *lafẓ* (plural *alfāẓ*) and *ma'nā* (plural *ma'ānī*), the two other key concepts of al-Jurjānī's theory, be translated simply as 'words' and 'senses'. For a word, al-Jurjānī uses the term *kalima*, and for the sense of a statement, independent of the given linguistic form expressing it, he writes *maḍmūn*. The best translation for *lafẓ* generally seems to be 'expression', since it connotes the material, perceptible aspect of the linguistic sign. *Ma'nā* is more difficult. It can sometimes be rendered as 'content' (i.e., the signified of a linguistic sign), but often it stands for a poetic 'image' or theme, a motif, or even for syntactic-semantic categories that are not called content in English, as in the expression *ṣūrat al-ma'nā*, 'the form of the meaning', or *ma'ānī n-naḥw*, 'grammatical meanings'). The latter term in particular regularly causes confusion in the literature (when it is not simply avoided). What it means is something like this: a grammatical construction, such as a verb phrase, gives rise to 'meaning' all by itself, independently of its contextual message. If we were to invent a sentence such as 'The troarco spatly briggles the brult', which obviously has no meaning – in the ordinary sense, at least – but at the same time is not fully devoid of significance (that is, we understand that something does something to something else), conveying something, producing 'meanings' solely by the grammatically correct arrangement of words – those 'meanings' are *ma'ānī n-naḥw*. In contemporary linguistics, the concept of 'semantic syntax' refers to this phenomenon.

The preceding example is sufficient to show that translations such as 'content', 'sense' or 'meaning', at least in their familiar usage, do not really correspond to the concept of *ma'nā* in al-Jurjānī (and other Arabic poeticists). Ritter was no doubt aware of this while working on his brilliant translation of the 'mysteries of eloquence', which he did almost throughout his academic life. He decided to translate *ma'nā* as 'Sinninhalt' ('sense content') or 'Sinnmotiv' ('sense motif'), which does little to elucidate the concept: what exactly are 'sense contents'? A more significant alternative is 'dichterischer Gedanke' ('poetic idea'), which Heinrichs proposes in his dissertation *Arabische Dichtung und griechische Poetik* (Arabic poetry and Greek poetics) while admitting that it does not match the Arabic *ma'nā* in every case. 'Meaning' is a possible translation precisely because it is a very general term. 'Intention', in the sense in which it is used in textual linguistics, is more precise in many cases, as is 'idea' in Lotman's sense.

In any case, it is practically unavoidable to translate *maʿnā* variously depending on the context.[115] To avoid misunderstandings in the discussion that follows, we will use the Arabic terms, or at least include them in parenthesis, where an unambiguous English translation is lacking. Ultimately, however, the principal cause of the lexical difficulty, as we shall explain in more detail in this section, is this: although the dualism of form and content that is fundamental to Classical European rhetoric is in principle not contradicted by Arabic theory[116] and is still frequently thought and assumed in everyday usage, it is not applicable to *maʿnā* and *lafẓ*: in al-Jurjānī's theory: neither exists independently of the other; neither can take precedence over the other; there can be no content without form, no meaning without its linguistic expression. This concept anticipates a fundamental insight of modern linguistic and literary studies. To al-Jurjānī, *iʿjāz* lies not in the beauty of the ideas (*ḥusn al-maʿānī*), not in the linguistic expressions (*alfāẓ*), not in the individual words (*kalim*) or in their expressiveness, not in the letters and the resulting prosody, not in occlusive consonance or metaphor, not in the odd words (*ġarā'ib*), the diacritical marks or in the general flawlessness of the diction – all of these opinions were held, and he strove to refute each of them individually.[117] Al-Jurjānī sees the *iʿjāz* of the Quran in the verses' inimitable *naẓm*, and that means in their 'structure', the meaningful combination of lexical signs to convey an intention. This is the central thesis of the book, running through the various lines of argument throughout the text.

> We say that the qualitative surplus (*mazāyā*) appeared to them [Muhammad's contemporaries] in the *naẓm* of the Quran, that the qualities they found in the combination of linguistic expressions (*alfāẓ*) were what made them incapable of any response, any resistance. We say that the figures of words and meanings (*badāʾiʿ*) in the individual parts of the verses were what filled them with awe, and that every expression was in its place and in harmony with the others, as was the use of every idiom and the position of every predicate and the form of every threat, admonition, information, reminder, encouragement and warning; and that everything had a reason and a proof, an attribute and an explanation. All that confused and fascinated them. They examined surah by surah, section by section and verse by verse, and they found no word that was not in its proper place, no expression that would have been better placed elsewhere or could have been replaced by a different, similar or better one, one that would have been more appropriate or suitable. They found a well-structuredness that overwhelmed their minds by its magnificence, and all people were petrified by its linguistic order and harmony, by its inner perfection and the consistency of its composition. No orator felt the ambition to contend against it; no matter how they racked their brains, they had no ideas; no tongue was able to say anything or to make a demand, and even the greatest among the opponents had to admit defeat and abstain from all rebuttal.[118]

Al-Jurjānī is not the first to locate the miracle of the Quran in its *naẓm*. Among others before him, al-Jāḥiẓ, al-Khaṭṭābī, al-Bāqillānī and, most importantly, ʿAbduljabbār advanced this view. Naturally al-Jurjānī knows that, and he takes their achievements – which are by no means humble – for granted, even if he does not cite them by name but refers to them generally as 'rhetoricians' (*bulaġāʾ*). (Al-Jāḥiẓ is an exception: al-Jurjānī quotes him repeatedly, sometimes refuting and sometimes agreeing with him.) Such allusions are significant in regard to ʿAbduljabbār in particular, and no doubt strategic: the *Dalāʾil* is in large part a combative reply to him. ʿAbduljabbār had gone the farthest in the direction that al-Jurjānī took, but as a Mu'tazili he had drawn – in the Ash'arite's view – the wrong dogmatic conclusions from his many undeniably correct and original observations, and therefore urgently needed to be corrected.[119] His predecessors, al-Jurjānī charged at the beginning of his book, had had only a vague notion of what constituted the Quran's *naẓm*. His ambition was therefore to advance beyond their achievements by developing a general theory of poetic discourse. To attain that goal, al-Jurjānī starts at the beginning: with an explanation of fundamental principles of textual linguistics, a clarification of what human discourse is made up of, namely, not a simple succession of arbitrary words, even in the simplest case, but meaningful combinations of subject and predicate. Even when the predicate is unspoken, it implicitly underlies the utterance: where the basic linguistic unit, the sentence, seems to contain only a noun and a particle, as in a simple appeal (*nidāʾ*), it also contains an implicit verb (*fiʿl muḍmar*). The speaker of the utterance 'O ʿAbdullah!' (*yā ʿAbdallāh*) cannot help instinctively adding in his mind an 'I mean' (*aʿnī*), 'want' (*urīdu*) or 'call' (*adʿū*), which he expresses indirectly by the particle *yā*.[120] Octavio Paz formulated the same idea in other words:

> Before language can be produced, the signs and sounds must be associated in such a way that they will imply and transmit a meaning. . . . Thus, it is not the word, but the phrase or sentence, that constitutes the simplest unit of speech. The phrase is a self-sufficient whole; as in a microcosm, all language dwells therein. Like the atom, it is an organism separable only by violence. And indeed, only by the violence of grammatical analysis is the phrase broken up into words. Language is a universe of meaningful units, that is, of phrases.[121]

Only after al-Jurjānī has presented and discussed the three possible types of Arabic sentences and their variants in full detail (all Arabic sentences consist of a noun in combination with another noun, a verb or a verb *and* a particle) does he turn to his subject proper: identifying what characterizes poetic expression in order to determine the specific nature of the quranic miracle. His project is to find the basis of every single merit of the Quran, documenting each one in turn in the text, so that his argument does not rest on mere feelings of taste and sentiment. It is a difficult, laborious endeavour (if it were not so arduous, he taunts, the urgency of the task would not be denied by so many people) and ultimately an impossible one, but he, al-Jurjānī, wants to guide the reader and distinctly explain one thing after another.[122] It is not enough just to say that the eloquence and verbal artistry of the Quran are 'a particular quality of the form of its composition (*naẓm*) and a special kind of structure (*tarkīb*)', as one might say that the qualitative difference between two rugs arises from the carpet-weavers' combining colours and patterns with one another, and perfection is the degree of quality at which an ordinary person 'gives up his ambitions to achieve it, and no longer knows how, and is exhausted and is caught in his inability (*'ajz*)'.[123] No, al-Jurjānī writes, one must also be able to say wherein lies the surplus of quality, the *mazīya*, that distinguishes one discourse from another. One must be able to identify and define this special quality exactly and describe it by examples and comparisons, just as one would like to ask an artist how he produced a precious silk brocade, and would request a demonstration so that one might see with one's own eyes 'how he interweaves the warp and weft and floating threads on this side and that, how he makes these threads form certain patterns in the length and breadth, and which colour he introduces first and which second and which third.'[124] Starting from the principle that it is possible to distinguish right and wrong and the beautiful from the bad in every art, and to prefer one beautiful thing to another and to distinguish degrees of artistry, it must also be possible, given two verses, to analyse precisely why one of them is better than the other; it must be possible to understand poetry and the Quran as well as the master carpet-weaver understands where each silk thread belongs in the brocade; just as the artisan knows why he places each individual piece of an inlay where he does and not somewhere else; just as the master builder can explain the position of each brick in a wondrous building. In other words, al-Jurjānī's project was nothing less than to investigate God's plan – or, shall we say, His poetics. He does not say it in so many words, but he leaves no doubt that his interest is in knowing why God spoke as He did and not otherwise and that the language of God's word is no different – that is, it is subject to the same rules and mechanisms as the human language of the poets and the rhetoricians – it is just better.

In a way, al-Jurjānī goes still farther in literary exegesis, in *tafsīr adabī*, than Amīn al-Khūlī and his successors would do almost a thousand years later (and a number of them fell into the clutches of a modern Inquisition for propounding similar views to those al-Jurjānī had proclaimed long before). Al-Jurjānī treated the language of the Quran as a human language, one accessible to mortals; he advocated applying literary scholarship to the study of the Quran and understanding it in the light of Arabic poetry. Moreover, he conceived literary and aesthetic analysis not only as an indispensable tool but also as a kind of religious duty. Diametrically opposed to the Augustinian principle that reading the Bible requires only true humility, not scholarship and literary culture,[125] al-Jurjānī demands poetic sensitivity and literary scholarship in the truly devout, since only the study of poetics gives access to the Quran, its message and its miraculous nature. If the Quran stands out and is recognizable as divine by its eloquence, he argues, the Arabs were able to perceive this *ḥujja*, this proof of Muhammad's prophethood, only because they were familiar with poetry, because poetry was their divan and their moral standard (*'unwān al-adab*), because their culture was founded entirely on verbal beauty, and they even held contests in which they competed in poetry and rhetoric.[126] Anyone who wanted to divert the Muslims' attention from poetry and the study of eloquence was no better than an enemy of the faith preventing them from memorizing and reciting the Quran and keeping God's commandments. Such a person violated the duty to protect the Quran from alteration and corruption so that its validity might endure and be manifest for all time. 'He is as one who would make us forget and would remove the Quran from our hearts', al-Jurjānī writes, 'who takes away and destroys the medicine that is necessary for your recovery and your continued life.'[127]

After devoting the first chapters of his book to systematically rebuking those who would deny or question the value of poetry, grammar (*naḥw*) and the 'science of rhetoric' (*'ilm al-bayān*) or of academic endeavours in general ('reviling' might be a more apt expression to describe the scornful, lecturing tone of these pages, which are even more sarcastic than the author's otherwise polemical style), al-Jurjānī turns his argument against another position. The opinion is widely held, he complains, probably thinking of an intellectual tradition that descends from Ibn Qutayba (d. 889)[128] through Abū Hilāl al-'Askarī (d. after 1015)[129] to Ibn Khaldūn (d. 1406),[130] that the eloquence of a speech, including the Quran, is due to *alfāẓ*, and its beauty arises from such factors as the choice and arrangement of the most elegant words. This view, and especially the purely schematic dualism of expression (*lafẓ*) and idea (*ma'nā*) that it implies, is what al-Jurjānī hammers at throughout the book, exaggerating it in his polemical paraphrases, attacking it and developing his own arguments in contradistinction to it. His central purpose is to show that individual words are neutral, that there is *a priori* no difference between *rajul* (man) and *faras* (mare), no more than between *rajul* and the corresponding Persian word, for example; that neither possesses greater eloquence, and that beauty is generated only by the *naẓm* of the ideas in a given expression (*lafẓ*);[131] to demonstrate that the relation between meaning and linguistic expression is by no means only a matter of convention and hence arbitrary, as the linguists of his day assumed.[132] For al-Jurjānī, an individual word has no aesthetic property or quality. Nor does an idea exist without linguistic expression, however; ideas cannot be evaluated in isolation from their expression. The eloquence of a discourse is thus due neither to the mere content of what is said nor to the choice of words, but to its specific composition or artistic structure, which is not at all arbitrary but determined by its meanings. Al-Jurjānī supports this thesis by discussing numerous examples, both from the Quran and from poetry. In verse 11:44 (*wa-qīla yā arḍu bla'ī mā'aki*... ; 'And it was said, 'Earth, swallow thy waters...'),[133] for example, the miracle lies only in the combination (*irtibāṭ*) of the words, in the inimitable way in which the first joins with the second and the second with the third and the third with the fourth to form a perfect, immutable unit.[134] The complex linguistic structure of the complete verse is the source of its irresistible excellence (*faḍīla qāhira*) and evident quality (*mazīya ẓāhira*). There is nothing miraculous about any individual word in it, such as the particle *yā* ('O'), for example; we find 'these properties that fill you with the awe of *i'jāz*' only in its combination with the word *arḍ*, 'earth' (which al-Jurjānī finds incomparably more brilliant and precise in the context of this verse than the apparently semantically identical *ayyuhā l-'arḍ*), and in the interconnection of all the words.[135]

Both in the Quran and in the verses of many poets, al-Jurjānī demonstrates how the same word appears perfect in one place and unfitting in another: if the opponents' opinion were correct that the specific quality of a discourse comes from the individual words, then a given word must be beautiful or ugly in every case – but it is not. Consequently, to take up al-Jurjānī's comparison, the composition (*naẓm*) of a discourse is like the weaving of a rug and the combination of its differently coloured threads and yarns. Blue is not in itself more beautiful than red, but only in the context of a specific pattern, in combination with other colours, and in relation to the artistic idea on which the carpet is based. In this image, however, it is not the letters (*ḥurūf*) but the words (*kalim*) that correspond to the weaver's material. Al-Jurjānī was only marginally interested in the auditory and musical dimensions of Quran recitation, like most other classical rhetoricians (but unlike the Sufis and unlike many modern authors who have written on *i'jāz*). He did not theorize about onomatopoeia:

> if the Creator of language had said *rabaḍa* instead of *ḍaraba* (for the verb 'strike'), no defect would have resulted from it. The same cannot be said of the combination (*naẓm*) of words, for it is in their combination that you follow the trail of the thoughts (*ma'ānī*) and you arrange them according to the way in which they are arranged in your mind (*nafs*). Thus it can only be a combination that does justice to the condition of a word in its constellation with the others; it is not a combination in which one part is joined to another haphazardly.[136]

In this concept of *naẓm*, it is not letters or words as mere sounds that are joined together in the speaker's mind, but individual signifieds whose signifiers in combination produce a certain message. Any change in their structure, however inconspicuous, must yield a different meaning: *Zaydun ka-l-asad* ('Zayd is like a lion') is not the same as *ka-anna Zaydani l-asadu* ('as if Zayd were a lion'),[137] and the Quran verse *wa-ja'alū li-llāhi shurakā'a l-jinna* ('Yet they ascribe to God, as associates, the jinn')[138] would only superficially say the same thing if *shurakā'* ('associates') preceded *li-llāh* (God's): because *shurakā'* follows *li-llāh*, the statement has a totality and an aesthetic appeal, 'its beauty and force' (*ḥusn wa-raw'a*). If *shurakā'* were prefixed (as in *wa-ja'alū l-jinna shurakā'a li-llāhi*, 'Yet they made the jinn associates of God'), not only would the verse lose its elegance, but its meaning too would be different: one might then see the reprehensible nature of the act in the fact that the unbelievers made *the jinn* and not someone else God's associates. The emphasis is actually, as al-Jurjānī shows in one and a half pages of minute analysis, on the reproach that the unbelievers gave God *any* associates, whether the jinn or any other beings. This is achieved by placing the word *shurakā'* as the first object of the verb *ja'ala* ('made'), while *allāh* is placed where the second object (*al-jinn*) would be expected. Because the second object is moved back, it takes on an explanatory character; it is not the substance of the statement.[139] Similarly, the author analyses the verse *wa-la-tajida annahum aḥraṣa n-nāsi 'alā ḥayātin* ('You will find them, of all mankind, those most attached to life'),[140] demonstrating how strongly the meaning would be altered and the beauty, splendour and suppleness of the expression diminished if only the noun *ḥayāt* ('life') were in the determinate state. As another example of the insight, known since Aristotle, that the aesthetic effect arises from breaking the probabilistic order of the language, al-Jurjānī discusses verse 19:4, in which Zacharias says, *wa-shta'ala r-ra'su shaybā* ('and my head is all aflame with hoariness').[141] Too many saw and praised only the metaphor (*isti'āra*) in this formulation, but the 'majestic dignity, the excess of loftiness, the fascinating awe that penetrates souls at this speech' are caused, al-Jurjānī writes, by the unusual and unexpected way in which the individual words are interlocked. The verb (*ishta'ala*) refers to a noun (*ra's*, 'head') but at the same time depends on the last word (*shayb*, 'hoariness'), which denotes the cause in relation to the first word. All three words are thus inseparably linked to one another. Although the verb *ishta'ala* refers to *ar-ra's*, the combination by itself makes no sense. The sense comes only with the connection between *ra's* and the appended *shayb*. The noun with which the verb is grammatically linked is in the nominative case, while the noun that determines the sense of the verb is in the accusative. Thus the verb *ishta'ala* belongs to *ra's*, the first noun, only because of the second noun. On the level of the verbal expression, *lafẓ, ishta'ala* is connected with *ra's*, but semantically, on the level of *ma'nā*, it belongs to *shayb*: as a result, all three words are inseparably and inimitably interlocked. If, al-Jurjānī goes on, *ishta'ala* were directly linked with *shayb* (as in *ishta'ala shaybu r-ra'si*, 'The hoariness of my head is aflame', or *ishta'ala sh-shaybu fī r-ra'si*, 'The hoariness on my head is aflame'), the beauty, glory (*fakhāma*) and force (*raw'a*) that the speech has would be lost. Only this exact arrangement fully expresses the glare of the old man's white head, giving the image a totality (*shumūl*) and making it a symbol of age: the listener imagines a man who has not had a single black hair on his head for as long as anyone can remember. In the variations mentioned, the image loses its absoluteness and its force; we don't know whether all or only some of the speaker's hair is white. Furthermore, the word *ar-ra's*, the head, has the meaning 'my head', without the need for a possessive pronoun: this concision adds to the elegance of the verse.[142] Al-Jurjānī finds a similar effect in verse 54:12: *wa-fajjarnā l-arḍa ʿuyūnan* ('We made the earth burst out in gushing springs'). The verb *fajjara*, 'let (something) burst forth', 'let (something) gush', is semantically related to *ʿuyūn* ('springs') – it is the springs that gush and that burst forth out of the earth – but in *lafẓ*, in the 'outward' verbal expression, the verb is connected to *arḍ* ('earth'). Again, it is this interlocking of the three words in a complex reciprocal relation that creates the totality, al-Jurjānī says: we see how the water gushes out everywhere on earth as out of springs, as if all earth were one great spring, or as if God had made the earth burst with many springs (this is the reading chosen in the translation above). But if the verse had been *wa-fajjarnā ʿuyūna l-arḍi*, 'We made the springs of the earth gush forth', or *wa-fajjarnā l-ʿuyūna fīl-ʿarḍi*, 'We made the springs on earth gush forth', the listener would understand merely that water gushed forth out of the earth from springs in various places.[143]

Al-Jurjānī considered it a widely held misconception that the same facts could be expressed, more or less eloquently, in two different ways. Such an idea could only be based on a superficial view of language. While it is true that one might refer to the same matter or object (*maḍmūn*) by two different phrases, as one sees for example in comparing a verse with its paraphrase in the commentary (*tafsīr*), the meaning (*maʿnā*) must necessarily change with the altered wording (*lafẓ*), since the two are an inseparable unit. There is no such thing, al-Jurjānī said, as a bare *maʿnā* that has yet to be dressed in an outer *lafẓ*, and he realized what semioticians and aestheticians of the twentieth century would strive to explain: meaning and expression are not like the body and its clothes; two utterances cannot have different styles and the same content.[144] Poetic form is not an ornamentation with which one might decorate an utterance that could just as well be made in simple words; it is inherent in the message being communicated and unthinkable without it.[145] Paraphrasing a verse in prose not only destroys its structure but also yields a different meaning; the text is no longer the same; *ishtaʿala r-ra'su shayban* does not express the same thing as *ibyaḍḍa ra'sī kulluhū*, 'My head has turned all white'.[146] And here, in particular, al-Jurjānī takes great pains to distil the subtlest differences in meaning out of two variants of a verse – shifts in meaning caused by the different placement of a word or the choice of a certain particle, such as *yā* instead of *ayyuhā* (for the vocative 'O...!'), or the substitution of an apparent synonym for a word. In such microscopic analyses, al-Jurjānī displays great rigour and his book makes captivating reading. He seems to anticipate many of the findings of modern semiotics and literary studies about the connection between sign and meaning, such as – to name just one obvious example – Lotman's thesis that an idea does not exist outside the linguistic structure that is adequate to express it, that there are ideally no synonyms from the reader's perspective, and that the substitution or even the repetition of a single word in a text creates not a variation of the same content but a new content.[147]

The central idea of *Dalā'il al-i'jāz fī l-Qur'ān* is that the composition or structure (*naẓm*) of a sentence follows from the idea (*ma'nā*) that the speaker has in mind, and no expression (*lafẓ*) can be found fitting or unfitting except with regard to the idea. Al-Jurjānī expressed this thesis clearly in his *Mysteries of Eloquence*, where he writes that

> it is not the speaker who leads the idea to wordplay and rhyme; on the contrary, the idea leads him to these two stylistic devices and makes him hit upon them; so much so that, if he had wanted to substitute an expression without assonance, the sense would have fought against it, and he would have been forcing something strange upon it, and the speaker would have been just as much subject to censure as one who put together tasteless puns and repulsive rhymes. You will find no method that is more felicitous and better from beginning to end, and no course that better leads to a good form of expression and more reliably commands applause, than to leave the ideas free to follow their own disposition and let them find the words themselves.[148]

This does not imply, however, that the poet merely follows the formal law of the *alfāẓ*, and that the words of a sentence are like a continuous silk thread, making creative acts superfluous. Al-Jurjānī vehemently contests such a view. To him, collocations of *alfāẓ* make sense only if they express an intention of the speaker or poet and, strictly speaking, not the expressions but the individual ideas or intentions (*ma'ānī*) are connected together. To al-Jurjānī, the act of composition (*naẓm*) always refers to the totality of the *ma'ānī* to be expressed. Merely concatenating words, if they do not function as vehicles of the speaker's intended *ma'ānī*, is nothing creative that would justify calling the speaker an author (*mu'allif*). To use the analogy of carpet-weaving once again for the composition of a verse, it is the master weaver who must put together the silk threads and tie them to produce an intended pattern.[149] Because the *naẓm* of an oration is something that the poet ultimately creates by joining together his poetic ideas (*ma'ānī*), like an artist who combines different colours and so composes a painting, it is impossible, al-Jurjānī finds, to imitate it (*ḥikāya fī n-naẓm*), since an imitation could at best refer to the wording of the individual expressions (*alfāẓ*) and the sound of the letters, and so would be only superficial. 'It is impossible to imitate or plagiarize a writer whose art is the word', Karl Kraus said in the twentieth century, and his reasoning is altogether in keeping with al-Jurjānī's poetics: 'Words that stand by themselves, that stick in the average mind, and hence do not have the greatest value, can be copied. But how stale and empty they seem in their new surroundings. Unrecognizable!'[150] A person who wants to imitate a writer, Kraus says, must take the trouble to copy the whole work. Al-Jurjānī writes that plagiarism has more to do with the work of a reciter (*rāwī*) than that of a poet. The imitation cannot be mistaken for something artistically creative any more than the singer (*munshid*) of a poem by Imra' al-Qays (d. 550) could be mistaken for the poet himself.[151] That and similar misconceptions arise because the listeners naturally receive the ideas only through the expressions. But that does not imply that the individual *alfāẓ* only join together to form a meaning afterwards, in the listener's ear, and not before, in the speaker's mind.[152]

It goes without saying that al-Jurjānī the Ash'arite theologian has as much to do with the formulation of such ideas as al-Jurjānī the literary theorist. Even though he does not mention the Quran in this connection, we have a definite impression that the author is interested less in the relation between singer and poem than in that between God and the reciter of His words: he is interested in what happens in the moment of the recitation. As explained in chapter 3, Ash'arite theology even before al-Jurjānī had defined the act of recitation as an 'imitation' (*ḥikāya*), and so had overcome the conflict between the premise that the Quran is God's direct speech and the inadmissible presumption that it is God Himself who speaks during a Quran recitation by means of human tongues and lips. Similar theological considerations no doubt moved al-Jurjānī to point out that, while a speech (*kalām*) can be attributed to a speaker, the words are no more identical with that speaker than silk with the weaver or gold and silver with the jeweller.[153] Analogously, although al-Jurjānī does not say so explicitly here, God's word would be – in keeping with Ash'arite dogma – an accidental property of God, not an essential one. Although he does not place it in the foreground, the author at no time denies his theological position. It is present even when he does not mention the Quran – not because the theologian al-Jurjānī sometimes meddles with the work of the literary scholar al-Jurjānī, as Margaret Larkin suggests.[154] Rather, we must realize that his interests in theology and in literary studies coincide. They are indivisible: al-Jurjānī *formulates his poetics*, not as a neutral observer or a mere aesthete but *as a theologian*, one of the eminent ones of his time, and on the basis of a clearly defined position on the revelation. Every poetic idea, he continues, carries its perfect expression in it, and there is ultimately only one wording that fits it. The poet's business is to approach that perfect language. If the order of the various ideas were absolutely clear, the expressions would compose themselves.[155] That may sound, if we erroneously take *alfāẓ* and *ma'nā* as exact counterparts of form and content as they are traditionally understood, as if the artistic means were demoted to mere accessories of the message to be communicated. That is not the intention, however. In the hundreds of lines of poetry and verses of the Quran that he interprets, al-Jurjānī is never interested in the content; he never discusses the value or the deeper truth of the ideas. Nor does he hold with pitting the content against the form: he explicitly decries the person who evaluates a poem only for its sense, who considers it praiseworthy only for the ideas, wisdom or aphorism it contains, ignoring the aesthetic function of the linguistic signs, as we might say today. Al-Jurjānī has even sharper words for a person who values only the ideas than for one who thinks a poem can be evaluated with no regard for its meaning:

> He is swayed only by the outer appearance of things, only by the bare phrases, and is like someone who thinks he is offering merchandise for sale. All he is interested in is getting it sold. He imagines he has perfected his art and his ability and achieved his ultimate goal when he goes on about taking and stealing, saying, 'This is from such a person, and such another had this to say about that.'[156]

To al-Jurjānī, the expression is the linguistic aspect of a given meaning, and the one is unthinkable without the other. The expression has no intrinsic value as a merely verbal or acoustic entity. But as a vehicle or, more exactly, as the outer form of an idea, it can have a poetic function; it does not simply serve to communicate a message that is extrinsic to it, but is in the ideal case itself a part of the message. As a consequence, the listener is not generally moved by the content of the utterance, but rather by the perfect realization of a certain message in the form appropriate to it. Again and again al-Jurjānī demonstrates that one of two sentences with apparently identical meaning leaves one cold, while the other is delightful. The *mazīya*, the specific quality of a line of poetry or a verse from the Quran, lies not in pure verbal acrobatics or in the semantic meaning: it arises from the realization of the *ma'nā* in the linguistic structure that is ideal for it, that expresses it perfectly. Al-Jurjānī's discussion of the acoustic dimension of poetry makes it plain that this *ma'nā* is more than just discursive content. The moment the relation of the *ma'ānī* to one another is clear and they have ordered themselves in the speaker's consciousness, he writes, there is no need to think about the rhyme, or the euphony in general, or even the metre of a line of verse.[157] It would make no sense to read *ma'ānī* here as merely a conceptual 'content' or the 'non-linguistic referent' of the discourse, with an existence independent from its linguistic form. Why should two 'contents' sound good if they fit together? *Ma'nā* must generally be understood in such contexts as an artistic idea, of which a certain linguistic expression is an essential part. This is also clear in al-Jurjānī's comparison of *ma'nā* with the intention of a carpet-weaver, a miniaturist or an architect: these artists are interested not in communicating a conceptual statement but in sending an aesthetic message in the semiotic sense – a shape, a pattern of colours, an image. Al-Jurjānī's aim is not to subordinate content to form or vice versa. Rather, building on the premise that a fitting, unique expression (*lafẓ*) is inherent in every idea, and that every idea is realized in a certain linguistic structure (*naẓm*), he sees the poet's task as finding the ideal form, whatever it may be, of a given message. Here in particular we are justified in translating *naẓm* as 'composition': the individual words are interconnected like the notes of a song. Just as a single tone is not a harmony, an individual *lafẓ* does not make a trope – al-Jurjānī prizes tropes as one of the most precious essences of eloquence – but can only become one in a meaningful, intentional combination with other *alfāẓ*.[158] In the best case, the words of a sentence are arranged so that they form a unit in which they cannot be thought and evaluated individually, because they are interlocked like the bricks of a building.

> You are like a master builder who puts one brick in its place with his right hand and at the same time puts another brick in another place with his left. Moreover, he sees even as he places the first bricks where the third and fourth belong, and then puts them there.[159]

The remarks of the Brazilian poet Vinicius de Moraes (d. 1980) may underscore the fact that al-Jurjānī's simile and the poetics behind it have something to do with the practice of poetry:

> A construction worker has nothing but a heap of bricks, which have no other significance besides being bricks, to build a house under the supervision of a master builder, who in turn only follows the calculations of an engineer, who follows the design of an architect. A heap of bricks is a heap of bricks. But a house can be quite beautiful if a good architect's design is supported by a good engineer's calculations and the execution is entrusted to the hands of a good master builder and a good worker.
>
> Substitute words for the bricks and give the poet the fourfold duties of the architect, the engineer, the master builder and the worker, and what you get is what poetry is. This comparison may sound presumptuous, at least from the poet's perspective, but on the contrary it seems to me to put poetry in its real place among the arts: that of true humility.[160]

The essential criterion for the *faṣāḥa* of a sentence, what makes it effective, beautiful and ultimately inimitable, is thus the relation between the intended *maʿnā* and the *naẓm* realized in the *alfāẓ*. Language is perfected where the composition of individual linguistic expressions is appropriate to and most exactly expresses the intended idea. The act of composition here refers to the individual ideas (*maʿānī*),[161] not to the *alfāẓ*, which are nothing but their outward form. Al-Jurjānī sets this conception in opposition to the notion (which he attributes to al-Jāḥiẓ)[162] that eloquence is whatever sounds pleasant and flows lightly from the tongue: by that logic, the miraculous aspect of the Quran would be its absolute acoustic purity and the absence of all sequences of words and letters that are difficult to pronounce or sound unpleasant. Al-Jurjānī finds this position extremely weak because it limits eloquence to something external and detaches it from the foundation of verbal art (*balāġa*). Eloquence would then consist 'no longer in clarity of meaning (*dalāla*), correctness of designation (*ishāra*), justness of proportions, beauty of arrangement and composition, originality in the use of metaphor and allegory, no longer in the principle of proceeding from the general to the particular, no longer in the connection and separation of the parts of the sentence in the proper place, and no longer in the fulfilment of the conditions of ellipsis, intonation, and placement of the parts before or after one another'[163] – all of these properties would then no longer be signs of the miraculous nature of the Quran. Al-Jurjānī does not deny the importance of proportionality (*tanāsuq*) and harmony (*talā'um*), which must prevail in the acoustic sequence of the letters, but sees them less as a criterion than as a natural condition for any kind of elevated utterance, whether in poetry or in everyday speech.

Since al-Jurjānī defines the quality of a discourse by the accuracy with which it communicates the speaker's intention and his message's richness of meaning, it is logical that he considers the greater communicative value of a figurative manner of speaking a reason to prefer it to literal speaking. Common sense would suggest the opposite: that a figurative expression is more beautiful but less exact than a literal one. On the contrary, al-Jurjānī writes that tropes in poetry reinforce and elucidate the meaning far more than an immediate expression of the same facts.[164] One peculiarity of metaphorical expression, indeed its 'chief honorary distinction', he writes in the *Mysteries of Eloquence*, is 'that it gives you a great deal of sense with few words, so that you draw as it were a multitude of pearls from one oyster, pluck different kinds of fruits from one branch'.[165] Al-Jurjānī demonstrates here an astounding sensitivity for the essence of poetic language – as Lotman said, the complex artistic structure of poetic language offers a unique way to condense information[166] – but the same statements by al-Jurjānī, read in the light of his 'Evidence of Miraculous Inimitability', also attest to the peculiar nature of the notion that he, or the culture that produced him, had of language and poetry – peculiar from a contemporary Western perspective, of course. In fact, the precision with which he determines how a message changes if one chooses a slightly different metaphor, for example, or uses a metonymy instead, if one states the subject first or elides the predicate in a verbal sentence – in short, his whole immense rule book of poetic expression – is hardly reproducible in a modern European language. We feel that it is not by chance that Paul Celan says, 'Nicht an meinen Lippen suche deinen Mund' ['Not on my lips seek your mouth'], and not 'An meinen Lippen suche deinen Mund nicht' ['On my lips seek your mouth not'] – that is, we know intuitively that the first variant sounds more pleasant, is aesthetically more attractive than the second, but no one would try to propose a universal law that says what happens to the sense when one begins a line of a poem with a negative complement instead of appending the negation at the end of the line. To find a comparably nuanced grammatical, semantic distinction, we might think of the '*Sprachlehren*', or language lessons, of Karl Kraus, whom we have cited above, and his explanation, for example, of the distinction between '*nur noch*' and '*nur mehr*'* or the mysteries of the word '*ohne*' [without].[167]

* Both German adverbial phrases meaning 'no longer anything but' – Trans.

Karl Kraus, who was not an academic, yet whose notes on the German language are invaluable reports from the writer's studio (like the essays of Octavio Paz, also cited in this chapter),[168] came to mind again and again during my study of al-Jurjānī: this too is an indication that the Persian's findings are related to, were developed in, the practice of poetry. Little about them is abstract. Kraus's guiding principle of composition seems as if drawn from the theory of *naẓm*: 'Words that have served before for all kinds of tasks are placed so that they yield that interpenetration in which the thing and the sound, the idea and the image cannot have existed one without the other, nor one before the other.'[169] Kraus does not go as far as al-Jurjānī in trying to define the meanings of even minimal variations of a discourse – it would have been absurd to do so in German. Even with perfect mastery of all the syntax and lexical rules, there are still plenty of cases that cannot be decided by those rules and are left to the speaker's intuitive sense of the language. In Arabic, on the other hand, or at least in Arabic as al-Jurjānī conceives it, practically nothing is left to chance or intuition, and the reason why some freedom is left to the critic in judging a line of poetry is because poetic language is so complex that it exceeds human ability to draw up rules to cover every imaginable utterance[170] – although the rules potentially exist: after all, the 'branches and shades' in the sphere of linguistic composition are 'numerous and without limit'.[171] No matter what a speaker may want to say, in al-Jurjānī's view there is for exactly that statement an ideal expression which is theoretically explainable, which is based on the correct application of fixed syntactic-semantic structures (*ma ʿānī n-naḥw*), which takes into account the nuances of meaning of the individual expressions, and which yields the most precise formulation of the intended message. It is not left to the author's whim or poetic feeling to choose a verbal or a nominal sentence, to negate the sentence with *mā* or with *lā* or to introduce a conditional phrase with *in* or with *iḏā*, to join a compound sentence asyndetically or with *fa*, *wa*, *thumma* or another conjunction (*ḥarf al-ʿaṭf*), to say *bal* or *lākin* for 'but', to say *aw* or *am* for 'or', to move a phrase back or forward (*ta'khīr wa-t-taqdīm*), to omit it (*ḥaḏf*), repeat it (*takrār*), show it (*iẓhār*) or 'hide' it (*iḍmār*), to use a metaphor (*istiʿāra*), a metonym (*kināya*) or an allegory (*tamthīl*). Every construction, every rhetorical element says something definite; no word is where it is by chance. Al-Jurjānī must therefore clash with the view of the philosopher al-Kindī (d. 866), who says there are 'filler words' in Arabic, and that the sentences *ʿAbdullāhi qā'imun*, *Inna ʿAbdallāhi qā'imun* and *Inna ʿAbdallāhi la-qā'imun* ('ʿAbdallāh stands') are equivalent. Al-Jurjānī points out that the first sentence expresses the simple fact of ʿAbdallāh's standing, the second is an answer to a prior question, and the third a reaction to the assertion that ʿAbdullāh does not stand. He demonstrates in detail all the functions of the emphatic particle *inna* ('truly'), where it occurs, how it joins sentences, how it relates to indefinite and definite nouns, in what cases *inna* is obligatory and in what cases one must decide based on the context whether the predicate should be omitted because *inna* is used. He explains how *inna* is used in the answer to a preceding or implicit question, and how it is used according to the opinion of the addressee, whether the speaker potentially supports, rejects or has an indeterminate attitude towards the statement. All of these conditions follow clear, insightful laws (*qawānīn*) that al-Jurjānī exposes in detail – the discussion of syntactic and stylistic distinctions between words fills almost a third of the book – although he does not seem to aspire to completeness but, rather, takes specific observations as opportunities for deeper reflections on certain linguistic issues. Discourse attains perfection where it not only solidly and correctly follows these rules but also surprises the listener by applying them and expertly combining them with one another, so that, although he can detect exactly why it pleases him, even the greatest poet must admit he is not able to produce anything like it, but only to copy it at best: that is *i'jāz*, miraculous inimitability.

In my study of the aesthetic reception of the Quran, it was in reading al-Jurjānī that I first realized the full magnitude of the miracle that is the Quran in the Arab Muslim perspective. When one follows, over hundreds of pages, how al-Jurjānī determines the semantic weight of even minimal linguistic differences, how he painstakingly defines which of the apparently negligible variations must be used in which cases, when one discovers what an 'almost magical' effect (*shabīh bi-s-siḥr*)[172] an ellipsis, for example, can have when used in the right place, or when one looks at his chapters on moving phrases forward or back in a sentence[173] and studies the syntactical functions of such shifts (subdivided according to whether or not the case of the prepended words changes), when one learns about the differences in meaning that result from placing either the predicate or the independent personal pronoun that stands for the predicate in front of it – al-Jurjānī explains the effect for two cases, namely in an affirmative clause and in an interrogative clause introduced by the particle *a*-, and the shift in meaning also depends on whether the speaker's intention is a negative or affirmative position with respect to something already said – when one learns how the meaning of an interrogative clause changes depending on whether the preceding verb is an imperfective or present form, and whether it is an imperfective with a present or future meaning, and whether the preceding phrase is a subject or an object, and whether it is a complete predicate or one expressed by a personal pronoun; when similarly detailed specifications of eloquent usage are given for relative clauses, for the emphatic particle *inna*, for nominal sentences, for metaphor and for many other questions of grammar, syntax and rhetoric, then one can understand how miraculous the Quran is in the eyes of someone like al-Jurjānī. As an outsider one may question the laws he postulates; one may even doubt whether the Quran really applies them perfectly in all details, as al-Jurjānī says it does, but, to him, both the consistency of the standards he sets and their perfect conformance with the linguistic reality of the Quran are verified, objective scientific findings, proven by text citations and corroborated by the text's reception history and his own aesthetic experience. And if we put ourselves in his place for a moment, and grant the same validity he does to the correctness of his analysis, then the Quran must indeed be something quite astonishing, almost inexplicable – in a word, miraculous. For Muhammad, who, according to al-Jurjānī's perspective, was not a poet and had not assimilated the fine points of rhetoric in long years of training, who did not know the secrets of syntax (*naḥw*), diction (*luġa*), tradition (*riwāya*) or metre (*'arūḍ*), who had no notion of rhetorical figures (*badī'*), who did not even master writing (this was taken to be synonymous with a lack of literary training)[174] – for such a literary layman to apply, spontaneously and without ever having shown any propensity to poetic expression, the entire system of poetic language, which no normal person could ever master in all its details; for this layman, his soul inspired, to create out of the known material of words, figures of speech and rules of syntax and style something completely new, previously unknown and never even approached since, in such an inimitable, unprecedented and hence unlearnable way – this historic fact, verifiable and demonstrable and obvious to anyone, must appear miraculous.

To form an impression of the subjective astonishment that al-Jurjānī and the other authors describe, we may imagine the reaction to a person who sits down at a piano for the first time and spontaneously produces the most beautiful, refined, brilliantly composed étude, or, since the significant competitions of our time are no longer waged in the artistic field, we may imagine common fantasies from our world: someone who has never been to school but discovers and gives an exact physical description of quantum theory; someone who has never driven a car but takes the wheel and immediately wins a Formula 1 race; and so on. For Muhammad's contemporaries, the argument goes, such a feat must be performed in the field of poetry, for that was their *maydān*, their arena, where one had to prove oneself.[175] That is the logic of the miraculous proof in practically all the *i'jāz* authors. The Andalusian Ibn 'Aṭīya (d. 1151) expresses it in these words: although the poet or rhetor has absolved years of training and thinks he knows all the tricks, 'you see how he polishes a qasida or a speech for a year, and still changes it; but if you take an expression from God's book and circulate it among the Arabs to find a more a beautiful expression – you will find nothing.'[176] It is not, or not only, that Muhammad's discourse is considered so perfect, but there is another inexplicable fact: he had never learned the laws of beautiful oratory, which in the Arabic literary tradition is at least as much a science (*'ilm*) as an art (*ṣinā'a*); he had never studied under a poet, had never acquired the poetic skills that were considered even more important than intuition for composing a good text, and indeed for producing a poetic idea (in contrast to the modern European tradition with its invocation of the poetic *ingenium*),[177] and yet, they said, everything was right, no word was out of place, every idea was optimal and, very importantly, flawlessly expressed according to the rules of *'arabīya*. Numerous Orientalists in the wake of Nöldeke have vehemently contested the latter claim, the correct use of the language, but, to Arabic literary critics and *i'jāz* scholars, it was all an incontrovertible fact; the miracle was as clear as a physical phenomenon, as soundly proven as a scientifically measurable force and as visible as the transformation of a staff into a snake. Where the Quran deviated from the rules of *'arabīya* as they were known from ancient Arabic poetry, they did not deem it a fault, as the Orientalist discourse did, but as the particular quality of the quranic use of the language. These different perceptions of the same phenomenon are one reason why Western and Muslim judgements of the quranic style are often so extremely contradictory.

Al-Jurjānī's ideal of beauty and that of his time was different from ours, and it seems to us premodern inasmuch as it places severe restrictions on the subjectivity of aesthetic feeling. Yet it does not entirely exclude subjectivity. Although al-Jurjānī unstintingly talks about the science of rhetoric (*'ilm al-bayān*), he is nonetheless aware that literary culture and knowledge about the nature of language are not sufficient by themselves to do justice to a poem or to produce a masterpiece oneself. Ultimately poetry depends on intuition and inspiration, even for one as obsessed with rules as al-Jurjānī. Observing the laws of grammar, syntax and rhetoric is a necessary condition, but it does not make up the *mazīya*, the abundant quality of an oration. *Mazīya* occurs only when the composition (*naẓm*) of a speech is the optimal and unique arrangement of the most beautiful and most precise expressions chosen from all possible alternatives. In al-Jurjānī's poetics, this can be explained by laws and linguistic mechanisms to a degree that must sometimes appear absurd to the speaker of a modern European language and could hardly be applied even in the literary Arabic of today. But even al-Jurjānī declares that something more is necessary in addition to this learnable knowledge: the poet's creative imagination and spontaneity.[178] It seems to have been a general aesthetic opinion of his time that the fetters of the system of rules about figures of speech, thematic progressions and other structural elements were balanced by the artist's unpredictable creativity, and the appeal for the recipient consisted in the constant creation of new, unexpected, stirring verbal images and harmonies out of the familiar patterns. 'If we dealt only with a rigid system of rules', Lotman remarks, referring to an 'aesthetics of identity' such as we have seen in connection with Quran recitation, 'each new work would be only a copy of its predecessor; redundancy would suppress entropy, and the work of art would lose its informational value.'[179] For classical Arabic poetry, which Western observers have often described as unbearably formulaic, affected and full of clichés,[180] this ideal of a dialectical, suspenseful relation between the system of rules and the poet's individual creativity and imagination is immediately apparent,[181] and al-Jurjānī applies it to the Quran, which uses the familiar forms and patterns much more freely.

On another level, the principle that the mastery of all linguistic and rhetorical rules is worthless if the poet lacks inspiration, talent and creativity holds for the recipient as well. We can interpret al-Jurjānī's words as saying one cannot appraise a poetic text coldly using reason alone; one must experience it, one must give in to it completely and, following its curving path, progress through one's own emotions. The ideal listener is one

> to whom his soul speaks when something shows him a hint of the source of the beautiful and the good, so that he immerses himself in the discourse, and sometimes finds bliss (*aryaḥīya*) and then lets it go again, and he is astonished when you surprise him, and he takes notice when you call his attention to the places of linguistic merit (*mazīya*). But to converse about such matters with someone for whom two different states and variants of a discourse amount to the same thing and who inspects a linguistic composition (*naẓm*) only for correct syntax and the outward inflection of the words, that is extremely rarely profitable.[182]

Thus the listener, if not a poet himself or herself, must have a creative potential, must be willing and able to 'respond' to the text. Or, in the words of Octavio Paz: 'There is one note common to all poems, without which they would never be poetry: participation. Each time the reader truly relives the poem, he reaches a state that we can call poetic.'[183] Several times in the course of his book, al-Jurjānī emphasizes the need for sensitivity (*iḥsās*), taste (*ḏawq*), a feeling for language (*luṭf aṭ-ṭab'*) and talent (*qarīḥa*) in order to penetrate the subtleties of the language, to discover its spiritual ideas and to be able to talk scientifically about a discourse, whether it is the Quran or poetry.[184] He quotes the famous poet al-Buḥturī (d. 897) as saying that people such as Abū l-'Abbās ath-Tha'lab – a prominent man of letters and critic of the time – who studied the 'science of poetry' (*'ilm ash-shi'r*) but had written no noteworthy poetry themselves, were not competent to judge great poets such as Abū Nuwās (d. 813) or Muslim ibn al-Walīd al-Anṣārī (d. 823).[185] He also mentions al-Jāḥiẓ, who said that the orators and verbal artists among the Arabs realized the *i'jāz* of the Quran the fastest and the most clearly.[186] In view of those remarks, it is certainly with a deeper purpose that al-Jurjānī closes his preface with a long poem that, apart from the premise that the miracle of the Quran lies in its *naẓm*, mainly repeats what the preface has already said. It seems as if al-Jurjānī wanted to present his qualifications to write a book about the eloquence of the Quran. Like his diction in general, which is polished, sometimes artistic, not always easily understandable, but never careless, the poem identifies him as someone who, according to his own standards, has the stylistic competence to judge other authors' texts and even the revelation; as someone who has absorbed the language of the Quran into his flesh and blood, as Muḥammad 'Abduh would later demand.[187] Weisweiler aptly remarks about al-Jurjānī's style:

> Because he knows how to proffer the dry subject matter in a pleasing form, captivating the reader, he is also able to impose on the reader of this work

> the unusual burden of negotiating sometimes long sentences. It would be unjust to see this propensity of al-Jurjānī's towards long sentences as a stylistic weakness. It is not a fortuitous quirk but a purposely intended stylistic ideal. This stylistic form corresponds to his aesthetic notion that a sentence in which the clauses are aligned like pearls on a string can shine perhaps by its idea but not by its expression, whereas in a perfect complex sentence the parts mesh and intertwine, joining together to form not an outward but an inward unity, as if formed of one piece, even though such a structure is much more difficult to produce. As a fine stylist, he knows that the listener's or reader's vigour is maintained by being forced to a certain degree to work out the sense.[188]

Although this observation refers to individual sentences, the overall structure of the book is analogous: it shows only a rudimentary composition, and the sequence of topics seems to betray a certain aimlessness. For all the systematic and integral character of al-Jurjānī's theory of *naẓm*, its presentation is scarcely ordered by any recognizable system. After a preface about the basic conditions of human speech, he first explains, over twenty dense pages, wherein the value of the science of eloquence (*ʿilm al-balāġa*) in general and of poetry and syntax (*naḥw*) in particular lies, before going on to mention the miraculous nature of the Quran and to develop his poetics. Up to this point, the first quarter of the book, the subject matter seems to be on the whole fairly structured. But then the author suddenly embarks on a thorough study of general syntactical phenomena and poetic devices,[189] which he interrupts temporarily to return to the topic of *naẓm*, *maʿnā* and *lafẓ*. After the discussion of syntax, he then returns definitively to the fundamental theme of the relation between linguistic expression and poetic idea, discussing it again and again with reference to the Quran. To the contemporary reader, however, the discussion of this topic appears anything but systematic: the leaps from one idea to another are glaring; some topics are returned to repeatedly, even repetitiously, while others are touched on only briefly and discussed as if parenthetically. At times one cannot help turning back to see whether a section is only a paraphrase of something already said or whether it adds new details. Especially where the author thinks of new possible objections to his thesis (which he does throughout the book, presenting them in full detail before refuting them in all particulars), the volume has the feel of a lecture transcript rather than a textbook designed for silent study; it is as if the author were spontaneously responding to the ever-changing, sometimes counterproductive interjections of an imaginary audience. At one point al-Jurjānī even says himself that everything must have been said about a topic and, if he nonetheless goes on and discusses further aspects of it, he is only taking unnecessary trouble, but his conscience compels him to dispel every trace of doubt and suspicion and to rebut absolutely everything.[190]

But what is sometimes tiring for the contemporary reader, the seemingly endless pursuit of more and more subordinate and parenthetical trains of thought, will hardly have seemed a fault to al-Jurjānī's original addressees, since it is wholly in keeping with the scholastic discourse of his time, and hence within his readers' and listeners' horizon of expectations. More importantly, however, it is in keeping with al-Jurjānī's poetics, which takes only the sentence, or the Quran verse or line of poetry, as the basis for assessment. The surah as a compositional unit of text is never mentioned, much less the total structure of the Quran. Al-Jurjānī's own style also demonstrates that the basis of aesthetic judgement is the sentence: the composition of his sentences is captivating; their clauses are intertwined in ways that make Thomas Mann's syntax look as simple as a comic book; yet he attaches little importance to the structure and proportions of longer sections of the text. If we remember that it was usually individual verses that drew cries of rapture from the listeners in the accounts of the reception of the Quran, and that the other classical books on *iʿjāz* also present the verse and not the surah as the important unit to examine, al-Jurjānī's attitude emerges as a view of the Quran that is very different from Western poetics and from possible aesthetic receptions of the Bible, but is representative of his culture. A literary appraisal of the Bible based on the sentence as a fundamental unit would hardly be imaginable: the stories and the narrative parables are what fascinate and delight the reader. There is no reason to assume that the listener of a surah would not be moved by its overall composition and discern an aesthetic value in it, yet it is remarkable that this aspect of the text has been largely ignored by Arab rhetoricians. Only once does al-Jurjānī call attention to the category of the complete work – although without mentioning the Quran: some verses, he writes, do not appear beautiful until one hears them in context with the poet's other verses; whereas with some verses

> you see how their beauty overwhelms you at one stroke; they give you something so wondrous that your eyes directly fill with tears, so that after a single line you realize the poet's outstanding quality and skill and profess the power and permanence of his art, to the point that, even if you did not know who the author of the verses was, you would discern that they were the work of a great poet and artist. These are the verses in which, as you recite them, you place your finger on a word and say, Yes, this is it, only this. Where this is the case, the poem is that of a true poet, the discourse is full of splendour and the style is of the highest and noblest quality. Such a poem is rare, and you find it only in the greatest and most experienced masters, those graced by God (*al-maṭbūʿūn*), to whom the word must truly have been given as an inspiration. Even so, you must nevertheless examine several poems, or even study the whole collection, to collect a number of lines [that show these qualities].[191]

To judge a poet we can and must examine the work. Yet the work is not a relevant category for analysis or the basic unit of literary assessment: the quality of a work is determined by the quality of its individual verses, lines or sentences; it is their composition of various components that is essential in al-Jurjānī's valuation.[192] This concentration on the line of verse or the sentence as a fundamental unit seems strange at first from the contemporary Western point of view, but was indeed known in older European literatures and is not at all rare in modern poetry.[193] It apparently expresses an aesthetic norm that is also present in the frequently mentioned, sometimes too one-sidedly emphasized but unmistakable 'molecular' structure of classical Arabic poetry (not until the tenth century does a tendency appear, in al-Mutanabbī, for example, to give more importance to the overall composition and to connect the parts by a stricter logical thematic progression).[194] Although most surahs of the Quran are more clearly composed of interrelated parts than the conventional qasida, the text is perceived and evaluated using the same complex of norms that are applied to poetry. Although al-Jurjānī praises the whole Quran as a miracle, and at one point cites Ibn Mas'ūd's enthusiasm over the *ḥa-mīm* surahs,[195] what he analyses is always an individual verse, considering at most its connection to the preceding and the following verse. The structure of the work is not relevant; the quality of the Quran is judged from the findings on its individual verses. In the 'Mysteries of Eloquence' too, which deals primarily with the potential of figurative language, the poetic image is the elementary unit, and the relation between individual images is only of interest where they appear as the components of a larger image.[196] If we could ask al-Jurjānī, he would no doubt assure us that the overall composition of the Quran, or at least the structure of sections recognizable as units, such as the surah of Joseph (no. 12) or the surah 'The All-Merciful' (no. 55), are of inimitable quality, but evidently this aspect did not interest him – nor did it interest most of the Muslim rhetoricians of his epoch.[197] Al-Khaṭṭābī touches on the issue in discussing the harmony (*talā'um*) of the motifs and themes within a surah.[198] Al-Bāqillānī is one of the few to discuss the surah as a literary unit and to accord great importance to the overall composition. His analysis of longer sections of surahs, however, which he compares with the poems of Imra' al-Qays' and al-Buḥturī,[199] had little influence in the *i'jāz* literature. Al-Bāqillānī himself rejects the view, held by some unnamed Mu'tazili, that the individual verses are not a miracle in themselves but only sequences of several verses. For his part, he considers every surah and every verse of the Quran a miracle.[200] Several other scholars go beyond those whom al-Bāqillānī criticizes to hold that *i'jāz* is manifested only in the long surahs, and then in their overall composition,[201] but such views and aesthetic norms were marginal – or, at least, they were rarely followed to their logical conclusion of analysing the surah's structure as a whole. Az-Zarkashī recounts that a certain Abū Bakr an-Nīshābūri[202] was the first to ask, every time he heard the Quran, why this verse was next to that and why a given surah followed another, and he publicly called the scholars of Baghdad ignorant because they paid no attention to the connections between the individual verses and surahs. According to az-Zarkashī, the issue was ignored all the more after an-Nīshābūri, perhaps because it was too difficult.[203] A more likely reason is that it was simply not considered particularly important. Ibn Khaldūn mentions the connection between the verses, but insists that each verse was created by itself and must be considered separately.[204] As-Suyūṭī devotes a chapter of his encyclopaedic work to 'the referential character of the verses and surahs',[205] but it is only in recent decades that a fundamental change of attitude has occurred. Modern Arabic authors' books on the miraculous character of the composition of the surahs and the relations between them, such as that of ʿAbdulmutaʿāl as-Saʿīdī,[206] and on the 'narrative art of the Quran', such as that written in the mid-twentieth century by Muḥammad Aḥmad Khalafallāh,[207] must indirectly reflect a contact with aesthetic categories and norms carried over from a Western context (which need not diminish their prestige and importance from a Muslim perspective – after all, as Ṣādiq ar-Rāfiʿī says, every age and every society discovers different miraculous properties of the Quran because it 'is the book of all times and every time has its own proof of its miraculous nature').[208] The opposite conclusion, which is occasionally drawn in the Western literature and is likewise only possible from today's perspective, has not yet surfaced in the *iʿjāz* discourse: namely that of seeing the molecular structure of the Quran as a quality that has only recently been rediscovered in the greatest works of modern literature. The literary scholar Norman Brown, for example, said of the Quran, 'The whole texture is one of interruption (Joyce's "enterruption"); collision (Joyce's "collideorscape"); abrupt collage, or bricolage, of disconnected ejaculations, *disjecta membra*, miscellaneous fragments.'[209]

Naturally al-Jurjānī could not have arrived at such an opinion, although he was not interested in the overall composition, and the topic of the work as a category reminds us that we must be careful not to project our own aesthetic notions onto an eleventh-century Iranian 'Arabist'. Furthermore, al-Jurjānī's concept of 'beauty' turns out to denote primarily a precision of expression and does not necessarily correspond to what we would understand by the colloquial term today – that is, a form generally felt to be attractive and pleasant. Yet qualities such as 'attractive', 'pleasant', 'pleasant-sounding', 'admirable', 'captivating', 'overwhelming', 'stunning', 'brilliant', 'harmonious', 'well-proportioned', and the like, which are within the semantic field of the beautiful, can all refer to what al-Jurjānī calls *ḥusn*. There is no question that it is an aesthetic category, like all the other terms he uses to characterize the Quran. If we compare how the author describes poetry and how he describes the Quran, we find that he situates both in the same sphere, and sees the difference between them not in poeticity but in the perfection with which the Quran uses the resources and mechanisms of poetic language, forming them into a new, unprecedented and inimitable kind of text that exerts a unique power over its listeners. It is not only the fact that al-Jurjānī in developing his poetics implicitly suspends the concept of genre, applying his theory equally to the Quran and to poetry, drawing on both, trying and proving it on both – even using exactly the same terms to discuss individual Quran verses or lines of poetry. In the Quran and in brilliant poetry he finds *faṣāḥa* (eloquence), *balāġa* (verbal art), *luṭf* (sweetness), *faḍl* (merit), *bahr* (brilliance), *ḥusn* (beauty), *sharaf* ('elegance'), *fakhr* (grandeur), *ḥalāwa* (bliss), *siḥr* (magic), *qarīḥa* (talent), *ḏawq* (taste), *iḥsās* (feeling), and the like. There are no fundamental differences to be found; I can hardly recall any characterization of the Quran that does not also occur in the discussion of a poet's verse. The only detectable differences are in the appropriation of dogmatically relevant terms, such as *burhān* (argument), *khujja* (evidence) and *iʿjāz*, and in the description of the text's effects on the listeners. While al-Jurjānī does mention poetry's 'action upon the soul and incitement of bliss',[210] if I am not mistaken he reserves the term *rawʿa*, denoting a profoundly moving splendour that engenders fascination and dread, for the Quran. *Rawʿa* (or the masculine form, *rawʿ*, which denotes the reaction it elicits) is often mentioned when Muslim scholars describe the Quran and is of central importance for the whole reception history of the Quran. It is often explained by reference to verse 39:23, which says 'the skins of those who fear their Lord shiver'.[211] Indeed *rawʿa* can perhaps be best translated as 'shiver', as long as we remember that this shivering connotes not only fear but also pleasure (which is why the term is often used in the same breath as *laḏḏa*, 'enjoyment', or *ḥalāwa*, 'delight').[212] The tension Rudolf Otto outlines between *mysterium tremendum* and *mysterium fascinosum* is exactly the setting of *rawʿ* and *rawʿa*. We first encountered this tension in chapter 1 in connection with the Quran's first listeners; in the last chapter of this book we will see that it is an important theme in the writings of the Islamic mystics in particular, who have reflected more than others on the emotional power of Quran recitation. The theological discourse in which al-Jurjānī participates mentions this power, sometimes calling it a miraculous property of the Quran, but does not dwell on it as the mystical discourse does. The theological discourse is more interested in what the Quran is objectively than in what it induces subjectively.

The other *iʿjāz* authors too, as even a casual glance in as-Suyūṭī's and az-Zarkashī's compilations on *iʿjāz* shows, describe the Quran using aesthetic categories such as *ṭalāwa* (grace) and *malāḥa* (loveliness), *ḥusn* and *faṣāḥa*, discuss its *balāġa* and its *naẓm*, and draw comparisons with poetry and other kinds of poetic language. But in al-Jurjānī more than in the others – and I rank this alongside the rigour of his analysis and the clarity of his linguistic and poetic thesis as one of the most striking aspects of his 'Arguments' – one feels the urgency of the aesthetic interest, especially in comparison with the other major work of the classical *iʿjāz* literature, Qāḍī Abū Bakr al-Bāqillānī's *Iʿjāz al-Qurʾān*. Where al-Bāqillānī pits the Quran against poetry, analysing a poem only in order to demonstrate the superiority of the revelation, ignoring in the process the value and the autonomy that poetry has, al-Jurjānī never lets the impression arise that he uses poetry only for purposes of theological demonstration. Nowhere does he devalue a line of poetry in favour of a Quran verse. Where he does make a comparison, his recourse to a line of poetry serves to explain the stylistic peculiarity of a Quran verse, or vice versa. Al-Jurjānī's *Dalā'il al-i'jāz* documents the importance of the aesthetic dimension in the reception of the Quran with a rare poignancy. The author is not a dogmatist, not a dry scholastic, not a pietistic defender of the faith. His book is the work of one obsessed with the beauty of language, one who loves poetry and is visibly aesthetically moved by the Quran; he is a man in search of the reason for his fascination. He is concerned not with proving *that* the Quran's beauty is inimitable – he takes that estimation for granted – but with explaining *why* it is so. Where the theologian al-Jurjānī waxes apologetic in his writings, he is an apologist of poetic language, whether in the Quran or in poetry. He has both of them equally in mind when he praises the potential of metaphoric language, for example:

> Its field extends so far, it has so many variations, it develops such marvellous beauties, it encompasses such a broad area, it is so inexhaustible and traverses in art so many heights and depths that all its branches and ramifications cannot be catalogued, its variations and kinds cannot be exhaustively listed. Indeed it has a truly magical power and embodies everything that can swell the breast, give pleasure to the mind, revive the soul and instil true comfort. It always knows the way to bring you maidens of choice beauty, endowed with the greatest perfection, and can bring up pearls from its sea that, when other gems rival them, have no small degree of quality and merit and display great beauty that no one can deny and that makes the others yellow with shame of their kinship with worthless stones. It can bring up ingots from the mines whose like has never been seen, and can form works of art from them that make all jewellery worthless and that show you at last what true jewels are; in a word, it can grant you delights to give joy to the religious and the secular worlds and grandeurs of the highest degree, so that it is impossible to describe them fittingly and to do justice to its full beauty.[213]

Not a single sentence in al-Jurjānī is aimed at convincing an undecided or ignorant reader of the special quality of the Quran; the speaker never has the attitude of one who has to prove that quality. To al-Jurjānī it goes without saying. This is a fundamentally different attitude from that displayed by al-Bāqillānī, who lived several decades earlier and, in contrast to al-Jurjānī, not on the fringes, but in the Islamic metropolis Baghdad.[214] Of course that difference in attitudes has to do with the different addressees at whom the two books are aimed, which is apparent in their respective introductions. Both authors clearly describe the ills of their times that have motivated them to write on *i'jāz*, but the kinds of ills they mention are completely different. A comparison will serve to illustrate them.

The Direction of the Discourse

One of the most important and most urgent tasks, al-Bāqillānī states in the introduction to his *I'jāz al-Qur'ān*, is to document the truth of Muhammad's claim to prophethood and the authenticity of his miracle. Although no one will ever be able to survey its miraculous properties entirely, he writes, every Muslim has the duty to know the true quality of the Quran and to be aware of its magnificence. Today, however, ignorance (*jahl*) has spread everywhere; it is flourishing and dominates the world; knowledge is declining, even dying out; it survives only here and there in hiding. The knowledgeable are exposed to the rudeness of a dark age; they cower before its gloom as one cowers on encountering a fierce lion. They are so intimidated that they neglect their duties and no longer follow God's path. People are divided into two groups: some abandon the truth and forget the Guidance, while others are deterred from helping and overtaxed in their own work.

> This has led the apostates (*mulḥidūn*) to question the foundations of the religion and plunge the weak into doubt about what they had been certain of. The followers of the religion have grown few, their helpers have allowed themselves to be distracted and the faithful have become resigned, so that they are now a target for anyone who wants to attack them. It is now once more as it was in the beginning when people ranted about the Quran. Some said it was magic, others considered it poetry, and others again claimed it contained only fables of the ancestors. If we wanted, they said, we could produce something like it.[215]

Indignantly, al-Bāqillānī points out that some compare the Quran with poetry and other forms of oratory and, worse still, even prefer those genres to the divine revelation. Such wickedness is not the invention of the heterodoxy of his time: the Quraysh and others – all comrades in heresy – made most of those statements in earlier days. In contrast to the new apostates, the earlier slanderers at least saw the Guidance afterwards and repented. The ignorance of the present day, al-Bāqillānī wrote, is much more unsettling, and the heterodoxy farther than ever from the Guidance. It would have behoved the scholars who wrote useful books about the meaning of the Quran, and the theologians in general, instead of digressing into subtle discussions of its accidents or exploring endless niceties of inflection or yet exposing the deepest mysteries of grammar, to demonstrate the miraculous nature of the Quran and show everyone the evidence of it, because 'that is more urgently needed and its study is a more important duty.' The failings of Muslim scholars in this matter are to blame, al-Bāqillānī writes, for the fact that some people have even adopted the view of the Brahmin and 'think they can conclude from their fellows' inability to confirm the miracle that the miracle need not be confirmed, and indeed has no signs'.[216] (The reference to the Brahmin is probably an allusion to the proponents of the *ṣarfa* theory, which was said to be imported from India.)[217] The situation is the worse, al-Bāqillānī continues, because these people have advanced quite far in laying the foundation of their reforms and distinguish themselves by the elegance of their writings, while the existing confirmations of the Quran's miraculous nature – he names al-Jāḥiẓ and his book on 'the composition of the Quran' – are incomplete, their arguments not compelling, their exposition and arrangement careless. In view of the lack of precedents and foundations, some negligence and awkwardness can be excused, but one must not simply sit back and abandon the field to heresy.

> And so someone asked me to treat this topic as a whole so that the suspicions of the ignorant can be eliminated and their doubts disappear, and the slanders that they invent and aim at the aspects of the miracle may have an end. We have acceded to that request in the hope of approaching God the Exalted, to Whom praises flow, trusting in Him, His aid and the happiness that He bestows.[218]

Even leaving aside the rhetorical ornamentation and hyperbole that were characteristic of Muslim scholarship at that time, the motives that led the theologian al-Bāqillānī to write his book and his perspective on the intellectual situation of his day are apparent. Evidently, growing doubts were being voiced about the miraculous nature of the Quran, and the consensus about its aesthetic properties that had existed among earlier generations, al-Bāqillānī implies, was in danger of collapsing. The memory of the Quran's triumph over all adversaries, and of the historic challenge to imitate it that no one had been able to meet, was obscured by bold attempts to find fault with its style, question its miraculous nature and so undermine the foundation of the religion. A number of scholars and poets of the ninth and tenth centuries are known to have disputed the stylistic superiority of the Quran, either because they followed the *ṣarfa* doctrine or because they were among those freethinkers whom Muslim tradition charges with so many transgressions. A good two hundred years before al-Bāqillānī, poets and men of letters such as Ibn al-Muqaffaʿ, Bashshār ibn Burd (d. 784), Ṣāliḥ ibn ʿAbdilquddūs (d. c. 777) and ʿAbdulḥamīd ibn Yaḥyā l-Kātib (d. 750) are said to have met regularly in Basra to criticize the style of the Quran and improve upon it in verses of their own.[219] Ibn al-Muqaffaʿ in particular is accused of the gravest offences in this regard, including having written a whole book against the Quran.[220] It is unlikely that all the accusations are true, but the fact that they were raised and believed in subsequent centuries indicates in itself that there were doubts and disputes. We also know that a number of Iranian secretaries (*kuttāb*) at the Abbasid court made it their business to point out errors and contradictions in the Quran, which irritated al-Jāḥiẓ, while the well-known apostate Ibn ar-Rāwandī allegedly compiled their arguments as a polemic against *iʿjāz* in his writings criticizing the Quran.[221] In the beginning there were scholars even among the clergy who, like al-Murdār (d. 840 or 841), denied there was anything miraculous about the Quran, rejecting even the theory of *ṣarfa*.[222] And poets and aesthetes such as Yaḥyā b. al-Ḥakam al-Ġazāl (d. second half of the ninth century), Abū ṭ-Ṭayyib al-Mutanabbī, Qabūs ibn Wushmgīr (d. 1012) and Abū l-ʿAlāʾ al-Maʿarrī (d. 1058) are said to have questioned the inimitability of the Quran even into the eleventh century. From its inception, *iʿjāz* was by no means undisputed.[223]

Although most accounts and documents of refutations of the quranic miracle date from the decades before al-Bāqillānī, the stylistic miracle does not yet seem to have attained dominance in the tenth century, as Heinz Grotzfeld surmises: otherwise the *qāḍī* al-Bāqillānī would hardly have felt it necessary to take such a vehement stand against the heterodoxy's *advance*.[224] If we understand the formation of the *iʿjāz* doctrine as the canonization of a tradition, a process leading towards a maximum of authority in substance and a high degree of formal definition, then al-Bāqillānī's treatise corroborates Assmann's thesis that the formation of canons occurs in 'times of *internal* cultural polarization, when traditions are broken and people must decide which order to follow'.[225]

Like al-Bāqillānī, al-Jurjānī several decades later also paints a gloomy picture of his world: he lives in a time, he writes at the beginning of his book, in which things and views have diverged from their natural and proper way and been turned upside down, so that the most powerless person is one who advances in science – which is a friend, and must be cared for as any other friend – and strives for knowledge.[226] But how different are the symptoms that al-Jurjānī identifies in his portentous diagnosis: there is no mention of serious challenges to the aesthetic quality of the Quran. Unlike al-Bāqillānī, who attaches great importance to refuting the proponents of the *ṣarfa* doctrine,[227] he has only a few scornful remarks for them, giving the impression that it is hardly worth his while to argue against something so patently absurd.[228] The dissension, doubt and delusion that al-Jurjānī considers important and mentions as the motivation for his work are connected, not with the miraculous stylistic inimitability of the Quran in itself – that is apparently undisputed among his readers, his book implies – but with the specifics of the Quran's style, and whether and how it can be explained. He criticizes the contempt his contemporaries have for linguistics and literary studies because they think they do not need them to confirm the miracle. There is no science 'that is so wronged, that must suffer so much injustice, about which so many falsehoods are circulated and about which such depraved ideas and nasty opinions prevail, that is treated with such violent ignorance and is the subject of such disastrous misunderstandings' as the science of rhetoric.[229] And elsewhere he writes about it: 'If someone says there is no science in the world that has been the subject of such terrible errors, horrible entanglements and the dissemination of such depraved opinions as this science has been – I believe he cannot be called a liar.'[230] Al-Jurjānī concurs with al-Bāqillānī in the bitter knowledge that the just and the reasonable are a dwindling minority and that many people are as if drowned,[231] but, while al-Bāqillānī would more likely place the rhetoricians and grammarians among those who have strayed from the Guidance, al-Jurjānī considers them the true defenders of the faith. Only poetry and the scientific study of language and literature, he affirms, open the gate to the *iʿjāz* of the Quran. There is no other science 'whose roots reach deeper and whose branches higher, whose fruits are sweeter and whose flowers more fragrant, whose harvest is more noble and whose sun shines brighter'.[232]

> Among all strange things, is there anything stranger than a nation of sensible people who recite God's word, 'Say: If men and jinn banded together to produce the like of this Koran, they would never produce its like, not though they backed one another',[233] and who believe and profess that the Quran is a miracle, and then, in spite of the proof of *iʿjāz* and its evidence, turn away and start to explain it another way? Truly, if they paid attention, they would see what a great offence they are committing.[234]

Unfortunately, al-Jurjānī writes, many people think it is enough to speak without committing solecisms, and they do not see that there are subtleties and secrets in the language that can be discovered only by striving on the path of knowledge and science, 'which alone constitute the merit of a discourse and allow one speech to rise above the others, which lead it to the highest levels and degrees, so high that it becomes unique, so high that it attains *iʿjāz* and exceeds human ability.'[235] The subtleties, particularities and joys of the language are unknown to those people: 'neither do they open up to them, nor do they desire them'.[236] As ill chance would have it, an opinion predominates among those very people that obstructs their access to these beautiful properties in the first place, namely their poor opinion of poetry, which is the source of all these subtleties and joys, and of grammar, which smoothens the path to them.

> As for poetry, they imagine that it is of no great usefulness and consists either of charming anecdotes and pleasantries or of weeping over the poet's lover, descriptions of ruins and characterizations of camels or of praises or curses, and that it is something neither religion nor the world needs. But, as for grammar, they have reached the opinion that it is mere affectation, a kind of aberration, and something that rests on no foundation and no reason.... If they recognized their foolishness and where it has led them, they would seek refuge in God.[237]

In the chapters that follow his preface, al-Jurjānī successively establishes the value and justification of poetry and grammar. He begins by refuting the three main arguments that were advanced against the recitation and the transmission of poetry: first, that its content is useless; second, that poems have rhyme and metre, which is reason enough for some to reject them; and, third, that the poets did not lead virtuous lives. Among al-Jurjānī's many counter-arguments, we may highlight one that is relevant once more in the Muslim world today: the insight that the poet is only an imitator or narrator (*ḥākin*) and cannot be identified with, or chastised for, what he narrates and quotes in his works, no more than one might chastise God for quoting the speech of the unbelievers in the Quran.[238] Otherwise, al-Jurjānī's reasoning is quite traditionalist. He mainly cites numerous hadiths and traditions to demonstrate how much the Prophet, his comrades and the early authorities prized and loved poetry. To interpret the Quran verses about the mendacious poets[239] as expressing contempt or even a prohibition of poetry is an error, he writes, and contradicts the whole history of Muslim scholarship. Al-Jurjānī admits that some people misuse poetry for mere amusement, but he stresses that there are truly noble reasons to concern oneself with it and to preserve it.

> I would like to study it to know the quality of eloquence and so to obtain a standard for the evaluation of a discourse, or to use it in the explanation of the Quran and the sunnah, and to study the composition of the poem and that of the Quran in detail and to compare them in order to discern the position of *iʿjāz* and to dwell in my examination on the place where it is visible.[240]

Still more reprehensible than contempt for poetry, in al-Jurjānī's view, is the growing indifference in regard to *ʿilm an-naḥw*, the science of grammar, which ultimately results in exclusion from the knowledge of the Quran and its meanings. No one who is in his right mind denies that one must master inflection in order to distinguish a correct speech from a false one, he says; there is no need to waste many words on things that can be taken for granted. But if some people have no fundamental objection to grammar, yet simply do not want to bother about its subtleties and fine points, seeing them only as a superfluous effort and a cause of confusion, then it is not unreasonable to ask them exactly which things they think are superfluous. If it is too much for them to study the system of derivation, word formation and metre, including the metre of loan words, to become aware of the inner structure of the language and its logic, to concern themselves with matters of vocalization, the conjugation of strong and weak verbs, the formations of the dual and plural forms, nunation and declension and their special cases – their excuses may be accepted, although they would do well to learn these things. But even in the fundamental questions of grammar, whose 'correctness and necessity' they admit,[241] they are so unsure that they grope in the dark when it comes to interpreting the Quran. They may be able to tell subject and predicate apart, al-Jurjānī suspects, but they run into trouble when it comes to vocalization, to say nothing of defining the individual constituents of a predicate or distinguishing the four kinds (*aḍrub*) of sentences. They are aware that the adjective declension must agree with the corresponding noun, but that there is a science behind that, and that the adjective sometimes specifies and sometimes explains something, and that there is a difference between the purposes of specification (*takhṣīṣ*) and explanation (*tawḍīḥ*), just as there is between the purposes of the evident and the ambiguous, and that sometimes the attribute (*ṣifa*) neither specifies nor explains but serves to emphasize, as in God's words *fa-iḏā nufikha fī ṣ-ṣūri nafkhatun wāḥidatun* ('So, when the trumpet is blown with a single blast'),[242] and that there is a qualitative difference between adjectives that express a price (*madḥ*) and those that express praise (*thanā'*), just as there is between the various adjectives that are used about the names of God – they are rather uncertain about all this. If such people would at least not interfere, al-Jurjānī concludes, and be content with what they know and stay away from Quran interpretation, that would be a big improvement: 'Even if they accomplished nothing, they would at least not make anything worse.'[243]

The contrast between al-Jurjānī's and al-Bāqillānī's descriptions of the status quo and the opposite directions of the polemics that open their treatises on *i'jāz* are obvious. After these diverging expositions, we can understand why the two authors adopt completely different lines of argument. One, al-Bāqillānī, aims to establish a thorough foundation for the quranic miracle with reference to all kinds of proofs and with rebuttals of all contrary evidence: his whole endeavour is to confirm the Quran as a miracle in the first place and to defend it against contestations; he compiles the most important indications of its miraculous nature in the literature and would reinforce them with his own arguments and evidence – the Quran's prophecies, its knowledge of the past, and its linguistic uniqueness (his chief argument, which he supports by ten signs); he strives to demonstrate the superiority of the divine oratory over all human discourse by means of detailed comparisons with ancient and contemporary poems, with the sayings of the Prophet himself and those of his comrades and his adversaries. The other, al-Jurjānī, aims not to establish *i'jāz* but to perfect it: he takes it for granted that the quranic miracle is accepted fact and has no ambitions to reiterate all the existing proofs in order to impress any doubters with the sheer mass of its miraculous properties; he concentrates instead on one single property of the Quran, its linguistic composition, and explains it in depth throughout the book from one angle after another, so that his argumentation is directed not against the deniers of the miracle, or even against those theologians who present other miraculous properties besides the linguistic one (in fact he almost ignores them), but against those Muslims who do not substantiate the Quran's linguistic uniqueness or who in his opinion do so fallaciously. Neither of the two books, and as far as I can see no other classic *i'jāz* compendium, indicates that the *i'jāz* scholars were primarily concerned with converting the followers of other religions. The only explanation for van Nieuwenhuijze's repetition of the common misconception that the *i'jāz* proof was aimed at Jews and Christians, 'whom it was meant to convince',[244] is that he did not read the sources. Almost all of them are documents of an intra-Islamic discourse addressed to fellow Muslims or to dissident elements within the community, intended to bolster them and ultimately motivated, like any development of dogma, by the community's search for identity. A collective identity is established and shaped by a sanctified canon of texts, values, conceptions and experiences. It is only natural that its formation involves a differentiation from other communities and that the resulting conceptions are introduced and applied in the interreligious discourse as well; it is unthinkable that they would not be. 'The sanctification of a particular tradition always leads to the sanctification of a particular community',[245] Jan Assmann wrote, and what he states here for the general case of canon formation can be observed in the formation of the *i'jāz* theory. Its development can be seen in some respects as the canonization, not of a text, but of an image of the past, a tradition and doctrine. That does not make *i'jāz* a helpless attempt by Muslim scholastics to construct a miracle of their own for use in discussions with the dogmatically superior Christians and Jews to win them over to Islam.

I'jāz and the Quran's Reception History

With all due caution, we may make some inferences from al-Jurjānī's and al-Bāqillānī's expositions about the discourse in which they arose and to which they contributed. The scholastic method of such treatises, the various forms of *qīla... wa-anā qultu...* ('It is said that... But I say...'), generally have the effect of telling the audience a good deal about the positions against which the author is arguing. The two *i'jāz* books at hand are no exception. At the time al-Jurjānī wrote, the basic outlines of the *i'jāz* doctrine had probably become definitively established in the form in which they are generally found today. His book is not written from a defensive position but was conceived as an extension of and enlargement upon a belief that was already accepted as valid. To my knowledge, the same is true of the works of authors who came after him. Qāḍī 'Iyāḍ, for example, is able to make the claim, which would not have occurred to al-Bāqillānī or al-Khaṭṭābī, that even the unbelievers admitted the miracle of the Quran, although they did not attribute it to God;[246] while Ibn Ḥajar al-'Asqalānī (d. 1458) writes in *Fatḥ al-bārī*, his commentary on the *Ṣaḥīḥ al-Bukhārī*:[247] 'There is no dispute among the wise that the book of God is a miracle, that no one was able to match it when the challenge was spoken.'[248] To al-Jurjānī, the danger of his time was not so much that the congregation might lose faith in *i'jāz*, but that they might blindly adopt it as a mere tradition, let it gel into mere dogma, and not be willing to experience it anew for themselves again and again. In the connection of 'the first-person singular to the first-person plural' that he examines in the process of canon formation,[249] Assmann focuses his attention clearly on the necessity of self-experience and individuation in the normative consciousness of the community.

Al-Bāqillānī, on the other hand, sees the foundations of faith being shaken and tries to compile as many of the most powerful arguments as possible to buttress the edifice of *i'jāz*, which in his day was not yet very robust, against the storm of heterodoxy. He goes about this effort a great deal more systematically and elaborately than his predecessor al-Khaṭṭābī, for example, although the direction of his discourse and the nature of his argument is not entirely in line with that author. Al-Khaṭṭābī also cites and refutes those who find the language of the Quran by no means unique and who criticize the doctrine of the linguistic miracle.[250] Al-Bāqillānī takes after him in describing, for the sake of evidence, the reactions of the first listeners, the rapture of the Meccans, and the helplessness of Muhammad's opponents against the quranic challenges, and this not as if claiming to present new information but rather as if reminding his listeners of a past of which they already knew and appealing to the community's collective memory. While he mentions the conversions of the poets Labīd ibn Rabī'a, Ka'b ibn Zuhayr and Hassān ibn Thābit in one sentence, invoking them as witnesses of *i'jāz*, he sees no need to explain who those poets were, how and why they converted, and what they said about the Quran. Al-Bāqillānī's treatment of the well-known conversion of 'Umar ibn al-Khaṭṭāb is also revealing, and in fact a prime example of the necessity of considering the intertextuality of such writings: 'Another hadith tells that 'Umar ibn al-Khaṭṭāb, God bless him, heard the surah *Ṭāhā* and converted to Islam.'[251] That is all al-Bāqillānī says. But his readers of course know the subtext: they know what he means; every one of them has heard the story of this most famous of all conversions – how 'Umar stormed into his sister's room when he heard a Quran reciter; how he knocked the page out of her hand, then regretted his brutality, picked up the pages and began to recite the Quran; how he was inspired and finally cried out, 'How beautiful, how sublime this oratory is!'[252]

Al-Bāqillānī's other references to the past are similarly abridged – like those of his predecessor al-Khaṭṭābī.[253] Without the authors' and the readers' shared memory of the early period of Islam, of the *founding events* of Muslim history, these references would seem obscure, incomplete, banal. Evidently they are not cited to convince an addressee outside the community but to appeal to shared memory of the community members, their identifying myths. Let me say once again, in using the word 'myths' I am not saying anything about the authenticity of the remembered events. In the sense explained in chapter 1, 'myth' denotes a form of remembrance. For example, Muhammad's Mecca with its Kaaba indubitably existed in the early seventh century, but in Muslim memory it is stylized as a commemorative space, and this is a normal process in cultural history. The remembrance of a community's founding history is a reconstruction, as cultural memory always operates by reconstruction, regardless of the factuality of the events.

The prior history that is reconstructed in the *iʿjāz* doctrine, and is indispensable for its acceptance and elaboration, is composed mainly of four phenomena. First, the ancient Arabs were masters of working with words; they were the very nation of poets. Second, Muhammad was illiterate, or in any case not versed in literary matters; he had never learned the extensive catalogue of rules that governed Arabic poetry. Third, the Quran had a tremendous aesthetic effect on the Meccans and on all subsequent generations. Fourth, neither Muhammad's adversaries, among whom were the best and most ambitious poets and orators of all time, nor any of the unbelievers of later times were able to meet the challenge issued in the Quran itself and match it stylistically. Those are the four fundamental myths of *iʿjāz*: the doctrine of the Quran's stylistic inimitability rests on them. As indicated in chapter 1, practically no work on *iʿjāz* fails to mention the uniqueness of Arab poetry and the high prestige it enjoyed at the time Muhammad preached the Quran. Even al-Jāḥiẓ in the ninth century knew that the Arabs, although they were masters of language and were highly motivated by their tribal honour and their hostility towards Islam, had had to admit defeat in the face of the quranic challenge. According to the argument repeated many times after al-Jāḥiẓ, if ever a people should have been capable of meeting the challenge, it was the Arabs, with the purity 'of their language, which is the master of their action; with their overflowing eloquence welling up in their breast, their dominating capacity for beautiful language – after all, they are able to speak of snakes, scorpions, wolves, dogs, scarabs, dung beetles, asses, doves; about everything that crawls and walks; about what they see with their eyes and about what they conceive in their hearts.'[254] As poets they were unmatched. In the collective memory, the ancient Arabs' oratory combines 'the merits of the Bedouins' language, with its forceful, epigrammatic style and its coarse straightforwardness, and the beautifully polished speech and cultivated language of the city-dwellers', as Tor Andrae remarks with reference to al-Bāqillānī and Ījī (d. 1355).[255] On the Arabs' stylization of their own past, which is still mentioned with unabated emphasis in support of *iʿjāz* in the twentieth century,[256] Andrae writes:

> In the interest of proof they take full advantage of the admiration that the ancient Arabs' eloquence and poetry enjoyed among later generations. They indulge in broad descriptions of how the ancient Arabs were capable of anything by their oratory: making the coward bold, the miser generous, the defective perfect, the famous forgotten.[257]

As part of the image of the past, the greatest achievements of later generations are said to have only approached or barely reached the level of olden times, but never exceeded it.[258] Again and again, the interpretation presented in chapter 1[259] is repeated: the prophets' miracles are fitting for the peoples they must convince, and Muhammad's sign must be a linguistic one because he is the prophet of a people that prides itself most of all on its poets. The Meccans' reactions to Muhammad's recitation of the Quran are likewise often mentioned: The Meccans' amazement and confusion was all the greater because Muhammad's oratory outshone all the poets' verse, even though he was not a poet. Muhammad's lack of literary education, the silence of his opponents, the conversions of ʿUmar ibn al-Khaṭṭāb, Muṭʿim ibn ʿAdī and others, and the colourful descriptions of the fervour of Muhammad's faithful listeners – all of these become *figures of memory* in works such as al-Bāqillānī's. Likewise the adversaries' attempts to meet the challenge to match the Quran, which are described as pitiful. Al-Bāqillānī derisively quotes a sample from Musaylima ibn Ḥabīb and does not fail to mention the prophet Sajāḥ, who emerged immediately after Muhammad's death:[260] all of them 'fools' (*sukhafāʾ*) according to Qāḍī ʿIyāḍ, for only the fools among the Arabs did not see that the eloquence and persuasiveness of the Quran could not be matched by any human oratory. Others named as challengers during Muhammad's lifetime include Manham ʿAbhala ibn Kaʿb, Ṭulayḥa al-Asadī and an-Naḍr ibn al-Ḥārith. The names of Ibn al-Muqaffaʿ, Bashshār ibn Burd, al-Maʿarrī and al-Mutanabbī are mentioned again and again as later challengers[261] by authors who proudly report their failure. 'It is told of each one who has tried to challenge the Quran', Qāḍī ʿIyāḍ writes, 'that he was stricken with awe (*rawʿa*) and terror (*hayba*), so that they abandoned their attempts.' Ibn al-Muqaffaʿ, for example, who 'was among the most eloquent of his day',[262] walked past a boy who recited the Quran verse *wa-qīla yā ʾarḍu blaʿī māʾaki* ('And it was said, "Earth, swallow thy waters"').[263] On hearing it, the man of letters went home to tear up his imitation, crying, 'I avow this cannot match that; that is no human word.' Another episode that Qāḍī Iyāḍ recounts in this connection is that of Yaḥyā b. al-Ḥakam al-Ġazāl, 'in his day the rhetorician of Andalusia'. He set himself the task of imitating the surah *al-Ikhlāṣ* (no. 112), but on looking at it he was so stricken with 'fear (*khaya*) and emotion (*riqqa*)' that he longed for repentance and atonement.[264]

At the time al-Bāqillānī wrote his book, the history had long since been reconstructed: the events are recounted in detail in the hadith collections, the biographies of the Prophet and the Quran commentaries, and are thematically organized in the *nubūwa* compilations of Abū Nuʿāym and al-Bayhaqī, for example, both younger contemporaries of al-Bāqillānī, and in Qāḍī ʿIyāḍ's *Shifāʾ*, which is still extremely popular in the Islamic world today. To study the Muslim community's cultural memory, one must refer to these texts, whose function is to evoke and represent the salvation history. Contrary to what one might expect, the extant *iʿjāz* surveys, the earliest of which date from the late tenth century, contain only isolated and often fragmentary stories of the first Quran listeners, even though in the Muslim perspective these are the most striking proof of the Quran's miraculous power. Nevertheless, the remembered history is present in these writings too – only in a different form, more sketchy or schematic than in the *nubūwa* works. Members of the community are expected to know at least its rough outlines. That is why al-Bāqillānī and the other *i'jāz* authors do not need to reconstruct the events of the founding period and can instead simply evoke the memory of them by reference to shared knowledge and use them as evidence in support of their own theories.

The four myths mentioned – the status of language and poetry among the Arabs, Muhammad's lack of literary knowledge, the power of the Quran and the challenge to its opponents – are contained in the cultural memory and present as axioms both in al-Bāqillānī and in al-Jurjānī. Yet the two theologians differ in the way in which they refer to them and in the degree of detail in their references. Al-Bāqillānī, whose work has the character of the formative phase of the doctrine, finds it necessary to point to the past far more often and to invoke the past as evidence of the miraculous nature of the Quran. The reason he does so – because the memory seems to be dissolving, so that belief in the miracle is endangered – is easy to infer from his exposition; his wording reveals it. An example:

> *Do you not see* that their poets disliked one another and that there are *famous* anecdotes, *well-known* reports and *frequently retold* recollections of their mutual dislike, and that they competed with one another, boasting and priding themselves on linguistic eloquence, rhetoric and skill. In view of these circumstances, it would have been unthinkable for them not to try to match the Quran if they had been able, whether or not they had been challenged.... And so, if we see that they did not contend by any of the traditional forms of oratory, the usual speeches, familiar messages or ornate poems, and presented nothing in opposition to the Quran, but all said, 'That is more eloquent (*afṣaḥ*) and more unusual (*aġrab*) than everything I have ever created; it is an example', then we know that they were unable and there was nothing that could have matched the Quran. If they had achieved something comparable, it would have come down to us and we would know it, just as we know the poems of the Jahiliyyah and the words of the eloquent and the wise among the ancient Arabs, and as the words of the soothsayers and the poets of *rajaz*, *saj'* and *qaṣīda* and their other forms of verbal art and forms of eloquence have come down to us.[265]

The facts al-Bāqillānī relates to his readers are not new. He is reminding them of something they already know in order to reinforce the confirmatory miracle. Because al-Jurjānī, on the other hand, intends not to defend *i'jāz* but to elucidate its grounds in greater depth, he hardly needs to remind the reader at such length. Most of all, however, he changes the style of such references to the past. It is true that he repeats al-Jāḥiẓ's and al-Bāqillānī's argument that the Meccans never would have chosen to fight Muhammad, and so chosen death, if they had not felt their inability (*'ajz*) to produce a speech that could even approach the brilliant wording of the Quran and so bring their rival to his knees;[266] he also touches on the myth of the Arabs as a nation of poets and quotes al-Jāḥiẓ's statement that every one of their orators (*khuṭabā'*) and verbal artists (*bulaġā'*) immediately recognized the unique linguistic quality of the Quran and realized their inability to produce anything comparable;[267] and he refers to the commentaries of Muhammad's contemporaries and several early Islamic authorities such as Ibn Mas'ūd on the beauty of the Quran. Unlike al-Bāqillānī, however, he does not present all these references in the form of precise indications to conjure up memories but takes the presence of the founding history as given and invokes it in support of his own view of the Quran. This tendency to interpret the past to further his own ideas rather than recalling and referring to it simply as evidence of *i'jāz* can be seen in al-Jurjānī's treatment of all four of the premises mentioned. For example, his primary interest in mentioning the Prophet's 'innocence' of all literary education, which the reader is assumed to know, is not to present an argument for *i'jāz* but to warn the reader against inferring from this information that all literary education is prohibited. The quranic statement that God did not teach the Prophet the art of poetry[268] does not signify a disdain for that art, al-Jurjānī writes. The meaning is rather: although Muhammad never studied the rules and techniques of poetry, his oratory is the most perfect and the most eloquent, 'so that the proof is the more shining and crushing and the evidence still stronger and clearer and to silence the deniers more definitively, to humble the obstinate still more, to teach a lesson to those who spread suspicions, and to prevent disbelief from arising in the first place.'[269]

Another example of how al-Jurjānī weaves in a reference to Muslims' shared history to reinforce his own arguments is found in a section in which he rebuts the view that the miracle of the Quran is its acoustic beauty:

> We have seen the experts when they mentioned the Arabs' inability to match the Quran. They said the Prophet challenged them, and there were poets and orators among them and people who were famous for the eloquence of their tongue, for their way with words, their rhetoric and their intellectual talents, people with the gift of wisdom and cleverness in public speech. We have not heard those experts say that the Arabs took the Prophet's challenge to mean they should produce a speech that was free of sounds difficult to pronounce.[270]

Al-Jurjānī cites the statements of the authorities as evidence of the absurdity of the view he criticizes, showing that it is not consistent with the historic events as they are present in the community's memory. The immediate addressee is clearly not an uninformed or a doubting reader who needs to be convinced of the power of the Quran. The following reference to the first Quran listeners' reactions is similar:

> Who is it that claimed that the evidence that was shown to them, and the fact that enraptured them, and the longing that filled their breast, and the awe that struck them and moved them, so that they said, 'There is a sweetness in it and an elegance; its branches bear plentiful fruit, and much water springs from its ground' – that all of this which fascinated and shook them was just the placement of the vocalization marks and their arrangement in relation to the voiceless markings between two consonants, or the rhymes at the ends of the verses? Where did such characterizations and comparisons originate?[271]

The meaning of this passage is not that the Quran had a great effect on Muhammad's contemporaries. If it were, the sentence would have taken the form *The Quran enraptured the Meccans, filled their breasts with longing*, and so on. Rather, the sender assumes the Quran's effect is already known, and the meaning is that a certain interpretation of that effect is false: *Do you think the Quran enraptured the Meccans and filled their breasts with longing only because...?* The same intention can be observed in all of al-Jurjānī's references to the Quran's reception history. On the same page, he cites two statements by Ibn Mas'ūd and a hadith:

> Or do you think Ibn Mas'ūd, in describing the Quran with the words, 'Its sweetness never ends, and its spring never runs dry', or when he said, 'When I contemplate the *ḥā'-mīm* surahs, it is as if I were walking in evergreen gardens with soft and delightful meadows. I go forever more in search of them' – that is, of the beauty of those gardens – do you think he said that because of the metre of the words and the rhyme of the verses? Do you think that is what they meant when they said, 'Its wonders have no end, and no matter how often one repeats the recitation, it never grows dull'?[272]

Al-Jurjānī can safely assume that the educated reader knows the sense of both the statements by Ibn Mas'ūd, or can at least classify them immediately: they are part of a store of general culture and are often repeated by Muslim authors.[273] The same is true of the quotations about the never-ending wonders of the Quran, its incomparable sweetness and elegance, its branches bearing plentiful fruit and the water that springs from its ground. Al-Jurjānī does not mention the source of these quotations, or even quote them completely; his readers, familiar with the tradition, know that the first quotation is a common hadith of the Prophet[274] and the second is the famous cry of al-Walīd ibn al-Muġīra on hearing the Quran for the first time.[275]

All four of al-Jurjānī's quotations mentioned here are based in a memory that is shared between the author and the reader and forms the ground on which he builds his theory. As in al-Bāqillānī's book, the discourse on *iʿjāz* is unthinkable except in the context of the collective memory. Because he is afraid people are forgetting, al-Bāqillānī refers to the past much more frequently than al-Jurjānī, who describes a different situation in his exposition and gets by with relatively few allusions and quotations, which he uses mainly to support his own argumentation, not to refresh the reader's memory. In both books, however, and in the *iʿjāz* literature generally, the founding history of the Muslim community as canonized in the biography of the Prophet, the hadith collections and the exegetic works – that is, the remembered history of the Quran's reception – is the indispensable underpinning. It is present to the immediate addressee as an intertextuality; outsiders must make the effort to bear it in mind.

Cultural memory is reconstructive; it conserves the past not as past but only as an image of the community's history which the community constructs at a certain time under certain circumstances for reasons that are usually understandable. This image can be closer to what is called historic reality, as in the case of the Holocaust for today's Jews, or pure fiction, as in the case of the Christian topography. The question *to what degree* the Muslim community's memory coincides with the historic events in the first decades of Islam is intentionally excluded from the scope of this book. But *the fact that* such a relation exists between the remembered history and the Quran's reception as it actually transpired must be recognized and kept in mind, not least because the situations of reception continue during the phase of reconstruction. That is, while the collective memory of the earlier reception of the Quran is still being shaped, the same Quran is still being heard, and new accounts of the wondering responses it causes are continually being brought into circulation. This constitutes a certain measure of verifiability which, although it is not comparable with the verifiability of more recent historic events, nonetheless makes the event real, current and, last but not least, subjectively understandable for the remembering community in the reception experience. In a slightly different sense from that which Jan Assmann intended in introducing the terms, one might say that the first Quran recitations and their effect are remembered both in the *cultural memory* and in the *communicative memory*, which is constituted in day-to-day interaction and goes back no farther than eighty or a hundred years.[276]

The inference that the Muslims did not simply project the Quran as a source of aesthetic experience back into their own salvation history, but that it actually played an outstanding role in the *formative phase* of Islam, a role that made such a projection possible, is supported not only by the numerous legends about listeners in that phase and later centuries who professed Islam, swooned or died. At least equally significant are other texts which were not intended to praise the power of the Quran and are not suspected of religious romanticism: I am referring to such texts as conservative theologians' criticisms of the overly ecstatic reactions of Quran listeners, and biographical testimony that is interesting precisely for the incidental character of its information about the reception of the Quran. We encounter such documents often enough in all kinds of contexts. The history *The Shining Stars among the Kings of Egypt and Cairo* by Abū l-Maḥāsin ibn Taġribirdī (d. 1412), for example, contains a report, recounted by Goldziher, that the Quran reciter and singer Muḥammad ibn Jaʿfar al-Adamī (d. 960) once undertook a pilgrimage to Mecca together with some other respected scholars. Near Medina they met a *qaṣṣās*, a blind story-teller, who, in the middle of a circle of other pilgrims, entertained the crowd with pleasing but spurious traditions and anecdotes from the life of the Prophet. One of the group 'wanted to stop the impostor', according to the story,

> but the Koran reader disapproved of such action, fearing lest it would cause the mob to defend the story-teller and to turn against his critics. He hit on an appropriate measure: he began to recite the Koran himself and, hardly did the blind man's audience hear his beautiful recitation, than they left the teller of traditions and gathered around the Koran reader instead.[277]

Quran recitations are frequently mentioned in the accounts of Muslim travellers as well. The Andalusian Ibn Jubayr (d. 1217), for example, recorded his impressions of a Ramadan night in the mosque of Mecca in the following words:

> There was hardly a niche or a corner in the mosque where there was not a reciter with a group praying behind him. The mosque trembled with the voices of the reciters in every corner, so that the eyes saw a sight and the ears heard melodies that filled the senses with excitement.[278]

The classic works on *iʿjāz* reveal that the context in which they were written had an extremely high aesthetic appreciation of the Quran. The best illustration of that appreciation is found where it is contested. Al-Bāqillānī, for example, complaining frequently of disparaging appraisals of the Quran by some of his contemporaries, depicts them as a *novel* phenomenon. He is most indignant about the news that some impudent apostates *have begun* to prefer poetry to the Quran: 'I have heard tell of one of the ignorant that he began to compare it with some lines of poetry and measure it against other oratory, and not even content with that, he actually preferred them to the Quran.'[279] Reading between the lines, the wording and the thrust of the argument permit inferences about al-Bāqillānī's thought and that of his addressees on the stylistic quality of the Quran. We might paraphrase the quotation as follows: 'Imagine, there are people who do not regard the Quran as inimitable, as we do and our fathers before us did; and not only that, but one of them is said to have gone so far as to compare it with other discourses, and even found them better and more beautiful than the Quran.' The tone indicates that such a view was felt to be an astounding, incomprehensible, outrageous, very recent and, most of all, rare error: *this is how far things have gone*. He also indicates that his warning is addressed to readers who have experienced the aesthetic attraction of the Quran before reading his book. Al-Bāqillānī is trying not to persuade the reader of the Quran's beauty (if so, the line of argumentation would be: *See, the Quran is so beautiful because*...) but to prove that the beauty his addressees already perceive is *muʿjiz*, a miracle. The basic pattern of his discourse is therefore: *The beauty of the Quran, of which you have heard much and everyone is aware, is inimitable and hence a miracle, because*.... This does not imply that all of al-Bāqillānī's contemporaries considered the Quran a linguistic masterpiece, but it does indicate that the author had reason to expect such an appreciation on the part of the majority of his readers – who are not the entire population, or even the Muslim population, of his society, but the educated circles, versed in questions of religion and dogma – that is, the readers of a theological treatise that is not exactly easily comprehensible.

Other reports of stylistic contestations of the Quran also indicate that they contested an established view – that is, they arose in a context in which the revelation was aesthetically received and appreciated by some kind of community. One of the most thorough of the extant critiques of the quranic rhetoric is the letter of a Christian named ʿAbdulmasīḥ ibn Isḥāq al-Kindī, who lived at the court of the caliph al-Ma'mūn (d. 833). Another courtier, ʿAbdullāh ibn Ismāʿīl al-Hāshimī, in a written appeal to him to embrace Islam, had pointed proudly to the stylistic inimitability of the Quran. Al-Kindī replied with a long letter in which, alongside remarks on its dubious authenticity and the content, he criticized the style of the Quran.[280] This correspondence is significant for our present topic because the Muslim distinctly invites the Christian to Islam with the idea that the linguistic superiority of the Quran is plainly visible and that it must be a missionary's best argument. Even if this estimation on al-Hāshimī's part is wrong, or at least one-sided, we cannot imagine that he simply made it up out of thin air: it must have been shared by a certain group and inferred from some kind of empirical evidence. Ibn al-Jawzī's rebuttal to the writings of Ibn ar-Rāwandī several centuries later contains similar indications:

> But it is a sign of his foolishness that he undertakes to criticize the Quran, which reached the ears of the Arab princes and amazed them all, and which the people of pure language were unable to imitate; but he in his ignorance of language dares to find fault with it – all that he has revealed is his own disgrace....Then he starts to quibble with the Quran and says it contains solecisms. This querulous person thinks he can teach even the well-spoken enemies [of God] a lesson who [even they] have admitted the purity of the Quran's language![281]

Ibn al-Jawzī spares himself the trouble of a refutation: the mere reference to the Quran's reception history and the consensus of the community, with which his readers are familiar, is sufficient to expose Ibn ar-Rāwandī's criticism as ridiculous.

A more remarkable phenomenon in the earlier history of Arabic literature is that many of the best-known prose authors and poets tried at least once in their lives to compete stylistically with the Quran. Even disregarding how these reports end (the authors invariably admit that the task is impossible), it is significant that the protagonists evidently regarded the Quran as a real challenge against which to test and prove themselves. At the meetings of Muslim and non-Muslim freethinkers and men of letters in eighth-century Basra, mentioned above,[282] the best recited poems were characterized in the following way: 'Your poem is better than this or that verse of the Koran; this line is better than that other verse of the Koran; etc.'[283] A particularly libertarian member of that circle, Bashshār ibn Burd, on hearing a poem of his that he particularly liked recited by a singer in Baghdad, said it was as beautiful as the surah *al-Ḥashr* (no. 59). He must have thought the surah was not bad. Al-Bāqillānī's book also suggests that even people who did not consider the language of the Quran unsurpassable did not find it atrocious either. 'Our opponents', the theologian complains, deny that the Quran in all its parts is a masterpiece of language; in addition to the 'noble words joined with novel meanings' they find other phrases that detract from its 'beauty of expression'.[284] These unspecified deniers of *iʿjāz*, we cannot help concluding, consider the Quran a serious literary monument and concede it has linguistic quality, although not inimitability. Such an attitude, which is also found by the way in a modern critic of the Quran such as the Iranian ʿAlī Dashtī (d. 1981),[285] is fundamentally different from that shown by the known critiques of the biblical style. Nietzsche, for example, who accused the Holy Ghost of writing poor Greek, considered the poetry of the Bible not a 'challenge' but wretched and contemptible. Voltaire was similarly dismissive: 'Nulle politesse, nulle science, nul art perfectionné dans aucun temps chez cette nation atroce' [No politeness, no science, no perfection of any art at any time among this atrocious nation].[286] Those Christian believers who attained prominence as despisers of biblical language, such as the secretary of the papal court Lorenzo Valla (d. 1457) and his countryman the poet and cardinal Pietro Bembo (d. 1547), were not provocateurs undermining the firm conviction of an overwhelming majority. On the contrary, they were expressing agreement with an opinion widely held in the learned circles of their time, probably with a view to directing the full attention of the faithful to the content of the doctrine.[287] By contrast, the intent, the tone and the wording of the extant reports on critics of the quranic language reveals that they were nonconformists, 'iconoclasts' who opposed or 'challenged' a judgement held by a majority of their community which they felt, as such dissidents always do, to be obsolete and blindly inherited. By their rebellion they attest to the aesthetic appreciation of the Quran by the community of the faithful during the formative period of Islam and during the formation of the *iʿjāz* doctrine.

That such an aesthetic appreciation is not something to be taken for granted in the history of religion can hardly be better demonstrated than by a comparison with the aesthetic appraisals of the Bible in Western Christianity. Of course both testaments of the Christian Bible were aesthetically received, and many people praised their *beauty*, in spite of *sermo humilis*, their plain human language. Even the early Christian audience showed such a preference for rhetorical skill that listeners applauded specific passages of a sermon,[288] and the groundbreaking achievements of translators, such as St Jerome's Vulgate and Luther's German Bible, had an influence as stylistic models that was by no means limited to ecclesiastical circles. There were repeated theological efforts to attribute literary qualities to the Bible and to build dogma on them. The tradition of linking biblical and secular poetry in argument extends from the Church Fathers to the present day.[289] Where these efforts resulted in an extensive literature – and this qualifier is important if we do not want to ignore the Christian congregations' sensory delight in the reading of scripture in church, which existed throughout Christian history – we can discern three major waves of aesthetic enthusiasm for the Bible: in the Church Fathers, during the Renaissance and during the Enlightenment. However, the documents of all three periods attest that they originated in a context of reception that was completely different from that which saw the emergence of the *iʿjāz* compendia, and that the hostile attitude in early Christianity, for example, was nothing like that in the centres of Islamic scholarship during the Abbasid period, as Josef van Ess suggests.[290] In all three periods, authors *point out* the beauty of the scriptures, addressing readers who, they feel, have not yet devoted sufficient attention to this quality of the Bible. Their writings are those of an elite who would like to bring the poetry of the holy scripture to the attention of their community. The first of the three waves mentioned, the Church Fathers, are a special case. As Dieter Gutzen notes in his work on the poetry of the Bible, the earliest attempts to demonstrate the presence of rhetorical devices in the Bible must be 'understood as an answer to the criticism that educated opponents of Christianity made against the style of the biblical scriptures: it was offensive to these educated persons that ideals of the greatest moment that pretended to historic influence were propounded not in the expected "stilus gravis", but in a "stilus humilis", which was accorded and reserved to the comic sphere.'[291] We know that the linguistic mixture of the *koine* Greek scripture, which was hardly written by native speakers, seemed nothing less than barbaric to educated Latin speakers. Even the early Latin translations always appeared to the Roman heathens, in Erich Auerbach's judgement, to 'have about them something awkward, half-educated, and heavily pedantic'.[292]

> They found this literature gross and vulgar, awkward in syntax and choice of words, and, to make matters worse, riddled with Hebraisms. Certain passages

> which to us seem undeniably powerful were looked upon as a turbid jumble; the product of fanatical, half-educated sectaries. The educated pagan public reacted with ridicule, contempt, and horror. How could the profoundest of problems, the enlightenment and redemption of mankind, be treated in such barbarous works?[293]

The extremely peculiar style of the first translations, made by inexperienced Latin writers, was not corrected by Christian literary scholars, as one might have thought, to conform to the norms of classical rhetoric and so eliminate the annoyance. Very early on, the texts of the *Vetus Latina* gained such an authority among the congregations that they had soon become part of the established tradition, and a Bible text after the classical taste would have had no chance of becoming popular. St Jerome's new edition was not created until around 400 and did not revise all parts of the text with equal thoroughness. Where it deviated significantly from the customary wording, it was difficult to impose it on the congregations. The corpus of holy scripture thus remained a foreign object amid Latin literature of classical origin.

In this situation two largely independent lines of defence formed among the Christian authors of late antiquity. One group, historically the more successful one, acknowledged the 'humility' of the biblical style and found a form of grandeur in it that was different from the accustomed kind. The concept of *sermo humilis*, 'humble speech', took shape. 'This dialectical position, in which the problem of translation was ignored, carried force because of its inner truth', Auerbach writes; it was 'at once offensive and defensive'.[294] Another, less common rebuttal that early Christian authors, including Cassiodorus (d. c. 583) and Isidore of Seville (d. 636), made to the criticism of the Roman pagans did not prevail as easily: their argument claimed that the holy scripture was artistically perfect, and they detected in the Bible the tropes and figures of speech of the traditional rules, those of the traditional poetry and rhetoric of classical antiquity, in order to explain that 'all the nations had derived not only their eloquence but all the true wisdom in their possession from the Old Testament, which was far older than the heathen cultures.'[295] This argument was not particularly effective in regard to stylistic matters, however, since it was difficult to present the Latin text of the Bible as a document of classical discursive culture. Hence the stylistic argument gained little acceptance among the educated class and was eclipsed by the doctrine of *sermo humilis*. It was not until the feeling for the classical tradition had died out – Auerbach dates this development to about 700 – that the Bible was praised somewhat successfully, by the English Benedictine the Venerable Bede (d. 735) for example, as a model of classical style. And it was not until late in the Renaissance that more voices attested to the poetic radiance of the Bible, in part because of Christian scholars' increasing familiarity with Hebrew. The anti-clericalist Roger Bacon (d. 1294) had insisted as early as the thirteenth century that the Hebrew text was untranslatable. During the

Renaissance, this intellectual current was represented primarily by the school of 'Christian Hebraists', of which the Swabian humanist Johannes Reuchlin (d. 1522) was the principal pioneer. But here, once again, what happened was not the theological treatment and dogmatic formulation of a general reception experience, reinforced by cultural memory and carried by a broad consensus of the community. It was individuals at first who demonstrated the poetic power of the Bible to a relatively naive majority, and they were for the most part, unlike the authors of the *iʿjāz* compendia, not representatives of an orthodoxy or of any dogmatic school; in fact many of them were poets. One of the most important and earliest among them was Boccaccio (d. 1375), who pointed to the poetic quality of the Bible in his defence of poetry.[296] His contemporary Petrarch (d. 1374), like Jewish poets before him and many Christian authors after him, cited the example of the 'shepherd poet' David to support the idea of a common ground of poetry and the Bible.[297] The magnitude of the difference between this discourse, which also perceives the revelation as a literary monument, and the theory of *iʿjāz* is underscored by Petrarch's judgement that secular and sacred poetry complement one another as 'those I prefer for style and those I prefer for substance'.[298] In addition to his honest admiration, Petrarch's motive, and that of most authors who praised biblical poetry in that period, was not so much to defend the Bible from its detractors as to support poetry against an orthodoxy that was sceptical of it. These efforts continued during the Baroque period, although the standard of stylistic appreciation was still the rules of Classical rhetoric. Joachim Dyck writes:

> The poets of the seventeenth century judge the value of poetry by normative laws and defend the magnificence of holy scripture with the standards that were handed down to them from 'pagan' antiquity. They are not yet able to defend the linguistic autonomy of the Bible because they would then forfeit the ability to praise it by reference to examples and received authorities: the claim of originality can only be upheld by contempt for authority and by renunciation of traditional ties. The writers of the German Baroque were not predecessors of Husband or Herder. To them, David is still an *ancient Cicero*, and the Song of Songs is a *genus bucolicum* or a *drama*.[299]

Those who referred to the poetic power of the Bible in the Renaissance and in the Baroque were often humanitarians, poets, musically inclined theologians – that is, not representatives of orthodoxy and popular piety; but in Islam in every century it was the conservative preachers and scholars who zealously held fast to the aesthetic quality of the Quran and vaunted and praised its linguistic facets (while those who rejected *iʿjāz* are found rather among the poets, freethinkers and those notorious as heretics).[300] In the eighteenth century too, when Christian authors free themselves from ancient stylistic models and begin to accord the Bible a value of its own, in its quality as an exotic, 'enthusiastic' poetry, as a 'rich collection of authentic natural poetries', as the Göttingen theology professor Johann Gottfried Eichhorn exclaimed,[301] this takes place in a reception context completely different from those which al-Bāqillānī and al-Jurjānī subjectively portray in reference to the Quran.[302] Because they were the first to perceive the particular nature of biblical poetry, the eighteenth-century authors saw themselves even more than those of the Renaissance as making a 'discovery', as the subtitle of Gutzen's book indicates – as an elite uncovering a quality, thanks to their philological education and their poetic sensitivity, that had long been buried. As early as 1661, the scientist Robert Boyle had explicitly devoted his book *Some Considerations Touching the Style of the H. Scriptures* to the *defence* of the Bible as a work of outstanding literary quality and the *refutation of all objections* that had been raised against its style, pointing out the necessity of judging it only in the original, not in its translations.[303] In the eighteenth century, growing numbers of scholars took up the cause of restoring the dignity of what Eichhorn called the 'despised and derided'[304] biblical scriptures. But even that important advocate of biblical poetry was far from placing it on a level with the great poetry of later eras. If it were applied to the Quran, his lukewarm apology would have seemed to a Muslim theologian an outright slander of the divine word:

> Those who would despise it because it comes from a nation that had not attained a high level of culture, and had exercised its intellectual abilities only in one direction, must have met its most important merits either with ingratitude or with such injustice as to demand the full light of noon from the first dim rays of dawn.[305]

The continued defensive attitude of the argument is unmistakable. The Hebrews' scriptures are considered remarkable as literature on account of their age (even Greek literature sinks 'to low youth, compared with them')[306] and their resulting documentary value: 'What other books would have preserved for us such pure tales from the childhood of mankind, disappearing in the mists of time?'[307]

Yet the devotees of biblical poetry soon abandoned their defensive posture. The new poetic theories of the early eighteenth century, which rehabilitated the irrational facets of Classical rhetoric and emphasized subjective and psychological factors over scholastic norms, contributed to the perception of the Bible as a literary monument among larger circles of readers. The 'Orientals' poetry of nature'[308] should, Herder demanded, be experienced in their 'original nature and beauty', without borrowing 'from foreign models and arts of poetry',[309] for 'it is mere folly, also, to judge of this whole class of words and images among the Hebrews by the caprices of our customs.'[310] While the revealed substance of the Bible declined in authority over the course of the Enlightenment, its poetic character gained in importance, in keeping with the advances of an 'aesthetics of the heart': 'The exhibition of art in the poetry of the Greeks is but tawdry ornament compared with this child-like and pure simplicity.'[311] Hamann sees the Gospel as ideal poetry: 'the strongest, most sensual and exuberant revelation of the nature of the divine will'.[312] To quote Joachim Dyck again:

> The followers of emotional aesthetics discovered the Old Testament as a most precious and autonomous poetry after its own laws, and made it their standard, a shining example of their 'new' literary concept. In doing so they relieved it of its function as a mere argument representing the worthiness of the poets and poetry. It takes its place in the canon of secular literature, which has meanwhile acquired an unrestricted franchise and no longer requires a biblical advocate.[313]

A wave of enthusiasm for biblical poetry – for its impassioned language and enthusiastic diction, its bold metaphors and its enigmatic, irregular style – was provoked by Herder, Hamann, and indirectly, through his concept of religious feeling, Schleiermacher[314] too in Germany, by scholars such as Bishop Robert Lowth in his 1741 *Lectures on the Sacred Poetry of the Hebrews* in the English-speaking countries, and by Augustin Calmet (d. 1757) with *Commentaire littéral sur tous les livres de l'Ancien et du Nouveau Testament* in France. Goethe is only the most famous of the many poets of that time who found poetic inspiration in the world of biblical language and ideas.[315] In philosophy, the 'aestheticization of religion' was first manifested in the writings of the Romantic authors and later developed into a concept in the systematic theories of Schelling and Hegel, the philosophers of Idealism.[316] In the wake of the Enlightenment, aesthetics had first stood out from logic and ethics as something autonomous and in many respects had become the dominant element of the philosophical view of the world. The protest by Kierkegaard cited at the outset of this chapter must be seen in the context of this period. He was opposing what appeared to him as a new view that was rapidly spreading and threatening the foundations of faith.

None of the three phases sketched above of the Bible's aesthetic reception in Europe shows significant similarities with the context in which the doctrine of *iʿjāz* developed in the ninth century: the very air is different; the circumstances are not comparable. When Thomas Aquinas explained the uniqueness of the Bible by its divine inspiration, he was thinking of its literary form among other things, but it never occurred to him, or to any other Christian author, to see in it a miraculous proof of God or a perfect use of language, transcending the *stylistic* abilities of even the greatest poets.[317] That in no way implies a general lack of aesthetic sense in the religious world of Christianity. But the aesthetic processes are of a different kind: both in the cult and in the theology, they refer not so much to the beauty of the scripture as primarily to the revelation of the living God, which, as Hans Urs von Balthasar writes, must be conceived 'not only in its aspect of truth and goodness, but just as much in its inconceivable glory'[318] and forms the 'source of Christian and therefore all aesthetics'.[319] Balthasar's large-scale, three-volume endeavour to define the aesthetics of Christianity and describe the broad abundance of aesthetic experiences also revolves around such terms as beauty, splendour and glory, but the ideas, associations and themes that he and the authors he discusses mean by these terms are diametrically opposed to what al-Jurjānī means when he talks of *ḥusn*, *bahr* or *fakhr*. The glory of the divine revelation mentioned in the Gospel of John, the beauty of God's self-statement, manifests itself for Christians not primarily in the scripture, as for Muslims, but in the occurrence of the living God: 'And the Word was made flesh, and dwelt among us (and we beheld his glory, the glory as of the only begotten of the Father), full of grace and truth.'[320] It is no wonder therefore that no absolute claim has ever been made in regard to the poetic nature of the Bible like that which Muslim scholars assert as dogma for the Quran, and that the revealed text as a literary monument or an acoustic work never even came close to fulfilling the central, identifying and stabilizing function that it did in the Arab-Islamic world – that no structure as far-reaching and as essential for theology as *iʿjāz* has been constructed anywhere in the Christian world.

The theological point of departure alone would have sufficed to ensure that no such construct arose. It would not have had the foundation of reception with its two components – the historic reception in the cultural memory and the current reception as the individual believer's auditory experience – in other words, it would have had neither footing nor continuity. The discourse on *iʿjāz* is distinctly identifiable as a treatment and interpretation of a memory and experience shared by both the authors and the addressees. It is addressed directly to Muslim readers, who do not need to be told of the aesthetic qualities of the Quran, with the aim of explaining to them how those qualities constitute a miracle. The Muslim authors emphasize the dialectic of memory and experience as the foundation of *iʿjāz* again and again, although in different words and to different purposes. They do so when they say, as al-Jurjānī does, that the history of the quranic challenges, which is known to all, confirmed by all authorities and seriously denied by no one – the inability of all opponents, including the greatest poets and rhetoricians of all time, to match the Quran – is already sufficient evidence of the miracle. At the same time, al-Jurjānī maintains, every believer has the duty to comprehend the Quran independently in its full divine splendour. To be content with knowing that no one answered the challenge, and to take that as sufficient evidence for the divine nature of the Quran, would be just as inadequate as learning to repeat other people's opinions by rote. To trust in the judgement of the ancestors and practise mere *taqlīd*, 'imitation', is not enough: one must discover the metaphysical beauty by one's own research to verify the Quran's *iʿjāz* for oneself. Only personal experience, personal knowledge, is a lasting safeguard against error.[321] Al-Jurjānī writes:

> What kind of a person are you that you forswear the knowledge of the divine proof and prefer ignorance to knowledge and darkness to light? In this of all matters, then, you prefer blind imitation, and you find it more profitable to concern yourself with other sciences? Separate yourself from this conceit; remember your reason, and be honest with yourself. See the abhorrence of your error and the ugliness of the delusion you are under. Do you know any weaker opinion or uglier decision than the choice to abhor the knowledge of God's proof which, when one has recognized it, could not be more brilliant and beautiful, more strong and compelling, and to prefer that the power of that proof should not triumph over idolatry and tower over all disbelief?[322]

Other authors also underscore the necessity of verifying the founding history by one's own knowledge – which in this case is nothing more or less than a subjective aesthetic experience made possible by literary education. 'We know', says the rhetorician Abū Hilāl al-ʿAskarī, for example,

> that when people do not strive for knowledge of the artistic language and disdain the knowledge of the pure language, they do not recognize the *iʿjāz* of the Quran by the qualities with which God has distinguished it, such as the beauty of its diction and so forth... but only by the fact that the Arabs are incapable of that. But what a shame for the legal scholar (*faqīh*) whose example the others follow, for the Quran reciter whose instructions people obey, for the theologians whose speculation people refer to, for the Arabs with their tribal pride, and for the Quraysh of noble lineage, if they can only recognize the miracle of the holy book as an African or a Nabataean could, if they need the same indirect evidence as an illiterate person.[323]

Al-Bāqillānī takes a similar view, although his reference to the indispensability of literary studies is less emphatic, and he more acerbically points out that non-Arabs and uneducated people, who lack the necessary linguistic skills, can and must be content to recognize Muhammad's miracle by the Arabs' historic inability to meet the challenge of the Quran.[324]

The factors that contributed to the development of *iʿjāz* are of many kinds, as mentioned at the beginning of this section, and apologists' ambitions to attribute a miracle to the Prophet Muhammad were undoubtedly among them, but that alone could never have led to such a peculiar theory, indeed a unique one in the history of religion – how would they have thought of it? – nor could mere scholastic sophistry have carried it so quickly to such an overwhelming acceptance among Muslims (and especially Arabs). That was possible only thanks to the community's already existing collective memory of the power of the recited Quran and to their own aesthetic reception of the recitation, which, external influences such as religious veneration notwithstanding, was part of the individual believer's concrete experience. In a word: *i'jāz* was born in the theologians' studies, but it was conceived by the Quran reciters and their listeners; they were its source, and such an unusual theory would have been inconceivable without them. The dogma is the expression and the theological interpretation of a reception history. A theory such as that of *i'jāz*, which is not written in the Quran but *arose* over the course of Islamic history and became one of the most important foundations of Islamic faith, cannot be understood except in the light of that reception history. Otherwise it would just be apology, vulnerable and weak in its argumentation, as Gustave Edmund von Grunebaum described it.[325] From that point of view, the fact that Muslims persist in believing in it seems like an insignificant quirk. Yet Grunebaum's own explanation of the origin of *i'jāz* – namely that the Quran, unlike the Bible in the early Christian West, was not preceded by any major literature or set of stylistic rules, and was therefore not subjected to any comparison with a better literature by existing literary criteria[326] – reveals only the trammels of his own cultural perceptions. Even the relatively early *i'jāz* author ar-Rummānī compares the Quran to ancient models of style in his *Nukat fī i'jāz al-Qur'ān*. Moreover, Grunebaum's simplistic explanation completely ignores the connection between collective memory, subjective experience and theological dogma. Tossing around attributes such as 'weakness of the aesthetic argument' and 'vulnerability of a proof based on historical incident and subjective judgement',[327] which were typical of Western *i'jāz* scholarship for long enough,[328] makes one blind to the specific insight that the doctrine offers into the world of Islamic faith and to this fascinating phenomenon in intellectual history: the aesthetic proof of a religion's truth, a community's claim to have found humanity's dream of a perfect language realized in its sacred text. Instead one persists in value judgements or, as Rudi Paret calls them, 'objective observations'.[329] Everyone is free to judge as they please, but to understand *i'jāz* and the culture that produced it, it is more important to discover what the Quran was and is *to the Muslims*: to study its 'phenomenology', not its 'ontology'. This is not to say one has to put on a galabiya and sway to the rhythm of the Quran recitations. In many cases it is enough to read texts and explore the world that appears in them. What is extraordinary is also familiar: 'My delight (*volupté*) was so great and so fearful that I decided to determine the grounds for it and to transfer my delight into knowledge', Baudelaire wrote about a performance of *Tannhäuser*.[330] That is the beginning of all aesthetics, even the aesthetics of theologians.

5

The Prophet among the Poets

The poet is the transcendental physician.

Novalis

The doctrine of *iʿjāz* maintains that the Quran is formally too good to have been composed by a human being: too artistic to be a work of art, too original in its style to have been invented, too beautiful to be explicable by anything but divine action. This argument, which has been the central pillar of the confirmatory miracle of Islam down to the present day, is essentially based on aesthetic premises and places the Quran in a difficult relation to Arabic poetry: an antipodean one certainly, but not in the sense that they are merely different in kind (as the Gospel of Luke is different from the poetry of Ovid, for example) – that is, in a relation of being unrelated. The relation is rather a dynamic tension between a text that is unfamiliar to the community of listeners and the existing complex of norms, manifested in poetry, on which it impinges. It is a dialectical relation: the repudiation of poetry by the Quran is a sublation [*Aufheben*] in Hegel's threefold sense: negation, preservation, transformation. From the inside perspective of the first audience, the salient aspect of this relation is that the Quran is not like poetry (that is, not like any known form of verse). Yet, when we look at the relation from outside, we notice that the audience spontaneously compared the Quran with poetry, that poetry provided the standard by which they judged it and, in the Muslim memory, poetry is what it transcended.

What about the Prophet and his inspiration? If the text is situated in such an ambivalent, complex relation to poetry and unites elements that other cultures distribute among the categories of poetry and revelation, we might expect to see the image of its first receiver – as the faithful conceive him, or its author in the eyes of other recipients – treated similarly. This is exactly what Kierkegaard saw as the danger of an aesthetic approach to revelation: 'If the sphere of paradox-religion is abolished, or explained away in aesthetics, an Apostle becomes neither more nor less than a genius, and then – good night, Christianity!'[1] There is no corresponding paradox in Islam, and for precisely the reason Kierkegaard mentioned: it is explained away in aesthetics, because the proof of authenticity of the revealed scripture, evident to every sensible person, is its stylistic supremacy. Does that make the Islamic apostle a genius? The question seems to be not entirely absurd. After all, the well-known Egyptian author ʿAbbās Maḥmūd al-ʿAqqād (d. 1964) wrote a whole book, following an idea of Thomas Carlyle, on 'the genius of Muhammad'.[2] While the two contemporary Iranian scholars Mortażā Motahharī (d. 1979) and Sayyed Mojtabā Mūsawī Lārī vehemently deny that a prophet such as Muhammad is anything like a genius,[3] the discussion of these various positions is not very fruitful, since the Arabic *ʿabqarī* and the Persian *nubūġ* do not correspond to Kierkegaard's notion of a genius. Al-ʿAqqād writes about Muhammad's military genius and his administrative genius, for example, and his book also contains chapters about Muhammad as an ingenious husband and his qualities as a father, while Moṭahharī and Lārī, in writing about genius, refer rather to an outstanding thinker and scholar. They also use 'genius' in the customary present-day sense of an extraordinary gift. When Kierkegaard, on the other hand, writes about a genius, he is thinking primarily of a person of very great artistic talent. His image of a genius, or rather that of his time, originates in the aesthetics of the German Enlightenment, which shaped the ideal of the artist in modern Europe and continued to influence it into the twentieth century.[4] If we base the comparison between an apostle and a genius on this concept, we can make some surprising observations in regard to Islam. While there is practically no doubt in Western Christian culture that an apostle has fundamentally different properties from those of an artistic genius (in regard to speech, inspiration and personality), Muslim conceptions of the revelation (*waḥy*) show startling similarities with ideas about inspiration and the nature of the artist in the aesthetics of genius. Notions about how and under what circumstances the revelation took place are relevant to the topic of this book, the aesthetic experience of the Quran, inasmuch as they communicate a certain concept of its origin, which is of course related to the perception of the text itself. Just as the receiving community situated the text, as I have tried to show in chapter 2, within the horizon of the familiar poetic and divinatory texts (whose functions were not strictly separated from one another) and then distinguished it from them, its origin too, and hence the centre of the salvation history, is conceived as a process, as I hope to explain in this chapter, that stands in a dialectical – that is, in the threefold sense a *sublating* – relation to the inspirations of the poets and soothsayers. Muhammad's revelation was identified by distinction from those inspirations. It is not the purpose of this book to examine the extent to which the concept of Muhammad's revelation coincides with real events. In any case, however, the sources that tell us how Muhammad received an inspiration, and what was the specific nature of that prophecy of which he and, with time, more and more of his compatriots were convinced, are mainly post-quranic sources – that is, the hadith collections and biographies of the Prophet and the treatises on the prophethood (*nubūwa*), on the kinds and circumstances of revelation (*kayfīyat al-waḥy*) generally, and on the specific occasions of revelation (*asbāb an-nuzūl*). And the image that the Quran's recipients formed of its origins is a view shaped by their sociocultural milieu, their ways of seeing the world, their convictions and mythic beliefs, their *imagination*; it is their concept of the revelation; it tells us little about the historic Muhammad.[5] By contrast, the quranic statements about Muhammad's inspiration are relatively general. Even the archangel Gabriel, who plays a key role in the Muslim concept of revelation, is mentioned only once in the Quran as a transmitter of the divine word.[6] It is the traditions that furnish the outlines of the Prophet's image and the circumstances of his revelations. To mention just one example, Muhammad's initial fear that what he had experienced was a poet's or soothsayer's initiation is an important element in his biography, but it is mentioned only briefly in the Quran and is narrated in detail only in the biographical literature (*sīra*) – that is, at least a hundred years later. Accordingly, the Prophet's whole psychological development – the dramatic events up to and including his thoughts of suicide, his attempt to throw himself off a cliff and the appearance of the angel bringing him the redeeming confirmation that he was a prophet sent by God[7] – is of dubious authenticity. As Angelika Neuwirth writes, a closer familiarity with the literary genre of *sīra*, the biography of the Prophet, is all one needs 'to recognize the pattern, which was typical of exegesis in that genre, of the elevating narrative development of a Quran verse that was felt to be too dry'.[8] In her analysis of the information that the Quran provides about the historic Muhammad, she also points out that there is little confirmation for the Prophet's propensity to trance-like states, which is so stirringly described in the *sīra* and the hadiths. While the Quran itself mentions an ecstatic aspect of at least some of Muhammad's experiences of revelation, as for example when it refutes the insinuation that he was *majnūn*, possessed by a jinn, we can also cite some Quran passages in which a revelation in an unexpected state of ecstasy appears improbable, such as the openings of the 73rd and 74th surahs, in which the Prophet is called upon to *prepare* to receive new revelations during the night. Some passages seem to allude to nocturnal worship in the form of a vigil, emphasizing the chanting that Muhammad expected. There are no references to a deep sleep, the state which precedes inspiration in the ancient Oriental conception of prophecy. All in all, the Quran has little to say about the specific circumstances of Muhammad's revelations: it tells more about the modes of communication between God and Man in general.[9] In the Muslim exegesis, on the other hand, and in Oriental studies, the notion of a revelation received in a trance or in a dream is projected onto this vague image – that is, Muhammad's inspiration is represented as an occurrence that is familiar from the inspiration of the pre-Islamic poets and seers.

An especially well-known formulation of the Muslim concept of revelation and one which is based on the traditional representation of revelation events, unlike the rationalistic prophecy theories of the Muslim philosophers, is the sixth introductory discussion in Ibn Khaldūn's *Muqaddima*.[10] Noteworthy among the many Muslim authors of the twentieth century who have examined the event of revelation are Manāʿ al-Qattān,[11] Moḥammad Ḥoseyn Ṭabāṭabāʾī,[12] Muḥammad Rashīd Riḍā,[13] Moḥammad Taqī Sharīʿatī-Mazīnānī,[14] Maḥmūd Rāmiyār,[15] Naṣr Ḥāmid Abū Zayd[16] and Muḥammad Shaḥrūr.[17] From their discussions, and of course from the traditional narratives, a general idea of the Muslim Prophet and his revelation emerges that is for the most part representative. A striking feature of this image is that the Muslim imagination attributes a great many qualities to the Messenger of God that in modern European intellectual history have been reserved to the artist. These coincidences are a prominent indication of the close relationship between poetry and revelation in the world of Muslim thought.

The Islamic Prophet and the Aesthetics of Genius

In eighteenth-century German poetry and philosophy up to the Romantic period, the artist – and the category of genius was generally only applicable to artists – was an exceptional, a superior person.[18] The figure of the artist, inspired by English and French aesthetics (Shaftesbury, Batteux, Diderot), influenced by Hamann's religious-aesthetic theory of genius and garnished with classical ideas, heralds the ascendance of individualism. As philosophical aesthetics took shape, creative, immediate subjectivity became the focus of artistic production, and the artist became the symbol of the subject attaining emancipation in bourgeois society. Echoing a classical tradition, Schiller attributed the unconscious activity of the artist to 'inspirations of a god'. Schiller conceived genius as a creative 'naiveté',[19] and the early Nietzsche considered a childlike nature one of the principal sources of the ingenious work of art. Eichendorff's lines are characteristic of the time:

> Let good God in you hold sway
> Fill your breast and boldly sing!
> What's true in you will soon take shape,
> The rest remains a wretched thing.[20]

The most pronounced celebration of the irrational element of artistic activity was the *Sturm und Drang* movement. It transformed the concept of genius into an instrument in the struggle against the rationalism of the early Enlightenment, which was felt to be too schematic. The *Sturm und Drang* authors imagined genius as being completely unfettered, uncultivated, enthusiastic and unswayed by the rules of taste. During the same phase, about 1770, the cult of the genius reached its culmination.

What they talk and how they write
With every tenth word, on every third page
Incessantly of genius!

Klopstock complained,[21] and Herder, half in hindsight and half diagnosing the persisting fashion of glorifying the genius, sarcastically wrote in his treatise 'On the Cognition and Sensation of the Human Soul', published between 1774 and 1778:

> Our philosophy and language lacked so much when neither yet knew anything about '*Schenie*'; suddenly there was treatise upon treatise, essay after essay, about it and we probably still have a task 'about genius' to look forward to from one or another metaphysical academy in Denmark, Holland, Germany or Italy.[22]

This literature finds him 'completely dry, because I know nothing less in the world than what genius is – whether its gender be masculine, feminine or neuter.'[23] Herder does not completely reject the concept of genius but stresses the component of prudence and the necessity of regulating the creative genius, thus paving the way for the classic concept of genius developed primarily by Kant, Goethe and Schiller.[24] Although the ingenious artist continues to be understood as receiving an inspiration from the Absolute, Kant and Schiller more strongly emphasize the importance of conscious as well as unconscious activity. Kant has no time for the '*men of genius* (they are better called *apes of genius*)' who declare 'that difficult study and research are dilettantish and that they have snatched the spirit of all science in one grasp'.[25] In the nineteenth century the idea ultimately wins out, even in Hegel's rival Schopenhauer,[26] that the artist's inspiring emotion or enthusiasm must be joined with 'a concentration of his emotional life', as Hegel wrote.[27] Schopenhauer, however, citing classical authors, also reminds readers of the proximity of genius to madness.[28] In fact a number of ingenious people fell prey to madness (Hölderlin, Tasso, Nietzsche, Schumann and Lenau, to name just a few examples; Adrian Leverkühn's fate in *Doctor Faustus* also comes to mind).

Towards the end of the nineteenth century, a 'twilight of genius' finally sets in, a *Genie-Dämmerung*, in Gadamer's phrase.[29] It is most dazzling in Nietzsche's work: his collection of aphorisms *Human, All Too Human* (1886) and his settling of accounts with Wagner (*The Case of Wagner: Nietzsche* contra *Wagner*, 1888) are rejections of all the hopes that had been placed in genius over the course of the Enlightenment (and for a long time by Nietzsche himself). In mocking his former idol Wagner as 'God's ventriloquist', he associates the false, intentionally projected appearance of genius with fraud.[30]

In the twentieth century, the term genius loses its metaphysical and exclusively aesthetic meaning almost entirely. Musil's *Man without Qualities*, Hesse's *Steppenwolf* and, most of all, Thomas Mann's *Doctor Faustus* are the last major attempts to explore the potential of the creative genius under the specifically 'modern' conditions of the twentieth century – valedictions, as it were. The repudiation of the ideal of the genius, the abhorrence and even nausea that it evokes, is aggravated by the fact that Nazi ideology and the ideas that paved its way (Jünger, Spengler, Borchardt) turned it to authoritarian and totalitarian purposes. The association of genius with the idea of a *Führer*, which was current even before 1933, became a constant topos of panegyrics to Hitler in the Third Reich. The genius as he was portrayed especially in the writings of Josef Goebbels is the grotesque face of the Enlightenment's ideal person. To the statesman, Goebbels wrote before the Nazi takeover in his novel *Michael*, 'the nation is exactly what the stone is for the sculptor.' The Leader and the masses are like the painter and his paints. 'Geniuses use up people. That is simply the way things are.'[31]

The best-known example of an aesthetics of genius, treating nearly all the important motifs of the genius at once, is that of the early Schelling, who developed his concept primarily in the *System of Transcendental Idealism*. Schelling sees the purpose of transcendental philosophy as explaining how knowledge as 'the coincidence of an objective with a subjective' is possible, and hence finding 'the absolute certainty whereby all other certainty is mediated'.[32] Its goal is thus in a sense a knowledge of knowledge. Schelling is the first philosopher of idealism to offer a systematic history of consciousness of the self, and he does so in regard to the question of how the individual can gain consciousness of an external world that is independent of him. He combines two lines of argument: one traces the development of stages of self-mediation of the self-object, which initially has no unconsciousness of itself; the other systematically presents the capacities and acts of self-consciousness. The successive stages of these capacities correspond with the increasing penetration of the self-object with subjectivity, and the highest subjective self-presentation is the self which has shown itself to be pure subjectivity – yet this is the aesthetic intuition of the genius, which is necessarily productive – that is, produces works of art. In the aesthetic intuition, not only is the unity of conscious and unconscious, subjective and objective, free and necessary action present, as it is in nature, but the subject is also conscious of it. The work of art is the product both of free activity and of a higher necessity; intention is joined in the creative genius with a purposelessness that is granted to him through the bounty of a higher nature. To the mere mortal, this unconscious (the word is not used in the psychological sense) and unintending, which sets the objective and unconscious activity in an unexpected harmony, appears as purely external – as destiny – although in truth it is 'that absolute which contains the common ground of the preestablished harmony between the conscious and the unconscious'.[33] The feeling of emotion that accompanies the completion of the work of art 'is itself enough to show that the artist attributes that total resolution of his conflict'[34] between conscious and unconscious activity not to himself alone, but to a higher power: genius though he may be, he is moved by the Absolute; in his works of art the divine power attains objective reality; in them God is manifested.

> Just as the man of destiny does not execute what he wishes or intends, but rather what he is obliged to execute by an inscrutable fate which governs him, so the artist, however deliberate he may be, seems nonetheless to be governed, in regard to what is truly objective in his creation, by a power which separates him from all other men, and compels him to say or depict things which he does not fully understand himself, and whose meaning is infinite. Now every absolute concurrence of the two antithetical activities [that is, conscious and unconscious activity] is utterly unaccountable, being simply a phenomenon which although incomprehensible, yet cannot be denied; and art, therefore, is the one everlasting revelation which yields that concurrence, and the marvel which, had it existed but *once* only, would necessarily have convinced us of the absolute reality of that supreme event.[35]

If one were to substitute the word 'Prophet' for 'artist' and 'Quran' for 'art' in this quotation from Schelling, it would read almost word for word like a statement of the Islamic concept of revelation. In any case, the points of intersection between the idea of genius in modern philosophy and the Islamic conception of *nubūwa*, prophethood, are unmistakable. Like the Islamic Prophet (*nabīy*),[36] the artist in Schelling's concept is a medium of the Absolute. In the artist's as in the Prophet's work the divine power takes on objective reality: the work is, in Kant's words, a 'schema of the supersensible'.[37] The revelation is, in a phrase used often in the Muslim literature, an 'unveiling of what is hidden' (*kashf al-maḥjūb*);[38] and, in the concise wording of the contemporary author Abū Zayd, 'the Absolute unveils itself to Man' in the Prophet's *ru'yā*, his 'dream vision'.[39] Schelling's wording is almost identical when he writes that, in the aesthetic intuition of the genius, the Absolute 'laid aside the veil wherewith it shrouds itself in others'.[40] The prophetic inspiration, like that of the genius, is understood as an afflatus from God; it is not the result of conscious activity. In the words of Novalis, it is 'incomprehensible' even to the artist 'why it is just so and not otherwise'.[41] The immediate cause of artistic productions, Schelling wrote in his lectures on *The Philosophy of Art*, is 'the indwelling element of divinity in human beings'. In the same context he mentions the 'productiveness of God', and says that what is productive in the artist is 'a piece of the absoluteness of God'.[42] The Prophet likewise attributes the Quran to a higher power, one that could be compared to what Schelling sees as responsible for the work of artistic genius: the 'free bounty of nature', 'being inspired by an afflatus from without', or the 'objectivity' with which his product is endowed 'as if by no help of his own, that is, in a purely objective manner'.[43] In the moment of their inspiration and divine possession, the genius and the Prophet do not themselves act: they mediate the act of someone else; someone else acts through them. They are, as Novalis says, the 'mouth of God'[44] or, in the words of Rūmī, like the stone figures of men or birds in caravanserais and on the banks of pools: 'Out of their mouths the water comes and pours into the pool. All possessed of reason know that the water does not issue out of the mouth of a stone bird, it issues out of another place.'[45] What Nietzsche wrote about his inspirations for *Zarathustra* almost reads like a poetic account of Muhammad's experience:

> The idea of revelation in the sense of something suddenly becoming *visible* and audible with unspeakable assurance and subtlety, something that throws you down and leaves you deeply shaken – this simply describes the facts of the case. You listen, you do not look for anything, you take, you do not ask who is there; a thought lights up in a flash, with necessity, without hesitation as to its form – I never had any choice. A delight whose incredible tension sometimes triggers a burst of tears, sometimes automatically hurries your pace and sometimes slows it down; a perfect state of being outside yourself with the most distinct consciousness of a host of subtle shudders and shiverings down to the tips of your toes; a profound joy where the bleakest and most painful things do not have the character of opposites, but instead act as its conditions, as welcome components, as *necessary* shades within this sort of excess of light; an instinct for rhythmic relations that spans wide expanses of forms – the length, the need for a rhythm, that *spans wide distances* is almost the measure of the force of inspiration, something to balance out its pressure and tension… All of this is involuntary to the highest degree, but takes place as if in a storm, of feelings of freedom, of unrestricted activity, of power, of divinity.[46]

The Prophet too, when God speaks to him at the onset of the revelation, does not know what is happening to him. He goes away from his companions or covers his face with his shirt. A glow like the dawn often comes over him.[47] Like the artist Kant describes, he 'does not have it in his power to think up' his preaching 'at will or according to plan',[48] or to make a revelation occur by his own intention; it comes over him; he can at most passively 'expect' it. The Quran itself instructs the Prophet in verse 28:86:

> You yourself could not have expected the Scripture to be sent to you; it came only as a mercy from your Lord.[49]

The tradition records how Muhammad once asked Gabriel why he did not grant him revelations more often. He received the answer that the angels only come down at the behest of their Lord.[50] The Muslim tradition has a word, *fatra*, the 'hiatus', for the harrowing interval of waiting in vain for an inspiration: the word designates the relatively long time between the first and second revelations, during which Muhammad, not knowing whether God would ever speak to him again, waited restlessly for an inspiration 'until it became intolerable and filled him with grief', as Ibn Hishām writes.[51] Later in his mission a revelation often failed to appear when he expected it, and, conversely, revelations took him by surprise. A hadith describes how he once stopped in the middle of a conversation and

> stared into the sky for an hour. Then he slowly lowered his gaze until it was directed at the ground to his right. The Messenger of God avoided looking where the eyes of 'Uthmān [ibn Maẓ'ūm], whom he had been talking with, might meet his. Then he began to shake his head as if he were trying to understand something that had been said to him, turning his gaze back up to the sky as before.[52]

The tradition describes in rich detail how Muhammad's inspirations taxed his forces past their limits. He often began to shiver in spite of the blazing hot weather, or to sweat in spite of the icy cold. 'I saw how the revelation came down to him on a very cold day', 'Ā'isha reported. 'Then it abated, and his forehead was dripping with sweat.'[53] In another tradition, the Prophet's wife recounts:

> The Messenger of God did not move from his place when he was beset by God with what was wont to beset him. He was wrapped in his garment and a leather cushion was placed under his head.... Then the fit passed from the Messenger of God. He sat up, and beads of sweat ran down like drops of water on a winter day.[54]

By his own account, the Prophet often heard sounds like the buzzing of bees or the jingling of a bell, and said, 'That is the hardest for me to bear.'[55] Those who were present describe how, during a revelation, Muhammad's face turned pale; he began to breathe heavily or his teeth chattered; he fainted or fell into a lethargic state that lasted hours; and how he spoke the revealed words in pain, with trembling lips, but was afterwards delighted with the accomplishment and overjoyed with the beauty and perfection of the revelation.[56] The descriptions come close to the following one from *Doctor Faustus* by Thomas Mann:

> A genuine inspiration, immediate, absolute, unquestioned, ravishing, where there is no choice, no tinkering, no possible improvement; where all is as a sacred mandate, a visitation received by the possessed one with faltering and stumbling step, with shudders of awe from head to foot, with tears of joy blinding his eyes.[57]

Both concepts reproduce the topos familiar since classical antiquity of the productive rapture, divine possession or holy madness (*theia mania*), seen as a disease by the sufferer's surroundings. Nietzsche proclaims, 'One physiological precondition is indispensable for there to be art or any sort of aesthetic action or vision: intoxication.'[58] 'Thou, upon whom the Remembrance is sent down, thou art assuredly possessed!' the unbelievers said to Muhammad.[59] Noah and Moses too were called 'possessed' and, indeed, 'not a Messenger came to those before them but they said, "A sorcerer, or a man possessed!"'[60] Plato too observed that a person possessed by a god 'is admonished by the many for being disturbed, when his real state is one of possession, which goes unrecognized by the many'.[61] The belief that Muhammad was mentally ill or suffered from epilepsy persists into the Christian literature of the Middle Ages and early Oriental studies.[62] Such judgements can certainly be understood as conscious disparagements, whereas Hölderlin in his tower probably really was 'mad'. But something must have caused Muhammad's opponents to bring forward precisely this accusation (and even the ancient Arabic word *majnūn* had a pathological connotation of epilepsy or catalepsy):[63] there must have been a similarity in the phenomena; there must have been something quite disturbing to outside observers. According to the traditional accounts, the revelation sometimes made Muhammad break out in a sweat even on cold days; sometimes he foamed at the mouth, or fell into a trance, or fell to the ground as if struck by lightning and lay there for an hour without moving; his face might turn blue or red-hot; he might have a high fever that lasted days; his arms writhed so that his companions thought they were breaking; sometimes he screamed like a camel foal.[64] Averroes attributed such symptoms to the great strain placed on the Prophet's psyche in the moment of divine inspiration, which left him without the mental strength to control his physical organs.[65] According to aṭ-Ṭabarī's account, Muhammad at first thought he was possessed and wanted to kill himself, until Waraqa ibn Nawfal recognized him as a prophet and calmed him, saying, 'Thou art not, by the blessing of thy Lord, a man possessed.'[66] That is, the fits of rapture that coincided with his revelations could have been taken, or mistaken, for the outward signs of morbid possession or the ordinary frenzy of poetic inspiration;[67] even to his companions Muhammad seemed 'as if in a state of delirium' for hours.[68] But his possession and delirium are not ordinary: in the Muslim view, it is God who takes possession of the Prophet and so dictates to him the words, without his will or even his consciousness. In the same sense, Dostoevsky, himself an epileptic, turned the stereotypical notion of Muhammad's epilepsy around into a positive image. He once surprised his friends by saying:

> All you healthy people... don't even begin to understand what happiness is, the happiness that we epileptics experience during the instant before our attack. Muhammad maintains in his Koran that he saw Paradise and was in Paradise. All the clever fools are convinced that he was simply a liar and a fraud. Not at all! He was not lying. He actually was in Paradise in a fit of

epilepsy, which he suffered with just as I do. I don't know whether that bliss lasts for seconds or hours or months, but, believe me, I wouldn't exchange all the joys life can offer for that bliss![69]

Another striking parallel between the Prophet and the artist can be seen in the importance of dreams for their inspiration. 'My eyes sleep, but my heart wakes', Muhammad often said.[70] In the Muslim narrative, Muhammad received numerous revelations in dreams, including his first, and said, 'I saw what a sleeping person sees in a dream.'[71] Dreams are also accorded a prominent intuitive function in the modern conception of the artist. 'The state of poetic inspiration is a dream state', said Friedrich Hebbel,[72] and Goethe thought 'man dreams only so that he doesn't stop seeing.'[73] Although almost all cultures see dreams as a medium of transcendental knowledge, whether artistic, prophetic or mystical, it is noteworthy that the Islamic theoreticians who have discussed such knowledge philosophically – scholars such as al-Fārābī and Avicenna, and also Ibn Khaldūn – have used terms, models and concepts similar to those found in modern aesthetics, since the two currents are fed by a common spring: that of Greek philosophy. Both the Prophet and the artist experience in the moment of inspiration an aesthetic idea. The mental faculty that conceives the idea is the imagination, a concept derived from the Aristotelian notion of *fantasia* (in Arabic, *khayāl*, *mukhayyila* or *mutakhayyila*).[74]

Genius and prophecy are also both impossible without suffering. As Hamann says in *Clouds*, the sequel to his *Socratic Memorabilia*, 'Don't stare at me because I am so *black*, for the *genius* has burnt me so.'[75] Muhammad is quoted as saying the prophets suffer the hardest blows and, the more righteous they are, the harder their fate is.[76] Once when he read surah 37, *aṣ-Ṣaffāt*, to a delegation from Hadhramaut who had come to Mecca to find out about the Prophet, he was unable to get past the fifth line.

Then God's messenger was silent, and his soul was still, nothing in it moved, only the tears flowed over his beard. They said, 'We see you weep. Are you weeping out of fear of Him Who has sent you?'

'My fear of Him makes me weep. He has sent me on a *straight path* that is like the edge of a knife. If I were to stray from it, I would be destroyed.' Then he recited: 'If We willed, we could take away that We have revealed to thee...'[77] to the end of the surah.[78]

The association with melancholy has been an important component of the idea of genius throughout its history. Numerous artists' self-portraits are filled with the awareness that melancholy and torments of the souls are distinguishing signs and must accompany the process of artistic creation.[79] Or, in Hölderlin's words:

Yet, fellow poets, us it behoves to stand
Bareheaded beneath God's thunder-storms,
To grasp the Father's ray, no less, with our own two hands
And, wrapping in song the heavenly gift,
To offer it to the people.
For only if we are pure in heart,
Like children, and our hands are guiltless,
The Father's ray, the pure, will not sear our hearts
And, deeply convulsed, and sharing his sufferings
Who is stronger than we are, yet in the far-flung down-rushing storms of
The God, when he draws near, will the heart stand fast.[80]

The Prophet too bears a heavy burden in his nearness to God and in what he experiences through his inspiration – that is, what distinguishes him from other people; hence the existential grief that comes with the act of revelation.[81] 'We shall cast on thee a weighty word',[82] God says to Muhammad in the Quran. 'The prophethood is a heavy burden',[83] says his biographer too. 'Truly, I see what you do not see, and I hear what you do not hear', says Muhammad himself to his companions; 'If you knew what I know, you would laugh little and weep much.'[84] There are many similar accounts of the many different and deep sufferings of the genius, of people whose peculiar perception of the world makes them practically damned by God – Schopenhauer calls their lot the 'martyrdom of genius'.[85] Like the Prophet who feels himself to be walking on the razor's edge, Hamann says, quoting Horace, 'Incedo per ignes': I tread on fire.[86] The *Steppenwolf* Harry Haller quotes a sentence from Novalis: 'One ought to take pride in pain – all pain is a reminder of our exalted rank',[87] and then glosses it himself: 'Human life becomes a real hell of suffering only when two ages, two cultures and religions overlap.' That leads him to the fate of Nietzsche, who 'had to endure our present misery more than a generation in advance', and elicits the comment from the fictional editor of Haller's writings: 'Haller is one of those people who end up caught between two eras, deprived of all security and innocence; one of those fated to experience to an intense degree, as a personal torment and hell, all that is questionable about human life.'[88] The actual experiences of inspiration are what is described as painful. The tradition quotes Muhammad's companions as saying, 'When the revelation came down to the Prophet, it caused him great pain, so that we knew what was happening. Then he separated himself from his companions and stayed behind. He covered his head with his garment and suffered terribly.'[89] 'When the revelation came down to him, it was a torment to him, and his face turned pale', Ibn Saʿd notes.[90] Asked whether he noticed when the revelation came upon him, Muhammad answered: 'Yes, I hear a rattling, then I grow calm. No revelation takes place without making me think my soul is being torn from me.'[91]

The Absolute, Schelling writes, 'unrelentingly' sets the genius – like the Prophet – 'in conflict with himself', but at the same time it is 'gracious in relieving him of the pain of this contradiction'[92] and rewards him with the bliss, as the mystics in particular emphasized, of *visio beatifica*.[93] The pain of the inspiration and the calamities to which he is exposed are especially severe in the first phase of the revelation, then they subside with time and the prophetic event becomes quieter. In this regard we can see an interesting parallel between Schopenhauer's theory of genius and Ibn Khaldūn's theses on prophecy. Schopenhauer defines genius as

> the capacity to maintain oneself in a purely intuitive state, to lose oneself in intuition and to withdraw cognition that originally only existed in its service to the will from this service, i.e. temporarily to put one's interests, willing and purposes entirely out of mind, and consequently, fully to relinquish one's personality in order to remain as the *pure cognitive subject*, the clear eye of the world.[94]

The Prophet too, in Ibn Khaldūn's portrayal, temporarily relinquishes his personality: in the moment of the revelation, he casts off (*insilākh*) his humanity 'to attain an angelic perception and so hear the (wordless) speech of the soul (*kalām an-nafs*). This causes pain, because a being leaves his own being and moves from his own horizon to another.'[95] To Schopenhauer (and in most of conceptions of genius), while the genius maintains a purely intuitive state, at the same time he conserves 'as much clarity of mind as is necessary to repeat what has been grasped in the form of well-considered art and "what floats in wavering appearance to fasten down in enduring thoughts" (*Faust* I, lines 348–9)'.[96] Ibn Khaldūn draws a distinction between two forms of revelation. In one, the Prophet simply absorbs – that is, he has no consciousness of what is happening to him; one might say he is in a state of pure intuition. Only afterwards does he understand the meaning of the revealed discourse.[97] In the second form, where the Prophet is also Messenger, he is still in a state of intuition but remains conscious at the same time and understands the meaning of the revelation as he receives it. Such an inspiration troubles the Prophet less, and Ibn Khaldūn considers this form more perfect than the first. In Schopenhauer's terms, we may say it combines pure perception with clarity of mind. If we consider further that Muhammad, in Ibn Khaldūn's portrayal, grew accustomed to the inspirations, and so gradually became capable of the second form of revelation, which coincided with the increasing length and complexity of the verses,[98] we cannot help thinking of certain ingenious personalities who have crystallized into archetypes: from the Goethe of *Sturm und Drang* and the *Sufferings of Young Werther* to the classical Goethe, the wise councillor in Weimar whose well-ordered *Faust* symbolized the pinnacle of German poetry (from the pulsating rhythms of the early Meccan surahs, bursting with energy, to the extravagantly elaborating, serenely sermonizing long verses of the Medinan surahs that reflect everything in heaven and earth). In youth the genius bursts forth, seized with divine fervour, 'but only middle or old age can bring to perfection the genuine maturity of the work of art', Hegel teaches, citing Goethe and Schiller.[99]

The Prophet, like the genius, is driven to productive activity by an inner urge. Before his vocation, as the *sīra* recounts in detail, he feels a conflict 'which strikes at *the ultimate in him*, the root of his whole being', and 'sets in motion the whole man with all his forces'.[100] The *sīra* likewise relates, especially in relation to Muhammad's first revelation, that after his vocation Muhammad 'is driven into production involuntarily and even in spite of himself'.[101] In Islam, what Schelling describes as an incomprehensible destiny which holds sway over the artist and compels him to perform his artistic activity is the role of the angel Gabriel, who, in the frequently retold story of the revelation of surah 96,[102] shakes and chokes him and 'compels him to say or depict things which he does not fully understand himself, and whose meaning is infinite'.[103] Another topos common to the concepts of the Prophet and the genius is that both are at first misjudged and rejected by their milieu, and each is under the influence of 'a power which separates him from all other men',[104] driving him into isolation.

Like the ideal notion of the artist, the Prophet is merely the medium of a message that originates with God or the Absolute. To ensure that Muhammad is no more than the *bearer* of the divine communication, the later Islamic tradition must portray him as an *ummī*, an illiterate with no literary or philosophical training.[105] His condition is comparable with the 'creative naiveté' in the aesthetics of genius, the 'childlike' quality that is necessary for the Absolute to manifest itself in the work of the artistic genius. 'What in Homer compensates for his ignorance of the rules of art', Hamann asks, 'and what can a Shakespeare show to make good his ignorance or violation of those critical laws? The unanimous answer is: genius.'[106] The less prior education and skill the prophet or the artist brings to his role, the greater the amazement and the admiration they elicit from their fellows. When Lenz declares the *Opinions of a Layman* to be the 'cornerstone of all my poetry, all my truth, all my feeling',[107] he is putting aside all philosophical and other acquired knowledge and explaining genius by reduction to the artist's bare being. According to al-Jurjānī, one reason why God did not provide the Prophet with the literary education of the poets was to make the persuasive power of the Quran greater and the inexplicable nature of its beauty clearer.[108] Earlier authors too made Muhammad's lack of education a pillar of the miraculous proof.[109]

The verses of the Quran are 'exemplary' in the Kantian sense: 'while not themselves the result of imitation', they serve, to a greater extent than any other work in the history of Arabic literature, 'others in that way, i.e., as a standard or a rule for judging'.[110] The Prophet and the artistic genius are both unconscious of what constitutes the formal perfection of their works and are incapable of communicating to others the rules of production that might enable them to produce something similar. With no awareness or observance of the existing artistic or other norms, they create their own norms, by which future works are measured. Kant calls this 'exemplary originality'.[111] Even before the German aesthetics of genius, English and French philosophers attributed to genius 'the right and power to break the tablets of the law and to establish new rules by virtue of its own authority',[112] and this idea too has a parallel in the thesis of the *iʿjāz* scholars which says the Quran breaks free of all experience and is like no form of structured discourse known before, and yet it is the model for all future works of language. The parallel continues in Schelling's statement that the fundamental characteristic of a work of art is its ambiguity, which Muslims likewise praise in the Quran:[113] 'every one of them is capable of being expounded ad infinitum, as though it contained an infinity of purposes.'[114] Critics, especially among Muhammad's contemporaries, regularly perceived the Quran's unfathomable nature as incomprehensibility, as a 'muddle' (*aḍġāth*), in the Quran's own words.[115] Almost all innovators in literature since Aeschylus and Euripides have been called obscure. Their works are difficult for their contemporaries to understand because they transcend familiar horizons and penetrate into new worlds of linguistic creation. The aestheticians of genius observed the poets of the *Sturm und Drang* movement and the Romantic period as they experienced such a reception.

The distinction between prophecy (*nubūwa*), on the one hand, and ordinary soothsaying (*kahāna*) and poetry, on the other, is analogous to the distinction Schelling draws between 'art' as a learnable skill and 'poetry' as a 'poetic ability' given by nature. The motif is as old as Horace, who differentiated between *ars* and *ingenium*. Without ever having studied the rules of rhetoric – unlike the poet (*shāʿir*) – the Prophet uses them in his speech with a degree of perfection that exceeds the limits of human skill. And, unlike the soothsayer (*kāhin*), the Prophet does not learn certain techniques to summon inspiration but is chosen by God: in this regard he is what Kant would call a 'favourite of nature',[116] for the prophetic gift is innate, like the talent of the genius, and unlike the master craftsman's skill. In al-Bāqillānī's judgement, the rhymed prose (*sajʿ*) of the soothsayers, ascribed to their acquired skill, is 'among the discourses in which the sense follows the linguistic expression that leads to a rhyme':[117] it is a formal linguistic schema in which the message must fit – mere 'mechanical art', as Kant calls it, 'art of diligence and learning'.[118] The technically induced inspiration of the *kāhin* can result – to paraphrase Schelling – only in 'a semblance of revelation, which, by its superficiality and by many other indications, e.g. the high value it attaches to the mere mechanics of rhyming prose, the poverty of form in which it operates, etc., . . . in contrast to the unfathomable depth which the true prophet, though he labours with the greatest diligence, involuntarily imparts to his work, and which neither he nor anyone else is wholly able to penetrate',[119] is easily distinguishable from the verses of the Quran, which are the result of divine inspiration.

The prophet's role as the first recipient of the divine message can also be seen as analogous to the role of the artist in the theory of genius. Schelling sees the artist himself as the first recipient of satisfaction: in his aesthetic intuition, the artist is immediately aware of the resolution of his inner conflict and his self-completion. Furthermore, the productive activity is a defining aspect of the genius and of the prophet. Only his work makes the genius what he is, just as the prophet by definition must proclaim his revelation. The 'outward expression... of calm, and silent grandeur'[120] that characterizes the perfect work of art in Schelling's conception (although what Schelling has in mind, following Winckelmann, is Greek statues of the gods) comes very close to Muslims' most frequent descriptions of the divine discourse, *jalāl* and *jamāl*, still closer are the terms 'sublime' and 'beautiful', which are the essential attributes of the artistic work of genius in nearly all the aesthetic theories of the eighteenth and nineteenth centuries. The mystics in particular developed whole theories and systems of quranic attributes (divine attributes manifested in the Quran, to be exact), which centred on the terms *jalāl* and *jamāl*, and their respective fields of meaning and connotation largely overlap with those of the sublime and the beautiful in the German philosophical tradition.

The power 'to pacify our endless striving, and likewise to resolve the final and uttermost contradiction within us',[121] which Schelling reserves to art, would correspond to the promise that Muslims see in their faith. In contrast to Christianity, which tends to situate redemption in the next world, both the work of art and the Quran (especially in mystical reception) can create a rapturous ecstasy in the here and now. 'He who would ascend to the gardens of Paradise should recite the *ḥāmīm* surahs', the Prophet said.[122] Schopenhauer, influenced by Eastern spirituality, writes about the beatific experience of beauty, which he conceives as a mystical process, a nirvana:

> then suddenly the peace that we always sought on the first path of willing but that always eluded us comes of its own accord, and all is well with us. It is the painless state that Epicurus prized as the highest good and the state of the gods: for that moment we are freed from the terrible pressure of the will, we celebrate the Sabbath of the penal servitude of willing, the wheel of Ixion stands still.... It is then all the same whether we see the setting of the sun from a prison or from a palace.[123]

The relation between philosophy and art in Schelling is similar to that which many Muslim thinkers see between reason and revelation. The insights of reason and those of revelation are fundamentally related: both are approaches to the Absolute. But revelation – like art in Schelling's *System* – takes precedence over philosophy. Only the revelation gives philosophy access to absolute truth ('certainty', in Schelling's terms). The revelation is therefore 'the only true and eternal organ' of reason;[124] it is 'paramount to the philosopher, precisely because it opens to him, as it were, the holy of holies'.[125] Such a relation between reason and revelation is not specific to Islam or to Schelling: Christian scholasticism, for example, sees reason as similarly dependent on revelation. It is nonetheless remarkable that not only the substance of the Quranic revelation but even the mere sound of it can cause an intuition of the truth: the truth is not apprehended purely discursively, but aesthetically – that is, by *aisthesis* or sensory perception – just as the work of art in the aesthetics of genius holds an aesthetic truth (*veritas aesthetica*), a truth founded on sensory perception and feeling.[126] The Quran is 'the marvel which, had it existed but once only, would necessarily have convinced us of the absolute reality of that supreme event'[127] – like the work of art to Schelling, but unlike the Bible: in Christianity the miracle that proves God's existence is not a work but a person – Jesus Christ – and His acts. And just as Schelling says there is 'but one *absolute* work of art, which may indeed exist in altogether different versions, yet is still *only one*',[128] the divine revelation in the quranic conception is likewise a unique and eternal discourse, presented to the various peoples, through the various messengers, in their respective languages.

The list of analogies between the European artistic genius and the Islamic Prophet does not go on indefinitely, and the similarity in some of the aspects mentioned may have to be qualified on a closer examination. Of course there are significant differences between the two concepts. For example, the purpose of the work of art is inherent in the work; the genius produces not in order to guide people to the true path, but for the sake of the work itself. The Enlightenment philosophers demanded autonomy for art; it was to serve no other purpose outside itself. The preaching of the Prophet, on the other hand, is teleological in the strict sense of the word. Kierkegaard expresses the difference in these words: 'No genius has an *in order that*; the Apostle has, absolutely and paradoxically, an *in order that*.'[129] In this sense Muhammad is undoubtedly an apostle – although we may note that not all theories of genius see the purpose of art as inherent in the work. Hamann, for one, says that art has the character of a religious communication, and that the genius is completely dependent on God.[130] To Schelling too, and to other idealists, art ultimately has an ulterior purpose, an 'in order that'; its autonomy is challenged because it becomes the locus of a manifestation of the Absolute – something extrinsic to it – and it takes on a function as the organ of an extra-aesthetic insight, namely that of the philosopher. There are also distinct differences between the prophet and the artistic genius. The notions of a prophet as necessarily free of sin (*'iṣma*), or as a miracle-worker, for example, which have great importance in theology and in the popular veneration of the Prophet (although not in the Quran itself),[131] have no counterpart in the aesthetics of genius. Another important difference is that the prophet as a person is subordinate to the revealed work, unlike the artist, whose work is conceived as an expression of his outstanding individuality. Friedrich's assertion in Eichendorff's novel *Ahnung und Gegenwart*, 'The poet is the heart of the world',[132] is not applicable to the prophet. Another distinguishing characteristic, and a last example of the difference, is that the artist must have certain acquired abilities in order for the Absolute to express itself in him. He is *not only* a medium in the thrall of divine inspiration; he *also* creates as a conscious activity. 'The mental powers, then, whose union (in a certain relation) constitutes genius, are imagination and understanding', Kant said.[133] This is in contrast to the Islamic Prophet – although one might discuss whether he too combines conscious and unconscious activity, as, for example, when he is asked a certain question and then withdraws so that Gabriel can reveal to him God's judgement on it. But it is not my intention to blur the distinctions. If there were no differences, Muhammad would really be a genius, or, conversely, a genius would be a prophet. The present comparison with concepts and theories from the aesthetics of genius is not meant as a claim that the genius and the prophet are identical. Rather, I have tried to draw attention to some contours in the Muslim image of the Prophet that have rarely been discerned up to now. For the analogy between the two concepts is more than just a curiosity, and anything but coincidental: it allows us to see the obvious proximity of the prophet and the poet in the Arab imagination. The Muslim concept of the revelation (*waḥy*) unites characteristics in the Prophet that modern Western intellectual history has divided between two relatively clearly separate fields, art and religion.

Plato's Legacy

To get a clear picture of the different notions and concepts in the history of Oriental and European thought, we can look at how Classical ideas about the prophetic poet were very differently assimilated in the two intellectual currents. I have already hinted that the German aesthetics of genius built on models from classical antiquity, although its direct impetus came from England and France.[134] Schelling in particular alludes frequently to Plato, and mainly to his dialogue *Ion*, in which a famous passage deals with poets who sing 'not by virtue of a skill, but in a state of inspiration and possession'[135] and are 'nothing but the gods' interpreters, each possessed'.[136] Plato sees art as originating in enthusiasm, in being 'in company with god', one of many kinds of divine madness (*theia mania*) that he outlines in *Phaedrus*.[137] The other three kinds of *mania* are the cathartic (that of religious purification rituals), the philosophical and the prophetic. The Platonic theory of enthusiasm, which conceives the artist as related to the seer and the prophet, as an inspired proclaimer of divine words, was directly influential in Europe, beginning with the Renaissance,[138] continuing with Shakespeare,[139] and culminating in the aesthetics of genius. In Islamic philosophy, the Platonic concepts related to metaphysical knowledge were assimilated and developed much earlier by al-Fārābī (d. 950) and later by Avicenna and Averroes.[140] A noteworthy characteristic of this philosophical discourse is that it treats the question of prophecy as open and answers it in different ways, sometimes in the negative.[141] For the subject of the present discussion, what is important is that those who upheld the religious revelation as fact, including Avicenna and al-Fārābī, naturally developed a theory of prophecy from the Platonic and Neoplatonic theories of inspiration, which they combined with Aristotelian epistemology. The artistic component of the Platonic theory of inspiration did not resonate with the Islamic philosophers, except where they integrated it in the theory of prophecy. Fazlur Rahman explains this observation by saying that the Muslims had a revealed scripture in the strict sense, whereas the religious ideas of the Greeks had been influenced over centuries by Homer and Hesiod, so that poetry had become a kind of revelation to them.[142] By implication, this means that, because they had the Quran, the Muslim philosophers lacked the inducement to ascribe a metaphysical nature to works of poetry.

Of the Muslim philosophers, Avicenna was the one who developed the most detailed theory of prophecy. Influenced by Neoplatonic and Aristotelian ideas and building directly on Plato's *Timaeus*,[143] he tried to make the phenomenon of prophecy rationally comprehensible and to integrate it in his philosophical concept of the world.[144] Avicenna identifies prophecy as a human quality that, although it is extraordinarily highly developed in the prophet by virtue of his innate psychic structure, is not supernatural, but physiologically explainable. Among the innate predispositions of a prophet are a high intellectual capacity, a highly developed imagination and a particular energy of the soul. A prophet's knowledge is different in degree, but not in kind, from any other metaphysical knowledge; such knowledge is also considered to be possible outside the prophetic sphere.[145] Because of his intellectual gifts, the prophet has the extraordinary (but not supernatural) ability to receive transcendental knowledge from the active intelligence in the form of an intellectual insight. Such an insight is thus rooted in an intellectual act that is manifested to the prophet, due to his highly developed imagination, in the form of visions and auditory experiences that generally come to him in an ecstatic sleep. Prophetic insight in a waking state is possible only at the highest level of consciousness.

One might think that such physio-psychological explanations of prophecy, based on theories from classical antiquity, would have been met with strict rejection among Muslims. On the contrary: al-Ġazālī, in his famous (or notorious) refutation *The Incoherence of the Philosophers* (*Tahāfut al-falāsifa*), spared Avicenna's portrayal of prophetic insight from criticism.[146] Moreover, in his autobiographical work *The Rescuer from Error* (*Mal-Munqiḏ min aḍ-ḍalāl*), he explicitly classes the prophetic faculty (*khāṣṣīyat an-nubūwa*) as an organic faculty like the senses, the power of judgement (*at-tamyīz*) and reason (*ʿaql*):[147]

> As reason is a stage of human development in which the individual develops an inner eye for different kinds of intelligible knowledge (*maʿqūlāt*) that cannot be perceived by the senses, prophecy too refers to a stage in which the individual develops an eye to see what is hidden (*al-ġayb*).[148]

Ordinary people do not attain the stage of prophecy in their development, however. God has given them a model of the prophetic faculty instead, the faculty of dreaming. Yet the possibility of a divine inspiration occurring in a waking state through the mediation of an angel is not limited to prophets, al-Ġazālī finds: mystics too have this capacity. The mystics' inspiration is different from that of prophets only in that the angelic vision (*ilhām*) is absent.[149] Ibn Khaldūn holds a similar position. Although he does not stand directly in the Greek philosophical tradition, he adopts the philosophers' classification in attributing the prophetic dream vision (*ru'yā*) to the activity of the human imagination: in ordinary people this faculty is noticeable only during sleep, but poets and mystics have it in waking too. The imagination is most highly developed in prophets, and they are the people whose dreams are perfect and complete and altogether true. In this regard once again the difference between a prophet and a mystic or poet lies in the content of the inspiration and in the intensity of the experience, but not in the fact of inspiration itself.[150] Christian philosophy comes to a different conclusion: although the scholastics discussed intensely the ideas of the Muslim philosophers (and those of the Jewish Arab Maimonides [d. 1204]), who were a major influence on the scholastic theory of prophecy, alongside the Patristic authors (Augustine, Cassiodorus [d. c. 583], Gregory the Great [d. 604] and Isidore of Seville [d. 636]), they did not adopt those ideas wholesale by any means. Bruno Decker notes in his book *The Development of the Doctrine of Prophetic Revelation from William of Auxerre to Thomas Aquinas*:

> We must see the proponents of this [the Islamic] theory of the prophets not so much as material sources of the scholastic speculations on prophecy, but as opponents with whom the Christian theologians had to grapple. For this theory of prophecy, at least in the judgement of scholastic theologians, had a highly naturalistic and rationalistic character. They needed to repel that to avoid endangering the supernatural character of the revelation, but at the same time wanted to isolate what was really useful in the theory and incorporate it in their system.[151]

Scholars such as Alexander of Hales (d. 1245) and Thomas Aquinas (d. 1274) rejected major parts of the Arab theories of prophecy, and so indirectly refused the Platonic and Neoplatonic ideas that were present in these doctrines but not immediately available to Christian authors.[152] Unlike Islam, Christian scholasticism did not immediately adopt the Platonic concepts, but drew distinct boundaries between prophetic and ordinary knowledge and sought metaphysical explanations of the supernatural character of prophecy. The Aristotelian doctrine that knowledge of the concealed is attainable through the imagination and accessible to people with extraordinary gifts had less influence on the scholastics than on the Muslim philosophers, in spite of Thomas Aquinas's epistemological shift from Augustine to Aristotle. The Classical philosophers' conception of the prophet was not directly treated in Europe until the Renaissance. Yet it was used here not to develop the theory of prophecy, as it was in the Islamic world, but to shape the ideal of the artist. A brief comparison of al-Fārābī and Schelling, whom we discussed in the previous section, will illustrate the difference.

Al-Fārābī adopts Plato's theory of prophetic knowledge more unequivocally than the later philosophers, although sometimes in Neoplatonic variant forms.[153] In keeping with the Greek philosophy and way of thinking, but conflicting with the traditional beliefs in jinn and angels, he conceives divination and prophecy as an innate faculty of the soul rather than as a state of possession by supernatural forces. Both *kahāna* and *nubūwa* are located in the imagination, which is a link between the activities of sensation and *ratio* and is particularly active during sleep, when both sensation and reason are inactive and the imagination is released from them. No one who has his wits about him exercises 'true, inspired divination', Plato said, 'but sleep or illness has to have fettered and weakened his intellect, or he has to be possessed, in an altered state of consciousness.'[154] Al-Fārābī follows Plato, but adds that the imagination, at least in the greatest of the prophets, is completely active in daytime as well as in sleep, so that they could receive revelations both in dreams and in waking, as the traditions say Muhammad did. The imagination is the faculty innate in every person that allows the prophets – and, to a limited degree, the soothsayers, and other people too according to a specified decreasing scale – to attain metaphysical knowledge. This takes place by means of the activity of *mimesis* (*fi'l al-muḥākāt*), which occurs in the imagination and imitates the soul's impressions from the higher world, as if translating them into symbols. As a consequence, 'true visions' (*ru'yā ṣādiqa*)[155] can occur. Al-Fārābī sees even the highest form of prophecy as based on the mimetic activity of the imagination. It allows the prophet to translate the intelligibles (*ma'qūlāt*) of the higher world, which is not graspable in itself, into objects of prophetic vision. The imagination 'imitates the intelligibles of utmost perfection, like the First Cause (*as-sabab al-awwal*), the immaterial things and the heavens, with the most excellent and perfect sensibles (*maḥsūsāt*), like things that are beautiful to look at.'[156] During this operation, the prophet feels sensual pleasure:

> When it happens that the faculty of imagination imitates (*ḥākā*) those things with sensibles of extreme beauty (*jamāl*) and perfection, the man who has that sight comes to enjoy overwhelming and wonderful pleasure (*laḏḏa*), and

> he sees wonderful things which can in no way whatever be found among the other existents.[157]

These ideas are recognizable as Platonic and Neoplatonic: the higher world can only be interpreted as the sphere of Platonic Ideas, which we can only conceive mentally, according to Plato, thanks to our memory of the time before birth. In al-Fārābī's concept, the mimetic activity of the imagination makes it possible to translate the original images of the higher world into visual, verbal or musical symbols, to represent them, to realize sensations of them: all of this is part of the semantic field of the Greek *mimesis*, of which the translation 'imitation' suggests only one facet. Such a connection between creative *fantasia* and *mimesis* is characteristic of the philosophical tradition on which al-Fārābī builds. His portrayal of *nubūwa* as the result of mimetic activity in the soul's imagination has its closest parallels, as Richard Walzer points out, in the Neoplatonic *theory of art*.[158] It was not unusual to discuss art and prophecy together, since Plato had treated them as comparable phenomena in *Phaedrus*. In antiquity it was possible to apply the idea of mimesis to the prophetic *and* artistic activity; al-Fārābī translates and transfers it to a Muslim context while restricting it to prophetic insight, or divinatory insight in general. He does not mention artistic inspiration in this connection. The Greek topos of metaphysical cognition has also been integrated in modern European philosophy, but as a component of aesthetic theory, not of a theory of prophecy. Schelling, for example, says the aesthetic intuition is the highest subjective capacity of presentation and is accompanied by a feeling of 'infinite tranquillity'.[159] For Schelling, as for Goethe, the 'pleasure' takes on the religious-mystical meaning of participation in the supernatural made possible by the ecstatic communication.[160] Simplifying somewhat, we may say that the two different concepts were developed in the two intellectual contexts by building on the same principle, the Platonic and Neoplatonic idea of artistic and prophetic insight. Where the Muslims recognized their Prophet in the Greek ideas about the process of metaphysical knowledge, the modern philosophers found an explanation of the artist's act of creation. If it was possible to integrate the same idea in two apparently so different concepts, there must be a connection between those concepts – that is, between the Islamic Prophet and the Western artist. This is precisely where the parallels between the aesthetics of genius and *nubūwa* have their roots.

Al-Fārābī himself is clearly aware of the prophetic activity's aesthetic dimension. He would have known that the term *muḥākāt* is the usual translation of the Greek *mimesis*, which in antiquity denoted the activity of the artist. And in fact he writes that the Prophet can communicate his metaphysical experiences only encoded in 'imitating phrases (*aqāwīl muḥākāt*), in allegories (*rumūz*), in enigmatic phrases (*alġāz*)' – that is, only in poetic form.[161] By associating the Prophet's preaching with a poetic or metaphorical language, he sets the Prophet apart from the philosopher – whose status is superior! – and instead classes him with a type of person who, in a different conceptual context, would be called a poet. Although the activity of the visionary prophet as described by al-Fārābī cannot be reduced to the activity of the artist, it evidently does involve features that we would call artistic, as Richard Walzer notes in his commentary on this passage.[162]

We can amplify Walzer's suggestive remark with reference to Schelling's aesthetics of genius. Al-Fārābī discusses the relation between *prophet* and philosopher, while Schelling makes a nearly identical distinction between the intuition of the *artist* and that of the philosopher – although Schelling holds that art, because it uses poetic forms, is superior to abstract philosophy, while al-Fārābī gives philosophy precedence. Although Schelling sees the artist's *intellectual* intuition, like that of the philosopher, as the result of the productive activity of the imagination, the *aesthetic* intuition of the genius – the telos of Schelling's transcendental philosophy – is realized only in art, because only the artist produces external works, while in philosophy intuition remains internal. Philosophy conceives the Absolute as the absolutely identical which precedes and underlies all dichotomies, but philosophy itself remains bound up in the dichotomies because it cannot express the Absolute in its inner definition, and indeed the Absolute cannot be comprehended conceptually. Only the non-conceptual aesthetic intuition can reveal the highest truth, the Absolute, God. In the aesthetic intuition, the intellectual intuition does not remain interior but takes on objective reality in the work of art. The aesthetic intuition is thus 'the intellectual intuition become objective',[163] and art is the organ of philosophy. (Schelling does not explicitly say that art as the means is thus subordinate after all to philosophy as the end, but the implication is unavoidable.) Both Schelling and al-Fārābī concede to the philosopher and to the artist or the prophet a path to the Absolute, but while al-Fārābī, building on Plato, places the fourth *mania*, the philosophical, above all others and views it as a defect that the prophet can express his intuition only in a kind of poetic code, and not in abstract philosophical terms, Schelling sees the artist's 'poetic faculty' as the element that places him above the philosopher. The difference in valuation notwithstanding, the two philosophers are talking about similar kinds of phenomena, a comparable type of person; one calls him 'prophet', the other 'artist'. This does not mean that the Muslim Prophet and the modern artist are identical: the image of Muhammad as drawn by tradition or philosophy cannot be reduced to that of Schelling's poetic genius. But certain qualities that are attributed to the artistic genius in modern European culture, essential qualities, are regarded as characteristic of the Prophet in Muslim intellectual traditions.

Poetry and Prophecy

In examining the possible reasons for the analogies between genius and *nabīy* – and, by implication, the reasons why Muslim conceptions of the revelation include descriptions and topoi that are associated in other cultures with the genesis of works of art – the first one to consider is of course the conscious use of religious terminology by the aestheticians of genius. Such terminology reinforced the metaphysical pretensions of art, which was to take the place of religion (for a time Friedrich Schlegel and Novalis entertained the idea of 'writing a new Bible and following in Muhammad's and Luther's footsteps').[164] But there is something more beyond the terminology. The deeper reason why these two concepts are comparable, although they seem so remote from one another today, is that artistic inspiration per se is related to religious revelation, and their similarities, and their symbiosis, are the rule in cultural history rather than the exception. The prophetic poets and the poetic prophet – both possessed by an outside power, whether it is a *daemon*, after the common notion in the aesthetics of genius, or a jinn or an angel – can be numbered among the fundamental topoi of human culture.[165] 'Over a wide area of the earth poetry and prophecy are the two essential elements in the co-ordination and synthesis of thought and its transmission', Nora K. Chadwick writes.[166] 'Poetry and prophecy are the expression of human thought at its most intense and concentrated moments, stimulated by excitement, and expressed in artistic form.'[167] Poets and prophets were no more considered fundamentally different in ancient Arab culture than they were in Greek antiquity, where the poet Hesiod is venerated as a prophet and the two roles are united in such figures as Orpheus, Musaeus and Linus.[168] In all cases, divinatory preaching, the spontaneous poetry of the seer in an ecstatic state, has an aesthetic effect on its listeners, and, conversely, the poet has an extra-aesthetic function as a holder of concealed knowledge.[169] Novalis is not wrong, even if his inference seems too romanticized: 'In the beginning the poet and the priest were one, and only later ages have separated them. But the true poet has always remained a priest, just as the true priest has always remained a poet.'[170] The experience of inspiration has been expressed, probably in all religious traditions, in the form of an inspired language that is distinct from the colloquial language and often poetic, like the ceremonious words of the Buddha, the songs of the Chinese Shījīng, Akhnaton's sun hymn and the seventeen Gathas or hymns of Zoroaster.[171] 'God needs prophets to manifest Himself, and all prophets are necessarily artists', Fritz Medicus wrote: 'What a prophet has to say can never be said in prose.'[172] There are many formulations of this idea. Nizār Qabbānī said, 'From God's throat flows poetry',[173] and Johann George Hamann calls God 'the Poet at the beginning of days'.[174] The Muslim tradition too, in a somewhat different sense, says that the prophetic proclamation necessarily has an aesthetic element: 'God only sent messengers who had beautiful voices.'[175] The Gospel also testifies: 'But without a parable spake he not unto them.'[176] The Sanskrit Vedas, the oldest Hindu scriptures, contain many parts that are designated as 'songs' and are sung. Their origins show a remarkable parallel to the Islamic concept of revelation: like Muhammad, the rishis (seers) experienced God as the Word (*vāc*).[177]

In cultural history, the numerous connections between art and revelation or between poetry and prophecy are explained by their shared origins in cult. Even today, many writers feel that association, including the Lebanese poet Adonis, who says poetry 'transcends the outward appearances and looks upon the inner truth of an object, or of the world as a whole'.[178] Likewise Octavio Paz, when he writes that the 'frequency with which poets yield to the frenzy of the dance of syllables and rhythmic sounds irreducible to concepts reveals, once more, the profound affinity, never wholly explained, between poetic and religious experience.'[179] Without necessarily adopting a religious interpretation, we can see that one of the fundamental purposes of poetry or art is to transcend realities, to create a new, personal reality out of them and in them, and so to attain perceptions that are not accessible to us in day-to-day contexts – that is, *to make the invisible visible*. That is of course metaphysics, in a way, and even today something prophetic seems to be inherent in the act of artistic creation.

Many of the lines we have traced connecting the artist in the aesthetics of genius with the *nabīy* in Islam could be extrapolated to prophets of all cultures. For example, the difference between the seer, who uses an acquired technique to discover what is concealed, and the prophet, whose prophetic gift is innate and who cannot bring on his ecstatic states intentionally, which we have compared with the distinction between *ars* and *ingenium*, is found in many contexts. Similarly, a highly excited inner state is always a condition of divinatory experiences, as it is of the inspiration of Schelling's ideal artist, whether that state is a kind of obsession or the feeling of being filled by a higher power – by God – which expresses itself through the prophet (or the prophetess, as in the case of Aeschylus's Cassandra).[180] The word of the Hebrew prophets was also in verse and had great aesthetic attraction for their contemporaries; those prophets too were perceived as poets by a large part of their milieu, as was Muhammad, who carries on their tradition in this regard especially. Ezekiel complains that his people see his prophecy 'as a very lovely song of one that hath a pleasant voice and can play well on an instrument'.[181] Other prophets are called madmen or poets; they often receive their revelations in dreams;[182] they have visions and auditory experiences; they cannot intentionally invoke the inspired state; they suffer punishment and ridicule, like Jeremiah,[183] and are at first misjudged and persecuted by their contemporaries, like Elijah.[184] And they too grow accustomed to the revelations, and the agitation of their experience diminishes.[185] But the Hebrew prophets especially can truly be called poets with regard to their historic significance – and with greater justification than Muhammad. Poetry is present, Johann Gottfried Eichhorn wrote, 'in all their utterances, whether they are moral, narrative or prophetic. And poetry was their most natural garb.'[186] The artistic form of the prophetic scriptures, their strictly observed metre and their generally regular strophes, is so dominant that prose passages are often suspected of being later insertions.[187] Of course, in referring to the 'poets' of the Old Testament we are speaking not of literary persons in the contemporary sense but of poet-prophets: they are concerned with communicating supernatural knowledge, not devising pleasing verses. Biblical Hebrew does not have a generic term for poetry.[188] We must bear this in mind in reading Robert Carroll's finding:

> Describing the figures usually called 'prophets' as poets is a relatively problem-free description in that there can be no disagreement that individuals such as Amos, Hosea, Jeremiah or Ezekiel were poets. The speakers of the oracles in the anthologies we call 'prophetic' literature were clearly poets. That is indisputable. All other descriptions are highly disputable.[189]

More than a few Bible scholars are certain that Israel's poets were made into 'conventional' prophets only by subsequent editors,[190] and the version that has come down to us contains only fragments of the lost poetic versions of the Bible.[191] There is not room here to summarize this debate, which has been carried on most extensively in the English-language literature. We can note, however, that the Hebrew prophets spoke 'poetically' and have been compared with and praised as poets in all ages, from Philo of Alexandria (d. 50) to the contemporary Canadian literary scholar Northrop Frye. Even in the extant versions of the texts, which are the result of successive revisions,[192] some revelations are recorded in verse, and prophecy and poetry clearly blend together in David and Isaiah, for example.[193] A reference to the Old Testament shows that 'the poetic' in Muhammad's inspirations and preaching is not a specific 'quality' of Islam but a natural facet of all prophecy, especially Semitic prophecy. At this point one might be tempted to reframe the question of the aesthetic dimension of the revelation in Islam, and ask instead why that dimension seems to have been all but lost in the modern Western conception of religion and prophecy, or at least relegated to the background and given attention only by isolated individuals, mainly artists and scholars who are particularly interested in aesthetic processes. In any case, the Muslim concept of revelation is not exceptional as far as its analogues with the process of artistic creation are concerned. We may see it rather as an example of a phenomenon that exists across multiple cultures and religions, and one that lends itself particularly well to study because it is thoroughly described in the traditions.

Muhammad and the Poets

Regardless of the justification for seeing the Muslim Prophet and his connections to poetry as conforming to a general rule in the history of religion, there can be no doubt that the aesthetic profile of the Muslim Prophet is particularly sharp. The outlines of the biblical prophets are not only more blurry and uneven, but a number of purely divinatory properties are also attributed to them which are not associated with Muhammad – mainly telepathic and telekinetic powers of all kinds, from rainmaking to healing the sick. Neither Muhammad nor the artistic genius shows anything analogous to such functions. At best, they can be found rather in the biographies of Muslim mystics.[194] The element of the typical prophetic miracle, which has a fundamental importance in most revelations, including those of the Bible,[195] and distinguishes the prophets of all ages from the poets, is only marginal in the Quran. The concept of the miracle is transposed in the Quran to a purely spiritual level, and then essentially limited in Muslim theology to the linguistic form of the Quran. It is nonetheless apparent that the aesthetic dimension of revelation that was originally inherent in the Old Testament was at least pushed into the background by later editors, and further neglected in both Christian and Jewish theology before being repeatedly 'rediscovered' in subsequent eras,[196] whereas in Islam the aesthetic dimension was from the outset a cornerstone not only of religious experience (that much could be said of biblical poetry too) but also of the discourse on dogma. The aesthetic dimension was the field of both positive argument, as the linguistic quality of the text became the critical miraculous proof of the revelation, and negative argument, since nothing required such definitive refutation as the claim that Muhammad was 'just' a poet. Nowhere in the books of the Old Testament, not even in Ezekiel, is the dissociation from poets such a central issue in the prophetic discourse, nowhere is the conflict with poetry carried out with such determination, as in the Quran – no doubt because the dividing line between prophet and poet was not particularly important to the ancient Hebrews. For the Islamic Prophet, however, because poetry had developed into something autonomous, yet without giving up its metaphysical aspirations, the conflict was clear. Evidently no objection plagued the Prophet as much, and none of his opponents' arguments is as vehemently rebuffed in the Quran, as the assertion that he was a poet. In a total of fifteen passages the Quran responds directly or indirectly to the accusation, which the unbelievers apparently raised again and again, that Muḥammad was a *sāḥir* (sorcerer), a *kāhin* (soothsayer), a *shāʿir* (poet) or generally *majnūn*, possessed by a jinn. The passages demonstrate how urgent it was to refute the accusations. While the rebuttal takes on a stereotypical character in later surahs, the thoroughness of the five early Meccan instances indicates at least that the accusations represented a real danger.[197] We must conclude that, because of certain actions, behaviours or words, especially in the first phase of his revelation, Muhammad *necessarily* had to struggle to avoid being mistaken for a poet. And if there had been nothing in his activity that suggested such an identification, then it would never have occurred to his opponents to discredit him as a poet: they would have found other ways of casting doubt on his claim to divine revelation.[198] But they said, 'Nay, he is a poet.'[199]

Muhammad is also called a sorcerer[200] and a soothsayer,[201] but the real polemic against his claim to prophethood stresses his identification as a poet. That may seem surprising at first: if any textual genre of the Jahiliyyah shows a formal similarity with Muhammad's revelation, it is the rhymed prose (*saj'*) of the soothsayers. The disparity with ancient Arabic poetry is too obvious (if we disregard the 111th surah, which comes close to the style of *hijā'*, the genre of invective poems) to make it plausible that Muhammad could have been confused with the poets. Nevertheless, the assertion that Muhammad is a poet is the principal issue in the dispute as it is reported in the Quran. What can explain the fact that many listeners perceived the Prophet's preaching against the horizon of ancient Arabic poetry? Michael Zwettler, who has addressed this question, sees the Quran's use of *'arabīya*, the inflected formal language reserved for poetic texts, as the reason for the poet polemics.[202] Without excluding this possibility, we should note that the Muslim tradition suggests another element of the revelation that corresponds with poetry as a reason for the alleged confusion: the occurrence of inspiration. If we start from the picture that the tradition paints of the Prophet's revelation, we cannot help seeing his ecstatic tendency as the essential reason why Muhammad would have been accused of being just a poet. His inspirations are described as something that bears a remarkable similarity to the inspirations of the ancient Arab poets. The wording of the Quran corroborates this interpretation: the Meccans quoted in it stress the element of 'possession'. That hardly suggests they were thinking of the authors of qasidas, which are long poems with a complex structure. The comparison is rather with the poets of the spontaneously improvised *hijā'* genre. It was chiefly this type of poet that was considered to be possessed by a personal demon (*jinn*, *shayṭān* or *tābi'*).[203] The *hijā'* poet shared a linguistic form with the seer: a rhyming aphorism composed of a few short lines with a parallel structure which, although restrained by a simple iambic metre, *rajaz*, betrayed the state of severe mental excitement in which the verses originated.[204] The crucial distinction that the tradition makes between the ordinary poets and Muhammad refers not to the kind of inspiration they received but to its source: jinn or satans in the poets' case;[205] the archangel Gabriel or the one almighty God in Muhammad's.

In Muhammad's first experience of revelation, for example, the angel appears to him (in the version recounted by al-Bukhārī)[206] and says,

'Recite!'

'I will not recite!' the Prophet replies.

Thereupon the angel seizes him and chokes him until he nearly loses consciousness. Then the angel releases him and says, 'Recite!'

Again the Prophet answers, 'I will not recite!'

The angel seizes him a second time and chokes him until he nearly loses consciousness. Then the angel releases him and says, 'Recite!'

'I will not recite!' the Prophet repeats.

The angel seizes him again and chokes him until he nearly loses consciousness. Then the angel releases him and pronounces the beginning of the Surah *'Alaq*:

Recite: In the Name of thy Lord who created,
created Man of a blood-clot.
Recite: And thy Lord is the Most Generous.[207]

In Ibn Hishām the tradition is not much different: the angel has a name, Gabriel, and he carries a silk cloth with writing on it and uses it to choke the Prophet.[208] These accounts show striking similarities to the legends of Ḥassān ibn Thābit's vocation to poetry. The vocation of Ḥassān ibn Thābit, who later became the eulogist of the Prophet, is also described as an unexpected possession by a personal spirit. In his case, however, it is not an angel but an ordinary female demon who encounters the unsuspecting young man in the streets of Mecca, seizes him, kneels on his chest and asks him whether it is he whom the people expect to be a poet. When Ḥassān answers in the affirmative, the demon forces him to recite three verses which explicitly mention the participation of demonic powers in his poetic creation – and from then on he is a poet.[209]

Possession by an external power, recitation under coercion of words that the speaker does not understand at first, and motifs such as suffocation by a personal spirit and involuntary vocation are not limited to the Prophet in the Muslim tradition. 'Abīd ibn al-Abraṣ too, who had never composed a poem before, dreamt he had a ball of hair put in his mouth and was told, 'Arise!' And he stood up and from then on was a *hijā'* poet.[210] This story recalls, at least remotely, the beginning of the 74th surah, in which Muhammad receives the exhortation: 'O thou shrouded in thy mantle, / Arise, and warn!'[211] (A number of scholars, diverging from the main stream of exegesis, have taken this to be the first revelation of the Quran.)[212] The principal difference consists in the message itself – that is, in the fact that Muhammad is called upon to glorify his Lord, while 'Abīd is merely empowered to compose invective verse against those who insult him. Muhammad himself is said initially to have mistaken his first experience of revelation for a poetic initiation. That means he recognized what had happened to him as a kind of event that was familiar from the biographies of the poets. Only later – and only after a second revelation, and after receiving the opinion of his cousin Waraqa ibn Nawfal and the encouragement of his wife Khadīja – did he become aware that it was not a jinn that had possessed him during the night but God's greatest familiar (*an-nāmūs al-akbar*), the archangel Gabriel.[213] If even Muhammad himself misinterpreted his trancelike state as a poetic *mania*, it is understandable that his milieu thought that his first and subsequent fits of ecstasy were signs of such a possession. The same can be said of his dream visions and auditory experiences, which were also a kind of event about which he and his contemporaries knew from the inspirations of poets. In the ancient Arab imagination, *ru'yā*, dream vision, is a setting for both prophetic and poetic inspiration. The Prophet himself says that, although prophecy would end with his death, people's dreams would remain as 'proclaimers' (*mubashshirāt*) of the prophecy.[214] Another hadith says, 'A Muslim's dream vision is one forty-fifth of prophecy.'[215] This idea is pursued farthest by the mystics, and especially by Ibn ʿArabī, who interprets dreams as a setting of divine revelations (*tanzīl*) and dialogues of the soul with God, of the lover with the beloved – 'and does not every lover seek to be alone with the beloved?'[216]

It is apparent from the Quran that the unbelievers doubted not Muhammad's inspiration per se but his claim in regard to the source of it. That is to say, they did not slander the Prophet as a liar, a fraud or a criminal, which would have been conceivable, and more disparaging, since poets enjoyed high prestige. They conceded that he had an inspiration, but not that of a messenger of God: 'Shall we forsake our gods for a poet possessed (by jinn; *shāʿir majnūn*)?'[217] The traditions confirm what the Quran hints at here and elsewhere: that the unbelievers saw Muhammad's revelations as the ordinary inspirations of a demon or a satan, like those that soothsayers and poets experienced. Once when everyone could see that the Prophet was waiting in vain for a revelation, a Quraysh woman said, 'His satan has stood him up.'[218] In this situation it is understandable and logical that the Quran does not appeal to the stylistic idiosyncrasy of its verses in its efforts to distinguish Muhammad from the poets – although such an argument would be accurate and at first glance more obvious. It is more urgent to disparage the poets' inspiration and the agency that causes it, differentiating it from Muhammad's revelations and their source. In regard to the dream visions, this difference is expressed in a terminological distinction between prophetic and poetic dreams: the first are *ru'yā* or *manām*, and the second are *ḥulm* (plural *aḥlām*), which is used pejoratively in the Quran. The Quran denies the opponents' assertion that the Prophet has only muddled dreams (*aḍġāthu l-aḥlām*), and is therefore a poet,[219] and persists in attributing *ru'yā* to Muhammad,[220] Abraham[221] and all the prophets.[222] This division continues in the hadiths: the Prophet is quoted as saying, 'I saw what a sleeping person sees in a dream (*manām*)',[223] and, 'The *ru'yā* is from God, and the *ḥulm* is from Satan.'[224]

The Quran and the sunnah concede that the poets are inspired, but the beings which inspire them, the satans (*ash-shayāṭīn*) and the jinn, are themselves misguided and in error. Muhammad is safe from them; 'by the grace' of his Lord he is not possessed by jinn (*majnūn*).[225] Muhammad and the unbelievers will see 'which of you is the demented (*maftūn*)'.[226] The 81st surah contains an oath by the planets, the night and the dawn that the Quran is the 'word of a noble Messenger / having power, with the Lord of the Throne secure' – that is, the word of Gabriel, not of an 'accursed satan'. This surah too says Muhammad is not possessed but saw the angel 'on the clear horizon'.[227]

The repudiation of the poets and the discrediting of those who prompt them is sharpest in the 26th surah, 'The Poets'. The Quran recalls the history of the pre-Islamic prophets, embedding Muhammad in it, when it says,

> Truly it is the revelation (*tanzīl*)
> of the Lord of all Being,
> brought down by the Faithful Spirit (*nazala bihī r-rūḥu l-amīn*)
> upon thy heart, that thou mayest be one of the warners,
> in a clear, Arabic tongue.[228]

Shortly thereafter, the idea that the Quran could have been brought down by satans is again negated:

> Not by the Satans has it been brought down (*wa-mā nazzalat bihī sh-shayāṭīn*), it behoves them not, neither are they able.
> Truly, they are expelled from hearing (*innahum ʿanis-samʿi la-maʿzūlūn*).[229]

After characterizing Muhammad's inspiration as divine, the speaker deals with the pseudo-revelation of the poets at the end of the surah.

> Shall I tell you
> on whom the Satans come down? (*ʿalā man tanazzala sh-shayāṭīn*)
> They come down on every guilty impostor.
> They give ear (*yulqawna s-samʿ*),
> but most of them are liars.
> And the poets – the perverse (*al-ġāwūna*) follow them;
> hast thou not seen how they wander in every valley
> and how they say that which they do not?
> Save those that believe,
> and do righteous deeds, and remember God oft,
> and help themselves
> after being wronged; and
> those who do wrong shall surely know
> by what overturning they will be overturned.[230]

The Quran underscores the interconnection of the three passages quoted in the surah by describing both the poets' and Muhammad's inspirations as the reception of a message with which someone – a satan in the one case, the 'faithful spirit' in the other – descends from a place portrayed as being above.[231] In both cases this operation is designated by the root *n-z-l* ('to descend', 'to come down'), as a verb of the first, second or fifth stem or as a verbal noun of the second stem (*tanzīl*). The angel passes on the words of the Lord to Muhammad faithfully, but satans (*most* satans, to be exact) can only spread lies. From another surah, which was probably revealed in Mecca about the same time, we learn that the satans are excluded from the exalted assembly of the angels. However hard they listen – and this is what the *yulqawna s-samʿ* in verse 223 of 'The Poets' refers to – they cannot hear it. If one of them happens to catch a few words, he is pursued by a bright firebrand.[232] But the Quran has harsh words not only for Gabriel's rivals the satans: in verses 224 to 226, it mentions the poets and their followers, and Zwettler does not exaggerate when he writes that it would be hard to imagine a 'more incisive, scathing, and irrefutable' taunt.[233]

In these verses, and in the context of the whole surah, whose seductive composition presents the history of the pre-Islamic prophets as a blueprint for Muhammad's mission, recounting how they appealed in vain to their peoples to fear God and follow them, and repeating their appeal *fa-ttaqū llāha wa-aṭīʿūni*, 'Fear God and obey me', like a refrain, it becomes clear that the conflict with the poets is at bottom a struggle for control. That is why the quranic polemics centre on the poets and not on the soothsayers, for example: among the inspired classes, only the poets claim leadership of the tribe; only they are an obstacle to Muhammad's mission to lead his people on the *Straight Path* – that is, to take command. The remark that only the *ġāwūn*, the misguided or the errant, follow the poets is thus directed precisely against their claim to power.[234] Likewise the prior statement that they received their inspirations from beings that knew nothing of the 'celestial assembly' and so could only spread lies, while Muhammad's heavenly message was brought to him by a faithful, reliable spirit (*ar-rūḥ al-amīn*), is aimed at undermining the poets' credibility as leaders whose power is derived from their supernatural knowledge. If their knowledge can be shown to be fragmentary and arbitrary, their authority will inevitably be doubted. Conversely, the opponents' polemic in verse 21:5 quoted above is aimed at discrediting Muhammad's dream visions as *muddled*: while conceding that he had visions in the first place, the adversaries dispute the *accuracy* of his knowledge of the concealed (*al-ġayb*). The poets' aptitude as leaders is also contested in the passage that ridicules them as 'wandering in every valley'. This may be an ironic allusion to a basic topos of the ancient Arabic qasida: the speaker's apparently aimless travel by camel. The Arabic phrase *annahum fī kulli wādin yahīmūna* has the pejorative connotation of straying, confusion, mindlessness. Finally, the statement that the poets 'say what they do not do' is not so much an accusation against the poets themselves, as is often written, as primarily a statement on what poetry is and what constitutes it. Verse 21:5 also explicitly mentions invention as a characteristic of poetry. The prophets, on the other hand, are portrayed as people who do not invent something themselves but communicate the message of a third party, the one God, and proclaim its absolute truth; people who stand up for their words, who make them the guiding principle of their own lives and so 'say what they do'.[235] The difference between religion and art discussed here, which concerns their different relations to reality, is a fundamental one and by no means new. It is revealing that Arab writers of later centuries use precisely the verses just quoted to defend the autonomy of poetry and the legitimacy of poetic fiction.[236] The speaker of these verses has a twofold purpose: first, to underscore the distinction between Muhammad and the poets, which was evidently often overlooked in Muhammad's milieu, and, second, to discredit those poets who heretically presumed to claim leadership, which was the Prophet's sole prerogative once the revelation had begun because of the special quality of his knowledge. Poetry is not declared illegitimate per se, and the text explicitly makes an exception in its verdict for those poets who 'believe, and do righteous deeds, and remember God oft' – that is, those who are within the Islamic value system and do not threaten the hierarchical structure of the community. To put it bluntly, the conflict with the poets is about ideology and power, not hostility to art, or issues of aesthetic criticism or aesthetic superiority.[237]

It is understandable that the traditions and the exegesis intensify this initial conflict, which is after all quite complex, and more hinted at in the Quran than clearly asserted – and which cannot be simply summarized in the sentence '*Le Coran a horreur du poète*'.[238] The escalation can occur in either direction: towards a total prohibition of poetry or the opposite, an ostensibly religious defence of poetry. Where fear of poetry rules, the commentators further disparage the source of the poets' inspiration, which merges with that of the soothsayers. The Prophet is supposed to have said, 'The angels converse in the clouds about the things that will happen on Earth. The satans catch a word of their talk and pour it in the soothsayer's ear, as if pouring out a bottle, and in the process they add a hundred lies.'[239] According to other hadiths, he also said it would be better for a person to be plagued with a belly full of pus than to fill his insides with poetry,[240] and that poetry is the Quran that God gave Satan (Iblīs) when he expelled him from Paradise.[241] Immediately after his conversion, the poet ʿAbdullāh ibn az-Zibaʿrā confesses in a poem of remorse that he had followed Satan on the path of error.[242] ʿUbaydullāh ibn Ziyād is said to have left off composing poetry because he did not want to bring the words of God together in his heart with those of Satan,[243] and other well-known poets too, including Labīd ibn Rabīʿa, are said to have renounced poetry after converting to Islam.[244] We can state in more general terms that the whole mechanism of assimilation of transcendental knowledge had suddenly been cast into doubt.[245] With the end of the revelation, several theologians said, all inspiration must come to an end, most of all the poetic, which comes not from God but from another source. Of course, the harsh deprecation of poetry that occurs in the hadiths and traditions cited has not gained ascendancy. The first caliphs' relations to poets seem to have been defined more by a pragmatic 'cultural policy', as the following anecdote attests. The caliph ʿUmar wanted to prohibit the poet al-Ḥuṭay'a from composing other insulting poems (*hijā'*) – not for religious reasons, but because they caused agitation in the society. But the poet argued that *hijā'* was the source of his livelihood, and that if he were to stop composing it his family would starve. So they reached an agreement that al-Ḥuṭay'a would at least refrain from comparing people with one another in his poems, which incited them to animosity.[246]

Poetry prevailed. Its flourishing has 'happily never been diminished' by Islam, Tilman Nagel finds;[247] on the contrary, Annemarie Schimmel writes, the 'love of poetry' became 'a hallmark of traditional Muslim culture'.[248] Like those who despise poetry, its apologists too refer to remarks and suggestions from the Prophet's biography. They appeal to poets such as Ḥassān ibn Thābit, ʿAbdullāh ibn Rawāḥa and Kaʿb ibn Mālik who, the traditions say, belonged to Muhammad's inner circle, and they quote the many praises of poetry and music (the two are discussed together) attributed to the Prophet.[249] 'In some poetry is wisdom', he is reported to have said,[250] and, 'Among the most beautiful of beauties (*ajmal al-jamāl*) are the beautiful poem and the singing of a beautiful voice'.[251] The Prophet called to a group of singing and dancing women and children coming from a wedding, 'God knows you are the dearest people to me.'[252] He joyfully attended poets' recitations, selecting verses for them himself;[253] he was delighted and moved by them. At a recitation of a hundred verses of Umayya ibn Abī s-Salṭ, he cried after every verse, 'One more! And one more!'[254] Poems were recited regularly even in the *ḥaram* of Mecca[255] and during the building of the mosque in Medina, where a minbar was set up especially for the poet Ḥassān.[256] It is striking that neither the Quran nor the Prophet (as far as is handed down in the hadiths) denies the supernatural origin of the poets' words. Both sources take pains only to devalue the origin of poetry as not divine and as unreliable – and only in reference to those poets who oppose Muhammad. Muhammad's eulogist Ḥassān, on the other hand, is supposed to have been supported in composing his poems by the archangel Gabriel himself.[257]

The defences of poetry that occur throughout the history of Muslim theology repeatedly point out that the 26th surah of the Quran explicitly makes an exception from its condemnation for those poets who 'believe and do righteous deeds'. While Nöldeke et al. and Régis Blachère believe this verse is a Medinan insertion,[258] Johann Christoph Bürgel ventures the opinion that Muhammad, purely for reasons 'of religious politics', surrounded himself with 'poets who reinforced his influence by the proven instrument of power' rather than waste the opportunity to exploit 'the powerful weapon [of poetry] for his goals'.[259] Furthermore, the hadiths that document Muhammad's enthusiasm for poetry have been discounted as inventions after the fact with the purpose of establishing a justification for poetry.[260] There is no historic evidence for theses such as these, however, and it would be appropriate to approach the hadiths that are unfavourable to poetry with the same scepticism that is justly shown towards those favourable to it.[261] The Prophet's biography is like many other sources: you can find in it any statement about poetry you want and put the rest on the chopping board of historical scepticism. And Muslim theologians are only negligibly more inclined than some Orientalists to use it in this way. Regardless of one's position in the debate surrounding Wansbrough and the historic credibility of the Quran, one should at least be sophisticated enough to show restraint in psychologizing the historic Muhammad and his ideas, motives and intentions. Similarly, it behoves us to be careful with judgements about the relation between *the* (true, original) Islamic religion and *the* art of poetry, and instead to limit our statements to the views of specific persons or groups at specific times. Even claiming the Quran as a historic source, and without completely denying the authenticity of the traditional literature, the only point on which consensus is possible is that Muhammad condemned the *blasphemous* poets (how could he do otherwise?) and found it necessary to combat those poets who composed verses vilifying him, because of the extraordinary importance of poets as the propagandists of their tribes. There is no evidence of a contempt for poetry in general, only an admission of the danger represented by the 'heathen poets', as the scholar of poetics Ibn Rashīq writes, 'who addressed their maledictive verse to the Messenger of God and aggrieved him'[262] – that is, who fought the Quran with its own weapon: with verse.

> It is said that the devil cried out three times: first when he was cursed and his form became different from that of the angels, then when he first saw Muhammad pray in Mecca, and again when Mecca was conquered. Then he gathered his retinue and said, 'There is no hope of turning Muhammad's people back to idolatry after today, so spread poetry and song (*nawḥ*) among them.'[263]

The Language of the Angels

The actual consequence that Muhammad's emergence had for poetry was not to eliminate it but to demystify it in a way: at first poetry abandoned its pretensions to compete with the revelation without becoming religious in its ideological orientation or in its choice of themes (a significant genre of religious poetry emerged centuries later among the mystics).[264] The notion of possession by personal demons gradually faded into the background, supplanted by the idea of the poet's craftsmanship. This development had already begun before the emergence of Islam but gained new momentum afterwards. In the long term, however, it did not lead to a reduction in the poets' sources of inspiration, since they soon endowed themselves once more, in Abbasid Baghdad if not earlier, with metaphysical authority and attributed their poetry to the agency of higher powers – at least in the more abstract sense of poetic inspiration as it had been described earlier by Plato and would be described again centuries later in the aesthetics of genius. They often clothed these notions in the terms of the old belief in the jinn, much as the aestheticians of genius revived such concepts as the muse or the artist's daemon, without regaining the corresponding mythic meanings. Although the notion of the jinn and the satans taking possession of poets became less current as an artistic motif, the greatest poets, the *fuḥūl*, continued to be thought of as inspired by celestial powers and revered for their supernatural talent throughout the history of classical Arabic literature and in the literature of other Muslim peoples. 'In the ranks of the great they march / The Prophet in the lead, the poets right behind', the Persian poet Neẓāmī (d. 1209) proclaimed.[265] The poets were still princes – 'princes of the spoken word' (*umarā' al-kalām*), as they were called.[266] The ancestral source of poetic inspiration was not so much replaced as expanded. This allowed societies that had become Muslim to persist in the old idea of inspiration by jinn and at the same time to accept new, non-Arabic doctrines of daemons, including the exorcistic rites of the Persian-Turkish *parīkh*^{w}*ān* or the African *zār*.[267]

The Islamic Middle Ages hardly saw a monism of inspiration like that which could be said to have existed in the Christian Middle Ages, when the artist was generally anonymous and worked for the glory of God. Perhaps some Muslim theologians demanded something comparable to the situation in the Christian Middle Ages, in which there could be no high art on non-religious themes and all legitimate enthusiasms must take the form of Christian apostolates – 'that is, post-pentecostal missions of speech that are ultimately nourished by the sole authoritative source of promulgations of truth: the gospels and the Christian mission according to Matthew 28:19', as Peter Sloterdijk puts it in his description of premodern culture.[268] But, in any case, such demands were hardly influential in the medieval cultures from Andalusia to India. Those cultures produced a number of poets who certainly could be called geniuses in the modern sense, inspired by higher powers: think only of the great Arab poets – some of whom were completely secular in their outlook, while others, such as Abū Nuwās, explicitly flirted with a satanic source of inspiration or, like al-Mutanabbī, styled themselves prophets – think of Ferdousī (d. 1020 or 1026) and ʿOmar Khayyām (d. 1131): none of these was a 'faithful tutor of sharia, mirror of the divine order and beauty', as all the recognized poets of the Islamic world must be, according to the logic of the sociologist Claus Leggewie, since 'the separation of art, religion and politics that is constitutive of modern societies has not been successfully carried out' in the Arab-Islamic region.[269] As misleading as it would be to say that these poets existed *because of* Islam, neither can we reduce them to the status of dissidents and say they existed *in spite of* Islam. In the face of an Orientalist tradition that tends, showing a suspicious affinity with modern Islamism, to explain all intellectual, social, political and artistic developments by Islam, or at least by their dialectical relation to Islam, we must insist that it is nonsensical to press the entire literature of the Islamic countries into a mould of *omnipotence and power*, much less to define them as *ḥalāl* or *ḥarām* – either approved and in the service of God or autonomous and therefore heretical, merely a minor branch of Oriental literature and history. One only has to open a good orthodox treatise by al-Jurjānī, Ibn Qutayba or ar-Rāzī (to say nothing of the Persian-language theological discourse, which contains as many lines of poetry today as a Persian rug has flowers and ornaments) to see that even those poets who claimed to be the medium of a higher power were not exactly relegated to the margins for all time. Poetry did not have to show religious credentials to all and sundry; it remained a source of legitimate enthusiasms, regardless of the undisputed precedence that has always been given to the revelation in religious circles. This 'pluralism of inspiration' is exemplified in a hadith that is frequently cited in the Islamic literature. It is probably a later invention, but the same can be said of other pronouncements of the Prophet on poetry. What is significant is that statements such as this one are referred to repeatedly in the Muslim literature, and in Muslim theology in particular, and reflect a real situation and a widely held opinion.

> A man entered the Messenger of God's house while there were people there reciting the Quran and people reciting poems. The man said, 'Messenger of God! The Quran and poetry?' He answered, 'Sometimes one, sometimes the other!'[270]

The revelation and its distinction from poetry eventually consolidated the special status of poetry. Although there could be no further *waḥy*, revelation, after God had spoken to Muhammad through a *waḥy* – the inspirations of the poets and the mystics were called *ilhām* – and although the strict distinction between poetic and prophetic inspiration was clear in the minds of the faithful (but not necessarily in the minds of all literary scholars), poetry was the only medium besides the revelation (and, later, mysticism) with an acknowledged claim to an association with a transcendental reality, an access to supernatural inspiration, even if that association and that access remained limited. Even those authors who reject poetry do so because they recognize its metaphysical association (otherwise they could disregard it as unimportant) but find it dangerous and sacrilegious; as Clifford Geertz circumscribed it, 'it stands as a kind of secular counterpoise, a worldly footnote, to the revelation itself.'[271] On the ambivalence of the poets' expression in an Islamic context, Geertz writes,

> They turn the tongue of God to ends of their own, which, if it is not quite sacrilege, borders on it; but at the same time they display its incomparable power, which, if not quite worship, approaches it. Poetry, rivalled only by architecture, became the cardinal fine art in Islamic civilization, and especially the Arabic-speaking part of it, while treading the edge of the gravest form of blasphemy.[272]

To be exact, the ambivalent relation Geertz is talking about is this: precisely because the revelation borders on poetry, there were efforts to suppress poetry from the beginning. It was morally suspect because it is not sacred enough to justify the power that it actually possesses and not secular enough to be treated on a par with ordinary eloquence. This intermediate status of poetry, the acknowledgement of its power by the religious leaders and their attempt to cope with it, is vividly demonstrated in an anecdote related by Saad Abdullah Sowayan. Among the inhabitants of the Arabian peninsula in centuries past, a person who had been bitten by a snake tried to remain awake until the morning star appeared in the sky. The belief was that the snake's venom would enter the bloodstream if the person who had been bitten went to sleep before the snake itself did. To help the victim stay awake, the inhabitants of the village or the tribe would gather around to sing and hold poetry duels through the night. If the victim was not better the next morning, the people believed the snake had 'turned over on its back'. In that case, the family and acquaintances sang and recited until dawn for seven nights. When the Wahhabi took power, public singing was generally prohibited by the religious authorities. So that the poets could nonetheless perform, their followers sometimes pretended to have been bitten by a snake: by this subterfuge they received the legal authorities' permission to sing and recite for the alleged victim.[273] The conception of the poetic act as one that rivals God and is therefore potentially sacrilegious – the 'ambivalence in the genius of language' that George Steiner mentions[274] – became a fundamental theme of Arabic literature. As long as literature remained secular, it was subject at most to political and moral constraints in Muslim cultures. But where the poets competed directly with religion, whether by reference to a celestial source of inspiration or simply by trying to imitate and outshine the style of the Quran, they were often subjected to religiously motivated criticism and sometimes to persecution. They have been largely undeterred, and in today's perspective the challenge of orthodox or even merely time-honoured faith connects them with 'the Promethean thrust of modern poetry', which consists, in Octavio Paz's outline, in the 'will to create a new "sacred," in contradistinction to the one that churches offer us today.'[275] Among those in the Arab world who have dedicated themselves to this old and new undertaking, the poet Adonis, whom we have quoted in the preceding chapters, holds an outstanding position. His work can be read as an impassioned exploration – sometimes violent, sometimes almost tender – of the Arab intellectual and aesthetic tradition. A religious current runs through it and at the same time makes it impious. It is not with religious poetry that Adonis has made his mark – that is, with poetry in the service of religion – but with a poetry that challenges the position of religion. He draws on the role of the poet in the Jahiliyyah, whose prophetic pretensions were rejected by Islam, yet at the same time on the mystical poets such as al-Ḥallāj (d. 922) and an-Niffarī (d. 965). The mystics had restored a metaphysical earnestness to poetry after it had been to some extent secularized as a result of Islam, and the invocation of demons, angels or Satan had become more a formula than a real perception. They made poetry into a prophetic contemplation. To create a linguistic and spiritual reality of their own, they broke with the traditional Arabic poets' canon of rules – just as the Quran had done before them, in Adonis's interpretation, and as he undertakes to do anew in his own poetry. His *nom de plume* can be understood as a manifesto: Adonis is the divinity famed for beauty, whose cult is devoted to a vegetation that blossoms profusely, dies off, and then regenerates itself. Unlike the mystical poetics who considered themselves Muslims and justified their transgression of the aesthetic and religious norms by religious arguments, Adonis rejects all Islamic associations. He casts off religion like an old skin – not ignoring it, as most poets of his time do, but addressing the very process of shedding it. His poems are neither situated in the shadow of Islam, like those of the mystics, nor necessarily directed against Islam. They affirm a world of their own. They are turned towards the heavens, yet not towards God.

> Today I burned up the mirage of Saturday,
> the mirage of Friday.
> Today, I cast off the house's mask.
> I exchanged the god of blind stone,
> And the god of the seven days,
> for a dead one.[276]

The hadith quoted above that says poetry (and, with it, music) is the Quran that God gave Satan (the fallen angel, Iblīs) on expelling him from Paradise attests to something corresponding to the Dionysian principle in the classical imagination, tracing its fascination to the real but forbidden and perilous influence of a power that is both transcendental and at the same time suspect. One of the principal defectors to the anti-poetry faction, Abū l-Ḥārith al-Awlāsī (d. 909 or 910), explained his renunciation of poetry and song by the following experience:

> I was very diligent at that time in the mystical ritual of 'listening' (*samāʿ*), when one night someone came to my cell and said, 'Some seekers of God have gathered and desire your presence.'
>
> I went out and followed him until finally we came to the group, who formed a circle, with an old man sitting at the end. When those assembled saw me, they greeted me with extraordinary reverence, and the old man said to me, 'If it please you, let us recite some verses.'
>
> As I expressed my assent, two people began to recite poems to beautiful melodies, poems about the anguish of parting. All fell into rapture, emitted sounds of joy and displayed gestures of delight, while I wondered at their behaviour. This euphoria went on until dawn, and then the old man asked me, 'O sheikh, are you not curious to know who I am and who these people are?'
>
> 'Your dignity prevented me from asking', I replied.
>
> Then he cried out that he, might God's curse strike him, was Iblīs, and the assembly were his children. Their gatherings and songs had two purposes: 'First, I lament the anguish of the separation and remember the days of my happiness; and, second, I tempt the devout and lead them astray.' From that

day on I never again felt the need to practise the ritual of listening, and I was cured of that great foolishness.[277]

The majority of the mystics have a completely different, extremely ambivalent relation to the character of Satan, respecting and sometimes revering him as a 'martyr of love': for them, the arts of poetry and song have never lost their attraction in spite of – and perhaps even because of – their suspect origins. 'Abū l-Ḥārith, I have obtained nothing with which I can tempt you except this', said Iblīs to the mystic al-Awlāsī in another version of their meeting. That version does not mention that al-Awlāsī renounced poetry after the encounter, quoting him instead as saying, 'The sweetness of the singing troubled me so that I wanted to jump off the roof.'[278]

As the reed-pipe laments because it has been cut off from the reed bed, music and poetry to the Sufis are an expression of nostalgia for the primal state, and for its language and sound. The concept of the original state as ideal implies that poetic and revealed language were one, or that poetry came into existence only with Satan's expulsion from Paradise. 'Iblīs was the first one to complain (*nāḥa*) and the first one to sing', the Prophet is supposed to have said according to Sufi tradition.[279] In heaven there is no need for poetry: there the angels sing, just as the Romantics imagined.[280] The only earthly manifestation of that original language is the Quran brought down by angels: it is so perfect that even the devils take their places in Heaven to listen to the revelation.[281] In that conception, poetry, Satan's Quran, would be the attempt – from its opponents' point of view, a sacrilegious and doomed attempt – to approximate the original (a 'shadow of the veil of prophecy', as Neẓāmī calls it),[282] to 'eat again from the Tree of Knowledge to fall back into the state of innocence', as Kleist writes in his essay 'The Puppet Theatre',[283] to traverse the potential of language and, at the end of the circle, to enter its Paradise again from the opposite side. 'In the realm of poetry', Neẓāmī says, 'no one but me has ever knocked on the door of [divine] majesty'.[284] Hafiz too says of his songs that they reached Paradise: the angels learn them by heart, Venus (Anāhīd in Persian), the musician of Heaven, plays them, and they move even the Messiah to dance.[285]

Anahid's lute has nothing more to do
Where your ghazal, o Hafiz, has poured out tones of love.[286]

The relation in Islam between art and religion, Quran and poetry, Prophet and poets is delicate and resists black-and-white generalizations; it has been portrayed often enough as simple antagonism, but it cannot be understood without an appreciation of the substantial proximity of the two poles. It is striking that Western researchers have failed to perceive or account for certain aspects of the Islamic cultural sphere – in this case, the aesthetic dimension of the revelation – because they were not familiar with them from their own cultural background. Stefan Wild has listed plausible reasons why Orientalists ignored the poetic function of the quranic language and its reception.[287] Yet there are obvious affinities not only between poetry and the Quran but also between the poets and the Prophet. If they have rarely been noticed,[288] it may be simply because they were not expected. In the nineteenth century, scholars (at least the well-meaning among them) looked for a historic hero in Muhammad; in the twentieth century, the social reformer increasingly came to the fore. The Prophet as a poet went unnoticed. The points of intersection between the image of the Prophet in Islam and that of the artist in the German aesthetics of genius are an indication that artistic and religious inspiration in Muslim cultures stand in a different relation to one another – a closer but at the same time an ambivalent relation – than the accustomed concepts of the Christian Middle Ages or our own time. The Islamic Prophet is neither a messenger nor an artistic genius as the modern mind conceives them: the Muslim concept of the Prophet brings together descriptions, topoi and ideas that have been divided in the course of Western history between two relatively clearly differentiated concepts, art and religion. The proximity of the two in the quranic revelation does not make Islam unique in cultural history: what is unusual is rather the importance of the aesthetic in the world of Islamic faith and its persistence down to the present day.

Friedrich Schleiermacher introduced the term *Kunstreligion*, 'a religion originating in art', by which he designated an interpenetration of religious and aesthetic phenomena.[289] Novalis and the Romantics adopted it enthusiastically; it was incorporated in the aesthetics of genius; Hegel put it to its most important use in his *Phenomenology of Spirit*. There is good reason to suppose that an exploration of Islam as a *religion of art* could be at least as fruitful as the studies that have customarily examined it as a *religion of law*.

The term *Kunstreligion* in Europe belongs both to the past and to the future. While Schleiermacher wishes for a religion of art to emerge, Hegel feels its realization has been accomplished once and for all in ancient Greece. To Hegel the *Kunstreligion* is a grand spiritual achievement, but one that is irretrievably past and not worthy of repeating. Islam can be interpreted as an assertion of its presence: the Quran would then be, in Hegel's terms (although without the tendency of his later works towards the sublation of art), the *absolute* work of art of Islamic culture.

6

The Sufi Listeners

> Is not my word like as a fire?
> saith the Lord; and like a hammer
> that breaketh the rock in pieces?
>
> Jeremiah 23:29

Once when Manṣūr ibn ʿAmmār ad-Dandānqānī (d. 839 or 840), a famous wise man who was particularly respected by the Sufis, came upon a ruin, he discovered a young man reciting the *ṣalāt al-khāʾifīn*, the ritual 'prayer of the fearful' that is composed of Quran verses. Manṣūr waited until the young man had finished his prayer before offering him a friendly greeting. The young man replied in kind. Manṣūr asked him whether he did not know that there is a valley in Hell of which it is said, 'it is a furnace / snatching away at the scalp, / calling him who drew back and turned away.'[1] The young man heaved a loud sigh and fainted. When he came to, he asked the sheikh to recite some more. So Manṣūr recited to him the phrase from verse 2:24, 'whose fuel is men and stones'. The young man dropped dead. But written on his chest were the words: 'So he shall be in a pleasing life / in a lofty garden, / its clusters nigh to gather.'[2]

They wept or uttered cries of horror and joy, fell into raptures, fell down wailing, and collapsed as if struck by lightning, or even died on the spot, like the young man in the episode just recounted, with which Abū Isḥāq ath-Thaʿlabī begins his *Book of Those Slain by the Noble Quran, Who Heard the Quran and Thereupon Died*:[3] no one reacted to the melody of the divine word more enthusiastically, or with more alarm, than the Sufis, the mystics of Islam. They must have experienced what André Breton suspected: 'Beauty will be CONVULSIVE, or it will not be at all.'[4] When someone recited the verse *lahum min jahannama mihādun wa-min fawqihim ġawāshin* ('Gehenna shall be their cradle, and above them coverings')[5] to ʿAbdullāh ibn Ḥanẓala, he broke out in such sobbing that the onlookers thought he was writhing in agony. After a while, ʿAbdullāh stood up again. The companions told him to sit down, but he screamed at them, 'The violence (*heybat*) of these verses won't let me sit.'[6] Ash-Shiblī (d. 945), the eccentric mystic of Baghdad, fainted on hearing verse 18:23 ('And mention thy Lord, when thou forgettest') and, when he came to, he cried, 'Astonishing the heart that hears His word and keeps its place; and astonishing the soul that hears His word and is not beside itself!'[7] On another occasion, when the verse 17:86 ('If We willed, We could take away that We have revealed to thee...') was read during prayers in the mosque, the sheikh gave out such a cry that his disciple Abū ṭ-Ṭayyib Aḥmad ibn Muqātil al-ʿAkkī thought he 'was out of his mind. I saw that his face had turned pale, and he shuddered and said, "Such words are addressed to friends." He repeated that many times.'[8]

The Quran has enraptured, delighted, dismayed and excited the Sufis more than any other text. The devout person who sinks to the ground 'struck' by the Quran is a frequent motif in their writings, and the image to them is a model of extinction. And it is well known that the Prophet himself, as virtually no Sufi treatise neglects to mention, broke out in tears, fainted, or had his hair suddenly turn grey on hearing a certain verse of the Quran, and even more severe reactions are ascribed to some of his companions and successors, up to and including sudden death. The form in which the mystical authors refer to the time of Muhammad is much like that of the *iʿjāz* compendia: abbreviated references to the memory shared by the authors and readers; appeals to the *founding events* of Muslim history to establish the legitimacy of the authors' own religious experience. The full text of Hojwīrī's reference to the story of the secret Quran listeners Abū Sufyān, Abū Jahl and al-Akhnas ibn Sharīq, for example, is: 'Its sweetness attained such a degree that the unbelieving Quraysh secretly went to the Prophet's house at night and listened to him saying his ritual prayer, and were amazed at his recitation.'[9] His readers know immediately what he means; they see the scene in their mind's eye, just as al-Bāqillānī's readers do when he mentions ʿUmar's conversion in a single sentence.[10] What is characteristic of treatises on the Sufis' listening is that Hojwīrī first recalls the Meccans' reactions to the recitation of the Quran – the well-known exclamations of ʿUmar, an-Naḍr, ʿUtba, Abū Jahl and others – before going on to discuss the mystics who listen to the Quran and the states they attain.[11] Such a reference to the shared salvation history is a method frequently used in Sufi writings to embed the accounts of Quran listeners who become ecstatic, faint or die in a general Islamic context, and to insert the enraptured protagonists in the chain of an unimpeachable tradition. As we remarked in chapter 1,[12] the mystics particularly emphasize the moments of dread, grief, and horror in the early history of the Quran's reception in order to claim the Prophet and his comrades as their own predecessor: they reinterpret the early period of Islam as the early period of Sufism, leading into the ascetic movement of the seventh and eighth centuries, since there are numerous accounts from this time too about enraptured Quran listeners. The tradition tells that Muslim ibn Yasār (d. c. 719), for example, who was even more respected among the devout in Basra than the forefather of mystical asceticism, al-Ḥasan al-Baṣrī (d. 728) himself,[13] did not move during a Quran recitation, even when a pillar collapsed in the mosque during the public *ṣalāt*; he didn't notice a thing even when a fire broke out in his house.[14] It is not surprising that we encounter the topos of conversion once again in this connection, only now with a Sufi element: in his hagiographic collection, ʿAṭṭār (d. 1220) relates how the blacksmith Abū Ḥafṣ al-Ḥaddād (d. 879), before he became one of the leading Sufis of his day, was sitting in his smithy one day when a man walked across the bazaar reciting a verse from the Quran.

> Al-Ḥaddād's heart was so filled by the verse that he lost consciousness, and, thrusting his hand into the forge instead of his tongs, he pulled out the red-hot iron and laid it on his anvil. The apprentices were about to hammer the iron when they saw that he was holding it with his hand.
>
> 'Master, what is the matter?' they cried.
>
> But he told them to strike the iron.
>
> 'But why should we strike it? The iron is already finished!'
>
> Then he cried out, dropped the piece of iron, and left his shop forever. 'I have wanted to give up this work voluntarily for so long, and never did until this happened and freed me from myself. No matter how long I tried to give up this work, I couldn't until the work abandoned me.'
>
> From that day on he undertook a strict asceticism and began to practise solitude and meditation.[15]

In view of such examples, and because the *enthusiasmos* brought on by the Quran was considered the noblest form of 'divine rapture', some devout persons in the ninth and tenth centuries may have been overly demonstrative in their emotion. But Ibn Sīrīn (d. 728 or 729) knew a sure way to tell a sham from a person truly under divine rapture. Asked for his opinion on those who fell down and flailed about on hearing the Quran, he answered, 'Take them up on a high rooftop, set them down on the parapet, and sing them the Quran from beginning to end. If they throw themselves off the roof, their swooning is sincere.'[16] The mystics are even said to have used Quran recitation as a treatment for the sick in the Prophet's day[17] and as a method of narcosis to anaesthetize patients for operations,[18] as mentioned in a poem written by the Persian poet Sanāʾī (d. 1131) about ʿAlī ibn Abī Ṭālib:

> At the Battle of Uḥud, ʿAlī the Prince, the impetuous Lion, received a grievous wound. The head of the arrow remained in his foot, and he knew that it was necessary to take it out, this being the only cure for him. As soon as the surgeon saw it, he said, 'We must cut it open with a knife; to find the arrowhead, a key must be applied to the closed wound.'
>
> But ʿAlī had no strength to bear the insertion of the forceps. 'Let it alone', said he, 'till the time of prayer.' So when he was engaged in prayer his surgeon

gently took out the arrow-head from his limb, bringing it clear away while ʿAlī was unconscious of any suffering or pain.[19]

The Quran even found use as a means of non-violent resistance: when his village was raided, Sheikh ʿAbdullāh ibn Yaḥyā b. Abī l-Haytham aṣ-Ṣaʿbī al-Yamanī (d. 1158 or 1159) was unaffected by the swords of his attackers while he recited the 'verses of protection' (*āyāt al-ḥifẓ*).[20] However, Quran recitation could also have rather alarming medical consequences. Yaḥyā l-Bakkā' (d. 747 or 748), for example, let out a cry while listening to the Quran 'that left him sick for four months, during which he received visitors from all over Basra'.[21] The therapeutic usefulness of the Quran is still more dubious for the protagonists of ath-Thaʿlabī's *Book of Those Slain by the Quran*. The nineteen cases described in it are by no means the only ones recorded in the Sufi literature.[22] The Quran has occasionally been used as a deadly weapon against competitors, as the account of ad-Duqqī (d. c. 977) suggests:

> Once I saw two sheikhs. One of them was named Jabala and the other Zurayq, and both of them had students and novices. One day Zurayq and his followers visited Jabala. One of Zurayq's followers recited from the Quran. One of Jabala's disciples let out a cry and died. The next morning, Jabala said to Zurayq, 'Where is your student who recited yesterday?' Zurayq called him and said, 'Recite!' He recited something, and then Jabala let out a cry, and the reciter died on the spot. Jabala said, 'One for one. He who started is the more sinister.'[23]

According to the explanation of this story, Jabala's student died because his heart was more pure and more illuminated than that of the reciter, so that when he listened the text penetrated him more deeply.[24] Al-Ġazālī also narrates an episode that demonstrates how dangerous Quran recitation can be:

> A man was performing ritual purification in the Euphrates when another man came walking along the riverbank reciting the Quran verse, 'Now keep yourselves apart, you sinners, upon this day!'[25] The first man immediately became so upset that he drowned.[26]

Listening to the Quran appears as the most dignified form of suicide in the story of the young man who greets the traditionist Aḥmad ibn Abī l-Ḥawārī (d. 844 or 845) with the following words: 'O Aḥmad, you have come just in time, for I must hear a Quran verse to give up the ghost.'[27] Jinn too have been slain by the Quran, as al-Ġazālī and as-Sarrāj report:

> The tale is told of a Sufi who said, 'One night as I recited the verse "Every soul shall taste of death",[28] and began to repeat it over and over, suddenly

an invisible speaker called to me, "How often are you going to repeat that verse? You have already killed four jinn who hadn't even raised their heads to heaven since their creation!" '[29]

Hojwīrī recounts a similar story, except that in this case the creatures slain by the Quran recitation are fairies (*parī*):

> A sheikh said, 'When I was reciting the words of God the Exalted, "And fear a day wherein you shall be returned to God",[30] a voice cried, "Sing more softly! Four fairies are already dead of the terror (*heybat*) of that verse." '[31]

Not only did listeners die of excitation, but apparently even the dead could not help reciting the Quran. Sheikh Rūzbehān Baqlī (d. 1209) of Shiraz, renowned as the man who preserved the writings of al-Ḥallāj, is said to have participated regularly from beyond the grave in a recitation duel with his disciple.[32] The power of Quran recitation sometimes had the opposite effect: instead of carrying on singing after death, some persons completely renounced recitation in life. An anonymous dervish quoted by Hojwīrī (d. 1071) confessed that, out of fear of the consequences, he had neither recited nor listened to the Quran, except the passages necessary for ritual prayer, for ten years.[33] Others could not even recite that much: as soon as they pronounced the word *Allāhu* that begins the call to prayer, they became so agitated that they could not say the next word, *akbar*.[34] Abū l-ʿAbbās ibn ʿAṭāʾ (d. 922), one of the outstanding personalities of mysticism in Baghdad, reported that he had used to recite the whole Quran twice a day and twice every night, but for fourteen years he got only as far as the eighth surah. Hojwīrī himself relates how he once visited Sheikh Abū l-ʿAbbās Shaqānī and heard him recite the verse 'God has struck a similitude: a servant possessed by his master, having no power over anything.'[35]

> In reciting, he wept and wailed so that I thought he was dying.
>
> 'O Sheikh, what is the state you are in?' I cried.
>
> 'After eleven years I have reached this passage in my Quran recitation, but I simply can't get any further.'[36]

Samāʿ and Quran Recitation

The reactions of the Sufi Quran listeners are spectacular and at the same time disturbing; they are unique in the Muslim literature, and perhaps in all religious literature. Naturally the theologians and linguists have thought more about the linguistic perfection of the Quran; they have striven with admirable diligence and sometimes with astonishing poetic sensitivity to analyse it, to explain it, to demonstrate it in their *iʿjāz* compendia; and there can be no doubt that the legal scholars and preachers, and guardians of the faith generally, have proclaimed these aesthetic qualities an incontrovertible miracle and expressed their awe and praise at every opportunity (although they were often sceptical as to whether the miracle could be explained rationally); and it is true that the chroniclers of the old and new schools, the 'Muslims' and the 'Orientalists' among them, have pointed to the delights that skilled Quran reciters evoke throughout the Arab world; but the subjective experience of the listener, the experience of an acoustic quality that is felt to be metaphysical, has nowhere been the focus of such attention, nowhere is the power of the Quran described as vibrantly, as in the mystical literature of Islam. The Sufis, in their search for the experience of God, knowing that truth is real only where words are left behind, only as something sensually experienced and never merely as something theoretically known – the Sufis have always been more sensitive than others to the transcendent beauty of the quranic recitation. A tenth-century handbook of mysticism says about the Sufi practice of listening (*samāʿ*):

> The Sufis are specially honoured with it. After they renounced this transient world, chose poverty, sacrificed their lifeblood to God and laboured in voluntary devotions after fulfilling their duties, God opened the eyes of their hearts so that they can see with pure aspiration and clear understanding and hear with the knowledge that God foreordained for them. They hear with real hearing, and they receive intimations of supernatural facts and follow the best of the Quran: the reality that has settled in their hearts beforehand, consisting in realities of love, of longings, of the precious manner of worship and wonderful gifts that God has laid inmost in them, and the right guidance that God has assured to those who hear.[37]

It has often been stressed that many Arabs and other Oriental peoples are particularly sensitive to sounds in general, whether musical or linguistic. It is no coincidence that for a long time music and tones were commonly applied, and studied by scientists, as a means of medical therapy in the Islamic world. We may recall the many incidents from *The Thousand and One Nights* in which the heroes and heroines fainted because the song of a female voice or the sound of a lute reached their ears: there is doubtless a kernel of truth behind the fiction.[38] In Sufism, this fine sensitivity for everything acoustic is raised to a power that hardly seems comprehensible today. If the legends sometimes seem to embellish devout Sufis' sensitivity in all too vivid colours, so that their usefulness as historic testimony is limited to the history of a mentality,[39] there is in principle, as Annemarie Schimmel explains, 'no reason to doubt…that a moving recitation of a line from the scripture or a worldly verse could cause people to faint, even to die from excitement.'[40] A quotation from a text, a verse, a tone from a musical instrument, even the call to prayer, the cry of the water-bearer or the pickle vendor in the marketplace, the bleating of a sheep or the rushing of the wind is said to have been enough in some cases to make a mystic ecstatic or unconscious. If the singing is especially masterful, it can be deadly.

Because music and singing are considered an echo of the primeval, divine sound, the Sufis attribute to them literally magical properties. Simply hearing a beautiful tune makes dead-tired camels feisty, crying children quiet and healthy people frantic, and cures sufferers of madness and melancholy.[41] The very incongruity of the anecdotes that have been handed down about such effects provides a realistic impression of the power that the Sufis ascribe to music. For example, Abū Bakr Muḥammad ibn Dāwud ad-Dīnawarī, better known as ad-Duqqī, recounts how he once encountered a Bedouin tribe travelling in the steppes and was invited into the tent of a member of the tribe:

> In the tent I saw a bound black slave, and in front of the living area I saw dead camels. I saw an emaciated camel wasting away as if it was about to die. The bound slave said to me: 'You are my master's guest tonight, and you are dear to him. Intercede for me and ask him to take these shackles from me! He will not refuse you.' When food was put before me, I refused to eat. That grieved my host sorely. When he asked what was the matter, I answered, 'I will only eat when you have forgiven this slave his offence and taken off his shackles.' 'O thou!' he replied, 'that slave has made me poor and ruined all my property, and brought harm to me and my family.' I asked him what he had done. He replied, 'This slave has a beautiful voice. These camels were my livelihood, but he saddled them with heavy loads and drove them with his singing so that they walked three days' journey in one night, so sweet was his singing as he drove them. When they arrived here and we unpacked their burdens, they all died except this one camel. But you are my guest. In honour and in consideration of you I will forgive him.' Then he released the slave from his shackles and we ate our meal. But in the morning I wanted to hear the singer's voice. My host ordered the slave to sing on a camel that pulled the water out of a well that was there. The slave went and began to drive the camel and to sing. But when he raised his voice the camel went wild and broke its tether. I fell down on my face. I believe I have never heard a more beautiful voice than his. His owner screamed, saying, 'Man, what do you want from me? You have ruined my camel. Go away from me!'[42]

In the literature of Islamic mysticism, the place of anecdotes such as this one about the power of music, poetry and the Quran is usually in treatises and chapters on *samā'*, the practice of 'listening'.[43] The Sufis use this term to denote all practices using forms of artistic expression, or the experience of aesthetic phenomena in general, to attain a condition of ecstasy and, if possible, to achieve their own annihilation (*fanā'*) or *unio mystica*. In such a state, the most venerable sheikhs look like 'a flock of sheep when the wolves have invaded them'.[44] *Samā'* could include listening to instrumental music, singing, poetry or the Quran, and also dance and – in a later era – the sight of comely youths or beautiful sights in general. The terms and concepts of hearing and seeing often overlap. Listening, *samā'*, can be understood as an inner vision, or, conversely, vision can be conceived as an acoustic process. Al-Makkī (d. 996), for example, writes:

> Fitting recitation (of the Quran) is his who is truly faithful. For when God gives him the reality of faith, he gives him, equal to it in and like in measure and origin, a reality of vision, so that his recitation is founded on his vision.[45]

Although the term *samā'* can be used in reference to all kinds of aesthetic experiences, in the treatises of the classical Sufi theoreticians such as as-Sarrāj (d. 998), Hojwīrī, al-Qushayrī (d. 1074), al-Ġazālī, Abū Ḥafs 'Umar as-Suhrawardī and Abū l-Mafākhir Bākharzī (d. 1335 or 1336), it usually means specifically listening, whether to poetry, the Quran or other musical forms – musical because all authors conceive both Quran and poetry recitation as melodic and describe them using a terminology that originates in the field of music, regardless of whether they consider it permissible to recite the Quran to secular melodies or instrumentation, as *qirā'a bi-l-alḥān* or *qawwālūn* singing. Simply reading or speaking the Quran is practically never mentioned.

The mystics' practices, whose popular forms were part of the folk culture, were notoriously suspect to members of the orthodoxy. The founders of the four schools of legal thought in particular are infamous among mystics for their rejection of poetry, dance, music and excessively musical Quran recitation. 'Abū Ḥanīfa has not taught love, / Shāfi'ī has no traditions about it', was Sanā'ī's answer to such criticism from the bookish scholars,[46] and 'Umar as-Suhrawardī remarked drily:

> Those who are naturally dull and unfeeling also reject listening. To them is said: An impotent man knows not the bliss of sexual intercourse, and a blind man cannot enjoy splendid beauty, and he who has not suffered misfortune does not say, 'We belong to God, and to Him we shall return.'[47]

In their defence, the Sufis cited the innate ability of all living things to enjoy beautiful sounds,[48] saying, 'The beautiful voice is a refreshment from God for a heart that dwells in the love of God.'[49] In addition to rational arguments, the mystics invoked dozens of Quran verses and hadiths as evidence that singing and dancing were permissible. All the Quran verses that mention listening were interpreted as sanctioning *samā'*, and the Prophet himself was portrayed as an enthusiastic music and poetry listener.[50] The Sufis' opponents sharply contested the Quran interpretations and the authenticity of the hadiths, however. But what roused them still more was the fact that some Muslims apparently indulged in the pleasures of their uninhibited senses – often under the influence of drugs – as part of *samā'*, and hence under the pretext of spirituality. The orthodoxy could not endorse such actions, especially since some sheikhs engaged in erotic, and primarily homoerotic, versions of the contemplation of beauty. More moderate mystics such as 'Umar as-Suhrawardī and al-Ġazālī repudiated such practices as distortions of *samā'* and symptoms of decadence. Not everyone 'who practises listening and throws up their arms and whirls belongs to the community of the initiates (*ahl-e asrār*)', writes Shamshoddīn Lāhījī (d. 1506),[51] and Bākharzī rails that in his day listening had declined 'to a name without meaning and a form without a soul and a ritual without authenticity'; no sooner had it evolved from a strictly guarded ritual into a public spectacle than it was corrupted.[52] Such complaints must not obscure the fact that *samā'* has remained down to the present a form of religious experience that is affirmed in principle by even the strictest mystics and widespread among the people. Disagreement within Sufism is over specific forms of *samā'*. Many non-Sufi legal scholars reject it altogether, however, and Iran as an Islamist-oriented state has seen attacks against Sufis and rigid suppression of their meetings.

The word *samā'* can also refer to the set ritual of the mystics in the *khāneqāh*s and *samā'khāne*s, the dervishes' cloisters, meeting-places and auditoriums, which have been in existence since the ninth century, or to the mystic's listening in general, regardless of the place and the sounds concerned. As for the Quran, it is recited primarily at the beginning and end of the regular *samā'* sessions, as the Prophet is said to have recommended to ad-Duqqī (d. 911 or 912) in a dream,[53] not as part of the actual practices of music and dance that induce a state of trance in the participants.[54] In any case, practically none of the traditions about Sufis becoming enraptured while listening to the Quran is set in such a ritual meeting. Yet nowhere is a distinction drawn between the ecstasy induced in a *samā'* session and that attained by the *maqāri'*, the Quran reader, for example, on other occasions. Those Sufis are held in the highest respect who can be sent into the trance of absolute love of God, anywhere and at any time, by melodious sounds or even by chance tones, and who in certain cases remain enraptured for weeks, months or even years. Bākharzī writes that, when the mystic has attained the highest stage of the path, his heart

> is fixed on that listening in which the word of God is heard in every sound he hears. His listening does not stop at human harmonies and melodies, in keeping with the declaration of Abū 'Uthmān Maġribī: 'Whoever claims to practise listening but does not listen to the twittering of the birds, the creaking of the door or the throbbing of his breathing – know that his claim is a

fiction and a lie.' The true listener reaches a point where his listening takes place inside him, and he does not need to hear anything outside.[55]

The testimony about the reception of the Quran among Sufis presented at the beginning of this chapter and in the sections that follow must be viewed both in the light of the mystics' *samāʿ* practice and in the more general context of the highly developed sensitivity to music – and indeed all sounds in their cultural milieu. What we observed in regard to the traditions from the Prophet's time is equally applicable here: the reactions to the sound of the Quran should not be analysed in isolation from the equally spectacular reactions to other texts and tones. Studied in the context of other auditory experiences, they do not seem nearly as incredible, or as implausible, as they may at first appear to an observer of today. Like all miracles, these wonders are related to the reality in which we find them: they are an escalation of the ordinary, an extrapolation along the same lines. This does not make miracles explicable, but it does make them understandable. When we consider the discourse in which these accounts arise, what is astonishing is not the quality of the responses to a text but, rather, the intensity and quantity of the evidence of those responses: even al-Ġazālī in his day was moved to remark on the multitude of stories about mystics – whom he called 'possessors of hearts' (*arbāb al-qulūb*) – who fell into raptures (*wajd*) on listening to the Quran, and, over a century earlier, Abū Naṣr as-Sarrāj, in his *Kitāb alluma*ʿ, one of the earliest textbooks of Sufism, could only demur: if he were to mention those among the Prophet's contemporaries and their successors and those who came after down to our time who listened to the Quran and 'swooned and wept, who died, who lost a limb or fell unconscious – then the book would be too long and would no longer be a concise outline'.[56]

Although the great number of accounts about Sufi Quran listeners attests that as-Sarrāj's claim is not exaggerated, I will attempt in the following section to define their experience more exactly and to determine whether it is an aesthetic one. This seems to be not only due and necessary for the purposes of the present book but also desirable with regard to broader themes in view of the existing research: the reception of the Quran in Islamic mysticism is mentioned only marginally in the Western literature, if at all. The two Leiden manuscripts of ath-Thaʿlabī's text cited at the beginning of this chapter offer a starting point for this investigation. As far as I can see, it is the only text of Islamic mysticism that is devoted exclusively to the reactions of Quran listeners. Since the author abstains almost completely from commentary on the stories he relates, however, and displays all the concision, brevity and formulaic style that are typical of this genre of Muslim literature,[57] we must refer to the appropriate works of Sufi masters such as al-Ġazālī, Hojwīrī, and Khʷāge ʿAbdullāh Anṣārī (d. 1089), which discuss in detail the states induced by listening, in order to understand the ideological and psychological background of the reports.[58] Richard Gramlich's German translations, with their numerous cross-references and sources, are vitally helpful in this endeavour, as is a work published a number of years ago by Najīb Māyel Harawī in Teheran. It contains, in addition to a knowledgeable introduction, the most important *samā'* treatises and *samā'* chapters from broader works that have been written in or translated into Persian, including some texts that are almost unknown and some that had never been printed before.[59]

The Listeners Slain by the Quran

Abū Isḥāq Aḥmad ibn Muḥammad ath-Tha'labī is not remembered as a mystic in the history of Muslim scholarship. He is renowned as a Shafi'i Quran commentator and a reliable traditionist, and most of all as the author of an edifying little book of lives of the prophets. But the nineteen Quran listeners he presents (alongside jinn and the pre-Islamic sage Luqmān) are mainly devout Muslims of the eighth and ninth centuries, almost all of whom have backgrounds in early Islamic asceticism, which was already mystically oriented. Their actions and their vocabulary identify them as Sufis or predecessors of the Sufis, or, in the case of the Prophet's contemporaries among them, as Muslims to whom particularly ascetic attitudes and abilities can be ascribed. The action is usually set in Basra, Kufa or Nishapur: these were the centres of the ascetic movement in early Islam, and the first two were also known for the mastery of their Quran reciters.

Ath-Tha'labī is not concerned in his text with praising the beauty or the grandeur of God's word. He takes the Quran's majesty and its magical power over its listeners as self-evident and not requiring any particular explanation. Unlike numerous authors of the *i'jāz* literature, and unlike the mystic Hojwīrī,[60] he is not interested in setting forth the irresistible power of the Quran as an argument for its miraculous nature, although the narratives he presents would be ideally suited for that purpose. His objective is, rather, to present the people slain by the Quran as models of piety for every Muslim. Ath-Tha'labī leaves no doubt that his intentions are God-fearing and have absolutely nothing to do with reception aesthetics:

> I have written this book in the hope that God may have mercy on us if we honour their memory and that he may let the power of his blessing (*baraka*) reach us. For, as the hadith says, 'Compassion comes down with the remembrance of the righteous.'[61]

God has chosen those slain by the Quran, ath-Tha'labī writes, distinguished them with His blessing and made them glad with His light. By killing them, He granted them the bounty of the most glorious blood testimony (*ash-shahāda al-'uẓmā*), so that they are now with their Lord, rewarded and surrounded by radiant light; they are 'the most admirable martyrs and the most honourable scholars who have attained the (mystical) stations (*manāzil*) and the most resplendent degrees (*marātib*)'.[62] In the accounts themselves, ath-Tha'labī also mentions, and certainly not without educational aims, that some of the wise men appeared to some witness after death and proclaimed the bliss that God gave them in the afterlife. For example, in the episode recounted at the beginning of this chapter, Manṣūr ibn 'Ammār ad-Dandānqānī saw the young man who had died as a result of his recitation one night in a dream, seated on a throne with a crown on his head.

> 'What has God done with you?' Manṣūr asked him.
> 'He gave me the reward of the fighters of Badr, and more.'
> 'Why?'
> 'Because they died by the swords of the unbelievers, but I was slain by the sword of the all-forgiving King.'

Several lines later, ath-Tha'eabī himself exhorts his reader: 'Follow them therefore, you who study our book, in the performance of good deeds, and love them with your heart and your tongue, and you will be with them, if God on high wills.'[63]

Such devout teaching is worlds apart from the aesthetic fascination that marks al-Jurjānī's study of the Quran's miraculous qualities. The introduction announces edifying literature. And if we examine the occurrences that ath-Tha'labī recounts, all poetry seems to have vanished: the devout die because they fear hellfire, not because they experience the Quran as beautiful. It is nearly always verses about hellfire, threats or impending trials that cause the tremors in the listeners' hearts: verses that announce the Day of Judgement, warn against hellfire, or describe its torments.

> Manṣūr ibn 'Ammār said: I often wandered at night through the streets of Kufa, and once, late at night, I heard a reciter speaking. He wept as he recited the Quran. I stopped by the door of his house and listened. Finally I called through the cracks of the door: 'Then fear the Fire, whose fuel is men and stones, prepared for unbelievers.'[64] And he fell down dead.[65]

The story of Zurāra al-Ḥarashī of Basra, who recited the Quran in prayer, is equally terse: 'When he came to the verse "For when the trump is sounded",[66] he fell down dead'.[67] The same thing happened to a Quran listener who is introduced only as the brother of the traditionist and ascetic Muḥammad ibn al-Munkadir (d. 748), who recited the verse 'God will show them something they had not reckoned with':[68] 'Then he cried, "O woe," and continued crying it until he finally died, God have mercy on him.'[69] And, in the eighth or ninth century, a certain Asad ibn Ṣulhab was sleeping on the bank of the Euphrates in Kufa, woke with a start when he unexpectedly heard a reciter speak the verse 'But the evildoers dwell forever in the chastisement of Gehenna'[70] and reeled. 'When the reciter then said, "That is not abated for them and therein they are sore confounded",[71] he fell in the water and died, God have mercy on him.'[72]

It would be presumptuous to draw conclusions about the subjective experience of the recipients from these altogether minimalist accounts, reduced to the bare essentials. But this much is plain: death is caused not by an excess of bliss, but by verses whose content is perceived as threatening. There are no heart attacks due to excessive pleasure, no aesthetic overload, but panic in the face of the impending Judgement. Ath-Tha'labī himself explicitly names the quite 'unpoetic' cause of death in his introduction: God 'made them die from the fear of Him'. This interpretation is reinforced by some of his more detailed accounts. The eighteenth story, for example, is about a devout young man highly esteemed by Caliph 'Umar who once met a woman after leaving evening prayers – and not only that, but the woman – o terrible stroke of fate – 'exhibited' herself to the devout young man, in ath-Tha'labī's restrained words. Enamoured, the young man followed her to her door. When she disappeared into her house, he was left in a daze, until he suddenly recalled the words of the Lord: 'The godfearing, when a visitation of Satan troubles them, remember, and then see clearly.'[73] Reciting it, he fell down unconscious. The woman noticed it and called her maid, and together they carried the young man back to his parents' house, where they laid him in front of the door. His father found him there, carried him inside, and treated him until he came to his senses. His father asked him what happened, and after some urging the young man told him, and recited the verse that had crossed his mind as he stood outside the woman's house. But before reaching the end of the verse, 'he sighed loudly and gave up the ghost'.

Ath-Tha'labī does not explain the cause of the young man's death – whether it was shock at the unaccustomed sight of the woman, fright at his own transgression, or the content of the Quran verse about the godfearing who remember in the face of Satan's temptation and see. Perhaps what he saw was not as comforting as the translation of the Quran verse suggests; perhaps it was something threatening: the hellfire prepared for him, the sinner. Especially in the context of the other stories, and the detachment from the world that their protagonists manifest, his death clearly cannot be imagined as a gentle passing away, intoxicated by blissful sounds and at peace with himself and the world, but rather as a consequence of the fear (*khawf*) that so dominated the lives of the early Islamic ascetics. Traces of the ascetic movement are found well into classical mysticism, and it has a great fascination for cultural historians, both because of the unsurpassed radicalism of its attitudes and life projects and because it united extravagant behaviours and notions that seem rather bizarre to us with a perception of the world that seems strangely modern, familiar to readers of Büchner and Beckett, as, for example, when the bleakness and transience of human existence are remarked upon with the utmost severity (ash-Shiblī calls this world 'a privy to be filled up'),[74] or when human suffering under God's aloofness is expressed in sometimes gruff, sometimes pathetic laments. Al-Ġazālī summarizes this view in the observation that He is there, but He is far away; we fear Him because we 'know Him and His qualities and know that, if He were to let all humanity perish, it would not bother Him and no one would stop Him.'[75] Ibn Qayyim al-Jawzīya quotes a man who takes his quarrel with God (*at-taẓallum ʿalā r-rabb*) to extremes as saying, 'Nothing is more destructive to creatures than the Creator',[76] and al-Qushayrī remarks:

> It is said that after the well-known calamity had befallen Iblīs, Gabriel and Michael wept for a long time. Then God imparted to them the question: Why do you weep so much? They said, Lord, we do not feel safe from Your malice (*makr*). Then God spoke, That is as it should be! You should not feel safe from My malice.[77]

The verse epics of ʿAṭṭār in particular include numerous characters and historic figures from the spectrum of early Islamic asceticism, and the poet himself seems not unmoved by their gloomy view of human existence. He compares God with a puppeteer, for example, who plays with his creatures and delights in their complaints, and with a potter 'who first makes pots with great skill and then smashes them Himself'.[78] Danton too asks in Büchner's play: 'But we're the poor musicians and our bodies the instruments. Do we wring these awful yowlings from them only to have them rise higher and higher and fade away into a voluptuous sigh in the ears of heaven?'[79] The 'damned argument: something cannot become nothing, there's the misery!'[80] stated in *Danton's Death* has a forerunner in the insight of Ibn ash-Shibl (d. 1081): 'The torment for us is that we've been called into existence!'[81] Even death offers little hope: 'In this ditch, in this prison (the grave) we're far more helpless than you', ʿAṭṭār has a sheikh say from the grave to his novice in a dream.[82] Al-Fuḍayl ibn ʿIyāḍ says, in view of misery on every hand, 'I envy neither a Prophet sent by God nor an angel close to God nor a devout servant of God; I envy only those who were never created.'[83] Another time, he is supposed to have called out weeping to a group of traditionists: 'You there, this is no time for retelling hadiths! This is a time for weeping and pleading and humbling yourselves and begging as if you were drowning. This is the time to hold your tongue, conceal your place, strive to heal your heart, take what you know and leave what you know not.'[84] When al-Ḥasan al-Baṣrī was asked how he was, he smiled and said,

> 'You ask me about my condition? What would you say about people who go to sea in a ship but are then shipwrecked at sea, so that each of them is left clinging to a plank? What is their condition?' The man answered, 'They are in a dire state.' Al-Ḥasan said, 'My condition is worse than theirs.'[85]

A companion describes his condition:

> God have mercy on Abū Saʿīd: by God, when he faced you he looked as if he were coming from a relative's burial, and when he turned his back he looked as if hellfire dangled over his head, and when he sat down he looked like a prisoner going to be beheaded, and in the morning he looked as if he had returned from beyond the tomb, and in the evening he looked like a sick man worn out by his illness.[86]

The ascetic's fear, the feeling that 'hellfire was made just for him',[87] can take on grotesque forms. A tradition recounts that Sarī as-Saqaṭī (d. 865 or later) looked at his nose several times a day because he was afraid his face might have turned black.[88] Ibrāhīm ibn Adham (d. 778), after ritual prayers, held 'his hands in front of his face out of fear that God could bash him over the head with his prayers',[89] and ʿAbdullāh ibn al-Mubārak walked up to his companions one day and said, 'I acted brazenly towards God yesterday: I asked Him for Paradise.'[90] The advice of Ḥātim al-Aṣamm (d. 851 or 852) expresses the radical scepticism of the ascetics in a nutshell:

> Don't let a good place fool you! No place is better than Paradise, and yet Adam's well-known perdition befell him there. Do not be fooled by many acts of worship! For what befell Satan happened after he had served God a long time. Do not be fooled by great knowledge! For Balʿam knew well the greatest name of God, yet look at what happened to him. Do not be fooled by the fact that you see the devout! For none has ranked higher with God than the chosen one, yet it did not help his relatives and enemies that they encountered him.[91]

The ascetics' and early mystics' extremely negative view of the world, their extreme detachment from the world and the unadulterated distrust with which they regarded every glimmer of hope, and sometimes even God himself, whom they felt to be all-punishing, all-avenging and all-cunning, one Who torments His creatures 'with destruction after having previously built them up'[92] or, as al-Ḥallāj says, Who bound his loving Satan and threw him into the sea, 'saying: / Be careful that the water does not wet you',[93] – their pessimism has been wisely and thoroughly discussed by other authors, including Tor Andrae,[94] Margaret Smith,[95] Louis Massignon,[96] Annemarie Schimmel,[97] Richard Gramlich[98] and of course Hellmut Ritter,[99] so that there is no need to describe them here. To understand ath-Thaʿlabī's treatise, however, it is essential to know that the persons whose stories he presents belonged to this circle, or at least had attributes that are characteristic of this circle. This is especially evident in the episode of the famous grammarian Abū Saʿīd ʿAbdulmalik al-Aṣmaʿī's encounter with a Bedouin, who is introduced as a 'coarse fellow, sitting barefoot on a camel, girded with a sword and with a bow in his hand'.[100]

'Where are you coming from?' the Bedouin asks him.

'From a place where people recite the word of the All-Merciful', al-Aṣmaʿī replies.

'Does the All-Merciful have a word that people recite?'

'Yes.'

'Recite some of it to me.'

'First dismount from your camel', al-Aṣmaʿī requests. After the Bedouin has dismounted, the grammarian recites the 51st surah. When he comes to the 22nd verse, 'And in heaven is your provision (*rizq*), and that which you are promised', the Bedouin interrupts him and asks if that is the word of the All-Merciful. Al-Aṣmaʿī answers in the affirmative, adding that God has sent it down through his messenger Muhammad. The Bedouin says,

> 'That is enough for me.' Then he went to his camel, slaughtered it and cut it in pieces, hide and all. 'You do the distributing', he said.
>
> So we distributed the meat to everyone who came along. Then he took his sword and his bow, broke them and buried them in the sand. Then he turned around and fled in the direction of the desert, saying, 'And in heaven is your provision and that which you are promised.'

This story touches on a number of important characteristics of the ascetic lifestyle, including the renunciation of worldly goods (*zuhd*), which is a condition for the state of perfect trust in God (*tawakkul*) to which the ascetic aspires. The converted Bedouin renounces his possessions and buries the weapons that under normal circumstances would assure his survival, before fleeing into the desert, alone with no provisions and with no other preparations. The underlying view of the ascetics is that God is ultimately the only one Who acts, and the truly devout believer must surrender completely to His will. Money and property are therefore sinful.[101] The crucial Quran verse about *rizq* is understood in its literal sense and seen as proof that only God provides one's livelihood, and all action by the seeker to secure his life or sustenance is a presumption upon God's omnipotence.[102] Completely occupied with praying, honouring God, lamenting and weeping (many of their masters were known as *bakkāʾūn*, 'those who constantly weep'),[103] these men and women only slept, drank and ate the bare minimum, trusting in God to grant their survival – if such was His will. Many a Sufi was said to have exchanged his wool garment for an elegant robe so that his fellows would not be provoked to charity and so interfere in God's providence. In extreme cases, their passiveness went as far as to include refusing medical treatment or even clean water, dissembling an illness, and tarrying in the area of an epidemic.[104] A dervish who fell in the Tigris was asked whether he wanted to be rescued.

> 'No!' he cried.
>
> Then did he want to die?
>
> 'No! What have I to do with wanting?'[105]

If Sufism can be defined as a 'hatred of this world and a love of listening', as Abū l-Ḥusayn an-Nūrī (d. 907) says,[106] then ath-Tha'labī's protagonists are true Sufis. They are constantly in fear and grief, in keeping with the ascetic ideal. The more moderate among them spend the night praying and reciting the Quran instead of sleeping,[107] are constantly ashamed of their wrongdoings,[108] lead a life of poverty,[109] eat little,[110] care little for the things of this world,[111] warn against God's wrath and the desires of the instinctive soul,[112] and are itinerant, 'dressed in a long outer garment of wool, a staff in their hands'.[113] Others apparently advocate more extreme attitudes: at least, they are described as emaciated figures, as 'a slight young man exhausted by praying'[114] or as someone who looks like 'an old worn-out water skin, but with his face full of light'.[115] The Bedouin from the story quoted above hardly seems more at ease after his conversion: when by chance al-Aṣma'ī meets him later in Mecca, the Bedouin can call to him only in a 'thin voice' and is, according to the grammarian's words, 'no more than skin and bones, and deathly pale'. When at his request al-Aṣma'ī once more recited the beginning of the 51st surah up to the verse about *rizq* and the next verse after it, the Bedouin departed this world. Like the Bedouin in this story, many ascetics of that time were forever wandering: they went from place to place, restless, sad, solemn, naked or dressed only with a cloth. Ḏū n-Nūn describes their state of mind in the following words:

> They are people driven away from their homes by worry and anxiety. Sorrow is rooted deep in their souls. Their anxious thoughts seek God and their hearts fly with longing to meet. Fear lays them low in the bed of sickness, and distress butchers them with the knife of punishment. Their plentiful weeping makes their heart's blood burst from them, and their spirits perish out of bitter sorrow for their Friend's sake. Their food is dry herbs and their drink is pure water. They rejoice in the words of the Merciful One and bewail their sins before Him with sorrowful voices like doves. They seek refuge in deserts and mountain gorges. They keep watch over the evening star, as it goes to its rest. With struggle and effort they endure the hours of the night watch. To flee from their fellow men is the innermost desire of their hearts.[116]

Ath-Tha'labī's text is a document of great significance for the study of the ascetic movement in early Islam and is well worth reading as an introduction to their intellectual world. Although the topic of the present book does not encompass this issue, it is indispensable to observe that the attitude towards life underlying these stories is grounded in the extraordinary metaphysical fear and grief of the early Islamic ascetics, and their spiritual movement is the frame of reference in which the stories have their reality. The devout Muslims of whom ath-Tha'labī tells have internalized what al-Ġazālī recommends: they do not dare to relate 'the verses of promise and praise that are addressed to the righteous' to themselves; on the contrary, they feel God threatens them personally in the 'verses of loathing and rejection of those who have gone astray'.[117]

In this light we can understand ath-Thaʿlabī's report that Sheikh al-Miswar (d. 683) was 'unable, because of his great fear, to listen to the Quran':

> When, as sometimes happened, someone recited a word or a verse of the Quran to him, he uttered a shrill cry and was out of his senses for days afterwards. Finally a man from the tribe Khathʿam caused his death. The man recited to him: 'On the day that We shall muster the godfearing to the All-merciful with pomp and drive the evildoers into Gehenna herding'.[118]
>
> 'I am one of the evildoers and not the godfearing!' al-Miswar cried. 'Quran reader, recite it to me again!'
>
> The man recited it again. Then he sighed loudly and departed this world.[119]

Ath-Thaʿlabī abstains from any explanation of the subjective experience that befalls the fearful listeners. To understand it, we must refer to the theoretical treatises of mysticism, which discuss in depth the psychological processes that take place during listening and – usually in a separate chapter – investigate the causes, consequences and background of *khawf* ('fear') as one of the mystic states or stations. The systematic theoretician of Sufism, Khʷāje ʿAbdullāh Anṣārī, defines *khawf* as the 'loss of carefree sureness due to knowledge of the message (*khabar*)',[120] and al-Ġazālī explains it as 'the heart's suffering and burning as a result of the anticipation of future adversity'.[121] It is al-Ġazālī too who offers what may be the most precise description of the condition and its symptoms:

> When the knowledge is complete, it creates the state of fear and the burning of the heart. The effect of the inflammation then passes from the heart to the body, the limbs and the characteristics. In the body it appears in the form of emaciation, jaundice, fainting, wailing and weeping, and sometimes the gall bladder bursts, which results in death. Or the condition rises to the brain and shatters the mind. Or it becomes overwhelming and causes hopelessness and desperation.... In the character [the effect of the fear manifests itself] by suppressing the instinctive desires and clouding the sensations of pleasure so that the sins that a person would like to have become odious, as honey becomes odious to one who desires it the moment he learns that there is poison in it. Then the instinctive desires are burnt by the fear and the limbs become well mannered, and the heart is filled with ordinariness, humility, littleness and submission, and pride, hate and envy leave it; it is filled with care because the person is afraid and sees the peril of his end. He devotes himself to nothing else, and all his activity is keeping his eyes on God, calling himself

> to account, struggling spiritually, stinting with his breaths and glances and holding the soul responsible for incidents, steps and words. He is like one who has been caught in the claws of a ravenous beast and does not know whether it will let him go, so that he escapes, or whether it will devour him, so that he dies. His outside and inside are completely filled with what he fears, so that there is no room left for anything else. That is the condition of those whom the fear has conquered and overpowered, and that was the condition of several of the Prophet's comrades and successors.[122]

The Terror of God

The state of fear that is present in ath-Thaʿlabī's accounts and described by al-Ġazālī has an established place in the theory and religious practice of Sufism, but it is not specific to the sphere of Islamic faith. Non-Muslims too, and certainly non-Sufis, have known and experienced that the faithful can be overwhelmed in the moment of religious excitement not only by feelings of gratitude, confidence, serenity or love but also by unforeseen, extraordinary grief, excessive dread and unbearable fear. This is nothing other than the *mysterium tremendum* that Rudolf Otto has aptly described as a universal experience of faith, the feeling of horrible mystery, 'a terror fraught with an inward shuddering such as not even the most menacing and overpowering created thing can instil'.[123] This experience is found in the Quran;[124] the Old Testament is rich in expressions for it.[125] 'Like a gentle tide', Otto writes, it can pervade one's mind 'with a tranquil mood of deepest worship',[126] a long-lasting, gentle inclination of the soul, yet sometimes 'almost unobserved..., a mere fleeting shadow passing across his mood'.[127] It can be purified to a fine state and manifest itself, transfigured, as humble trembling and silence. But the *mysterium tremendum* can also be so strong that it 'seems to penetrate to the very marrow, making the man's hair bristle and his limbs quake';[128] it can

> burst in sudden eruption up from the depths of the soul with spasms and convulsions, or lead to the strangest excitements, to intoxicated frenzy, to transport, and to ecstasy. It has its wild and demonic forms and can sink to an almost grisly horror and shuddering. It has its crude, barbaric antecedents and early manifestations...[129]

Otto attributes the moment of *tremendum*, shuddering fear, to what he calls 'creature-feeling': 'It is the emotion of a creature, submerged and overwhelmed by its own nothingness in contrast to that which is supreme above all creatures.'[130] In the face of the divine or the numinous, man becomes conscious of his own createdness, nothingness and complete dependence.

The kind of feeling that Otto puts into words, with a good deal of pathos, as the core of all religious experience is, we might irreverently add, not reserved to religious threshold experiences. The boundaries between what is a momentous and singular formative experience for the subject and what, seen from the outside or in retrospect, is banal or even inflated are more flexible than Otto pretends. 'Look, sir, just look at the stars!' says Tonio Kröger's fellow passenger on the Baltic Sea ferry.

> 'Twinkling away up there; by God, the whole sky's full of them. And when you look up at it all and consider that a lot of them are supposed to be a hundred times the size of the earth, well, I ask you, how does it make one feel! We men have invented the telegraph and the telephone and so many wonders of modern times, yes, so we have. But when we look up there we have to realize nevertheless that when all's said and done we are just worms, just miserable little worms and nothing more – am I right or am I wrong, sir? Yes', he concluded, answering his own question, 'that's what we are: worms!' And he nodded toward the firmament in abject contrition. Oh, Lord, thought Tonio Kröger. No, he's got no literature in his system. And at once he recalled something he had recently read by a famous French writer, an essay on the cosmological and the psychological world view; it had been quite a clever piece of verbiage.[131]

In working with Rudolf Otto's text, one cannot help – and not only from a contemporary standpoint, as the excerpt from Thomas Mann's story suggests – tempering his emphasis and his idealizations and relativizing some of the absolutes that he reserves only to the highest human impulses. This discretion need not lead to the opposite conclusion, however, of declaring his model of religious experience unfounded in reality and therefore useless. His model does reflect an essential insight. That the theoreticians of Sufism, the builders of its sturdy, sometimes perhaps too rigidly constructed intellectual framework, arrive at explanations of the *mysterium tremendum* that resemble one another down to the choice of diction[132] supports the validity of Otto's interpretation, and would not have surprised him – after all, he never limited his remarks to Christianity. It also suggests that Sufi knowledge has a currency that transcends individual cultures. To designate the emotion they mean, both Otto and the Muslim mystics use the term 'fear': the Latin *tremor* or the Arabic *khawf*. But Otto was just as well aware as the Sufi master ʿAnṣārī that a word taken from day-to-day life is merely a shell; that it is at best the least inexact designation for something that cannot really be comprehended in a single term. The term 'tremor', Otto writes, 'is taken, aptly enough but still only by analogy, to denote a quite specific kind of emotional response, wholly distinct from that of being afraid, though it so far resembles it that the analogy of fear may be used to throw light upon its nature.'[133] To ʿAnṣārī, the spiritual state (*ḥāl*) of *khawf* is divided into three degrees (*daraja*), of which ordinary fear, *khawf al-ʿāmma*, is only the lowest. This form of fear occurs at the station of the base instincts and of absence (*maqām an-nafs wa-l-ġayba*) and relates, as a necessary corrective of faith, to such perils as the punishments of the afterlife. It is elicited 'by the acceptance of the quranic threats as true, the memory of one's transgressions and reflection on the consequences'.[134] At the 'station of the heart and of presence (*ḥuḍūr*)', the seeker reaches a higher degree of *khawf*, 'the fear of the divine malice (*makr*), which occurs when one is intoxicated with the sweet air of [spiritual] awakening'.[135] As ʿAnṣārī's commentator ʿAbdorrazzāq Kāshānī (d. 1330) explains, this fear is the apprehension that the sweetness and pleasure of being with God could turn out to be only a ruse of the Almighty to deceive the seeker.[136] Only at the 'station of mystery and contemplation' (*maqām assirr wa-l-mushāhada*), which is reserved to the chosen, is 'the terror of fear (*waḥshat al-khawf*) nothing but a trembling before the Awe-inspiring (*haybat al-ijlāl*)', or, according to another version of the text, 'trembling before the Majestic (*al-jalāl*)'.

> But this is the highest station on which there is information in regard to fear. It is a trembling that befalls him to whom the unveiling is granted, in the moments of secret dialogue, and protects him who contemplates while God speaks to him, and shatters the witness by the impact of divine power.[137]

Otto sees something similar when he refers to the 'depreciation of the *subject* in his own eyes' before the 'absolute superiority'[138] of the numinous. He also describes the numinous as 'unapproachable',[139] however, which is not applicable to the ultimate degree of the Sufis' mystical experience: in the moment of annihilation, *fanā'*, the mystic dissolves in God; he is in Him, filled with Him, one with Him. When Anṣārī mentions the shattering of the eyewitness, he is referring to this relinquishment of one's personality. But, in Otto's theory too, the *fearful* is supplanted by the *majestic* at the highest level of religious experience, which, all the mystics agree, exceeds human strength. The Quran verses that Kāshānī quotes in explaining this passage from Anṣārī's *Sharḥ manāzil as-sā'irīn* ('Explanation of the wanderers' stations') give the quality discussed here its most powerful expression:

> And when Moses came to Our appointed time
> and his Lord spoke with him, he said,
> 'Oh my Lord, show me, that I may behold Thee!'
> Said He, 'Thou shalt not see Me; but behold
> the mountain – if it stays fast in its place, then thou shalt see Me.
> And when his Lord revealed Him to the mountain
> He made it crumble to dust; and Moses fell down swooning.[140]

Najmuddīn al-Kubrā (d. 1221), another theoretician of Sufism, also connects the sometimes lethal fear that occurs in *samā*ʿ with Moses' state after the revelation when God said to him: 'O Moses, We have spoken to you what ten thousand men together would not have had the strength to withstand, and if We had said more to you, surely you would be dead.'[141] Such a prophetic dread has nothing to do with the fear of punishment for one's own transgressions: according to the definition in one lexicon of mysticism, it is 'a fear of the Authentic'.[142] Muhammad is said to have suffered such fear, according to a Sufi legend. When Gabriel appeared to him and the Prophet was filled with a fear such as he had never before imagined, he asked the angel what kind of condition it was. It was not a chance occurrence and not something that would pass, the angel answered. Dread was the constant companion of all beings who had been touched by the hand of heavenly Power: all angels, saints and prophets. 'None of us in the hermitages of holiness lives with himself in peace and harmony in the world; we are all afraid that this condition will occur again.'[143] The fourth imam of the Shiites, ʿAlī Zayn al-ʿĀbidīn, is said to have turned pale every time at his ritual ablutions before prayer. 'What is it that happens to you at every ritual washing?' his family asked him. He replied, 'Do you know before Whom I am about to stand [in prayer]?'[144] Mystics also often quote the explanation of the sixth imam, Jaʿfar aṣ-Ṣādiq (d. 765), who fainted during his ritual prayers: 'I repeated the Quran verse so many times in my heart that I heard it from Him Who spoke it, and my body could no longer withstand the sight of His omnipotence.'[145] The imam here declares a claim to a kind of revelation – that he was spoken to directly by God – occurring in the moment of Quran recitation. This is not unusual in Islam, and not necessarily presumptuous even for an ordinary believer. As I have tried to explain in chapter 3, reciting the Quran is generally understood as reproducing the initial situation of its revelation. In mysticism, this idea becomes very concrete: the enraptured listener no longer merely represents that situation as part of a ritual; his recitation is not just a mimesis (*ḥikāya*) of the divine speech, as it is to the theologians. Potentially, at least, he sees and hears God really, not just symbolically. 'The veil of wisdom', ʿUmar as-Suhrawardī teaches, is withdrawn 'before his deep sight'; his hearing of the Quran verse 'Am I not your Lord?'[146] becomes an 'unveiling and contemplation'.[147] At the highest stage, the listening Sufi experiences what the prophets experienced when God spoke to them: the prophets' fear, their torment, their terror were the same, or at most greater in degree. Ibn ʿArabī negates even the difference in degree between the experience of prophets and mystics when he proclaims as God's words: 'It is I Who recite My book for him with his tongue while he listens to Me. It is My nightly conversation (*musāmara*) with him.'[148] Just as God spoke to the Prophet in a nocturnal dialogue, the mystics seek a nocturnal conclave for the soul's dialogue with God – for 'Does not every lover seek to be alone with the beloved?'[149] They spend the night reciting His word and opening their ears for what He says to them with His word. When He says, 'O ye people!'[150] they prick up their ears and say, 'We are the people! What do You want of us, that You now call on us, o Lord?'

The Almighty to Whom praises flow speaks with their tongues when they recite the word He has sent down: '"Fear your Lord! The earthquake of the hour is a mighty thing",[151] o ye people!'

And they say, 'Here we are and at Your service (*labbayka*), o Lord!'

And He says, 'O ye people, fear your Lord, "who assigned you the earth for a couch, and heaven for an edifice, and sent down out of heaven water, wherewith He brought forth fruits for your provision; so set not up compeers to God wittingly."'[152]

And they say, 'O Lord! You have spoken to us, and we have heard; You have made us understand, and we have understood. O Lord! Lead us and use us for what You desire from us, Your servants.'[153]

In the recitation, the servant experiences anew the *Laylat al-Qadr*, the 'Night of Revelation', in his soul; he becomes himself an *ummī*, which means not that he is ignorant of reading and writing, but that he has the necessary immaculateness to receive the divine word.[154] Even the moderate mystic al-Ġazālī sees the possibility of contemplating God unveiled in the Quran recitation:

The steps of the recitation are three. The lowest is that the servant thinks he recites the Quran standing before God, seen by Him, heard by Him. His state should be one of entreaty, praise, supplication and appeal. The second step is that he witnesses with his heart that God sees him and speaks to him with His words, whispers to him thanks to His favour and His bounty; his station is shame (*ḥayā'*), glorification, attention (*iṣġa'*) and understanding. The third step is that he sees the Speaker in the recitation and His attributes in the words; he no longer perceives himself, or his recitation, and no longer perceives that he enjoys a favour that has been granted to him; instead his whole comprehension is directed at the Speaker, Who takes possession of his thinking as if he were sunken in the contemplation of the Speaker and absent from everyone else, and blind to everything else.[155]

As-Suhrawardī too evokes the revelation that takes place during listening to the Quran:

When the forelock of the tawhid appears to the Sufi, and he opens his ears, while he hears the menace and the promise and opens his heart by ridding himself of ungodliness, then he becomes present before God and an eyewitness, so that he sees his own or another's tongue in recitation as the Bush of Moses, inasmuch as God spoke to him from it: 'I am God.'[156] When his

> hearing is thus a hearing of God and his listening a listening to God, then his hearing will become seeing and his seeing hearing, his knowledge action and his action knowledge, and his last will become his first and his first his last.[157]

Because such a Quran recitation leads the human listener to a scorching nearness to God, it is literally an existential experience: it can lead to spiritual annihilation or, as we see in the accounts of ath-Thaʿlabī, to physical extinction. It is not for everyone, Ibn ʿArabī writes:

> Immerse yourself in the sea of the Quran, if your breath is strong enough. And, if not, then be content to study the commentaries on its outward meaning; in such a case do not immerse yourself, for you would drown. The sea of the Quran is deep, and if he who plunges into it does not keep close to the shore, he never returns. The prophets and those who preserve their legacy undertake the pursuit of remote places out of compassion for the universe. Those who are gone (*al-wāqifūn*), however, who reached their destination but remained there and never returned again, are of no use to anyone, and no one is of any use to them: they aspired to reach the middle of the sea – no, the middle of the sea aspired to reach them – and they are immersed forever and will never come back out of the sea.[158]

The Sufis were aware, as was the later Christian theologian Rudolf Otto, of the burden that the proximity to God brings with it, whether for the prophet to whom God speaks or for the devout believer who listens to the Quran and so hears His words. The Sufis experienced the reality of the quranic saying, 'Those of His servants fear God who have knowledge.'[159] But they also knew that the *tremendum* that confuses the senses is only *one* facet of what the listener experiences, and that the powers of the numinous, as Otto calls it, also include 'that in it which bewilders and confounds . . . captivates and transports . . . with a strange ravishment, rising often enough to the pitch of dizzy intoxication; it is the Dionysiac-element',[160] the *fascinans*. Abū l-Ḥusayn al-Ḥusri (d. 981) says about listening, 'There must be everlasting thirst and everlasting drink, so that, the more one drinks, the greater his thirst',[161] and Otto writes:

> The daemonic-divine object may appear to the mind an object of horror and dread, but at the same time it is no less something that allures with a potent charm, and the creature who trembles before it, utterly cowed and cast down, has always at the same time the impulse to turn to it, nay even to make it somehow his own. The mystery is for him not merely something to be wondered at [*das Wunderbare*] but something that entrances him [*das Wundervolle*].[162]

The horrible and the attractive, juxtaposed as the principal qualities of the ineffable numen on which Otto's exposition is based, correlate with the Sufi concepts of the divine *jalāl* ('majesty') and *jamāl* ('beauty'). To the German theologian, the *mysterium tremendum* incites fear and the *mysterium fascinans* bliss, rapture, exuberant joy. Likewise most of the mystics attribute the effect of *khawf* (or terror, *hayba*) to God's majesty and the effect of *faraḥ* or *surūr*, 'joy' or 'bliss', or sometimes *uns*, 'intimacy', to God's beauty.[163] 'In the bounty of God and in His mercy, in that let them rejoice', says a verse of the Quran that is often quoted in this connection.[164] Like Otto, who sees a qualitative leap from ordinary joy to religious beatitude, Anṣārī distinguishes the bliss of the mystic, which he terms *surūr*, from joy over worldly things, *faraḥ*: *surūr* is pure, unalloyed with other feelings. Furthermore, to the outside observer, the listener's fear and joy are often indistinguishable; both are expressed in weeping. To initiates, however, weeping for fear and weeping for joy are worlds apart. The Sufis postulated a system of tears that listed the characteristics, the background and the rank of every single form of weeping, including weeping for fear or joy, weeping out of longing, grief or desire, weeping on parting, and *wijdān*, the 'ecstasy of love', as it is usually translated.[165]

Where the religious thought of the early Islamic ascetics had been strongly centred on God's majesty, and hence on the human creature's fear, the transition to classical Sufism and the mysticism of love is precisely marked by the increasing emphasis on God's beauty and its corresponding attributes, such as 'kindness' (*luṭf*) and 'mercy' (*raḥma*). The fear remains, and the early ascetics' attitude towards life does not disappear, but something is added to it. 'In the beginning, the seekers (*sā'irūn*) experience God's majesty', the theologian Fakhruddīn ar-Rāzī writes about Quran-listening mystics. 'When they glimpse the world of the majestic, they seem lost and perplexed, and then, when something from the world of beauty shines on them, it is as if they begin a new life.'[166] Such statements reflect a paradigm shift that leads to a higher appreciation of the mystical joys and other states or stations that are associated with beauty, such as hope (*rajā'*) and familiarity (*uns*).[167] Although the early ascetics also knew hope, but explicitly ranked it below fear,[168] the mystic Bākharzī later explained: 'Of the kinds (*aqsām*) of weeping that we have explained, the highest is weeping for joy (*faraḥ*). It is as if one who has been long absent comes home and, since he has not seen his relatives and loved ones for so long, weeps because of the force of joy and the magnitude of rejoicing.'[169] The only form Bākharzī values more highly is 'weeping in the ecstasy of love', in which the other kinds of weeping – joy, fear and longing – join together and mutually suppress one another. The Prophet's weeping was of this kind when Abū ibn Ka'b recited to him from the fourth surah, 'The Women', and it was brought on by a kind of revelation or, more exactly, by the manifestations (*tajalliyāt*) and inspirations (*ilhāmāt*) that come down to friends of God from the world of true certainty (*ḥaqq al-yaqīn*).[170]

Like al-Ġazālī and other later Sufis, Bākharzī sees fear as a necessary stage, but one that must be transcended; it attests to a lack of contemplation and is a stage in which, in the words of al-Wāsiṭī (d. after 932), 'a curtain is between God and Man'.[171]

The re-evaluation of the states of the soul and the cautious relativizing of fear in classical Sufism explains why, in those of ath-Thaʿlabī's stories that contain comments on the death or on the victim, the protagonists speak to a living person from Paradise and appear as utterly fulfilled by and united with God[172] – although this does not necessarily imply that they have attained the 'most splendid stages' of the mystical path, as the author claims in the introduction. After all, as far as the text informs us, they die in the state of and as a consequence of fear – and they have nourished that fear by listening to the quranic threats and reflecting on their transgressions, which corresponds to the very first stage of *khawf* according to Anṣārī's system.[173] In only a few of ath-Thaʿlabī's stories do we find specific indications that the victim may have attained not ordinary fear, but the 'trembling of reverence' – the highest stage of fear, again according to Anṣārī. The Bedouin in the episode recounted above may have done so – he speaks of God as the Merciful and quotes the verse 'We have found that which our Lord promised us true',[174] before dying with the praise of God on his lips[175] – and so may a number of other saints that we will present in the rest of this chapter. In any case, some of the greatest Sufis looked rather contemptuously on the many people who were outwardly, and spectacularly, convulsed by listening to the Quran. They probably felt that the higher and more spiritual form of fear consists in what Otto calls 'the hushed, trembling, and speechless humility of the creature', and that the 'strangest excitements',[176] the intoxication and ostentatious ecstasy are a sign of weakness and immaturity. Those who attain the complementary states of *fanāʾ* ('annihilation') and *baqā* ('remaining in God after annihilation') have sobriety (*ṣaḥw*), not intoxication (*sukr*): Hojwīrī quotes his master's teaching, 'Intoxication is the playground of children, but sobriety is the death-field of men',[177] and elsewhere he refers to the Prophet, who grew accustomed to the revelations with time and showed less and less excitement.[178] In this connection many Sufis also quote the answer that Asmāʾ, the daughter of the caliph Abū Bakr, gave to her grandson when he asked her how the Prophet's contemporaries had responded to the recitation of the Quran: 'They were as God has described them in the Quran. Tears streamed from their eyes, their skin quivered, and a trembling came over them.' 'Nowadays I see people who faint when they hear the Quran', said her grandson. Asmāʾ merely replied, 'I take my refuge in God against Satan who was stoned.'[179]

Moses too is said to have opposed his listeners' rending their garments in their agitation,[180] as he was himself admonished by God not to fall into agitation at the 'station of ecstasy' (*maqām al-wajd*),[181] and a number ascetics' and Sufis' words of rebuke and anger have been handed down about listeners who lose consciousness. When ʿAbdullāh ibn ʿUmar, for example, came upon a man who lay unconscious on the ground because he had heard the Quran, he said: 'We too are in the fear of God and yet do not fall to the ground. It is the devil coming out of inside him who does this to him. The Prophet's companions never did such a thing.'[182] Al-Junayd calls the 'second sobriety', a person's regained self-awareness as one who is in God after a rapture, the highest and most noble state.[183] Asked why he no longer showed any excitement on listening to poetry or music, he recited the Quran verse 'And thou shalt see the mountains, that thou supposest fixed, passing by like clouds – God's handiwork, who has created everything very well. He is aware of the things you do.'[184] In introducing this anecdote, as-Sarrāj writes that al-Junayd 'probably wanted to suggest: 'You see the stillness of my limbs and the serenity of my exterior, but you do not know where I am with my Lord. That too is one of the qualities of perfection.'[185] Al-Junayd himself is said to have subsequently died of a Quran recitation.[186]

Sahl at-Tustarī (d. 896) spent years listening to the Quran without ever becoming delirious, a companion reports, but one day, near the end of his life, when someone recited a verse from the Quran to him, 'I saw him turn pale and tremble and nearly collapse. When he had returned to his sober state, I asked him about it. He said, "My friend, we have grown weak." '[187] Sahl gave the same answer on another occasion, again after he had 'become delirious and was excited and agitated' while listening to the Quran. His companions asked him, if that was weakness, then what is strength? 'Strength is', the wise man answered, 'that nothing can penetrate one without being swallowed by the strength of one's state, so that what penetrates one does not change one.'[188] After recounting this anecdote, ʿUmar as-Suhrawardī continues:

> The saying of Abū Bakr aṣ-Ṣiddīq on seeing someone weep at a Quran recitation is similar: 'We were like that too until our hearts grew hard.' His words 'grew hard' mean: solidified and surrendered to listening to the Quran and being familiar with its lights and no longer finding it so unusual that they underwent a change.[189]

Such statements do not reflect a consensus, however, or even a dominant opinion among Sufis, and we must not think the deceased Quran listeners of ath-Thaʿlabī's book were taken for novices on the mystic path, for dilettantes who could not cope with the powerful instrument of Quran recitation, because of the strong emotions they showed or because of their fear of the torments of the afterlife. Of course they were not. Stories of staunch believers who did not survive a Quran recitation appear often in the mystical literature of Islam, and their fate is reported to the present day – by the contemporary authors Ḥeydarkhānī and Harawī, for example – with sympathy and respect. Sufi thought is more unsystematic and flexible than a classical textbook such as Anṣārī's *Explanation of the Stations of the*

Wanderer would lead us to believe. No matter how much an author stresses that the fear of God's punishment is no proper state for a master of the mystic love of God, he may still honour the ascetic who dies of fright; he may write dismissively about the death and fainting of Quran listeners and yet not criticize Muḥammad ibn al-Munkadir's (d. 748) brother who departed this world crying, 'Woe, woe!',[190] or pull the halo off Sheikh al-Miswar (d. 683), who died of fright during a recitation.[191] And there is something more involved. While the religious experience of most of those slain by the Quran may have been dominated by the fear of God, on a closer look, fear is not everything: even in ath-Thaʿlabī's pleasure-hating, all-fearful ascetics, it is accompanied by an irrepressible excitability over the beauty of the text. Ath-Thaʿlabī's believers might have also said, directly or figuratively, with Thābit al-Bunānī (d. c. 741): 'For twenty years I suffered with the Quran, and for twenty years it was my pleasure.'[192] They experience God in the Quran recitation as an irresistible attraction: 'Such is the *jaḏb*', the third story says; *jaḏb* in Sufi terminology is the divine attraction that sets the mystic in turmoil and makes him seek union with God.[193] Although at first glance many of the episodes seem unambiguous and monopolar, the ambivalence, the devout believer's dithyrambic pleasure in the Quran that goes hand in hand with a fearful shiver, is visible between the lines. It is felt from the very beginning: what else but fascination can explain the fact that the young man in the episode narrated at the beginning of this chapter,[194] after he had fainted at the Quran recitation of Manṣūr ibn ʿAmmār, on coming to his senses immediately asked him to recite some more? That the *tremendum* and *fascinosum* of the sacred text maintain an equilibrium, as Stefan Wild remarked in reference to the history of the Quran's influence among Sufis,[195] seems to be true of the ascetics in ath-Thaʿlabī's work. In this regard, too, these early traditions once more corroborate Rudolf Otto's interpretation of the holy.

The Pleasure of Listening

But at this point we must note that our theme diverges significantly from Otto's interpretation. Although Otto quotes from the revealed scriptures and from numerous religious poetic texts which he feels express the numinous, and also refers to artistic means of expression of the numinous,[196] he says little about how horror and bliss actually arise in the believer. He notes that the 'ancient traditional expressions' of Luther's Bible are 'still retained despite their obscurity', and 'the only half intelligible or wholly unintelligible language of devotion' in the church service[197] can awaken the feeling of mystery, and also that 'he who "in the spirit" reads the written word lives in the numinous'[198] – but we learn nothing specific about what induces religious experience and what forms it is known to take. Yet Otto's reference to the conversion experiences collected by William James clearly indicates that he can in fact imagine the moments of religious excitement with which we are concerned occurring in all kinds of situations: during prayer, in day-to-day life, in moments of great psychological duress or moral reprobation. That does not mean, to be quite clear yet again at this juncture, that Otto or James, who called particular attention to the emotional and sensual aspects of faith, thought it impossible for a religious experience to be induced by the *beauty* of Bible verses or by a spiritual chorale or Raphael's Madonnas. But since they rarely mention beauty as an inductive impulse, we may at least assume they did not consider it central in the religious life of their community. At one point Otto quotes from one of James's conversion stories in which the religious experience is described as 'like the effect of some great orchestra, when all the separate notes have melted into one swelling harmony',[199] but music is used here only as a metaphor: the experience is actually caused by a crucial biographical event, such as the encounter with another person or a situation of acute spiritual or material distress.[200]

In the conversions of Muhammad's contemporaries, on the other hand, and indeed in those of the Sufis too (as perhaps in all mysticism, not just the Islamic variety), the aesthetic process, the enjoyment of listening to music, is by no means simply an analogy. It is literally true. Their religious experience often takes place during the reception of something musical: what induces the religious insight is the sound of the Quran (or of poetry), or a text recited in an artistic interpretation; it is through the Quran's 'bare sounds and tunes' that the rapture can be elicited, ʿUmar as-Suhrawardī writes.[201] 'It is known', Mostamlī-Bokhārī (d. 1042) remarks, 'that in the heart of a person who hears someone reciting the Quran – reciting it well – sensitivity and contrition emerge, no matter how vicious and hard-hearted the person is, and the contrition remains and the person enters a state of blessedness.'[202] The unbelievers become devout and beatified on listening to the Quran, but, to listeners who are very far advanced on the mystic path, God reveals Himself in His whole beauty and majesty.[203] Such an experience is aesthetic, in both an elementary and a more complex way – that is, both in the sense of 'sensual' and in the sense of a pleasant experience of a poetically structured text that the recipient finds beautiful. 'At this stage, delight (*ḥalāwa*) and the enjoyment of silent dialogue (*laḏḏat al-munāǧāt*) become overpowering', al-Ġazālī writes, and he goes on to quote the words of an anonymous master as an exemplary expression of aesthetic delight:

> I recited the Quran without experiencing any joy in it, until I recited as if I was hearing the Messenger of God reciting it before his companions. Then I was raised to a higher station, and I recited it as if I was hearing Gabriel conveying it to the Messenger of God. Then God brought on another station (*manzila*), so that I now hear it from Him who speaks it. And I experience an enjoyment and a contentment (*naʿīm*) that I can no longer do without.[204]

It is true that very few of ath-Tha'labī's accounts would lead us to infer that the listeners experience enjoyment and happiness. But even the terror that they assert seems to be not entirely devoid of pleasure. Sheikh al-Miswar, whom we have already mentioned, on hearing a verse about the impending Judgement Day, not only deplored his sins, but in the same breath he also asked the reciter to repeat the verse. We must assume it exerted some kind of sensual attraction upon him; his behaviour reveals the same ambivalent dread that emerged in connection with the reactions of the early Muslims, which were sometimes described as severe. That ambivalence has been known since antiquity and has been discussed by probably every theoretician who has examined catharsis, including Antonin Artaud and Hans Robert Jauss.[205]

Ath-Thalabī's traditions, or at least the majority of them, clearly reveal that the aesthetic properties of the text that the protagonist hears are what he perceives as enchanting and what brings about a religious insight. The story of Abū 'Uthmān al-Ḥīri (d. 911), one of the great mystics of his time, who fainted during a Quran recitation and had to be carried home, recounts that it was the voice of the reciter Abū l-Ḥasan al-Būshanjī (d. 958 or 959) that killed him (*qatalahū ṣawtu l-Būshanjī*):[206] that means it could not have been just the content of the surah recited that was so stunning, but the extraordinary acoustic quality of that particular singer's recitation must also be taken into account. Similarly, we must assume that the young, slender Kufan in ath-Tha'labī's eighth narrative did not confess out of pure piety that he longed for nothing as deeply as to hear the famous Quran reciter Ṣāliḥ al-Murrī (d. 792 or 793) again – the anecdote not only expresses 'something uniquely attractive and *fascinating*', which combines 'in a strange harmony of contrasts' with the repulsion of the *tremendum*, to use Otto's words;[207] it also makes plain that the attraction of the Quran is of an *aesthetic*, *musical* nature. If the young man had been only devout, and interested exclusively in the discursive message of the text, not its sensual fascination, he would have wished for any Quran recitation that fulfilled the pertinent norms, not for a particularly artistic one.

When the famous Quran reciter heard of the young man's wish, he made the trip to Kufa expressly, and there in the mosque he recited verses 101 to 108 of the 23rd surah (from 'For when the trumpet is blown' to 'Slink you into it, He shall say, and do not speak to Me'). Ṣāliḥ himself reports:

> The young man became agitated and lost his composure, until finally he fell down and died. Now there was a door that led from the young man's house into the mosque. Suddenly an old woman was standing there who had brought some food. She was his mother. When she saw her son, she asked, 'What has happened to my son?'
>
> I told her the story.
>
> 'Are you Ṣāliḥ al-Murrī?' she asked.

I said I was.

'May God give you your reward in this world and in the next for having fulfilled my son's wish. He longed for you incessantly, by almighty and majestic God.'[208]

Ṣāliḥ al-Murrī's Quran recitation must have been very special indeed. Alongside other cases of listeners fainting and dying, Abū Nuʿaym mentions that tears would flow from Ṣāliḥ's audiences' eyes on hearing the *ḥamdulillāh* with which he began his Quran recitations and sermons.[209] Al-Ġazālī tells of four believers who died on hearing Ṣāliḥ's recitation.[210] The blind sage Abū Juhayr aḍ-Ḍarīr, one of the great wise men of the *tābiʿūn*, the generation that succeeded the Prophet, also died on hearing the Quran, if we may believe the reciter's account as reported by ath-Thaʿlabī. Because of its particular dramatic structure, I must render this episode in some detail.

Ṣāliḥ the ascetic, together with four other well-known devout men of Basra, went to his house in the desert, far outside the city, to pray to God on their behalf. After they had waited until Abū Juhayr had completed his extensive noon prayers, one of the visitors, Muḥammad ibn Wāsiʿ (d. c. 740), went to him reverently to greet him. The wise man welcomed his visitor kindly and asked who he was. When Muḥammad said his name, Abū Juhayr remarked,

'The people of Basra say you are the most devoted to God of all of them, unless you pray to God that He might conceal it.' He was silent for a while, then he sat down. Then Thābit al-Bunānī came up and greeted him. Abū Juhayr returned his greeting and asked, 'Who are you, may God have mercy upon you?'

'I am Thābit.'

'Abū Muḥammad?'

'Yes.'

Then Abū Juhayr welcomed him and said, 'The people of Basra say you pray to God the most of all of them, unless you pray to God that He might conceal it.' He was silent for a while, then he sat down. Then Ḥabīb Abū Muḥammad [d. 772] stepped forward and greeted him. Abū Juhayr returned his greeting and asked, 'Who are you, may God have mercy upon you?'

'I am Ḥabīb.'

'Abū Muḥammad?'

'Yes.'

Then Abū Juhayr welcomed him and said, 'The people of Basra say your prayers are answered, unless you pray to God that He might conceal it.' He was silent for a while, then he sat down.

Then Mālik [ibn Dīnār Abū Yaḥyā, d. 749] stepped forward and greeted him. Abū Juhayr returned his greeting and asked, 'Who are you, may God have mercy upon you?'

'I am Mālik.'

'Abū Yaḥyā?'

'Yes.'

Then Abū Juhayr welcomed him and said, 'The people of Basra say you lead the most ascetic life of all of them, unless you pray to God that He might conceal it.' He was silent for a while, then he sat down. Then I stepped forward and greeted him. Abū Juhayr returned my greeting and asked, 'Who are you, may God have mercy upon you?'

'I am Ṣāliḥ.'

'The reciter?'

I said I was. Then he raised his hands in the air and said, 'Praise be to God Who has gathered you together on my behalf. I had prayed to God that He might gather you in my house. Praise be to God Who has heard my prayers. Truly, Ṣāliḥ, I long for your Quran recitation.' Then Muḥammad ibn Wāsiʿ said to him, 'But Abū Juhayr, we have come so that you might intercede for us with God.'

Abū Juhayr raised his hands in the air, and we ours, and he began to appeal to God. After a while, he said, 'Ṣāliḥ, recite!'

So I began to recite. And God gave me such a voice as I have never known myself to have, and such as I have never heard again in my life. I recited, 'The inhabitants of Paradise that day, better shall be their lodging, fairer their resting-place. Upon the day that heaven is split asunder with the clouds and the angels are sent down in majesty, the Kingdom that day, the true Kingdom, shall belong to the All-merciful.'[211] But Abū Juhayr uttered a violent, tormented cry and fell down unconscious. Although we thought he was already dead, we shook him incessantly and poured water on him until he finally came to. But after he had awoken and come to his senses, he seemed as if nothing could revive the spirits in his body.

'Ṣāliḥ, recite, for I cannot get enough of your Quran recitation', he said to me.

Then I recited, 'We shall advance upon what work they have done, and make it a scattered dust.'[212] But, by God, I had no sooner finished the verse than he was dead, God have mercy on him. We thought it was the same as the first time, and we shook him, until we suddenly noticed that he was stiff. Then we hurried to his wife and called her.

'What do you want?' she asked.

'We recited the Quran to Abū Juhayr, and he died', we answered.

'I am not surprised. But tell me: is Ṣāliḥ al-Murrī among you?'

'Do you know him?'

'I have never seen him.'

'Then why do you not ask to know more about him?'

'Abū Juhayr, God have mercy on him, often said, "I long for Ṣāliḥ al-Murrī's Quran recitation. Know that I will die when I hear his recitation." When you told me he had heard the Quran and died, I suspected that he had heard Ṣāliḥ's recitation and died during it.'

We confirmed that he had heard Ṣāliḥ's recitation and died during it. She said, 'Praise be to God Who has heard his prayers and fulfilled his wish.'[213]

The wise man's longing to hear Ṣāliḥ al-Murrī's Quran recitation is not conceivable without an element of aesthetic attraction. It would be absurd to say that just the referential content of the recited message excited him to such a degree that he first fainted and then, on the second recitation, dropped dead. The acoustic styling as an additional level of the text's complexity must be inferred to explain the extraordinary reception of it that the story describes. Abū Juhayr is famous as a devout Muslim who spends the greater part of the day in ritual prayers – that is, reciting the Quran softly; he must know the content of the text better than most. Although the passages that Ṣāliḥ recites to him are those called *wa'd* and *wa'īd* passages – that is, God's promises and threats – the reciter in this story evidently chooses them for their particular recitative qualities, not to instruct or admonish Abū Juhayr. Furthermore, Abū Juhayr's own announcement that he will die when he hears Ṣāliḥ's recitation demonstrates that his death is not due to mere fear of punishment or hope for a reward. He does not say, 'When I hear this or that verse' or 'when I hear Ṣāliḥ recite God's threats and promises', but 'when I hear Ṣāliḥ's recitation': that means it is not primarily the religious message contained in the verses but Ṣāliḥ's voice, which on this day moreover has a special quality – 'such a voice', the reciter himself feels, 'as I have never known myself to have, and such as I have never heard again in my life' – it is the reciter's voice that constitutes the special power of the Quran in this particular instance of recitation. In other stories from ath-Tha'labī's book, too, the recitations that cause the listener's death are characterized as especially good ones. The power is in the manner of the message's communication, not in its substance alone.

There is a consensus among Muslims even today, as a brief but perhaps illuminating look at the contemporary discussion of Quran recitation reveals, that the effect of the revelation on the listener is related to the quality of the recitation. The artistic treatment of the text is called *taṣwīr al-ma'nā*, 'illustration of the meaning', and is understood to be an essential component of the recitation. According to Labīb as-Sa'īd, a mastery of the technique of recitation results in a 'particular intonation (*talḥīn khāṣṣ*), which makes the quranic meanings (*ma'ānī*) evident and carries them in full ripeness into the hearts and minds' of the listeners.[214] The sayings of the Prophet praising the 'beautiful voice', which are frequently quoted in such contexts, are understood in the same sense as, for example, 'Embellish the Quran with your voices! The beautiful voice augments the beauty of the Quran',[215] and 'Everything has an ornament: the ornament of the Quran is the beautiful voice.'[216] The classical theologian Ibn Qayyim al-Jawzīya writes that the 'ornamentation' (*tazyīn*), the 'embellishment of the voice' (*taḥsīn aṣ-ṣawt*) and the 'musical entrancement' (*taṭrīb*) increase the power of the recitation because only they allow the meaning truly to penetrate into the listeners' hearts.[217] Others say, 'When the Quran is recited with a beautiful voice, it affects the soul more strongly and is better heard by the heart.'[218] If one follows the rules for an ideal recitation as outlined by Sufi authors such as al-Ġazālī and al-Makkī, the musical rendition is not only 'ornament' in the ordinary sense of the term – an element that is pleasing but ultimately extrinsic to the understanding of the essential part, the content – on the contrary, it is basic to the actualization of the message. All the Muslim doctrines of Quran recitation suggest that it should be a comprehensive religious experience that touches the senses, the mind and the spirit. It should not be the mere transmission of information or, of course, the opposite, pure entertainment.[219] Such a total experience would hardly be produced, people realize, simply by reading the Quran correctly: the 'beauty of the voice' in the perfect recitation, as-Saʿīd writes, 'has the higher purpose of moving the audience emotionally'.[220] There is no doubt even today that a recitation that is correct, but not perceived as beautiful in the sense of a musical aesthetic, normally does not induce the desired sensual and spiritual experience. One of the reciters interviewed by Nelson, Sheikh Muḥammad Salāma, explains that he learned music 'for the sake of the Quran, in order to take possession of the hearts [of his listeners]'.[221] The idea that only ornament and the beautiful voice, which are human contributions, allow the message of the Quran to unfold and magnify its effect may appear to contradict the dogma that the text is formally perfect and unsurpassable, but in fact it follows from the Muslim concept of revelation, which is founded on the oral nature of the scripture. The text is realized only in the oral *performance*, or, as Kristina Nelson puts it, 'melody is the means by which the divine is comprehended. At that point great art happens.'[222]

If the listeners' different responses to one and the same verse depend on the manner of the recitation, that implies that the *aesthetic function* – that element in the transmitted message that refers not to information about extralingual signifieds but to the lexical signs themselves – is critically important to the communication that takes place in the recitation. Looking in this light at the story of Abū Juhayr presented above, we can say that the recitation's highly developed aesthetic function, which derives both from the arrangement of the lexical signs themselves and from the manner in which the reciter renders them phonetically and musically, makes the recitation resonate with the recipient in a way that the simple discursive content cannot explain. To put it more simply: if someone had merely *informed* Abū Juhayr of what the verse said, or if someone had merely read it to him in an ordinary voice, or if Ṣāliḥ with his beautiful voice had delivered a statement of the same import but without the poetic expression of the Quran verses concerned – Abū Juhayr would not have died. What killed him was neither the text alone nor the reciter's vocal interpretation of it, and certainly not the referential content of the verses: it was the recitation as a complex organization of different layers of interwoven information or, in Lotman's terms, the *artistic structure* of the message communicated to him.

The words of Abū Juhayr himself indicate that the reception situation brings together different kinds of components in a specific constellation. For while he does not say that a certain text – that is, this or that verse of the Quran – will kill him, he says that he will die by the voice of Ṣāliḥ. Yet Ṣāliḥ will not recite just *anything*; it is not just his admirable voice that Abū Juhayr longs to hear, but 'his Quran recitation'. Both the *specific* text and the *specific* singer must come together in order for his listening to have the presaged consequences. That means the elements necessary for the reception cannot be separated – no more than a lover of Glenn Gould's fanatically worshipped recording of the *Goldberg Variations* could give an exact answer to the question whether he or she finds it magical because it is Bach's *Goldberg Variations* or because it is Glenn Gould playing them. To a true fan, the same score interpreted by someone else loses some of its enchantment, but the magic would be gone completely if the pianist were to perform the *Radetzky March*, or even another Bach piece, instead of the *Goldberg Variations*.

The reception of a given piece is of course different from one person to another, and even from one instance of listening to the next, and is influenced by an infinite number of factors, including external ones such as the surroundings, the atmosphere and prior judgements. Yet, even discounting such extra-aesthetic influences, it is often difficult for the recipient, to say nothing of an outside observer, to be aware of what dominates in his or her perception of a piece of music (or an artistically spoken text) and is responsible for the pleasure in it: whether it is the melody, for example, the sound pattern, the style of musical rendering, the voice of the performer or, in a composition that the listener knows well, the interpretation of a certain artist. In ath-Thaʿlabī's stories, the causes are likewise difficult to isolate. Sometimes the believers encounter a verse to which they are particularly sensitive during prayer; sometimes it is completely irrelevant whether a good, trained voice recites it; and sometimes they can hear the same verse again and again without losing their composure, but then on hearing an outstanding singer recite it they fall down dead or unconscious. The Sufis, who doubtless loved the Quran but were apparently little concerned with its *iʿjāz* as a dogma of Muslim teaching (the subject rarely comes up in their writings), knew that 'listening', including listening to the Quran, is something altogether idiosyncratic. By no means did they claim that the Quran inevitably induced ecstatic enthusiasm in its listeners, nor did they present evidence that its power was greater than that of other texts. The number of Sufis who are supposed to have died listening to music or poetry is probably only insignificantly fewer than the number slain by the Quran.[223] To give just one example in which the effects of poetry are every bit as extreme as those of the Quran, we may cite the death of Abū l-Ḥusayn an-Nūrī of Baghdad, who was one of the most renowned Sufis of his time. It is said that he attended a singing performance and, on hearing a certain verse about love, stood up, enraptured, and wandered aimlessly about.

> He wandered into a mown field of reeds where the stubble was as sharp as swords. He began to walk around in it, repeating the verse until daybreak, while the blood flowed from his feet. His feet and calves then swelled, and he died a few days later.[224]

Even a great holy man, Ḏū n-Nūn (d. 859), is said to have fallen on his face while listening to poetry so that blood dripped from his forehead.[225] Ash-Shiblī, who claimed to have recited the Quran thirteen thousand times in his own prayer room,[226] and whose intense reactions to the recitations of others are described by many authors,[227] used to react no less impulsively whenever he heard a certain line by the poet Abū l-ʿAbbās (d. after 808).[228] Even the Prophet is alleged to have become so euphoric when a Bedouin recited a line of poetry to him with a beautiful voice that 'his cloak fell from his shoulder'.[229] Several authors also cite, with evident sympathy, the story of the famous sheikh Yūsuf ibn al-Ḥusayn ar-Rāzī (d. 916) of Ray, who broke out weeping on hearing two lines of a poem and said to the reciter, 'My dear son! Do you upbraid the people of Ray who say Yūsuf is a heretic? Since morning prayers I have been reading the Quran, and not a drop has come to my eyes, but two verses have sounded the resurrection in me.'[230]

Some authors go so far as to explain why the effects of poetry are often greater than those of the Quran. Al-Ġazālī, for example, argues that many people know the Quran by heart and repeat its verses many times a day in their hearts, while a poem when recited is generally new to the listeners, and the less familiar a text is, the stronger 'its effects on the heart'. It is also true of a poem that 'its effect grows weaker' the second time one hears it, 'and the third time it ceases almost entirely'.[231] Hojwīrī, on the other hand, says that the Quran listener is so shaken and captivated that he can no longer stir, whereas the word of a poet relaxes the listener and sets him in motion.[232] In contrast to the theologians' teaching, according to which the miracle of inimitability is specific to the Quran, the Sufis felt that other revelations, such as those of Moses and David, could also exercise an overpowering charm on the listener.[233] Hellmut Ritter recounts the following story from ʿAṭṭār's *Book of Suffering* (*Muṣībatnāme*):

> David sang the psalter so beautifully for twenty years that reason no longer remained in its place, the foot forgot how to walk, the leaves of the trees all became ears, water ceased to flow, birds stopped flying. But everyone experienced only joy from the singing and went on living happily. One day, however, he was struck by the arrow of pain and now he sang sorrowful songs. Then everyone who heard him died so that in the end 40,000 people lost their life in this way, and God Himself had to reproach him.[234]

To the mystics, the sound of the Quran is not the only source of auditory delights, and the effect that a verse, whether from the Quran or a poem, will have in a given situation depends on the listener and his individual condition. Al-Ġazālī expressed this thought in his *Alchemy of Happiness* with the term *monāsabat*, the 'relation' or 'proportionality' which exists between the text and the recipient and depends on the listening experience. He also wrote 'that not all Quran verses have a relation to the state of the lover' – that is, the mystic; it is difficult to imagine that the verses about inheritance law might 'fan the flames of love, unless someone is at the highest stage of love and everything they hear evokes a state of ecstasy in them.'[235]

The awareness that al-Ġazālī expresses here is that of reception aesthetics: a knowledge that the perception of a text or a melody is significantly influenced by the recipient's individuality and the specific context and situation of the reception. 'Listening is an affliction (*fitna*) for those who aspire to it and a solace for those who find it', says al-Junayd.[236] The actualization of an aesthetic message, the Quran included, cannot be isolated from the recipient and defined independently of his or her experience. Rüdiger Bubner writes, 'What the aesthetic experience undergoes is constituted in the experience and by the experience, so what the content of that experience is cannot be objectivized independently of it, in a work for example.'[237] Expanding on Kant, who said the grounds that determine a judgement of taste 'cannot be other than subjective',[238] Bubner writes that the aesthetic experience is not a purely passive acceptance of external effects but must also be described as performance on the part of the person experiencing it.[239] The Sufis expressed something similar, to a certain extent, in their language. ʿUmar as-Suhrawardī, for example, writes that a piece of music, a poem or even the Quran 'does not give rise, in the heart, to anything which is not already there'.[240] What enters a person through listening could just as easily lead him to truth as to heresy, Ḏū n-Nūn says,[241] and Hojwīrī finds that *ṣamā*ʿ is like a sun 'that shines on all things and affects all things according to their quality: it scorches one, it sets another ablaze; it caresses one, it melts another.'[242] A proverb compares *samā*ʿ to a rain which only makes buds grow that are already present inside a person,[243] and Sarī as-Saqaṭī, one of the first to systematize the mystic states (*aḥwāl*), suggests, 'The hearts of lovers become enraptured in *samā*ʿ, and the hearts of the remorseful become afraid, and the hearts of those who yearn are inflamed.'[244] His predecessor Abū Sulaymān ad-Darānī (d. 830) says more plainly, 'The beautiful voice does not bring anything into the heart. It only sets in motion what is in the heart.'[245] Similarly, Abū Najīb as-Suhrawardī (d. 1168) writes:

> And it is said: Listening (*samā*ʿ) evokes the joy and grief, fear, hope and longing that lies concealed in the heart. Sometimes it makes one weep, and sometimes it moves one to ecstasy (*ṭarab*). And it is said: Listening touches all elements in a person, so that a person sometimes weeps and sometimes

cries, sometimes claps their hands together, sometimes dances, and sometimes faints.[246]

Al-Ġazālī, too, sees music's 'miraculous effect' on the soul in the fact that some voices and songs 'make you happy and some make you sad, some lull you to sleep, some induce laughter and merriment and some make you move your hands and body and head to the rhythm.'[247] Al-Ġazālī recounts the following anecdote that points to the dynamic relation between text and recipient in the mystical experience of listening. When ʿUtba al-Ġulām (eighth century) heard someone reciting the poet's verse 'Praise the Almighty of Heaven / The lover is truly in need', he cried, 'I confirm it!' Someone else cried, 'I deny it!' And a third person who had observed the other two cried: 'They are both right!'[248] Another episode that al-Ġazālī cites also demonstrates how the aesthetic experience, as Kant showed in the *Critique of the Power of Judgement*, takes place in the tension between sensual emotion and creative action, and 'meaning' emerges for the experiencing subject only when the aesthetic object correlates with his or her person and condition. Ad-Darrāj (d. 932) was once walking along the bank of the Tigris with Ibn al-Fuwaṭī when they saw how a slave singer (*jāriya*) recited a verse of poetry ('Every day you show a different face / It would be better for you were it otherwise') and a young man called to her, 'O singer, by God and by your master's life, recite that verse again!' When she had repeated the verse, the young man said, 'That is in fact the state I am in.' Then he cried out and passed away. The population of Basra immediately came out of their houses to pray, and a short time later they carried the deceased to his grave with great sympathy. But the slave singer was given her freedom, and her master gave away his palace and all his possessions and left the city weeping, and was never seen again.[249]

Rudolf Otto would protest, if he could, against any attempt to explain the cases of religious excitement he describes using aesthetic theories: he kept religious and aesthetic experience strictly apart, writing, 'Religious feelings are not the same as aesthetic feelings.'[250] In connection with the *mysterium fascinans* he mentions beatitude and joy, but not enjoyment and pleasure. Otto does not include categories such as 'the beautiful' or 'the sublime' in the religious sphere; they are at best 'but a pale reflexion' of the *mysterium*;[251] the irrational quality of music is not to be confused with the irrational quality of the numinous. Yet we may doubt whether religious and aesthetic experience can be as strictly differentiated as Otto thinks, regardless of which religion is concerned.[252] The Sufi texts referred to in this chapter in any case are based on a different perspective. They are concerned explicitly with aesthetic phenomena such as 'beauty' (*jamāl* or *ḥusn*), 'majesty' (*jalāl*), 'enjoyment' (*ladda*), 'listening' (*samāʿ*) and beautiful melodies (*laḥn ṭayyib* or *ṣawt ḥasan*, often used in the sense of 'music'). ʿEbādī quotes an unknown teacher as saying, 'Pure enjoyment can only be found in listening.'[253] When as-Sarrāj writes that the Sufis, in listening to the Quran and qasidas, were '*not only* after the beauty of the melody and the sweetness of the voice and the delight and enjoyment in them',[254] he seems to feel it goes without saying that they *were* after those things, whether exclusively or not. Throughout the works of the Sufis, the absence of a line of demarcation between the reception of music, poetry and revelation is striking. In their treatises, authors such as as-Sarrāj, al-Qushayrī, al-Ġazālī and 'Umar as-Suhrawardī generally discuss the phenomenon of Quran listening in the chapter on *samā'*. In Arabic and Persian, the term is understood in the strict sense as 'listening to music'. Rudolf Gramlich translates it accordingly as '*Musikhören*' and Annemarie Schimmel as 'mystical dance', 'concert' and often as 'music' – and for good reasons, if we bear in mind that the Quran and poetry are understood to be musical in nature. In the *samā'* chapters, didactic anecdotes about listening to the Quran, listening to music and listening to poetry are narrated in succession to reinforce a given thesis. Bākharzī, for example – we could say the same of many other authors – quite naturally weaves hadiths and anecdotes about Quran listening into a discussion of the permissibility of singing and music.[255] That does not mean the Sufis considered poetry and revelation to be one and the same, but the distinction between them is one that they make within a single objective field; they belong to the same discourse. And that distinction refers primarily – and this is what is actually surprising, and remarkable from a modern perspective – to the difference between the texts and their 'authorship', not to a difference in how people listen to the texts. The fundamental difference between the Quran and poetry is found, as we discovered in chapter 2, in the sender and the message sent, not in the recipient and his or her reception. The stories of listeners slain by poetry are discussed in exactly the same context as the stories of those slain by the Quran, and, if the theory and practice of *samā'* is mentioned, it generally refers equally to listening to poetry, to music and to the Quran. Ath-Tha'labī's treatise could also be mentioned among the examples, although poetry is discussed in it only once. But that one case is revealing enough.

Aḥmad ibn Abī l-Khawārī (d. 860 or 861), a traditionist and an ascetic, reports that on his way to Basra he suddenly heard a cry. When he went to look where it had come from, he found a man lying on the ground unconscious. When he asked what had happened, one of the people present said, 'He was a man with "presence of heart" (*ḥāḍir al-qalb*). He heard a verse from God's book and fainted.'[256] *Ḥāḍir al-qalb* is a Sufi term that indicates the sole presence of God in the mystic's heart. The verse that the man had heard before fainting was: 'Is it not time that the hearts of those who believe should be humbled to the Remembrance of God and the Truth which He has sent down?'[257] The narrative continues:

> When the man heard our words, he came to, stood up, and immediately began to recite: 'Is it not time for the parting to pass away, / And for the branch, the branch of the moringa, to branch? / For the love-stricken, pining and writhing, / Is it not time to weep for him and have pity on him? / I wrote

> a book of the longing in my breast, / Its likeness is that of an ornate brocade.' Then he cried, 'Dark, dark, dark (*ishkāl, ishkāl, ishkāl*)!'[258] and fell down unconscious. And lo, he was dead.[259]

The similarity between the reception of the Quran and that of poetry is palpable. The sheikh, to whom a higher mystical status is ascribed by the attribute *ḥāḍir al-qalb*, hears thematically related quranic and poetic verses in succession and in a single reception situation (that is, without interrupting his initial *samāʿ*, as far as we can tell from the text, but continuing it immediately on coming to his senses), and each time he is stunned by what he hears. And, as if to underscore how little room there is for didactic and dogmatic thinking in such episodes, poetry in this case has the greater effect.

Although the Quran and poetry largely share the same reception context in Islamic mysticism, the Quran is not poetry to Sufis, and they do not conceive it as poetry, consciously or unconsciously. Rather than situating the Quran in the sphere of art because it is mentioned in the same breath with poetry and music, we should ascribe both kinds of texts, and music too, to the religious sphere. To the mystics, all three are an organ of religious insight, not – or, at least, not only – of aesthetic enjoyment. The beautiful voices, Ḏū n-Nūn said, including those that recite the Quran, are 'appeals and allusions to God, which He has placed in every good man and every good woman'.[260] At another point he calls them an 'impulse towards truth that drives hearts to God'.[261] Other Sufis conceive listening to poetry, music or the Quran as a state 'that makes the orientation towards the mysteries visible by its ardour',[262] or as an 'unveiling of the mysteries that lead to the contemplation of the Beloved'.[263] All of these quotations indicate that listening is not an end in itself but is directed towards achieving an insight, a 'finding' (*wajd*), as the word for the ecstasy aimed at in listening indicates. That does not mean, however, that the insight occurs 'unaesthetically', if we imagine the concept of aesthetic experience as broader than the perception of 'the beautiful' and not strictly bound 'to the phenomenon in its visibly presented plasticity', and imagine the religious experience as transcending this field of sensory presentation, looking 'through things in a sense', in Ernst Rothacker's formulation of a widely held opinion.[264] But such a distinction ultimately degrades the aesthetic experience into mere 'satisfaction', a pleasant persistence in gazing at an outward appearance; it does not do justice to the phenomenon of aesthetic experience because it does not take into consideration that works of art too implicitly claim to offer insight; they too claim to open up new and deeper realities to their recipients. Where aesthetics does not become 'culinary' and 'fail its task', in Adorno's goading phrase, it is more than pleasure: 'Artworks are understood only when their experience is brought to the level of distinguishing between true and not true or, as a preliminary stage, between correct and incorrect.'[265] Elsewhere he writes:

> Actually, the more they [works of art] are understood, the less they are enjoyed. Formerly, even the traditional attitude to the artwork, if it was to be absolutely relevant to the work, was that of admiration that the works exist as they do in themselves and not for the sake of the observer. What opened up to, and overpowered, the beholder was their truth, which as in works of Kafka's type outweighs every other element. They were not a higher order of amusement.[266]

In almost all philosophical theories of art, and most distinctly in those that are descended from Hegel, aesthetic experience results in truth; it reveals that which outward appearances conceal.[267] That is what it has in common with religious experience, and hence the explanations that Western philosophers propose for the reception of an *artistic text* can in many respects be applied to the mystics' listening – at least, they are the most accurate descriptions available in the Western literature to understand such events. A *theologian* such as Otto in any case has nothing useful to offer; except for a few platitudes, he presents little reflection on the production of *tremendum* and *fascinans* in listening to music, poetry or the recited scripture, as maintained in the *samāʿ* treatises – that is, on their involvement in aesthetic experience.

Aesthetic experience need not produce only, or even primarily, 'enjoyment': what happens to those slain by the Quran cannot be explained by the Kantian concept of *disinterested satisfaction*.[268] We can see it rather as an insight which the experiencing subject interprets as absolutely true and absolutely crucial for his life and religious practice, and which is received aesthetically. The subjectively dramatic experience of the Quran verses is not induced primarily by their discursive content (which is familiar to the devout listeners from prior reception situations) but by their sensual manner of appearance – that is, their linguistic-musical structure or, in more general terms, their acoustic and expressive qualities. Not all mystics would agree with Ibn ʿArabī that, once one attains a certain degree of understanding, the individual words in the Quran are unimportant and one understands the message by the sound alone;[269] yet there can be no doubt that the truth communicated in *samāʿ* is not thought of in a discursive sense but lies in what Adorno calls – in the Hegelian tradition – the text's *Gehalt*, its substance. Because it transcends the discursive, this substance exists only in the aesthetic experience of sensory constellations or, to use Kant's words once more, in the 'presentation of aesthetic ideas', meaning those 'representations of the imagination' which give rise to thought but for which no adequate concept exists that could be communicated in language.[270] Adorno too says, 'Understanding has as its idea that one become conscious of the artwork's content [as a spiritual content] by way of the full experience of it.'[271]

In the listening Sufis, such an experience can induce, as we have seen, both enjoyment (*laḏḏa*) and dread and terror (*hayba*). The truth of the Quran is by no means pure pleasure, no more so than the truth of many works of art, especially those Adorno praises: just as the Quran claims to be a message of joy (*bushrā*) and a warning (*nidār*), so the experience of its substance can lead both to intoxicating feelings of happiness and to panic and horror at the afterlife scenarios it announces. The sentence 'So give thou good tidings to My servants'[272] is offset not only by terrifying descriptions of the impending inferno but also by the Prophet's saying quoted in chapter 5: 'If you knew what I know, you would laugh little and weep much.'[273] In listening to the revelation that Muhammad promulgated, the faithful seem to realize this knowledge; it seems to illuminate them, fascinating and horrifying at the same time, like 'lightning that flashes and then goes out; lights that appear and then vanish', as a Sufi quoted by al-Qushayrī says: 'How sweet they would be if they would only remain for a moment with the one who possesses them!'[274] Adorno's dictum that fireworks are prototypical of works of art[275] is confirmed in the accounts presented above. What he writes about the experience of a work of art is also true of these Quran listeners:

> The experiencing subject, from which aesthetic experience distances itself, returns in aesthetic experience as a transaesthetic subject. The aesthetic shudder once again cancels the distance held by the subject. Although artworks offer themselves to observation, they at the same time disorient the observer who is held at the distance of a mere spectator; to him is revealed the truth of the work as if it must also be his own. The instant of this transition is art's highest. It rescues subjectivity, even subjective aesthetics, by the negation of subjectivity. The subject, convulsed by art, has real experiences; by the strength of insight into the artwork as artwork, these experiences are those in which the subject's petrification in his own subjectivity dissolves and the narrowness of his self-positedness is revealed. If in artworks the subject finds his true happiness in the moment of being convulsed, this is a happiness that is counterposed to the subject and thus its instrument is tears, which also express the grief over one's own mortality. Kant sensed something of this in his aesthetic of the sublime, which he excluded from art.[276]

The moment in which the subject in the aesthetic experience, surrendering to an object, loses himself, and in that very loss true subjectivity is rescued and returns – we could call precisely this moment as the essence of the ecstasy that the mystics pursue in *samā'*, which is an absorption in contemplation, a relinquishment of one's subjectivity. For, as Bākharzī says, the *wājid*, the 'finder' through listening, is 'in truth a *fāqid*', a loser of himself.[277] The listener absorbs the recitation 'into himself with mind and heart and soul and substitutes it for his whole being', 'Umar as-Suhrawardī writes. 'The word embraces and encloses him, and every hair on him becomes hearing and every atom of him vision, so that he hears the whole thing with his whole being and sees the whole thing with his whole being.'[278]

Schopenhauer conceives the experience of art similarly, so that it is almost indistinguishable from mystical experience. The state that is essential for the listener's or spectator's 'cognition of the Idea', he writes, is 'pure contemplation, absorption in intuition, losing oneself in the object, forgetting all individuality, abolishing the mode of cognition that follows the principle of sufficient reason and grasps only relations'.[279] Essential to both Schopenhauer and as-Suhrawardī is the unreserved contemplation that Walter Benjamin compared with the 'image of (a painter's) vanishing in a picture (painted by himself) – an image borrowed from the tradition of Chinese folktales'.[280]

After the petrification of his subjectivity has dissolved in the state of 'annihilation' (*fanā'*), the experiencing subject in the state of 'abiding in God' (*baqā'*) becomes aware of himself again in the Other, in the Divine, and his qualities are returned to him in a new, spiritual shape.[281] The subject's happiness is opposed to the subject, as Adorno says; it is born of the convulsion that releases the subject from himself. The Sufis too know that the organ of that convulsion is weeping, which also expresses grief (*ḥuzn*) over one's own frailty – for this reason 'Umar as-Suhrawardī calls the ecstasy of the mystic an 'outcry of the spirit',[282] and Thābit al-Bunānī is reported to have said, 'There is not a pillar left in the Friday mosque at which I have not recited the whole Quran and wept.'[283] Qoṭbeddīn Manṣūr 'Ebādī outlined in his *Virtues of Sufism* how Sufis see the subjective expression of the process of annihilation and abiding in God – as a renewal of the primal covenant between God and man.

> The great ones of the mystic path (*ṭarīqat*) have spoken thus: listening is penetration (*wārid'*) of the Authentic into a heart, to make known the concealed states and to renew the Adamic covenant. Such a penetration is perceived in two ways, however: there are some for whom the strength of their aspiration and determination dominates over the acceptance of life, and they preserve all that comes to them secretly and in concealment. Their interior is disturbed by the power of what they hear, and their exterior is still. And there are others for whom the terror of love and the sorrow of madness take possession of their hearts. Because what they hear glitters like the flashing of lightning in the pores of their heart, the power of sorrow dominates the silence of reverence. They are set in motion by the effect of the lightning. Excitement fills their mind and carries over to their exterior. Their eyes weep at the splendour that flashes before them and overcomes them. After a time, their emotion has become stronger and makes their tongue raise a racket. After a time it has become more perfect, and the preponderance of the external confusion joins with the inner discomposure.[284]

In a certain sense, the terminology mystics use in describing their experience of God is more aesthetic than that which Adorno uses in talking about the experience of art. Adorno felt uncomfortable grasping works of art and their reception with the traditional categories of art theory such as 'enjoyment', 'beauty', 'happiness', 'pleasing', 'taste' and 'sublimity': he sensed that they were no longer adequate. Rather than simply ignoring them and inventing new terms, he struggled with them and, by reflecting on them, stripped away all naiveté in his use of them. By mistrusting them, he preserved what appeared to him salvageable of aesthetics after Auschwitz. He held it as a 'strict antinomy' that 'the beautiful is no more to be defined than its concept can be dispensed with'.[285] He almost entirely eschewed a word such as '*Genuß*' ('enjoyment'), which the Sufis used emphatically; attributes such as '*Ohrenschmaus*' ('a feast to the ears') sounded jarring to him. He saw artistic experience as autonomous only where it repudiated the taste of enjoyment.

Such mistrust, rooted in historic and intellectual developments, is unknown to the Sufis quoted in this chapter. In their writings, they represent the experience of God as an enjoyable experience of beauty, and they interpret God's words, 'Shall the reward for the beautiful be anything but beautiful?'[286] as addressed to them. Sarī as-Saqaṭī quotes those who are granted the contemplation of God as saying, 'We deem all torments more desirable than to be veiled from Thee. When Thy beauty is revealed to our hearts, we take no thought of affliction.'[287] Through listening, the Sufi is guided through 'one of the arenas of beauty', in ad-Darrāj's image, and 'out to the vast meadows of repose'.[288] ʿEbādī too says, 'Perfect enjoyment lies only in listening.'[289] Even those slain by the Quran experience God not only as something true (and hence causing terror or bliss) but also, in listening to the Quran, as something beautiful, as ath-Thaʿlabī explicitly states in his fourteenth story, about a relative of the Umayyad governor Muhallab ibn Abī Sufyān (d. 702) – apparently an older man, since he is called *shaykh.*

Together with two servants, a man and a woman, he was returning by boat on the Tigris to his home in Basra from a business journey. During his boat journey he saw a young man standing on the riverbank in the simple wool garment of an ascetic. He had pity on the man and offered to take him along to Basra in the boat. In the course of the journey, the emissary invited the ascetic to eat with him, which he accepted only after considerable urging. The host wanted to do more for his guest and ordered his servant to get out her lute and sing.

Afterwards he asked his guest, 'Young man, can you sing as beautifully?'

'I can do something that is much more beautiful than that', the young man replied, and he recited with 'a beautiful voice' the verses 4:77–8, which speak of the death that awaits everyone. Then the Sheikh threw his cup in the water and said,

> 'I confess that is the most beautiful thing I have ever heard. Is there any more than that?'

The young man said there was, and then recited: 'Say: "The truth is from your Lord; so let whosoever will believe, and let whosoever will disbelieve." Surely we have prepared for the evildoers a fire, whose pavilion encompasses them; if they call for succour, they will be succoured with water like molten copper, that shall scald their faces – how evil a potion, and how evil a resting-place!'[290]

That made a deep impression upon the sheikh's heart. He called for a pot and threw it in the water; he took the lute and broke it. Then he asked, 'Young man, is there also something joyful here?'

'Yes', the young man answered, and recited: 'Say: "O my people who have been prodigal against yourselves, do not despair of God's mercy; surely God forgives sins altogether; surely He is the All-forgiving, the All-compassionate."'[291]

The Sheikh uttered a loud cry and fainted. When they examined him, he had already died.

The emissary was carried home and buried and widely mourned; meanwhile his servant led an ascetic life after this occurrence. She was wrapped in hair, and over it she wore the typical wool garment of the seekers of God. She spent the days fasting and the nights praying. One night she heard someone reciting the verse, 'Say: The truth is from your Lord...'. The story ends: 'When people came in the morning, they found her dead.'

Of course it is not simply delight that the young man's Quran recitation induces in the sheikh and his servant but also a terrifying knowledge. Yet the act of convulsion in which they and the other Quran listeners realize the truth is described as one of pleasure, and the message, disconcerting as it is, is described as beautiful: the young man announces an especially beautiful recitation and then selects verses that tell of the death that awaits everyone; and the host, far from crying out in horror, declares that it is the most beautiful thing he has ever heard. 'There are a hundred thousand pleasures in listening', says Rūzbehān Baqlī in explaining the connection between insight and pleasure, and 'knowledge for a thousand years of insights, which cannot be attained by any worship, can be cut from every pleasure'.[292] The connection is found in al-Ġazālī too, when he mentions the 'enjoyment that the sense of hearing causes when it receives the knowledge appropriate to it'.[293]

The experience of listening affords pleasure, but the Sufi term of *ladda*, and others such as *tarwīḥ* ('refreshment') or *taṭrīb* ('delight'), certainly do not mean 'taking pleasure in art, modelled on real enjoyment', which Adorno considered an impertinence.[294] If one were to name a central phenomenon in ath-Thaʿlabī's or other authors' narratives about Sufi Quran listeners, it would certainly not be the 'culinary' pleasure of listening to the Quran and delighting in the beauty of its language – that is, the 'disinterested satisfaction' which Kant imagined, and which Adorno rightly found inadequate in view of the reality of works of art.[295] What makes this pleasure so special, and what leaps out at the reader of these stories, is that it is mingled with the fear, with the physical horror, that the Quran awakens in those who hear it recited. They cannot get enough of it even though they know they will not survive its powerful effect.

> You walk upon the dead with scornful glances,
> Among your gems Horror is not least fair;
> Murder, the dearest of your baubles, dances
> Upon your haughty breast with amorous air.[296]

The simultaneity of pleasure and horror that Baudelaire extols is especially prominent in the last episode presented. It also recalls the blind man Abū Juhayr, one of several mystics mentioned in the Sufi literature who know that a certain Quran recitation will kill them, and yet wish for nothing as longingly as to hear exactly that.[297] And whatever death wishes or other psychological or religious motives may be revealed in, or interpreted into, these anecdotes, they begin with a desire to hear the Quran – more precisely, as we have seen, a desire that is quite obviously rooted in aesthetic fascination. Nonetheless, what happens to Abū Juhayr and the other Quran listeners cannot be caught in attributes such as 'enjoyment', 'satisfaction' or 'refreshment', although the real fear with which they respond to the proclamation of doom is a kind of resistance that is closer to desire than to disinterest.[298] Perhaps the *lad̲d̲a* of the Sufi treatises about listening should be translated not with the word 'enjoyment' [*Genuß*], which suggests an *ars poetica* that would be completely inadequate to the Sufi experience, but with a term such as 'pleasure' [*Lust*], which Adorno preferred. 'Pleasure' is also more likely to offer a path to 'ecstasy', the state described by the Sufis; and, for that, 'the meagre concept of enjoyment is hardly adequate, other than to produce disgust for enjoying anything.'[299] Enjoyment in the ordinary sense is in any case not what Ruwaym (d. 915 or 916) was referring to when he said, in answer to the question what the Sufis experience in listening,

> They contemplate the substance that others overlook, and they exhort it: To me, to me! They are beatified with joy over it. Afterwards the veil falls, and then their joy turns to weeping, and one tears his clothes and another cries out, a third weeps, each according to what is apportioned to him.[300]

The conceptual difficulties that arise are inherent in the matter under consideration: it resists concepts. 'The Sufis have states that languages cannot grasp and that cannot be explained by verbal expression', says the 'Life of Kings', a ninth- or tenth-century manual of Islamic mysticism.[301] Adorno expressed this idea in a simile:

> Artworks speak like elves in fairy tales: 'If you want the absolute, you shall have it, but you will not recognize it when you see it.' The truth of discursive

knowledge is unshrouded, and thus discursive knowledge does not have it; the knowledge that is art, has truth, but as something incommensurable with art.[302]

Adorno's cognitive utopia, 'to unseal the nonconceptual with concepts, without making it their equal',[303] could serve as an epigraph before the mystics' endeavours to bear witness to their experience. It is utopian because the knowledge revealed defies all linguistic expression, and the happiness that it gives has its reality only as an experience: 'one does not have it, but is in it.'[304] Their realization is aesthetic in nature. Or mystical: in relation to the listeners slain by the Quran, the terms seem to be almost interchangeable. The converse is also true: just as we can understand the mystics' listening aesthetically, we can also read Adorno's aesthetic theory (and, *a fortiori*, Schopenhauer's aesthetics discussed in it) as a secular or a negative mysticism. Hence the analogies. 'For him who has a genuine relation to art, in which he himself vanishes, art is not an object; deprivation of art would be unbearable for him, yet he does not consider individual works sources of joy', Adorno writes.[305] If we replace the term 'art' in that sentence with *samāʿ*, it could just as well be the words of a Sufi. Unlike many of his interpreters, Adorno was doubtless aware that aesthetic and mystical experiences ultimately converge. The fundamental difference between them lies in the definition of their content as artistic-aesthetic or religious-mystical knowledge, and perhaps in the existential nature of the convulsion they involve, but not in how they occur and how they are immediately perceived. Adorno did posit a transcendence – which, unlike the Sufis, he interpreted non-religiously: he called the transcendental not God, but the 'completely other' or the 'non-identical'. To him the transcendental was shrouded in black, and the work of art was not its revealed scripture, as the Quran is to the mystics, but its mirror-writing. That is theology backwards.

Just as the 'autonomous work of art', in Adorno's view, tends to express nothing, the Sufis knew that, at the end of the mystic path and at the highest stage of listening, silence remains; all sensations cease; fear and weeping, horror and enjoyment no longer exist, and even beauty and majesty can no longer express what the seeker contemplates: Anṣārī defines such a 'listening of the extraordinary among the extraordinary' as 'a listening that purifies the unveiling (*kashf*) of all deficiencies, in which the origin meets eternity and the end arrives at the beginning',[306] and Ibn ʿArabī writes:

Al-Junayd was asked about the insight of the mystic (*al-ʿārif*). 'The colour of his original state is the colour of water', he said. Now if a mystic is asked about the Quran and about the heart which has received a revelation, he must give that same answer.[307]

That which is known, 'contemplated', through listening can only be thought without images[308] – that is, it can only be defined abstractly, as the perfection (*kamāl*) in which the divine beauty and majesty are realized, or the negation of everything conceivable. 'The Old Testament prohibition on images has an aesthetic as well as a theological dimension', Adorno remarks. 'That one should make no image, which means no image *of* anything whatsoever, expresses at the same time that it is impossible to make such an image.'[309] The beauty that is proper to the divine perfection cannot 'be perceived by the senses or discerned by analogical reasoning', ʿUmar as-Suhrawardī writes; 'to reason, it has no How, and to comprehension it is inexplicable.'[310] Imam ʿAlī is also invoked as a witness to this knowledge: 'I saw nothing except that I saw God before, after and with it.'[311] Such is the splendour of God's beauty that only the strongest can bear it, as a Sufi legend illustrates. When Moses came down from Mount Sinai, everyone who looked at him was blinded by the divine radiance that was on his face.[312] The Absolute is not visible precisely because it is revealed to the eye absolutely bare: the overpowering nearness blinds the eye; the unshaded light is absolute blackness (*nūr-e siyāh*) and the knowledge of the absolute Existence brings with it the knowledge of the absolute Nothingness (*nisti-ye moṭlaq*) – an idea that the mystics have often expressed.[313] Nothing more can then be said about the contemplated Other, only how it is revealed in the subject disappearing in it. Many Sufis can only conceive that as music. The idea of an imageless truth leads Adorno as if spontaneously to music as the true locus of abstract truth,[314] and we find the similar idea in Islamic mysticism that the highest manifestation of God is only conceivable in tones – not in words, not in images, only in pure sound. In the listening of the spiritually perfect, says ʿUmar as-Suhrawardī, 'God reveals himself unveiled through music'.[315] Rūzbehān Baqlī compares the state of *unio mystica* to a 'dance with God',[316] and Rūmī writes, 'the House of Love is made completely of music, of verses and songs'; the 'heavenly beloved circumambulates this house', playing his rebab 'and singing intoxicating tunes'.[317]

Such notions are not so foreign to Western thought. In the philosophy of the bourgeois era, the most perfect expression of the beautiful was long situated in the field of plastic rather than musical art, but an important current emerged in aesthetic philosophy in the course of the nineteenth century, especially with Schopenhauer and Nietzsche, and extended into the twentieth century, most significantly in Adorno, which elevated music to the organ of an abstract cognition. In this tradition music becomes, in Nietzsche's words, 'the true metaphysical activity of this life'.[318] Schopenhauer in particular, who conceived the Absolute as will, comes close to the notions of some Sufis in his remarks on music; he seems to be much more aware than Adorno, or even Hegel, of the latent mysticism of his philosophy. He writes, for example:

> In fact, music is an *unmediated* objectivation and copy of the entire *will*, just as the world itself is, just as in fact the Ideas themselves are, whose multiplied appearance constitutes the world of particular things. Therefore,

> unlike the other arts, music is in no way a copy of the Ideas; instead, it is a *copy of the will itself*, whose objecthood the Ideas are as well: this is precisely why the effect of music is so much more powerful and urgent than that of the other arts: the other arts speak only of shadows while music speaks of the essence.[319]

Sufis too see music, not as the representation of the Absolute, but as its authentic medium. Perhaps most pay attention only to the material sound, but he who is among the extraordinary hears the spiritual in it; he 'hears everything as it really is', Hojwīrī teaches.[320] When Schopenhauer says music expresses 'the inner essence, the in-itself of the world',[321] or that 'on the whole the music is the melody to which the world is the text',[322] that is not far removed from Rūmī's now proverbial metaphor in which the human being is an instrument in God's hand and his existence the music that God plays: 'We are the harp You pluck' (*Mā 'o angīm wa to nākhūn mīzanī*). In the Sufi view of the world, God created all creatures to praise Him in their respective languages, so that all the world is one divine harmony, one great hymn in His honour. In the beginning was not the word, but music – and music will be when the soul ascends to its Lord, for music is, in the saying attributed to Rūmī, 'the creaking of the gates of Paradise'.[323] He and many other Sufis, like some of the German Romantics, can imagine this original language only as something musical, 'a wondrous song', as Novalis wrote in his novella *The Novices of Sais*, whose 'irresistible tones penetrated deep into the inwardness of nature and split it apart.'[324] When al-Junayd was asked how dignified and respectable people could suddenly become enraptured on hearing a beautiful voice, he replied that it was because they heard the sweet primordial melody of the divine Adamic covenant, in which God asked the children of Adam, 'Am I not your Lord?' (*a-lastu bi-rabbikum*), and they said, 'Yes, we testify':[325] 'The sweetness of that speech and the bliss of that word remained in the souls' organs of hearing.'[326] It is no coincidence that this recalls Socrates' speech in praise of Eros in Plato's *Phaedrus*: in the face of earthly beauty, the true lover is overwhelmed by the recollection of the beautiful that he contemplated before birth in the celestial place; however, this convulsion is experienced only by one who is still capable of that recollection: the philosopher. He seems to grow wings; he wants to soar upwards, but he cannot. He looks up at the heavens and pays no more heed to earthly things. He does not understand what is happening to him; he is like a bird that cannot fly and flaps its wings in vain. They condemn him as a madman, but in truth his is the highest enthusiasm. When the person intoxicated by beauty partakes of the divine, it must appear to the many as madness. This enthusiasm is the best thing for the one affected, and also for one in community with him, and a person in this madness who loves the beautiful is called a lover. The earthly forms of the Ideas are no longer luminous, for beauty was only luminous in the beginning. But, to the lover, it glows under every being.[327]

It is this Platonic concept of memory of the Beautiful in the beginning which al-Junayd and other Sufis, surely influenced by Neoplatonic ideas, although without knowing the *Phaedrus*, so elegantly transposed into an Islamic context, and which was also a strong influence in European aesthetics even after the Romantics – recall Hegel's definition of the beautiful as the 'appearance of the Idea to sense'[328] or Schelling's concept of art as 'the representation of the archetypes'.[329] It may serve as the backdrop before which the following story becomes real: the last and, I find, the most heart-rending case I will present from the *Book of Those Slain by the Quran*. Perhaps we must really think in mythic, or at least in Platonic, Sufi, or otherwise transcendental dimensions and world views if we want to situate ʿAlī ibn al-Fuḍayl ibn ʿIyāḍ's feverish desire for the sound of the Quran anywhere but in the field of mere curiosity, or even religious fanaticism. He had just recovered from a severe illness (the account does not say explicitly what his illness was, but hints that it was probably a consequence of Quran listening) and was so utterly and completely at the mercy of his passion that his father, on hearing that a 'man from Basra who mastered recitation outstandingly' had come to town, immediately sent for him to prevent him from reciting to his son.

> But, before the messenger reached him, he had already recited to him as follows: 'In the name of God, the Merciful, the Compassionate: If thou couldst see when they are stationed before their Lord!'[330] Then ʿAlī sank to the ground, heaved a loud sigh and gave up the ghost.

According to another version mentioned by ath-Thaʿlabī, ʿAlī dies of a Quran recitation by his own father, Abū ʿAlī al-Fuḍayl (d. 803), who became famous himself as an ascetic and a lover of the Quran. Unaware that his son was nearby, he recited verse 23:106: 'Our Lord, our adversity prevailed over us: we were an erring people.' ʿAlī fell down unconscious and only came to his senses when his mother, who had been urgently summoned, poured water over his head. 'You're killing this boy!' she shouted at his father.

> The father tarried as long as God wanted. Without knowing that his son was standing behind him, he recited: 'There would appear to them from God that which they never reckoned with.'[331] The son fell down dead, and his father broke off his recitation.
>
> Someone went to his mother and said to her, 'Go to him.' She came and poured water on her son, but he was dead.[332]

The reader will have noticed that I have often looked for analogies from other contexts and cultures for the events, texts and perceptions discussed, not in order to claim they are equal, but rather as an approach to a phenomenon that can at first seem disconcerting, strange or simply quirky, to make it more understandable, more conceivable; and, most of all, to point out the part of reality that the texts have for us – to identify them as documents of an experience whose relevance goes beyond their originating context of Islam. Yet I am obliged to confess that I can hardly name anything comparable to the magnitude of attraction to a text that is demonstrated in this episode and those presented earlier in this section, whether in religious or in secular literature. One would have to recall the great ecstatic lovers, whether from the verses of Neẓāmī or of Shakespeare, to find a comparable *enthusiasmos*. And indeed the Sufis themselves, who felt themselves primarily to be lovers, found this kind of illustration of their mystical experience the most familiar and the most natural. The listening seekers (*sālek-e samā'gar*), Ḥoseyn Ḥeydarkhānī writes in a modern treatise on *samā'*, feels nothing 'of the cold of his own disbelief, or the heat of his infatuation, just as the guests of Sulayha did not notice that they cut their own hands instead of the citrus fruit offered when Joseph entered.'[333] Even al-Junayd, who was known as particularly 'sober', drew an analogy with Joseph's beautiful appearance.

> One day when I came to as-Sarī and saw him with an unconscious man, I asked what had happened to him. As-Sarī said, 'He heard a verse from God's book.' I replied, 'Let it be recited a second time!' It was done, and the man came to his senses. Sarī asked me how I had known that. I said, 'By Joseph's shirt Jacob lost his eyesight, and by it his sight returned again.'[334]

Ḥeydarkhānī, quoted above, would no doubt not have agreed with al-Junayd's advice: one who has been made 'drunk and unconscious by the vision of the perfect beauty of the divine Beloved', he writes, after the rather ecstatic tradition in Sufism, should not be disturbed before he awakens of himself, since such an experience is of the highest degree and worth.

> It is here that all of the listening seeker's habits and qualities are annihilated before the Light of all lights. His fate is not without similarity to that of Sulayha in the story from the *Thousand and One Nights* in which Sulayha burns with love for Joseph for seven years and loses herself in that love. When she was cold, she said 'Joseph!' (and she grew warmer); when she was warm, she said 'Joseph!' and she felt cool; when she was hungry, she said 'Joseph!' and she was sated; when she was thirsty, she slaked her thirst with 'Joseph!' As Ibn Sīrīn has said, the seeker of God, when he has reached this stage, feels nothing, even if he is thrown down to the ground from the roof.[335]

Like Plato, the Sufis conceive the most extreme perfection possible to humans only as an encounter with the Beautiful – not with the Idea of the Good, or of Being, or the like. 'God is beautiful', says one of the most frequently quoted hadiths in the Sufi literature:[336] coming from a philosopher, that statement would be interesting enough for its directness and because it defines the Absolute aesthetically, but coming from the founder of a religion it is altogether remarkable. The divine is beautiful, says Socrates in the *Phaedrus*.[337] Likewise in Diotima's speech in *The Symposium*, it is something beautiful and wondrous that awaits the lover of beauty at the end of the path.[338] In Plato it is a beautiful *figure*, an object, that induces the divine enthusiasm; in the Sufis, on the other hand, it is a figure of sound; the experience is auditory, not visual (although some Sufis too experienced *samāʿ* as the sight of a beautiful body). This seems familiar from Schopenhauer and those who came after him, but at the same time unique: I could not name any other *text* that is ascribed an attraction as strong and as musical as that of the Quran in these episodes. And, as much as the Sufis loved the sounds of music and poetry, the Quran to them is 'the most beautiful of things, and things that are thought beautiful cannot be found beautiful beside its beauty', as-Sarrāj writes.[339] There is nothing 'that moves the heart more and brings on sadness more strongly than reciting the Quran', says the ascetic and preacher of repentance Wuhayb ibn al-Ward (d. 770),[340] and Hojwīrī proposes what is perhaps the prettiest praise of the Quran by a mystic:

> Its instruction is more enchanting than all instructions, its expression is more wonderful than all expressions, its commandments are sweeter than all commandments, its prohibitions are more peremptory than all prohibitions, its promises are more seductive than all promises, its threats are more harrowing than all threats, its stories are more exhaustive than all stories, its parables are more poignant than all parables. It has captured a thousand hearts that heard it; it has captivated a thousand souls with its stories. It can lower the most powerful people in the world down to the most common and raise the most common up to the most powerful.[341]

Naturally such statements are not the result of sound, objective literary analysis, and the legends collected by ath-Thaʿlabī are not factual documents: there is no reason not to attribute to them a high degree of imagination and stylization. But the same must be said of Plato's allegory, of Neẓāmī's and Shakespeare's love stories: they are not faithful accounts of real events, but poetry – and yet we can certainly take them seriously and relate them to our own reality. But the simple fact that such an attraction is ascribed to the Quran, that these pious legends of the dying Quran listeners have currency, that they are retold and collected – that alone is, as far as I can see, unparalleled. There may be differences of opinion as to whether the Quran is the world's most beautiful text, as Muslims claim, but there can be little doubt that the beauty they attribute to it is claimed for no other poetic or revealed text. This phenomenon, if we would secularize it and grasp it as a historic singularity and a scientific conundrum, is the actual miracle of Islam. Just as in Christianity, to submit one last analogy, it is not the Crucifixion itself that is unique and inexplicable – Jesus Christ was one of many who were hung on crosses in his day – but the belief in Christ's resurrection – that is, the response of his contemporaries and later generations. That is what makes his death on the Cross, and that is what makes the language of the Quran, a miracle.

Romanization of Arabic and Persian Words

Technical Notes

’	Glottal stop before a vowel at the onset of a syllable, as in the second syllable of English ‘uh-oh’.
aw	(Only in Arabic) Diphthong, similar to ‘ou’ in English ‘out’.
‘	Voiced fricative that sounds like an ‘a’ pressed out of the throat. It is produced by constricting the pharynx (in Persian, as ‘’’).
ā, ī, ū	Long vowels (in Persian, vowels are not lengthened in pronunciation; ‘ā’ in Persian is a back ‘a’, similar to the Swedish ‘å’).
č	(Only in Persian) Like ‘ch’, as in ‘much’.
ḏ	(Only in Arabic) Like a voiced ‘th’ in English, as in ‘that’.
ḍ	(Only in Arabic) An emphatic, palatal, pharyngealized ‘d’.
ġ	A velar ‘r’, like the French ‘r’ (in Persian, a soft, as if hinted, voiced uvular ‘r’).
j	A soft ‘g’, as in English ‘giant’.
h	Like ‘h’ in English, but always distinctly pronounced as a consonant, even at the end of a syllable.
ḥ	An aspirated h, between the ‘h’ in English ‘help’ and the ‘ch’ in Scottish ‘loch’ (in Persian, as ‘h’).
kh	Like ‘ch’ in Scottish ‘loch’.
kh^{w}	(Only in Persian) As ‘kh’. The letter ‘w’ here is only written, not pronounced.
ou	(Only in Persian) Diphthong, similar to the ‘o’ in English ‘hello’.
q	An unvoiced, guttural ‘k’ (in Persian, as ‘ġ’).
s	Unvoiced ‘s’, as in ‘bus’.
sh	Unvoiced ‘sh’, as in ‘sheep’.
ṣ	Emphatic, palatal, pharyngealized s (in Persian, as ‘s’).
s̱	(Only in Persian) As ‘s’.
ṭ	An emphatic, palatal, pharyngealized t (in Persian, as ‘t’).
th	(Only in Arabic) Like unvoiced ‘th’ in English, as in ‘thing’.
w	Like w in English ‘wonder’ (in Persian, like English ‘v’, as in ‘vocal’).
y	Like consonantal ‘y’ in English, as in ‘young’.
z	Like ‘z’ in English, as in ‘zoo’.
ż	(Only in Persian) As ‘z’.
ẕ	(Only in Persian) As ‘z’.
ž	(Only in Persian.) Like ‘j’ in French, as in ‘Jacques’.

Persian words, names and text are transcribed as Persian: thus Sorūsh, for example, rather than Surūsh). The names of authors who wrote all or most of their works in Persian are transcribed as Persian. The Arabic titles of Persian books are transcribed as Arabic, however.

Other Notes

The following were variously used in translations of Quran passages:

Hazrat Mirza Bashir-ud-Din Mahmud Ahmad (ed.), *Der heilige Qur-ân*. 2nd rev. edn, Zurich, 1959.
Arthur J. Arberry, *The Quran Interpreted*. New York, 1955.
Richard Bell, *The Qur'ān Translated*, 2 vols. Edinburgh, 1937–9.
Régis Blachère, *Le Coran*, 3 vols. Paris, 1947–50.
M. A. S. Abdel Haleem, *The Qur'an: A New Translation*. Oxford, 2004.
Max Henning, *Der Koran*. Stuttgart, 1980.
Tarif Khalidi, *The Qur'an: A New Translation*. London, 2009.
Rudi Paret, *Der Koran*. 5th edn, Stuttgart, Berlin and Cologne, 1989.
Muhammad Ahmad Rassoul, *Die ungefähre Bedeutung des Al-Qur'ān Al-Karīm in deutscher Sprache*. 3rd rev. edn, Cologne, 1988.
Friedrich Rückert, *Der Koran*, ed. Hartmut Bobzin. Würzburg, 1995.

All Quran commentaries are cited by the corresponding Quran verse. In the case of particularly long commentaries on individual verses, page numbers are given in parentheses.

Hadiths are cited in accordance with the system of A. J. Wensinck's *Handbook of Early Muhammadan Tradition* (Leiden, 1971). Because the arrangement of the individual sections (*abwāb*) in contemporary print editions does not always match the numbers in Wensinck's concordance, the currently customary numbering has been added.

Bible quotations, except where indicated, are given after the King James Version.

All encyclopaedia and dictionary entries are cited by headword.

All emphasis and quotation marks within quotations are present in the original text except where otherwise indicated.

Spelling, capitalization and transcription of quoted translations have been adapted to the present text.

Glossary

ādāb at-tilāwa: The codes of behaviour for Quran recitation.

'arabīya: The standard literary register of Arabic, associated with the pre-Islamic Arabs.

asbāb an-nuzūl: The historic occasions of the revelation of the Quran to Muhammad and the traditional Islamic science that studies these occasions.

Ash'ari (Arabic: *Ash'arīyūn*, after Abū l-Ḥasan 'Alī al-'Ash'arī): A theological school in Sunni Islam that is generally sceptical of the knowledge attainable through reason.

faṣāḥa: Eloquence.

Hadith (Arabic: *ḥadīth*, pl. *aḥādīthu* 'narrative'): A traditional, normative saying or deed of Muhammad, or the corpus of such traditions.

hijā': The ancient Arabic genre of invective or satirical poetry.

Hijra: Muhammad's emigration from Mecca to Yathrib, which was then renamed Medina, in September 622; the beginning of the Islamic calendar.

i'jāz: The Quran's inimitability, or its miraculous nature in general (literally: 'incapacitation').

Jahiliyyah (Arabic: *jāhilīya*, 'time of ignorance'): Arabian antiquity before the revelation of the Quran.

kahāna: Soothsaying.

kāhin (pl. *kuhhān*): Soothsayer.

kitāb: Book; used in the Quran in reference to the celestial original of the revealed text.

lafẓ: Expression.

ma'nā: Meaning.

maqām (pl. *maqāmāt*): A melodic mode in Arabo-Persian classical music.

mujawwad: A musical form of Quran recitation based on the melodic modes of Arabo-Persian vocal art.

murratal: An austere or meditative form of Quran recitation.

muṣḥaf: The Quran as a written or printed material object.

Mu'tazili (Arabic: *Mu'tazila*, from *i'tazala*, 'to withdraw'): An early school of Sunni theology, strongly oriented towards rationalism, which exerted a strong influence on later Shiite theology.

nabī: Prophet.

naẓm: The linguistic structure or composition of a text (literally: 'order').

nubūwa: Prophethood.

qāri' (pl. *qurrā'*): A Quran reciter (also called *muqri'*, *tālī* or *murattil*).

qirā'a (pl. *qirā'at*): A Quran recitation, or one of the possible variant readings of the Quran.

Quraysh (Arabic: *al-Quraysh*): The Arab tribe in Mecca to which Muhammad belonged.

rasm: The written Quran in unpointed and unvocalized Arabic, codified under the third caliph, ʿUthmān.

rasūl: Apostle; envoy.

rāwī (pl. *ruwāt*): Rhapsode; a reciter and transmitter of ancient Arabic poetry.

shāʿir (pl. *shuʿarā*): Poet.

ṣalāt: Islamic ritual prayer, consisting of recitation from the Quran and fixed liturgical phrases.

samāʿ: The ritual 'listening' of the mystics; mystical dance.

shayṭān (pl. *shayāṭīn*): In early Arabic, a kind of demon; later used to refer to the fallen angel Iblīs – that is, Satan in the biblical sense.

shiʿr: Poetry.

sīra: A biography of the Prophet Muhammad, or the body of biographical traditions about him.

Sufism (Arabic: *taṣawwuf*, possibly from *ṣūf*, 'wool'): Islamic mysticism.

tafsīr: Exegesis or commentary on the Quran.

tajwīd: Standards for enunciation of the Quranic text and guidance for the audience's emotional attitude to the recitation (literally: 'embellishment').

Traditionist (Arabic: *muḥaddith*): A collector of the traditions of the Prophet's acts and words (*aḥādīth*).

umma: The community of Muslims.

waḥy: Revelation or inspiration.

Zahiri (Arabic: *ẓāhirīyūn*): A school of Quran exegesis which adheres strictly to the literal sense.

Notes

The following abbreviations have been used:

EI[1] *Enzyklopädie des Islam*, 4 vols. Leiden and Leipzig, 1913–34; Supplementary vol., 1938.

EI[2] *The Encyclopaedia of Islam*. New edn, Leiden, 1954–.

Preface

1 'Das islamische Dogma der "Unnachahmlichkeit des Korans"', p. 166.
2 Ibid., p. 167.
3 Gramlich, 'Der Urvertrag in der Koranauslegung', p. 205.
4 Müller, *Untersuchungen zur Reimprosa im Koran*, p. 9.

Chapter 1 The First Listeners

1 With few exceptions, the people named in this chapter were contemporaries of Muhammad. Because their exact dates are generally uncertain, to say the least, while the approximate historic period in which they lived is known, I am omitting the year of death where these persons are named. The names of those concerned are marked in the index.
2 Lane, *Selections of the Ḳur-án with an Interwoven Commentary*, p. 88; Sell, *Faith of Islam*, p. 8; Smith, *Mohammed and Mohammedanism*, p. 179.
3 See, e.g., Hojwīrī, *Kashf*, p. 76; Ġazālī, *Kīmiyā*, p. 148; Sarrāj, *Schlaglichter*, p. 229.
4 Quoted in Hojwīrī, *Kashf*, p. 76; also in Ġazālī, *Kīmiyā*, p. 148; Sarrāj, *Schlaglichter*, p. 409.
5 The 'Book of Those Slain by the Quran' and the effects of the Quran on Muslim mystics are the focus of chapter 6.
6 Rāfiʿī, *Iʿjāz*, pp. 212–13. On ar-Rāfiʿī's life and works, see Brockelmann, *Geschichte*, Supp. 3, pp. 71ff.
7 With regard to Labīd's conversion, Theodor Nöldeke has stated in the introduction to his 1864 *Beiträge zur Kenntnis der Poesie der alten Araber* [Contributions to the knowledge of the poetry of the ancient Arabs] that the whole framing story of the episode is historically incredible, and that there is little reason to assume that the best of the early Arab poets actually hung their

poems on the doors of the Kaaba. See also the extensive references in Kister, *Studies in Jāhiliyya and Early Islam*, no. XVI.

8 The heated debate in Islamic studies on the authenticity of the traditions collected in the *sīra* (the Prophet's biography) is summarized by Gregor Schoeler, *The Biography of Muhammad: Nature and Authenticity*, pp. 3ff. In his own investigation, Schoeler comes to the conclusion that, with all due prudence, at least the main outlines of the *sīra* and, in particular, the accounts from Muhammad's Medinan period can be accepted as historically credible. Ibid., pp. 114ff.

9 See, e.g., Quṭb, *At-Taṣwīr al-fannī*, pp. 11ff; Rāmiyār, *Tārīkh-e Qor'ān*, pp. 213ff; Abū Zahra, *Al-Mu'jiza al-kubrā*, pp. 59ff.; Riḍā, *Al-Waḥy al-muḥammadī*, pp. 148ff.

10 Abū Nu'aym, *Dalā'il*, p. 158.

11 Jan Assmann, *Cultural Memory*, p. 5.

12 Ibid., p. 4.

13 Ibid., p. 3.

14 Ibid.

15 Ibid., p. 72.

16 Ibid., p. 61.

17 Ibid., p. 47.

18 Ibid., p. 59.

19 Ibid., p. 33. Assmann refers here to the work of the French sociologist Maurice Halbwachs, who developed the concept of '*mémoire collective*' in the 1920s. See the English translations of his books, *On Collective Memory* and *The Collective Memory*.

20 Assmann, *Cultural Memory*, p. 59.

21 Ibid., p. 38.

22 Ibid., p. 60.

23 Quran 2:23; 10:38; 11:13; 17:88; 52:34.

24 Nöldeke et al., *History of the Qur'ān*, p. 44; Wansbrough, *Quranic Studies*, pp. 78–9; Cantarino, *Arabic Poetics*, p. 13; Radscheidt, '"I'jāz al-Qur'ān" im Koran?'; Radscheidt, *Die koranische Herausforderung*; van Ess, *Theologie und Gesellschaft*, vol. 4, p. 607.

25 Assmann, *Cultural Memory*, p. 60.

26 Sellheim, 'Prophet, Chalif und Geschichte', esp. pp. 89f; Arafat, 'Early Critics of the Authenticity of the Poetry of the Sīra'. On the contemporary debate over the authenticity of the traditional literature in general, see Juynboll, *Authenticity of the Tradition Literature*.

27 Quoted in Goldziher, *Muslim Studies*, vol. 2, pp. 145f.

28 Ibid., pp. 154ff. For a critique of the *quṣṣāṣ* that also describes their practices, see Ibn al-Jawzī's *Kitāb al-quṣṣāṣ*.

29 Quoted in Goldziher, *Muslim Studies*, vol. 2, p. 56.

30 Ḥusayn, *Fī sh-shi'r al-jāhilī*, p. 53. See also the critique by 'Abdulmuta'āl aṣ-Ṣa'īdī, *Naqd kitāb ad-duktūr Ṭāhā Ḥusayn*, esp. pp 40ff.

31 *Shifā'*, vol. 1, p. 258.

32 *Al-Mu'jiza al-kubrā*, p. 57.

33 Rāfi'ī, *I'jāz*, p. 157.

34 Bāqillānī, *I'jāz*, p. 229.

35 Jāḥiẓ, *Hujaj an-nubūwa*, pp. 278ff. Often cited, for example by Ibn Qutayba, *Ta'wīl mushkil al-Qur'ān*, p. 10; Jurjānī, *Dalā'il*, p. 302/475; Bayhaqī, *Dalā'il*, pp. 12f.; Zarkashī, *Burhān*, vol. 2, p. 107; Suyūṭī, *Itqān*, vol. 2, p. 119; Rāfi'ī,

I'jāz, p. 166. (The book *Dalā'il al-i'jāz fī l-Qur'ān* by 'Abdul-qāhir al-Jurjānī, which we will examine more closely in chapter 4, is well known in two editions that differ in their chapter divisions. In my references, the first page number is that of the edition edited by Muḥammad 'Abduh and Rashīd Riḍā, which is still the more common one; the second page number is that of the newer, more reliable edition edited by Maḥmūd Muḥammad Shākir.)

36 Abū Zahra, *Al-Mu'jiza al-kubrā*, p. 58.

37 *Qiṣṣatī ma'a sh-shi'r*, p. 16.

38 *History of the Arabs*, p. 91.

39 *Über Poesie und Poetik der Araber*, p. 1.

40 'Wansbroughians' would of course object, because they set the establishment of the Quran text in the third century of the Hijra. Even they must accept that the Quran's statements on its own reception have some value, however, and in any case they are documents of remembered history. Among the many things that weaken Wansbrough's thesis is the fact that the quranic statements about its reception, as I will show, do not by any means accord with the version of the Quran's reception history that emerges from the *ṣīra* literature. Indeed, the Quran at times adamantly resists that version. If the *ṣīra*, the sunnah and the Quran were as interdependent as Wansbrough claims, we would expect the Quran to confirm what the biographical literature – which Wansbrough says was established earlier – says about its effects. But what the Quran has to say on this subject evidently belongs to a different discourse, to a different and earlier phase. On the significance of the Quran as a historic source, see also Angelika Neuwirth's notes in 'Erste Qibla', pp. 269–70; also Paret, 'Der Koran als Geschichtsquelle'; Peters, 'The Quest of the Historical Mohammed'.

41 'Medinensische Einschübe in mekkanische Suren', p. 62.

42 Berque, *Relire le Coran*, p. 122. Marshall G. S. Hodgson uses the same argument in opposition to a typically Orientalist statement by Arthur Jeffery to the effect that the Quran has neither theological nor literary value, but merits study only because of the Muslims' special appreciation of it: 'Its prestige he tries to explain as resulting from its unique theological status, but he does not say that that status itself must be explained – that the Qur'ān must have won considerable prestige on internal grounds before serious persons would be willing to assign it so unique a theological status' (*Venture of Islam*, vol. 1, p. 367, n. 4).

43 39:23 (trans. Haleem).

44 Rāzī, *Tafsīr*, commentary on 39:23.

45 Schiller, 'The Artists'.

46 12:4 (trans. Arberry).

47 Quran 25:33.

48 In his commentary on verse 12:3, Paret himself interprets the passage – quite rightly– as an aesthetic statement: 'The sense of the whole is roughly: *"We tell you in the most beautiful way, more beautifully than any human source could do".*'

49 Plotinus, *Beauty*, p. 52.

50 Quran 4:69.

51 E.g., 16:96–7; 17:35; 18:7.

52 Trans. Arberry.

53 Zamakhsharī, *Kashshāf*, commentary on 95:4. See also Quran 4:86; 16:125; 18:31; 25:33; 25:76; 33:29; 39:23 et al.

54 5:83, trans. Arberry; *Iḏā sami'ū mā unzila ilā r-rasūli tarā a'yunahum tafīḍu mina d-dam'i mimmā 'arafū mina l-ḥaqq* (this verse seems to refer specifically to the Quran's Christian listeners). Paret's German translation, 'ihre Augen auf Grund der Kenntnis, die sie (durch ihre eigene Offenbarung) von der Wahrheit (bereits) haben, von Tränen überfließen', is speculative. The Quran does not state which truth causes the listeners mentioned here to weep: the truth of the Quran, or the one they already had. The verse merely states that they weep because they recognize a truth as a consequence of the recitation. In most of the documents that attest to the effect of Quran recitation, the occurrence of an insight caused by an aesthetic experience is, directly or indirectly, the fundamental motion of the receptive act. We will undertake a closer examination of this act primarily in chapter 6.

55 *Der Sprachstil des Koran*, p. 78.

56 Thomas Mann, *Doctor Faustus*, pp. 78–9.

57 Rubin, 'The Ka'ba'.

58 5:83; 84:21; 32:15; 17:107–9. It is uncertain whether verse 19:58, which describes a similar reaction, refers to the proclamations of earlier prophets or to the Quran (see Paret's commentary on these verses). Verse 3:113 seems to refer to Christians who listen to the Bible, but on a closer look it is ambiguous. It could also refer, as several exegetes have suggested, to Muslims who have converted from Christianity. See, e.g., the commentaries on 3:113 in Rāzī, *Tafsīr*, and Ṭabarsī, *Majma'*.

59 See, e.g., verses 11:16; 34:43; 37:36; 38:6; 74:24.

60 For a complete analysis of this scenario, see Neuwirth, 'Vom Rezitationstext über die Liturgie', pp. 82ff.

61 *Kashshāf*, commentary on 12:3.

62 See, e.g., the commentaries on 39:23 in Rāzī, *Tafsīr*, and Ṭabarsī, *Majma'*.

63 The corpus of early texts which forms the foundation for the present chapter includes, in addition to the Quran, the canonical hadith collections of al-Bukhārī, Muslim, ad-Dārimī, at-Tirmiḏī and Ibn Māja, the Shiite *al-Kāfī*, and the historic works of al-Wāqidī, Ibn Hishām, Ibn Kathīr, Ibn Sa'd and aṭ-Ṭabarī.

64 The texts on which I draw from this 'classical' phase, in which the essential doctrines and history of Islam have already been established, are the *nubūwa* treatises of al-Bayhaqī and Abū Nu'aym al-Iṣfahānī, Ibn Sallām's *Faḍā'il al-Qur'ān*, and the encyclopedic works *Iḥyā' 'ulūm ad-dīn* by al-Ġazālī, *Ash-Shifā'* by Qāḍī 'Iyāḍ, *Al-Burhān fī 'ulūm al-Qur'ān* by az-Zarkashī, and *Al-Itqān fī 'ulūm al-Qur'ān* by as-Suyūṭī. In isolated cases I refer to other works without having systematically analysed them for this chapter. Such works include the Quran commentaries cited, of which Rāzī's *At-Tafsīr al-kabīr* in particular (better known in the West as *Mafātīḥ al-ġayb*) offers a wealth of pertinent information. Because of the multitude of relevant traditions, any method not based on a clearly defined corpus would have resulted in more material than can be discussed in one chapter. Surprisingly, the classical *i'jāz* works, which also form part of the theological discourse of this phase, contain relatively little material on the early history of the Quran's reception. The reasons for this are explained in chapter 5.

65 These include books by Rāmiyār, Abū Zahra, Rāfi'ī, Sharī'aṭī-Mazīnānī, Labīb as-Sa'īd, Riḍā, Haykal and the early Sayyid Quṭb, well-known Egyptian and Iranian scholars, all of whom represent a traditionally oriented Quran scholarship and are hardly controversial within the Islamic world. For

this chapter I have intentionally left aside the works of modernist authors and those who are generally disputed in religious circles, such as Bint ash-Shāṭi', Naṣr Abū Zayd and ʿAlī Sarīaṭī.

66 See ʿIyāḍ, *Shifā'*, vol. 1, p. 247.

67 See Ibn Hishām, *Sīra*, p. 383.

68 We cannot determine conclusively what is meant in the *sīra* by *ṣalāt* and the corresponding verb *yuṣallī*, and to what extent it is the same as the customary ritual prayer of today. It seems almost certain, however, that it was a kind of ritualized Quran recitation in some form.

69 Ibn Kathīr, *Sīra*, vol. 3, p. 705. In several other cases too, an 'explanation' or 'proposal' of Islam by the Prophet himself or one of his comrades is sufficient. (Ṭufayl, for example, says about the conversion of his father, *ʿaraḍtu ʿalayhi l-islāma fa-aslama*. Ibn Hishām, *Sīra*, vol. 1, p. 384.)

70 See e.g. Ibn Hishām, *Sīra*, vol. 1, p. 442. The translation of the term *qur'ān* is a problem. We know that, in the Quran itself, it usually occurs not as the title of a collection of texts but in the common sense of 'recitation' (see also the more detailed discussion in chapter 3). Later, however, the term became firmly established as the title of the revelation recited by Muhammad and recorded in writing. Since then, the title of the Quran is retrospectively read into the term *qur'ān*. Such 'projections' are of course a topic of this book, so that we cannot simply translate the term in its etymological sense, disregarding the history of Quran interpretation. In the prophetic traditions, which are right on the threshold of the shift in meaning, *qur'ān* occurs both in the simple sense of 'recitation' and as a proper name. In many cases it is difficult to determine which meaning is appropriate. The problem becomes even more complicated when a later text quotes the Quran: the speaker in the Quran uses *qur'ān* to mean a 'recitation', yet the speaker of the later text understands it as *al-Qur'ān*, the name of the holy scripture. The problem is probably not solvable in translation, except by using the Arabic transliteration *qur'ān* throughout instead of the conventional English title Quran or Koran. This would hardly facilitate reading, however, as each occurrence still needs to be interpreted. For the sake of readability, I have simply written Quran wherever *qur'ān* occurs in the Arabic sources. The reader must bear in mind, however, that the word in Quran quotations usually means 'oration, recitation'.

71 Ibn Saʿd, *Ṭabaqāt*, I/i, 146; recounted similarly in Ibn Hishām, *Sīra*, vol. 1, p. 428.

72 See Ibn Kathīr, *Sīra*, vol. 1, 428.

73 Ibn Saʿd, *Ṭabaqāt*, I/i, 115.

74 ʿIyāḍ, *Shifā'*, p. 262.

75 Ibn Hishām, *Sīra*, vol. 1, pp. 427–8; Ibn Kathīr, *Sīra*, vol. 2, p. 174; Ṭabarī, *Tārīkh*, vol. 1, pp. 1208–9; Ibn Saʿd, *Ṭabaqāt*, III/ii, 15.

76 Bayhaqī, *Dalā'il*, vol. 2, p. 17; also mentioned in Ibn Kathīr, *Sīra*, vol. 1, p. 452; Ibn Saʿd, *Ṭabaqāt*, I/ii, 44.

77 Abū Nuʿaym, *Dalā'il*, p. 163.

78 Ibn Hishām, *Sīra*, vol. 1, p. 427; translation quoted after *The Life of Muhammad*, pp. 196–7. The event is also mentioned in Ibn Kathīr, *Sīra*, vol. 1, p. 174; Ṭabarī, *Tārīḫ*, vol. 1, p. 1208.

79 By Usayd ibn al-Ḥuḍayr, for example, whose conversion is examined later in this section (see pp. 19–20), and by the poet Hawḏa ibn ʿAlī (see Ibn Saʿd, *Ṭabaqāt*, I/ii, 18).

80 Quran 15:94 (trans. Haleem).

81 Qāḍī ʿIyāḍ, *Shifā'*, vol. 1, p. 262.
82 That ʿUmar loved poetry before his conversion is known from Ṭabarī, *Tārīkh*, vol. 1, pp. 1144–5. His confession to a passion for wine is quoted by Ibn Saʿd: one of the hardest obligations of Islam, the caliph said on his deathbed, is that of eschewing wine. *Ṭabaqāt*, III/i, 261; see also Juynboll, 'The Position of Qur'an Recitation in Early Islam', p. 244.
83 Ibn Hishām, *Sīra*, vol. 1, p. 342.
84 See also Bukhārī, *Ṣaḥīḥ*, LXIII/35 (no. 3863).
85 Ibn Hishām, *Sīra*, vol. 1, pp. 343ff; Ibn Kathīr, *Sīra*, vol. 2, pp. 33ff.
86 Ibn Hishām, *Sīra*, vol. 1, pp. 346ff; Ibn Kathīr, *Sīra*, vol. 2, pp. 37–8.
87 Ibn Hishām, *Sīra*, vol. 1, p. 252.
88 On this topic, see Bāqillānī, *Iʿjāz*, p. 272.
89 Ibn Hishām, *Sīra*, vol. 1, p. 382; translation quoted after *The Life of Muhammad*, p. 175.
90 Rāmiyār, *Tārīkh-e Qor'ān*, pp. 214–15.
91 Ibn Hishām, *Sīra*, vol. 1, p. 383.
92 Ibid., translation quoted after *The Life of Muhammad*, p. 176; also mentioned in Ibn Kathīr, *Sīra*, vol. 2, p. 73; Ibn Saʿd, *Ṭabaqāt*, IV/i, 175.
93 Rāmiyār, *Tārīkh-e Qor'ān*, p. 213–14.
94 Bāqillānī, *Iʿjāz*, p. 43.
95 Abū Nuʿaym, *Dalā'il*, p. 164.
96 Wāqidī, *Maġāzī*, p. 128; also mentioned in ʿIyāḍ, *Shifā'*, vol. 1, p. 274.
97 Ibn Ḥanbal, *Musnad*, I/318 (no. 2922).
98 Ibn Hishām, *Sīra*, vol. 1, pp. 435ff., translation quoted after *The Life of Muhammad*, pp. 200–1; also mentioned in Ibn Kathīr, *Sīra*, vol. 2, pp. 181ff.; Ṭabarī, *Tārīḫ*, vol. 1, pp. 1214ff. Another version of Usayd's conversion is given in Ibn Saʿd, *Ṭabaqāt*, II/i, 68.
99 *Al-Muʿjiza al-kubrā*, p. 67.
100 Ibn Saʿd, *Ṭabaqāt*, I/i, 146, 148ff.; Khaṭṭābī, *Bayān iʿjāz al-Qur'ān*, p. 71.
101 Ibn Hishām, *Sīra*, vol. 1, p. 392, translation quoted after *The Life of Muhammad*, p. 179; see also Rāmiyār, *Tārīkh-e Qor'ān*, p. 220; Haykal, *The Life of Muhammad*, p. 133.
102 Ibn Hishām, *Sīra*, vol. 1, p. 336, translation quoted after *The Life of Muhammad*, p.152.
103 Abū Nuʿaym, *Dalā'il*, p. 171.
104 ʿIyāḍ, *Shifā'*, vol. 1, p. 274. Recounted similarly by al-Jāḥiẓ, who attributes the statement to the Jewish physician and translator Māsarjawayh: cf. *Ḥayawān*, vol. 4, p. 192.
105 ʿIyāḍ, *Shifā'*, vol. 1, pp. 262–3.
106 *Al-Muʿjiza al-kubrā*, p. 88.
107 *Iʿjāz al-Qur'ān*, pp. 46–7.
108 *At-Taġannī*, pp. 67ff.; *Al-Jamʿ as-sawṭī*, pp. 221ff.
109 *Waḥy wa-nobūwat*, pp. 420–1.
110 *Eslām wa-honar*, pp. 242ff.
111 *An-Naṣṣ al-qur'ānī*, pp. 24–5.
112 Rāmiyār, *Tārīkh-e Qor'ān*, p. 221.
113 Ibn Hishām, *Sīra*, vol. 1, p. 422.
114 72:1–2; cf. ʿIyāḍ, *Shifā'*, vol. 1, p. 277.
115 Bayhaqī, *Dalāi'l*, vol. 2, p. 15.
116 I assume the anecdote originated with the account of aṭ-Ṭufayl's conversion already cited (see pp. 18–19).

117 The most famous of the later converts to Islam who were ostensibly persuaded by the poetic quality of the Quran is probably ʿAlī ibn Rabbān aṭ-Ṭabarī, who wrote about himself in his *Kitāb ad-dīn wa-d-dawla* (pp. 44–5). When one asks Muslims or people who have dealings with Muslims about this phenomenon, many of them know of cases of such conversions among their acquaintances. Kristina Nelson, who conducted research in Cairo for her book *The Art of Reciting the Qur'an*, reports, 'One of several such stories which were told to me is that of an American who, hearing a five minute excerpt of Shaykh Rifʿat's reciting over the radio, was so moved that he came to Egypt, took instruction, and became a Muslim (*The Art of Reciting*, p. 94). See also Saʿīd, *Al-Jamʿas-sawṭī*, p. 255.

118 Acts 9:1ff; 23:3ff; 26:12ff.

119 Augustine, *Confessions*, Book 8, pp. 127–47.

120 See 'The Memorial' in Pascal, *Pensées*, p. 285; for a discussion, see Guardini, *Pascal for Our Time*, pp. 19–44.

121 See Holl, *Gesammelte Aufsätze*, pp. 27ff.; Lilje, *Luther*, pp. 67–8.

122 See Wenzel, *Hören and Sehen*; Mukařovský, *Aesthetic Function, Norm and Value as Social Facts*, pp. 16ff. The most prominent present-day example is probably the Russian Orthodox Church, whose enormous growth in popularity since the end of the Soviet Union is explained not least by the sensual splendour of its worship services and rituals. See the report by Kerstin Holm in the illustrated supplement of *Frankfurter Allgemeine Zeitung*, 11 April 1998.

123 Dilthey, 'Johann Georg Hamann', p. 54.

124 'Thoughts about My Life' (*Gedanken über meinen Lebenslauf*). Quoted in Ronald G. Smith, *A Study in Christian Existence*, New York: Harper, 1960, pp. 42–3.

125 On Hamann's conversion, see also Sievers, *Johann Georg Hamanns Bekehrung*; Unger, *Hamann und die Aufklärung*, vol. 1, pp. 123ff.

126 James, *The Varieties of Religious Experience*, pp. 157–209.

127 Ibid., p. 193.

128 Augustine, *Confessions*, Book 8, ch. 11, pp. 143–4.

129 James, *The Varieties of Religious Experience*, p. 194.

130 Bukhārī, *Ṣaḥīḥ*, X/105 (no. 771).

131 Wāqidī, *Maġāzī*, p. 397.

132 Ṭabarī, *Tārīkh*, vol. 1, pp. 2095, 2294–5.

133 Ibn Saʿd, *Ṭabaqāt*, IV/ii, 9–10.

134 Ġazālī, *Iḥyā'*, p. 170; Rāmiyār, *Tārīkh-e Qor'ān*, p. 234.

135 Kulaynī, *Gozīde-ye Kāfī*, 'K. Faḍl al-Qur'ān/B. Tartīl al-Qur'ān', no. 12 (in the Persian explanation of the hadith that is printed below the Arabic text in this annotated selection of Kulaynī's work).

136 Sharīʿaṭī-Mazīnānī, *Waḥy wa-nobūwat*, p. 421.

137 ʿAbdullāh subsequently turned away from Islam and claimed that Mohammed had taken this phrase from him. Zamakhsharī, *Kashshāf*, commentary on 6:93; Nöldeke et al., *History of the Qur'ān*, p. 37; van Ess, *Theologie und Gesellschaft*, vol. 4, p. 622.

138 Ġazālī, *Iḥyā'*, vol. 1, p. 169 (the same statement is also attributed to al-Walīd ibn al-Muġīra: see p. 34 in this chapter).

139 Ibn Ḥajar al-ʿAsqalānī, *Fatḥ al-bārī*, vol. 2, p. 164 ('K. Al-Āḏān/B. Ahl al-ʿilm').

140 Ibid.; also mentioned in Ṭabarī, *Tārīkh*, vol. 1, p. 1809.

141 Van Ess, *Gedankenwelt des Muḥāsibī*, p. 198.
142 Quoted ibid.
143 Jurjānī, *Dalā'il*, p. 251/388.
144 Surahs 40 to 46, which are prefaced with the two letters *ḥm*.
145 Ibn Sallām, *Faḍā'il al-Qur'ān*, p. 137 (XLI, 4); Jurjānī, *Dalā'il*, p. 251/388.
146 Muslim, *Ṣaḥīḥ*, VI/36 (no. 796).
147 Ġazālī, *Iḥyā'*, vol. 1, 169; almost verbatim in the earlier Ibn Māja, *Sunan*, V/186 (no. 1338).
148 Bukharī, *Ṣaḥīḥ*, XCVIII/52 (no. 7544); a variation that reads '. . . singing the Quran (*taġannā bi-l-Qur'ān*)' is found in Dārimī, *Sunan*, XXIII/33 (no. 3493).
149 Muslim, *Ṣaḥīḥ*, VI/35 (no. 794); Bukhārī, *Ṣaḥīḥ*, XCVIII/50 (no. 7540).
150 Bukhārī, *Ṣaḥīḥ*, X/102 (no. 768).
151 Kulaynī, *Kāfī*, 'Faḍl-al-Qur'ān/Tartīl al-Qur'ān', nos. 10–11.
152 Ibid., no. 4; see also the Shiite mystic Sabzewārī's explanation in *Tuḥfat al-'abbāsīya*, p. 415.
153 See, e.g., Muslim, *Ṣaḥīḥ*, VI/40 (no. 800); Bukhārī, *Ṣaḥīḥ*, LXVI/32 (no. 5049); ibid., LXVI/35 (no. 5055).
154 Tirmiḏī, *Al-Jāmi'*, XLIII/14 (no. 3070).
155 Dārimī, *Sunan*, XXIII/33 (no. 3504); without the subordinate clause in Ibn Māja, *Sunan*, V/186 (no. 1342).
156 Dārimī, *Sunan*, XXIII/1 (no. 3311); see also ibid., no. 3318.
157 Bukhārī, *Ṣaḥīḥ*, LXIV/39 (no. 4232).
158 Ġazālī, *Iḥyā'*, vol. 1, 173; almost verbatim in Ibn Māja, *Sunan*, V/176 (no. 1338).
159 Quoted in Makkī, *Die Nahrung der Herzen*, p. 222. It appears without Abū Mūsā's response in the earlier Muslim, *Ṣaḥīḥ*, VI/34 (no. 793); Bukhārī, *Ṣaḥīḥ*, LXVI/31 (no. 5048); Dārimī, *Sunan*, XXIII/33 (no. 3495). Cf. variants in Ibn Qayyim al-Jawzīya, *Zād al-ma'ād*, p. 165, and al-Qurṭubī, *Jāmi'*, Introduction, vol. 1, p. 12. In Ibn Māja (*Sunan*, V/176 [no. 1341]) and Dārimī (*Sunan*, XXIII/33 [no. 3502]), it is 'Abdullāh ibn Qays who says the Prophet has been given one of David's flutes.
160 Juynboll has collected several. See 'The Position of Qur'an Recitation', pp. 245–6.
161 Nawawī, *At-Tibyān*, p. 81.
162 'Umar as-Suhrawardī, *Die Gaben der Erkenntnisse*, p. 165.
163 Ibn Sa'd, *Ṭabaqāt*, III/i, 223.
164 Ṭabarī, *Tārīh*, vol. 1, p. 2755.
165 Muslim, *Ṣaḥīḥ*, VI/47 (no. 817).
166 Ibn Sa'd, *Ṭabaqāt*, III/i, 202.
167 Rāmiyār describes the central position of Quran recitation in the social and religious life of the early Muslims in detail (*Tārīkh-e Qor'ān*, pp. 226ff.); see also Riḍā, *Al-Waḥy al-muḥammadī*, pp. 162ff.; Juynboll, 'The Position of Qur'an Recitation'.
168 Bukhārī, *Ṣaḥīḥ*, LXVI/36 (Nr. 5058).
169 G. H. A. Juynboll has compiled several accounts in 'The Qur'ān Reciter on the Battlefield'.
170 Wāqidī, *Maġāzī*, p. 355; Ibn Hishām, *Sīra*, vol. 2, p. 169.
171 Ibn Sa'd, *Ṭabaqāt*, I/i, 148.
172 *Al-Waḥy al-muḥammadī*, p. 162.
173 Muslim, *Ṣaḥīḥ*, VI/34 (no. 792).
174 Ġazālī, *Iḥyā'*, vol. 1, p. 173.

175 Quoted in al-Qurṭubī, *Jami'*, Introduction, vol. 1, p. 13; Ibn al-'Arābī is quoted in similar words in the article '*taġannī*' in *Lisān al-'Arab*; this version also appears in Talbi, 'La qirā'a bi-l-alḥān', p. 185.
176 E.g., 21:5; 37:36; 52:30; 69:41.
177 Abū Zahra, *Al-Mu'jiza al-kubrā*, p. 62; 'Iyāḍ, *Shifā'*, vol. 1, p. 266.
178 Abū Zahra, *Al-Mu'jiza al-kubrā*, p. 60.
179 Ibn Hishām, *Sīra*, vol. 1, p. 300.
180 Ibid., vol. 1, p. 358.
181 Quṭb, *At-Taṣwīr al-fannī*, p. 26.
182 8:31 (trans. Arberry). See also 23:83; 27:68; 46:17; 16:24; 25:5; 68:15; 83:13. On the expression *asāṭīru l-awwalīna*, see Paret's commentary on 6:25.
183 'Iyāḍ, *Shifā'*, vol. 1, p. 263.
184 Vodička, 'Die Rezeptionsgeschichte literarischer Werke', p. 76.
185 Ibid., p. 77.
186 Mukařovský, *Aesthetic Function, Norm and Value as Social Facts*, p. 5.
187 Vodička, 'Die Rezeptionsgeschichte literarischer Werke', p. 77.
188 Guyau, *Problems of Contemporary Aesthetics*, pp. 32–3, quoted in Mukařovský, 'The Place of the Aesthetic Function', p. 36.
189 See Jauss, *Aesthetic Experience and Literary Hermeneutics*, p. 62.
190 See, e.g., Muslim, *Ṣaḥīḥ*, VI/40 (no. 800).
191 Ibn Sallām, *Faḍā'il al-Qur'ān*, p. 64 (XIII/3).
192 Ibid. (XIII/4); Hojwīrī, *Kashf*, p. 73.
193 I.e., surahs 56, 69, 77, 81 and 101.
194 Sarrāj, *Schlaglichter*, p. 408. Sarrāj also provides further references for this tradition and those mentioned above. Also mentioned in Ḥojwīrī, *Kashf*, p. 75.
195 Abū Nu'aym, *Dalā'il*, p. 165.
196 E.g., Quran 17:106–9.
197 Ibn Sallām, *Faḍā'il al-Qur'ān*, p. 64 (XIII/2); Nawawī, *Tibyān*, p. 82. We should bear in mind, however, that such expressions of weeping are to a certain degree idiomatic and are not always necessarily meant in a literal sense (see Müller, *'Und der Kalif lachte'*, under *'bakā'* in the index). Analogous usage can also be seen in modern Arabic literature (see Guth, '*Fa-ġrawraqat 'uyūmihum bi-d-dumū'*').
198 Ġazālī, *Iḥyā'*, vol. 1, p. 174.
199 Hojwīrī, *Kashf*, p. 73; see also Nawawī, *Tibyān*, 81.
200 Ġazālī, *Lehre von den Stufen zur Gottesliebe*, p. 388.
201 In later discussions of Quran recitation, sadness is also treated as an aesthetic quality. Al-Jawzīya quotes a scholar as saying, 'I do not like recitation of the Quran to secular melodies (*al-qirā'a bi-l-alḥān*), except when there is sadness in it – that is, when it is recited with the sadness that Abū Mūsā (al-Ash'arī) had in his voice': *Zād al-ma'ād*, p. 165.
202 See p. 9 above.
203 See Aristotle, *Poetics*, 1449b; Schadewaldt, *Tübinger Vorlesungen*, p. 17; also Schadewaldt, *Hellas und Hesperien*, vol. 1, p. 203.
204 *Poetics*, 1459a; Helmut Flashar (Ritter, *Historisches Wörterbuch*, 'Katharsis') translates the expression as 'spezifische Lust'; Manfred Furhmann renders *oikeia hedone* as 'besonderes Vergnügen'.
205 Muslim, *Ṣaḥīḥ*, VI/40 (no. 800); Buḫārī, *Ṣaḥīḥ*, LXVI/32 (no. 5049); ibid., LXVI/35 (no. 5055).
206 Jauss, *Aesthetic Experience and Literary Hermeneutics*, p. 92 (emphasis added).

207 Ibid., p. 67.
208 *Duino Elegies*, 1.
209 59:21.
210 *Shifā'*, vol. 1, p. 274.
211 Riḍā, *Al-Waḥy al-muḥammadī*, p. 157.
212 Ibn Kathīr, *Sīra*, vol. 2, pp. 498–9; also mentioned in Bayhaqī, *Dalā'il*, vol. 1, 445–6; Suyūṭī, *Itqān*, vol. 2, p. 117.
213 This and other versions of this episode in Bayhaqī, *Dalā'il*, vol. 1, p. 446; verbatim in ʿIyāḍ, *Shifā'*, vol. 1, p. 262; cf. Abū Zahra, *Al-Muʿjiza al kubrā*, pp. 61–2.
214 Abū Nuʿaym, *Dalā'il*, p. 162.
215 Rāmiyār, *Tārīkh-e Qor'ān*, p. 217.
216 Ibid.
217 Ibid.
218 Suyūṭī, *Bāb an-nuqūl fī asbāb an-nuzūl*, pp. 693ff.; Rāzī, *Tafsīr*, commentary on 74:11ff.
219 74:11–27 (trans. Arberry).
220 Almost the same words are attributed to Naḍr: see Ibn Hishām, *Sīra*, vol. 1, p. 300.
221 Ibn Hishām, *Sīra*, vol. 1, p. 270; cf. ʿIyāḍ, Shifā', vol. 1, p. 265.
222 Abū Nuʿaym, *Dalā'il*, p. 179; also in Bayhaqī, *Dalā'il*, vol. 1, pp. 454ff.; Muslim, *Ṣaḥīḥ*, XLIV/27 (no. 2473). Another version appears in Ibn Kathīr, *Sīra*, vol. 1, pp. 446ff. See also Naḍr's similar statement in Ibn Hishām, *Sīra*, vol. 1, p. 300, and Bayhaqī, *Dalā'il*, vol. 1, p. 448.
223 Bukhārī, *Ṣaḥīḥ*, LXIII/33 (no. 3861).
224 Bayhaqī, *Dalā'il*, pp. 455–6.
225 Rāfiʿī, *Iʿjāz*, p. 189.
226 25:30–3 (trans. Arberry). See also 23:66 and Paret's commentary on it.
227 Bāqillānī, *Iʿjāz*, p. 154; see also Ṭabarī, *Jāmiʿ*, commentary on 6:93.
228 *Al-Muʿjiza al-kubrā*, p. 65.
229 17:88 (trans. Arberry).
230 11:13 (trans. Arberry).
231 10:38 (trans. Arberry). Other verses cited in support of *iʿjāz* are 6:93, 16:103, and 8:31.
232 2:24 (trans. Arberry).
233 *Dalā'il*, vol. 1, p. 158.
234 Hujaj an-nubūwa, p. 274.
235 Bāqillānī, *Iʿjāz*, p. 33.
236 Rāfiʿī, *Iʿjāz*, p. 189.
237 Bāqillānī, *Iʿjāz*, p. 43.
238 Rāmiyār, *Tārīkh-e Qor'ān*, p. 218.
239 The traditions contain several versions; the events are recounted here after Ibn Hishām, *Sīra*, vol. 1, p. 293. Cf. Ibn Kathīr, *Sīra*, vol. 1, pp. 501ff.; Bayhaqī, *Dalā'il*, pp. 449ff.; Abū Nuʿaym, *Dalā'il*, pp. 161–2; ʿIyāḍ, *Shifā'*, vol. 1, pp. 274–5.
240 Wāqidī, *Maġāzī*, pp. 357–8.
241 Ṭabarī, *Tārīkh*, vol. 1, p. 1231.
242 Riḍā in particular develops this aspect: see *Al-Waḥy al-muḥammadī*, p. 158.
243 Quoted in Suyūṭī, *Itqān*, vol. 2, pp. 117–18.
244 Bukharī, *Ṣaḥīḥ*, XCVIII/32 (no. 7490).
245 Ibid., LXIII/29 (no. 3854).

246 Bayhaqī, *Dalā'il*, vol. 2, p. 50.
247 40:28.
248 Bayhaqī, *Dalā'il*, vol. 2, p. 52; Ṭabarī, *Tārīkh*, vol. 1, p. 1186.
249 Ibn Hishām, *Sīra*, vol. 1, p. 299, translation quoted after *The Life of Muhammad*, p. 135; Ibn Kathīr, *Sīra*, vol. 1, pp. 464–5; see also the variations on this story in Bayhaqī, *Dalā'il*, vol. 1, pp. 438ff.
250 Ibn Hishām, *Sīra*, vol. 1, p. 373, translation quoted after *The Life of Muhammad*, p. 171.
251 Abū Zahra, *Al-Mu'jiza al-kubrā*, p. 63; see also Quran 23:66 and Paret's commentary on that verse.
252 41:2–5 (trans. Haleem); see also 8:20.
253 Rāmiyār, *Tārīkh-e Qor'ān*, p. 217.
254 Ibn Hishām, *Sīra*, vol. 1, p. 313.
255 Ibn Kathīr, *Sīra*, vol. 1, p. 508; see also Haykal, *The Life of Muhammad*, p. 100.
256 Ibn Hishām, *Sīra*, vol. 1, p. 315.
257 Rāmiyār, *Tārīkh-e Qor'ān*, p. 214.
258 Hamadānī, *Sīrat*, pp. 127–8; cf. commentary on 15:90 in Ṭabarsī, *Majma'*, and Qurṭubī, *Jāmi'*. Some of the exegetes think the verses *kamā anzalnā 'alā l-muqtasimīna llaḏīna ja'alū l-qur'āna 'iḍīna* (15:90–1) refer to this episode. The literal sense of this apparently fragmentary passage is still not firmly established (see Paret's commentary). Most of the Muslim commentators read it either as 'As we send down punishment on those who divide into bands and call the Quran a bunch of lies', or as 'As we send down punishment on those who divide the Quran (into parts they believe and parts they do not believe)'. Some exegetes (such as Maḥalli and Suyūṭī, *Tafsīr al-jalālayn*) hold the opinion that this passage refers to the Christians and Jews. Aṭ-Ṭabarsī enumerates two and al-Qurṭubī seven existing interpretations of the verses.
259 Bayhaqī, *Dalā'il* , vol. 1, pp. 444–5; Quran 36:9 (trans. Arberry).
260 6:25; cf. 8:20–3; 30:58–9.
261 *Al-Mu'jiza al-kubrā*, p. 67.
262 Ibn Hishām, *Sīra*, vol. 1, p. 361, translation quoted after *The Life of Muhammad*, p. 164.
263 Bayhaqī, *Dalā'il*, vol. 1, pp. 452–3; see also Ibn Hishām, *Sīra*, vol. 1, p. 315; Ibn Kathīr, *Sīra*, vol. 1, pp. 505–6.
264 Rāmiyār, *Tārīkh-e Qor'ān*, p. 216.
265 *Burhān*, vol. 2, p. 114.
266 *Shifā'*, vol. 1, p. 274.
267 Haykal, *The Life of Muhammad*, p. 134. On this book, see Wessels, *A Modern Arabic Biography of Muḥammad.*
268 17:47.
269 To demonstrate this, it is sufficient to open any Western biography of the Prophet or history of the Arabic world. One of the few exceptions is, surprisingly, Essad Bey's *Mohammed* (Munich, 1993): although it is based on the same sources as Oriental studies, this rather literary biography makes no claim to so-called scientific accuracy. In writing his novel *Mohammed* just a short time earlier, the poet Klabund, unlike Bey, lacked the necessary language skills to refer to the sources and so was limited to the publications of the day in Oriental studies. It is revealing that he hardly addressed the aesthetic effects of Quran recitation, although he in particular would certainly have been interested in it.

270 Rāfiʿī, *Iʿjāz*, p. 167; cf. ibid., p. 171, where Rāfiʿī attributes a similar statement to al-Jāḥiẓ.
271 *Kitāb ad-dīn wa-d-dawla*, p. 90.
272 Kraus, 'Beiträge zur islamischen Ketzergeschichte', p. 369.
273 Rāmiyār, *Tārīkh-e Qor'ān*, p. 214.
274 *At-Taṣwīr al-fannī*, p. 11.
275 *Al-Muʿjiza al-kubrā*, p. 64.
276 *Al-Waḥy al-muḥammadī*, p. 154.
277 *An-Naṣṣ al-qur'ānī*, p. 21.
278 Ibn Hishām, *Sīra*, vol. 1, p. 422.
279 Ibn Saʿd, *Ṭabaqāt*, I/i, 146.
280 Trans. Arberry.
281 Maḥallī and Suyūṭī, *Tafsīr al-jalālayn*, commentary on 41:26.
282 Riḍā, *Al-Waḥy al-muḥammadī*, pp. 159ff.; Rāmiyār, *Tārīkh-e Qor'ān*, p. 217.
283 Rāzī, *Tafsīr*, commentary on 41:26.
284 Quran 28:55; 23:3; 25:72.
285 *Al-Muʿjiza al-kubrā*, pp. 62–3.
286 11:5 (trans. Arberry).
287 Rāmiyār, *Tārīkh-e Qor'ān*, p. 218.
288 'Kollektives Gedächtnis und kulturelle Identität', p. 13.
289 Ibn Hishām, *Sīra*, p. 421; Ṭabarī, *Tārīḥ*, vol. 1, p. 1201.
290 Rāmiyār, *Tārīkh-e Qor'ān*, p. 214.
291 Another example is Rashīd Riḍā's commentary on the anecdote presented on p. 41 in this chapter about the effect of Abū Bakr's Quran recitations on Ibn ad-Duġunna's followers: see *Al-Waḥy al-muḥammadī*, pp. 158–9.
292 'The Concretization of the Literary Work', p. 119.
293 Ibid.
294 Vodička, 'Die Rezeptionsgeschichte literarischer Werke', p. 71.
295 See Adorno, *Introduction to the Sociology of Music*, p. 61.
296 See Kermani, *Offenbarung als Kommunikation*, pp. 17–18.
297 'Die Rezeptionsgeschichte literarischer Werke', p. 81.
298 Mukařovský, *Aesthetic Function, Norm and Value as Social Facts*, pp. 26ff.
299 *Abhandlungen*, p. 25; but see also Fahd, *La Divination arabe*.
300 *Walter Benjamins Theorie der Sprachmagie*, p. 19.
301 'The Name of God'.
302 *Language and Myth*.
303 See the essays in Benjamin, *Sprache und Geschichte*.
304 See the selections edited by Heinrich Fischer, *Magie der Sprache* and *Über die Sprache*.
305 See *Philosophical Investigations*, esp. §§79, 183 (pp. 41–2, 80).
306 George Steiner provides a brief history of ideas on the origin of language in *After Babel*, pp. 51ff. The best-known discussion of this question, which has interested people in every era, is probably Herder's essay *On the Origin of Language*; a more detailed one is Borst, *Turmbau von Babel*.
307 *Kritische Schriften*, vol. 2, p. 229, quoted in Menninghaus, *Walter Benjamins Theorie der Sprachmagie*, p. 29.
308 Herder, *On the Origin of Language*, p. 136.
309 *Ash-Shiʿr qindīl akhḍar*, p. 60.
310 Ibid., pp. 62–3.
311 Ibid., p. 60.
312 'Aesthetica in Nuce', p. 63.

313 Vico, *New Science*, 'Introduction', no. 32 (p. 23); cf. no. 432 (pp. 172–3); nos 928ff (pp. 402ff.) et al.
314 Ibid., no. 446 (pp. 183–4).
315 Eco, *The Search for the Perfect Language*, pp. 90–1; Scheible, *Wahrheit und Subjekt*, pp. 59–71; Auerbach, *Literary Language and its Public*, pp. 7ff.
316 Frye, *Great Code*, p. 6.
317 'Umgangssprache entsteht, wenn sie mit der Sprache nur so umgehn; wenn sie sie wie das Gesetz umgehen; wie den Feind umgehen; wenn sie umgehend antworten, ohne gefragt zu sein.' *Über die Sprache*, p. 7.
318 Van der Leeuw, *Einführung*, p.155; Izutsu, *Language and Magic*, p. 20; Guillaume, *Prophecy and Divination*, p. 173.
319 Van der Leeuw, *Religion in Essence and Manifestation*, p. 408.
320 Van der Leeuw, *Einführung*, p. 159.
321 Lehmann, 'Biblical Oaths'.
322 Neuwirth, 'Der Horizont der Offenbarung', pp. 4–5. Lamya Kandil critically examined Angelika Neuwirth's arguments: see 'Schwüre in den mekkanischen Suren' [Oaths in the Meccan surahs] and her dissertation *Untersuchungen zu den Schwüren im Koran* [Studies on the oaths in the Quran]. See also Smith, 'Oaths in the Qur'ān', pp. 126ff; Heiler, *Erscheinungsformen*, pp. 311–14.
323 Ibn ʿArabī, *Futūḥāt*, vol. 3, pp. 69–70; see also Chodkiewicz, *An Ocean Without Shore*, p. 19.
324 *Metaphysics*, p. 4.
325 Cassirer, *Language and Myth*, p. 36.
326 Quran 2:31.
327 Cassirer, *Language and Myth*, p. 82.
328 Ibid., pp. 45ff.; Eliade and Couliano, *Handbuch der Religionen*, p. 84. On this topic in general, see Usener, *Götternamen*.
329 Graham, *Beyond the Written Word*, p. 64 (see other references there).
330 *An-Naṣṣ al-qur'ānī*, p. 31.
331 Izutsu, *Language and Magic*, p. 22.
332 Isaiah 55:10–11.
333 *Einführung*, p. 156.
334 3:61; 24:7. On the status of the oath in Islam, see Pedersen, *Der Eid bei den Semiten*, pp. 194ff.; Wellhausen, *Reste arabischen Heidentums*, pp. 187ff.
335 Van der Leeuw, *Religion in Essence and Manifestation*, p. 409.
336 Frye, *Great Code*, pp. 6ff.
337 Izutsu, *Language and Magic*, p. 26.
338 Cassirer, *Language and Myth*, p. 52.
339 Psalms 57:4; see also Isaiah 49:2.
340 *Asrār al-balāgha*, p. 306.
341 Ibid., pp. 369–70.
342 Paz, *The Bow and the Lyre*, p. 97.
343 Izutsu, *Language and Magic*, p. 40; Cassirer, *Language and Myth*, pp. 98–9.
344 Rilke, 'For Nike, Christmas 1923', in *Selected Poems*, trans. Susan Ranson and Marielle Sutherland. Oxford: OUP, 2011.
345 Mukařovský, *On Poetic Language*, p. 45; Jakobson, 'What Is Poetry?', p. 378.
346 *Language and Magic*, p. 13.
347 Horkheimer and Adorno, *Dialectic of Enlightenment*, p. 133. See also Scholem's remarks in 'The Name of God', pp. 79–80.
348 On the category of silence in literature, see Hauser, *Sociology of Art*, pp. 753ff.; Paz, *The Bow and the Lyre*, pp. 26ff., 97–8.

349 See Cassirer, *Language and Myth*, pp. 73–4; Heiler, *Erscheinungsformen*, pp. 334–9.
350 Paz, *Early Poems*, p. 5.
351 See, e.g., his *Letters to Milena*.
352 *Language and Silence*, p. 50. The most powerful notes on the transformation of language in the Third Reich are still those in Victor Klemperer's *Language of the Third Reich*.
353 'Literary History as a Challenge', p. 23.
354 According to Weisgerber, the semantic analysis of a word and the way it is used in a specific context, what connotations it has, what associations it evokes, the criteria by which it designates an object, and the like, can help us to understand the world view of the people who speak the given language. See, e.g., his book *Vom Weltbild der deutschen Sprache*. The American linguists Sapir and Whorf formulated a similar theory around the same time, but independently from Weisgerber. According to the 'Sapir–Whorf hypothesis' (which Whorf called 'the principle of linguistic relativity'), a language determines how its speakers think and perceive the world. Language, according to Whorf, is not merely a means of expressing thoughts but rather forms the thoughts themselves. See, e.g., his *Language, Thought, and Reality*. For criticism and correction, see Gipper, *Gibt es ein sprachliches Relativitätsprinzip?*. On the history of linguistic theories of this kind, see Steiner, *After Babel*, pp. 89ff; Paz, 'Reading and Contemplation', pp. 35ff.
355 Some Muslim scholars have drawn a distinction between *aʿjamī* and *ʿajamī*. The first word refers to people who cannot express themselves clearly and distinctly, while the second designates non-Arabs. Not all Arabic lexicographers share this view. See Izutsu, *God and Man*, pp. 187–8.
356 On the term *aʿjamī*, see Goldziher, *Muslim Studies*, vol. 1, pp. 98–136; Izutsu, *God and Man*, pp. 187–8; Zwettler, *Oral Tradition*, pp. 163–4.
357 The concept of *ʿarabīya* as a separate language of poetry that was distinct from the tribal dialects has been widely affirmed by scholars of Islam. See, e.g., Kahle, 'The Qur'an and the ʿArabiya'; EI^2, 'ʿArabīya'; Fischer, 'Das Altarabische in islamischer Überlieferung'; but most importantly, for a summary of *ʿarabīya* and the history of its study, Zwettler's *Oral Tradition*, pp. 100ff., and Versteegh's *Arabic Language*, pp. 37ff. See also Johann Fück's arguments disputing the diglossic situation in *Arabiya*, and further Spitaler's review as a representative of the critical responses to Fück's thesis.
358 *Studies in Islamic History*, p. 6.
359 Hitti, *History of the Arabs*, p. 91.
360 Goldziher, *Abhandlungen*, pp. 19–20; Cantarino, *Arabic Poetics in the Golden Age*, p. 20; Nicholson, *Literary History of the Arabs*, p. 73.
361 Cf. Goldziher, *Abhandlungen*, p. 24.
362 Quoted in Cantarino, *Arabic Poetics in the Golden Age*, p. 24.
363 In connection with the acquisition of spiritual knowledge, Chadwick prefers to speak of 'mantic' rather than 'prophetic' persons and poetry, since 'prophetic' today is usually associated with prediction, while 'mantic' also includes knowledge about the past and present. Furthermore, 'prophecy' indicates only the proclamation of knowledge, while the 'mantic' includes the acquisition and possession of such knowledge. *Poetry and Prophecy*, pp. xiii–xiv.
364 Goldziher, *Abhandlungen*, p. 17; Fahd, *La Divination arabe*, p. 117; Guillaume, *Prophecy and Divination*.
365 Chadwick, *Poetry and Prophecy*, p. 72.

366 Ibid., p. 1.
367 Ibid., p. xiii.
368 See Goldziher, *Abhandlungen*, pp. 19ff; Hitti, *History of the Arabs*, pp. 94–5.
369 Suyūṭī, *Itqān*, vol. 1, p. 119.
370 Wagner, *Grundzüge der klassischen arabischen Dichtung*, vol. 1, p. 30.
371 Eichler, *Die Dschinn, Teufel und Engel im Koran*, pp. 25ff.
372 Wagner, *Grundzüge*, vol. 1, p. 33.
373 *'Umda*, pp. 40–52.
374 As Goldziher has shown, this notion was a reference to a type of poet who spontaneously produced invective verse (*hijā'*), who, like the seers, composed in *rajaz*, a poetic form of short, rhyming lines in simple iambic meter and parallel construction. Only later was the poet possessed by jinn identified with the author of long, intricately structured qasidas. See Goldziher, *Gesammelte Schriften*, vol. 3, pp. 400–5, and *Abhandlungen*, pp. 1ff., 24–5; Neuwirth, 'Der historische Muhammad', pp. 86ff. On the ancient Arab notion of the jinn and the concept of poetic inspiration in general, see Izutsu, *God and Man*, pp. 168ff.; Eichler, *Die Dschinn, Teufel und Engel im Koran*; Zbinden, *Die Djinn des Islam*, pp. 75–99; Henninger, 'Geisterglaube'; EI^2, 'Djinn'; Kermani, *Offenbarung als Kommunikation*, pp. 42ff. This notion lives on in the Islamic era as a literary topos, just as the expression 'the poet's muse' recalls a relationship that was originally conceived as real.
375 Cf. Eichler, *Die Dschinn, Teufel und Engel im Koran*, pp. 23ff.; Neuwirth, 'Der historische Muhammad', pp. 87–8, n. 10; Shahid, 'Contribution to Koranic Exegesis', pp. 577ff.
376 E.g., 15:6; 26:27; 37:36; 51:52; 52:29.
377 Goldziher, *Abhandlungen*, p. 24; see also the arguments in Izutsu, *God and Man*, pp. 172ff. The notion that a person can be possessed by jinn persists even today in the folk beliefs of some countries, as does the custom of exorcising the jinn by reciting the Quran. See Wieland, *Studien zur Djinn-Vorstellung im heutigen Ägypten.*
378 14:24–6 (trans. Arberry).
379 Izutsu, *Language and Magic*, pp. 27ff. The Arabic words for 'soul' (*nafs*) and 'breathe' (*nafasa*) are derived from the same root. The connection between the soul and breath is quite clear in the quranic phrase *iḏā nafakhtu fīhi min rūḥī* (when I have breathed My spirit into him), referring to God's act of creation. See 15:29, 38:72, 32:9; and similar expressions in 21:91, 66:12.
380 Goldziher, *Abhandlungen*, pp. 48ff.
381 See van der Leeuw, *Religion in Essence and Manifestation*, pp. 405–6.
382 Quoted in Goldziher, *Abhandlungen*, p. 30.
383 Bukhārī, *Ṣaḥīḥ*, LXXVIII/3 (no. 5973).
384 Goldziher, *Abhandlungen*, p. 30.
385 Quoted ibid., p. 31.
386 Van der Leeuw, *Religion in Essence and Manifestation*, p. 404.
387 Quoted in Heiler, *Erscheinungsformen*, p. 276; see also Dieterich, *Eine Mithrasliturgie*, pp. 39–40.
388 Goldziher, 'Verheimlichung des Namens', p. 2.
389 Cassirer, *Language and Myth*, pp. 50–1.
390 Isutzu, *Language and Magic*, p. 22.
391 Van der Leeuw, *Religion in Essence and Manifestation*, p. 404.
392 Leviticus 19:12.
393 Matthew 18:20.

394 Dieterich, *Eine Mithrasliturgie*, pp. 114–15.
395 Shakespeare, *Julius Caesar*, Act 3, scene 3.
396 Goldziher, 'Verheimlichung des Namens', p. 1.
397 Izutsu, *Language and Magic*, p. 23; Goldziher, *Gesammelte Schriften*, vol. 5, pp. 167–9.
398 Goldziher, *Gesammelte Schriften*, vol. 5, pp. 45ff.
399 Chadwick, *Poetry and Prophecy*, p. 49.
400 Sowayan, 'Tonight My Gun Is Loaded'; Geertz, 'Art as a Cultural System', pp. 1495ff.
401 Hitti, *History of the Arabs*, p. 94.
402 *Abhandlungen*, p. 26; on *hijā'*, see also van Gelder, *The Bad and the Ugly*.
403 Quoted in Goldziher, *Abhandlungen*, pp. 95ff.
404 Ibn Sa'd, *Ṭabaqāt*, I/ii, 18.
405 Robson, 'Magical Use of the Koran', p. 55.
406 Ibn Rashīq, *'Umda*, vol. 1, p. 31; Bukhārī, *Ṣaḥīḥ*, LXXVII/91 (nos 6152–3).
407 *Sīra*, vol. 2, p. 173.
408 Quoted in EI², 'Siḥr'; also quoted by Naguib Mahfouz (Najīb Maḥfūẓ) in his *Echoes of an Autobiography*, p. 48; see also Wagner, *Grundzüge*, vol. 1, p. 33.
409 Wagner, *Grundzüge*, vol. 1, p. 33.
410 Ṭabarī, *Tārīkh*, vol. 1, pp. 1144–5; Goldziher, *Abhandlungen*, p. 59.

Chapter 2 The Text

1 *Manāhij tajdīd*, pp. 279–336. On the author, see Speicher, 'Einige Bemerkungen zu al-Khūlīs Entwurf'.
2 On the formal characteristics of ancient Arabic poetry, see Bloch, *Vers und Sprache im Altarabischen*; Müller, *Ich bin Labīd*; Bauer, *Altarabische Dichtkunst*; Abu Deeb, 'Towards a Structural Analysis of Pre-Islamic Poetry'.
3 'What Is Poetry?' p. 369.
4 'Towards an Impure Poetry', p. 51.
5 Mukařovský, *Aesthetic Function, Norm and Value as Social Facts*, pp. 2–3.
6 *Ash-Shi'r qindīl akhḍar*, pp. 66–7.
7 Kadkanī, *Musīqī-ye she'r*, pp. 226–7.
8 Jakobson, 'What Is Poetry?', pp. 370ff.
9 *Aesthetic Theory*, p. 10. See also Iser, 'Wirklichkeit der Fiktion'.
10 Cantarino, *Arabic Poetics*, p. 89.
11 *Al-Fann al-qaṣaṣī fī l-Qur'ān al-karīm*. On this question, see Wielandt, *Offenbarung und Geschichte*, pp. 134–52. Before Khalafallāh, Ṭāhā Ḥusayn advanced a similar thesis in his book on pre-Islamic poetry (*Fī sh-shi'r al-jāhilī*).
12 'What Is Poetry?', p. 369. On this topic, see also Octavio Paz's seminal remarks in *The Bow and the Lyre*, pp. 3ff.
13 Kugel, *The Idea of Biblical Poetry*, pp. 69–95, 302ff.
14 Nöldeke et al., *History of the Qur'ān*, p. 117, n. 1.
15 Jauss, 'Literary History as a Challenge', p. 23.
16 Wild, 'We Have Sent Down to Thee', p. 140.
17 The 'poetic function' is actually Jakobson's term; Mukařovský himself used the more general term 'aesthetic function'. In reference to linguistic texts, however, I will use Jakobson's term, since it has become established in literary theory, and because it is more precise in that it permits a distinction between the functions of linguistic and non-linguistic texts.

18 Mukařovský, 'Über die gegenwärtige Poetik', p. 89.
19 Morris, *Signs, Language and Behavior*, p. 194.
20 Mukařovský, *Aesthetic Function, Norm and Value as Social Facts*, pp. 76–7.
21 'Prosa und Feuilletons aus dem Nachlass' (unpublished); quoted in *Lektüre für Minuten*, vol. 2, p. 133.
22 'Rezensionen aus dem Nachlass' (unpublished); quoted in *Lektüre für Minuten*, vol. 2, p, 167.
23 *The World as Will and Representation*, vol. 1, pp. 256–7.
24 Lotman, *Structure of the Artistic Text*, pp. 17–18.
25 Roman Jakobson later added two more functions of language to Mukařovský's model: the metalinguistic and the phatic functions (Jakobson, 'Linguistics and Poetics', pp. 62ff.). These are not important for our study, however, which is concerned primarily with the poetic function, the fourth in Mukařovský's model, which Jakobson adopted. On the process of the gradual extension of Bühler's organon model of language, see Elmar Holenstein's introduction to Jakobson, *Poetik*, pp. 7–60.
26 Mukařovský, 'Zum Begriffssystem der tschechoslovakischen Kunsttheorie', p. 17; *Aesthetic Function, Norm and Value as Social Facts*, pp. 1–2; and 'The Place of the Aesthetic Function among the Other Functions', pp. 35ff.
27 'What Is Poetry?' p. 378.
28 Mukařovský, *Aesthetic Function, Norm and Value as Social Facts*, pp. 9ff., 54ff.
29 Jacobi, 'Die Altarabische Dichtung', p. 26.
30 On this particular surah, see Neuwirth and Neuwirth, 'Sūrat al-Fātiḥa'. On the '*qul* verses', see Radscheit, 'Word of God or Prophetic Speech?'
31 Richter, *Sprachstil des Koran*, p. 78.
32 *Mafhūm an-naṣṣ*, p. 65.
33 See, e.g., Quran 4:7–12; 2:226–42; 2:183–5.
34 Ġazālī, *Kīmiyā*, p. 179.
35 See p. 17 in chapter 1.
36 Lotman, *Structure of the Artistic Text*, pp. 10–11.
37 Sells, 'Sound, Spirit and Gender', p. 241.
38 Eco, *Opera aperta*, pp. 31–2.
39 'Zum Begriffssystem der tschechoslovakischen Kunsttheorie', p. 18; see also *Aesthetic Function, Norm and Value as Social Facts*, p. 28.
40 On competing functions in text, see also Mukařovský, 'Poetic Designation and the Aesthetic Function of Language', pp. 65ff.
41 Zwettler, *Oral Tradition*, pp. 101–2. Vollers, and in a milder form Kahle after him, argued that the Quran was originally promulgated in Muhammad's mother tongue, the Meccan colloquial dialect, and was later cast in a high Arabic dialect (Vollers, *Volkssprache and Schriftsprache im alten Arabien*; Kahle, 'The Qur'an and the "Arabiya"' and 'The Arabic Readers of the Qur'an'). This assumption has not prevailed in Arabic studies, however. See, e.g., Nöldeke, 'Zur Sprache des Korāns', pp. 1ff.; EI², ''Arabīya'; Watt, *Bell's Introduction to the Qur'an*, pp. 82ff.; Zwettler, *Oral Tradition*, pp. 117–18; Neuwirth, 'Koran', p. 113.
42 See pp. 60–1 above.
43 Eco, *La struttura assente*, p. 64.
44 Vodička, 'Die Rezeptionsgeschichte literarischer Werke', p. 73.
45 'Recite: In the name of thy Lord who created, created Man of a blood-clot', Quran 96:1 (trans. Arberry).

46 See Geyer, 'The Strophic Structure of the Koran'; Neuwirth, *Studien zur Komposition*.
47 See Nöldeke et al., *History of the Qur'ān*, pp. 29ff.; Neuwirth, *Studien zur Komposition*, pp. 65ff., and 'Symmetrie und Paarbildung'.
48 See Crapon de Caprona, *Le Coran*, pp. 215–487.
49 See Neuwirth, 'Zur Struktur der *Yūsuf*-Sure', p. 150.
50 See Johns, 'Quranic Presentation of the Joseph Story'.
51 See Richter, *Sprachstil des Koran*, pp. 4ff.
52 See Sister, 'Metaphern und Vergleiche im Koran'; Sabbagh, *La Métaphore dans le Coran*; Lohmann, 'Die Gleichnisreden Muhammeds'; Lichtenstädter, 'Origins and Interpretation', pp. 426–36; Mir, 'The Qur'an as Literature', pp. 54ff.; Buhl, 'Über Vergleichungen und Gleichnisse'; Neuwirth, 'Images and Metaphors'.
53 Neuwirth, 'Der historische Muhammad', pp. 103ff.
54 See Neuwirth, 'Horizont der Offenbarung' and 'Der historische Muhammad'; Kandil, 'Schwüre in den mekkanischen Suren' and *Untersuchungen zu den Schwüren*.
55 See Rippin, 'Poetics of Qur'ānic Punning'.
56 See Müller, *Untersuchungen zur Reimprosa*, but also Wansbrough's critical review of that work (*Bulletin of the School for Oriental and African Studies* 33 (1970), pp. 389–91).
57 Neuwirth, 'Symmetrie und Paarbildung', p. 470.
58 See Richter, *Sprachstil des Koran*; Sells, 'Sounds, Spirit and Gender' and 'Sound and Meaning'. See chapter 3 for a discussion of the acoustic features of the Quran.
59 Farūqī, 'Tartīl al-Qur'ān', p. 109.
60 Neuwirth, 'Der historische Muhammad', pp. 105ff.
61 Ibn Manẓūr, *Lisān*, vol. 7, p. 183 ('ʿ-r-ḍ'); also quoted in Graham, *Beyond the Written Word*, p. 94.
62 'Symmetrie und Paarbildung', p. 475.
63 Abū Zayd, *Islam und Politik*, p. 204.
64 Abū Zayd, *Mafhūm an-naṣṣ*, p. 160.
65 Suyūṭī, *Itqān*, vol. 1, p. 119.
66 Ibid., vol. 1, pp. 119ff.
67 Ibn Rashīq, *ʿUmda*, vol. 1, p. 30.
68 *Mafhūm an-naṣṣ*, p. 160; see also Neuwirth, 'Gotteswort und Nationalsprache', pp. 25–6.
69 More on this in chapter 4.
70 Ibn Qayyim al-Jawzīya, *Zād al-maʿād*, p. 166.
71 Ibn Hishām, *Sīra*, vol. 1, p. 356.
72 Vodička, 'Rezeptionsgeschichte literarischer Werke', p. 72. See also Mukařovský, *Aesthetic Function, Norm and Value as Social Facts*, p. 33.
73 Quran 8:38.
74 *Erscheinungsformen*, p. 273.
75 See Jacobi, 'Anfänge der arabischen Ġazalpoesie', p. 246; Wagner, *Grundzüge*, vol. 1, pp. 34–5.
76 Abū Zayd, *Mafhūm an-naṣṣ*, pp. 38ff.
77 See Quran 2:225; 5:89.
78 Goldziher, *Abhandlungen*, pp. 48ff.
79 Zwettler, *Oral Tradition*, p. 158.
80 'Literary History as a Challenge', pp. 23–4.

81 Ibid., p. 25.
82 Ibid.
83 Ibid.
84 *Waḥy wa-nobūwat*, p. 420.
85 *An-Naṣṣ al-qur'ānī*, p. 21.
86 *Itqān*, vol. 2, p. 120.
87 *Nukat*, p. 111. On the expression *naqḍ al-ʿāda* and the related sense of *kharq al-ʿāda*, see Antes, *Prophetenwunder*, pp. 40–6, and van Ess, *Theologie und Gesellschaft*, vol. 4, pp. 641–2.
88 Ibn Kathīr, *Sīra*, vol. 1, p. 499.
89 ʿIyāḍ, *Shifā*, vol. 1, p. 265.
90 Grunebaum, *Kritik und Dichtkunst*, pp. 136–7.
91 *Aesthetic Theory*, p. 273.
92 Nöldeke's influential study 'Zur Sprache des Korāns', uncritically reprinted by Régis Blachère in his *Histoire de la littérature arabe* (3 vols, Paris, 1952–66) and more recently praised by Miklos Muranyi ('Neue Materialien zur *tafsīr*-Forschung', p. 225), is a paradigm of this tendency. For a critical appraisal, see Neuwirth, *Studien zur Komposition*, pp. 67ff. and 171ff., and 'Koran', p. 114; Wild, 'Schauerliche Öde'; Wansbrough, *Quranic Studies*, pp. 112ff.
93 Nöldeke, 'Zur Sprache des Korāns', p. 9.
94 'Rezeptionsgeschichte literarischer Werke', p. 81.
95 Fück, *Arabiya*, p. 1.
96 *Arabs in History*, p. 132.
97 'Das islamische Dogma der "Unnachahmlichkeit des Korans"', p. 169.
98 'The Influence of the Arabic Language', p. 285.
99 Fück, *Arabiya*, p. 1. Versteegh has shed new light on the connection between grammar and Quran exegesis in his *Arabic Grammar and Qur'ānic Exegesis in Early Islam*, demonstrating that grammatical thinking among the community of Arabic speakers actually has its origins in the early Quran commentaries. See also Wansbrough, 'Arabic Rhetoric and Qurānic Exegesis'.
100 'What Is Poetry?' p. 369.
101 See Chejne, *Arabic Language*, pp. 38ff.
102 'Art as a Cultural System', p. 1490.
103 Ferguson, 'Diglossia' and 'The Arabic Koine'; Shouby, 'The Influence of the Arabic Language', pp. 285–6; Kaye, 'More on Diglossia in Arabic'; Diem, *Hochsprache und Dialekt im Arabischen*; Altoma, *Problems of Diglossia in Arabic*; Versteegh, *The Arabic Language*, pp. 189ff. The diglossic situation in China is no doubt comparable.
104 *Iʿjāz*, pp. 74–92.
105 *Manāhij tajdīd*, p. 303.
106 Stetkevych, *Abū Tammām and the Poetics of the ʿAbbāsid Age*, p. 287.
107 Such singing perfomances of spontaneously created poetry are the subject of a dissertation by Ḍirghām Ḥ Sbait: *The Improvised-Sung Folk Poetry of the Palestinians*. See also 'Palestinian Improvised-Sung Poetry' by the same author.
108 Shouby, 'Influence of the Arabic Language', p. 295. See also Chejne, *Arabic Language*, pp. 5–6.
109 Goldziher, *Gesammelte Schriften*, vol. 1, pp. 8–9.
110 Ibid., p. 8.
111 Chejne, *Arabic Language*, pp. 18ff.
112 Introduction to the second edition of Rāfiʿī, *Iʿjāz*, pp. 9–22, at p. 22. As-Saʿīd expresses a similar sentiment in *al-Jamʿ as-sawṭī*, pp. 376ff.

113 This is not to say that the standard Arabic of today is identical with the Arabic of the Quran. But the critical fact is that it is considered to be identical. A person who speaks *fuṣḥā* does so with the intention of using a language that – in spite of some differences in detail that have become conscious – is basically the same as classical Arabic; a person who listens to him instinctively links his speech to the chain of other texts and norms of standard Arabic, by which he attempts to understand, assess and evaluate it. And he considers this chain to reach unbroken from the Arabic of the Quran to the standard Arabic of today.

114 On the political speech in modern Arabic countries in general, and on the use and effect of a code change such as the shift between standard Arabic and dialect in particular, see Mazraani, *Aspects of Language Variation in Arabic Political Speech*, especially pp. 215ff.

115 Kermani, *Offenbarung als Kommunikation*; Speicher, 'Einige Bemerkungen zu al-Khūlīs Entwurf'.

116 Van Nieuwenhuijze, 'Qur'an as a Factor', p. 222. This topic will be treated in more detail in chapter 3.

117 See Qāḍī, 'Impact of the Qur'ān on the Epistolography of ʿAbd al-Ḥamīd'.

118 Graham, *Beyond the Written Word*, pp. 106, 171–2; Piamenta, *Islam in Everyday Speech*; Petit, *Présence de l'Islam dans la langue arabe*.

119 'Art as a Cultural System', pp. 1491–2.

120 Farrukh, *Bild des Frühislam*; Khan, *Vom Einfluß des Qur'āns*; Bellamy, 'Impact of Islam'; Zwettler, *Oral Tradition*, pp. 165ff. Grunebaum, on the other hand, finds that the Quran had relatively little influence on early Islamic poetry; see 'Von Muhammad's Wirkung'.

121 Zaġlūl Salām, *Athr al-Qur'ān*; Heinrichs, 'Literary Theory', esp. pp. 28ff.; Grunebaum, *Kritik und Dichtkunst*, pp. 87ff.

122 Brockelmann, *Geschichte*, vol. 2, pp. 526; Aleem, 'Iʿjazu 'l-Qur'an', p. 82.

123 Kratschkovsky, 'Die arabische Poetik', p. 28; Bürgel, 'Die beste Dichtung', pp. 66ff. On *muḥdath* poetry in general, see Wagner, *Grundzüge*, vol. 2, pp. 89–113; Adūnīs, *Ath-Thābit wa-l-mutaḥawwil*, vol. 2, pp. 173–202; Stetkevych, *Abū Tammām*, pp. 5–48; Heinrichs, *Arabische Dichtung und griechische Poetik*, pp. 83ff., and '"Manierismus" in der arabischen Literatur'.

124 See Ibn al-Muʿtazz, *Kitāb al-badīʿ*. Similarly, although less often and less systematically, the other great theoretician of *badīʿ*, Ibn Rashīq, also draws on the Quran as an example of the proposed new style. See, e.g., his *ʿUmda*, vol. 1, p. 299; vol. 2, pp. 61–5.

125 Adūnīs, *Ash-Shiʿrīya al-ʿarabīya*, pp. 50–1.

126 See Farūqī, 'Die Islamische Kunst'; Burckhardt, 'Perennial Values in Islamic Art' and *The Art of Islam*; Nasr, *Islamic Art and Spirituality*. On calligraphy in particular, see Lings, *The Quranic Art of Calligraphy*; Anwari-Alhosseyni, 'Das Kunsthandwerk der persischen Kalligraphie'.

127 Abbott, *Rise of the North Arabic Script*, pp. 5–14; Hitti, *History of the Arabs*, p. 88.

128 *Mafhūm an-naṣṣ*, p. 11. Cf. Adonis's similar statement, *An-Naṣṣ al-qur'ānī*, p. 36.

129 On this topic, see Khorramshāhī, *Qor'ān-shenākht*, pp. 17–44.

130 Nasr, 'Oral Transmission'.

131 'Linguistics and Poetics', p. 85.

132 '[L]'être même de la littérature, porté à son paroxysme': *On Racine*, p. ix.

133 *Die Geheimnisse der Wortkunst*, p. 62.

134 *Schools of Koranic Commentators*, p. 118. See the interpretation by the mystic Mas'ūd Bek Bokhārā'ī for a relatively moderate example of mystical hermeneutics. He relates the verse to *samā'*, the mystics' ritual 'listening', and sees the oil, for example, as symbolizing beautiful voices and sounds that ignite the light of love in the soul (*Al-Kashf fī bayān*, p. 385).
135 Eco, *La struttura assente*, p. 64. See also Eco, *The Open Work*, p. 58.
136 *Kashshāf*, commentary on 3:7.
137 *Die Geheimnisse der Wortkunst*, p. 157.
138 Eco, *The Open Work*, p. 25.
139 Zamakhsharī, *Kashshāf*, commentary on 3:7.
140 *The Sectarian Milieu*, p. 45; see also Wansbrough, *Quranic Studies*, p. 131.
141 'Tafsīr from Ṭabarī to Ibn Kathīr', p. 115.
142 *Relire le Coran*, p. 125.
143 Hämeen-Antilla, 'We Will Tell You the Best of Stories'.
144 Thomas Carlyle, *Heroes and Hero Worship*, London, 1872, p. 40; quoted in Brown, 'The Apocalypse of Islam', p. 69, and in Wild, 'Die schauerliche Öde', p. 434.
145 Wild, 'Die schauerliche Öde', p. 434.
146 *Ideals and Realities*, p. 48.
147 *Islam*, Dublin, 1903, p. 16; quoted in Zwemer, *Studies in Popular Islam*, p. 82.
148 *Understanding Islam*, p. 40.
149 Luther, *Werke*, vol. 19, p. 350.
150 *The Apology of al-Kindy*, pp. 78–9, 81. On the author and text, see chapter 4, p. 242.
151 Suyūṭī, *Itqān*, vol. 1, p. 113.
152 Ibid.
153 Quoted in Adūnīs, *An-Naṣṣ al-qur'ānī*, p. 44.
154 Abū 'Abdirraḥman Sulamī, *Nasīm al-arwāḥ*, in *Majmu'-e-ye khaṭṭī-ye Aḥmadīye-ye Shīrāz* (manuscript collection at the University of Teheran), nos 87, 100; quoted in Pourjavady, 'Zwei alte Werke über *samā'*', part 2, p. 42.
155 To name just one example, the expression *ummuhū hāwiyatun* in verse 101:9 is translated in seven different ways by six different European translators and commentators: '*um den ist es geschehen*' [he is lost, finished] (Paret); '*seine Mutter wird der Höllenschlund sein*' [the mouth of Hell will be his mother] (Henning); '*Verderben*' [ruin, doom] (Torrey; see Paret's concordance); '*Des Mutter ist die Tiefe*' [his mother is the depths] (Rückert); '*Fühlt von Hawiyas Arm sich umschränkt*' [feels enclosed by Hawiya's arm] (Grimme); '*dessen Mutter geht zu Grunde*' [his mother perishes] and '*wird kinderlos*' [becomes childless] (Fischer; see Paret's concordance). On the difficulty of understanding the Quran literally, see Fischer, *Der Wert der vorhandenen Koran-Übersetzungen*, pp. 7–8.
156 Quran 21:5.
157 E.g., Quran 51:12; 70:1; 75:6; 78:1–2; 79:42. On this topic, see Neuwirth, 'Koran', p. 121.
158 See Sells, 'Sounds, Spirit and Gender' and 'Sound and Meaning'.
159 Ibn Manẓūr, *Lisān*, vol. 8, 262b–270a ('q-r-'').
160 Likewise surah *al-Qadr* (no. 97) first introduces the expression *laylat al-qadr*, then asks the question *mā adrāka mā laylatu l-qadr*, 'What makes you know what the night of *qadr* is?'
161 *On Racine*, p. 11.

162 Birkenhauer, *Beckett*, p. 8.
163 *Der Koran*, p. 8.
164 *Aesthetic Theory*, p. 163.
165 Quoted in Suyūṭī, *Itqān*, vol. 2, p. 120.
166 *Ästhetische Erfahrung*, p. 42.
167 Later, however, through an idealization of the Prophet's status, a contrary thesis also emerged which holds that Muhammad was able to interpret even those verses (*al-mutashābihāt*) that are cryptic to other people. Even this view does not deny the actual ambiguity of the Quran, however: it only sets the Prophet above ordinary people; ordinary interpreters are still unable to grasp the ultimate meaning of God's word.
168 *Schlaglichter*, pp. 132–3.
169 Tillich, 'Die Idee der Offenbarung', p. 406.
170 For a critical reflection, see Smith, *What is Scripture*, p. 78; Jeffery, *The Qur'ān as Scripture*, p. 69.
171 Buhl, 'Über Vergleichungen und Gleichnisse', pp. 9–10; EI[1], 'Allāh' (D. B. Macdonald), p. 318. See also Lohmann, 'Die Gleichnisreden Muhammeds im Koran', pp. 262ff.
172 Bertolt Brecht, *Poems 1913–1956*, ed. John Willett and Ralph Mannheim, London, 1976, p. 439.
173 See Eco, *The Open Work*, pp. 3–4; Iser, 'Appellstruktur der Texte', pp. 234ff.
174 'The Apocalypse of Islam', p. 89.
175 Graham, 'Schriftprinzip', p. 212.
176 See Eco, *Opera aperta*, p. 16.
177 Plato, *The Sophists*, 235d ff.
178 Eco, *The Open Work*, pp. 5ff.
179 'Were the Prophets Poets?', p. 219.
180 Eco, *The Open Work*, p. 9.
181 Trans. Arberry.
182 Khorramshāhī, *Qor'ān-pažūhī*, pp. 37–43 and 732–45.
183 See, e.g., the commentary on 3:7 in aṭ-Ṭabarī, *Tafsīr*, and az-Zamakhshari, *Kashshāf*. On aṭ-Ṭabarī's hermeneutic method and his interpretation of this verse, see McAuliffe, 'Quranic Hermeneutics'.
184 Cf. 12:36–7 and 12:44.
185 36:69; see also 15:1.
186 26:195; see also 16:103.
187 Kermani, 'Appelliert Gott an den Verstand?'
188 See Izutsu, *God and Man*, pp. 35ff.; Abū Zayd, *Mafhūm an-naṣṣ*, pp. 35ff., 79–80; Kermani, *Offenbarung als Kommunikation*, pp. 39ff.
189 Ibn Manẓūr, *Lisān*, 'w-ḥ-y' (vol. 15, 381a). On the doctrine of *iʿjāz*, see also the sceptical comments of Ibn ʿArabī, who notoriously admits no doubt about his admiration of the Quran's beauty (*Al-Futūḥāt al-makkīya*, vol. 1, pp. 227–8; vol. 3, pp. 384ff.).
190 *Die Geheimnisse der Wortkunst*, p. 423.
191 Iser, 'Die Appellstruktur der Texte', pp. 234ff.
192 Goldziher, *Schools of Koranic Commentators*, pp. 163ff.
193 *Al-Futūḥāt*, vol. 3, p. 94. On Ibn ʿArabī's concepts of hermeneutics and the Quran recitation, see Abū Zayd, *Falsafat at-ta'wīl*; Michael Chodkiewicz, *An Ocean Without Shore*, pp. 19–33; Chittick, *The Sufi Path of Knowledge*, pp. 231–52. On the principles of mystical Quran exegesis in general, see Lory, *Les Commentaires ésotériques*, esp. pp. 9ff., 28ff.

194 Chodkiewicz, *An Ocean Without Shore*, p. 28.
195 *Al-Futūḥāt*, vol. 4, p. 25.
196 In February 1979, the Egyptian parliament resolved to prohibit the publication and distribution of *Al-Futūḥāt al-makkīya*. Although the decree was soon rescinded, it is still difficult today to obtain Ibn ʿArabī's works on the Egyptian book market (Chodkiewicz, *An Ocean Without Shore*, p. 22). In some other Sunni states they are banned even without an act of parliament.
197 *Burhān*, vol. 1, p. 537; Ġazālī, *Iḥyā'*, p. 254.
198 *Shifā'*, vol. 1, p. 264.
199 Goldziher, *Schools of Koranic Commentators*, pp. 55–6.
200 Rāfiʿī, *Iʿjāz*, p. 126.
201 ʿIyāḍ, *Shifā'*, vol. 1, p. 280.
202 *Première leçon du cours de poétique*, quoted in Eco, *Opera aperta*, p. 17.
203 *Dalā'il al-iʿjāz fī l-Qur'ān*, pp. 18–19/p. ix.
204 *Relire le Coran*, p. 122.
205 *Iʿjāz*, p. 267.
206 Ibn Sallām, *Faḍā'il al-Qur'ān*, pp. 67–8 (XV/1ff.).
207 Ibn Kathīr, *Sīra*, vol. 1, p. 502.
208 See chapter 1 above, pp. 43–4.
209 *Dalā'il al-iʿjāz fī l-Qur'ān*, p. 266.
210 Ibid., p. 265.
211 Eco, *The Open Work*, p. 37.
212 Quran 39:22.
213 Quran 20:114.
214 *Al-Futūḥāt*, vol. 3, pp. 128–9.
215 Jauss, *Aesthetic Experience and Literary Hermeneutics*, pp. 35ff.
216 Quoted in Schimmel, *Deciphering the Signs of God*, p. 165.
217 Eco, *The Open Work*, pp. 37–8.
218 Ibn Sallām, *Faḍā'il al-Qur'ān*, p. 63 (XIII/10).
219 Bukhārī, *Ṣaḥīḥ*, LXVI/37 (no. 5060–1); Dārimī, *Sunan*, XXIII/7 (no. 3364).
220 Ġazālī, *Kīmiyā*, p. 179, and *Iḥyā'*, vol. 2, p. 180.
221 *Kashf*, p. 72.
222 *Burhān*, vol. 2, p. 114.
223 *Shifā'*, vol. 1, p. 276. The quotation of the Prophet refers to a hadith that at-Tirmiḏī collected in his *Al-Jāmiʿ* (XLIII/14 [no. 3070]).
224 Eco, *The Open Work*, pp. 38.
225 *Iḥyā'*, vol. 1, pp. 174–5.
226 Ibid., vol. 1, pp. 168–9.
227 Ibid., vol. 1, p. 174.
228 Ibid., vol. 1, p. 179.
229 Ibid.
230 Ibid., vol. 1, pp. 175, 179.
231 Ibid., vol. 1, p. 179.
232 Ibid., vol. 1, p. 174.
233 *West–East Divan*, p. 25 (Book of Hafiz).
234 Ġazālī, *Iḥyā'*, vol. 1, p. 173.
235 Ibid., vol. 1, p. 174; also, almost verbatim, in Zarkashī, *Burhān*, vol. 1, p. 536.
236 See, for example, al-Makkī's remarks in the chapter on the Quran in his *Qūt al-qulūb* (*Nahrung des Herzens*, pp. 171–90), which is devoted largely to the same themes as al-Ġazālī's work.

237 *Discourses*, p. 124.
238 *The Pleasure of the Text*, p. 63.
239 *Islam und Politik*, p. 204.
240 Ibid.
241 *Manāhij tajdīd*, p. 296.
242 *Mafhūm an-naṣṣ*, p. 11.
243 See his book *Hermenūtīk, ketāb wa-sonnat* (Teheran, 1375/1996).
244 *Naqd al-khiṭāb ad-dīnī*, p. 93.
245 Adūnīs, for example: see *An-Naṣṣ al-qur'ānī*, pp. 40–1. I have discussed this theme in more detail in *Offenbarung als Kommunikation*, pp. 9ff.
246 Kafka, 'The Silence of the Sirens', p. 143.
247 *Waḥy wa-nobūwat*, p. 421.
248 Lotman, *The Structure of the Artistic Text*, p. 11.
249 Ibid.
250 Ibid., p. 12. On the inadequacy of the form/content scheme, see also Mukařovský, 'Über die gegenwärtige Poetik', pp. 86ff.; Adorno, *Aesthetic Theory*, esp. pp. 198–202.
251 On this word, see Rubin, *'Al-Ṣamad* and the High God'.
252 Eco, *The Open Work*, pp. 32–3.
253 Jakobson, 'On Linguistic Aspects of Translation', p. 434.
254 See Paret's own assessment of his work: 'Since the translation is not intended for edifying purposes but very simply aimed at making the meaning contained in the original understandable, I have abstained from an elevated form of expression' (*Der Koran*, p. 6).
255 Lotman, *The Structure of the Artistic Text*, pp. 10–11.
256 Quran 8:58.
257 Quran 18:11.
258 Ibn Fāris, *Ṣāḥibī*, pp. 41–2. Almost verbatim in the earlier Ibn Qutayba, *Ta'wīl Mushkil al-Qur'ān*, p. 16; also in Suyūṭī, *Muzhir*, vol. 1, p. 188.
259 Rāzī, *At-Tafsīr al-kabir*, commentary on surah 1 (vol. 1, pp. 209–17).
260 Ibid., pp. 211ff.
261 *The Structure of the Artistic Text*, p. 29.
262 See the interpretation by Schadewaldt in *Hellas und Hesperien*, vol. 1, pp. 763ff.
263 *Die Briefe an Gräfin Sizzo*, p. 29.
264 *West–East Divan*, p. 281.
265 'The Task of the Translator', p. 78; cf. Kermani, 'Appelliert Gott an den Verstand?' pp. 64–5.
266 Werner Diem in the encyclopedia article 'Koran' in *Lexikon der islamischen Welt*. As far as I can see, only Wild has been firmly critical of Paret's translation: see 'Die schauerliche Öde', pp. 445–6.
267 Ibid.
268 Trans. Khalidi.
269 See Kermani, 'Appelliert Gott an den Verstand?', pp. 57ff.
270 Tilman Seidensticker too (*Das Herz im Altarabischen*, dissertation, Giessen, 1990, p. 84) interprets the verses in question in the same way as Paret: see Kermani, 'Appelliert Gott an den Verstand?' p. 58, n. 11.
271 50:37.
272 *Die Geheimnisse der Wortkunst*, p. 391–2.
273 Paz, *The Bow and the Lyre*, p. 35.
274 *Die Geheimnisse der Wortkunst*, p. 392.

275 *Iʿjāz*, p. 48.
276 *The Art of Reciting the Qur'an*, p. 13.
277 *The Meaning of the Glorious Koran*, p. vii.
278 *Kann der Koran übersetzt werden?*, p. 13.
279 Andrae, *Mohammed*, pp. 97–8. See also Horovitz, *Koranische Untersuchungen*, pp. 45ff.
280 Lotman, *The Structure of the Artistic Text*, p. 18.
281 Quran 12:1–2 (trans. Haleem, slightly modified). Cf. 13:37; 20:112; 39:28; 41:3; 42:7; 43:3.
282 Quran 41:44 (trans. Haleem).
283 Quran, 26:198–9 (trans. Haleem, modified). Paret interprets the second hypothesis (*fa-qara'ahū ʿalayhim*) as reciting 'in his own language'. It is not clear from the context, however, in what language the non-Arab (*aʿjamī*) would have recited the Quran. The verse can also be understood as implying that the non-Arab would have preached the message in Arabic, and the Arabs would not have believed him because of the imperfection of his language. In connection with the emphasis on the clarity that is inherent in the Quran's language, this interpretation seems more plausible to me. That Arabs would not have believed a prophet who spoke to them in Greek, for example (which is what Paret's translation amounts to), would be a bit too simple: how could they have believed him if they did not even understand him? Izutsu (*God and Man*, pp. 186–7) explains this verse in exactly the sense I suggest, and he also shows that *aʿjamī* is not necessarily an ethnic term but refers to all persons who are unable to speak clear and well-formed Arabic. See also Goldziher, *Muslim Studies*, vol. 1, pp. 98ff. On the word *aʿjam*, see chapter 1, p. 60.
284 16:103 (trans. Haleem); see also 25:5.
285 26:195 (trans. Arberry); see also 46:12. On the problem of the 'Arabic Quran', see Izutsu, *God and Man*, pp. 185ff.; Zwettler, *Oral Tradition*, pp. 161–4; Cragg, *The Event*, pp. 54ff., and *Readings*, pp. 46–7; Rāfiʿī, *Iʿjāz*, pp. 82ff.
286 33:40. On this passage, see Horovitz, *Koranische Untersuchungen*, pp. 53–4; Jeffery, *The Qur'ān as Scripture*, pp. 78–9; Colpe, 'Das Siegel der Propheten'; Roest Crollius, *The Word in the Experience of Revelation*, pp. 123ff.
287 John 14:16, 26; 16:7. See also Paret's commentary on Quran 61:6.
288 7:158.
289 81:27.
290 *Mohammed*, vol. 1, pp. 122ff.
291 *Mohammedanism*, pp. 47–9, 52–3.
292 Buhl, 'Fasste Muhammed seine Verkündigung als eine universelle, auch für Nichtaraber bestimmte Religion auf?'
293 *Vorlesungen*, vol. 1, pp. 9–10.
294 See his review of Caetani's *Annali dell'Islām*, *Wiener Zeitschrift für die Kunde des Morgenlandes* 21 (1907), p. 307.
295 Goitein, *Studies in Islamic History*, p. 8.
296 Chejne, *The Arabic Language*, p. 12.
297 Yāqūt, *Mu'jam al-udabā'*, vol. 1, p. 84.
298 *Risāla*, p. 48.
299 Kulaynī, *Kāfī*, 'Faḍl-al-Qur'ān/Anna al-Qur'ān yurfaʿ', no. 1. A similar statement is attributed to Bukayr ibn al-Aḥnas: 'When the non-Arab recites something that is not in the Quran, the angels write it down as it was revealed' (Ibn Sallām, *Faḍā'il al-Qur'ān*, p. 47 [VII/5]).
300 Acts 2:3–4.

301 See Chouraqui, *Reflexionen*, pp. 15ff.; Lanczkowski, *Sacred Writings*, p. 33.
302 Steiner, *After Babel*, p. 258.
303 See Salmāsīzāde, *Tārīkh-e tarjome-ye Qor'ān*, pp. 73ff.
304 See Tibawi, 'Is the Qur'ān Translatable?'; Rāmiyār, *Tārīkh-e Qor'ān*, pp. 648ff.
305 Zarkashī, *Burhān*, vol. 1, pp. 548ff.
306 *Studies in Popular Islam*, p. 98.
307 'Ein Same, der gedeiht auf allen Triften', in Rückert, *Werke*, vol. 1, p. 232. Original:

Den Christenbüchern ist ein großer Vorzug eigen,
Vor dem beschämet die des Islams müssen schweigen;
Der Vorzug, daß sie leicht in alle Volksmundarten
Zu übertragen sind auf allen Weltumfahrten.
Des Korans Redeschmuck geht rettungslos verloren,
Der Bibel Einfalt wird dadurch neu geboren.
Daher mag eher die, als jener, Segen stiften,
Gleich einem Samen, der gedeiht auf allen Triften.

308 Rahman, 'Translating the Qur'an', p. 25.
309 *Tafsīr al-Qur'ān*, vol. 1, p. 31 (Introduction). See also ʿAbduh's discussion of this issue in his commentary on the surah *Aʿrāf* (verses 153–7; vol. 9, pp. 293–339). See also Jomier, *Le Commentaire coranique du Manâr*, pp. 338–47; Zwemer, *Studies in Popular Islam*, p. 98; Jansen, *Interpretation of the Koran in Modern Egypt*, pp. 10–11.
310 Rahman, 'Translating the Qur'an', p. 26.
311 Zwemer, *Studies in Popular Islam*, p. 99.
312 In Iran alone, for example, there are at least eight widely distributed translations – all with parallel Arabic text. See the reviews in Khorramshāhi, *Qor'ān-pažūhī*, pp. 362–457. Compared with translations of the Bible, however, the number of languages in which the Quran is available is still minuscule. In his *History of the Quran*, published in the 1980s, Rāmiyār counts thirty-five languages (*Tārīkh-e Qor'ān*, p. 645). Although this figure now seems too low, the difference is still striking.
313 *Islam und Politik*, p. 204.
314 Zarkashī, *Burhān*, vol. 1, pp. 548, 550; van Ess, *Theologie und Gesellschaft*, vol. 2, pp. 491–2; Grunebaum, *Medieval Islam*, 34ff.; EI[2], 'Ḳur'ān/Translations of the Ḳurān', p. 429. In the beginning of the Islamization of the Persian-speaking regions such as Khorasan, it seems to have been customary to read at least excerpts of the Quran in Persian: see Narshakhī, *History of Bukhara*, p. 48.
315 Van Ess, *Theologie und Gesellschaft*, vol. 4, p. 571.
316 Sorūsh, 'Ẕātī wa ʿarabī dar dīn'. On the author, see Amirpur, 'Ein iranischer Luther?'
317 See Goldziher, *Muslim Studies*, vol. 1, pp. 137–200.
318 Ibn Fāris, *Ṣāḥibī*, pp. 41ff.; Suyūṭī, *Muzhir*, vol. 1, pp. 19ff.
319 Suyūṭī, *Muzhir*, vol. 1, pp. 188–9.
320 *Risāla*, p. 42; cf. Suyūṭī, *Muzhir*, vol. 1, p. 41.
321 Shāfiʿī, *Risāla*, p. 42; Suyūṭī, *Muzhir*, vol. 1, pp. 157ff.; Ibn Fāris, *Ṣāḥibī*, pp. 57ff.

322 Suyūṭī, *Muzhir*, vol. 1, p. 21. As a consequence of the supposed superiority of Arabic as the language of Paradise, many scholars feel the Quran must be untranslatable simply because it is an Arabic book. 'No translator is capable of translating it into another language, as the Gospel can be translated from Syrian into Ethiopian and Greek or the Torah and the Psalms and all divine scriptures can be translated into Arabic, for the languages of the non-Arabs are not as rich in tropes as that of the Arabs', says the philologist Ibn Qutayba in *Ta'wīl mushkil al-qur'ān*, p. 16. Exactly the same statement is found in Ibn Fāris, *Ṣāhibī*, p. 41, and Suyūṭī, *Muzhir*, vol. 1, p. 187. Al-Jāḥiẓ too, in *Kitāb al-ḥayawān*, p. 75, writes that translation from the Arabic is problematic in itself, not only in the case of the Quran. See also Rāzī, *At-Tafsīr al-kabīr*, commentary on surah 1 (vol. 1, pp. 209–17), and ʿAlī aṭ-Ṭabarī, *Kitāb ad-dīn wa-d-dawla*, pp. 194–5.
323 Suyūṭī, *Itqān*, vol. 1, p. 45.
324 On the Muslim discussion of the original language and the Tower of Babel, see Geiger, *Judaism and Islam*, pp. 87ff.; Borst, *Turmbau von Babel*, vol. 1, pp. 325ff.; Weiss, 'Medieval Muslim Discussions'.
325 See Borst, *Turmbau von Babel*; Eco, *The Search for the Perfect Language*.
326 See Eco, *Opera aperta*, p. 21.
327 Quran 36:69–70 (after Khalidi; emphasis added).
328 See 16:35, 82; 24:54; 29:18; 64:14.
329 Mukařovský, 'Zum Begriffssystem der tschechoslovakischen Kunsttheorie', p. 17, and 'Structuralism in Aesthetics and Literary Studies', p. 73.
330 Quran 26:226; 69:40–51.
331 Jakobson, 'What is Poetry?', p. 370.
332 See Kott, *Shakespeare Our Contemporary*.
333 Ġazālī, *Iḥyā'*, vol. 1, p, 179.
334 Abū Zayd, *Ishkālīyāt al-qirā'a*, p. 43.
335 *Al-Futūḥāt*, vol. 3, p, 128.
336 Nelson, *The Art of Reciting the Qur'an*, pp. 153–87.
337 *Schlaglichter*, pp. 411–12.
338 Eco, *The Open Work*, p. 35ff.
339 See Wenzel, *Hören und Sehen*, pp. 95–127; Balthasar, *Herrlichkeit*, vol. 1, pp. 42ff.

Chapter 3 The Sound

1 *Selected Poems*, trans. Albert Ernest Flemming. New York: Routledge, [1985] 2011.
2 Also printed in *Majallat al-Azhar*, Shawwāl 1378/April 1959.
3 Rich in important references and objective analyses, the book is indispensable for Western research on Quran recitation as well. Furthermore, as the product of an orthodox pen, as-Saʿīd's book offers an authentic insight into the Muslim conception of writing (the author was not only a professor at ʿAyn Shams University but also taught for years at Azhar and at Saudi universities, was director of Quranic affairs in the Ministry of Religious Endowments (*awqāf*), and was considered in Egyptian religious circles as an authority on Quran studies). The English edition of *al-Jamʿ aṣ-ṣawtī* is in large part more a revision and condensation than a translation: the original with its complete references is much more comprehensive and more exact. Because

the English text was produced by two American Orientalists and an Egyptian theologian in close cooperation with the author, and can therefore be considered as his authentic work, I will quote from it where its revised text is more concise. On the book and its author, see also Weiss, *'Al-Muṣḥaf al-murattal'*.

4 96:1. The consensus has since become established in Oriental studies that, contrary to previous assumptions (reflected, by the way, in Rilke's poem 'Muhammad's Calling'), the word does not mean 'Read!'

5 See Neuwirth, *Studien zur Komposition*, pp. 1–2; Graham, *Beyond the Written Word*, pp. 79–115, and '*Qur'ān* as Spoken Word'; Roest Crollius, *The Word in the Experience of Revelation*, pp. 17–79.

6 7:204.

7 For more on this topic, see Kermani, 'Appelliert Gott an den Verstand?' pp. 53ff.

8 9:6.

9 41:26.

10 See, e.g., 17:78; 75:16–18; 54:17, 22, 32, 40; 20:114; 73:4; 28:85. Cragg offers what may be the most precise explanation of the word *qur'ān*: 'It could almost mean "Quranize", if we are careful to clarify what "Quranize" is. As "read" is to "reading", so *iqrā'* is to *Qur'ān*' (*The Event of the Qur'ān*, p. 27). See also Graham, 'Earliest Meaning' and *Beyond the Written Word*, pp. 88–95; Nöldeke et al., *History of the Qur'ān*, pp. 26–7; Juynboll, 'The Qurrā' in early Islamic History'.

11 'Schreiben und Veröffentlichen', p. 19. The Muslim tradition of the codification of the text under the third caliph, Uthmān, is not historically verifiable and is vehemently contested by such researchers as Burton (*Collection*) and Wansbrough (*Quranic Studies*). Angelika Neuwirth states the current understanding in Oriental studies, which is also the concept underlying the present work, as follows: 'In view of the chronologically documented activities in quranic philology of the 2nd/8th century, however, an early consolidation of the corpus "Quran", if only in the form of a consonantal framework... is still the most plausible hypothesis in comparison with other models' ('Vom Rezitationstext über die Liturgie zum Kanon', p. 78, n. 24; see also Neuwirth's reviews of Wansbrough, *Quranic Studies*, and Burton, *Collection of the Qur'ān*).

12 Suyūṭī, *Itqān*, vol. 1, p. 57.

13 See 2:185; 6:19; 9:111; 12:3; 15:87; 20:73; 27:6.

14 Suyūṭī, *Itqān*, vol. 1, p. 57.

15 As-Sa'īd, *The Recited Koran*, p. 20. See also as-Sa'īd, *Al-Jam' aṣ-ṣawtī*, pp. 31–3.

16 See Quran 2:121; Graham, *Beyond the Written Word*, pp. 80, 91–2; Schoeler, 'Schreiben und Veröffentlichung', p. 23.

17 Assmann, *Cultural Memory*, pp. 70–81; Assmann and Assmann, 'Schrift, Tradition und Kultur'.

18 See Neuwirth, 'Vom Rezitationstext über die Liturgiezum Kanon', pp. 77ff.

19 Sa'īd, *Al-Jam' aṣ-ṣawṭī*, p. 110, and *The Recited Koran*, p. 56.

20 See Sa'īd, *Al-Jam' aṣ-ṣawṭī*, pp. 108–9, 171–2, and *The Recited Koran*, pp. 55–6.

21 See Schoeler, 'Schreiben und Veröffentlichen', pp. 2–3; Abbott, *Rise of the North Arabic Script*, pp. 5–14.

22 See Graham, *Beyond the Written Word*, p. 89.

23 Isaiah 8:1 (trans. David H. Stern, *Complete Jewish Bible*).
24 6:7 (trans. Arberry).
25 87:6–8 [after Kermani].
26 Bukhārī, *Ṣaḥīḥ*, I/5 (no. 6).
27 *Al-Qur'ān: Ādāb tilāwatihī wa-samā'ihī*, Cairo, 1963, quoted in Kellermann, *Koranlesung im Maghreb*, p. 14. The tradition took a similar form as early as the eleventh century: see Denny, 'Exegesis and Recitation', p. 117.
28 Van Ess, *Theologie und Gesellschaft*, vol. 4, p. 624.
29 Quran 3:7; 13:39; 43:4; 85:22. On the concept of the celestial scripture, which is also known in other religions, see Heiler, *Erscheinungsformen*, pp. 351–2; Jeffery, *The Qur'ān as Scripture*, pp. 10–17; Widengren, *Ascension of the Apostle* and *Muḥammad*, pp. 115–39; Graham, *Beyond the Written Word*, pp. 50–1; Shaḥrūr, *Al-Kitāb wa-l-Qur'ān*, pp. 103–35.
30 17:105–6 (trans. Arberry).
31 25:32 (trans. Haleem).
32 56:77–80 (trans. Haleem, modified).
33 Sa'id, *The Recited Koran*, p. 74. See also Sa'id, *Al-Jam' aṣ-ṣawṭī*, pp. 73–4.
34 Sa'id, *Al-Jam' aṣ-ṣawṭī*, p. 110, and *The Recited Koran*, p. 56. See also Schoeler, 'Schreiben und Veröffentlichen', p. 34.
35 Ibn Sallām, *Faḍā'il al-Qur'ān*, p. 160 (IL/20).
36 'Koranlesung in Kairo', pp. 10–11.
37 *Beyond the Written Word*, p. 111. See also Smith, *What is Scripture?* pp. 65–91.
38 Hauser, *Sociology of Art*, pp. 455–6.
39 Angelika Neuwirth has thoroughly studied and described these stylistic devices in various essays and in her *Studien zur Komposition der mekkanischen Suren*. See especially Neuwirth, 'Zur Struktur der Yūsuf-Sure'; 'Symmetrie und Paarbildung'; 'Vom Rezitationstext über die Liturgie zum Kanon'. See also Crapon de Caprona, *Le Coran*; Johns, 'Quranic Presentation of the Joseph Story'; Sells, 'Sounds, Spirit and Gender' and 'Sound and Meaning'.
40 Wild, 'Die schauerliche Öde', pp. 441–2. See also Neuwirth, 'Das islamische Dogma der "Unnachahmlichkeit"', p. 168; Graham, 'The *Qur'ān* as Spoken Word', pp. 24–5, and 'Das Schriftprinzip', pp. 209–10.
41 What Denny wrote about this verse seems plausible: 'It is evident, then, that *tartīl* means more than simple reading aloud. Notice that both Arberry and Pickthall translate the imperative form (*rattil*) in 73:4 as "chant". I prefer this rendering, also, but feel that it must be used advisedly. It does not mean musical chanting, or singing, although the line between the two is sometimes very difficult to draw. The term "chanting" is often used indiscriminately with reference to recitation of the Qur'ān. There are technical terms in Arabic which were developed to distinguish the different types of Qur'ān recitation; applying the word "chanting" to them all does not take the varieties in account' ('Exegesis and Recitation', p. 96). *Tartīl* has undergone several shifts in meaning during its history. Today it is used to designate a form of recitation that is slow and vocally smooth, while the more musical recitation is called *tajwīd*, a word that is not used in this sense in the Quran. Other terms for Quran recitation are *qirā'a*, *tilāwa* and occasionally *taghīr*. On the terminology of recitation and its evolution, see Farūqī, 'Tartīl al-Qur'ān', pp. 106ff.
42 See, e.g., Bukhārī, *Ṣāḥīḥ*, LXVI/31 (no. 5048), III/44 (no. 7527), XCVIII/52 (no. 7544); Muslim, *Ṣaḥīḥ*, VI/34 (nos 792–3); Ibn Māja, *Sunan*, V/186 (nos 1341–2).

43 Muslim, *Ṣaḥīḥ*, VI/34 (no. 792); Bukhārī, *Ṣaḥīḥ*, LXVI/19 (no. 5023), XCVIII/32 (no. 7482); Ibn Māja, *Sunan*, V/176 (no. 1337). On the term *taġannā*, see the introduction to Qurṭubī, *Jāmi'*, vol. 1, pp. 13ff.
44 Bukhārī, *Ṣaḥīḥ*, LXVI/30 (no. 5047), XCVII/50 (no. 7540). On the term *tarjī'*, see Nelson, *The Art of Reciting the Qur'an*, p. 79.
45 Bukhārī, *Ṣaḥīḥ*, LXVI/29 (nos 5045–6).
46 Ibn Qayyim al-Jawzīya, *Zād al-ma'ād*, p. 164.
47 Kulaynī, *Kāfī*, 'Faḍl-al-Qur'ān/Tartīl al-Qur'ān', no. 3; Suyūṭī, *Itqān*, vol. 1, p. 107. A more detailed version of this hadith appears in the introduction to Qurṭubī, *Jāmi'*, vol. 1, p. 17, and Ibn Sallām, *Faḍā'il al-Qur'ān*, p. 80 (XVIII/16–17). The meaning of the term *luḥūn* is uncertain: in this context it may mean something like 'inflection'. For a general discussion of the root *l-ḥ-n* in Arabic, see Manfred Ullmann, *Wa-khairu l-ḥadīthi mā kāna laḥnan*, Munich, 1979.
48 Bukhārī, *Ṣaḥīḥ*, LXVI/28 (no. 5043); Muslim, *Ṣūḥīḥ*, VI/49 (no. 822). Compare 'Alī's statement in Kulaynī, *Kāfī*, 'Faḍl-al-Qur'ān/Tartīl al-Qur'ān', no. 1.
49 Ibn Māja, *Sunan*, V/176 (no. 1339). Dārimī, *Sunan*, XXIII/33 (no. 3492).
50 Bukhārī, *Ṣaḥīḥ*, LXVI/17 (no. 5020), XCVIII/57 (no. 7560); Dārimī, *Sunan*, XXIII/8 (no. 3365); Kulaynī, *Kāfī*, 'Faḍl al-Qur'ān/Faḍl al-ḥāmil', no. 6.
51 'There can be no doubt that the first Muslims sang the Quran to very simple melodies known only to them. After all, hadn't the holy book supplanted poetry in their lives? They therefore became accustomed to reeling off the verses of the Quran to the same melodies with which they had formerly embellished the poets' verses' (Talbi, 'La Qirā'a bi-l-alḥān', p. 185).
52 See Talbi, 'La Qira'a bi-l-alḥan'; Sa'īd, *at-Taġannī*, pp. 35ff., and *Al-Jam' as-sawṭī*, pp. 253–66; Nelson, *The Art of Reciting the Qur'an*, pp. 156–7.
53 Ibn Qutayba, *Ma'ārif*, p. 232.
54 Talbi, 'La Qirā'a bi-l-alḥān', p. 189.
55 *Kitāb al-Quṣṣāṣ*, pp. 118ff.
56 Aṭ-Ṭurṭūshī, *Kitāb al-ḥawādith wa-l-bida'*, pp. 75–86. See also the passages collected by Fierro Bello, 'The Treatises against Innovations', pp. 211ff.
57 Sa'īd, *At-Taġannī*, pp. 48–9.
58 Sa'īd, *Al-Jam' aṣ-ṣawṭī*, p. 263.
59 Quoted in Farmer, 'The Religious Music of Islam', p. 63; also cited in Farmer, *A History of Arabian Music*, p. 33; Shiloah, 'L'Islam et la musique', p. 419.
60 The earliest work on *'ilm at-tajwīd* is attributed to Mūsā ibn 'Ubaydillāh ibn Khaqān al-Baġdādī (d. 936).
61 *Nihāyat al-qawl al-mufīd fī 'ilm at-tajwīd.*
62 *At-Tibyān fī ādāb ḥamalat al-Qur'ān.*
63 *At-Tamhīd fī 'ilm at-tajwīd* and *Matn al-jazarīya fī fann at-tajwīd.* On the *'ilm at-tajwīd*, see Nöldeke et al., *History of the Qur'ān*, pp. 568–73; Sell, *Faith of Islam*, pp. 376–405; Wensinck and Kramers, *Handwörterbuch des Islams*, 'Tad̲jwīd'; Semaan, 'Tajwīd as a Source in Phonetic Research'; Denny, 'Qur'ān Recitation' and 'The *Adab* of Qur'an Recitation'; Nelson, *The Art of Reciting the Qur'an*, pp. 14–31; Boubakeur, 'Psalmodie coranique'; and Kellermann, *Koranlesung im Maghreb*, pp. 14–132, which includes a comprehensive bibliography.
64 Nelson, *The Art of Reciting the Qur'an*, p. 14. Muḥammad Quṭb offers a modern theological discussion of what constitutes a correct Quran recitation in his *Dirāsāt qur'ānīya* ('Kayfa naqra'u l-Qur'ān', pp. 487–507).
65 Sa'īd, *Al-Jam' aṣ-ṣawtī*, pp. 111ff.

66 'The *Adab* of Qur'an Recitiation', p. 146. See also Nelson, *The Art of Reciting the Qur'an*, p. xviii; Graham, *Beyond the Written Word*, p. 98.
67 Lotman, *The Structure of the Artistic Text*, pp. 155–6; Kellermann, *Koranlesung im Maghreb*, p. 133.
68 See Shafī'ī-Kadkanī, *Mūsīqī-ye she'r*, pp. 32–3; Rāfi'ī, *I'jāz*, p. 214.
69 *Lektüre für Minuten*, vol. 2, p. 171 (no. 897).
70 Surah 100 (trans. Rückert, slightly amended) [Arberry's English translation is provided here as a guide to the sense].
71 'Horizont der Offenbarung', pp. 6ff.
72 Steiner, *Language and Silence*, pp. 41–2.
73 Goldziher, *Abhandlungen*, p. 15.
74 Nelson, *The Art of Reciting the Qur'an*, pp. 70–1.
75 *Sunan*, XXIII/33.
76 *Zād al-Ma'ād*, pp. 165–9.
77 As-Sa'īd, *At-Taġannī*, pp. 5–17.
78 Ibn Khaldūn, *Muqaddima*, p. 270.
79 Ḍayf, *Al-Fann wa-maḏāhibuhū*, pp. 41–90; Kadkanī-Shafī'ī, *Mūsīqī-ye she'r*, pp. 31ff.; Farmer, *A History of Arabic Music*, pp. 17ff.; Bustānī, *Eslām wa honar*, pp. 42ff., 55ff.
80 Ibn Māja, *Sunan*, V/176 (no. 1340).
81 Sharī'atī-Marīnānī, *Waḥy wa-nobūwat*, pp. 420–1.
82 *Sprachstil des Korans*, e.g., pp. 2ff., 11ff., 17, 28–9, 33–4, 38ff., 62, 73–4. In its form and its approach, Richter's analysis, which has been largely forgotten today, is well within the current of traditional Orientalist Quran studies, although it shows a sense of the particularities of quranic oratory that is lacking in Nöldeke and others, including more recent authors such as Blachère and Wansbrough, who evaluated the Quran's style primarily against their own standards.
83 Steiner, *Language and Silence*, p. 43.
84 See Quran 2:159, 5:44; for variants with *anzalnāhū*, see 12:2; 44:3; 97:1.
85 'Sounds, Spirit and Gender', p. 247.
86 On the 'occasion of this revelation', see Bukhārī, *Ṣaḥīḥ*, LXV/111 (nos 4971ff.); EI^2, 'Abū Lahab'; Rubin, *Eye of the Beholder*, pp. 139ff.
87 Nelson, *The Art of Reciting the Qur'an*, p. 65.
88 See August Fischer, *Der Wert der vorhandenen Koran-Übersetzungen*, pp. 11–49; Rubin, 'Abū Lahab and Sūra CXI'; Horovitz, *Koranische Untersuchungen*, p. 88; and Paret's commentary on surah 100.
89 Sa'īd, *The Recited Koran*, p. 57. See also his *Al-Jam' aṣ-ṣawtī*, pp. 255–61.
90 Farūqī, 'Tartīl al-Qur'ān', p. 107.
91 See Denny, 'Qur'ān Recitation', p. 15; Nelson, *The Art of Reciting the Qur'an*, pp. 170ff.; Sa'īd, *At-Taġannī*, pp. 67ff.
92 Johns, 'The Quranic Presentation of the Joseph Story', p. 38.
93 Bergsträsser, 'Koranlesung in Kairo', p. 132.
94 See the remarks by K. Huber in Bergsträsser's 'Koranlesung in Kairo', p. 125; Kellermann, *Koranlesung im Maghreb*, pp. 148–9; Touma, 'Die Koranrezitation', p. 90.
95 Touma, 'Die Koranrezitation', p. 90; Kellermann, *Koranlesung im Maghreb*, p. 145; Nelson, *The Art of Reciting the Qur'an*, pp. 173ff.
96 Nelson, *The Art of Reciting the Qur'an*, pp. 37, 168–9.
97 Talbi, 'La qirā'a bi-l-alḥān', p. 187.

98 Nelson, *The Art of Reciting the Qur'an*, pp. 156ff; Farūqī, 'Tartīl al-Qur'ān', p. 110.
99 Nelson, *The Art of Reciting the Qur'an*, pp. 52ff., 136ff.
100 Nelson, *The Art of Reciting the Qur'an*, pp. 169–70; Sa'īd, *At-Taġannī*, pp. 68–9.
101 Quoted in Shiloah, 'L'Islam et la musique', p. 418. A similar version appears in Farmer, 'Religious Music of Islam', pp. 62–3.
102 *The Art of Reciting the Qur'an*, p. 154. On the listeners' reactions, see also Nelson's essay 'Reciter and Listener'.
103 *Majallat kull ash-shay' wa-d-dunyā*, no. 554; quoted in Sa'īd, *At-Taġannī*, p. 41. On the various occasions and forms of public Quran recitation in 1950s Egypt, and on the popularity of radio broadcasts of Quran recitation, see Jomier, 'La Place du Coran', pp. 142ff.
104 Sa'īd, *At-Taġannī*, pp. 102–3.
105 *Kitāb al-Quṣṣāṣ*, p. 118.
106 Ibid., p. 96.
107 Kellermann, *Koranlesung im Maghreb*, p. 16.
108 Jakobson, 'What is Poetry?' p. 378.
109 *Tafsīr al-Qur'ān*, commentary on verse 2:105 (vol. 1, p. 412).
110 Sa'īd, *At-Taġannī*, p. 100.
111 *Koranlesung im Maghreb*, p. 149.
112 Ibid., pp. 143ff. See also Suyūṭī, *Itqān*, vol. 1, pp. 101–2.
113 *Jāmi'*, vol. 1, pp. 16–17.
114 *At-Taġannī*, p. 50.
115 *I'jāz*, p. 46. Ar-Rāfi'ī's poetic description of a Quran recitation that he experienced as a child conveys the musical dimension of the event particularly forcefully: see his autobiographical work *Waḥy al-qalam* (vol. 3, pp. 28–31). A French translation of the chapter can be found in Jomier, *L'Islam vécu en Égypte*, pp. 107–110.
116 *Al-Mu'jiza al-kubrā*, vol. 1, p. 122.
117 *An-Naṣṣ al-qur'ānī*, p. 25.
118 Sa'īd, *Al-Jam' aṣ-ṣawtī*, p. 261.
119 Ibid., p. 255; see also Sa'īd, *At-Taġannī*, p. 66.
120 Nelson, *The Art of Reciting the Qur'an*, pp. 171ff.
121 Kāmil Abū l-'Aynayn, 'Al-Mūsīqā fī l-Qur'ān al-karīm', in *Al-Majalla al-mūsīqīya* (1974), no. 1 (January), p. 25; quoted in Nelson, *The Art of Reciting the Qur'an*, p. 94.
122 Sa'id, *At-Taġannī*, pp. 65–6, 94, and *Al-Jam' aṣ-ṣawtī*, p. 271.
123 Quoted in Nelson, *The Art of Reciting the Qur'an*, p. 178.
124 *Lektüre für Minuten*, vol. 2, p. 171. Even in the nineteenth century, Rückert held a similar opinion, and he was then the German poet most often set to music (Fricke, 'Rückert und das Kunstlied'). On setting poetry to music, see Frye, *Anatomy of Criticism*, p. 255; Nänny, 'Moderne Dichtung und Mündlichkeit', pp. 222ff.
125 Valéry, *The Art of Poetry*, p. 162.
126 Nagel, *Autonomy and Mercy*, pp. 73–4.
127 *The Art of Poetry*, p. 162.
128 Quoted in Ṭabarī, *Tārīkh*, vol. 1, p. 3353. Also recounted in Imam 'Alī ibn Abī Ṭālib's *Nahj al-balāġa*, Beirut, n.d., vol. 2, p. 5.
129 'Literary History as a Challenge to Literary Theory', p. 21.

130 Farūqī, 'Tartīl al-Qur'ān', p. 114; Kellermann, *Koranlesung im Maghreb*, pp. 6ff.
131 Goldziher, *Schools of Koranic Commentators*, pp. 2ff. Goldziher provides numerous examples of different scholars' divergent readings of one and the same sequence of letters. See also Beck, 'Der ʿuthmānische Kodex'.
132 Nöldeke et al., *History of the Qurʾān*, p. 38.
133 'Vom Rezitationstext über die Liturgie zum Kanon', p. 72.
134 Van Ess, *Theologie und Gesellschaft*, vol. 4, pp. 623–4.
135 Nöldeke et al., *History of the Qurʾān*, p. 38.
136 Kulaynī, *Kāfī*, 'Faḍl-al-Qur'ān/Tartīl al-Qur'ān', no. 3.
137 Zwettler, *Oral Tradition*, pp. 4ff., 24ff.; Monroe, 'Oral Composition in Pre-Islamic Poetry'.
138 *Aṭ-Ṭuruq al-ḥukmīya*, pp. 21–2. On the compilation of the Quran and its textual history, see the still authoritative account in Nöldeke et al., *History of the Qurʾān*, pp. 209ff. See also Jeffery, *The Qur'ān as Scripture*, pp. 89–103; EI², 'al-Ḳu'rān', pp. 403ff.
139 See the traditions and opinons in chapter 18 of Suyūṭī's *Itqān*, esp. pp. 59–60.
140 Endress, 'Arabische Schrift', pp. 171–2; Nöldeke et al., *History of the Qurʾān*, pp. 402–7; Neuwirth, 'Koran', p. 106; Beck, 'Der ʿuthmānische Kodex', pp. 367ff.; Saʿīd, *Al-Jamʿ aṣ-ṣawtī*, pp. 44ff.
141 Beck, 'Der ʿuthmānische Kodex', p. 360.
142 *Schools of Koranic Commentators*, p. 22.
143 Ibid., p. 1.
144 Ibid., p. 2.
145 Ibid.
146 On the study of Quran reading, see the still authoritative account by Bergsträsser and Pretzl in Nöldeke et al., *History of the Qurʾān*, pp. 471–584. Labīb as-Saʿīd's observations in *Al-Jamʿaṣ-ṣawtī*, pp. 126–220, are also helpful. See also Goldziher, *Schools of Koranic Commentators*, pp. 1–36; Pretzl, 'Wissenschaft der Koranlesung'; Paret, 'Ḳirā'a', in EI²; Neuwirth, 'Koranlesung'; Fażlī, *Tārīkhe qerāʾāt*. The two best-known classical works in which Quran surahs are discussed with regard to the variant readings of specific verses are al-Makkī's *Al-Kashf ʿan wujūh al-qirāʾāt assabʿ* and Ibn al-Jazarī's *An-Nashr fī l-qirāʾāt al-ʿashr*.
147 'Koranlesung', p. 315; verbatim in Neuwirth, 'Koran', p. 110.
148 Bukhārī, *Ṣaḥīḥ*, LXVI/5 (no. 4992), 27 (no. 5041); Muslim, *Ṣaḥīḥ*, VI/48 (no. 818).
149 Muslim, *Ṣaḥīḥ*, VI/48 (no. 820).
150 Suyūṭī, *Itqān*, vol. 1, p. 80. On the number seven in Sunni Islam, see Angelika Hartmann-Schmidt's dissertation *Die Zahl Sieben im sunnitischen Islam*, esp. pp. 98ff.
151 On the various explanations, see Nöldeke et al., *History of the Qurʾān*, pp. 39–41; Goldziher, *Schools of Koranic Commentators*, p. 25; Saʿīd, *Al-Jamʿ aṣ-ṣawtī*, p. 129. Among Shiites, the tradition of the seven *aḥruf* is sometimes called a lie that originated with the 'enemies of God'; Kulaynī, *Kāfī*, Faḍl al-Qur'ān/An-Nawādir, no. 12.
152 Nöldeke et al., *History of the Qur'ān*, p. 39.
153 *Schools of Koranic Commentators*, p, 27.
154 'Koranlesung', p. 316.
155 Ṭabarī, *Tārīḥ*, vol. 1, p. 2952; quoted in Schoeler, 'Schreiben und Veröffentlichen', p. 25.

156 Ibn Abī Dāwūd, *Kitāb al-Maṣāḥif*, quoted in Schoeler, 'Schreiben und Veröffentlichen', p. 25.
157 'Schreiben und Veröffentlichen', p. 24.
158 'Ganz grosse Freiheit': Beck, ''Arabiyya, Sunna und 'Āmma in der Koranlesung', p. 208.
159 On the developments outlined here, see Nöldeke et al., *History of the Qur'ān*, pp. 429–566; Beck, ''Arabiyya, Sunna und 'Āmma in der Koranlesung'; Neuwirth, 'Koran'; Kellermann, *Koranlesung im Maghreb*, pp. 1ff.
160 Bergsträsser, 'Koranlesung in Kairo', pp. 36ff.; Sa'īd, *At-Taġannī*, pp. 73ff.; Kellermann, *Koranlesung im Maghreb*, p. 4.
161 Kellermann, *Koranlesung im Maghreb*, p. 6.
162 Nawawī, *Tibyān*, pp. 155ff.
163 'Alī's criticism of his enemies' behaviour is revealing: see Ṭabarī, *Tārīkh*, vol. 1, pp. 3352–3.
164 See Robson, 'Magical Use of the Koran'; Donaldson, 'Koran as Magic'; Nasr, *Ideals and Realities of Islam*, p. 52; Schimmel, *Deciphering the Signs of God*, pp. 113ff. The reservations against printing the Quran that continued to be expressed long after the introduction of printing in the Muslim world are also significant in this connection: even today, some believers feel it is important to possess a handwritten copy. See Snouck Hurgronje, 'Islam und Phonograph', p. 432.
165 Quran 56:79.
166 Ibn Sallām, *Faḍā'il al-Qur'ān*, p. 58 (X/14).
167 Ibid., pp. 57 (X/11–12), 101ff. (XXVII, 1ff.); see also Zwemer, *Studies in Popular Islam*, p. 80.
168 From an essay that appeared in 1992 in the South African Muslim periodical *The Majlis*, quoted in Schimmel, *Deciphering the Signs of God*, p. 159.
169 Ibid.
170 Sa'īd, *Al-Jam' aṣ-ṣawṭī*, pp. 80ff., and *The Recited Koran*, pp. 65ff. A similar criticism was raised as early as 1926 in Rāfi'ī, *I'jāz*, p. 243, n. 1.
171 *Naqd al-khiṭāb ad-dīnī*, p. 98.
172 *Mafhūm an-naṣṣ*, p. 337. See also Abū Zayd's review of Graham's *Beyond the Written Word*.
173 *Phaedrus*, 275d–276e.
174 See Sellheim, 'Muhammeds erstes Offenbarungserlebnis'; Andrae, 'Legenden von der Berufung Muhammads'; Pedersen's review of Meyer, *Ursprung und Geschichte*; Bell, 'Mohammed's Call'; Buhl, *Das Leben Muhammeds*, pp. 134–8; Horovitz, *Koranische Untersuchungen*, p. 74; Watt and Welch, *Der Islam*, vol. 1, pp. 53–8. On the chains of transmission of the various versions, see Schoeler, *The Biography of Muhammad*, pp. 38ff.
175 Bukhārī, *Ṣāḥīḥ*, I/3 (no. 3); Ṭabarī, *Tārīkh*, vol. 1, p. 1148; Ibn Kathīr, *Sīra*, vol. 1, p. 385; Zarkashī, *Burhān*, vol. 1, pp. 263ff.; Suyūṭī, *Itqān*, vol. 1, p. 23.
176 Ibn Hishām, *Sīra*, vol. 1, pp. 236–7; Ṭabarī, *Tārīkh*, p. 1150; Suyūṭī, *Itqān*, vol. 1, p. 24.
177 See, e.g., Haikal, *Das Leben Muhammads*, pp. 82–3; Riḍā, *Al-Waḥy al-muḥammadī*, p. 112ff.; Rāmiyār, *Tarīkh*, pp. 53–7; and even Hamadānī's thirteenth-century Persian translation of Ibn Hishām's *Sīra* (*Sīrat-e rasūl allāh*, p. 110).
178 See Geertz, *Islam Observed*, pp. 56–89.
179 Nelson, *The Art of Reciting the Qur'an*, p. 182.

180 Boubakeur, 'Psalmodique coranique', p. 389; Nelson, *The Art of Reciting the Qur'an*, p. 181; Sa'īd, *Al-Jam' aṣ-ṣawtī*, p. 266.
181 Kellermann, *Koranlesung im Maghreb*, pp. 7–8; Farūqī, 'Qur'ān Reciters in Competion in Kuala Lumpur', p. 221.
182 Farmer, 'The Religious Music of Islam', p. 63.
183 *Koranlesung im Maghreb*, p. 7.
184 See Lotman, *The Structure of the Artistic Text*, pp. 290ff.
185 See Nelson, *The Art of Reciting the Qur'an*, p. 66; Kellermann, *Koranlesung im Maghreb*, p. 7.
186 'Koranlesung in Kairo', pp. 128–9.
187 Nelson, *The Art of Reciting the Qur'an*, pp. 110–11.
188 On the Indonesian case, see also Pacholczyk, 'Music and Islam in Indonesia', pp. 8–9; on Morocco, Kellermann, *Koranlesung im Maghreb*, pp. 9–10; on Nepal, Hoerburger, 'Gebetsruf und Qor'an-Rezitation in Kathmandu'; on the Balkan countries, Hoerburger, *Volksmusik in Afghanistan*, p. 96.
189 Kellermann, *Koranlesung im Maghreb*, p. 10.
190 See Snouck Hurgronje, 'Islam und Phonograph', pp. 434ff. See also the fatwa by the rector of Azhar University, 'A Fatwa on Broadcasting the Koran', *Muslim World* 24 (1934), pp. 190–1.
191 See also Kellermann, *Koranlesung im Maghreb*, p. 7. On the recitation of Sheikh 'Abdulbāsiṭ in particular, Józef Marcin Pacholczyk wrote a dissertation (which I have not been able to obtain) in 1970 at UCLA titled *Regulative Principles in the Koran Chant of Shaikh 'Abdu'l-Bāsiṭ 'Abdu'ṣ-Ṣamad.*
192 Graham, 'The *Qur'ān* as Spoken Word', p. 28. See also Graham, *Beyond the Written Word*; Widengren, *Religionsphänomenologie*, pp. 546–73; Kugel, *The Idea of Biblical Poetry*, pp. 111ff.; Koch, *Die Propheten*, vol. 1, pp. 39ff.; Roest Crollius, *The Word in the Experience of Revelation.*
193 Izutsu, *God and Man*, p. 152; Caspar, 'Parole de Dieu et langage humain en Christianisme et en Islam'.
194 Paradoxically, applications of computing technology at theological colleges and universities throughout the Islamic world (especially in those parts with 'fundamentalist' governments) are leading to a new kind of focus on the Quran's recitative character: in addition to the Arabic text and translations in numerous languages, CD-ROM editions today allow the user to play the text shown on screen, choosing among the voices of numerous reciters.
195 The first to make this observation was probably Nathan Söderblom: see his *Einführung in die Religionsgeschichte*, p. 65. Cf. Andrae, *Die Person Muhammeds in Lehre und Glauben seiner Gemeinde*, p. 117; Massignon, *Situation de l'Islam*, p. 9; Frick, *Vergleichende Religionswissenschaft*, pp. 68ff.; Smith, 'Some Similarities and Differences between Christianity and Islam'; Hodgson, 'Une comparaison entre l'islam et le christianisme en tant que structures de la vie religieuse'; Cragg, *The Call of the Minaret*, pp. 272ff.; Antes, 'Schriftverständnis im Islam', p. 179; Graham, *Beyond the Written Word*, pp. 96ff.; Abū Zayd, *Naqd al-khiṭāb ad-dīnī*, p. 196; Caspar, 'Parole de Dieu et langage humain en Christianisme et en Islam', pp. 39ff.; Schimmel, *And Muhammad Is His Messenger*, pp. 24–5; Zirker, *Christentum und Islam*, pp. 72–93; van Ess, *Theologie und Gesellschaft*, vol. 4, pp. 604–5.
196 Tirmiḏī, *Al-Jāmi'*, XLIII/17 (no. 3078).
197 Zarkashī, *Burhān*, vol. 1, p. 514.
198 Muslim, *Ṣaḥīḥ*, VI/42 (no. 804).
199 Ġazālī, *Iḥyā'*, vol. 1, p. 169.

200 Van Ess, *Theologie und Gesellschaft*, vol. 4, p. 628.
201 Schimmel, *Deciphering the Signs of God*, p. 199.
202 Dārimī, *Sunan*, XXIII/1 (no. 3324).
203 Ġazālī, *Iḥyā'*, vol. 1, p. 168. The term *ḥabl Allāh* to designate the Quran is a reference to a hadith recorded by ad-Dārimī; cf. *Sunan*, XXIII/1 (no. 3320).
204 Dārimī, *Sunan*, XXIII/23 (no. 3359).
205 Makkī, *Die Nahrung der Herzen*, p. 210.
206 Ġazālī, *Iḥyā'*, vol. 1, p. 169. A similar statement is found in a prophetic saying quoted by al-Qurṭubī in his introductory commentary on surah 40 (vol. 15, p. 288).
207 Quoted in Makkī, *Die Nahrung der Herzen*, p. 210.
208 Quoted in Andrae, *Die Person Muhammeds in Lehre und Glauben seiner Gemeinde*, p. 177. Over time, however, the personal veneration of the Prophet has grown to ever greater proportions, making him an inspiring figure of light to the mystics, a model of the perfect human being to philosophers, and the author of numerous miracles, although this is explicitly contested by the Quran (see, for example, surah 6:37, with the parallels mentioned in Paret's *Der Koran: Kommentar*, and Rahman, *Major Themes of the Qur'ān*, p. 77). On this topic, see primarily Schimmel, *And Muhammad Is His Messenger*; van Ess, *Theologie und Gesellschaft*, vol. 4, p. 630ff.; and Andrae's book on Mohammed.
209 Schimmel, *Deciphering the Signs of God*, p. 187.
210 Quran, surah 97.
211 John 21:25.
212 18:109 (trans. Arberry); cf. 31:27. There is a similar statement in Judaism about the Torah: see Graham, 'Das Schriftprinzip', p. 220.
213 Ibn Hishām, *Sīra*, vol. 2, p. 604.
214 Matthew 27:46; Mark 15:34.
215 Luke 23:46.
216 John 19:30.
217 The comparison between Jesus and the Quran is taken partially from Frick, *Vergleichende Religionswissenschaft*, pp. 68ff.
218 Ibn Hishām, *Sīra*, vol. 2, p. 656.
219 Ibid., vol. 2, pp. 660–1.
220 The statement is attributed both to Ibn 'Abbās and to Muḥammad ibn al-Ḥanafīya: see Bukhārī, *Ṣaḥīḥ*, LXVI/16 (no. 5019).
221 *Iḥyā'*, vol. 1, p. 183. In the early period of Islam, and even in the ninth century, *ḏikr* seems to designate a form of non-liturgical Quran recitation (see van Ess, *Die Gedankenwelt*, p. 201).
222 See Muslim, *Ṣaḥīḥ*, VI/35 (no. 795); Bukhārī, *Ṣaḥīḥ*, LXV/48 (no. 4839), LXVI/15 (no. 5018) and XCVIII/33 (no. 7486). The term *sakīna* can also refer to Muhammad's revelations and is generally associated with a special kind of tranquillity. In essential aspects it corresponds to the Jewish concept of *shekhinah*: see Goldberg, *Untersuchungen über die Vorstellung von der Schekhinah in der frühen rabbinischen Literatur*; Scholem, *On the Mystical Shape of the Godhead*, pp. 140–96.
223 *Herrlichkeit*, vol. 2, p. 11; see also ibid., vol. 1, pp. 38ff.
224 More on this in chapter 4.
225 See Werlen, *Ritual und Sprache*, p. 189; Wenzel, *Hören und Sehen*, p. 119.
226 Ġazālī, *Iḥyā'*, vol. 1, p. 169.

227 *Innakum lan tarji ʿū ilā llāhi bi-afḍali mimmā kharaja minhū yaʿnī l-Qurʾāna*; Tirmiḏī, *Al-Jāmiʿ*, XLIV/17 (no. 3079).
228 Ġazālī, *Iḥyā'*, vol. 1, p. 169; a slightly different version appears in Zarkashī, *Burhān*, vol. 1, p. 514.
229 The key verse for the institutionalization of Friday prayers is 62:9. On Islamic cult, see Becker, *Islamstudien*, pp. 472–500.
230 See Neuwirth, 'Vom Rezitationstext über die Liturgie zum Kanon', pp. 80ff.
231 Ġazālī, *Iḥyā'*, vol. 1, p. 169.
232 Van Ess, *Die Gedankenwelt*, p. 197.
233 Ibn ʿArabī, *Muḥāḍarat al-abrār wa-musāmarat al-akhyār*, vol. 1, p. 4; quoted in Andrae, *Die Person Muhammeds in Lehre und Glauben seiner Gemeinde*, p. 185.
234 See Nawawī, *Tibyān*, p. 71; Ibn Sallām, *Faḍā'il al-Qurʾān*, p. 55 (IL/4).
235 A statement by Yazīd ibn Abī Mālik, quoted in Ibn Sallām, *Fadā'il al-Qurʾān*, p. 55 (X/3).
236 Van Ess, *Theologie und Gesellschaft*, vol. 4, p. 623.
237 *Burhān*, vol. 2, p. 114.
238 ʿAbdalwahāb ash-Shaʿrānī, *Aṭ-Ṭabaqāt al-kubrā*, Aleppo, 1954, vol. 1, p. 62, quoted in Saʿīd, *At-Taġannī*, p. 96; also cited in Massignon, *Essai sur les origines du lexique technique de la mystique musulmane*, p. 46, n. 1.
239 Quoted in Rashīd Riḍā's preface to Rāfiʿī, *Iʿjāz*, p. 21.
240 Zwemer, *Studies in Popular Islam*, p. 80. Others held the opinion that it was permitted for Muslim teachers to teach the Quran to Jewish and Christian children since they already read 'from God's book' in the Bible and the Torah. See Ibn Sallām, *Faḍā'il al-Qur'ān*, p. 102 (XXVII/3).
241 Angelika Neuwirth takes a different position on this issue in 'Vom Rezitationstext über die Liturgie zum Kanon', p. 81.
242 Ġazālī, *lḥyā'*, vol. 1, p. 274.
243 See Nawawī, *Tibyān*, pp. 69ff.; Zarkashī, *Burhān*, vol. 1, pp. 554ff.; Denny, 'Islamic Ritual', pp. 75–6. See also Ibn Baṭṭūṭa's very detailed description of the recitation ritual in the mosque of Mecca: *Travels of Ibn Baṭṭūṭa*, vol. 1, pp. 238ff.
244 *Burhān*, vol. 1, p. 531.
245 Kulaynī, *Kāfī*, Faḍl al-Qur'ān/An-Nawādir, no. 10.
246 Bukhārī, *Ṣakhīḥ*, LIX/66 (no. 3220).
247 Zarkashī, *Burhān*, vol. 1, p. 555; Bukhārī, *Ṣaḥīḥ*, LXVI/7 (no. 4998).
248 Ibn Sallām, *Faḍā'il al-Qur'ān*, p. 47 (VIII/2).
249 Bukhārī, *Ṣaḥīḥ*, LIX/6 (no. 3221).
250 *Die Gaben der Erkenntnisse*, 41.
251 Ġazālī, *Iḥyā'*, vol. 1, p. 169. Ibn Sallām reports similar sayings in *Faḍā'il al-Qurʾān*, p. 53 (IL/7).
252 Qurṭubī, *Jāmiʿ*, Introduction, vol. 1, 5; Bāqillānī, *Iʿjāz*, p. 276.
253 Dārimī, *Sunan*, XXIII/1 (no. 3325); See also the versions in Ibn Sallām, *Faḍā'il al-Qur'an*, p. 21 (I/7), and in Zarkashī, *Burhān*, vol. 1, p. 539.
254 Ġazālī, *lḥyā*, vol. 1, p. 176.
255 Quoted in van Ess, *Die Gedankenwelt*, p. 209.
256 *Al-Muʿtamad fī uṣūl ad-dīn*, Beirut, 1974, quoted in Böwering, *Mystical Vision of Existence*, p. 95.
257 Goldziher, *Gesammelte Schriften*, vol. 5, p. 78; van Ess, *Die Gedankenwelt*, pp. 208ff.

258 Hasso Hoffmann, *Repräsentation: Studien zur Wort- und Begriffsgeschichte von der Antike bis ins 19. Jahrhundert*, Berlin, 1974, p. 65, quoted in Wenzel, *Hören und Sehen*, p. 122. See also Hubert Jedin, *Geschichte des Konzils von Trient*, vol. 3, pp. 32–52ff., 268–91; Kantorowicz, *The King's Two Bodies*, pp. 194–5; Dieterich, *Eine Mithrasliturgie*, pp. 106ff.
259 Wenzel, *Hören und Sehen*, p. 114. See also Balthasar's criticism of the Protestant 'de-aesthetization of theology' in *Herrlichkeit*, vol. 1, pp. 42ff. On the relation between religious and aesthetic experience in modern Christian theology in general, see Hoeps, *Bildsinn und religiöse Erfahrung*.
260 Saʿīd, *Al-Jamʿ aṣ-ṣawtī*, pp. 278–88; Rāfiʿī, *Iʿjāz*, pp. 242–3; Eickelman, 'The Art of Memory'.
261 Neuwirth, 'Der Koran – Mittelpunkt des Lebens', p. 73.
262 Ġazālī, *Iḥyā'*, vol. 1, p, 169.
263 Saʿīd, *Al-Jamʿ aṣ-ṣawṭī*, p. 279, and *The Recited Koran*, p. 58.
264 The status of memorization is also reflected in numerous hadiths: see, for example, Bukhārī, *Ṣaḥīḥ*, LXVI/22–3 (nos 5030–3).
265 Dārimī, *Sunan*, XXIII/1 (no. 3312).
266 Kulaynī, *Kāfī*, 'Faḍl al-Qur'ān/Al-Buyūt allatī yuqra'u fīhā l-Qur'ān', no. 2.
267 *The Mind of the Qur'ān*, p. 30.
268 Kulaynī, *Kāfī*, 'Faḍl-al-Qur'ān/Tartīl al-Qur'ān', no. 7.
269 *The Mind of the Qur'ān*, p. 30.
270 Quoted in Schimmel, *Deciphering the Signs of God*, p. 163.
271 See Jomier, 'La Place du Coran'; van Nieuwenhuijze, 'The Qur'an as a Factor in the Islamic Way of Life', p. 222.
272 Graham, *Beyond the Written Word*, p. x.
273 Denny, 'Exegesis and Recitation', p. 117.
274 Kellermann, *Koranlesung im Maghreb*, p. 18.
275 *Iḥyā'*, vol. 1, p. 174.
276 *Al-Futūḥāt*, vol. 3, pp. 127–8.
277 Ibid., vol. 3, p. 93.
278 Bukhārī, *Ṣaḥīḥ*, LXVI/36 (no. 5058) and XCVIII/58 (no. 7563).
279 Quran, 26:193.
280 *Al-Futūḥāt*, vol. 3, p. 93.
281 Kulaynī, *Kāfī*, 'Faḍl-al-Qur'ān/Tartīl al-Qur'ān', no. 2.
282 Ġazālī, *Iḥyā*, vol. 1, p. 171; similar versions in Suyūṭī, *Itqān*, vol. 1, p. 107; Makkī, *Die Nahrung der Herzen*, p. 179.
283 Ibn Sallām, *Faḍā'il al-Qur'ān*, pp. 63–4 (XIII/1). A shorter version appears in Ibn Māja, *Sunan*, V/176 (no. 1337).
284 Nelson, *The Art of Reciting the Qur'an*, p. 99.
285 Nawawī, *Tibyān*, p. 78; Zarkashī, *Burhān*, vol. 1, pp. 532ff.; Ibn Sallām, *Faḍā'il al-Qur'ān*, pp. 73ff. (XVII/1ff.).
286 Suyūṭī, *Itqān*, vol. 1, p. 106.
287 *Schlaglichter*, p. 412.
288 Ibid., pp. 407ff.; ʿEbādī, 'Taṣfiya', p. 217.
289 Ġazālī, *Iḥyā'*, vol. 1, p. 173.
290 'Art as a Cultural System', p. 1490.
291 Van Ess, *Die Gedankenwelt*, p. 205.
292 The question whether God has a voice and in what form Muhammad received the Quran – intuition or human speech – has been debated in Muslim theology many times. Van Ess gives an extremely clear presentation with the major

references in *Theologie und Gesellschaft*, vol. 4, pp. 612–25. See also Paret, 'Der Standpunkt al-Bāqillānī's in der Lehre vom Koran'; Kermani, *Offenbarung als Kommunikation*, pp. 58–66.

293 See Abū Zayd, *Mafhūm*, p. 49; van Ess, *Theologie und Gesellschaft*, vol. 3, pp. 283–4, vol. 4, pp. 61–2, 214ff., 612ff., and 'Verbal Inspiration', p. 182. See also Weiss, 'Medieval Muslim Discussions', pp. 38ff.; Watt, 'Early Discussions about the Qur'an', pp. 96–105; Wolfson, *The Philosophy of the Kalam*, pp. 268–74; Bouman, 'The Doctrine of ʿAbd al-Djabbār', pp. 80ff.; Peters, *God's Created Speech*, pp. 388–97.

294 The Hanbalite Ibn al-Farrā' explicitly rejected the theory: see his *Kitāb al-muʿtamad*, p. 89.

295 See Walzer's comment in the translation of al-Fārābī's *Mabādi' ārā ahl al-madīna al-fāḍila* (*Al-Farabi on the Perfect State*, p. 416); ʿUṣfūr, *Mafhūm ash-shiʿr*, pp. 154–86. Because the term *ḥikāya* has the Greek *mimesis* as a connotation, I think it is false to translate it, as Peters and van Ess do, as 'reproduction'. What humans are capable of is not reproduction – repetition of the creative act, in a sense; production in its own right – but 'imitation', as Wolfson and Watt correctly translate it, or 'representation', another possible reading of *mimesis*. Unlike *mimesis*, which cannot be more than an approximation, the word 'reproduction' suggests the production of an identical copy. This would be a reversal of the idea underlying the theory of *ḥikāya*, however.

296 *Aesthetic Theory*, pp. 172–3.

297 Quoted in Kellermann, *Koranlesung im Maghreb*, p. 14.

298 75:16–18 (trans. Arberry).

299 Husayn Muḥammad Maḥlūf, *Al-Qur'ān: Ādāb talāwatihī wa-samāʿlhī*, Cairo, 1963, p. 44, quoted in Kellermann, *Koranlesung im Maghreb*, p. 16, n. 56.

300 Fārūqī, 'Tartīl al-Qur'ān', p. 114.

301 Saʿīd, *Al-Jamʿ aṣ-ṣawtī*, p. 255, and *At-Taġannī*, p. 69; Nelson, *The Art of Reciting the Qur'an*, p. 63; Kellermann, *Koranlesung im Maghreb*, p. 134.

302 ʿAbdulwahhāb Ḥamūda, 'Mūsīqā l-Qur'ān', in *Liwā' al-Islām*, quoted in Saʿīd, *At-Taġannī*, p. 69.

303 Sheikh Ibrāhīm ash-Shaʿshāʿī, talking to Kristina Nelson about his father's recitation: Nelson, *The Art of Reciting the Qur'an*, p. 64.

304 Saʿīd, *Al-Jamʿ aṣ-ṣawtī*, p. 255.

305 Johns, 'The Quranic Presentation of the Joseph Story'.

306 See Adorno, *Aesthetic Theory*, p. 391.

307 Ibid., p. 165.

308 *Iḥyā'*, vol. 1, p. 174.

309 *Schlaglichter*, p. 405.

310 *Futūḥāt*, vol. 1, p. 239.

311 *Aesthetic Theory*, p. 172.

312 Ibid.

313 Ibid., p. 99.

Chapter 4 The Miracle

1 *System of Transcendental Idealism*, trans. Peter Heath. Charlottesville, VA, 1978, p. 225.

2 'Of the Difference Between a Genius and an Apostle', p. 109.

3 Ibid., p. 120.
4 Ibid., p. 119.
5 Ibid., p 104.
6 Ibid.
7 Ibid., p. 105.
8 Ibid., p. 118.
9 Ibid., p. 104.
10 *The Book on Adler*, p. 47.
11 Ibid., p. 39 (emphasis in original).
12 'Kierkegaard noch einmal', pp. 255–6.
13 Kierkegaard's enormous influence, especially on Protestant theology, began only after his thinking had been brought up to date by Karl Barth with his concept of a dialectical theology, from about 1920 to 1960. Interest in Kierkegaard has declined since then, although he is still a frequently cited author, and hardly a controversial one today. On the history of Kierkegaard's reception, we may cite Adorno's late essay 'Kierkegaard noch einmal' (Kierkegaard again): 'In barely a hundred years, Kierkegaard has been... smoothed over, swallowed up by the normal bourgeois awareness no less than, to cite Kierkegaard's own thesis, Christianity after nearly two millennia. Stimulating force, greatness like that of a Bismarck monument, world history – just what Kierkegaard despised – was the glorified legacy that remained of him. The solitary man has been turned into the mendacious chatter that boasts that others are inauthentic and given over to chatter. His fate was sealed in Germany before 1933 when the National Socialist Emanuel Hirsch laid claim to him: victory as defeat' ('Kierkegaard noch einmal', p. 244). See also Niels Thulstrup and Marie Mikulová (eds), *Kierkegaard's View of Christianity*, Copenhagen, 1978, and *Theological Concepts in Kierkegaard*, Copenhagen, 1980.
14 Bense, *Hegel und Kierkegaard*; Balthasar, *Herrlichkeit*, vol. 1, pp. 46ff.
15 On this issue, see Berning, 'Zur pietistischen Kritik an der autonomen Ästhetik'; Gutzen, *Poesie der Bibel*, pp. 42–63.
16 *Einige treue und deutliche Anleitung oder Unterricht, wie man die Bibel... mit Nutzen und Erbauung lesen soll*, Frankfurt and Leipzig, 1720, p. 137, quoted in Gutzen, *Poesie der Bibel*, pp. 50–1.
17 *Rubriken der Akten des Archivs der Brüder Unität*, IIA, 10.1, 40, quoted in Berning, 'Zur pietistischen Kritik an der autonomen Ästhetik', p. 106. See Bettermann, *Theologie und Sprache bei Zinzendorf*; Reichel, *Dichtungstheorie und Sprache bei Zinzendorf*.
18 Zinzendorf, *Die Öffentlichen Gemein-Reden*, p. 7.
19 Luther, *Werke*, vol. 38, p. 76; see also Luther, *Tischreden*, vol. 1, p. 44; *Werke*, vol. 34, p. 486.
20 Gutzen, *Poesie der Bibel*, pp. 29–30.
21 Quoted in Balthasar, *Herrlichkeit*, vol. 1, p. 46.
22 See, e.g., Luther, *Werke*, vol. 22, p. 378; *Tischreden*, vol. 3, p. 614.
23 See, e.g., Luther, *Werke*, vol. 38, p. 11; vol. 40, p. 361.
24 Calvin, *Institutes of the Christian Religion*, p. 36.
25 *Epistolae*, class III, 137, 18 (letter to Volusianus); quoted in Auerbach, *Literary Language and its Public in Late Latin Antiquity and in the Middle Ages*, p. 50.
26 See especially 1 Corinthians 1:18–21.
27 Auerbach, *Literary Language and its Public*, p. 51. See also Norden, *Die antike Kunstprosa*, pp. 521ff.; Dyck, *Athen und Jerusalem*, pp. 119–20.

28 Frye, *The Great Code*, pp. 1ff.
29 See Norden, *Die antike Kunstprosa*, pp. 526ff.; Kugel, 'Poets and Prophets', pp. 12ff. (and further references there).
30 'Of the Difference between a Genius and an Apostle', p. 111.
31 Ibid., p. 122.
32 Aṭ-Ṭabarī, ʿAlī ibn Rabbān, *Kitāb ad-dīn wa-d-dawla*, pp. 44–5. The translation is that of Alphonse Mingana: aṭ-Ṭabarī, *The Book of Religion and Empire*, pp. 50–1.
33 Kierkegaard, 'Of the Difference between a Genius and an Apostle', pp. 110–11.
34 Ibid., p. 104.
35 Ibid., p. 108.
36 Ibid.
37 *Shifā'*, vol. 1, p. 267.
38 Bukhārī, *Ṣaḥīḥ*, XCVII/1 (no. 7274).
39 Bāqillānī, *Iʿjāz*, p. 230.
40 Ibid. Suyūṭī quotes ar-Rummānī in the same sense: cf. *Itqān*, vol. 1, p. 122.
41 The arguments presented here are found in earlier authors, beginning probably with al-Jāḥiẓ (cf. *Hujaj an-nubūwa*, pp. 273ff., and the quotations in Suyūṭī, *Itqān*, vol. 2, pp. 117–18), and were raised again and again after Bāqillānī as well.
42 Much current scholarship surmises that these verses were invented by Muslims after the fact to demonstrate the superiority of the Quran. It may be assumed, however, that al-Bāqillānī considered them authentic and argued accordingly.
43 Andrae, *Die Person Muhammeds*, p. 94.
44 Neuwirth, 'Das islamische Dogma', pp. 170–1.
45 *Iʿjāz*, pp. 30, 47.
46 *Itqān*, vol. 2, p. 117.
47 Andrae, *Die Person Muhammeds*, p. 96.
48 *An-Nukat fī iʿjāz al-Qur'ān*, p. 111.
49 Valéry, *The Art of Poetry*, p. 215.
50 'Pharaoh said, "O Council, I know no other god for you than me. O Haman, fire some clay for me, and build me a tower..."' (trans. Khalidi).
51 The *ḥurūf al-qalqala*, /j/, /ṭ/, /d/, /q/ and /b/, are considered to have a reverberating effect when they occur in a final position.
52 Rāfiʿī, *Iʿjāz*, pp. 233–4.
53 Quoted in Suyūṭī, *Itqān*, vol. 2, p. 117.
54 *Dalā'il*, p. 36/25.
55 *Iʿjāz*, p. 191.
56 Wild, 'Die schauerliche Öde', p. 445.
57 *Die Weisheit des Brahmanen: ein Lehrgedicht in Bruchstücken*, p. 120.
58 'Die schauerliche Öde', p. 443.
59 See van Ess, 'Some Fragments', pp. 159–60, and *Theologie und Gesellschaft*, vol. 2, p. 35; vol. 4, p. 608. Van Ess considered the statement attributed to al-Muqaffaʿ authentic.
60 The Arabic text after Yūsuf al-Badīʿī's *As-Subḥ al-munabbī ʿan haythīyat al-Mutannabī* is quoted in Fischer, *Der 'Koran' des Abu l-'Alā' al-Maʿarrī*, p. 5; quoted in Wild, 'Die schauerliche Öde', p. 444; also quoted in Goldziher, *Gesammelte Schriften*, vol. 1, p. 368. On the dubious authenticity of the

legend, see Kremer, *Über die philosophischen Gedichte des Abū-l-'Alā Ma'arry*, pp. 76, 91; Goldziher, *Muslim Studies*, vol. 2, p. 364.

61 *Vermischte Bemerkungen*, p. 518.

62 *The Sociology of Art*, p. 463; see also Wild, 'Die schauerliche Öde', p. 443.

63 *The Sociology of Art*, p. 462.

64 Neuwirth, 'Das islamische Dogma der "Unnachahmlichkeit"', p. 170.

65 Ibid., pp. 172ff.

66 On the dogmatic background of the doctrine, see Andrae, *Die Person Muhammeds*, pp. 94ff.; Antes, *Prophetenwunder in der Ash'arīya*, esp. pp. 21–39; Gramlich, *Die Wunder der Freunde Gottes*, pp. 16–37.

67 Van Ess, *Theologie und Gesellschaft*, vol. 4, p. 605; Larkin, 'The Inimitability of the Qur'an' and *Theology of Meaning*, pp. 29ff.

68 Grotzfeld, 'Der Begriff der Unnachahmlichkeit des Korans', p. 71.

69 Among the many works on *i'jāz* by modern Muslim authors that could be cited in this connection, I list here those on which I drew in composing this chapter: Rāfi'ī, *I'jāz*; Abū Zahra, *Al-Mu'jiza al-kubrā*; Ṭabāṭabā'ī, *Mīzān*, commentary on 2:21–5; 'Abdurraḥmān, *Al-I'jāz al-bayānī*; Ḥusaynī, *Asālīb al-bayān*.

70 See Abū Zayd, *Mafhūm an-naṣṣ*, pp. 155ff., and *Ishkālīyāt al-qirā'a*, pp. 185–223.

71 See Jāḥiẓ, *Ḥujaj an-nubūwa*, pp. 270ff., and *Arabische Geisteswelt*, pp. 78ff.; Suyūṭī, *Itqān*, vol. 2, p. 117; Radscheit, *Die koranische Herausforderung*, pp. 2ff.

72 On the *ṣarfa* theory, see Aleem, 'I'jazu 'l-Qur'an', pp. 222, 227; Boullata, 'The Rhetorical Interpretation of the Qur'ān', pp. 141–2; 'Abdurraḥmān, *Al-I'jāz al-Qur'ān*, pp. 72ff.; Abū Zayd, *Mafhūm an-naṣṣ*, pp. 164ff.; Abū Zahra, *Al-Mu'jiza al-kubrā*, pp. 99–111; Khaṭṭābī, *Al-Khaṭṭābī et l'inimitabilité du Coran*, pp. 80–1; van Ess, *Theologie und Gesellschaft*, vol. 3, p. 412, vol. 4, pp. 609–10.

73 Andrae, *Die Person Muhammeds*, p. 97; Schreiner, 'Zur Geschichte der Polemik zwischen Juden und Muhammedanern', pp. 664ff.

74 See 'Abduljabbār, *I'jāz*.

75 See al-Jaḥiẓ's statements on *ṣarfa* in *Ḥujaj an-nubūwa*, p. 270, and in *Kitāb al-ḥyawān*, vol. 4, pp. 89–90, and vol. 6, p. 269. See also van Ess, *Theologie und Gesellschaft*, vol. 3, p. 411, and vol. 4, pp. 111–12, 609; the French translator Audebert in Khaṭṭābī, *Al-Khaṭṭābī et l'inimitabilité du Coran*, pp. 58–9, 62–3. Audebert overlooks al-Jāḥiẓ's affirmation of *ṣarfa*, however, and reads him as having been a proponent of stylistic *i'jāz*, which van Ess doubts. What is certain is that, while al-Jāḥiẓ did not use the term *i'jāz* in the extant texts, he did consider the Quran linguistically inimitable, and he stressed the Arabs' verbal prowess as few others have done. He was one of the first to advance the well-known ethno-psychological theory that Muhammad's sign must be a linguistic one because the ancient Arabs were a nation of poets. Furthermore, the title of his book on the Quran, *Naẓm al-Qur'ān*, of which only excerpts have survived, indicates that al-Jāḥiẓ attached great importance to the language of the revelation. In general, the dividing line between the followers and the opponents of the *ṣarfa* theory must not be drawn too firmly.

76 *An-Nukat fī i'jāz al-Qur'ān*, p. 75; Suyūṭī, *Itqān*, vol. 2, p. 122.

77 Suyūṭī, *Itqān*, vol. 2, 119–20.

78 Rāfi'ī, *I'jāz*, p. 144.

79 Van Ess, *Theologie und Gesellschaft*, vol. 3, p. 412; Schreiner, 'Zur Geschichte der Polemik zwischen Juden und Muhammedanern', p. 665. The opinion that the Quran is not perfect by human standards is held by Ibn Ḥazm: he argues that the language of the Quran must not be judged by ordinary criteria, since parts of it would it have to be found not particularly eloquent (ibid., p. 670). In the Arabic poetry of the ninth and tenth centuries, the openness of the message is not only observed, as in the case of the Quran, but also intentionally pursued: see al-Wād, *Al-Mutanabbī*, pp. 135ff.
80 See Suyūṭī, *Itqān*, vol. 2, p. 118; Zarkashī, *Burhān*, vol. 2, pp. 104–5.
81 Suyūṭī, *Itqān*, vol. 2, p. 120.
82 On the *wujūh al-iʿjāz*, see especially Suyūṭī, *Itqān*, vol. 2, pp. 116ff.; Zarkashī, *Burhān*, vol. 2, pp. 105ff.; Abū Zahra, *Al-Muʿjiza al-kubrā*, pp. 111ff.; Aleem, 'Iʿjazu l-Qur'an', pp. 220ff.; Boullata, 'The Rhetorical Interpretation of the Qur'ān', pp. 141ff. On *kharq al-ʿāda* in particular, see Antes, *Prophetenwunder*, pp. 40–6; Gramlich, *Die Wunder der Freunde Gottes*, pp. 16ff.
83 See, e.g., Zarkashi, *Burhān*, vol. 2, p. 109; Suyūṭī, *Itqān*, vol. 2, p. 120.
84 *Shifā'*, vol. 1, p. 280.
85 Quoted in Suyūṭī, *Itqān*, vol. 2, pp. 121–2. Az-Zarkashī voices a similar opinion: see *Burhān*, vol. 2, p. 114.
86 *Iʿjāz*, p. 155.
87 See Jansen, *Interpretation of the Koran in Modern Egypt*, pp. 51ff. For a critique of 'scientific *iʿjāz*', see al-Khūlī, *Manāhij tajdīd*, pp. 290ff. Jansen, with a perspective completely different from al-Khūlī's, comments, '[O]ne cannot help admiring the courage of certain scientific exegetes of the Koran. Whereas in Christianity it took centuries before the Churches "admitted" certain scientific truths, often after bloody struggles, many modern Muslim scientific exegetes of the Koran boldly claim that the Koran, the backbone of Islam, already contains the modern sciences and their principles, and all this with a courage and vigour that deserves a nobler aim' (*Interpretation of the Koran in Modern Egypt*, p. 54).
88 Rashad Khalifa, for example, the author of an 'authorized' (by whoever authorized it, at least) 'English version' of the Quran, finds *iʿjāz* in a mathematical code in the Quran based on the number 19 (*Quran: Visual Presentation of the Miracle*). On this issue, see Boullata, 'The Rhetorical Interpretation of the Qur'ān', pp. 148–9.
89 *Al-Muʿjiza al-kubrā*, p. 116.
90 Khaṭṭābī, *Bayān*, p. 70; Suyūṭī, *Itqān*, vol. 2, p. 121; Zarkashī, *Burhān*, vol. 2, p. 114; ʿIyāḍ, *Shifā*, vol. 1, pp. 273–4.
91 Quoted in Suyūṭī, *Itqān*, vol. 2, p. 120; similar statements are found in Zarkashī, *Burhān*, vol. 1, p. 387, vol. 2, p. 109. Aleem quotes al-Qummī as saying almost the same thing: see 'Iʿjazu 'l-Qur'an', pp. 223–4.
92 *Bayān*, pp. 24–5.
93 *Iʿjāz*, p. 230.
94 *Die Imâla*, p. 5.
95 Aleem, 'Iʿjazu l-Qur'an', pp. 79–80; Zaġlūl Salām, *Athar al-Qur'ān fī taṭawwur an-naqd al-arabī*; Cantarino, *Arabic Poetics in the Golden Age*, pp. 9–19; Heinrichs, 'Contacts between Scriptural Hermeneutics and Literary Theory' and 'Poetik, Rhetorik, Metrik und Reimlehre', pp. 180ff.; Adūnīs, *Ash-shiʿrīya al-ʿarabīya*, pp. 33–55. On Arabic literary criticism and theory in general, see in addition especially the following works: Heinrichs, *Arabische Dichtung und griechische Poetik* and 'Literary Theory'; Grunebaum, *Kritik*

und Dichtkunst; van Gelder, *Beyond the Line*; Bencheikh, *Poétique arabe*; Kanazi, *Studies in the Kitāb aṣ-Ṣināʿatayn*; Bohas et al., *The Arabic Linguistic Tradition*; Stetkevych, *Abū Tammām*. Of the countless Arabic works on this topic, I will mention here only the two most important books by Iḥsān ʿAbbās, *Tārīkh an-naqd al-adabī* (Beirut, n.d.) and *Mafhūm ash-shiʿr* (4th edn, Nicosia, 1990), both of which contain extensive bibliographies.

96 Heinrichs, 'Literary Theory'.

97 *Burhān*, vol. 1, p. 387.

98 See the biographical notes in Ritter's translation of *Asrār al-balāġa*, pp. 4ff. See also Abu Deeb, *Al-Jurjānī's Theory of Poetic Imagery*, pp. 18ff.; Ait el Ferrane, *Die Maʿnā-Theorie bei al-Jurjānī*, pp. 23ff.; Larkin, *The Theology of Meaning*, pp. 1ff.

99 Weisweiler, ''Abdalqāhir al-Curcāni's Werk über die Unnachahmlichkeit des Korans', p. 77.

100 Ritter, in Jurjānī, *Geheimnisse der Wortkunst*, p. 11.

101 Jurjānī, *Dalā'il*, p. 18/ix.

102 See Ait el Ferrane, *Die Maʿnā-Theorie bei al-Jurjānī*, p. 9.

103 See Riḍā's preface to Jurjānī's *Dalā'il*, pp. 5ff.

104 Abū Zahra, *Al-Muʿjiza al-kubrā*, p. 110.

105 Quṭb, *At-Taṣwīr al-fannī*, pp. 30–1.

106 Khalafallāh, ''Abdalqâhir's Theory'. See also Abu Deeb's panegyric in *Al-Jurjānī's Theory of Poetic Imagery*, p. 17 and elsewhere.

107 Abū Zayd, *Ishkālīyāt al-qirā'a*, pp. 149–83.

108 Bohas and his co-authors (in *Arabic Linguistic Tradition*, pp. 16–17) share this opinion.

109 Quoted in the introduction to the edition I have cited; see Rāfiʿī, *Iʿjāz*, p. 23; on the author, see Brockelmann, *Geschichte*, vol. S. 3, p. 215.

110 For one of the rare exceptions, see his discussion of verse 28:38 (*Iʿjāz*, pp. 233–4).

111 *At-Taṣwīr al-fannī*, pp. 33–4.

112 Max Weisweiler has already done that ('Al-Curcānī's Werk über die Unnachahmlichkeit des Korans'), but no more than that, for not exactly crucial sections of *Dalā'il*.

113 Kamal Abu Deeb has set himself this task in *Al-Jurjānī's Theory of Poetic Imagery*. Other studies in Western languages on al-Jurjānī's poetics include Khalafallāh, ''Abdalqâhir's Theory in His "Secrets of Eloquence"'; Abu Deeb, 'Al-Jurjānī's Classification of *Istiʿāra*'; Heinrichs, *Arabische Dichtung und griechische Poetik*, pp. 69–79; Ait el Ferrane, *Die Maʿnā-Theorie bei al-Jurjānī*; Larkin, *The Theology of Meaning*. For the most important studies on al-Jurjānī by Arab authors, the references in Abu Deeb, *Al-Jurjānī's Theory of Poetic Imagery*, pp. 1–2; and *Encyclopaedia Iranica*, ''Abd al-Qāher J̌urǰānī'. See also the essay by Abū Zayd in *Ishkālīyāt al-qirā'a* (pp. 149–83), which contains further references.

114 In the introduction to Jurjānī, *Geheimnisse der Wortkunst*, p. 6.

115 On the complexity of the concept of *maʿnā* and the difficulty of translating the word, see also Ait el Ferrane, *Die Maʿnā-Theorie bei al-Jurjānī*, pp. 13ff.; EI^2, 'Maʿnā'; Larkin, *The Theology of Meaning*, pp. 44ff.

116 Heinrichs says so in *Arabische Dichtung und griechische Poetik*, p. 69, although, curiously, when he turns to al-Jurjānī a few pages later, he fairly clearly develops the idea that that dualism no longer exists in al-Jurjānī (cf. pp. 76ff.).

117 *Dalā'il*, pp. 249ff./385ff.

118 Ibid., p. 44/39.

119 On the relation between the two theologians, see Abū Zayd, *Ishkālīyāt al-qirā'a*, p. 130; Larkin, 'The Inimitability of the Qur'an' and *The Theology of Meaning*, pp. 12ff. On the precursors of the *naẓm* theory, see Bohas et al., *The Arabic Linguistic Tradition*, pp. 115ff.; Khaṭṭābī, *Al-Khaṭṭābī et l'inimitabilité du Coran*, pp. 2ff.

120 *Dalā'il*, pp. 15ff./4ff.

121 *The Bow and the Lyre*, pp. 38–9. Paz counters the objection that some languages have pronouns that are meaningful units in themselves with the same argument as al-Jurjānī: each such word is an implicit sentence ('Those pronouns are phrase-words'; ibid., p. 39).

122 *Dalā'il*, pp. 59–60/64–5.

123 Ibid., pp. 42–3/35–6.

124 Ibid., p. 43/36.

125 Auerbach, *Literary Language and its Public*, pp. 50–1.

126 Jurjānī, *Dalā'il*, p. 24/pp. 8–9.

127 Ibid., p. 25/9.

128 See Ibn Qutayba, *Ash-Shi'r wa-sh-shu'arā'*, vol. 1, pp. 12ff.

129 See Kanazi, *Studies in the Kitāb aṣ-Ṣinā'atayn*, p. 42.

130 See *Muqaddima*, p. 357.

131 See also Jurjānī, *Dalā'il*, pp. 237ff./365ff.

132 On the proponents of this view, see Bohas et al., *The Arabic Linguistic Tradition*, pp. 110ff.

133 Trans. Arberry.

134 Jurjānī, *Dalā'il*, pp. 47ff./45–6, 77ff./99ff.

135 Ibid., p. 48/45.

136 Ibid., p. 51/49.

137 Ar-Rāzī later reproduced al-Jurjānī's discussion of this example almost verbatim: see Carter, 'Remarks on M. B. Schub'.

138 6:100 (trans. Arberry).

139 *Dalā'il*, pp. 192–3/286ff.

140 2:96 (trans. Khalidi).

141 Trans. Arberry.

142 *Dalā'il*, pp. 82–3/100–1.

143 Ibid., p. 83/102. This verse is one of al-Jurjānī's favourite examples and is discussed in a total of seven places.

144 Ibid., pp. 304ff./481ff. Al-Jurjānī ascribes the view that *ma'nā* and *lafẓ* are like body and clothes to the philologist 'Abdurraḥmān ibn 'Īsā l-Hamadāni. On that author and his book *Kitāb al-alfāẓ al-kitābīya*, see Brockelmann, *Geschichte*, vol. 1, p. 133; Sezgin, *Geschichte*, vol. 8, p. 193, vol. 9, p. 316.

145 See the section 'Idea and Structure' in chapter 2, pp. 114ff.

146 *Dalā'il*, pp. 270ff./428ff.

147 Lotman, *The Structure of the Artistic Text*, pp. 28–9. To find other aspects of al-Jurjānī's theory that are still current in view of present-day linguistics and literary studies, one may consult Abu Deeb's study *Al-Jurjānī's Theory of Poetic Imagery*: the author's whole ambition is to show how closely al-Jurjānī's findings and insights resemble those of modern authors. Although he does so with a certain persistence, it is indeed uncanny to see how similar the passages he quotes are, even down to the wording. Such anticipatory echoes are found almost to a greater degree in al-Jurjānī's theses on tropic expressions, which form the focus of Abu Deeb's study and are also discussed

in detail by Margaret Larkin (*The Theology of Meaning*, pp. 72–109), than in his theory of *naẓm* discussed here.

148 *Geheimnisse der Wortkunst*, pp. 20–1.
149 *Dalā'il*, pp. 240–1/370ff.
150 *Über die Sprache*, p. 13.
151 *Dalā'il*, p. 234/pp. 359–60. Imitating a particular style (*uslūb*), al-Jurjānī writes, is something different: this occurs often, in relations between master and student for example, and is quite normal. *Dalā'il*, pp. 298ff./470ff. This distinction reveals quite clearly that the term *naẓm* as al-Jurjānī uses it cannot be translated simply as 'style'.
152 *Dalā'il*, p. 242/pp. 372–3.
153 Ibid., pp. 236–7/362–3.
154 Larkin, 'The Inimitability of the Qur'an', pp. 38ff. Larkin qualifies this statement herself elsewhere: cf. *The Theology of Meaning*, p. 171.
155 *Dalā'il*, pp. 50ff./49ff.
156 Ibid., p. 171/252.
157 Ibid., pp. 87–8/109–10.
158 Ibid., pp. 196ff./293ff.
159 Ibid., p. 78/94.
160 De Moraes, *Saravá*, p. 106.
161 Jurjānī, *Dalā'il*, pp. 51–2/49–50.
162 Ibid., p. 55/57.
163 Ibid., p. 56/59.
164 Ibid., pp. 62ff./70ff.
165 *Geheimnisse der Wortkunst*, p. 62.
166 Lotman, *The Structure of the Artistic Text*, p. 23.
167 *Die Sprache*, pp. 18ff.; also collected in *Magie der Sprache*, pp. 323ff.
168 See Walter Benjamin's authoritative essay on Karl Kraus in *Illuminationen*, pp. 353–410.
169 Kraus, *Über die Sprache*, p. 78.
170 *Dalā'il*, p. 78/93.
171 Ibid., p. 74/87.
172 Ibid., p. 106.
173 Ibid., pp. 85–106.
174 Wensinck, 'Muhammad und die Propheten', p. 192. Al-Jāḥiẓ contests the view that Muhammad was uneducated and illiterate, however. Muhammad, he says, could have been the most eloquent and erudite man among the Arabs if he had wanted to, but he deliberately abstained from these arts so that his recalcitrant contemporaries 'had no pretext to desist from that which he calls on him to do'. Because he had neglected 'to make poems and pass them on, his tongue could no longer express itself in poetry, for habit is the twin of aptitude' (*Kitāb al-bayān wa-t-tabyīn*, vol. 4, ed. A. M. Hārūn, Cairo, 1950, quoted in *Arabische Geisteswelt*, p. 178). To al-Jurjānī, however, it is clear that, although he was the 'most eloquent among the Arabs', Muhammad was illiterate (*Dalā'il*, p. 37/pp. 26–7).
175 Ibid., p. 24/9.
176 Quoted in Suyūṭī, *Itqān*, vol. 2, p. 119.
177 On the position of poetry between science and art, and on the skills that Arabic literary critics expected a poet to master, see Heinrichs, *Arabische Dichtung und griechische Poetik*, pp. 49ff., 82ff.; Cantarino, *Arabic Poetics*, pp. 55ff.

178 E.g., *Dalā'il*, pp. 75/88, 234–5/357–8.
179 *The Structure of the Artistic Text*, p. 290.
180 A typical example is Grunebaum's essay 'Die aesthetischen Grundlagen der arabischen Literatur', in *Kritik und Dichtkunst*, pp. 130–50. See also Bauer, *Altarabische Dichtkunst*.
181 See the structural analysis of the classical Arabic quasida in Müller, *Ich bin Labīd*, pp. 21–110.
182 *Dalā'il*, p. 195/291.
183 *The Bow and the Lyre*, p. 14.
184 E.g., *Dalā'il*, pp. 170/250–1, 195–6/291–2, 348/547.
185 Ibid., p. 171/pp. 252–3.
186 Ibid., p. 170/251; Jāḥiẓ, *Hujaj an-nubūwa*, p. 229.
187 *Inna li-kalāmi llāhi uslūban khāṣṣan ya'rifuhū ahluhū wa-man imtazaja l-Qur'āna bi-laḥmihī wa-damihī*; quoted in Rashīd Riḍā's preface to Rāfi'ī, *I'jāz*, p. 21.
188 ''Abdalqāhir al-Curcānī's Werk über die Unnachahmlichkeit des Korans', pp. 79–80. See also Jurjānī, *Geheimnisse der Wortkunst*, p. 157.
189 *Dalā'il*, pp. 87ff./109ff.
190 Ibid., p. 240/370.
191 Ibid., p. 75/78.
192 Ibid., pp. 77–8/p. 93.
193 Paz, *The Bow and the Lyre*, pp. 39–40.
194 Van Gelder, *Beyond the Line*, pp. 14–22 and passim; Kanazi, *Studies in the Kitāb aṣ-Ṣinā'atayn*, pp. 100ff.; Heinrichs, *Arabische Dichtung und griechische Poetik*, pp. 12–31.
195 *Dalā'il*, p. 251/pp. 388–3. That is, surahs 40 to 46; see chapter 1, note 143.
196 See his analysis of verse 10:25 of the Quran in *Geheimnisse der Wortkunst*, p. 122.
197 It is a mystery to me how Abu Deeb (in his 'Studies in Arabic Literary Criticism', p. 57; see also his *Al-Jurjānī's Theory of Poetic Imagery*, pp. 294ff.) comes to the conclusion that al-Jurjānī of all people is the only one among the Classical Arabic literary critics to evaluate a poetic text in its overall composition. In any case, van Gelder's comparative study (*Beyond the Line*, esp. pp. 135–6, 160–1) reaches the opposite finding: evidently by intention, al-Jurjānī does not adopt the incipient view of the composition of a whole work that can be found in his predecessors and that some of the literary critics who followed him went on to develop. See also Heinrichs, 'Poetik, Rhetorik, Metrik und Reimlehre', pp. 181–2.
198 *Bayān*, pp. 27, 40–1, 54.
199 *I'jāz*, pp. 152–228. Grunebaum has translated this section (*A Tenth-Century Document*, pp. 56–115).
200 Bāqillānī, *I'jāz*, p. 232.
201 See van Gelder, *Beyond the Line*, p. 99; van Ess, *Theologie und Gesellschaft*, vol. 4, p. 610.
202 On his identity, see van Gelder, *Beyond the Line*, p. 100, n. 214.
203 *Burhān*, vol. 1, p. 62.
204 *Muqaddimah*, p. 353.
205 *Itqān*, vol. 2, pp. 108–14.
206 As-Sa'īdī, *An-Naẓm al-fannī fī l-Qur'ān*, Cairo, n.d.
207 *Al-Fann al-qaṣaṣī fī l-Qur'ān*.
208 Rāfi'ī, *I'jāz*, p. 154.

209 Brown, 'The Apocalypse of Islam', p. 89. See also van Gelder, *Beyond the Line*, p. 201.
210 *Dalā'il*, p. 355/557.
211 Trans. Arberry (slightly modified). The verse is cited, in connection with the *raw'a* that the Quran evokes, by Qāḍī 'Iyaḍ (*Shifā'*, vol. 1, p. 274) and by as-Suyūṭī (*Itqān*, vol. 2, p. 121).
212 See, e.g., Suyūṭī, *Itqān*, vol. 2, p. 121.
213 *Geheimnisse der Wortkunst*, p. 62.
214 On al-Bāqillānī's biography, see Bouman, *Le Conflit autour du Coran et la solution d'al-Bāqillānī*, pp. 54ff.; EI^2, 'Al-Bāqillānī'.
215 Bāqillānī, *I'jāz*, p. 20.
216 Ibid., p. 21.
217 See Abū Zahra (*Al-Mu'jiza al-kubrā*, p. 69), who quotes Abū Rayḥān al-Bīrūnī's book on India (*Mā li-l-Hind*), among others.
218 Bāqillānī, *I'jāz*, p. 21.
219 Goldziher, *Muslim Studies*, vol. 2, p. 363; Aleem, 'I'jazu l-Qur'an', pp. 229ff.
220 There is only one reference that points to the existence of such a book, however: a Zaidi imam from Yemen, al-Qāsim ibn Ibrāhīm, had written a book with the title *Kitāb ar-radd 'alā z-zindīq al-la'īn Ibn al-Muqaffa'*. It is highly doubtful, however, whether the book al-Qāsim refers to was written by Ibn al-Muqaffa' and, if so, whether it was really his mysterious *mu'āraḍa*, as the editor Michelangelo Guidi assumed (see Bergsträsser's review of Guidi, *La lotta tra l'Islām e il manicheismo*'; Aleem, 'I'jazu 'l-Qur'an', pp. 230–1; EI^2, 'Ibn al-Muḳaffa'', p. 885). Al-Bāqillānī himself quotes unnamed sources who claim that Ibn al-Muqaffa' had attacked the Quran but ultimately repented and tore his book apart (see his *I'jāz*, pp. 48–9). Van Ess has explained, based on some fragments that were found several years ago, that Ibn al-Muqaffa' had written on the Quran, but the work appeared to have the character of a parody of the quranic style rather than the attack of a heretic (see 'Some Fragments'; *Theologie und Gesellschaft*, vol. 2, p. 35).
221 Van Ess, *Theologie und Gesellschaft*, vol. 4, p. 608. Van Ess qualifies the view advanced by Kraus (in 'Beiträge zur islamischen Ketzergeschichte') and adopted by many others, however, that the historic Ibn ar-Rāwandī was really the 'picture-book' heretic that the Muslim history has made him into: see van Ess, *Theologie und Gesellschaft*, vol. 4, pp. 292–349.
222 Ibid., vol. 4, p. 608, vol. 3, p. 139, vol. 5, p. 339; EI^2, 'Murdār'.
223 See Aleem, 'I'jazu l-Qur'an', pp. 228ff.
224 Grotzfeld, 'Der Begriff der Unnachahmlichkeit des Korans', p. 64.
225 Assmann, *Cultural Memory and Early Civilization*, p. 106 (emphasis added).
226 *Dalā'il*, p. 41/33.
227 Bāqillānī, *I'jāz*, p. 45.
228 *Dalā'il*, pp. 252/390, 336/526.
229 Ibid., p. 23/6.
230 Ibid., p. 240/369.
231 Ibid., p. 23/6.
232 Ibid., pp. 22–3/p. 5.
233 17:88 (trans. Arberry).
234 *Dalā'il*, p. 240/369.
235 Ibid., p. 24/8.
236 Ibid.
237 Ibid.

238 Ibid., p. 27/12.
239 26:224–6.
240 *Dalā'il*, p. 36/26.
241 Ibid., p. 39/30.
242 69:13 (trans. Arberry).
243 *Dalā'il*, p. 40/31.
244 'The Qur'an as a Factor in the Islamic Way of Life', p. 245.
245 Assmann, *Cultural Memory*, p. 108.
246 *Shifā'*, vol. 1, p. 254.
247 Brockelmann, *Geschichte*, vol. 1, p. 165.
248 Quoted in Suyūṭī, *Itqān*, vol. 2, p. 117.
249 *Cultural Memory*, p. 108.
250 See, e.g., *Bayān i'jāz al-Qur'ān*, pp. 31ff., 40.
251 *I'jāz*, p. 43.
252 Ibn Hishām, *Sīra*, vol. 1, p. 345.
253 See al-Khaṭṭābī's discussion of various conversions caused by the sound of the Quran (*Bayān*, pp. 28, 70–1).
254 *Arabische Geisteswelt*, p. 143; cf. Suyūṭī, *Itqān*, vol. 2, pp. 117–18.
255 Andrae, *Die Person Muhammeds*, p. 95.
256 See, e.g., Rāfi'ī, *I'jāz*, p. 157; Abū Zahra, *Al-Mu'jiza al-kubrā*, pp. 84ff.
257 Andrae, *Die Person Muhammeds*, p. 95.
258 Bāqillānī, *I'jāz*, p. 229.
259 See pp. 7–9.
260 *I'jāz*, pp. 153–4. On Sajāḥ, see EI[1], 'Sājāh'.
261 See Suyūṭī, *Itqān*, vol. 2, p. 119; Rāfi'ī, *I'jāz*, pp. 173ff.
262 'Iyāḍ, *Shifā*, vol. 1, p. 275.
263 11:44 (trans. Arberry).
264 'Iyāḍ, *Shifā*, vol. 1, p. 275.
265 Bāqillānī, *I'jāz*, p. 39 (emphasis added).
266 *Dalā'il*, p. 44/38.
267 Ibid., pp. 251–2/p. 389.
268 36:69.
269 *Dalā'il*, p. 37/27.
270 Ibid., p. 302/475.
271 Ibid., pp. 250–1/p. 388.
272 Ibid., p. 251/pp. 388–9; the hadith is found in Tirmiḏī, *Al-Jāmi'*, XLIII/14 (no. 3070).
273 E.g., Ibn Sallām, *Faḍā'il al-Qur'ān*, p. 137 (XLI/4); Qurṭubī, *Al-Jāmi'*, introductory commentary on surah 40.
274 Tirmiḏī, *Al-Jāmi'*, XLIII/14 (no. 3070).
275 Ibn Kathīr, *Sīra*, vol. 1, pp. 498–9.
276 See Assmann, 'Der zweidimensionale Mensch', pp. 20ff., 'Kollektives Gedächtnis und kulturelle Identität', p. 10., and *Cultural Memory*, pp. 34ff.
277 Goldziher, *Muslim Studies*, vol. 2, p. 150.
278 Ibn Jubayr, *Tagebuch eines Mekkapilgers*, p. 101.
279 *I'jāz*, p. 20; the reference is probably to Bashshār ibn Burd.
280 *The Apology of al-Kindy*, pp. 78ff. The text has also been translated into French and Latin (see bibliography). For a detailed summary of the contents, see Graf, *Geschichte der christlichen arabischen Literatur*, vol. 2, pp. 135–41, and Abel, 'L'Apologie d'al Kindi'. It is uncertain whether the correspondence actually took place between the authors named, but it is considered probable.

See the introductions to the translations cited and Brockelmann, *Geschichte*, vol. S. 1, pp. 344–6; EI[2], 'al-Kindī, 'Abd al-Masīḥ', pp. 120–1; Kraus, 'Beiträge zur islamischen Ketzergeschichte', esp. p. 337.

281 Quoted in Ritter, 'Philologika VI', pp. 11–12.

282 See p. 228.

283 Goldziher, *Muslim Studies*, vol. 2, p. 363.

284 Bāqillānī, *I'jāz*, p. 260.

285 See the second chapter of his book *Bīst-o-se sāl resālat*, which is banned in Iran but widely circulated in clandestine and foreign printings. (There is an unsatisfactory German translation titled *23 Jahre: die Karriere des Propheten Muhammad*, Aschaffenburg, 1997.) A rebuttal to it is Moṣṭafā Ḥoseynī Ṭabāṭabā'ī, *Khiyānat dar gozāresh-e tārīkh*, 2 vols, 1363/1984.

286 Voltaire, *Essai sur les mœurs*, in *Œuvres complètes*, Paris, 1877–85, vol. 11, p. 209; quoted in Lessenich, *Dichtungsgeschmack und althebräische Bibelpoesie*, p. 5.

287 Gutzen, *Poesie der Bibel*, p. 26.

288 Auerbach, *Literary Language and its Public*, p. 28.

289 Dyck, *Athen und Jerusalem*, p. 7.

290 Van Ess, *Theologie und Gesellschaft*, vol. 4, p. 698.

291 Gutzen, *Poesie der Bibel*, p. 25. See also ibid., pp. 28ff.; Auerbach, *Mimesis*, pp. 50ff.

292 Auerbach, *Literary Language and its Public*, p. 59.

293 Ibid., p. 45. On the texts of early Christianity in the context of Greek literature, see Norden, *Antike Kunstprosa*, pp. 478–528.

294 *Literary Language and its Public*, p. 47.

295 Ibid., p. 46. Cf. Curtius, *European Literature and the Latin Middle Ages*, pp. 41–4, 74–5; Norden, *Antike Kunstprosa*, pp. 526ff.

296 Boccaccio, *Life of Dante*, pp. 45ff.

297 On this idea and on the reception of biblical poetry in the Renaissance in general, see Kugel, *The Idea of Biblical Poetry*, pp. 204ff.; Dyck, *Athen und Jerusalem*, pp. 64ff.; Rhu, 'After the Middle Ages'; Bachern, *Dichtung als verborgene Theologie*, pp. 22ff.

298 *Epistolae de rebus familiaris*, 22:10, quoted in Kugel, *The Idea of Biblical Poetry*, p. 214.

299 Dyck, *Athen und Jerusalem*, p. 87; but see also Dyck's qualification in regard to the discussion of biblical metre in the subsequent pages.

300 Tor Andrae, *Die Person Muhammeds*, p. 97; Goldziher, *Muslim Studies*, vol. 2, pp. 363ff.

301 *Einleitung ins Alte Testament*, vol. 1, p. 15.

302 On the aesthetic reception of the Bible in the eighteenth and nineteenth centuries, see Gutzen, *Poesie der Bibel*; Dyck, *Athen und Jerusalem*, pp. 91ff.; and on the English-speaking countries in particular, Lessenich, *Dichtungsgeschmack und althebräische Bibelpoesie*; Wojcik and Frontain, *Poetic Prophecy in Western Literature*.

303 *Some Considerations Touching the Style of the H. Scriptures: Extracted from Several Parts of a Discourse (Concerning Divers Particulars Belonging to the Bible); Written Divers Years Since to a Friend*, London, 1661. On this text, see Dyck, *Athen und Jerusalem*, pp. 73ff.

304 Eichhorn, *Einleitung ins Alte Testament*, vol. 1, p. 15.

305 Ibid., p. 14.

306 Ibid., p. 18.

307 Ibid., p. 16.
308 *Vom Geist der Ebräischen Poesie*, p. 751 ['*Die Naturpoesie der Morgenländer*', rendered without the reference to nature as 'the poetry of the Orientals' in Marsh's English translation (vol. 1, p. 73) – Trans.].
309 Ibid., p. 1195.
310 *The Spirit of Hebrew Poetry*, p. 112.
311 Ibid., p. 210. To praise biblical poetry, even Herder refers to the idea of 'humble' discourse: 'But it was only in this simple form that they could be apprehended moreover by the most simple and undisciplined understanding, and seize upon the heart of man, when most depressed and most in need of their influence' (ibid., p. 211).
312 *Sämtliche Werke*, vol. 1, p. 226.
313 Dyck, *Athen und Jerusalem*, p. 8.
314 See *On Religion*, esp. pp. 150ff.
315 See Niggl, 'Biblische Welt in Goethes Dichtung'.
316 Bachern, *Dichtung als verborgene Theologie*, pp. 49–74.
317 Thomas Aquinas, *Summa Theologica*, vol. 1, Question 1, Article 10.
318 *Herrlichkeit*, vol. 2, p. 9.
319 Ibid., vol. 1, p. 27.
320 John 1:14.
321 *Dalā'il*, pp. 45–6/49–50.
322 Ibid., pp. 25–6/p. 10.
323 *Kitāb aṣ-ṣināʿatayn al-kitāba wa-sh-shiʿr*, ed. M. al-Bajawī and Abdulfaḍl Ibrāhīm, Cairo, 1952, pp. 3–4; quoted in Grotzfeld, 'Der Begriff der Unnachahmlichkeit des Korans', pp. 71–2.
324 Bāqillānī, *Iʿjāz*, pp. 40–1, 118.
325 EI[2], 'Iʿdjāz'.
326 Grunebaum, *A Tenth-Century Document*, p. xv.
327 Grunebaum in EI[2], 'Iʿdjāz', pp. 1018–19.
328 The view survives in milder form in van Ess, *Theologie und Gesellschaft*, vol. 4, p. 608.
329 *Mohammed und der Koran*, p. 90.
330 Quoted in Hauser, *Sociology of Art*, p. 471.

Chapter 5 The Prophet among the Poets

1 'Of the Difference between a Genius and an Apostle', p. 103.
2 *ʿAbqarīyat Muḥammad*. On the author, see Wielandt, *Offenbarung und Geschichte*, pp. 100ff.; Wessels, *A Modern Arabic Biography of Muḥammad*, pp. 14ff.
3 Moṭahharī, *Waḥy wa-nobūwat*, 16–17; Lari, *The Seal of the Prophets*, pp. 61ff.
4 I use the term 'Enlightenment' here not in the strict sense of the historical period in philosophy (considered to have begun in Germany in the eighteenth century and culminated in Kant, who transcended it) but in the general sense, designating the cultural and intellectual movement that replaced religion with reason as the chief authority. In this sense idealism too is an Enlightenment philosophy.
5 On the *Muslim* notions of the revelation (that is, notions fed not only by the Quran), see Pautz, *Muhammed's Lehre von der Offenbarung*; EI[1], 'Waḥy'; Nieuwenhuijze, 'Prophetic Function in Islam'; Bell, 'Mohammed's Call' and

'Muhammad's Visions'; Graham, *Divine Word and Prophetic Word*, pp. 9–48; Kermani, *Offenbarung als Kommunikation*, pp. 30–7, 58–90 (with extensive references on the present topic of Muhammad's revelation).

6 Quran 2:97.

7 See, e.g., Ṭabarī, *Tārīkh*, vol. 1, pp. 1147–56.

8 'Der historische Muhammad im Spiegel des Koran', p. 94.

9 See especially Quran 42:51–2. On the *quranic* concept of revelation in particular, see Izutsu, *God and Man*, pp. 151–93; Jeffery, *The Qur'ān as Scripture*, pp. 51–63; Kermani, *Offenbarung als Kommunikation*, pp. 51–8.

10 Pp. 67–82; in Rosenthal's English translation, pp. 184–245. For summaries, see Rahman, *Prophecy in Islam*, pp. 105–8; Guillaume, *Prophecy and Divination*, pp. 197–213.

11 *Mabaḥith fī 'ulūm al-Qur'ān*, pp. 27–45.

12 *Al-Mīzān*, commentary on verses 41:51–3; see also the transcripts of Ṭa-bāṭabā'ī's lectures in Seyyed Ṭehrānī, *Mehr-e tābān*, Teheran, n.d., pp. 207–13.

13 *Al-Waḥy al-muḥammadī*, pp. 43–7.

14 *Waḥy wa-nobūwat.*

15 *Tārīkh-e Qor'ān*, pp. 33–210.

16 *Mafhūm an-naṣṣ*, pp. 35–65.

17 *Al-Kitāb wal-l-Qur'ān*, pp. 145–76.

18 On the aesthetics of genius, see Schmidt, *Die Geschichte des Geniegedankens*; Ritter, *Historisches Wörterbuch*, 'Genie'; Zilsel, *Die Entstehung des Geniebegriffes*; Cassirer, *The Philosophy of the Enlightenment*; Gadamer, *Truth and Method*, esp. pp. 39–55 and the index.

19 *On Naïve and Sentimental Poetry*, p. 189.

20 From 'Ahnung und Gegenwart', in *Werke*, p. 741. [Original: Den lieben Gott laß in dir walten, / Aus frischer Brust nur traulich sing! / Was wahr in dir, wird sich gestalten, / Das andre ist erbärmlich Ding.]

21 *Ausgewählte Werke*, p. 183. [Original: Was schwatzen und wie schreiben sie / Nach jedem zehnten Wort, auf jedem dritten Blatt / Nur immer vom Genie!]

22 'On the Cognition and Sensation of the Human Soul', p. 232.

23 Ibid., p. 231.

24 Schmidt, *Die Geschichte des Geniegedankens*, vol. 1, pp. 141ff.

25 *Anthropology from a Pragmatic Point of View*, p. 121.

26 Cf. Schopenhauer, *The World as Will and Representation*, p. 209.

27 Hegel, *Aesthetics: Lectures on Fine Art*, vol. 1, p. 283.

28 *The World as Will and Representation*, p. 214ff.

29 Gadamer, *Truth and Method*, p. 84. See also Schmidt, *Die Geschichte des Geniegedankens*, vol. 2, pp. 169ff.; Adorno, *Aesthetic Theory*, pp. 232ff.; Valéry, *The Art of Poetry*, pp. 212ff.

30 Schmidt, *Geschichte des Geniegedankens*, vol. 2, p. 154.

31 Josef Goebbels, *Michael: Ein deutsches Schicksal in Tagebuchblättern*, 2nd edn, Munich, 1931, pp. 60ff.; quoted in Schmidt, *Geschichte des Geniegedankens*, vol. 2, p. 207. [The translation is that of Joachim Neugroschel: *Michael: A Novel*, New York: Amok Press, 1987, pp. 14, 31.]

32 *System of Transcendental Idealism*, pp. 5, 10. On Schelling's aesthetics of genius, see Düsing, 'Schellings Genieästhetik'; Schmidt, *Geschichte des Geniegedankens*, pp. 390–403; Baumgartner and Korten, *Schelling*, pp. 68–78.

33 *System of Transcendental Idealism*, p. 221.

34 Ibid. p. 223.

35 Ibid.

36 Muhammad is both *rasūl* and *nabīy*, messenger (apostle) and prophet, and there is controversy both in Muslim theology and in Islamic studies as to what makes him *rasūl* and what makes him *nabīy* (see Bijlefeld, 'A Prophet and More Than a Prophet?'; Wensinck, 'Muhammad und die Propheten'; Jeffery, *The Qur'ān as Scripture*, pp. 118ff.; Rāmiyār, *Tārīkh-e Qor'ān*, pp. 174ff.; Shaḥrūr, *Al-Kitāb wa-l-Qur'ān*, pp. 101–11; Kermani, *Offenbarung als Kommunikation*, pp. 83–4). In the analogies between the Enlightenment concept of genius and the concept of prophethood and divine mission in Islam in this section, I should therefore refer to Muhammad each time as *nabīy* (prophet) and *rasūl* (messenger). But, for the sake of simplicity, I will use the term *nabīy*, principally because the Islamic thinkers (such as Ibn Khaldūn, Avicenna and al-Farābī) have discussed mainly Muhammad's 'prophethood' (*nubūwa*) and less his 'mission'. I would also like to use the Arabic term *nabīy*, at least alongside its translation, because the translation 'prophet' does not exactly convey the sense and evokes some false associations (see van Nieuwenhuijze, 'The Prophetic Function in Islam', pp. 119ff.). Today, for example, we ordinarily think of a prophet as someone who foretells the future (although predicting the future was originally not an essential characteristic of the major scriptural prophets: see Kittel, *Theologisches Wörterbuch*, 'Prophet'). The *nabīy*, on the other hand, is only – and this is the literal translation – a 'transmitter of messages', and there is no consensus among Muslims that Muhammad's attributes included telling the future. In medieval Christian polemics, the fact that Muhammad did not claim to predict the future was seen as evidence that he was not a true prophet (see Hagemann, *Propheten*, p. 191).

37 *Critique of the Power of Judgement*, p. 204.

38 See the articles under 'Kashf' in Sajjādī, *Farhang-e eṣṭelāḥāt wa-ta'bīrāt-e 'erfānī*, and in Ullmann, *Wörterbuch*.

39 *Mafhūm an-naṣṣ*, p. 64.

40 *System of Transcendental Idealism*, p. 222.

41 *Philosophical Writings*, pp. 162–3.

42 Schelling, *The Philosophy of Art*, p. 84.

43 *System of Transcendental Idealism*, p. 223.

44 Quoted in Kuhn, *Schriften zur Ästhetik*, p. 147.

45 Rūmī, *Discourses*, p. 52.

46 'Ecce Homo', pp. 126–7.

47 EI[1], 'Waḥy'.

48 *Critique of the Power of Judgement*, p. 187.

49 Trans. Haleem.

50 Bukhārī, *Ṣaḥīḥ*, LIX/6 (no. 3218); cf. Quran 19:64.

51 Ibn Hishām, *Sīra*, vol. 1, p. 241. See also Buḥārī, *Ṣaḥīḥ*, I/3 (no. 4).

52 Ibn Ḥanbal, *Musnad*, I/318 (no. 2922).

53 Bukhārī, *Ṣaḥīḥ*, I/2 (no. 2).

54 Ibn Hishām, *Sīra*, vol. 2, p. 302; a similar version is found in Bukhārī, *Ṣaḥīḥ*, LII/15 (no. 2661).

55 Bukhārī, *Ṣaḥīḥ*, I/2 (no. 2), ILX/6 (no. 3215); Muslim, *Ṣaḥīḥ*, XLIII/23 (no. 2333); Ibn Sa'd, *Ṭabaqāt*, I/1, 132.

56 These phenomena are documented in Muslim, *Ṣaḥīḥ*, VI/46 (no. 814), XLIII/23 (no. 2334); Tirmiḏī, *Sunan*, XLIV/23 (no. 3222); Ibn Ḥanbal, *Musnad*, I/34 (no. 223); Suyūṭī, *Itqān*, vol. 1, p. 45; Ibn Sa'd, *Ṭabaqāt*, I/1, 131–2; Rāmiyār, *Tārīkh-e Qor'ān*, pp. 108ff.

57 Thomas Mann, *Doctor Faustus*, p. 237.
58 'Ecce Homo', pp. 195.
59 Quran 15:6 (trans. Arberry).
60 Quran 51:52 (trans. Arberry).
61 Plato, *Phaedrus*, 249d.
62 See, e.g., Weil, *Das Leben Muḥammeds*, pp. 42ff. The view that Muhammad suffered from epilepsy is critically discussed in Otto Pautz, *Muhammed's Lehre von der Offenbarung*, pp. 35ff., and Tor Andrae, *Mohammed*, p. 51.
63 See Fischer, '*Majnūn* "epileptisch"'.
64 These phenomena are all documented in Ibn Sa'd, *Ṭabaqāt*, I/1, 131–2; Nöldeke et al., *History of the Qur'ān*, p. 20.
65 Decker, *Entwicklung der Lehre von der prophetischen Offenbarung*, p. 28.
66 Quran 68:2; Ṭabarī, *Tārīkh*, vol. 1, pp. 1147–8.
67 The accusation that Muhammad was possessed (*majnūn*) is closely connected with the suspicions that he was only a soothsayer (52:29) or a poet (37:36). See Kermani, *Offenbarung als Kommunikation*, pp. 47ff.
68 Ibn Sa'd, *Ṭabaqāt*, I/1, 131.
69 Quoted in the memoirs of the mathematician Sofya Kovalevskaya (d. 1891), who knew Dostoevsky in her childhood and youth: *A Russian Childhood*, p. 178.
70 Ibn Hishām, *Sīra*, vol. 1, p. 400.
71 Quoted in Wensinck, *Concordance*, vol. 1, p. 504a. See also Quran 48:27; Abū Zayd, *Mafhūm an-naṣṣ*, pp. 56–7; Kermani, *Offenbarung als Kommunikation*, pp. 73ff., 112–13.
72 Quoted in Kiessig, *Dichter erzählen ihre Träume*, p. 277.
73 Quoted ibid., p. 286.
74 See, e.g., Kant, *Critique of the Power of Judgement*, p. 192; Ibn Khaldūn, *Muqaddima*, vol. 1, pp. 70–1 (in the translation, pp. 198–9).
75 *Sämtliche Werke*, vol. 2, p. 107.
76 Tirmiḏī, *Al-Jāmi'*, XXXIV/45 (no. 2509).
77 Quran 17:86 (trans. Arberry).
78 Abū Nu'aym, *Dalā'il*, vol. 1, p. 165.
79 Schmidt, *Die Geschichte des Geniegedankens*, vol. 1, pp. 105ff.
80 Hölderlin, 'As on a holiday…'.
81 Ibn Sa'd, *Ṭabaqāt*, I/1, 131.
82 Quran 73:5 (trans. Arberry).
83 Ibn Hishām, *Sīra*, p. 240.
84 Tirmiḏī, *Al-Jāmi'*, XXXIV/7 (no. 2414).
85 *The World as Will and Representation*, p. 214. An enthralling representation of the tormented and driven genius, next to Büchner's novel *Lenz*, is Stefan Zweig's book about Kleist, Hölderlin and Nietzsche, *The Struggle with the Daemon*.
86 Quoted in Nadler, *Johann George Hamann*, p. 411.
87 Hesse, *Steppenwolf*, p. 16.
88 Ibid., pp. 23–4.
89 Ibn Ḥanbal, *Musnad*, I/464 (no. 4421).
90 *Ṭabaqāt*, I/1, 131.
91 Ibn Ḥanbal, *Musnad*, I/222 (no. 7071).
92 *System of Transcendental Idealism*, p. 223.
93 More on this in chapter 6.
94 *The World as Will and Representation*, p. 209.

95 *Muqaddima*, p. 71.
96 *The World as Will and Representation*, p. 209.
97 See *Muqaddima*, p. 71.
98 Ibid., pp. 71–2.
99 *Aesthetics: Lectures on Fine Art*, vol. 1, p. 283.
100 Schelling, *System of Transcendental Idealism*, p. 222.
101 Ibid., p. 223.
102 See Andrae, 'Die Legenden von der Berufung Muhammads'; Sellheim, 'Muhammeds erstes Offenbarungserlebnis'.
103 See p. 258 above.
104 Ibid.
105 On this aspect of the tradition and on the original meaning of the word *ummī*, see Goldfeld, 'The Illiterate Prophet'; Zwemer, *Studies in Popular Islam*, pp. 100–20; Cragg, *The Event of the Qur'ān*, pp. 57ff.
106 *Sämtliche Werke*, vol. 2, p. 75.
107 *Notizen und Fragmente*, pp. 283–4.
108 *Dalā'il*, p. 37.
109 Van Ess, *Theologie und Gesellschaft*, vol. 1, pp. 31–2, vol. 4, pp. 611–12.
110 *Critique of the Power of Judgement*, pp. 186–7.
111 Ibid., p. 195.
112 Cassirer, *The Philosophy of the Enlightenment*, p. 256.
113 See pp. 105ff. in chapter 2.
114 *System of Transcendental Idealism*, p. 225.
115 Quran 21:5.
116 *Critique of the Power of Judgement*, p. 196.
117 *I'jāz al-Qur'ān*, p. 77.
118 *Critique of the Power of Judgement*, pp. 185, 188.
119 Cf. Schelling, *System of Transcendental Idealism*, p. 224: the original has 'poetry' in the place of 'revelation', 'artist' for 'prophet', and 'art' for 'rhyming prose'.
120 Ibid., p. 225.
121 Ibid., p. 222.
122 Qurṭubī, *Jāmi'*, introductory commentary on surah 40 (XV, 288).
123 *The World as Will and Representation*, p. 220.
124 *System of Transcendental Idealism*, p. 231.
125 Ibid.
126 Cf. Adorno, *Aesthetic Theory*, p. 175ff. More on this in chapter 6.
127 See p. 258 above.
128 *System of Transcendental Idealism*, p. 231.
129 'Of the Difference between a Genius and an Apostle', p. 127.
130 Hamann, *Sämtliche Werke*, vol. 2, p. 260; see also Schmidt, *Die Geschichte des Geniegedankens*, vol. 1, pp. 98–9.
131 See, for example, Ibn Khaldūn, *Muqaddima*, pp. 67–8.
132 Eichendorff, *Werke*, p. 740.
133 *Critique of the Power of Judgement*, p. 194. On the union of inspiration and poetic technique, see Ruthven, *Critical Assumptions*, pp. 51–82.
134 See Zilsel, *Die Entstehung des Geniebegriffes*, pp. 7–105.
135 *Ion*, 533e. See also Bubner, 'Die Entdeckung Platons durch Schelling'.
136 *Ion*, 534e.
137 See *Phaedrus*, 249b–250e. On this topic, see also Pieper, *Enthusiasm and Divine Madness*.

138 Curtius, *European Literature and the Latin Middle Ages*, pp. 474–5.
139 Nietze, 'A Midsummer Night's Dream'.
140 See Davidson, *Alfarabi, Avicenna, and Averroes on Intellect*; Walzer, *Greek into Arabic*, pp. 236ff.
141 See Walzer's comment in al-Fārābī, *Mabādi' ārā' ahl al-madīna al-fāḍila*, p. 423.
142 Rahman, *Prophecy in Islam*, p. 62.
143 *Timaeus*, esp. 70d–72d.
144 On Avicenna's theory of prophethood, which is mentioned in several of his works, see Fazlur Rahman's *Prophecy in Islam*, which deals in detail with al-Fārābī and Avicenna while also discussing orthodox positions, and Louis Gardet's *La Pensée religieuse d'Avicenne* (Paris, 1951), pp. 109–41. For a briefer survey, see Davidson, *Alfarabi, Avicenna, and Averroes on Intellect*, pp. 116–23; Decker, *Die Entwicklung der Lehre von der prophetischen Offenbarung*, pp. 13–29; Sharif, *History of Muslim Philosophy*, vol. 1, pp. 498–501.
145 While this interpretation is in contradiction to Horten (*Texte zu dem Streite zwischen Glauben und Wissen im Islam*, pp. 7ff.), it is persuasively demonstrated with textual references by Rahman (*Prophecy in Islam*, pp. 30ff. et al.) and Davidson (*Alfarabi, Avicenna, and Averroes on Intellect*, pp. 116ff.). Averroes refined the thesis of comparability and explicitly refuted the view that the various forms of human inspiration are qualitatively different (see Davidson, *Alfarabi, Avicenna, and Averroes on Intellect*, pp. 341ff.).
146 On this dispute, see also Bello, *The Medieval Islamic Controversy*. In another work, however, *Ma'ārij al-quds*, al-Ġazālī emphasizes the supernatural and miraculous qualities of prophecy, and finally, in his *Mi'rāj as-Sālikīn*, he calls the philosophers unbelievers because of their theory of prophecy: see Rahman, *Prophecy in Islam*, pp. 94–9.
147 The distinction between *tamyīz* and *'aql* here corresponds roughly to the distinction between understanding [*Verstand*] and reason [*Vernunft*] in Kant and other German philosophers.
148 Ġazālī, *Munqiḏ*, p. 42. On the function of dreams in Islamic culture, see Grunebaum, 'The Cultural Function of the Dream'; Rahman, 'Dream, Imagination, and *'Ālam al-mithāl*'; Fahd, 'Les Songes et leur interprétation', p. 137.
149 Cf. van Ess, *Theologie und Gesellschaft*, vol. 4, p. 621.
150 *Muqaddima*, pp. 69ff.
151 Decker, *Die Entwicklung der Lehre von der prophetischen Offenbarung*, p. 13. On the relation of Islamic philosophy to Christian scholasticism, see also Ernst Bloch's little noted study *Avicenna und die Aristotelische Linke*.
152 While the Christian scholastics had only parts of the *Timaeus* in direct translation, the Muslim scholars had access to the entire work in various translations. Furthermore, they had the complete text of the *Republic*, the *Laws* and at least excerpts of numerous other dialogues of Plato, including the *Phaedrus*, which is important alongside the *Timaeus* for the concept of enthusiasm, and the *Ion*, to which al-Fārābī refers explicitly in this work on Plato, *Falsafat Aflāṭūn*. See the English translation in *The Philosophy of Plato*, pp. 56, 61–2; Walzer, *Greek into Arabic*, p. 238, and 'Arabische Übersetzungen aus dem Griechischen', pp. 180ff.; Decker, *Die Entwicklung der Lehre von der prophetischen Offenbarung*, p. 6.
153 I refer in this discussion to chapter 14 of al-Fārābī's work on the 'principles of the views of the citizens of the best state' (*Mabādi' ārā' ahl al-madīna al-fāḍila*), which has been edited, translated and annotated by Richard Walzer

(*Al-Farabi on the Perfect State*; Arabic text and translation, pp. 210–27; commentary, pp. 413–23). In Friedrich Dieterici's better-known German edition (*Alfārābīs Abhandlung Der Musterstaat*, Hildesheim, 1985), the text comprises chapters 24 and 25 (pp. 47–53). For a more detailed interpretation of al-Fārābī's theory of prophecy, see Walzer, *Greek into Arabic*, pp. 206–19.

154 *Timaeus*, 71e (p. 71).
155 Fārābī, *Mabādi' ārā'*, p. 220.
156 Ibid., p. 219.
157 Ibid., pp. 220ff.
158 Walzer, *Greek into Arabic*, pp. 213–14.
159 *System of Transcendental Idealism*, p. 221.
160 Schmidt, *Die Geschichte des Geniegedankens*, vol. 1, pp. 193–4.
161 Fārābī, *Mabādi' ārā'*, p. 224. See also Walzer's commentary: ibid., p. 422.
162 Ibid., p. 416.
163 *System of Transcendental Idealism*, p. 229.
164 Schlegel in a letter to Novalis, 20 October 1798 (quoted in Bachern, *Dichtung als verborgene Theologie*, p. 70); Novalis mentions the idea several times in his replies to Schlegel.
165 See Goldammer, *Formenwelt des Religiösen*; van der Leeuw, *Sacred and Profane Beauty*, pp. 145ff.; Heiler, *Erscheinungsformen und Wesen der Religion*, p. 275; Lewis, *Ecstatic Religion*.
166 *Poetry and Prophecy*, p. xiii.
167 Ibid., p. xi.
168 Nagy, 'Ancient Greek Poetry, Prophecy, and Concepts of Theory'; Sikes, *The Greek View of Poetry*.
169 Chadwick, *Poetry and Prophecy*, pp. 46ff.
170 *Philosophical Writings*, p. 36.
171 Heiler, *Erscheinungsformen*, pp. 552ff.
172 Medicus, *Grundfragen der Ästhetik*, p. 14.
173 *Ash-Shi'r qindīl akhḍar*, p. 70.
174 'Aesthetica in Nuce', p. 78.
175 Kulaynī, *Kāfī*, 'Faḍl-al-Qur'ān/Tartīl al-Qur'ān', no. 10.
176 Mark 4:34.
177 On this parallel between the Hindu and Islamic concepts of revelation, see Roest Crollius, *The Word in the Experience of Revelation*; Crapon de Caprona, *Le Coran*, pp. 42–3; Graham, *Beyond the Written Word*, pp. 67ff.
178 *Muqaddima lī sh-shi'r al-'arabī*, p. 125.
179 Paz, 'Reading and Contemplation', pp. 7–8. See also Ruthven, *Critical Assumptions*, pp. 51ff.; Wojcik and Frontain, *Poetic Prophecy in Western Literature*.
180 On these two phenomena, see Chadwick, *Poetry and Prophecy*, pp. 58ff.; van der Leeuw, *Einführung in die Phänomenologie der Religion*, pp. 109ff.
181 Ezekiel 33:32.
182 Wensinck, 'Muhammad und die Propheten', p. 188.
183 Jeremiah 20:7.
184 1 Kings 19:10.
185 Andrae, *Die Person Muhammeds*, pp. 19–20. On the forms and characteristics of Israelite prophecy in general, see Neumann, *Das Prophetenverständnis in der deutschsprachigen Forschung*; Koch, *Die Propheten*; Westermann, *Basic Forms of Prophetic Speech*.
186 *Einleitung ins Alte Testament*, vol. 4, pp. 30–1.

187 Auerbach, 'Die Prophetie', p. 239.
188 Kugel would prefer for this reason to set the term 'biblical poetry' in quotation marks. The linguistic structure of the text is also not conducive to a distinction between poetry and prose, which would imply too strict a polarity. See *The Idea of Biblical Poetry*, pp. 69–70, and also Kugel's criticism of the 'excesses' of literary analyses of the Bible, 'On the Bible and Literary Criticism'.
189 Carroll, 'Poets not Prophets', p. 26. See also Guillaume, *Prophecy and Divination*, p. 243.
190 Carroll, 'Poets not Prophets', pp. 28–9; Auld, 'Prophets through the Looking Glass'.
191 Albright, *Yahweh and the Gods of Canaan*, pp. 2–3, 30ff.; Myers, *The Linguistic and Literary Form of the Book of Ruth*; Frye, *The Great Code*, p. 210. For a critical reflection on this discussion, see Kugel, who opposes the inference that every instance of parallelism in Genesis is a fragment of a long-lost original version (*The Idea of Biblical Poetry*, pp. 76ff.).
192 On the versions of the prophetic traditions in the Old Testament, see Westermann, *Basic Forms of Prophetic Speech*.
193 Kugel, 'David the Prophet'; Wojcik, 'The Uncertain Success of Isaiah's Prophecy', pp. 31ff.; Geller, 'Were the Prophets Poets?'.
194 Widengren, *Literary and Psychological Aspects of the Hebrew Prophets*, pp. 98ff.
195 Heiler, *Erscheinungsformen*, pp. 496ff.
196 Geller, 'Were the Prophets Poets?'; Kugel, *The Idea of Biblical Poetry*, pp. 96ff.
197 52:29–34; 68:1–6, 44–5; 69:38–52; 81:19–29. On this topic, see Neuwirth, 'Der historische Muhammad', pp. 88ff.
198 See Izutsu, *God and Man*, pp. 170ff.; Cragg, *The Event of the Qur'ān*, p. 40; Abū Zayd, *Mafhūm an-naṣṣ*, pp. 158ff.
199 21:5 (trans. Arberry).
200 10:2; 38:4; 51:52.
201 52:29; 69:42.
202 Zwettler, *Oral Tradition*, pp. 158ff.
203 Goldziher, *Abhandlungen*, pp. 10ff.
204 Neuwirth, 'Der historische Muhammad', p. 87.
205 *Shayāṭīn* refers in such contexts not to Satan in the biblical sense, who also appears in later surahs of the Quran, but to the ancient Arab concept of a daemon associated with a specific poet, possessing and inspiring him.
206 *Ṣaḥīḥ*, I/3 (no. 3).
207 Quran 96:1–3 (trans. Arberry).
208 *Sīra*, vol. 1, p. 236.
209 Goldziher, *Abhandlungen*, p. 3.
210 Goldziher, 'Die Jinnen der Dichter', p. 685.
211 Trans. Arberry.
212 See Watt, *Muḥammad's Mecca*, p. 54.
213 Ṭabarī, *Tārīkh*, vol. 1, pp. 1150–1.
214 Buḫārī, *Ṣaḥīḥ*, XCI/5 (no. 6990).
215 Muslim, *Ṣaḥīḥ*, XLII/0 (no. 2263). The same statement is repeated with different numbers in the subsequent hadiths in Muslim.
216 Ibn ʿArabī, *Futūḥāt*, vol. 1, p. 237.
217 Quran 37:36.

218 Bukhārī, *Ṣaḥīḥ*, XIX/4 (no. 1125).
219 21:5.
220 17:60.
221 37:105.
222 48:27.
223 Muslim, *Ṣaḥīḥ*, XLII/0 (no. 2261).
224 Bukhārī, *Ṣaḥīḥ*, LIX/11 (no. 3292).
225 Quran 68:2.
226 68:6.
227 81:19ff. (after Arberry).
228 26:192–5 (trans. Arberry).
229 26:209–12 (trans. Arberry).
230 26:221–7 (trans. Arberry). The discussion of the 26th surah that follows makes heavy use of Zwettler's brilliant essay 'A Mantic Manifesto' yet does not entirely coincide with his analysis.
231 On the quranic concept of the revelation as 'sending down', see Wild, 'We Have Sent Down to Thee the Book with the Truth…'; Shaḥrūr, *Al-Kitāb wa-l-Qur'ān*, pp. 145–76.
232 37:8–10.
233 'A Mantic Manifesto', p. 113.
234 My interpretation of this term follows the customary Muslim exegesis (see, e.g., Zamahsharī, *Kashshāf*; Maḥallī and Suyūṭī, *Tafsīr al-Jalālayn*) and Zwettler's arguments ('A Mantic Manifesto', p. 111, n. 146; see also Paret's commentary on 26:224; Schub, 'Qur'ān 26:224'). Shahid ('A Contribution to Koranic Exegesis', p. 566), on the other hand, understands *ġāwūn* in an active sense as 'the beguilers' and associates it with the *shayāṭīn*. Bürgel ('Die beste Dichtung ist die lügenreichste', p. 28) and Heinrichs (*Arabische Dichtung und griechische Poetik*, p. 33) follow his reading.
235 Zwettler, 'A Mantic Manifesto', pp. 113ff.
236 See Bürgel, 'Die beste Dichtung ist die lügenreichste'; Jacobi, 'Dichtung und Lüge'.
237 Shahid's proposal to situate this passage in the narrower context of the *taḥaddī* verses (see 'Another Contribution to Koranic Exegesis', pp. 9ff.) is unconvincing.
238 'The Quran abhors poets': Fahd, *La Divination arabe*, p. 75.
239 Bukhārī, *Ṣaḥīḥ*, LIX/11 (no. 3288).
240 Ibid., LXXVIII/92 (no. 6155).
241 Goldziher, *Abhandlungen*, p. 7.
242 Ibn Hishām, *Sīra*, vol. 2, p. 419.
243 Meier, 'Some Aspects of Inspiration by Demons in Islam', pp. 425ff.
244 Wagner, *Grundzüge*, vol. 2, p. 4.
245 Heinrichs, 'The Meaning of *Mutanabbī*', p. 121. For a survey of Islam's relation to poetry and the discussion of it in Oriental studies, see Wagner, *Grundzüge*, vol. 2, pp. 1ff.; van Gelder, *The Bad and the Ugly*, pp. 13–34 (this is concerned specifically with Islam's relation to 'invective poetry' [*hijā'*]).
246 Ibn Rashīq, *'Umda*, vol. 2, p. 170.
247 Nagel, *Der Koran*, p. 49.
248 *Deciphering the Signs of God*, p. 129.
249 A typical example of such an 'answer to the statements of those who disapprove of poetry' is Ibn Rashīq, *Al-'Umda fī maḥāsin ash-shi'r*, vol. 1, pp. 27ff.
250 Bukhārī, *Ṣaḥīḥ*, LXXVIII/90 (no. 6145).

251 Kulaynī, *Kāfī*, 'Faḍl-al-Qur'ān/Tartīl al-Qur'ān', no. 8.
252 Quoted in Ḥeydarhānī, *Samā'-e 'ārefān*, p. 50. See also Ibn Māja, *Sunan*, V/125 (nos 1307ff.); 'Ebādī, *Manāqib aṣ-ṣūfīya*, p. 148.
253 Ibn Ḥanbal, *Musnad*, III/91, IV/91.
254 Ġazālī, *Iḥya*, vol. 2, p. 164; Makkī, *Die Nahrung der Herzen*, p. 515.
255 Abū 'Abdirraḥmān an-Nasā'ī, *Sunan an-Nasā'ī* (Beirut, n.d.), XXIV/109, 121.
256 Ġazālī, *Iḥyā'*, vol. 2, pp. 163–4; Bukhārī, *Ṣaḥīḥ*, LIX/6 (no. 3212). In another hadith, however, the Prophet explicitly prohibits poetry recitals in the mosque: Ibn Māja, *Sunan*, IV/5 (no. 749).
257 Bukhārī, *Ṣaḥīḥ*, LXXVII/91(nos 6152–3). Qurṭubī offers a detailed presentation of the relation between Islam and poetry, illustrated with many examples, in his commentary on the Quran passage 26:224–7 (*Al-Jāmi' li-aḥkām al-Qur'ān*, vol. 13, pp. 145–54). A poem from the divan of Ibn 'Arabī that Peter Bachmann has written about ('Ein Gedicht zur "Sure der Dichter"') gives a mystic's view of the verses.
258 Nöldeke et al., *History of the Qur'ān*, pp. 104–5; Blachère, 'La Poésie dans la conscience de la première génération musulmane', p. 95.
259 *Allmacht und Mächtigkeit*, p. 232. See also Bürgel, 'Die beste Dichtung ist die lügenreichste', p. 26.
260 Bonebakker, 'Religious Prejudice against Poetry in Early Islam'.
261 Ḥeydarhānī expresses the same sentiment in *Samā'-e 'ārefān*, pp. 47ff.
262 Ibn Rāshiq, *Al-'Umda fī maḥāsin ash-shi'r*, vol. 1, p. 31.
263 Wāqidī, *Kitāb al-maġāzī*, pp. 841–2. In fact, the first apostasy in the history of Islam is said to have been caused by the skilled tongue of the soothsayer al-Aswad: Ṭabarī, *Tārīkh*, vol. 1, p. 1796.
264 Ewald Wagner writes on this development (in *Grundzüge*, vol. 2, p. 10): 'Early Islamic poetry is a long way from the development of an autonomous genre of religious poetry like that which we find in the later poetry of the mystics.' Francesco Gabrieli shows (in 'Religious Poetry in Early Islam') that, although religious poetry existed in the early period of Islam, it was limited largely to poets from marginal and oppositional religious groups, mainly the Kharijites. See also Farrukh, *Das Bild des Frühislam in der arabischen Dichtung*; Khan, *Vom Einfluß des Qur'āns auf die arabische Dichtung*; Bellamy, 'The Impact of Islam on Early Arabic Poetry'.
265 *Makhzan al-asrār*, p. 19.
266 Cantarino, *Arabic Poetics in the Golden Age*, p. 18.
267 Meier, 'Some Aspects of Inspiration by Demons', p. 429.
268 'Der mystische Imperativ', p. 9–10.
269 Leggewie, 'Der Dichter als Prophet', p. 79 (the author follows portrayals by Bürgel and Grunebaum). Sloterdijk expresses similar sentiments: see 'Der mystische Imperativ', p. 11.
270 'Umar as-Suhrawardī, *Die Gaben der Erkenntnisse*, p. 169.
271 Geertz, 'Art as a Cultural System', p. 1493.
272 Ibid., p. 1490.
273 Sowayan, 'Tonight My Gun Is Loaded', pp. 164–5.
274 Steiner, *Language and Silence*, p. 39.
275 *The Bow and the Lyre*, p. 102; see also ibid., pp. 213ff.
276 Adonis, *Mihyar of Damascus, His Songs*, p. 70. Adonis has not only expressed the idea presented here in his poems but also formulated it in a number of theoretical works: see *Muqaddima, li-sh-shi'r al-'arabī* (esp. pp. 99–143); *Ath-Thābit wa-l-mutaḥawwil*; *Ash-Si'rīya al-'arabīya*; *As-Ṣūfīya wa-s-sūryālīya*.

See also Stefan Weidner's afterword to his German translation *Die Gesänge Mihyârs des Damaszeners* (Zurich, 1998) and his article 'Adonis'; Boullata, 'Adonis: Towards a New Arab Culture'; Khayrallah, 'Prophetic Vision in Modern Arabic Poetry'.

277 Hojwīrī, *Kashf*, p. 88.
278 Qushayrī, *Das Sendschreiben*, p. 479.
279 Bākharzī, *Awrād al-aḥbāb*, p. 342. *Nāha* can also mean 'to sing' (a lament).
280 See, for example, Novalis's early poem 'Geschichte der Poesie' (History of poetry), in *Schriften*, vol. 1, pp. 536–7.
281 Ibn Ḥanbal, *Musnad*, I/323 (no. 2979).
282 *Makhzan al-asrār*, p. 19.
283 Kleist, 'The Puppet Theatre', 416.
284 *Ganjīne-ye Ganjawī* (divan), Teheran, 2nd edn, 1335SH/1957, p. 117; quoted in Bürgel, *Allmacht und Mächtigkeit*, p. 240.
285 *Gedichte aus dem Diwan*, closing verses of the poems 17, 29, 43 and 47.
286 *Ghaselen*, no. 44.
287 Wild, 'Die schauerliche Öde', pp. 440ff.
288 Exceptions include Tor Andrae (*Mohammed: The Man and His Faith*, p. 48) and primarily Kenneth Cragg (*The Event of the Qur'ān*, pp. 39ff.).
289 *On Religion*, p. 139. On the term *Kunstreligion*, see Rohls, 'Sinn und Geschmack fürs Unendliche'; Ritter, *Historisches Wörterbuch*, 'Kunstreligion'.

Chapter 6 The Sufi Listeners

1 Quran 70:15 (trans. Arberry).
2 Quran 69:21–3 (trans. Arberry).
3 The two manuscripts of *Kitāb mubārak yuḏfīhi qatlā l-Qur'ān al-ʿaẓīm allaḏīna samīʿū l-Qur'ān wa-mātū bi-samāʿihī raḥmat allāh ʿalayhim wa-ʿalā jamīʿ al-muslimīn* (also called *Kitāb fīhi qatlā l-Qur'ān*) of which I have copies are held by the Oriental Manuscripts Collection of Leiden University Library (Or. 520[5] and Or. 998[2]; cf. Brockelmann, Geschichte, vol. 1, pp. 350–1). I am grateful to Dr van de Velde for supplying the copies. As part of a master's degree thesis at the University of Cologne in 1996, Beate Wiesmüller submitted an edition with commentaries and a German translation, which she kindly allowed me to use for the present chapter. I have diverged here from her translation occasionally (and routinely in regard to Quran verses, which she presents in Khoury's version). Because the master's thesis had not been published at the time, I refer to ath-Thaʿlabī's text by the order of the chapters in the manuscripts. On the author ath-Thaʿlabī, see Wiesmüller's introduction and EI[1], 'Thaʿlabī'; Nöldeke et al., *History of the Qur'ān*, pp. 141ff.; Calder, 'Tafsīr from Ṭabarī to Ibn Kathīr', pp. 118, 125–6.
4 Breton, *Nadja*, p. 160.
5 7:41 (trans. Arberry).
6 Hojwīrī, *Kashf*, p. 73.
7 Ibid.
8 Sarrāj, *Schlaglichter*, p. 410.
9 Hojwīrī, *Kashf*, p. 72. For the whole history, see chapter 1, pp. 43–4.
10 See chapter 4 above, p. 234.
11 Hojwīrī, *Kashf*, p. 72.

12 See p. 33.
13 Reinert, *Die Lehre vom tawakkul*, p. 315.
14 Van Ess, *Die Gedankenwelt des Muḥāsibī*, p. 198.
15 Farīdoddīn ʿAṭṭār, *Taḏkirat al-awliyā'* , Teheran 1373/1984, pp. 460–1. A shorter version appears in Hojwīrī, *Kashf*, p. 124; see also Gramlich, *Alte Vorbilder des Sufitums*, vol. 2, pp. 116–17.
16 Bākharzī, *Awrād al-aḥbāb*, p. 343.
17 Bukhārī, *Ṣaḥīḥ*, XXXVII/16 (no. 2276); LXVI/9 (no. 5007).
18 Ritter, *The Ocean of the Soul*, p. 548.
19 Sanā'ī, *The First Book of the Hadīqatu' l-ḥaqīqat*, pp. 115–16.
20 Gramlich, *Die Wunder der Freunde Gottes*, pp. 389–90. The verses 2:255, 12:64, 37:7, 15:17, 41:12, 86:4 and 85:12–22 are called *āyāt al-ḥifẓ*.
21 Ġazālī, *Lehre von den Lehre von den Stufen zur Gottesliebe*, p. 385.
22 Ritter, *The Ocean of the Soul*, p. 141.
23 Sarrāj, *Schlaglichter*, p. 414. Also found almost verbatim in Qushayrī, *Das Sendschreiben al-Qushayrīs über das Sufitum*, p. 472.
24 See Zakarīyā l-Anṣārī's commentary in Qushayrī, *Das Sendschreiben al-Qushayrīs über das Sufitum*, p. 473.
25 36:59 (trans. Arberry).
26 Ġazālī, *Iḥyā'*, p. 179.
27 Hojwīrī, *Kashf*, p. 76.
28 3:185.
29 Sarrāj, *Schlaglichter*, p. 410. Ġazālī, *Iḥyā'*, p. 149.
30 2:281.
31 Hojwirī, *Kashf*, p. 73.
32 Gramlich, *Die Wunder der Freunde Gottes*, pp. 359–60. Thābit al-Bunānī too is said to have recited the Quran in his tomb: see Gramlich, *Alte Vorbilder*, vol. 1, p. 44.
33 *Kashf*, p. 74.
34 Schimmel, *Mystical Dimensions of Islam*, p. 152.
35 16:75 (trans. Arberry).
36 Hojwirī, *Kashf*, p. 74.
37 Anonymous, *Lebensweise der Könige*, p. 130.
38 Nicholson, *Mystics of Islam*, p. 63.
39 Gronke, 'Lebensangst und Wunderglaube'.
40 Schimmel, *Mystical Dimensions of Islam*, p. 180. See also Ḥeydarkhānī, *Samāʿ-e ʿārefān*, pp. 470ff.; Ritter, *The Ocean of the Soul*, pp. 141, 533; Nicholson, *Mystics of Islam*, p. 64.
41 See, e.g., Hojwīrī, *Kashf*, p. 49; Nasafī, *Ādāb-e taṣawwof*, p. 258; Abar-Qūhī, *Majmaʿ al-Baḥrayn*, p. 290; Sarrāj, *Schlaglichter*, p. 393.
42 Sarrāj, *Schlaglichter*, pp. 393–4 (other references there).
43 For a general description of the *samāʿ* writings and a sketch of their history, see Pourjavady, 'Zwei alte Werke über *samāʿ*'. For more on this topic, see also Harawī, *Andar ġazal-e khʷīsh*, pp. 6–44; Ḥeydarkhānī, *Samāʿ-e ʿāre-fān*. On the practice of *samāʿ*, see Meier, 'The Dervish Dance'.
44 Ruwaym, quoted in Sarrāj, *Schlaglichter*, p. 416.
45 Makkī, *Die Nahrung der Herzen*, vol. 1, p. 209.
46 Quoted in Schimmel, *Mystical Dimensions of Islam*, p. 18.
47 ʿUmar as-Suhrawardī, *Die Gaben der Erkenntnisse*, p. 173.
48 *Iḥyā*, vol. 2, p. 161.
49 Sarrāj, *Schlaglichter*, p. 393.

50 For a critique, see Ḥeydarkhānī, *Samā'-e 'ārefān*, p. 47. The Sufis' arguments for *samā'* have been compiled by Harawī: see *Andar ġazal-e khʷīsh*, pp. 11ff.
51 Commentary on Maḥmūd Sabestarī, *Golshan-e raz*; quoted in Ḥeydarkhānī, *Samā'-e 'ārefān*, p. iv.
52 Bākharzi, *Awrād al-aḥbāb*, p. 314.
53 'Umar as-Suhrawardī, *Die Gaben der Erkenntnisse*, p. 169.
54 See Harawī, *Andar ġazal-e khʷīsh*, pp. 16–17; Ḥeydarkhanī, *Samā'-e 'ārefān*, p. 36; Abū Najīb as-Suhrawardī, *Kitāb ādāb al-murīdīn*, p. 64; Farġānī, *Manāhij al-'ibād*, p. 271. See also Gramlich's description of the rites of contemporary Iranian orders in *Die schiitischen Derwischorden Persiens*, vol. 3, pp. 33ff. I have also witnessed this procedure myself at meetings of the Ne'matollāhī and the Khāksār orders in Isfahan.
55 Bākharzī, *Awrād al-aḥbāb*, p. 368.
56 Sarrāj, *Schlaglichter*, p. 409.
57 On the genre, see Andrae, *In the Garden of Myrtles*, pp. 55–6.
58 Of course, it is not quite precise to talk of Islamic mysticism as if there was only one such institution: in fact, the term groups together many different positions and currents. With the exception of Ibn 'Arabī, however, the authors cited in this chapter, including Hojwīrī, al-Ġazālī, al-Qushayrī and as-Sarrāj, share a common stock of stories, ideas, concepts and values that makes them emerge as members of *one* tradition of thought – which we may call the main stream of classical mystical literature. The views and tendencies that appear in their writings form what can be and often is discussed as a coherent, if not always uncontradictory, intellectual concept (see, e.g., Meier, *Vom Wesen islamischer Mystik*; Nicholson, *The Mystics of Islam*).
59 Many of the anecdotes quoted in this chapter have multiple sources. In such cases I have indicated the various references but without aspiring to the kind of systematic catalogue of all existing sources that Gramlich strives to supply, since the declared purpose of these reflections is not a philological one, and they build explicitly on the philological work of other researchers. In some cases I have been able to add to Gramlich's very extensive information. I quote the *samā'* chapter of *Kashf al-maḥjūb* as it appears in Harawī's anthology. I have been able to obtain the other chapters of that work, which are less relevant to the present chapter, only in Nicholson's English translation, which I cite as *The Kashf.*
60 Cf. *Kashf*, p. 73.
61 *Qatlā l-Qur'ān*, introduction. The hadith referred to is not canonical.
62 Ibid.
63 Ibid. See also the 18th chapter of Tha'labī's treatise.
64 Quran 2:24 (trans. Arberry).
65 *Qatlā l-Qur'ān*, ch. 2.
66 74:8 (trans. Arberry).
67 *Qatlā l-Qur'ān*, ch. 5. Also mentioned in Hojwīrī, *Kashf*, p. 76; Ġazālī, *Kīmiyā*, p. 148; Sarrāj, *Schlaglichter*, p. 229.
68 39:47 (trans. Haleem).
69 *Qatlā l-Qur'ān*, ch. 7.
70 43:74 (trans. Arberry).
71 43:75 (trans. Arberry).
72 *Qatlā l-Qur'ān*, ch. 17.
73 7:201 (trans. Arberry).
74 Quoted in Gramlich, *Alte Vorbilder*, vol. 1, p. 601.

75 Ġazālī, *Lehre von den Stufen zur Gottesliebe*, p. 327. See also Ritter, *The Ocean of the Soul*, pp. 133–50, 165–87.
76 *Iġāthat al-lahfān*, pp. 319–20, quoted in Ritter, *The Ocean of the Soul*, p. 169. The saying is attributed to Abū Ṭālib al-Makkī: cf. Makkī, *Die Nahrung der Herzen*, vol. 1, p. 12.
77 *Das Sendschreiben al-Qushayrīs über das Sufitum*, p. 195 (other references there).
78 *Elāhīnāme*, 17/5, quoted in Ritter, *The Ocean of the Soul*, p. 43.
79 *Danton's Death*, Act 4, scene 5 (p. 67).
80 Ibid., Act 3, scene 7 (p. 56).
81 Quoted in Ritter, *The Ocean of the Soul*, p. 136.
82 *Manṭiq aṭ-ṭayr*, 43/5, 155–6, quoted in Ritter, *The Ocean of the Soul*, p. 145.
83 Ġazālī, *Lehre von den Stufen zur Gottesliebe*, p. 387.
84 Ibid., p. 389.
85 Ibid., p. 391.
86 Ibn al-Jawzī, *Ādāb al-ḥasan*, Cairo, 1931, p. 15, quoted in Ritter, 'Studien zur Geschichte der islamischen Frömmigkeit', pp. 18–19; cf. Ġazālī, *Lehre von den Stufen zur Gottesliebe*, p. 392.
87 Ritter, 'Studien zur Geschichte der islamischen Frömmigkeit', p. 15.
88 Ġazālī, *Lehre von den Stufen zur Gottesliebe*, p. 386.
89 'Aṭṭār, *Muṣībatnāme*, 36/3, quoted in Ritter, *The Ocean of the Soul*, p. 142.
90 Ġazālī, *Lehre von den Stufen zur Gottesliebe*, p. 386.
91 Ibid.
92 *Talbīs*, pp. 416–17, quoted in Ritter, *The Ocean of the Soul*, p. 168.
93 'O Leute, rettet mich vor Gott', p. 25.
94 *In the Garden of Myrtles*.
95 *Studies in Early Mysticism*, esp. pp. 153–243.
96 *La Passion d'al-Hallaj*, esp. vol. 2, and *Essai sur les origines du lexique technique*.
97 *Mystical Dimensions of Islam*, esp. pp. 23–41.
98 Especially *Alte Vorbilder*.
99 In addition to *The Ocean of the Soul*, cited above, see his work on al-Ḥasan al-Baṣrī ('Studien zur Geschichte der islamischen Frömmigkeit').
100 *Qatlā l-Qur'ān*, ch. 6.
101 Schimmel, *Mystical Dimensions of Islam*, p. 119.
102 Reinert, *Die Lehre vom tawakkul*, p. 35.
103 Schimmel, *Mystical Dimensions of Islam*, p. 31.
104 Ġazālī, *Lehre von den Stufen zur Gottesliebe*, p. 611.
105 Quoted ibid., p. 175.
106 Anonymous, *Lebensweise der Könige*, p. 132.
107 *Qatlā l-Qur'ān*, chs 2, 3 and 14.
108 Ibid., ch. 3.
109 Ibid.
110 Ibid.
111 Ibid., ch. 9.
112 Ibid., ch. 10.
113 Ibid., ch. 14.
114 Ibid., ch. 8.
115 Ibid., ch. 15.
116 Abū Nu'aym, *Ḥilyat al-awliyā'*, vol. 9, pp. 385–6; translation quoted here after Andrae, *In the Garden of Myrtles*, trans. Brigitta Sharpe, p. 55.

117 *Iḥyā'*, vol. 1, p. 253.
118 19:85–6 (trans. Arberry).
119 *Qatlā l-Qur'ān*, ch. 12; also in Ġazālī, *Lehre von den Stufen zur Gottesliebe*, p. 384.
120 *Sharḥ*, p. 65; *khabar* here may also mean 'tradition'.
121 *Lehre von den Stufen zur Gottesliebe*, p. 326.
122 Ibid., pp. 328–9.
123 Otto, *The Idea of the Holy*, p. 14. Otto's theory of the holy has stirred passions as few other works in the history of religion in the twentieth century. Gerardus van der Leeuw has aptly described the text and its reception: '*The Idea of the Holy* is one of the oddest books that have ever been written. Organized as an *essay*, ingeniously tossed off, it took on monstrous proportions, both in size (much of it had to be published later as parerga) and in the weight of its subject matter. The more often one reads it (and one cannot help reading it again and again!), the more strikingly the reader notices the inconsistencies, the ambiguities, the anacolutha in the train of thought. The book can well be called a philosophical miscarriage, a psychological aberration or a one-sided history of religion. And it has been called all that. There has even been a whole book of criticism of *The Idea of the Holy*, and that book was a prize-winner. And, although the critic was often right, still one couldn't help feeling that, when kings build, carters are in work. For in spite of its many methodological and logical errors, in spite of its formlessness, *The Idea of the Holy* opened up a new understanding of religion and religious phenomena to the post-war generation, and the book will probably continue to perform that service for many generations to come' ('Rudolf Otto und die Religionsgeschichte', pp. 80–1).
124 See, e.g., Quran 5:83; 16:50; 17:107–9; 35:28; 39:23.
125 See, e.g., Exodus 23:27; Job 9:34, 13:21; Jeremiah 10:10.
126 Otto, *The Idea of the Holy*, p. 12.
127 Ibid., p. 16.
128 Ibid.
129 Ibid., pp. 12–13.
130 Ibid., p. 10.
131 Mann, *Tonio Kröger*, pp. 40–1.
132 Annemarie Schimmel was probably the first to point out the parallels between Otto's theological system and Sufi teaching. According to her, Otto has 'expressed in scientific language a truth that had been known to every Sufi in the world of Islam for centuries' (*Mystical Dimensions of Islam*, p. 44).
133 Otto, *The Idea of the Holy*, p. 13.
134 Anṣārī, *Sharḥ*, p. 65.
135 Ibid.
136 Ibid., p. 66. On the fear of God's malice, see Schimmel, *Mystical Dimensions of Islam*, pp. 127–8.
137 Anṣārī, *Sharḥ*, p. 65.
138 Otto, *The Idea of the Holy*, pp. 11, 21.
139 Ibid., p. 19.
140 7:143 (trans. Arberry).
141 Al-Kubrā, Najmuddīn, *Fāwā'iḥ al-jamāl wa-fawātiḥ al-jalāl*, Wiesbaden, 1957, p. 67 (a non-canonical hadith).
142 Sajjādī, *Farhang*, article 'Khawf'.
143 Ibid.

144 Ġazālī, *Lehre von den Stufen zur Gottesliebe*, p. 384.
145 Ġazālī, *Iḥyā'*, vol. 1, p. 178; also quoted in Makkī, *Die Nahrung der Herzen*, vol. 1, p. 181; 'Umar as-Suhrawardī, *Die Gaben der Erkenntnisse*, p. 41.
146 Quran 7:172.
147 Suhrawardī, *Die Gaben der Erkenntnisse*, p. 41.
148 Ibn 'Arabī, *Futūḥāt*, vol. 1, p. 239.
149 Ibid., vol. 1, p. 237.
150 Quran 22:1.
151 Ibid.
152 Quran 2:22 (trans. Arberry).
153 Ibn 'Arabī, *Futūḥāt*, vol. 1, p. 238.
154 Ibn 'Arabī develops this idea in his *Kitāb al-isfār 'an natā'ij al-asfār*, the 'Book of the unveiling of the results of the journey'; see Chodkiewicz, *An Ocean without Shore*, p. 31.
155 *Iḥyā'*, vol. 1, p. 178.
156 28:30.
157 *Die Gaben der Erkenntnisse*, p. 41.
158 *Futūḥāt*, vol. 1, p. 76/vol. 1, p. 328.
159 Quran 35:28 (trans. Arberry).
160 Otto, *The Idea of the Holy*, p. 31.
161 Sarrāj, *Schlaglichter*, p. 397 (other references there).
162 Otto, *The Idea of the Holy*, p. 31.
163 See, e.g., Hojwīrī, *The Kashf*, pp. 376–7; Ibn 'Arabī, 'On Majesty and Beauty', pp. 6–7. This division reflects a strong tendency in Sufi theory but is not necessarily encountered in this form in every single author. Often the second step of fear, fear of the divine malice, is associated with God's beauty, for example: see the articles 'Khawf', 'Farah', 'Surah', 'Jamāl' and 'Jalāl' in Sajjādī, *Farhang*.
164 10:58 (trans. Arberry); quoted in, e.g., Anṣārī, *Sharḥ*, p. 254.
165 Ḥeydarkhānī, *Samā'-e 'ārefān*, pp. 452ff.; 'Umar as-Suhrawardī, *Die Gaben der Erkenntnisse*, p. 184.
166 *Tafsīr*, commentary on 39:23.
167 The Sufis have held different views on whether *khawf*, *faraḥ*, *rajā'* and other feelings are states (*ḥāl*) or stations (*maqām*): see Schimmel, *Mystical Dimensions of Islam*, p. 127 (where *maqām* is translated as 'station').
168 Ritter, 'Studien zur Geschichte der islamischen Frömmigkeit', p. 14.
169 Bākharzī, *Awrād al-aḥbāb*, p. 348.
170 Ibid., pp. 348–9. On the term *ḥaqq al-yaqīn*, see Schimmel, *Mystical Dimensions of Islam*, p. 142.
171 See Ġazālī, *Lehre von den Stufen zur Gottesliebe*, p. 326.
172 See *Qatlā l-Qur'ān*, ch. 3, episode 2; chs 5 and 16.
173 Anṣārī, *Sharḥ*, p. 65.
174 Quran 7:44 (trans. Arberry).
175 *Qatlā l-Qur'ān*, ch. 3.
176 Otto, *The Idea of the Holy*, pp. 12–13.
177 *The Kashf*, p. 186.
178 Hojwiri, *Kashf*, p. 85.
179 Bākharzī, *Awrād al-aḥbāb*, p. 342. Quoted in many sources, e.g., 'Umar as-Suhrwardī, *Die Gaben der Erkenntnisse*, p. 179; also by the scholar Ibn al-Jawzī, who generally rejects the mystics' *samā'* practice: see *Kitāb al-Quṣṣāṣ*, p. 96.

180 Ġazālī, *Iḥyā'*, vol. 2, p. 182; Qushayrī, *Das Sendschreiben al-Qushayrīs über das Sufitum*, p. 473; Sarrāj, *Schlaglichter*, p. 287; Bākharzī, *Awrād al-aḥbāb*, p. 343.
181 'Ebādī, *At-Taṣfiya fī aḥwāl al-mutaṣawwifa*, p. 219.
182 Bākharzī, *Awrād al-aḥbāb*, p. 343.
183 Schimmel, *Mystical Dimensions of Islam*, pp. 58–9.
184 27:88 (trans. Arberry). Sarrāj, *Schlaglichter*, p. 422; variants in, e.g., Qushayrī, *Das Sendschreiben al-Qushayrīs über das Sufitum*, p. 115, Ġazālī, *Iḥya'*, vol. 2, p. 183; Hojwīrī, *Kashf*, p. 91; Bākharzī, *Awrād al-aḥbāb*, p. 311.
185 *Schlaglichter*, p. 422.
186 Gramlich, *Alte Vorbilder*, vol. 1, p. 486.
187 Quoted after Qushayrī, *Das Sendschreiben al-Qushayrīs über das Sufitum*, p. 476; also in Bākharzī, *Awrād al-aḥbāb*, p. 367; Ġazālī, *Iḥya'*, vol. 2, p. 183; Sarrāj, *Schlaglichter*, p. 420 (other references there); a similar version is found in Umar as-Suhrawardī, *Die Gaben der Erkenntnisse*, p. 183.
188 Quoted in Ġazālī, *Iḥya'*, vol. 2, p. 183; also found in Suhrawardī, *Die Gaben der Erkenntnisse*, p. 184; Bākharzī, *Awrād al-aḥbāb*, pp. 367–8; Sarrāj, *Schlaglichter*, p. 420 (other references there).
189 Suhrawardī, *Die Gaben der Erkenntnisse*, p. 184.
190 *Qatlā l-Qur'ān*, ch. 7.
191 Ibid., ch. 12; Ġazālī, *Lehre von den Stufen zur Gottesliebe*, p. 384.
192 Makkī, *Die Nahrung des Herzens*, vol. 1, p. 188 (other references there).
193 EI[2], 'Madjdkhūb'; Sajjādī, *Farhang*, 'Jaḏbe'.
194 See p. 293 above.
195 'Die schauerliche Öde', p. 438.
196 Otto, *The Idea of the Holy*, pp. 65ff.
197 Ibid., pp. 64–5.
198 Ibid., p. 61.
199 James, *The Varieties of Religious Experience*, quoted in Otto, *The Idea of the Holy*, p. 37.
200 See James, *The Varieties of Religious Experience*, pp. 157–209.
201 Suhrawardī, *Die Gaben der Erkenntnisse*, p. 182.
202 Quoted in Mostamlī-Bohārī, *Sharḥ at-ta'arruf*, p. 52.
203 Ibn 'Arabī, 'On Majesty and Beauty', p. 8; Suhrawardī, *Die Gaben der Erkenntnisse*, pp. 34ff.; Schimmel, *Mystical Dimensions of Islam*, p. 182.
204 Ġazālī, *Iḥyā'*, vol. 1, p. 178. Also quoted in Makkī, *Die Nahrung der Herzen*, vol. 1, p. 188; a similar statement is attributed to Muslim ibn Maymūn al-Khawwāṣ (see p. 172 above).
205 See p. 32 in chapter 1 and also Kermani, 'Katharsis und Verfremdung'.
206 *Qatlā l-Qur'ān*, ch. 9.
207 Otto, *The Idea of the Holy*, p. 31.
208 *Qatlā l-Qur'ān*, ch. 8.
209 *Hilyat al-awliyā*, vol. 4, pp. 164–77, here p. 169.
210 Ġazālī, *Lehre von den Stufen zur Gottesliebe*, pp. 388ff.
211 25:24–6 (trans. Arberry).
212 25:23 (trans. Arberry).
213 *Qatlā l-Qur'ān*, ch. 15. Many authors mention that Abū Juhayr died listening to the Quran. See, e.g., Hojwīrī, *Kashf*, p. 76. Cf. Ġazālī, *Kīmiyā*, p. 148; Sarrāj, *Schlaglichter*, p. 409.
214 Sa'īd, *At-Taġannī*, p. 90.

215 Dārimī, *Sunan*, XXIII/33 (no. 3504).
216 Kulaynī, *Kāfī*, 'Faḍl-al-Qur'ān/Tartīl al-Qur'ān', no. 9; quoted in, e.g., Qushayrī, *Das Sendschreiben al-Qushayrīs über das Sufitum*, p. 464, cf. Bukharī, *Ṣaḥīḥ*, XCVIII/52.
217 Ibn Qayyim al-Jawzīya, *Zād al-ma'ād*, p. 167.
218 Quoted by al-Qurṭubī in the introduction to his *Jāmi'*, vol. 1, p. 11.
219 Nelson, *The Art of Reciting the Qur'an*, p. 99.
220 *Al-Jam' as-sawṭī*, p. 242.
221 *The Art of Reciting the Qur'an*, p. 66; see also ibid., p. 116.
222 Ibid., p. 191.
223 See, e.g., Hojwīrī, *Kashf*, pp. 85ff.; Sarrāj, *Schlaglichter*, pp. 413ff.; Ḥeydarkhānī, *Samā'-e 'ārefān*, pp. 470ff.
224 Sarrāj, *Schlaglichter*, pp. 323–4, 418. Also mentioned in Qushayrī, *Das Sendschreiben al-Qushayrīs über das Sufitum*, p. 422; Bākharzī, *Awrād al-aḥbāb*, p. 316.
225 'Umar as-Suhrawardī, *Die Gaben der Erkenntnisse*, p. 169. Also mentioned in Hojwīrī, *Kashf*, p. 65.
226 Gramlich, *Alte Vorbilder*, vol. 1, p. 529.
227 See pp. 293–4 above.
228 Sarrāj, *Schlaglichter*, p. 419.
229 Quoted after 'Umar as-Suhrawardī, *Die Gaben der Erkenntnisse*, p. 192. As-Suhrawardī does not consider this hadith particularly reliable, although the traditionalists had called it authentic. Bākharzī writes later that the scholars disagreed on the authenticity of the hadith (*Awrād al-aḥbāb*, p. 374); Aḥmad Ṭūsī quotes it with no mention of any doubt (*Al-Hadīya as-sa'dīya*, p. 363).
230 Sarrāj, *Schlaglichter*, pp. 411–12 (other references there). See also Ritter, *The Ocean of the Soul*, p. 530.
231 *Iḥyā'*, vol. 2, p. 180.
232 *Kashf*, p. 64. Aḥmad Jām Žande-Pīl offers a different explanation in his *Uns at-tā'ibīn*, pp. 198–9.
233 Ġazālī, *Iḥyā'*, vol. 2, p. 182; Hojwīrī, *Kashf*, p. 81; 'Ebādī, *Manāqib aṣ-ṣūfīya*, p. 150. The ritual prayer (*ṣalāt*) of Zacharias mentioned in the Quran (3:39), to which the angels listen, is also seen by mystics as exerting an attraction: see Abu Nu'aym, *Ḥilyat al-awliyā'*, vol. 2, p. 320; Gramlich, *Alte Vorbilder*, vol. 1, p. 41.
234 Ritter, *The Ocean of the Soul*, p. 533; cf. Ġazālī, *Iḥyā'*, vol. 2, p. 162.
235 *Kīmiyā*, p. 179; see also *Iḥyā'*, vol. 2, p. 187.
236 Kāshānī, *Miṣbāh al-hidāya*, p. 367.
237 Bubner, *Ästhetische Erfahrung*, p. 35.
238 *Critique of the Power of Judgement*, p. 89.
239 Bubner, *Ästhetische Erfahrung*, p. 36.
240 Quoted in Schimmel, *Mystical Dimensions of Islam*, p. 182.
241 Qushayrī, *Das Sendschreiben al-Qushayrīs über das Sufitum*, p. 467; also mentioned in Ġazālī, *Ihya'*, vol. 2, p. 175; Abū Najīb as-Suhrawardī, *Kitāb ādāb al-murīdīn*, p. 61; Bākharzī, *Awrād al-aḥbāb*, p. 303; Hojwīrī, *Kashf*, p. 82; Farġānī, *Manāhij al-'ibād*; Abar-Qūhī, *Majma' al-Baḥrayn*, p. 271.
242 *Kashf*, p. 84.
243 Ibid.
244 Abū Najīb Suhrawardī, *Kitāb ādāb al-murīdīn*, p. 61; Bākharzī, *Awrād al-aḥbāb*, p. 303.

245 Qushayrī, *Das Sendschreiben al-Qushayrīs über das Sufitum*, p. 478 (other references there).
246 Abū Najīb as-Suhrawardī, *Kitāb ādāb al-murīdīn*, p. 62.
247 *Iḥyā'*, vol. 2, p. 165.
248 Ibid., vol. 2, p. 173. Also mentioned in Qushayrī, *Das Sendschreiben al-Qushayrīs über das Sufitum*, p. 475; Sarrāj, *Schlaglichter*, p. 417.
249 *Iḥyā'*, vol. 2, pp. 172–3; other versions of this story are found in Hojwīrī, *Kashf*, p. 87; Qushayrī, *Das Sendschreiben al-Qushayrīs über das Sufitum*, p. 474; Sarrāj, *Schlaglichter*, pp. 413–14. In *Iḥyā'* (and only there), the name of one of the observers is given as Ibn ad-Darrāj, but it must have been Abū l-Ḥusayn ad-Darrāj, the disciple of Ibrāhīm al-Khawwāṣ.
250 Otto, *The Idea of the Holy*, p. 41, n. 1.
251 Ibid.
252 Erich Rothacker has pointed out that the aesthetic impulse implicitly figures in Otto's own conception, which makes no sense without it: see *Probleme der Kulturanthropologie*, pp. 111ff.
253 'Ebādī, *Manāqib aṣ-ṣūfīya*, p. 150.
254 Sarrāj, *Schlaglichter*, p. 424; emphasis added.
255 Bāḥarzī, *Awrād al-aḥbāb*, p. 341ff.
256 In the mystic understanding, which is founded on the Quran itself (see Kermani, 'Appelliert Gott an den Verstand?', pp. 57ff.), the heart is the organ of a higher kind of knowledge, and 'presence of heart' (*ḥuḍūr al-qalb*) is very important for listening and a deeper understanding of the Quran. See Louis Massignon, *La Passion d'al-Hallaj*, pp. 488ff.; EI^2, 'Kalb'.
257 57:16 (trans. Arberry).
258 This could also be read as *ashkāl* instead of *ishkāl*, in which case his cry would be something like, 'Forms, forms, forms!'
259 *Qatlā l-Qur'ān*, ch. 16.
260 Sarrāj, *Schlaglichter*, p. 393; Bākharzī, *Awrād al-aḥbāb*, p. 366.
261 Sarrāj, *Schlaglichter*, p. 395; Gramlich generally translates the term *wārid* as '*Anwandlung*', 'impulse' or 'mood', which lends it an active sense; literally it means 'penetration', and so signifies a kind of reception.
262 Qushayrī, *Das Sendschreiben al-Qushayrīs über das Sufitum*, p. 467.
263 Ibid., p. 471.
264 Rothacker, *Probleme der Kulturanthropologie*, p. 119.
265 Adorno, *Aesthetic Theory*, p. 457.
266 Ibid., p. 16.
267 Although the concept of truth has become problematic and is little used in major theories of art and perception today (see, e.g., the texts in Barck et al., *Aisthesis*), we cannot abandon it in regard to the reception of the Quran without doing violence to the object of our discussion. For all its affinity with art, the Quran is, in character, in its self-conception and in the minds of its recipients, not a work of art but the revealed text of a religion. Art may be able to do without the concept of truth, but religions cannot. This is why the categories and terminologies of postmodern theories of art are not applicable in reflecting on the Quran, whereas the last great conception of an aesthetics as a philosophy of art that upheld the concept of truth, in and against the tradition of Western bourgeois philosophy, Adorno's *Aesthetic Theory*, can help us better to understand the aesthetic experience of the Quran.
268 *Critique of the Power of Judgement*, pp. 91ff.
269 Ibn 'Arabī, *Futūḥāt*, vol. 3, pp. 93–4.

270 *Critique of the Power of Judgement*, p. 192.
271 *Aesthetic Theory*, p. 457. See also ibid., pp. 120–1.
272 Quran 39:17 (trans. Arberry).
273 Tirmiḏī, *Al-Jāmi'*, XXXIV/7 (no. 2414).
274 Qushayrī, *Das Sendschreiben al-Qushayrīs über das Sufitum*, p. 478.
275 *Aesthetic Theory*, p. 112.
276 Ibid., pp. 363–4.
277 *Awrād al-aḥbāb*, p. 367.
278 *Die Gaben der Erkenntnisse*, p. 38.
279 *The World as Will and Representation*, p. 220.
280 'Kierkegaard', p. 704.
281 Schimmel, *Mystical Dimensions of Islam*, pp. 58–9.
282 *Die Gaben der Erkenntnisse*, p. 181.
283 Abū Nu'aym, *Hilyat al-awliyā'*, vol. 2, p. 321.
284 'Ebādī, *Manāqib aṣ-ṣūfīya*, p. 146.
285 Adorno, *Aesthetic Theory*, p. 70.
286 Quran 55:60. See, e.g., Makkī, *Die Nahrung der Herzen*, vol. 1, pp. 343, 405, 502; Ġazālī, *Lehre von den Stufen zur Gottesliebe*, p. 727.
287 Hojwīrī, *The Kashf*, p. 111.
288 Sarrāj, *Schlaglichter*, p. 395.
289 *Manāqib aṣ-ṣūfīya*, p. 150.
290 18:29 (trans. Arberry).
291 39:53 (trans. Arberry).
292 Ḥeydarkhānī, *Samā'-e 'ārefān*.
293 *Iḥya*, vol. 2, p. 162.
294 *Aesthetic Theory*, p. 16.
295 Ibid., pp. 15–16.
296 Beaudelaire, 'Hymn to Beauty', p. 30. [Original: Tu marches sur des morts, Beauté, dont tu te moques; / De tes bijoux l'Horreur n'est pas le moins charmant, / Et le Meurtre, parmi tes plus chères breloques, / Sur ton ventre orgueilleux danse amoureusement.]
297 See pp. 323ff. above.
298 Adorno, *Aesthetic Theory*, p. 16.
299 Ibid., p. 17.
300 Qushayrī, *Das Sendschreiben al-Qushayrīs über das Sufitum*, p. 469. A similar version is found in Suhrawardī, *Die Gaben der Erkenntnisse*, p. 167.
301 Anonymous, *Lebensweise der Könige*, p. 138.
302 *Aesthetic Theory*, p. 173.
303 *Negative Dialectics*, p. 10.
304 Adorno, *Minima Moralia*, p. 112.
305 *Aesthetic Theory*, p. 16.
306 Anṣāri, *Sharḥ*, p. 58.
307 *Al-Futūḥāt*, vol. 3, p. 128.
308 Cf. Adorno, *Negative Dialectics*, p. 207.
309 *Aesthetic Theory*, p. 93.
310 *Die Gaben der Erkenntnisse*, p. 174.
311 Anṣārī, *Sharḥ*, p. 171.
312 Ritter, *The Ocean of the Soul*, p. 533.
313 Izutsu, 'Paradox of Light and Darkness', pp. 300ff./55ff., and *A Comparative Study of the Key Philosophical Concepts in Sufism and Taoism*, vol. 1, pp. 29ff.

314 See Martin Zenck, *Kunst als begrifflose Erkenntnis: Zum Kunstbegriff der ästhetischen Theorie Adornos*, Munich, 1977, pp. 93ff.
315 Quoted in Schimmel, *Mystical Dimensions of Islam*, p. 182.
316 Ibid.
317 *Diwān-i kabīr*, ed. B. Forūzānfar, 7 vols, Teheran, 1956–, quoted in Schimmel, *Mystical Dimensions of Islam*, p. 183.
318 Nietzsche, 'The Birth of Tragedy', p. 14. This phrase from the 'Foreword to Richard Wagner' in his debut work, *The Birth of Tragedy*, refers initially to art in general, but the subsequent interpretation of Schopenhauer's aesthetics makes plain that music is meant in a particular sense. See also Pothast, *Die eigentlich metaphysische Tätigkeit*, p. 104.
319 Schopenhauer, *The World as Will and Representation*, p. 285.
320 *Kashf*, p. 81.
321 *The World as Will and Representation*, p. 292.
322 Schopenhauer, *On the Metaphysics of the Beautiful*, p. 430.
323 Quoted in Rückert, *Werke*, vol. 2, p. 29.
324 Novalis, *The Novices of Sais*, p. 113.
325 Quran 7:172.
326 Kāshānī, *Miṣbāh al-hidāya*, p. 366. Cf. the versions in Bokhārā'ī, *Al-Kashf fī bayān ḥaqīqat as-samā'*, p. 384; Qushayrī, *Das Sendschreiben al-Qushayrīs über das Sufitum*, p. 466; Suhrawardī, *Die Gaben der Erkenntnisse*, p. 41.
327 *Phaedrus*, 243e–257b.
328 Hegel, *Aesthetics*, vol. 1, p. 111.
329 Schelling, *The Philosophy of Art*, p. 32.
330 Quran 6:30 (trans. Arberry).
331 39:47 (trans. Arberry, modified).
332 *Qatlā l-Qur'ān*, ch. 1.
333 *Samā'-e 'ārefān*, p. 469.
334 Quoted after Qushayrī, *Das Sendschreiben al-Qushayrīs über das Sufitum*; also mentioned, sometimes slightly modified, in Ġazālī, *Iḥya'*, vol. 2, p. 179; 'Ebādī, *Manāqib aṣ-ṣūfīya*, p. 131; Sarrāj, *Schlaglichter*, p. 410.
335 Ḥeydarkhāni, *Samā'-e 'ārefān*, pp. 468–9.
336 Handed down in various forms from several companions of the Prophet. See Wensinck, *Concordance*, vol. 1, p. 373.
337 *Phaedrus*, 246e. Plotinus continues the thought, emphasizing 'that in the Soul's becoming a good and beautiful thing is its becoming like to God' ('Beauty', in *The Enneads*, p. 52). In modern philosophy it is found in Shaftesbury and Boileau (see Cassirer, *The Philosophy of the Enlightenment*, p. 314) and later in Hegel (see *Aesthetics*, vol. 1, p. 111), whose thinking is in many ways Platonic. In the modern era, however, it is not God Who is called beautiful, but Truth.
338 Plato, *The Symposium*, 210e – 212a.
339 Sarrāj, *Schlaglichter*, p. 411.
340 Ibid., p. 151.
341 *Kashf*, p. 73.

References

Where two dates of publication are given, e.g., 1373/1954, the first is the year according to the Islamic Hijri calendar; SH is the solar Hijri calendar.

Abar-Qūhī, Ebrāhīm, *Majma' al-baḥrayn* (excerpt), in Najīb Mayel Harawī (ed.), *Andar ġazal-ekhʷīsh*. Teheran, 1372SH/1993, pp. 291–301.

Abbott, Nabia, *The Rise of the North Arabic Script and its Ḳur'ānic Development, with a Full Description of the Ḳur'ān Manuscripts in the Oriental Institute*. Chicago, 1939.

'Abduh, Muḥammad, and Riḍā, Rashīd, *Tafsīr al-Qur'ān al-ḥakīm ash-shahīr bi-tafsīr al-manār*, 12 vols. 2nd edn, Cairo, 1373–81/1954–61.

'Abduljabbār, Abū l-Ḥasan, *I'jāz al-Qur'ān*. Cairo, 1380/1960.

'Abdurraḥman, 'Ā'isha (Bint ash-Shāṭi'), *Al-I'jāz al-bayānī li-l-Qur'ān wa-masā'il Ibn al-Azraq* [The Quran's nature as a linguistic miracle], Cairo: Dār al-ma'ārif, 1971.

Abel, Armand, 'L'Apologie d'al Kindi et sa place dans la polémique islamo-chrétienne' [The apology of al-Kindi and its place in Islamic-Christian polemics], in *L'Oriente Cristiano nella storia della civiltà*. Rome: Accademia Nazionale dei Lincei, 1964, pp. 501–23.

Abu Deeb, Kamal, 'Al-Jurjānī's Classification of *Isti'āra* with Special Reference to Aristotle's Classification of Metaphor', *Journal of Arabic Literature* 2 (1971), pp. 48–75.

—— *Al-Jurjānī's Theory of Poetic Imagery*. Warminster: Aris & Phillips, 1979.

—— 'Studies in Arabic Literary Criticism: The Concept of Organic Unity', *Edebiyat* 2/1 (1977), pp. 57–90.

—— 'Towards a Structural Analysis of Pre-Islamic Poetry', *International Journal of Middle Eastern Studies* 6 (1975), pp. 148–84.

Abū Nu'aym, Aḥmad ibn 'Abdillāh ibn Aḥmad al-Iṣfahānī, *Ḥilyat al-awliyā*, 10 vols. Cairo, 1351–7/1932–8.

Abū Zahra, Muḥammad, *Al-Mu'jiza al-kubrā: Al-Qur'ān*. Cairo: Dār al-fikr al-'arabī, undated.

Abū Zayd, Naṣr Ḥāmid, *Falsafat at-ta'wīl: Dirāsa fī ta'wil al-Qur'ān 'inda Muḥyīddīn Ibn 'Arabī*. Beirut, 1403/1983.

—— *Ishkālīyāt al-qirā'a wa-ālīyāt at-ta'wīl*. 2nd edn, Beirut, 1412/1992.

—— *Mafhūm an-naṣṣ: Dirāsa fī 'ulūm al-Qur'ān* [The concept of the text: a study of the qur'anic sciences]. Cairo, 1410/1990.

—— *Naqd al-khiṭāb ad-dīnī*. Cairo, 1412/1992 = *Islam und Politik: Kritik des religiösen Diskurses* [Islam and politics: critique of the religious discourse], trans. Chérifa Magdi. Frankfurt am Main, 1996.

Adonis/Adūnīs, *Mihyar of Damascus, His Songs: Poems by Adonis (Ali Ahmad Sa'id)*, trans. Adnan Haydar and Michael Beard. Rochester, NY: BOA, 2008.
—— *Muqaddima li-sh-shiʿr al-ʿarabī* [An introduction to Arabic poetry]. 5th edn, Beirut, 1406/1986.
—— *An-Naṣṣ al-qur'ānī wa-āfāq al-kitāba*. Beirut, 1413/1993.
—— *Ash-Shiʿrīya al-ʿarabīya*. Beirut, 1405/1985.
—— *Aṣ-Ṣūfīya wa-s-sūryālīya* [Sufism and surrealism]. Beirut and London, 1412/1992; Eng. trans. as *Sufism and Surrealism*, trans. Judith Cumberbatch. London: Saqi Books, 2005.
—— *Ath-Thābit wa-l-mutaḥawwil: Baḥth fī l-ittibāʿ wa-l-ibdāʿ ʿinda l-ʿarab* [The fixed and the changing: a study of confirmity and originality in Arab culture], 3 vols. 4th edn, Beirut, 1403/1983.
Adorno, Theodor W., *Aesthetic Theory*, trans. Robert Hullot-Kentor. London and New York: Bloomsbury, 2004.
—— *Introduction to the Sociology of Music*, trans. E. B. Ashton. New York: Continuum, 1988.
—— 'Kierkegaard noch einmal' [Kierkegaard again], in *Gesammelte Schriften*, vol. 2. Frankfurt am Main: Suhrkamp, [1979] 1997.
—— *Metaphysics: Concepts and Problems*, trans. E. F. N. Jephcott. Stanford, CA: Stanford UP, 2002.
—— *Minima Moralia*, trans. E. F. N. Jephcott. London and New York: Verso, 2005.
—— *Negative Dialectics*, trans. E. B. Ashton. New York: Continuum, [1973] 2007.
Ahlwardt, Wilhelm, *Über Poesie und Poetik der Araber* [On the poetry and the poetics of the Arabs]. Gotha, 1856.
Ait el Ferrane, Mohamed, *Die Maʿnā-Theorie bei ʿAbdalqāhir al-Jurjānī (gestorben 471/1079): Versuch einer Analyse der poetischen Sprache*. Frankfurt am Main, 1990.
Albright, William Foxwell, *Yahweh and the Gods of Canaan*. London, 1968.
Aleem, Abdul, 'Iʿjazu 'l-Qur'an', *Islamic Culture* 7 (1933), pp. 64–82, 215–33.
Altoma, Salih J., *Problems of Diglossia in Arabic: A Comparative Study of Classical and Iraqi Arabic*. Cambridge, MA: Harvard UP, 1969.
Amirpur, Katajun, 'Ein iranischer Luther? ʿAbdolkarīm Sorūshs Kritik an der schiitischen Geistlichkeit' [An Iranian Luther? ʿAbdolkarīm Sorūsh's critique of the Shiite clergy], *Orient* 37 (1996), pp. 465–81.
Andrae, Tor, *In the Garden of Myrtles: Studies in Early Islamic Mysticism*, trans. Brigitta Sharpe. Albany: SUNY Press, 1987.
—— 'Die Legenden von der Berufung Muhammads' [The legends of Muhammad's vocation], *Le Monde orientale* 6 (1912), pp. 5–18.
—— *Mohammed: The Man and His Faith*, trans. Theophil Menzel. London: George Allen & Unwin, 1936; repr., New York: Routledge, 2008.
—— *Die Person Muhammeds in Lehre und Glauben seiner Gemeinde* [Muhammad the man in the doctrine and faith of his congregation]. Stockholm, 1918.
Anonymous, *Die Lebensweise der Könige (Adab al-mulūk): Ein Handbuch zur Islamischen Mystik*, trans. and ed. Richard Gramlich. Stuttgart, 1993.
Anṣārī, Khʷāje ʿAbdullāh, *Sharḥ manāzil as-sā'irīn* [Explanation of the stations of the wanderer]. Arabic with Persian commentary throughout by ʿAbdorrazzāq Kāshānī, ed. ʿAlī Shīrwānī. Teheran, 1373/1994.
Antes, Peter, *Prophetenwunder in der Ashʿarīya bis al-Ġazālī (Algazel)* [Miracles of the Prophet in Ash'arism up to al-Ġazālī]. Freiburg im Breisgau, 1969.

—— 'Schriftverständnis im Islam' [The concept of scripture in Islam], *Theologische Quartalschrift* 161 (1981), pp. 179–91.

Anwari-Alhosseyni, Shams, 'Das Kunsthandwerk der persischen Kalligraphie' [The artistic craft of Persian calligraphy], in Werner Diem and Abdoldjavad Falaturi (eds), *XXIV. Deutscher Orientalistentag vom 26. bis 30. September 1988 in Köln: Ausgewählte Vorträge*. Stuttgart, 1990, pp. 581–92.

al-ʿAqqād, ʿAbbās Maḥmūd, *ʿAbqarīyat Muḥammad*. Cairo: Dār al-hilāl, n.d. (*c*. 1382/1962).

Aquinas, Thomas, *Summa Theologica*, vol. 1. 3rd rev. edn, Salzburg and Leipzig, 1934 [Latin and German].

Arafat, W., 'Early Critics of the Authenticity of the Poetry of the Sīra', *Bulletin of the School of Oriental and African Studies*, 21 (1958), pp. 453–63.

Aristotle, *Poetics*, trans. Anthony Kenny. Oxford: OUP, 2013.

Asad, Muhammad, *Kann der Koran übersetzt werden?* [Is the Quran translatable?] Geneva, 1964.

Assmann, Jan, *Cultural Memory and Early Civilization: Writing, Remembrance, and Political Imagination*, Cambridge: CUP, 2011.

—— 'Kollektives Gedächtnis und kulturelle Identität' [Collective memory and cultural identity], in Assmann and Tonio Hölscher (eds), *Kultur und Gedächtnis* [Culture and memory]. Frankfurt am Main, 1988, pp. 9–19.

—— 'Der zweidimensionale Mensch: Das Fest als Medium des kollektiven Gedächtnisses' [The two-dimensional person: the feast as a medium of collective memory], in Assmann and T. Sundermeier (eds), *Das Fest und das Heilige: Religiöse Kontrapunkte zur Alltagswelt*. Gütersloh, 1991, pp. 13–33.

Assmann, Jan, and Assmann, Aleida, 'Schrift, Tradition und Kultur' [Writing, tradition and culture], in Wolfgang Raible (ed.), *Zwischen Festtag und Alltag*. Tübingen: Narr, 1988, pp. 25–49.

Auerbach, Elias, 'Die Prophetie' [Prophecy], in Peter Neumann (ed.), *Das Prophetenverständnis in der deutschsprachigen Forschung*. Darmstadt, 1979, pp. 220–51.

Auerbach, Erich, *Literary Language and its Public in Late Latin Antiquity and in the Middle Ages*, trans. Ralph Mannheim. London: Routledge & Kegan Paul, 1965.

—— *Mimesis: The Representation of Reality in Western Literature*, trans. Willard R. Trask. Princeton, NJ: Princeton UP, 1953.

Augustine of Hippo, *The Confessions of St Augustine*, trans. E. B. Pusey. London: J. M. Dent; New York: Dutton, 1907.

Auld, A. Graeme, 'Prophets through the Looking Glass: Between Writings and Moses', *Journal for the Study of the Old Testament* 27 (1983), pp. 3–23.

Bachern, Rolf, *Dichtung als verborgene Theologie: Ein dichtungstheoretischer Topos vom Barock bis zur Goethezeit und seine Vorbilder*. Bonn, 1956.

Bachmann, Peter, 'Ein Gedicht zur "Sure der Dichter" aus dem "Dīwān" von Ibn al-ʿArabī' [A poem on the surah 'The Poets' from the divan of Ibn al-ʿArabī], *Zeitschrift für arabische Linguistik* 25, pp. 24–49.

Bākharzī, Abū l-Mafāḫer Yaḥyā, *Awrād al-aḥbāb wa-fuṣūṣ al-ādāb* (excerpt), in Najīb Mayel Harawī (ed.), *Andar ġazal-e ḫʷīsh*. Teheran, 1372/1993, pp. 302–21.

Balthasar, Hans Urs von, *Herrlichkeit* [Glory], 3 vols. Einsiedeln, 1961–9.

al-Bāqillānī, Abū Bakr Muḥammad ibn aṭ-Ṭayyib, *Iʿjāz al-Qurʾān* [The miraculous nature of the Quran]. Beirut: ʿĀlam al-kutub, 1988; partial trans. as *A Tenth Century Document of Arabic Literary Theory and Criticism*, trans. Gustave Edmund von Grunebaum. Chicago, 1950.

Barck, Karlheinz et al. (eds), *Aisthesis: Wahrnehmung heute oder Perspektiven einer anderen Ästhetik* [Aisthesis: perception today; or perspectives of a different aesthetics]. Leipzig, 1991.

Barthes, Roland, *On Racine*, trans. Richard Howard. BerkeleyUniversity of California Press, 1992.

—— *The Pleasure of the Text*, trans. Richard Miller. New York: Farrar, Straus & Giroux, 1975.

Baudelaire, Charles, 'Hymn to Beauty', trans. Dorothy Martin, in *The Flowers of Evil*. New York: New Directions, 1955, pp. 30–1.

Bauer, Thomas, *Altarabische Dichtkunst: Eine Untersuchung ihrer Struktur und Entwicklung am Beispiel der Onagerepisode* [Ancient Arabic poetry: a study of its structure and development as reflected in the onager episode], 2 vols. Wiesbaden, 1992.

Baumgartner, Hans Michael, and Korten, Harald, *Friedrich Wilhelm Joseph Schelling*. Munich, 1996.

al-Bayhaqī, Abū Bakr Aḥmad ibn Ḥusayn, *Dalā'il an-nubūwa* [Signs of prophethood], 2 vols, ed. ʿAbdurraḥmān Muḥammad ʿUṯmān. Cairo, 1389/1969.

Beck, Edmund, ''Arabiyya, Sunna und ʿĀmma in der Koranlesung des zweiten Jahrhunderts' [ʿArabiyya, sunna and ʿāmma in second-century Quran reading], *Orientala* n.s. 15 (1947), pp. 180–224.

—— 'Der ʿuṯmānische Kodex in der Koranlesung des zweiten Jahrhunderts' [The Uthmanic codex in second-century Quran reading], *Orientalia* n.s. 14 (1945), pp. 355–73.

Becker, Carl Heinrich, *Islamstudien: Vom Werden und Wesen der islamischen Welt* [Islamic studies: on the development and essence of the Islamic world], vol. 1. Leipzig, 1924; repr. Hildesheim, 1967.

Bell, Richard, 'Mohammed's Call', *Muslim World* 24 (1934), pp. 13–19.

—— 'Muhammad's Visions', *Muslim World* 24 (1934), pp. 145–54.

Bellamy, James A., 'The Impact of Islam on Early Arabic Poetry', in Alfred T. Welch and Pierre Cachia (eds), *Islam, Past Influence and Present Challenge* (*in honor of W. M. Watt*). Edinburgh, 1979, pp. 141–67.

Bello, Iysa A., *The Medieval Islamic Controversy between Philosophy and Orthodoxy: Ijmāʿ and Ta'wīl in the Conflict between al-Ghazālī and Ibn Rushd*. Leiden, 1989.

Bencheikh, J. E., *Poétique arabe: essai sur les votes d'une création*. Paris, 1975.

Benjamin, Walter, *Illuminationen: Ausgewählte Schriften*, vol. 1. Frankfurt am Main, 1974.

—— 'Kierkegaard: The End of Philosophical Idealism', trans. Rodney Livingstone, in *Selected Writings: 1931–1934*. Cambridge, MA: Harvard UP, 2005, pp. 703–5.

—— *Sprache und Geschichte: Philosophische Essays* [Language and history: philosophical essays]. Stuttgart: Reclam, 1992.

—— 'The Task of the Translator', in *Illuminations*, trans. Harry Zohn. New York: Fontana, 1970, pp. 69–82.

Bense, Max, *Hegel und Kierkegaard: Eine prinzipielle Untersuchung* [Hegel and Kierkegaard: a study of principles]. Cologne and Krefeld, 1948.

Bergsträsser, Gotthelf, 'Koranlesung in Kairo' [Quran recitation in Cairo] (with a contribution by K. Huber), *Der Islam* 20 (1932), pp. 1–42; 21 (1933), pp. 110–40.

—— Review of Guidi, *La lotta tra l'Islām e il manicheismo, Islamica* 4 (1931), pp. 295–321.

Berning, Stephan, 'Zur pietistischen Kritik an der autonomen Ästhetik' [On the Pietist critique of autonomous aesthetics], in Helmut Koopmann and Winfried Woesler (eds), *Literatur und Religion*. Freiburg: Herder, 1984, pp. 91–119.

Berque, Jacques, *Relire le Coran* [Re-reading the Quran]. Paris: Albin Michel, 1993.

Bettermann, Wilhelm, *Theologie und Sprache bei Zinzendorf* [Theology and language in Zinzendorf]. Gotha, 1935.

Bijlefeld, Willem A., 'A Prophet and More Than a Prophet? Some Observations on the Qor'anic Use of the Term "Prophet" and "Apostle"', *Muslim World* 59 (1969), pp. 1–28.

Birkenhauer, Klaus, *Beckett*. Reinbek, 1971.

Blachère, Régis, 'La Poésie dans la conscience de la première génération musulmane' [Poetry in the consciousness of the first generation of Muslims], *Annales islamologiques* 4 (1963), pp. 93–103.

Bloch, Alfred, *Vers und Sprache im Altarabischen: Metrische und syntaktische Untersuchungen* [Verse and language in ancient Arabic: studies in metre and syntax]. Basel, 1946.

Bloch, Ernst, *Avicenna und die Aristotelische Linke* [Avicenna and the Aristotelian left]. Frankfurt am Main, 1963.

Bobzin, Hartmut, 'Friedrich Rückert und der Koran', in *Der Koran*, trans. Rückert. Würzburg, 1995, pp. vii–xxxiii.

Boccaccio, Giovanni, *Life of Dante*, trans. Philip Wicksteed. Richmond, Surrey: Oneworld, 2009.

Bohas, Georges, Guillaume, Jean-Patrick, and Kouloughli, Djamel Eddine (eds), *The Arabic Linguistic Tradition*. London and New York, 1990.

Bokhārā'ī, Mas'ūd Bek, *Al-Kashf fī bayān ḥaqīqat as-samā'* (excerpt), in Najīb Mayel Harawī (ed.), *Andar ġazal-e khʷīsh*. Teheran, 1372/1993, pp. 378–88.

Bonebakker, S. A., 'Religious Prejudice against Poetry in Early Islam', *Medievalia et humanistica* n.s. 7 (1976), pp. 93–103.

Borst, Arno, *Der Turmbau von Babel: Geschichte der Meinungen über Ursprung und Vielfalt der Sprachen und Völker* [The tower of Babel: history of opinions on the origin and diversity of languages and peoples], 4 vols. Stuttgart, 1957–63.

Boubakeur, Si Hamza, 'Psalmodie coranique' [Quranic psalmody], in J. Porte (ed.), *Encyclopédie des musiques sacrées*, 4 vols. Paris, 1968–1970, vol. 1, pp. 388–403.

Boullata, Issa J., 'Adonis: Towards a New Arab Culture', *International Journal of Middle Eastern Studies* 20 (1988), pp. 109–12.

—— 'The Rhetorical Interpretation of the Qur'ān: i'jāz and Related Topics', in Andrew Rippin (ed.), *Approaches to the History of the Interpretation of the Qur'an*. Oxford, 1988, pp. 139–57.

Bouman, Johan, *Le Conflit autour du Coran et la solution d'al-Bāqillānī* [The conflict over the Quran and al-Bāquillāni's solution]. Amsterdam, 1959.

—— 'The Doctrine of 'Abd al-Djabbār on the Qur'ān as the Created Word of Allāh', in T. P. van Baaren (ed.), *Verbum: Essays on Some Aspects of the Religious Function of Words, Dedicated to Hendrik Willem Obbink*, Domplein and Utrecht, 1964, pp. 67–86.

Böwering, Gerhard, *The Mystical Vision of Existence in Classical Islam: The Qur'ānic Hermeneutics of the Ṣūfī Sahl At-Tustarī (d. 283/896)*. Berlin and New York, 1980.

Breton, André, *Nadja*, trans. Richard Howard. London: Penguin, 1999.

Brockelmann, Carl, *Geschichte der arabischen Litteratur* [History of Arabic literature]. 2nd edn, vols 1–2, Leiden, 1943–9; supplementary vols 1–3, Leiden, 1937–42.

Brown, Norman, 'The Apocalypse of Islam', in *Apocalypse and/or Metamorphosis*. Berkeley, CA, 1991, pp. 69–94.

Bubner, Rüdiger, *Ästhetische Erfahrung* [Aesthetic experience]. Frankfurt am Main, 1989.

—— 'Die Entdeckung Platons durch Schelling' [Schelling's discovery of Plato], *Neue Hefte für Philosophie* 35 (1995), pp. 32–55.

Büchner, Georg, *Danton's Death, Leonce and Lena, and Woyzeck*, trans. Victor Price. Oxford, 1971.

Buhl, Frants, 'Fasste Muhammed seine Verkündigung als eine universelle, auch für Nichtaraber bestimmte Religion auf?' [Did Muhammad conceive his revelation as a universal religion to include non-Arabs?], *Islamica* 2 (1926), pp. 135–49.

—— *Das Leben Muhammads* [The life of Muhammad], trans. H. H. Schaeder. Leipzig, 1930.

—— 'Über Vergleichungen und Gleichnisse im Qur'ân' [On comparisons and parables in the Quran], *Acta Orientalia* 2 (1924), pp. 1–11; repr. in Rudi Paret, *Der Koran: Kommentar und Konkordanz*. Stuttgart, 1977, pp. 75–85.

al-Bukhārī, Muḥammad ibn Ismāʿīl, *Kitāb al-jāmiʿ aṣ-ṣaḥīḥ*, ed. Ḥasūna al-Nawawī, 9 vols. Cairo, 1378/1958.

Burckhardt, Titus, *The Art of Islam: Language and Meaning*. London, 1976.

—— 'Perennial Values in Islamic Art', *Studies in Comparative Religion* 1 (1967), pp. 132–41.

Bürgel, Johann Christoph, *Allmacht und Mächtigkeit: Religion und Welt im Islam* [Omnipotence and power: religion and the world]. Munich, 1991.

—— '"Die beste Dichtung ist die lügenreichste": Wesen und Bedeutung eines literarischen Streites des arabischen Mittelalters im Lichte komparatistischer Betrachtung' ['The best poetry is the most mendacious': essence and importance of a medieval Arabic literary dispute in the light of a comparative examination], *Oriens* 23–4 (1970–1), pp. 7–102.

Burton, John, *The Collection of the Qur'ān*. Cambridge, 1979.

Bustānī, Maḥmūd, *Eslām wa honar* (*Al-Islām wa-l-fann*), trans. Ḥoseyn Ṣāberī. Teheran, 1371/1992.

Calder, Norman, 'Tafsīr from Ṭabarī to Ibn Kathīr: Problems in the Description of a Genre, Illustrated with Reference to the Story of Abraham', in G. R. Hawting and Abdul-Kader A. Shareef (eds), *Approaches to the Qur'an*. London and New York, 1993, pp. 101–40.

Calvin, John, *Institutes of the Christian Religion*, trans. Henry Beveridge, vol. 1. London, 1949.

Cantarino, Vicente, *Arabic Poetics in the Golden Age*. Leiden, 1975.

Carroll, Robert P., 'Poets not Prophets: A Response to "Prophets through the Looking-Glass"', *Journal for the Study of the Old Testament* 27 (1983), pp. 25–31.

Carter, Michael G., 'Remarks on M. B. Schub: "A Sublime Subtlety"', *Zeitschrift für arabische Linguistik* 7 (1982), pp. 79–81.

Caspar, Robert, 'Parole de Dieu et langage humain en Christianisme et en Islam' [The word of God and human language in Christianity and Islam], *Islamochristiana* 6 (1980), pp. 33–60.

Cassirer, Ernst, *Language and Myth*, trans. Susanne K. Langer. New York: Dover, 1953.

—— *The Philosophy of the Enlightenment*, trans. Fritz C. A. Koelln and James P. Pettegrove. Princeton, NJ, 1951.

Chadwick, Nora Kershaw, *Poetry and Prophecy*. Cambridge, 1975.

Chejne, Anwar, *The Arabic Language: Its Role in History*. Minneapolis, 1969.

Chittick, William C., *The Sufi Path of Knowledge: Ibn al-ʿArabi's Metaphysics of Imagination*. Albany, NY, 1989.

Chodkiewicz, Michel, *An Ocean Without Shore: Ibn Arabi, the Book, and the Law*, trans. Ruth Fisher. New York, 1993.

Chouraqui, André, *Reflexionen über Problematik und Methode der Übersetzung von Bibel und Koran* [Reflections on the problems and methods of translating the Bible and the Quran], ed. Luise Abramowski. Tübingen, 1994.

Colpe, Carsten, 'Das Siegel der Propheten' [The seal of the prophets], *Orientalia Suecana* 33–5 (1984–6), pp. 71–83.

Cragg, Kenneth, *The Call of the Minaret*. New York, 1956.

—— *The Event of the Qur'ān: Islam in its Scripture*. London, 1971; repr. Oxford, 1994.

—— *The Mind of the Qur'ān: Chapters in Reflection*. London, 1973.

—— *Readings in the Qur'ān*. London, 1988.

Crapon de Caprona, Pierre, *Le Coran: aux sources de la parole oraculaire: structure rythmiques des sourates mecquoises* [The Quran: at the source of oracular speech: rhythmic structures of the Meccan surahs]. Paris, 1981.

Curtius, Ernst Robert, *European Literature and the Latin Middle Ages*. Princeton, NJ, 2013.

ad-Dārimī, Abū Muḥammad ʿAbdullāh ibn ʿAbdurraḥmān, *Sunan ad-Dārimī*, ed. As-Sayyid ʿAbdullāh Hāshim Yamānī al-Madanī, 2 vols. Medina, 1386/1966.

Davidson, Herbert Allen, *Alfarabi, Avicenna, and Averroes on Intellect: Their Cosmologies, Theories of the Active Intellect, and Theories of Human Intellect*. New York and Oxford, 1992.

Ḍayf, Shawqī, *Al-Fann wa-maḏāhibuhū fī sh-shiʿr al-ʿarabī*. 11th edn, Cairo: Dār al-maʿārif, n.d.

Decker, Bruno, *Die Entwicklung der Lehre von der prophetischen Offenbarung von Wilhelm von Auxerre bis zu Thomas von Aquin* [The development of the doctrine of prophetic revelation from William of Auxerre to Thomas Aquinas]. Breslau, 1940.

Denny, Frederick Mathewson, 'The *Adab* of Qur'an Recitation: Text and Context', in A. H. Johns (ed.), *International Congress for the Study of the Qur'an, Australian National University, Canberra, 8–13 May 1980*. Canberra, 1981, pp. 143–60.

—— 'Exegesis and Recitation: Their Development as Classical Forms of Qur'ānic Piety', in Frank E. Reynolds and Theodore M. Ludwig (eds), *Transitions and Transformations in the History of Religion: Essays in Honor of Joseph M. Kitagawa*. Leiden, 1980, pp. 91–123.

—— 'Islamic Ritual: Perspectives and Theories', in Richard C. Martin (ed.), *Approaches to Islam in Religious Studies*. Tucson, AZ: 1985, pp. 63–77.

—— 'Qur'ān Recitation: A Tradition of Oral Performance and Transmission', *Oral Tradition* 4 (1989), pp. 5–26.

Diem, Werner, *Hochsprache und Dialekt im Arabischen: Untersuchungen zur heutigen arabischen Zweisprachigkeit* [Standard language and dialect in Arabic: investigations of contemporary Arabic diglossia]. Wiesbaden, 1974.

Dieterich, Albrecht, *Eine Mithrasliturgie* [A Mithraic liturgy]. 2nd edn, Leipzig and Berlin, 1910.

Dilthey, Wilhelm, 'Johann Georg Hamann', in Reiner Wild (ed.), *Johann Georg Hamann*. Darmstadt, 1978, pp. 44–90.

Donaldson, Bess Allen, 'The Koran as Magic', *Muslim World* 27 (1937), pp. 254–66.

Düsing, Klaus, 'Schellings Genieästhetik' [Schelling's aesthetics of genius], in Annemarie Gethmann-Siefert (ed.), *Philosophie und Poesie: Otto Pöggeler zum 60. Geburtstag*, 2 vols. Stuttgart, 1988, vol. 1, pp. 193–213.

Dyck, Joachim, *Athen und Jerusalem: Die Tradition der argumentativen Verknüpfung von Bibel und Poesie im 17. und 18. Jahrhundert* [Athens and Jerusalem: the tradition of argumentative linking of the Bible and poetry in the 17th and 18th centuries]. Munich, 1977.

ʿEbādī, Qoṭbeddīn Abū l-Moẓaffar Manṣūr ebn Ardeshīr, *Manāqib aṣ-ṣūfīya* [Virtues of Sufism]. Teheran, 1362/1983.

—— *'At-Taṣfiya fī aḥwāl al-mutaṣawwifa'* (excerpt), in Najīb Mayel Harawī (ed.), *Andar ġazal-e khʷīsh*. Teheran, 1372/1993, pp. 215–20.

Eco, Umberto, *The Open Work*, trans. Anna Cancogni. Cambridge, MA: Harvard UP, 1989.

—— *Opera aperta: forma e indeterminazione nelle poetiche contemporanee* [The open work: form and indeterminacy in contemporary poetics]. Milan: Bompiani, 1993.

—— *The Search for the Perfect Language*, trans. James Fentress. Oxford: Blackwell, 1995.

—— *La struttura assente: la ricerca semiotica e il metodo strutturale* [The absent structure: semiotic studies and the structural method]. Milan: Bompiani [1968] 1994.

Eichendorff, Joseph von, *Werke in einem Band* [Works in one volume], ed. Wolfdietrich Rasch. Munich, 1985.

Eichhorn, Johann Gottfried, *Einleitung in das Alte Testament* [Introduction to the Old Testament], 5 vols. Göttingen, 1823–4.

Eichler, Paul Arno, *Die Dschinn, Teufel und Engel im Koran* [The jinn, devils and angels in the Quran]. Dissertation, Leipzig, 1929.

Eickelman, Dale F., 'The Art of Memory: Islamic Education and its Social Reproduction', *Comparative Studies in Society and History* 20 (1978), pp. 485–516.

Eliade, Mircea, and Couliano, Ioan P., *Handbuch der Religionen* [Guide to religions]. Zurich and Munich, 1991.

Endress, Gerhard, 'Die arabische Schrift' [The Arabic script], in Wolfdietrich Fischer (ed.), *Grundriss der arabischen Philologie* [Outline of Arabic Philology]. Wiesbaden, 1982, vol. 1, pp. 165–84.

Fahd, Toufic, *La Divination arabe: études réligieuses, sociologiques et folkloriques sur le milieu natif de l'Islam* [Arab divination: religious, sociological and folkloristic studies on the native environment of Islam]. Leiden, 1966.

—— 'Les Songes et leur interprétation selon l'Islam' [Dreams and their interpretation according to Islam], in A.-M. Esnoul, P. Garelli et al. (eds), *Les Songes et leur interprétation* [Dreams and their interpretation]. Paris: Seuil, 1959, pp. 125–57.

al-Fārābī, Abū Naṣr, *Al-Farabi on the Perfect State: Abū Naṣr al-Fārābī's Mabādi' ārā' ahl al-madīna al-fāḍila*, in Arabic and English, trans. and ed. Richard Walzer. Oxford, 1985.

—— *Alfārābīs Abhandlung Der Musterstaat* [Al-Fārābī's treatise 'The Model State' = *Mabādi' ārā' ahl al-madīna al-fāḍila*], ed. Friedrich Dieterici. Hildesheim, 1985.
—— 'The Philosophy of Plato' [= *Falsafat Aflāṭūn*], trans. Muhsin Mahdi, in al-Fārābī, *Alfarabi's Philosophy of Plato and Aristoteles*. New York, 1962, pp. 53–67.
Farġānī, Sa'īd, *Manāhij al-'ibād* (excerpt), in Najīb Mayel Harawī (ed.), *Andar ġazal-e khīsh*. Teheran, 1372/1993, pp. 265–73.
Farmer, Henry George, *A History of Arabian Music to the XIIIth Century*. London, 1973.
—— 'The Religious Music of Islam', *Journal of the Royal Asiatic Society* (1952), pp. 60–5.
Farrukh, Omar A., *Das Bild des Frühislam in der arabischen Dichtung von der Hijra bis zum Tode 'Umars* [The image of early Islam in Arabic poetry from the hijra to the death of 'Umar]. Dissertation, Erlangen, 1937.
al-Fārūqī, Lamyā', 'Die islamische Kunst: Eine Einführung' [Islamic art: an introduction], in Bayerische Landeszentrale für Politische Bildungsarbeit (ed.), *Weltmacht Islam*. Munich, 1988, pp. 561–73.
—— 'Qur'ān Reciters in Competition in Kuala Lumpur', *Ethnomusicology* 31 (1987), pp. 221–8.
—— 'Tartīl al-Qur'ān al-Karīm', in Khurschid Ahmad and Zafar Ishaq Ansari (eds), *Islamic Perspectives: Studies in Honour of Mawlānā Sayyid Abul A'lā Mawdūdī*. Leicester, 1979, pp. 105–19.
Fazlī, 'Abdolhādī, *Tārīh-e qerā'āt-e Qor'ān-e karīm*, ed. Seyyed Moḥammad Bāqer Hojjatī. Teheran, 1373/1994.
Ferguson, Charles A., 'The Arabic Koine', *Language* 35 (1959), pp. 616–30.
—— 'Diglossia', *Word* 15 (1959), pp. 325–40.
Fierro Bello, M. I., 'The Treatises against Innovations (*Kutub al-bida'*)', *Der Islam* 69 (1992), pp. 204–46.
Fischer, August, *Der 'Koran' des Abu l-'Alā' al-Ma'arrī* [The 'Quran' of Abu l-'Alā' al-Ma'arrī]. Leipzig, 1942.
—— '*Majnūn* "epileptisch"' [*Majnūn* in the sense of 'epileptic'], *Zeitschrift der Deutschen Morgenländischen Gesellschaft* 62 (1908), pp. 151–4.
—— *Der Wert der vorhandenen Koran-Übersetzungen und Sure 111* [The value of the existing Quran translations and Surah 111]. Leipzig, 1937.
Fischer, Wolfdietrich, 'Das Altarabische in islamischer Überlieferung: Das klassische Arabisch' [Ancient Arabic in Islamic tradition: classical Arabic], in Fischer (ed.), *Grundriss der arabischen Philologie* [Outline of Arabic philology]. vol. 1, Wiesbaden, 1982, pp. 37–50.
Frick, Heinrich, *Vergleichende Religionswissenschaft* [Comparative religious studies]. Berlin and Leipzig, 1928.
Fricke, Harald, 'Rückert und das Kunstlied: Literaturwissenschaftliche Beobachtungen zum Verhältnis von Lyrik und Musik' [Rückert and the art song: literary observations on the relation between lyric poetry and music], in H. Bobzin, W. Fischer anad M.-R. Uhrig (eds), *Rückert-Studien*. Wiesbaden, 1990, vol. 5, pp. 14–37.
Frye, Northrop, *Anatomy of Criticism*. Princeton, [1957] 2000.
—— *The Great Code: The Bible and Literature*. New York and London, 1982.
Fück, Johann, *Arabiya: Untersuchungen zur arabischen Sprach- und Stilgeschichte* [Arabiya: historical studies on Arabic language and style]. Berlin, 1950.
Gabrieli, Francesco, 'Religious Poetry in Early Islam', in Gustave von Grunebaum, *Arabic Poetry: Theory and Development*. Wiesbaden, 1973, pp. 5–17.

Gadamer, Hans-Georg, *Truth and Method*, trans. Joel Weinsheimer and Donald G. Marshall. 2nd edn, London: Bloomsbury, 2004.

al-Ġazālī, Abū Ḥāmid Muḥammad, *Iḥyā' 'ulūm ad-dīn* [The revival of the religious sciences], 4 vols. Cairo, 1358/1939.

—— *Kīmiyā* [*Kīmyāyé Sa'ādat*] [a shorter version, in Persian, of *Iḥyā'*]; Eng. trans. as *The Alchemy of Happiness*, trans. Claud Field. New York: Cosimo, 2007.

—— *Kitāb al-ḥyawān*, ed. 'Abdussalām Muḥammad Hārūn, 8 vols. Cairo, n.d.

—— *Mal-Munqiḏ min aḍ-ḍalāl* [The rescuer from error]. Beirut, 1389/1969.

—— *Muḥammad al-Ġazālīs Lehre von den Stufen zur Gottesliebe: Die Kapitel 31–36 seines Hauptwerkes*, trans. Richard Gramlich. Wiesbaden, 1984 [a partial German translation of *Iḥyā'*].

—— *Tahāfut al-falāsifa* [The incoherence of the philosophers], ed. Maurice Bouyges. Beirut, 1927.

Geertz, Clifford, 'Art as a Cultural System', *Modern Language Notes* 91 (1976), pp. 1490–9.

—— *Islam Observed: Religious Development in Morocco and Indonesia*. Chicago, 1971.

Geiger, Abraham, *Judaism and Islam: A Prize Essay*, trans. F. M. Young. Madras, 1898.

Geller, Stephen A., 'Were the Prophets Poets?', *Prooftexts* 3 (1983), pp. 211–21.

Geyer, Rudolf, 'The Strophic Structure of the Koran', in Ibn Warraq (trans. and ed.), *What the Koran Really Says*. Amherst, NY: Prometheus Books, 2002, pp. 635–46.

Gipper, Helmut, *Gibt es ein sprachliches Relativitätsprinzip? Untersuchungen zur Sapir–Whorf-Hypothese* [Is there a linguistic relativity principle? Studies on the Sapir–Whorf hypothesis]. Frankfurt am Main, 1972.

Goethe, Johann Wolfgang von, *West–East Divan*, trans. Martin Bidney and Peter Anton von Arnim. Albany: SUNY Press, 2010.

Goitein, Shlomo D., *Studies in Islamic History and Institutions*. Leiden, 1966.

Goldammer, Kurt, *Die Formenwelt des Religiösen: Grundriß der systematischen Religionswissenschaft* [The world of religion forms: outline of systematic religious studies]. Stuttgart, 1960.

Goldberg, Arnold M., *Untersuchungen über die Vorstellung von der Schckhinah in der frühen rabbinischen Literatur: Talmud und Midrasch* [Studies in the concept of shekhinah in early rabbinical literature: the Talmud and the Midrash]. Berlin, 1969.

Goldfeld, Isaiya, 'The Illiterate Prophet (*nabī ummī*): An Inquiry into the Development of a Dogma in Islamic Tradition', *Der Islam* 57 (1980), pp. 58–67.

Goldziher, Ignaz [Ignác], *Abhandlungen zur arabischen Philologie* [Discourses on Arabic philology], vol. 1. Leiden, 1896.

—— *Gesammelte Schriften* [Collected writings], 6 vols, ed. Joseph Desomogyi. Hildesheim, 1967–73.

—— 'Die Ginnen der Dichter', *Zeitschrift der Deutschen Morgenländischen Gesellschaft* 45 (1891), pp. 685–90.

—— *Muslim Studies*, 2 vols, trans. C. R. Barber and S. M. Stern, ed. S. M. Stern. London: George Allen & Unwin, 1971.

—— *Schools of Koranic Commentators*, trans. and ed. Wolfgang Behn. Wiesbaden: Harrassowitz, 2006.

—— 'Verheimlichung des Namens' [Concealing one's name], *Der Islam* 17 (1928), pp. 1–3.

—— *Vorlesungen über den Islam* [Lectures on Islam]. Rev. edn, Heidelberg, 1925.
Graf, Georg, *Geschichte der christlichen arabischen Literatur* [History of Christian Arabic literature], 5 vols. Vatican City, 1944–53.
Graham, William A., *Beyond the Written Word: Oral Aspects of Scripture in the History of Religion*. Cambridge, 1987.
—— *Divine Word and Prophetic Word in Early Islam: A Reconsideration of the Sources, with Special Reference to the Divine Saying or Ḥadīth Qudsī*. The Hague and Paris, 1977.
—— 'The Earliest Meaning of '"Qur'ān"', *Die Welt des Islams* 23–4 (1984), pp. 361–77.
—— 'The *Qur'ān* as Spoken Word: An Islamic Contribution to the Understanding of Scripture', in Richard C. Martin (ed.), *Approaches to Islam in Religious Studies*. Tucson, AZ: 1985, pp. 23–40.
—— 'Das Schriftprinzip in vergleichender Sicht' [The scriptural principle in a comparative perspective], in Alma Giese and J. Christoph Bürgel (eds), *Gott ist schön und Er liebt die Schönheit* [God is beautiful and He loves beauty]. Bern, 1994, pp. 209–26.
Gramlich, Richard, *Alte Vorbilder des Sufitums* [Early paragons of Sufism], 2 vols. Wiesbaden, 1995.
—— *Die schiitischen Derwischorden Persiens* [The Shiite dervish orders in Persia], 3 vols. Wiesbaden, 1965–81.
—— 'Der Urvertrag in der Koranauslegung' [The Adamic covenant in Quran exegesis], *Der Islam* 60 (1983), pp. 205–30.
—— *Die Wunder der Freunde Gottes: Theologien und Erscheinungsformen des islamischen Heiligenwunders* [The miracles of God's friends: theologies and forms of Islamic miracles of the saints]. Wiesbaden, 1987.
Grimme, Hubert, *Mohammed*, 2 vols. Münster, 1892.
Gronke, Monika, 'Lebensangst und Wunderglaube: Zur Volksmentatlität im Iran der Mongolenzeit' [Fear of life and belief in miracles: on the Iranian national mentality in the Mongol period], in Werner Diem and Abdoldjavad Falature (eds), *XXIV. Deutscher Orientalistentag vom 26 bis 30 September 1988 in Köln*. Stuttgart, 1990, pp. 391–9.
Grotzfeld, Heinz, 'Der Begriff der Unnachahmlichkeit des Korans in seiner Entstehung und Fortbildung' [The concept of the inimitability of the Quran in its origins and development], *Archiv für Begriffsgeschichte* 13 (1969), pp. 58–72.
Grunebaum, Gustave von, 'Introduction: The Cultural Function of the Dream as Illustrated by Classical Islam', in Gustave von Grunebaum and Roger Caillois, *The Dream and Human Societies*. Berkeley, CA, 1966, pp. 3–21.
—— *Kritik und Dichtkunst: Studien zur arabischen Literaturgeschichte* [Criticism and poetic art: studies on Arabic literary history]. Wiesbaden, 1955.
—— *Medieval Islam: A Study in Cultural Orientation*. Chicago, 1946.
—— 'Von Muhammads Wirkung' [On Mohammed's influence], *Wiener Zeitschrift für die Kunde des Morgenlandes* 44 (1937), pp. 38–40.
—— See also under al-Bāqillānī.
Grünert, Max T., *Die Imâla: Der Umlaut im Arabischen* [Imāla: the vowel shift in Arabic]. Vienna, 1876.
Guardini, Romano, *Pascal for Our Time*, trans. Brian Thompson. New York, 1966.
Guillaume, Alfred, *Prophecy and Divination among the Hebrews and Semites*. London, 1938.

Guth, Stephan, '*Fa-ġrawraqat ʿuyūnuhum bi-d-dumūʿ*: Some Notes on the Flood of Tears in Early Modern Arabic Prose Literature', in Lutz Edzard and Christian Szyska (eds), *Encounters of Words and Texts: Intercultural Studies in Honor of Stefan Wild on the Occasion of His 60th Birthday*. Hildesheim and Zurich, 1997, pp. 111–23.

Gutzen, Dieter, *Poesie der Bibel: Beobachtungen zu ihrer Entdeckung und ihrer Interpretation im 18. Jahrhundert*. Dissertation, Bonn, 1972.

Hāfeẓ [Hafiz], Moḥammad Shamsoddīn, *Gedichte aus dem Diwan* [Poems from the divan], ed. Johann Christoph Bürgel. Stuttgart, 1980.

—— *Ghaselen* [Gazels], trans. Friedrich Rückert. Zurich, 1988.

Hagemann, Ludwig, *Propheten: Zeugen des Glaubens: Koranische und biblische Deutungen*. Würzburg, 1993.

Halbwachs, Maurice, *The Collective Memory*, New York: Harper & Row, 1980.

—— *On Collective Memory*. Chicago, 1992.

Haleem, M. A. S. Abdel (trans.), *The Qur'an: A New Translation*. Oxford: OUP, 2004.

al-Ḥallāj [Al-Halladsch], Al-Ḥusayn ibn Manṣūr, *'O Leute, rettet mich vor Gott': Worte verzehrender Gottessehnsucht* ['O people, save me from God': words of consuming longing for God], trans. and ed. Annemarie Schimmel. Freiburg, 1985.

Hamadānī, Rafīʿoddīn Esḥāq ebn-e Moḥammad, *Sīrat-e rasūl Allāh*, ed. Jaʿfar Modarres Ṣādeqī. Teheran, 1373/1994.

Hamann, Johann Georg, 'Aesthetica in Nuce: A Rhapsody in Cabbalistic Prose', in Hamann, *Writings on Philosophy and Language*, trans. and ed. Kenneth Haynes. Cambridge: CUP, 2007.

—— *Sämtliche Werke: Historisch-kritische Ausgabe* [Complete works: historical and critical edition], 6 vols, ed. Joseph Nadler. Vienna, 1949–57.

Hämeen-Antilla, Jaako, '"We Will Tell You the Best of Stories": A Study on Sura XII', *Studie Orientalia* 67 (1991), pp. 7–32.

Harawī, Najīb Mayel, *Andar ġazal-e khʷīsh-e khʷīsh nehān khʷāham gashtan: Samāʿ-nāmehā-ye fārsī*. Teheran, 1372/1993.

Hartmann-Schmidt, Angelika, *Die Zahl Sieben im sunnitischen Islam* [The number seven in Sunni Islam]. Dissertation, Frankfurt am Main, 1989.

Hauser, Arnold, *Sociology of Art*, trans. Kenneth J. Northcott. Abingdon: Routledge, 2011.

Haykal, Muḥammad Ḥusayn [Muhammad Hussain Haikal], *Das Leben Muhammads* [The life of Muhammad], trans. S. M. Bleher. Siegen, 1987.

—— *The Life of Muhammad*, trans. Isma'il Ragi A. al Faruqi. Petaling Jaya: Islamic Book Trust, 2008.

Hegel, Georg Wilhelm Friedrich, *Aesthetics: Lectures on Fine Art*, trans. T. M. Knox, 2 vols. Oxford, 1975.

Heiler, Friedrich, *Erscheinungsformen und Wesen der Religion* [Manifestations and essence of religion]. Stuttgart, 1961.

Heinrichs, Wolfhart, *Arabische Dichtung und griechische Poetik: Ḥāzim al-Qarṭājannīs Grundlegung der Poetik mit Hilfe aristotelischer Begriffe* [Arabic poetry and Greek poetics: Ḥāzim al-Qarṭā-jannī's foundations of poetics in Aristotelian terms]. Beirut, 1969.

—— 'Contacts between Scriptural Hermeneutics and Literary Theory in Islam: The Case of *Majāz*', *Zeitschrift für Geschichte der arabisch-islamischen Wissenschaften* 7 (1991–2), pp. 253–84.

—— 'Literary Theory: The Problem of its Efficiency', in Gustave von Grunebaum, *Arabic Poetry: Theory and Development*. Wiesbaden, 1973, pp. 19–69.

—— '"Manierismus" in der arabischen Literatur' ['Mannerism' in Arabic literature], in Richard Granmlich (ed.), *Islamwissenschaftliche Abhandlungen: Fritz Meier zum 60. Geburtstag* [Treatises in Islamic studies in honour of Fritz Meier's 60th birthday]. Wiesbaden, 1974, pp. 118–28.

—— 'The Meaning of *Mutanabbī*', in James Kugel (ed.), *Poetry and Prophecy: The Beginnings of a Literary Tradition*. Ithaca, NY, 1991, pp. 120–39.

—— 'Poetik, Rhetorik, Metrik und Reimlehre', in Helmut Gätje (ed.), *Grundriss der arabischen Philologie* [Outline of Arabic philology], vol. 2: *Literaturwissenschaft*. Wiesbaden, 1987, pp. 177–207.

Henninger, Joseph, 'Geisterglaube bei den vorislamischen Arabern' [Belief in ghosts among pre-Islamic Arabs], in Henninger, *Arabia Sacra*. Freiburg, 1981, pp. 118–69.

Herder, Johann Gottfried, 'On the Cognition and Sensation of the Human Soul', trans. Michael N. Forster, in Herder, *Philosophical Writings*. Cambridge: CUP, 2002, pp. 187–246.

—— *On the Origin of Language*, in Herder and Jean-Jacques Rousseau, *On the Origin of Language*, trans. Alexander Code. Chicago and London, 1986, pp. 84–166.

—— *The Spirit of Hebrew Poetry*, trans. James Marsh, 2 vols. Burlington, VT, 1833.

—— *Vom Geist der Ebräischen Poesie: Eine Anleitung für die Liebhaber derselben, und der ältesten Geschichte des menschlichen Geistes*, in *Werke*, vol. 5: *Schriften zum Alten Testament*, pp. 661–1308, ed. Rudolf Smend. Frankfurt am Main, 1993.

Hesse, Hermann, *Lektüre für Minuten: Neue Folge* [Readings for minutes: new series], ed. Volker Michels. Frankfurt am Main, 1975.

—— *Steppenwolf*, trans. David Horrocks. London: Penguin, 2012.

Ḥeydarkhānī, Ḥoseyn, *Samāʿ-e ʿārefān: Bakhshī kāmel wa-farāgīr pīrāmūn-e samāʿ*. Teheran, 1374/1995.

Hitti, Philip K., *History of the Arabs: From the Earliest Times to the Present*. London and New York, 1958.

Hodgson, Marshall G. S., 'Une comparaison entre l'islam et le christianisme en tant que structures de la vie religieuse' [A comparison between Islam and Christianity as structures of religious life], *Diogène* 32 (1960), 60–89.

—— *Venture of Islam*, vol. 1: *The Classical Age of Islam*. Chicago, 2009.

Hoeps, Reinhard, *Bildsinn und religiöse Erfahrung* [Pictorial sense and religious experience]. Frankfurt am Main, 1984.

Hoerburger, Felix, 'Gebetsruf und Qor'an-Rezitation in Kathmandu (Nepal)' [The call to prayer and Quran recitation in Katmandu, Nepal], *Baessler-Archiv* n.f. 23 (1975), pp. 121–37.

—— *Volksmusik in Afghanistan, nebst einem Exkurs über Qor'an-Rezitation in Kabul* [Folk music in Afghanistan, with an excursus on Quran recitation in Kabul]. Regensburg, 1969.

Hojwīrī Ġaznawī, ʿAlī ebn ʿOsmān Jollābī, *Kashf al-maḥjūb* (excerpt), in Najīb Mayel Harawī (ed.), *Andar ġazal-e khʷīsh*. Teheran, 1372/1993, pp. 71–95.

—— *The Kashf al-Mahjúb: The Oldest Persian Treatise on Sufism*, trans. Reynold A. Nicholson. London, 1959.

Hölderlin, Friedrich, 'As on a Holiday …', in *Selected Poems and Fragments*, trans. Michael Hamburger, ed. Jeremy Adler. London: Penguin, 1998, pp. 175–7.

Holenstein, Elmar, 'Einführung: Von der Poesie und der Plurifunktionalität der Sprache' [Introduction: on poetry and the plurifunctionality of language], in Roman Jakobson, *Poetik: Ausgewählte Aufsätze 1921–1971*, ed. Elmar Holenstein and Tarcisius Schelbert. 3rd edn, Frankfurt am Main, 1993.

Holl, Karl, *Gesammelte Aufsätze zur Kirchengeschichte* [Collected essays on Church history], vol. 1: *Luther*. 6th edn, Tübingen, 1932.

Horkheimer, Max, and Adorno Theodor W., *Dialectic of Enlightenment: Philosophical Fragments*, ed. Gunzelin Schmid Noerr, trans. Edmund Jephcott. Palo Alto, CA: Stanford UP, 2002.

Horovitz, Josef, *Koranische Untersuchungen* [Quranic studies]. Berlin and Leipzig, 1926.

Horten, Max, *Texte zu dem Streite zwischen Glauben und Wissen im Islam: Die Lehre vom Propheten und der Offenbarung bei den islamischen Philosophen Farabi, Avicenna und Averroes* [Texts on the dispute between faith and knowledge in Islam: the doctrine of the Prophet and the revelation in the Islamic philosophers Al-Farabi, Avicenna and Averroes]. Bonn, 1913.

Ḥusayn, Ṭāhā, *Fī sh-shi'r al-jāhilī*. Cairo, 1926; repr. in *Al-Qāhira* 149 (April 1995), pp. 23–81.

al-Ḥusaynī, Sayyid Ja'far, *Asālīb al-bayān fī l-Qur'ān*. Teheran, 1363/1984.

Ibn 'Arabī, Muḥyīddīn, *Al-Futūḥāt al-makkīya* [The Meccan revelations], 4 vols. Cairo 1329/1911; new edn, ed. 'Uthmān Yaḥyā, Cairo 1392–/1972–.

—— 'On Majesty and Beauty: The *Kitāb al-Jalāl wa-l-jamāl* of Muhyiddin Ibn 'Arabī', *Journal of the Muhyiddin Ibn 'Arabī Society* 8 (1989), pp. 5–29.

Ibn Baṭṭūṭa, Muḥammad ibn 'Abdillāh, *Travels of Ibn Baṭṭūṭa*, ed. Sir Hamilton Gibb, 3 vols. London and Cambridge 1956–71.

Ibn Fāris, Abū l-Ḥusayn Aḥmad, *Aṣ-Ṣāḥibī fī fiqh al-luġā wa-sunan al-'arab fī kalāmihā*, ed. Muṣṭafā sh-Shuwaymī. Beirut, 1383/1963.

Ibn al-Farrā', Al-Qāḍī Abū Ya'lā, *Kitāb al-mu'tamad fī uṣūl ad-dīn*, ed. Wādī Z. Ḥaddād. Beirut, 1394/1974.

Ibn al-Jawzī, 'Abdurraḥmān, *Kitāb al-quṣṣāṣ wa-l-muḏakkirīn*, ed. Merlin L. Swartz. Beirut, 1391/1971.

Ibn Jubayr [Ibn Dschubair], Muḥammad ibn Aḥmad, *Tagebuch eines Mekkapilgers* [Diary of a Mecca pilgrim], trans. Regina Günther. Stuttgart, 1985.

Ibn Ḥajar al-'Asqalānī, Aḥmad ibn 'Alī, *Fatḥ al-bārī bi-sharḥ ṣaḥīḥ al-Bukhārī*, 13 vols + 1, ed. 'Abdul'azīz ibn 'Abdillāh ibn Bāz, Fu'ād 'Abdulbāqī and Muḥibbuddīn al-Khaṭīb. Beirut: Dār al-ma'rifa, n.d.

Ibn Ḥanbal, Aḥmad ibn Muḥammd, *Al-Musnad*, ed. Aḥmad Muḥammad Shākir, 15 vols. Cairo, 1375/1956.

Ibn Hishām, Abū Muḥammad 'Abdulmalik, *As-Sīra an-nabawīya*, 2 vols, ed. Muṣṭafā s-Saqqā, Ibrāhīm al-Abyārī and 'Abdulḥafīẓ Shalabī. Cairo, 1355/1937; repr. Beirut: Dār al-ma'rifa, n.d. [= Ibn Isḥāq, Muḥammad, *The Life of Muhammad: A Translation of Isḥāq's* Sīrat Rasūl Allāh, trans. Alfred Guillaume. London, 1955].

Ibn Kathīr, Abū l-Fidā' Ismā'īl, *As-Sīra an-nabawīya*, 4 vols, ed. Muṣṭafā 'Abdulwāḥid. Beirut, 1407/1987.

Ibn Khaldūn, Abdurraḥmān ibn Muḥammad, *Al-Muqaddima*, ed. Ḥujar 'Āṣī. Beirut, 1404/1984; Eng. trans. as *The Muqaddimah: An Introduction to History*, 3 vols, trans. Franz Rosenthal. New York, 1958.

Ibn Māja, Abū 'Abdillāh Muḥammad ibn Yazīd al-Qazwīnī, *Sunan*, ed. Muḥammad Fu'ād 'Abdulbāqī. Cairo: Dār iḥyā' al-kutub al-'arabīya, 1371/1952.

Ibn Manẓūr al-Ifrīqī al-Miṣrī, Abū l-Faḍl Gamāluddīn Muḥammad ibn Mukarram, *Lisān al-'arab*, 15 vols. Beirut, 1375/1956.

Ibn al-Mu'tazz, 'Abdullāh, *Kitāb al-badī'*, ed. Ignatius Kratchkovsky. London, 1935.

Ibn Qayyim al-Jawzīya, Shamsuddīn Abū 'Abdillāh Muḥammad, *Aṭ-Ṭuruq al-ḥukmīya fī s-siyāsa ash-shar'īya*, ed. Muḥammad Muḥyīddīn 'Abdulḥamīd. Cairo, 1380/1961.

—— *Zād al-ma'ād fī hudā khayr al-'ibād*, 2 vols, ed. Ṭaha 'Abdurru'ūd Ṭaha. Cairo, 1390/1970.

Ibn Qutayba, Abū Muḥammad 'Abdullāh ibn Muslim, *Al-Ma'ārif*, ed. Muḥammad Ismā'īl 'Abdullāh aṣ-Ṣawt. Beirut 1390/1970.

—— *Ash-Shi'r wa-shu'arā'*, 2 vols. Beirut: Dār ath-thaqāfa, n.d.

—— *Ta'wīl mushkil al-Qur'ān*, ed. Aḥmad Saqr. Cairo: Dār iḥyā' al-kutub al-'arabīya, *c.* 1373/1954.

Ibn Rashīq, Abū 'Alī al-Ḥasan, *Al-'Umda fī maḥāsin ash-shi'r*, ed. Muḥammad Muḥyīddīn 'Abdulḥamīd, 2 vols. 4th edn, Beirut, 1392/1972.

Ibn Sa'd, Muḥammad, *Aṭ-Ṭabaqāt al-kubrā* (*Biographien Muhammeds, seiner Gefährten und der späteren Träger des Islams bis zum Jahre 230 der Flucht*), ed. Eduard Sachau et al., 9 vols. Leiden, 1905–17.

Ibn Sallām, Abū 'Ubayd al-Qāsim, *Faḍā'il al-Qur'ān*, ed. Wahbī Sulaymān Khāwajī. Beirut: Dār al-kutub al-'ilmīya, 1411/1991.

Iser, Wolfgang, 'Die Appellstruktur der Texte' [The appeal structure of texts], in Rainer Warning (ed.), *Rezeptionsästhetik* [Reception aesthetics]. 4th edn, Munich, 1993, pp. 228–52.

—— 'Die Wirklichkeit der Fiktion', in Rainer Warning (ed.), *Rezeptionsästhetik* [Reception aesthetics]. 4th edn, Munich, 1993, pp. 277–324.

'Iyāḍ al-Yaḥṣubī, Al-Qāḍī Abū l-Faḍl, *Muhammad, Messenger of Allah: Ash-Shifa of Qadi 'Iyad*, trans. Aisha Abdurrahman Bewley. Granada: Madinah Press, 1992.

—— *ash-Shifā' bi-ta'rīf ḥuqūq al-muṣṭafā*, 2 vols in 1. Beirut: Dār al-kutub al-'ilmīya, n.d.

Izutsu, Toshihiko, *A Comparative Study of the Key Philosophical Concepts in Sufism and Taoism*, 2 vols. Tokyo 1966–7.

—— *God and Man in the Koran: Semantics of the Koranic Weltanschauung*. New York, 1980.

—— *Language and Magic: Studies in the Magical Function of Speech*. Tokyo, 1956.

—— 'Paradox of Light and Darkness in the *Garden of Mystery* of Shabestari', in Joseph P. Strelka (ed.), *Anagogic Qualities of Literature*. London, 1971, pp. 288–307; repr. in Izutsu, *Creation and the Timeless Order of Things: Essays in Islamic Mystical Philosophy*. Ashland, OR, 1994, pp. 38–65.

Jacobi, Renate, 'Die Altarabische Dichtung (6.–7. Jahrhundert)' [Ancient Arabic poetry (6th–7th centuries)], in Helmut Gätje (ed.), *Grundriss der arabischen Philologie* [Outline of Arabic philology], vol. 2: *Literaturwissenschaft*. Wiesbaden, 1987, pp. 20–31.

—— 'Die Anfänge der arabischen Ġazalpoesie: Abū Ḏu'aib al-Huḏalī' [The origins of Arabic Ġazal poetry: Abū Ḏu'aib al-Huḏalī], *Der Islam* 61 (1984), pp. 218–50.

—— 'Dichtung und Lüge in der arabischen Literaturtheorie' [Poetry and lies in Arabic literary theory], *Der Islam* 49 (1972), pp. 85–99.

al-Jāḥiẓ, Abū ʿUthmān ʿAmr ibn Baḥr, *Arabische Geisteswelt: Ausgewählte und übersetzte Texte von al-Jāḥiẓ (777–869)* [The Arabian intellectual world: selected and translated texts by al-Jāḥiẓ (777–869)], ed. Charles Pellat, trans. Walter W. Müller. Zurich and Stuttgart, 1967.

—— *Hujaj an-nubūwa*, in *Rasāʾil al-Jāḥiẓ*, 4 vols, ed. ʿAbdussalām Muḥammad Hārūn. Cairo, 1399/1979, vol. 3, pp. 223–81.

Jakobson, Roman, 'Linguistics and Poetics', in Jakobson, *Language in Literature*. Cambridge, MA: Harvard UP, 1987, pp. 62–94.

—— 'On Linguistic Aspects of Translation', in Jakobson, *Language in Literature*. Cambridge, MA: Harvard UP, 1987, pp. 428–35.

—— 'What is Poetry?', in Jakobson, *Language in Literature*. Cambridge, MA: Harvard UP, 1987, pp. 368–78.

James, William, *The Varieties of Religious Experience*. Cambridge, MA: Harvard UP, 1985.

Jansen, J. J. G., *The Interpretation of the Koran in Modern Egypt*. Leiden, 1974.

Jauss [Jauß], Hans Robert, *Aesthetic Experience and Literary Hermeneutics*, trans. Michael Shaw. Minneapolis: University of Minnesota Press, 1982.

—— 'Literary History as a Challenge to Literary Theory', in Jauss, *Toward an Aesthetic of Reception*, trans. Timothy Bahti. Minneapolis: University of Minnesota Press, 1982, pp. 3–45.

Jedin, Hubert, *Geschichte des Konzils von Trient*, vol. 3. Freiburg im Breisgau, 1970.

Jeffery, Arthur, *The Qur'ān as Scripture*. New York, 1952.

Johns, A. H., 'The Quranic Presentation of the Joseph Story: Naturalistic or Formulaic Language', in G. R. Hawting and Abdul-Kader A. Shareef (eds), *Approaches to the Qur'an*. London and New York, 1993, pp. 37–70.

Jomier, Jacques, *Le Commentaire coranique du Manâr: tendances modernes de l'exégèse coranique en Egypte*. Paris, 1954.

—— *L'Islam vécu en Égypte (1945–1975)* [Islam as it is lived in Egypt (1945–1975)]. Paris, 1994.

—— 'La Place du Coran dans la vie quotidienne en Égypte' [The position of the Quran in Egyptian day-to-day life], *Institut des Belles Lettres Arabes* [Tunis] 15 (1952), pp. 131–65; repr. in Jomier, *L'Islam vécu en Égypte*. Paris, 1994, pp. 185–219.

al-Jurjānī, ʿAbdulqāhir, *Asrār al-balāgha* (= The Mysteries of Eloquence of ʿAbdalqāhir al-Jurjānī), ed. Hellmut Ritter. Istanbul, 1954.

—— *Dalāʾil al-iʿjāz fī l-Qurʾān* [Arguments of the inimitability of the Quran], ed. Muḥammad ʿAbduh and Rashīd Riḍā. Beirut: ʿĀlain al-kutub, 1414/1994.

—— *Die Geheimnisse der Wortkunst des ʿAbdalqāhir al-Curcānī* [ʿAbdalqāhir al-Jurjānī's mysteries of eloquence], trans. Hellmut Ritter. Wiesbaden, 1959.

Juynboll, G. H. A., *The Authenticity of the Tradition Literature: Discussions in Modern Egypt*. Leiden, 1969.

—— 'The Position of Qur'an Recitation in Early Islam', *Journal of Semitic Studies* 19 (1974), pp. 240–51.

—— 'The Qur'ān Reciter on the Battlefield and Concomitant Issues', *Zeitschrift der Deutschen Morgenländischen Gesellschaft* 125 (1975), pp. 11–27.

—— 'The Qurrā' in Early Islamic History', *Journal of the Economic and Social History of the Orient* 16 (1973), pp. 113–29.

Kadkanī, Moḥammad Reżā Shafīʿī, *Musiqī-ye sheʿr*. Paris, 1368/1989.

Kafka, Franz, *Letters to Milena*, trans. Philip Boehm. New York: Schocken, 1990.

—— 'The Silence of the Sirens', in Kafka, *The Great Wall of China*, trans. Willa Muir and Edwin Muir. New York: Schocken, 1970.

Kahle, Paul, 'The Arabic Readers of the Qur'an', *Journal of Near Eastern Studies* 8 (1949), pp. 65–71.

—— 'The Qur'an and the 'Arabiya', in E. S. Löwinger and J. Somogyi (eds), *Ignace Goldziher Memorial Volume*, vol. 1. Budapest, 1948, pp. 163–82.

Kanazi, George J., *Studies in the* Kitāb aṣ-Ṣināʿatayn of *Abū Hilāl al-ʿAskarī*. Leiden, 1989.

Kandil, Lamya, 'Schwüre in den mekkanischen Suren' [Oaths in the Meccan surahs], in Stefan Wild (ed.), *The Qur'an as Text*. Leiden, 1996, pp. 41–57.

—— *Untersuchungen zu den Schwüren im Koran unter besonderer Berücksichtigung ihrer literarischen Relevanz für die Surenkomposition* [Studies of the oaths in the Quran with particular regard to their literary relevance in the composition of the surahs]. Dissertation, Bonn, 1996.

Kant, Immanuel, *Anthropology from a Pragmatic Point of View*, trans. and ed. Robert B. Louden. Cambridge: CUP, 2006.

—— *Critique of the Power of Judgement*, trans. and ed. Paul Guyer. Cambridge: CUP, 2000.

Kantorowicz, Ernst H., *The King's Two Bodies: A Study in Mediaeval Political Theology*. Princeton, NJ, 1997.

Kāshānī, ʿAbdorrazzāq. See under Anṣārī.

Kāshānī, ʿIzzuddīn Maḥmūd, *Miṣbāh al-hidāya wa-miftāḥ al-kifāya* (excerpt), Persian trans. Shādrawān Jalāloddīn Homāʾī, in Najīb Mayel Harawī (ed.), *Andar ġazal-e khʷīsh*. Teheran, 1372/1993, pp. 363–74.

Kaye, Alan S., 'Review Article: More in Diglossia in Arabic', *International Journal of Middle Eastern Studies* 6 (1975), pp. 325–40.

Kellermann, Andreas, *Koranlesung im Maghreb* [Quran reading in the Maghreb]. Dissertation, Berlin, 1996.

Kermani, Navid, 'Appelliert Gott an den Verstand? Eine Randbemerkung zum koranischen Begriff *ʿaql* und seiner Paret'schen Übersetzung' [Does God appeal to reason? A gloss on the Quranic term *ʿaql* and its translation by Paret], in Lutz Edzard and Christian Szyska (eds), *Encounters of Words and Texts: Intercultural Studies in Honor of Stefan Wild on the Occasion of His 60th Birthday*. Hildesheim and Zurich, 1997, pp. 43–66.

—— 'Katharsis und Verfremdung im schiitischen Passionsspiel' [Catharsis and alienation in the Shiite passion play], *Die Welt des Islams* 39/1 (1999), pp. 31–63.

—— *Offenbarung als Kommunikation: Das Konzept waḥy in Naṣr Ḥāmid Abū Zayds Mafhūm an-naṣṣ* [Revelation as communication: the concept of *waḥy* in Naṣr Ḥāmid Abū Zayd's *Mafhūm an-naṣṣ*]. Frankfurt am Main: Peter Lang, 1996.

Khalafallāh, Muḥammad, ''Abdalqâhir's Theory in His "Secrets of Eloquence": A Psychological Approach', *Journal of Near Eastern Studies* 14 (1955), pp. 164–7.

—— *Al-Fann al-qaṣaṣī fī l-Qur'ān al-karīm*. Cairo, 1372/1953.

Khalidi, Tarif (trans.), *The Qur'an: A New Translation*. London: Penguin, 2009.

Khalifa, Rashad, *Quran: Visual Presentation of the Miracle*. Tucson, AZ, 1982.

Khan, Muḥammad Rahatullah, *Vom Einfluß des Qur'āns auf die arabische Dichtung* [On the influence of the Quran on Arabic poetry]. Dissertation, Leipzig, 1938.

al-Khaṭṭābī, Abū Sulaymān Ḥamd ibn Muḥammad ibn Ibrāhīm, *Bayān iʿjāz al-Qur'ān*, in Muḥammad Khalafallāh and Muḥammad Zaġlūl Salām (eds), *Thalāth rasāʾil fī iʿjāz al-Qur'ān*. 2nd edn, Cairo, 1388/1968, pp. 19–72; French

trans. as *Al-Khaṭṭābī et l'inimitabilité du Coran: traduction et introduction au Bayān i'jāz al-Qur'ān*, trans. Claude-France Audebert. Damascus, 1402/1982.
Khayrallah, As'ad, 'Prophetic Vision in Modern Arabic Poetry', *Zeitschrift der Deutschen Morgenländischen Gesellschaft*, supplement 3, 2. Freiburg, 1975, pp. 700–8.
Khorramshāhī, Bahā'oddīn, *Qor'ān-pažūhī: Haftād baḥs wa-taḥqīq-e qor'ānī*. Teheran, 1372/1993.
—— *Qor'an-shenākht: Mabāḥesī dar farhang-āfannī-ye Qor'ān*. Teheran, 1375/1996.
al-Khūlī, Amīn, *Manāhij tajdīd fī n-naḥw wa-l-balāġa wa-t-tafsīr wa-l-adab*. Cairo, 1380/1961.
Kierkegaard, Søren, *The Book on Adler* (*Writings*, vol. 24), trans. Howard V. Hong and Edna H. Hong. Princeton, NJ, 1998.
—— 'Of the Difference Between a Genius and an Apostle', in *The Present Age and Of the Difference Between a Genius and an Apostle*, trans. Alexander Dru. London, 1962.
Kiessig, Martin (ed.), *Dichter erzählen ihre Träume: Selbstzeugnisse deutscher Dichter aus zwei Jahrhunderten* [Poets recount their dreams: personal testimony of German poets from two centuries]. Düsseldorf and Cologne, 1964.
al-Kindī, 'Abdulmasīḥ ibn Isḥāq, *The Apology of al-Kindy, Written at the Court of Al Mâmûn (circa a.h. 215; a.d. 830), in Defence of Christianity against Islam: With an Essay on its Age and Authorship Read Before the Royal Asiatic Society*, trans. William Muir. 2nd edn, London, 1887.
Kister, M. J., *Studies in Jāhiliyya and Early Islam*. London, 1980.
Kittel, Gerhard Friedrich (ed.), *Theologisches Wörterbuch zum Neuen Testament* [Theological lexicon of the New Testament], 10 vols. Stuttgart, 1933–78.
Klabund [Alfred Henschke], *Mohammed: Roman eines Propheten* [Mohammed: novel of a prophet], in *Romane der Leidenschaft*. Leipzig, 1990, pp. 65–113.
Kleist, Heinrich von, 'The Puppet Theatre', trans. David Constantine, in *Selected Writings*, London, 1997, pp. 411–16.
Klemperer, Victor, *The Language of the Third Reich: LTI – Lingua Tertii Imperii*, trans. Martin Brady. London and New York: Continuum, 2006.
Klopstock, Friedrich Gottlieb, *Ausgewählte Werke* [Selected works], ed. K. A. Schleiden. Munich, 1962.
Koch, Klaus, *Die Propheten* [The prophets], vol. 1: *Assyrische Zeit* [The Assyrian era]. 3rd rev. edn, Stuttgart, 1995.
Kott, Jan, *Shakespeare Our Contemporary*. New York: Norton, 1974.
Kovalevskaya, Sofya, *A Russian Childhood*, trans. and ed. Beatrice Stillman. New York: Springer, 1978.
Kratschkovsky, Ignats, 'Die arabische Poetik im IX. Jahrhundert' [Arabic poetics in the ninth century], *Le Monde orientale* 23 (1929), pp. 23–39.
Kraus, Karl, *Magie der Sprache* [The magic of language]. Frankfurt am Main, 1982.
—— *Die Sprache* [Language]. Frankfurt am Main, 1997.
—— *Über die Sprache* [On language]. Frankfurt am Main, 1982.
Kraus, Paul, 'Beiträge zur islamischen Ketzergeschichte' [Studies on the history of heresy in Islam], *Rivista degli studi orientali* 14 (1933), pp. 335–79.
Kremer, Alfred Freiherr von, *Über die philosophischen Gedichte des Abū-l-'Alā Ma'arry: Eine culturgeschichtliche Studie*. Vienna, 1888
Kugel, James, 'David the Prophet', in Kugel (ed.), *Poetry and Prophecy: The Beginnings of a Literary Tradition*. Ithaca, NY, 1991, pp. 45–55.
—— *The Idea of Biblical Poetry: Parallelism and its History*. New Haven, CT, 1981.

—— 'On the Bible and Literary Criticism', *Prooftexts* 1 (1981), pp. 217–36.

Kuhn, Helmut, *Schriften zur Ästhetik* [Writings on aesthetics]. Munich, 1966.

al-Kulaynī, Abū Ja'far Muḥammad ibn Ya'qūb ibn Isḥāq, *Gozīde-ye Kāfī*. Arabic and Persian, ed. K. Moḥammad Bāqer Behbūdī, 6 vols. Teheran, 1363/1984.

—— *Al-Kafī fī 'ilm ad-dīn*, ed. 'Alī Akbar Jaffārī, 7 vols. Teheran, 1372/1993.

Lanczkowski, Günter, *Sacred Writings: A Guide to the Literature of Religions*. New York: Harper & Row, 1966.

Lane, Edward William, *Selections of the Ḳur-án with an Interwoven Commentary*. London, 1843.

Lari, Sayyid Mujtaba Musavī [Sayyed Mojtabā Mūsawī Lārī], *The Seal of the Prophets and his Message*. Potomac, MD: Islamic Education Center, 1989.

Larkin, Margaret, 'The Inimitability of the Qur'an: Two Perspectives', *Religion and Literature* 20 (1988), pp. 31–47.

—— *The Theology of Meaning: 'Abd al-Qāhir al-Jurjānī's Theory of Discourse*. New Haven, CT, 1995.

Leggewie, Claus, 'Der Dichter als Prophet: Salman Rushdies jüngste Wende' [The poet as prophet: Salman Rushdie's latest turnaround], *Blätter* 8 (1991), pp. 1125–37; quoted in Leggewie, *Alhambra: Der Islam im Westen* [Alhambra: Islam in the West], Reinbek, 1993, pp. 77–91.

Lehmann, Manfred,'Biblical Oaths', *Zeitschrift für die alttestamentliche Wissenschaft* 81 (1969), pp. 74–92.

Lenz, Jakob Michael Reinhold, *Notizen und Fragmente aus der Zeit in Straßburg, Weimar und der Schweiz* [Notes and fragments from his time in Strasbourg, Weimar and Switzerland], in *Gesammelte Schriften* [Collected writings], ed. Franz Blei. Munich and Leipzig, 1910, vol. 4, pp. 281–91.

Lessenich, Rolf P., *Dichtungsgeschmack und althebräische Bibelpoesie im 18. Jahrhundert: Zur Geschichte der englischen Literaturkritik*. Cologne and Graz, 1967.

Lewis, Bernard, *The Arabs in History*. 2nd edn, London, 1954.

Lewis, I. M., *Ecstatic Religion*. Baltimore, 1971.

Lichtenstädter, Ilse, 'Origins and Interpretation of Some Koranic Symbols', in George Makdisi (ed.), *Arabic and Islamic Studies in Honor of Hamilton A. R. Gibb*. Leiden, 1965, pp. 426–36.

Lilje, Hans, *Luther*. Reinbek, 1965.

Lings, Martin, *The Quranic Art of Calligraphy and Illumination*. London, 1976.

Lohmann, Theodor, 'Die Gleichnisreden Muhammeds im Koran' [Mohammed's parables in the Quran], *Mitteilungen des Instituts für Orientforschung* 12 (1966), pp. 75–118, 241–87.

Lory, Pierre, *Les Commentaires ésotériques du Coran d'après 'Abd ar Razzâq al-Qashânî* [The esoteric commentaries on the Quran after *'Abd ar Razzāq al-Qashānī*]. Paris, 1980.

Lotman, Yuri M., *The Structure of the Artistic Text*, trans. Gail Lenhoff and Ronald Vroon. Ann Arbor, MI, 1977.

Luther, Martin, *Werke: Kritische Gesamtausgabe* [Works: complete critical edition]. Weimar, 1883–; repr. Weimar, 1966–.

McAuliffe, Jane Dammen, 'Quranic Hermeneutics: The Views of al-Ṭabarī and Ibn Kathīr', in Andrew Rippin (ed.), *Approaches to the History of the Interpretation of the Qur'an*. Oxford, 1988, pp. 46–62.

al-Maḥallī, Jalāluddīn, and as-Suyūṭī, Jalāluddīn, *Tafsīr al-jalālayn*. Beirut: Dār al-Qalam, n.d.

Maḥfūẓ, Najīb [Naguib Mahfouz], *Echoes of an Autobiography*, trans. Denys Johnson-Davies. New York: Doubleday, 1997.

al-Makkī, Muḥammad ibn ʿAlī Abū Ṭālib, *Die Nahrung der Herzen* [The nourishment of hearts], trans. Richard Gramlich, 4 vols. Stuttgart, 1992–5.

Mann, Thomas, *Doctor Faustus*, trans. H. T. Lowe-Porter. London: Vintage, 1999.

—— *Tonio Kröger*, trans. David Luke, in *Death in Venice, Tonio Kröger, and Other Writings*, ed. Frederick A. Lubich. New York: Continuum, [1999] 2003, pp. 1–55.

Massignon, Louis, *Essai sur les origines du lexique technique de la mystique musulmane* [Essay on the origins of the technical vocabulary of Muslim mysticism]. Paris, 1954.

—— *La Passion d'al-Hosayn-Ibn-Mansour al-Hallaj, martyr mystique de l'Islam, exécuté a Bagdad le 26 Mars 922: étude d'histoire religieuse* [The passion of Al-Husayn Ibn Mansur al-Hallaj, mystic martyr of Islam, executed March 26, 922, at Baghdad], 2 vols. Paris, 1922; repr. in 4 vols, Paris, 1976.

—— *Situation de l'Islam* [The situation of Islam]. Paris, 1939.

Mazraani, Nathalie, *Aspects of Language Variation in Arabic Political Speech*. Richmond, Surrey: Curzon, 1997.

Medicus, Fritz, *Grundfragen der Ästhetik: Vorträge und Abhandlungen*. Jena, 1917.

Meier, Fritz, 'The Dervish Dance: An Attempt at an Overview', trans. John O'Kane, in Meier, *Essays on Islamic Piety and Mysticism*. Leiden: Brill, 1999, pp. 23–48.

—— 'Some Aspects of Inspiration by Demons in Islam', in Gustave von Grunebaum and Roger Caillois, *The Dream and Human Societies*. Berkeley, CA, 1966, pp. 421–9.

—— *Vom Wesen der islamischen Mystik* [On the essence of Islamic mysticism]. Basel, 1943.

Menninghaus, Winfried, *Walter Benjamins Theorie der Sprachmagie*. Frankfurt: Suhrkamp, 1995.

Mir, Mustansa, 'The Qur'an as Literature', *Religion and Literature* 20 (1988), pp. 49–64.

Monroe, James, 'Oral Composition in Pre-Islamic Poetry', *Journal of Arabic Literature* 3 (1972), pp. 1–53.

Moraes, Vinicius de, *Saravá: Gedichte und Lieder*. Portuguese and German, trans. and ed. Kay-Michael Schreiner. Munich, 1989.

Morris, Charles William, *Signs, Language and Behavior*. New York: Braziller, 1955.

Mostamlī-Bohārī, Abū Ebrāhīm ebn Moḥammad, *Sharḥ at-taʿarruf li-maḏhab attaṣawwuf* (excerpt), in Najīb Mayel Harawī (ed.), *Andar ġazal-e khʷīsh*. Teheran, 1372/1993, pp. 47–57.

Moṭahharī, Mortażā, *Waḥy wa-nobūwat*. 2nd edn, Qom, 1357/1978.

Mukařovský, Jan, *Aesthetic Function, Norm and Value as Social Facts*, trans. Mark E. Suino. Ann Arbor, MI, 1979.

—— *On Poetic Language*, trans. and ed. John Burbank and Peter Steiner. Lisse: Peter de Ridder Press, 1976.

—— 'The Place of the Aesthetic Function among the Other Functions', in *Structure, Sign and Function: Selected Essays by Jan Mukařovský*, trans. and ed. John Burbank and Peter Steiner. New Haven, CT, and London, 1978, pp. 31–48.

—— 'Poetic Designation and the Aesthetic Function of Language', in Mukařovský, *The Word and Verbal Art*, trans. and ed. John Burbank and Peter Steiner. New Haven, CT, 1977, pp. 65–73.

—— 'Structuralism in Aesthetics and Literary Studies', trans. Olga Peters Hasty, in *The Prague School: Selected Writings, 1929–1946*, ed. Peter Steiner. Austin: Texas UP, 1982, pp. 65–82.

—— 'Über die gegenwärtige Poetik' [On contemporary poetics], in Mukařovský, *Studien zur strukturalistischen Ästhetik und Poetik*, trans. Herbert Grönebaum and Gisela Riff. Munich: Hanser, 1974, pp. 84–99.

—— 'Zum Begriffssystem der tschechoslovakischen Kunsttheorie' [On the conceptual system of Czechoslovakian art theory], in Mukařovský, *Studien zur strukturalistischen Ästhetik und Poetik*, trans. Herbert Grönebaum and Gisela Riff. Munich: Hanser, 1974, pp. 7–19.

Müller, Friedrun R., *Untersuchungen zur Reimprosa im Koran* [Studies on rhymed prose in the Quran]. Bonn, 1969.

Müller, Gottfried, *Ich bin Labīd und das ist mein Ziel: Zum Problem der Selbstbehauptung in der altarabischen Qaside* [I am Labīd and that is my goal: on the problem of self-assertion in the ancient Arabic qasida]. Wiesbaden, 1981.

Müller, Kathrin, *'Und der Kalif lachte, bis er auf den Rücken fiel': Ein Beitrag zur Phraseologie und Stilkunde des klassischen Arabischen* ['And the caliph laughed until he fell over backwards': a study of the phraseology and stylistics of classical Arabic]. Munich, 1993.

Muranyi, Miklos, 'Neue Materialien zur *tafsīr*-Forschung in der Moscheebibliothek von Qairawān' [New materials for *tafsīr* research in the library of the Qairawān mosque], in Stefan Wild (ed.), *The Qur'an as Text*. Leiden, 1996, pp. 225–55.

Muslim ibn al-Ḥajjāg al-Qushayrī an-Naysābūrī, Abū l-Ḥusayn, *Ṣaḥīḥ Muslim*, ed. Muḥammad Fu'ād 'Abdulbāqī, 5 vols. Cairo, 1374/1955.

Myers, Jacob M., *The Linguistic and Literary Form of the Book of Ruth*. Leiden, 1955.

Nadler, Josef, *Johann Georg Hamann 1730–1788: Der Zeuge des Corpus mysticum* [Johann Georg Hamann, 1730–1788: the witness of the corpus mysticum]. Salzburg, 1949.

Nagel, Ivan, *Autonomy and Mercy: Reflections on Mozart's Operas*, trans. Marion Faber and Ivan Nagel. Cambridge, MA, 1991.

Nagel, Tilman, *Der Koran: Einführung, Texte, Erläuterungen* [The Quran: introduction, texts and explanations]. Munich, 1983.

—— 'Medinensische Einschübe in mekkanische Suren: Ein Arbeitsbericht' [Medinan insertions in Meccan surahs: a report], in Stefan Wild, *The Qur'an as Text*. Leiden, 1996, pp. 59–68.

Nagy, Gregory, 'Ancient Greek Poetry, Prophecy, and Concepts of Theory', in James Kugel (ed.), *Poetry and Prophecy: The Beginnings of a Literary Tradition*. Ithaca, NY, 1991, pp. 56–64.

Nänny, Max, 'Moderne Dichtung und Mündlichkeit' [Modern poetry and orality], in Wolfgang Raible (ed.), *Zwischen Festtag und Alltag*. Tübingen, 1988, pp. 215–29.

Narshakhī, Muḥammad, *The History of Bukhara*, trans. Richard N. Frye. Cambridge, MA, 1954.

Nasafī, 'Azīz, *Ādāb-e taṣawwof* (excerpt), in Najīb Mayel Harawī (ed.), *Andar ġazal-e khīsh*. Teheran, 1972/1993, pp. 258–9.

Nasr, Seyyed Hoseyn, *Ideals and Realities of Islam*. Boston, 1972.

—— *Islamic Art and Spirituality*. Ipswich, 1987.

—— 'Oral Transmission and the Book in Islamic Education: The Spoken and the Written Word', *Journal of Islamic Studies* 3 (1992), pp. 1–14.

an-Nawawī ad-Dimashqī, Abū Zakarīyā Yaḥyā, *At-Tibyān fī ādāb ḥamalat al-Qur'ān*, ed. 'Abdulqādir al-Arnā'ūṭ. 3rd edn, Kuwait, 1409/1988.

Nelson, Kristina, *The Art of Reciting the Qur'an*. Austin, TX, 1985.

—— 'Reciter and Listener: Some Factors Shaping the Mujawwad Style of Qur'anic Recitation', *Ethnomusicology* 26 (1982), pp. 41–7.

Neruda, Pablo, 'Towards an Impure Poetry', trans. Dennis Maloney, in *Windows that Open Inward: Images of Chile*, ed. Dennis Maloney. Buffalo, NY: White Pine Press, [1935] 1999, pp. 49–53.

Neumann, Peter H. A. (ed.), *Das Prophetenverständnis in der deutschsprachigen Forschung seit Heinrich Ewald* [The concept of the Prophet in German research since Heinrich Ewald]. Darmstadt, 1979.

Neuwirth, Angelika, 'Erste Qibla – Fernstes Masjid? Jerusalem im Horizont des historischen Muḥammad' [The first qibla – the farthest masjid? Jerusalem in the view of the historic Muhammad], in F. Hahn, F.-L. Hossfeld, H. Jorissen and A. Neuwirth (eds), *Zion – Ort der Begegnung: Festschrift für Laurentius Klein zur Vollendung des 65. Lebensjahres*. Bonn, 1993, pp. 227–67.

—— 'Gotteswort und Nationalsprache: Zur Motivation der frühen arabischen Philologen' [God's word and national language: on the motivation of early Arabic philologists], in *Forschungsforum: Berichte aus der Otto-Friedrich-Unviersität Bamberg* 2 (1990), pp. 18–28.

—— 'Der historische Muhammad im Spiegel des Koran: Prophetentypus zwischen Seher und Dichter?' [The historic Muhammad as seen in the Quran: A type of prophet between the seer and the poet?], in Wolfgang Zwickel (ed.), *Biblische Welten: Festschrift für Martin Metzger zu seinem 65. Geburtstag*. Freiburg and Göttingen, 1993, pp. 83–108.

—— 'Der Horizont der Offenbarung: Zur Relevanz der einleitenden Schwurserien für die Suren der frühmekkanischen Zeit' [The horizon of the revelation: on the relevance of the introductory oath sequences to the surahs of the early Meccan period], in Udo Tworuschka (ed.), *Gottes ist der Orient – Gottes ist der Okzident: Festschrift für Abdoldjavad Falaturi zum 65. Geburtstag*. Cologne, 1991, pp. 3–39.

—— 'Das islamische Dogma der "Unnachahmlichkeit des Korans" in literaturwissenschaftlicher Sicht' [The Islamic dogma of the 'inimitability of the Quran' from the perspective of literary studies], *Der Islam* 60 (1983), 166–83.

—— 'John Burton, *The Collection of the Qur'an*', review, *Orientalische Literaturzeitung* 76 (1981), pp. 372–80.

—— 'John Wansbrough, *Quranic Studies*', review, *Die Welt des Islams* 23–4 (1984), pp. 539–42.

—— 'Koran', in Helmut Gätje (ed.), *Grundriss der arabischen Philologie* [Outline of Arabic philology], vol. 2: *Literaturwissenschaft*. Wiesbaden, 1987, pp. 96–135.

—— 'Der Koran – Mittelpunkt des Lebens der islamischen Gemeinde' [The Quran: the focus of the life of the Islamic community], in Bayerische Landeszentrale für Politische Bildungsarbeit (ed.), *Weltmacht Islam*. Munich, 1988, pp. 69–91.

—— 'Koranlesung zwischen Ost und West' [Quran reading between East and West], in Adel Sidarus (ed.), *Islāmo e arabismo a Península Ibérica*. Évora, Portugal, 1986, pp. 305–16.

—— *Studien zur Komposition der mekkanischen Suren* [Studies on the composition of the Meccan surahs]. Berlin and New York, 1981.

—— 'Symmetrie und Paarbildung in der koranischen Eschatologie: Philologisch-Stilistisches zu *Sūrat ar-Raḥmān* [Symmetry and pairing in the quranic eschatology: philological and stylistic observations on *Sūrat ar-Raḥmān*], *Mélanges de l'Université Saint-Joseph* [Beirut] 50 (1984), pp. 445–80.

—— 'Vom Rezitationstext über die Liturgie zum Kanon: Zu Entstehung und Wiederauflösung der Surenkomposition im Verlauf der Entwicklung eines islamischen Kultus' [From recitation text to liturgy to canon: on the origin and dissolution of the composition of surahs over the course of development of an Islamic cult], in Stefan Wild (ed.), *The Qur'an as Text*. Leiden, 1996, pp. 69–105.

—— 'Zur Struktur der Yūsuf-Sure' [On the structure of the Joseph Surah], in Werner Diem and Stefan Wild (eds), *Studien aus Arabistik und Semitistik: Festschrift Anton Spitaler*. Wiesbaden, 1980, pp. 123–52.

Neuwirth, Angelika, and Neuwirth, Karl, 'Sūrat al-Fātiḥa – "Eröffnung" des Text-Corpus Koran oder "Introitus" der Gebetsliturgie?' [The surah al-Fātiḥa: an 'opening' of the Quran as text corpus, or an 'introit' of the prayer liturgy?], in W. Groos, H. Irsigler and T. Seidl (eds), *Text, Methode und Grammatik: Wolfgang Richter zum 65. Geburtstag*. St Ottilien, 1991, pp. 331–57.

Neẓāmī Ganjawī, Ḥakīm, *Makhzan al-asrār*, in Neẓāmī Ganjawī, *Kollīyāt-e ḫamse-ye Neẓāmī*, ed. Parwīz Bābā'ī. Teheran, 1374/1995, pp. 1–121.

Nicholson, Reynold A., *A Literary History of the Arabs*. Cambridge, 1969.

—— *The Mystics of Islam*. London, [1914] 1989.

Nietze, William A. '"A Midsummer Night's Dream", v, i, 4–17', *Modern Language Review* 50 (1955), pp. 495–7.

Nietzsche, Friedrich, 'The Birth of Tragedy', trans. Ronald Speirs, in *The Birth of Tragedy and Other Writings*. Cambridge: CUP, 1999, pp. 1–116.

—— 'Ecce Homo: How to Become What You Are', trans. Judith Norman, in *The Anti-Christ, Ecce Homo, Twilight of the Idols and Other Writings*, ed. Aaron Ridley and Judith Norman. Cambridge: CUP, 2005.

Niggl, Günter, 'Biblische Welt in Goethes Dichtung' [The biblical world in Goethe's poetry], in Helmut Koopmann and Winfried Woesler (eds), *Literatur und Religion*. Freiburg: Herder, 1984, pp. 131–49.

Nöldeke, Theodor. 'Zur Sprache des Korāns' [On the language of the Quran]. In: *Neue Beiträge zur Semitischen Sprachwissenschaft*. Strasbourg 1910. pp. 1–30.

Nöldeke, Theodor, Schwally, Friedrich, Bergsträsser, Gotthelf, and Pretzl, Otto, *History of the Qur'ān*, trans. and ed. Wolfgang Rehn. Leiden: Brill, 2013.

Norden, Eduard, *Die antike Kunstprosa: Vom VI. Jahrhundert v. Chr. bis in die Zeit der Renaissance* [Ancient art prose: from the sixth century BC to the Renaissance]. 2nd edn, Leipzig and Berlin, 1909.

Novalis, *The Novices of Sais*, trans. Ralph Manheim. New York: Archipelago, 2005.

—— *Philosophical Writings*, trans. and ed. Margaret Mahony Stoljar. Albany: SUNY Press, 1997.

—— *Schriften* [Writings], ed. Paul Kluckhohn and Richard Samuel, 5 vols. 2nd edn, Darmstadt, 1960–88.

Otto, Rudolf, *The Idea of the Holy*, trans. John W. Harvey. Oxford: OUP, 1958.

Pacholczyk, Józef Marcin, 'Music and Islam in Indonesia', *World of Music* 28 (1986), pp. 3–11.

Paret, Rudi (trans. and ed.), *Der Koran* [The Quran]. Darmstadt, 1975.

—— 'Der Koran als Geschichtsquelle' [The Quran as a historic source], in Paret, *Der Koran*. Darmstadt, 1975, pp. 137–58.

—— *Der Koran: Kommentar und Konkordanz* [The Quran: commentary and concordance]. Stuttgart, 1977.

—— *Mohammed und der Koran: Geschichte und Verkündigung des arabischen Propheten* [Muhammad and the Quran: history and preaching of the Arab prophet]. Stuttgart, 1957.

—— 'Der Standpunkt al-Bāqillānī's in der Lehre vom Koran' [Al-Bāqillānī's position on the doctrine of the Quran], in *Studi Orientalistici in onore di Giorgio Levi Della Vida*, vol. 2. Rome: Istituto per l'Oriente, 1956.

Pascal, Blaise, *Pensées*, trans. A. J. Krailsheimer. London: Penguin [1966] 1995.

Pautz, Otto, *Muhammed's Lehre von der Offenbarung quellenmäßig untersucht*. Leipzig, 1898.

Paz, Octavio, *The Bow and the Lyre*, trans. Ruth L. C. Simms. Austin and London: University of Texas Press, 2009.

—— *Early Poems 1935–1955*, trans. Muriel Rukeyser et al. New York: New Directions, 1973.

—— 'Reading and Contemplation', in Paz, *Convergences: Essays on Art and Literature*, trans. Helen Lane. London: Bloomsbury, 1987, pp. 1–49.

Pedersen, Johannes, *Der Eid bei den Semiten* [The oath in Semitic culture]. Strasbourg, 1914.

—— Review of E. Meyer, *Ursprung und Geschichte der Mormonen: Mit Exkursen über die Anfänge des Islams und des Christentums, Der Islam* 5 (1914), pp. 110–13.

Peters, F. E., 'The Quest of the Historical Mohammed', *International Journal of Middle Eastern Studies* 23 (1991), pp. 291–315.

Peters, J. R. T. M., *God's Created Speech*. Leiden, 1976.

Petit, Odette, *Presence de l'Islam dans la langue arabe* [The presence of Islam in the Arabic language]. Paris, 1982.

Piamenta, Moshe, *Islam in Everyday Speech*. Leiden, 1979.

Pickthall, Muhammad Marmaduke (trans.), *The Meaning of the Glorious Koran*. London: Allen & Unwin, [1930] 1957.

Pieper, Josef, *Enthusiasm and Divine Madness: On the Platonic Dialogue 'Phaedrus'*, trans. Richard Winston and Clara Winston. New York: Harcourt, Brace & World, 1964.

Plato. *Ion*, trans. Trevor J. Saunders, *Early Socratic Dialogues*. London: Penguin, 2005.

—— *Phaedrus*, trans. Christopher Rowe. London: Penguin, 2005.

—— *The Symposium*, trans. Christopher Gill. London: Penguin, 1999.

—— Timaeus, in *Timaeus and Critias*, trans. Robin Waterfield. Oxford: OUP, 2008.

Plotinus, 'Beauty', in *The Enneads*, trans. Stephen MacKenna, ed. John Dillon. London: Penguin, 1991, pp. 45–55.

Pothast, Ulrich. *Die eigentlich metaphysische Tätigkeit: Über Schopenhauers Ästhetik und ihre Anwendung durch Samuel Beckett*. Frankfurt am Main, 1989.

Pourjavady, Nasrollah. 'Zwei alte Werke über *samā'*' [Two old works on samā'], *Spektrum Iran* 3/2 (1990), pp. 49–70; 3/3 (1990), pp. 36–61.

Pretzl, Otto, 'Die Wissenschaft der Koranlesung ('Ilm al-Qirā'a): Ihre literarischen Quellen und ihre Ausspracheregeln (Uṣūl)' [The science of Quran reading: its literary sources and their pronunciation rules (Uṣūl)], *Islamica* 6 (1933–4), pp. 1–47, 230–46, 290–331.

Qabbānī, Nizār, *Qiṣṣatī ma'a sh-shi'r*. Beirut, 1393/1973.

—— *Ash-Shi'r qindīl akhḍar*. Beirut, 1993.

al-Qāḍī, Wadād (ed.), 'The Impact of the Qur'ān on the Epistolography of 'Abd al-Ḥamīd', in al-Qāḍī, *Studia Arabica et Islamica: Festschrift for Ihsan Abbas*. Beirut, 1981, pp. 285–313.

al-Qattān, Manā', *Mabaḥith fī 'ulūm al-Qur'ān*. Cairo, 1391/1971.

al-Qurṭubī, Abū 'Abdillāh Muḥammad ibn Aḥmad al-Anṣārī, *Al-Jāmi' li-aḥkām al-Qur'ān*, ed. Mustafā s-Saqā. Beirut, 1387/1967.

al-Qushayrī, Abū l-Qāsim 'Abdulkarīm, *Das Sendschreiben al-Qushayrīs über das Sufitum*, trans. and ed. Richard Gramlich. Wiesbaden, 1989.

Quṭb, Muḥammad, *Dirāsāt qur'ānīya*. 4th edn, Beirut, 1402/1982.

Quṭb, Sayyid, *At-Taṣwīr al-fannī fī l-Qur'ān* [Artistic imagery in the Quran]. 9th edn, Beirut and Cairo, 1407/1987.

Radscheit, Matthias, '"I'jāz al-Qur'ān" im Koran?', in Stefan Wild (ed.), *The Qur'an as Text*. Leiden, 1996, pp. 113–23.

—— *Die koranische Herausforderung: Die taḥaddī-Verse im Rahmen der Polemikpassagen des Korans* [The quranic challenge: the *taḥaddī* verses in the context of the Quran's polemic passages]. Berlin, 1996.

—— 'Word of God or Prophetic Speech? Reflections on the Quranic *qul*-Statements', in Lutz Edzard and Christian Szyska (eds), *Encounters of Words and Texts: Intercultural Studies in Honor of Stefan Wild on the Occasion of His 60th Birthday*. Hildesheim and Zurich, 1997, pp. 33–42.

ar-Rāfi'ī, Muṣṭafā Ṣādiq, *I'jāz al-Qur'ān wa-l-balāġa an-nabawīya* [The miraculous nature of the Quran and the prophetic rhetoric]. Cairo, 1345/1926; repr. Beirut: Dār al-kitāb al-'arabī, 1401/1990.

—— *Waḥy al-qalam*, 3 vols. Beirut: Dār al-kitāb al-'arabī, n.d.

Rahman, Fazlur, 'Dream, Imagination, and *'Ālam al-mithāl*', in Gustave von Grunebaum and Roger Caillois, *The Dream and Human Societies*. Berkeley, CA, 1966, pp. 409–19.

—— *Major Themes of the Qur'ān*. Chicago, 1980.

—— *Prophecy in Islam: Philosophy and Orthodoxy*. London, 1958.

—— 'Translating the Qur'an', *Religion and Literature* 20 (1988), pp. 23–30.

Rāmiyār, Maḥmud, *Tārīkh-e Qor'ān* [History of the Quran]. Teheran, 1362/1983.

ar-Rāzī, Fakhruddīn, *At-Tafsīr al-kabīr*, 30 vols. Teheran: Dār al-kutub, n.d.

Reichel, Jörn, *Dichtungstheorie und Sprache bei Zinzendorf: Der 12. Anhang zum Herrnhuter Gesangbuch* [Theory of poetry and language in Zinzendorf: the 12th annex to the Herrnhut hymnal]. Berlin and Zurich, 1969.

Reinert, Benedikt, *Die Lehre vom* tawakkul *in der klassischen Sufik* [The doctrine of *tawakkul* in classical Sufism]. Berlin, 1968.

Rhu, Lawrence F., 'After the Middle Ages: Prophetic Authority and Human Fallibility in Renaissance Epic', in James Kugel (ed.), *Poetry and Prophecy: The Beginnings of a Literary Tradition*. Ithaca, NY, 1991, pp. 163–84.

Richter, Gustav, *Der Sprachstil des Koran* [The linguistic style of the Quran], ed. Otto Spies. Leipzig, 1940.

Riḍā, Muḥammad Rashīd, *Al-Waḥy al-muḥammadī*. Beirut, 1391/1971.

Rilke, Rainer Maria, *Die Briefe an Gräfin Sizzo, 1921–1926* [Letters to Countess Sizzo, 1921–1926], ed. Ingeborg Schnack. Expanded edn, Frankfurt am Main, 1977.

—— *Duino Elegies and The Sonnets to Orpheus*, trans. Stephen Mitchell. New York: Vintage, 2009.

Rippin, Andrew, 'The Poetics of the Qur'anic Punning', *Bulletin of the School for Oriental and African Studies* 57 (1994), pp. 193–207.

Ritter, Hellmut, *The Ocean of the Soul: Man, the World and God in the Stories of Farīd al-Dīn ʿAṭṭār*, trans. John O'Kane. Leiden: Brill, 2003.

—— 'Phililogika VI', *Der Islam* 19 (1931), pp. 1–17.

—— 'Studien zur Geschichte der islamischen Frömmigkeit, I: Ḥasan al-Baṣrī' [Studies in the history of Islamic piety I: Ḥasan al-Baṣrī], *Der Islam* 21 (1933), pp. 1–81.

—— See also under al-Jurjānī.

Ritter, Joachim (ed.), *Historisches Wörterbuch der Philosophie*, 13 vols. Basel: Schwabe, 1971–2007.

Robson, James, 'The Magical Use of the Koran', *Transactions of the Glasgow University Oriental Society* 6 (1934), pp. 51–60.

Roest Crollius, Ara A., *Word in the Experience of Revelation in Qur'ān and Hindu Scriptures*. Rome: Università Gregoriana, 1974.

Rohls, Jan, 'Sinn und Geschmack fürs Unendliche: Aspekte romantischer Kunstphilosophie' [Sense and taste for the infinite: aspects of Romantic philosophy of art], *Neue Zeitschrift für systematische Theologie und Religionsphilosophie* 27 (1985), pp. 1–24.

Rothacker, Erich, *Probleme der Kulturanthropologie* [Problems of cultural anthropology]. Bonn, 1948.

Rubin, Uri, 'Abū Lahab and Sūra CXI', *Bulletin of the School for Oriental and African Studies* 42 (1979), pp. 13–28.

—— *The Eye of the Beholder: The Belief of Muḥammad as Viewed by the Early Muslims*. Princeton, NJ, 1995.

—— 'The Kaʿba: Aspects of its Ritual Functions and Position in Pre-Islamic and Early Islamic Times', *Jerusalem Studies in Arabic and Islam* 8 (1986), pp. 97–131.

—— '*Al-Ṣamad* and the High God: An Interpretation of *Sūra* CXII', *Der Islam* 61 (1984), pp. 197–217.

Rückert, Friedrich, *Werke* [Works], ed. Annemarie Schimmel, 2 vols. Frankfurt am Main, 1988.

Rūmī, Jalāloddīn [Maulana Dschelaladdin Rumi], *Discourses of Rumi*, trans. A. J. Arberry. London: Curzon Press, 1993.

ar-Rummānī, Abū l-Ḥasan ʿAlī ibn ʿĪsā, *An-Nukat fī iʿjāz al-Qur'ān* [Remarks on the miraculous nature of the Quran], in Muḥammad Khalafallāh and Muḥammad Zaġlūl Salām (eds), *Thalāth rasā'il fī iʿjāz al-Qur'ān*. 2nd edn, Cairo, 1388/1968, pp. 73–113; French trans. as *Al-Khaṭṭābī et l'inimitabilité du Coran: traduction et introduction au Bayān iʿjāz al-Qur'ān*, trans. Claude-France Audebert. Damascus, 1402/1982.

Ruthven, Kenneth Knowles, *Critical Assumptions*. Cambridge, 1979.

Sabbagh, Toufic, *La Métaphore dans le Coran* [Metaphor in the Quran]. Paris, 1943.

Sabzewārī, Muḥammad ʿAlī, *Tuḥfat al-'abbāsīya* (excerpt), in Najīb Mayel Harawī (ed.), *Andar ġazal-e khʷīsh*. Teheran, 1372/1993, pp. 414–17.

ash-Shāfiʿī, Muḥammad ibn Idrīs, *Ar-Risāla li-l-Imām al-Muṭṭalibī*, ed. Aḥmad Muḥammad Shākir. Cairo, 1359/1940.

Shafīʿī-Kadkanī, Moḥammad Reżā, *Mūsīqī-ye sheʿr*. Paris, 1368/1989.

Sajjādī, Sayyed Jaʿfar, *Farhang-e eṣṭelāḥāt wa-taʿbīrāt-e ʿerfānī*. Teheran, 1370/1991.

Shaḥrūr, Muḥammad, *Al-Kitāb wa-l-Qur'ān*. 5th edn, Damascus, 1412/1992.

as-Saʿīd, Labīb, *Al-Jamʿ aṣ-ṣawtī al-awwal aw al-muṣḥaf al-murattal*. 2nd expanded and rev. edn, Cairo: Dār al-maʿārif, n.d.
—— *The Recited Koran: A History of the First Recorded Version*, trans. and ed. Bernard Weiss, M. A. Rauf and Morroe Berger. Princeton, NJ, 1975.
—— *At-Taġannī bi-l-Qur'ān*. Cairo, 1390/1970.
aṣ-Ṣaʿīdī, ʿAbdulmutaʿāl, *Naqd kitāb ad-duktūr Ṭāhā Ḥusayn, Fī sh-shiʿr al-jāhilī*. Cairo, 1344/1926.
Salmāsīzāde, Jawād, *Tārīkh-e tarjome-ye Qor'ān dar jahān*. Teheran, 1369/1990.
Sanā'ī, ʿAbū l-Majd Majdūd, *The First Book of the Hadīqatu' l-ḥaqīqat (The Enclosed Garden of Truth)*, trans. J. Stephenson. Calcutta, 1910.
as-Sarrāj, Abū Naṣr, *Schlaglichter über das Sufitum: Abū Naṣr as-Sarrājs Kitāb al-lumaʿ* [Highlights on Sufism: Abū Naṣr as-Sarrāj's *Kitāb al-lumaʿ*], trans. and ed. Richard Gramlich. Stuttgart, 1990.
Sbait, Ḍirghām Ḥ., *The Improvised-Sung Folk Poetry of the Palestinians*. Dissertation, University of Washington, Seattle, 1982.
—— 'Palestinian Improvised-Sung Poetry: The Genres of *Ḥidā* and *Qarrādī* – Performance and Transmission', *Oral Tradition* 4 (1989), pp. 213–35.
Schadewaldt, Wolfgang, *Hellas und Hesperien: Gesammelte Schriften zur Antike und zur neueren Literatur in zwei Bänden* [Hellas and Hesperia: collected writings on antiquity and on modern literature in two volumes], ed. Reimhol Thurow and Ernst Zinn. 2nd edn, Zurich and Stuttgart, 1970.
—— *Tübinger Vorlesungen* [Tübingen lectures], ed. Ingeborg Schudoma. Frankfurt am Main, 1991.
Scheible, Hartmut, *Wahrheit und Subjekt: Ästhetik im bürgerlichen Zeitalter* [Truth and subject: aesthetics in the bourgeois age]. Reinbek bei Hamburg, 1988.
Schelling, Friedrich Wilhelm Joseph, *The Philosophy of Art*, trans. Douglas W. Stott. Minneapolis: University of Minnesota Press, 1989.
—— *System of Transcendental Idealism (1800)*, trans. Peter Heath. Charlottesville: University Press of Virginia, 1978.
Schiller, Friedrich, 'The Artists', in *The Poems of Schiller, Complete: Including All His Early Suppressed Pieces*, trans. Edgar Alfred Bowring. London, 1851.
—— *On Naïve and Sentimental Poetry*, trans. Daniel O. Dahlstrom, in Schiller, *Essays*, ed. Walter Hinderer and Daniel O. Dahlstrom. New York: Continuum, 1993, pp. 179–260.
Schimmel, Annemarie, *And Muhammad Is His Messenger: The Veneration of the Prophet in Islamic Piety*. Chapel Hill: University of North Carolina Press, 1985.
—— *Deciphering the Signs of God: A Phenomenological Approach to Islam*. Albany: SUNY Press, 1994.
—— *Mystical Dimensions of Islam*. Chapel Hill: University of North Carolina Press, 1975.
Schleiermacher, Friedrich, *On Religion: Speeches to its Cultured Despisers*, trans. John Oman. London, 1893.
Schmidt, Jochen, *Die Geschichte des Geniegedankens in der deutschen Literatur, Philosophie und Politik, 1750–1945* [The history of the idea of genius in German literature, philosophy and politics, 1750–1945], 2 vols. 2nd edn, Darmstadt, 1988.
Schoeler, Gregor, *The Biography of Muhammad: Nature and Authenticity*. Abingdon: Routledge, 2011.
—— 'Schreiben und Veröffentlichen: Zu Verwendung und Funktion der Schrift in den ersten islamischen Jahrhunderten', *Der Islam* 69 (1992), pp. 1–43;

condensed English version as 'Writing and Publishing: On the Use and Function of Writing in the First Centuries of Islam', *Arabica* 44/3 (1997), pp. 423–35.

Scholem, Gershom, 'The Name of God and the Linguistic Theory of the Kabbala', trans. Simon Pleasance, *Diogenes* 79 (1972), pp. 59–80; 80 (1972), pp. 164–94.

—— *On the Mystical Shape of the Godhead: Basic Concepts in the Kabbalah*, trans. Joachim Neugroschel, ed. Jonathan Chipman. New York: Schocken, 1997.

Schopenhauer, Arthur, 'On Metaphysics of the Beautiful and Aesthetics', in *Parerga and Paralipomena: Short Philosophical Essays*, vol. 2, trans. E. F. J. Payne. Oxford, 1974, pp. 415–52.

—— *The World as Will and Representation*, trans. and ed. Judith Norman, Alistaire Welchman and Christopher Janaway. Cambridge: CUP: 2010.

Schreiner, Martin, 'Zur Geschichte der Polemik zwischen Juden und Muhammedanern' [On the history of the polemics between Jews and Mohammedans], *Zeitschrift der Deutschen Morgenländischen Gesellschaft* 42 (1888), pp. 591–675.

Schub, Michael, 'Qur'ān 26:224 /ġāwūna/ = "Fundamentally Disoriented": An Orientalist Note', *Journal of Arabic Literature* 18 (1987), pp. 79–80.

Schuon, Frithjof, *Understanding Islam*, rev. edn, Bloomington, IN: World Wisdom, 1998.

Sell, Edward, *Faith of Islam*. 3rd edn, Madras, 1907.

Sellheim, Rudolf, 'Muhammeds erstes Offenbarungserlebnis: Zum Problem mündlicher und schriftlicher Überlieferung im 1./7. und 2./8. Jahrhundert' [Muhammad's first experience of revelation: on the problem of oral and written transmission in the 1st/7th and 2nd/8th centuries], *Jerusalem Studies in Arabic and Islam* 10 (1988), pp. 2–16.

—— 'Prophet, Chalif und Geschichte: Die Muhammadbiographie des Ibn Isḥāq' [Prophet, caliph and history: Ibn Isḥāq's biography of Muhammad], *Oriens* 18–19 (1907), pp. 33–91.

Sells, Michael, 'Sound and Meaning in *Sūrat al-Qāriʿa*', *Arabica* 40 (1993), pp. 403–30.

—— 'Sounds, Spirit and Gender in *Sūrat al-Qadr*', *Journal of the American Oriental Society* 111 (1991), pp. 239–59.

Semaan, Khalil, 'Tajwīd as a Source in Phonetic Research', *Wiener Zeitschrift für die Kunde des Morgenlandes* 58 (1962), pp. 112–20.

Sezgin, Fuat, *Geschichte des arabischen Schrifttums* [History of Arabic literature]. Leiden, 1967–.

Shahid, Irfan, 'Another Contribution to Koranic Exegesis: The Sūra of the Poets (XXVI)', *Journal of Arabic Literature* 14 (1983), pp. 1–21.

—— 'A Contribution to Koranic Exegesis', in George Makdisi (ed.), *Arabic and Islamic Studies in Honor of Hamilton A. R. Gibb*. Leiden, 1965, pp. 563–80.

Sharīʿaṭī-Mazīnānī, Moḥammad Taqī, *Waḥy wa-nobūwat dar partou-e Qor'ān*. Mashhad, 1349/1970.

Sharif, M. M., *A History of Muslim Philosophy: With Short Accounts of Other Disciplines and the Modern Renaissance in Muslim Lands*, 2 vols. Wiesbaden, 1963.

Shiloah, Amnon, 'L'Islam et la musique' [Islam and music], in J. Porte (ed.), *Encyclopédie des musiques sacrées*, 4 vols. Paris, 1968–70, vol. 1, pp. 414–21.

Shouby, E., 'The Influence of the Arabic Language on the Psychology of the Arabs', *Middle East Journal* 5 (1951), pp. 284–302.

Sievers, Harry, *Johann Georg Hamanns Bekehrung: Ein Versuch, sie zu verstehen* [Johann Georg Hamann's conversion: an attempt to understand it]. Zurich and Stuttgart, 1969.

Sikes, Edward Ernest, *The Greek View of Poetry*. New York, 1969.
Sister, M., 'Metaphern und Vergleiche im Koran' [Metaphors and similes in the Quran], *Mitteilungen des Seminars für Orientalische Sprachen/Westasiatische Studien* 34 (1931), pp. 104–54.
Sloterdijk, Peter, 'Der mystische Imperativ: Bemerkungen zum Formwandel des Religiösen in der Neuzeit' [The mystical imperative: remarks on the changing form of religion in the modern period], Sloterdijk (ed.), *Mystische Weltliteratur: gesammelt von Martin Buber* [Mystical literature of the world: collected by Martin Buber], Kreuzlingen and Munich: Diederichs, 2007, pp. 9–37.
Smith, G. R., 'Oaths in the Qur'ān', *Semitics* 1 (1970), pp. 126–56.
Smith, Margaret, *Studies in Early Mysticism in the Near and Middle East*. London, 1931; repr. Amsterdam, 1973.
Smith, R. Bosworth, *Mohammed and Mohammedanism: Lectures Delivered at the Royal Institution of Great Britain in February and March 1874*. London, 1876.
Smith, Wilfried Cantwell, 'Some Similarities and Differences between Christianity and Islam', in James Kritzeck and R. Bayly Winder, *Studies in honour of Philip K. Hitti*. London, 1959, pp. 47–59.
—— *What is Scripture? A Comparative Approach*. London, 1993.
Snouck Hurgronje, Christiaan, 'Islam und Phonograph' [Islam and the phonograph], in Snouck Hurgronje, *Verspreide Geschriften II*. Bonn, 1923, pp. 419–47.
—— *Mohammedanism: Lectures on its Origin, its Religious and Political Growth, and its Present State*. New York, 1916.
Söderblom, Nathan, *Einführung in die Religionsgeschichte* [Introduction to the history of religion]. Leipzig, 1920.
Sorūsh, ʿAbdolkarīm, 'Ẕātī wa ʿaražī dar dīn', *Kiyān* 42 (Ḥordād–Tīr 1377/May–July 1988), pp. 4–20.
Sowayan, Saad Abdullah, '"Tonight My Gun Is Loaded": Poetic Dueling in Arabia', *Oral Tradition* 4 (1989), pp. 151–73.
Speicher, Katrin, 'Einige Bemerkungen zu al-Khūlīs Entwurf eines *tafsīr adabī*' [Some remarks on al-Khūlī's project of a *tafsīr adabī*], in Lutz Edzard and Christian Szyska (eds), *Encounters of Words and Texts: Intercultural Studies in Honor of Stefan Wild on the Occasion of His 60th Birthday*. Hildesheim and Zurich, 1997, pp. 3–21.
Spitaler, Anton, 'Review of Johann Fück, *Arabiya*', *Bibliotheca Orientalis* 10 (1953), pp. 144–50.
Steiner, George, *After Babel: Aspects of Language and Translation*. 3rd edn, Oxford: OUP, 1998.
—— *Language and Silence: Essays on Language, Literature, and the Inhuman*. New Haven, CT, 1998.
Stetkevych, Suzanne Pinckney, *Abū Tammām and the Poetics of the ʿAbbāsid Age*. Leiden and New York: Brill, 1991.
as-Suhrawardī, Abū Najīb ʿAbdulqāhir, *Kitāb ādāb al-murīdīn*, ed. Menahem Milson. Jerusalem, 1978.
as-Suhrawardī, Shihābuddīn ʿUmar Abū Ḥafs, *Die Gaben der Erkenntnisse des ʿUmar as-Suhrawardī* [The gifts of knowledge ofʿUmar as-Suhrawardī], trans. and ed. Richard Gramlich. Wiesbaden, 1978.
as-Suyūṭī, Jalāluddīn, *Bāb an-nuqūl fī asbāb an-nuzūl*, printed below the main text in al-Maḥallī, Jalāluddīn, and as-Suyūṭī, Jalāluddīn, *Tafsīr al-jalālayn*. Beirut: Dār al-Qalam, n.d.
—— *Al-Itqān fī ʿulūm al-Qurʾān*, ed. Aḥmad Saʿd ʿAlī. 3rd edn, Cairo 1370/1951.

—— *Al-Muzhir fī 'ulūm al-lūġa wa-anwā'ihā*, 2 vols. Cairo, 1958.

aṭ-Ṭabarī, Abū Ja'far Muḥammad ibn Jarīr, *Jāmi' al bayān 'an ta'wīl al-Qur'ān*, 30 vols (in 10 vols). Cairo, 1373/1954.

—— *Tārīkh ar-rusūl wa-l-mulūk*, ed. M. de Goeje, 15 vols. Leiden, 1879–1901; = *The History of al-Tabari*, trans. Franz Rosenthal et al., ed. Ehsan Yar-Shater et al., 39 vols. New York 1985–98.

aṭ-Ṭabarī, 'Alī ibn Rabbān, *The Book of Religion and Empire* (*Kitāb ad-dīn wa-d-dawla*), ed. Alphonse Mingana. Manchester, 1922.

aṭ-Ṭabarsī, Abū 'Ali al-Faḍl ibn al-Ḥasan, *Majma'al-bayān fī tafsīr al-Qur'ān*, 10 vols in 5. Beirut, 1358/1939.

Ṭabāṭabā'ī, Seyyed Moḥammad Ḥoseyn, *Al-Mīzān fī tafsīr al-Qur'ān*, 20 vols. 2nd edn, Beirut 1393/1973; Persian trans., 40 vols, Teheran 1365/1986.

Talbi, M., 'La qirā'a bi-l-alḥān', *Arabica* 5 (1958), pp. 183–90.

aṭ-Tha'labī, Abū Isḥāq Aḥmad ibn Muḥammad, *Kitāb mubārak yuḏkar fīhi qatlā l-Qur'ān al-'aẓīm allaḏīna samī'ū l-Qur'ān wa-mātū bi-samā'ihī raḥmat Allāh 'alayhim wa-'alā jamī' al-muslimīn* [The book of those slain by the noble Quran, who heard the Quran and thereupon died] (= *Die vom Koran Getöteten: Ath-Tha'labīs 'Qatlā l-Qur'ān' nach der Istanbuler und den Leidener Handschrifen* [Those slain by the Quran: Ath-Tha'labī's 'Qatlā l-Qur'ān' after the Istanbul and Leiden manuscripts]), trans. and ed. Beate Wiesmüller. Würzburg: Ergon, 2002.

Tibawi, A., 'Is the Qur'ān Translatable? Early Muslim Opinions', *Muslim World* 52 (1963), pp. 4–17.

Tillich, Paul, 'Die Idee der Offenbarung', *Zeitschrift für Theologie und Kirche* 8 (1927), pp. 403–12.

at-Tirmiḏī, Abū 'Īsā Muḥammad ibn 'Īsā b. Sahl, *Al-Jāmi' aṣ-ṣaḥīḥ*, 5 vols. ed. 'Abdulwahhāb 'Abdullaṭīf (vol. 1) and 'Abdurraḥmān Muḥammad 'Uthmān (Vols 2–5). Medina, 1384/1964.

Touma, Habib Hassan, 'Die Koranrezitation: eine Form der religiösen Musik der Araber' [Quran recitation: an Arab form of religious music], *Baessler-Archiv* 23 (1975), pp. 87–120.

aṭ-Ṭurṭūshī, Ibn Abī Randaqa, *Kitāb al-ḥawādith wa-l-bida'*. Tunis, 1959.

Ṭūsī, Aḥmad ibn Moḥammad, *Al-Hadīya as-sa'dīya* (excerpt), in Najīb Mayel Harawī (ed.), *Andar ġazal-e ḫʷīsh*. Teheran, 1372/1993, pp. 360–6.

Ullmann, Manfred (ed.), *Wörterbuch der klassischen arabischen Sprache* [Dictionary of classical Arabic], Wiesbaden, 1970.

Unger, Rudolf, *Hamann und die Aufklärung: Studien zur Geschichte des romantischen Geistes im 18. Jahrhundert* [Hamann and the Enlightenment: studies on Romantic intellectual history in the 18th century], 2 vols. Halle, 1925.

Usener, Hermann, *Götternamen: Versuch einer Lehre von der religiösen Begriffsbildung* [Names of gods: towards a theory of religious conceptualization]. Frankfurt am Main, 1948.

'Uṣfūr, Jābir, *Mafhūm ash-shi'r: Dirāsa fī t-turāth an-naqdī*. 4th edn, Nicosia, 1990.

Valéry, Paul, *The Art of Poetry*, trans. Denise Folliot. Princeton, NJ, [1958] 1985.

van der Leeuw, Gerardus, *Einführung in die Phänomenologie der Religion* [Introduction to the phenomenology of religion]. 2nd edn, Darmstadt, 1961.

—— *Religion in Essence and Manifestation: A Study in Phenomenology*, trans. J. E. Turner. Princeton, NJ, 1986.

—— 'Rudolf Otto und die Religionsgeschichte', *Zeitschrift für Theologie und Kirche*, n.f. 19 (1938), pp. 71–81; quoted in Günter Lanczkowski, *Einführung in die Religionswissenschaft*. Darmstadt, 1980, pp. 76–86.

—— *Sacred and Profane Beauty: The Holy in Art*, trans. David E. Green. Oxford: OUP, 2006.
van Ess, Josef, *Die Gedankenwelt des Ḥārith al-Muḥāsibī* [The world of ideas of Ḥārith al-Muḥāsibī]. Bonn, 1961.
—— 'Some Fragments of the *Muʿāraḍat al-Qurʾān* Attributed to Ibn al-Muqaffaʿ', in al-Qāḍī, *Studia Arabica et Islamica: Festschrift for Ihsan Abbas*. Beirut, 1981, pp. 151–63.
—— *Theologie und Gesellschaft im 2. und 3. Jahrhundert Hidschra: Eine Geschichte des religiösen Denkens* [Theology and society in the second and third centuries AH: a history of religious thought], 6 vols. Berlin and New York, 1991–7.
—— 'Verbal Inspiration? Language and Revelation in Classical Islamic Theology', in Stefan Wild (ed.), *The Qur'an as Text*. Leiden, 1996, pp. 177–94.
van Gelder, Geert Jan, *The Bad and the Ugly: Attitudes towards Invective Poetry (Hijāʾ) in Classical Arabic Literature*. Leiden, 1988.
—— *Beyond the Line: Classical Arabic Literary Critics on the Coherence and Unity of the Poem*. Leiden, 1982.
van Nieuwenhuijze, C. A. O., 'The Prophetic Function in Islam: An Analytic Approach', *Correspondance d'Orient: Études* 1–2 (1962), pp. 125–6; 5–6 (1964), pp. 99–119.
—— 'The Qur'an as a Factor in the Islamic Way of Life', *Der Islam* 38 (1963), pp. 215–57.
Versteegh, C. H. M., *Arabic Grammar and Qurʾānic Exegesis in Early Islam*. Leiden, 1993.
Vico, Giambattista, *New Science*, trans. David Marsh. 2nd edn, London: Penguin, 2001.
Vodička, Felix V., 'The Concretization of the Literary Work: Problems of the Reception of Neruda's Works', trans. John Burbank, in Peter Steiner (ed.), *The Prague School: Selected Writings, 1929–1946*. Austin: Texas UP, 1982.
—— 'Die Rezeptionsgeschichte literarischer Werke' [The reception history of literary works], in Rainer Warning (ed.), *Rezeptionsästhetik* [Reception aesthetics]. 4th edn, Munich, 1993, pp. 71–83.
Vollers, Karl, *Volkssprache und Schriftsprache im alten Arabien* [Popular language and written language in ancient Arabia]. Strasbourg, 1906.
Wagner, Ewald, *Grundzüge der klassischen arabischen Dichtung* [Outline of classical Arabic poetry], 2 vols. Darmstadt, 1988.
Walzer, Richard, 'Arabische Übersetzungen aus dem Griechischen' [Arabic translations from the Greek] (1962), in Paul Wilpert and Willehad P. Eckert (eds), *Antike und Orient im Mittelalter*. Berlin: de Gruyter, 2013.
—— *Greek into Arabic: Essays on Islamic Philosophy*. Oxford, 1963.
—— See also under al-Fārābī.
Wansbrough, John, 'Arabic Rhetoric and Qur'anic Exegesis', *Bulletin of the School of Oriental and African Studies* 31 (1968), pp. 469–85.
—— *Quranic Studies: Sources and Methods of Scriptural Interpretation*. Oxford, 1977.
—— *The Sectarian Milieu: Content and Composition of Islamic Salvation History*. Amherst, MA: Prometheus, 1978.
al-Wāqidī, Muḥammad ibn ʿUmar, *Kitāb al-maġāzī*, ed. Marsden Jones, 3 vols. London, 1966.
Watt, William Montgomery, *Bell's Introduction to the Qur'an*. Edinburgh, 1970.
—— 'Early Discussions about the Qur'an', *Muslim World* 40 (1950), pp. 27–40, 96–105.

—— *Muḥammad's Mecca.* Edinburgh. 1988.
Watt, William Montgomery, and Welch, Alford T., *Der Islam*, vol. 1: *Mohammed und die Frühzeit, Islamisches Recht, Religiöses Leben* [Muhammad and the early period, Islamic law, religious life], trans. Sylvia Höfer. Stuttgart, 1980.
Weidner, Stefan, 'Adonis', in *Kritisches Lexikon zur fremdsprachigen Gegenwartsliteratur* [Critical lexicon of contemporary foreign-language literature], ed. Heinz Ludwig Arnold. Munich, 1996 [41st supplement].
—— See also under Adonis.
Weil, Gustav, *Das Leben Muḥammeds (nach Ibn Hishām)* [The life of Muhammad, after Ibn Hishām]. Stuttgart, 1864.
Weisgerber, Leo, *Vom Weltbild der deutschen Sprache* [The German language's view of the world]. Düsseldorf, 1959.
Weiss, Bernard G., 'Medieval Muslim Discussions of the Origin of Language', *Zeitschrift der Deutschen Morgenländischen Gesellschaft* 124 (1974), pp. 33–41.
—— '*Al-Muṣḥaf al-murattal:* A Modern Phonographic "Collection" (*jamʿ*) of the Qur'ān', *Muslim World* 64 (1974), pp. 134–40.
Weisweiler, M., ''Abdalqāhir al-Curcānī's Werk über die Unnachahmlichkeit des Korans und seine syntaktisch-stilistischen Lehren' ['Abdalqāhir al-Jurjānī's work on the inimitability of the Quran and its syntactical-stylistic lessons], *Oriens* 11 (1958), pp. 77–121.
Wellhausen, Julius, *Reste arabischen Heidentums* [Vestiges of Arab paganism]. 3rd edn, Berlin, 1961.
Wensinck, A. J., *Concordance et indices de la tradition musulman*, 7 vols. Leiden, 1936–69.
—— 'Muhammad und die Propheten' [Muhammad and the prophets], *Acta Orientalia* 2 (1924), pp. 168–98.
Wensinck, A. J., and Kramers, J. H. (eds), *Handwörterbuch des Islams* [Concise dictionary of Islam]. Leiden, [1941] 1976.
Wenzel, Horst, *Hören und Sehen, Schrift und Bild: Kultur und Gedächtnis im Mittelalter* [Hearing and seeing, writing and pictures: culture and memory in the Middle Ages]. Munich, 1995.
Werlen, Iwar, *Ritual und Sprache* [Ritual and language]. Tübingen, 1984.
Wessels, Antonie, *A Modern Arabic Biography of Muḥammad: A Critical Study of Muḥammad Ḥusayn Haykal's Ḥayāt Muḥammad.* Leiden, 1972.
Westermann, Claus, *Basic Forms of Prophetic Speech*, trans. Hugh C. White. Cambridge: Lutterworth, 1991.
Whorf, Benjamin, *Language, Thought, and Reality: Selected Writings of Benjamin Lee Whorf.* Cambridge, MA: MIT Press, 1956.
Widengren, Geo, *The Ascension of the Apostle and the Heavenly Book.* Uppsala, 1955.
—— *Literary and Psychological Aspects of the Hebrew Prophets.* Uppsala and Leizig, 1948.
—— *Muḥammad, the Apostle of God, and his Ascension.* Uppsala and Wiesbaden, 1955.
—— *Religionsphänomenologie* [Phenomenology of religion]. Berlin, 1969.
Wieland, Almut, *Studien zur Djinn-Vorstellung im heutigen Ägypten* [Studies on the notion of jinn in present-day Egypt]. Würzburg, 1994.
Wielandt, Rotraud, *Offenbarung und Geschichte im Denken moderner Muslime* [Revelation and history in modern Muslim thought]. Wiesbaden, 1971.
Wild, Stefan, '"Die schauerliche Öde des heiligen Buches": Westliche Wertungen des koranischen Stils' ['The appalling tedium of the Holy Book': Western appreciations of the style of the Quran], in Alma Giese and J. Christoph Bürgel (eds),

Gott ist schön und Er liebt die Schönheit [God is beautiful and He loves beauty]. Bern, 1994, pp. 429–44.

—— '"We Have Sent Down to Thee the Book with the Truth ...": Spatial and Temporal Implications of the Qur'anic Concepts of *Nuzūl, Tanzīl*, and *Inzāl*', in Wild (ed.), *The Qur'an as Text*, Leiden, 1996, pp. 137–53.

Wittgenstein, Ludwig, *Philosophical Investigations*, trans. and ed. G. E. M. Anscombe, P. M. S. Hacker and Joachim Schulte. 4th edn, Chichester: Wiley-Blackwell, 2009.

—— *Vermischte Bemerkungen: Eine Auswahl aus dem Nachlass* [Miscellaneous remarks: a selection from the unpublished writings], ed. Georg Henrik von Wright and Heikki Nayman, in *Werkausgabe*, 8 vols. Frankfurt am Main, 1984, vol. 8, pp. 445–573.

Wojcik, Jan, 'The Uncertain Success of Isaiah's Prophecy: A Poetical Reading', in Wojcik & Raymond-Jean Frontain (eds), *Poetic Prophecy in Western Literature*, Rutherford, NJ, 1984, pp. 31–9.

Wojcik, Jan, and Frontain, Raymond-Jean (eds), *Poetic Prophecy in Western Literature*. Rutherford, NJ, 1984.

Wolfson, Harry Austryn, *The Philosophy of the Kalam*. Cambridge, MA, and London, 1976.

Yāqūt ar-Rūmī al-Ḥamawī, Shihābuddīn Abū ʿAbdillāh, *Muʿjam al-udabāʾ*, ed. D. S. Margoliouth, 20 vols. Leiden and London 1907–27.

Zaġlūl Salām, Muḥammad, *Athr al-Qurʾān fī taṭawwur an-naqd al-ʿarabī īlā ākhir al-qarn ar-rābiʿ al-hijrī*. 2nd edn, Cairo, 1961.

az-Zamakhsharī, Abū l-Qāsim Muḥammad Jārullāh Maḥmūd ibn ʿUmar, *Al-Kashāf ʿan ḥaqāʾiq at-tanzīl wa-ʿuyūn al-aqāwīl fī wujūh at-taʾwīl*, 4 vols. Qom, 1414/1992.

Žande-Pīl, Aḥmad Jām, *Uns at-tāʾibīn* (excerpt), in Najīb Mayel Harawī (ed.), *Andar ġazal-e ḫʷīsh*. Teheran, 1372/1993, pp. 188–200.

az-Zarkashī, Badruddīn Muḥammad ibn ʿAbdullāh, *Al-Burhān fī ʿulum al-Qurʾān*, 4 vols. Beirut, 1408/1988.

Zbinden, Ernst, *Die Djinn des Islam und der altorientalische Geisterglaube* [The jinn of Islam and ancient Oriental belief in ghosts]. Bern, 1959.

Zilsel, Edgar, *Die Entstehung des Geniebegriffes: Ein Beitrag zur Ideengeschichte der Antike und des Frühkapitalismus* [The origin of the concept of genius: on the intellectual history of classical antiquity and early capitalism]. Tübingen, 1926; repr. Hildesheim and New York, 1972.

Zinzendorf, Nikolaus Ludwig, *Die Öffentlichen Gemein-Reden im Jahr 1747: Erster und zweiter Teil, Ausgabe 1758/49* [The public general speeches in 1747: parts one and two, edition of 1748/49], in *Hauptschriften in sechs Bänden* [Principal works in six volumes], vol. 4, ed. Erich Beyreuther and Gerhard Meyer. Hildesheim, 1963.

Zirker, Hans, *Christentum und Islam: Theologische Verwandtschaft und Konkurrenz*. 2nd edn, Düsseldorf, 1992.

Zweig, Stefan, *The Struggle with the Daemon*, trans. Eden Paul and Cedar Paul. London: Pushkin, 2012.

Zwemer, Samuel M., *Studies in Popular Islam: A Collection of Papers Dealing with the Superstitions and Beliefs of the Common People*. London and New York, 1939.

Zwettler, Michael, 'A Mantic Manifesto', in James Kugel (ed.), *Poetry and Prophecy: The Beginnings of a Literary Tradition*. Ithaca, NY, 1991, pp. 75–120.

—— *The Oral Tradition of Classical Arabic Poetry: Its Character and Implications*. Columbus, Ohio State UP, 1978.

Index

* indicates a contemporary of Muhammad whose precise dates are unknown.